Additional copies of *Sport Pilot FAA Knowledge Test* are available from

Gleim Publications, Inc.
P.O. Box 12848 • University Station
Gainesville, Florida 32604

(352) 375-0772
(800) 87-GLEIM or (800) 874-5346
Fax: (352) 375-6940

www.gleim.com | avmarketing@gleim.com

The price is $19.95 (subject to change without notice). Orders must be prepaid. Call us, order online, or use the order form on page 327. Shipping and handling charges apply to all orders. Add applicable sales tax to shipments within Florida.

Gleim Publications, Inc., guarantees the immediate refund of all resalable texts, unopened and un-downloaded Test Prep Software, and unopened and un-downloaded audios returned within 30 days of purchase. Aviation Test Prep Online may be canceled within 30 days of purchase if no more than the first study unit has been accessed. Other Aviation online courses may be canceled within 30 days of purchase if no more than two study units have been accessed. This policy applies only to products that are purchased directly from Gleim Publications, Inc. No refunds will be provided on opened or downloaded Test Prep Software or audios, partial returns of package sets, or shipping and handling charges. Any freight charges incurred for returned or refused packages will be the purchaser's responsibility. Returns of books purchased from bookstores and other resellers should be made to the respective bookstore or reseller.

ALSO AVAILABLE FROM GLEIM PUBLICATIONS, INC.

Sport Pilot FAA Knowledge Test
Sport Flight Maneuvers and Practical Test Prep

Private Pilot and Recreational Pilot FAA Knowledge Test
Private Flight Maneuvers and Practical Test Prep

Pilot Handbook
Aviation Weather and Weather Services
FAR/AIM

Sport Pilot Syllabus
Private Pilot Syllabus
Instrument Pilot Syllabus
Commercial Pilot Syllabus

Flight Computer
Navigational Plotter
Pilot Logbook
Flight Bag

Advanced Pilot Training

Instrument Pilot FAA Knowledge Test
Instrument Pilot Flight Maneuvers and Practical Test Prep

Commercial Pilot FAA Knowledge Test
Commercial Pilot Flight Maneuvers and Practical Test Prep

Fundamentals of Instructing FAA Knowledge Test
Flight/Ground Instructor FAA Knowledge Test
Flight Instructor Flight Maneuvers and Practical Test Prep

Airline Transport Pilot FAA Knowledge Test

Flight Engineer FAA Test Prep Online

Gleim Pilot Training Kits

Sport Pilot
Private Pilot
Instrument Pilot
Commercial Pilot
Flight/Ground Instructor
Airline Transport Pilot
Sport Pilot Flight Instructor

Online Courses

Flight Review Ground Training (FAR 61.56)
Pilot Refresher Course
Instrument Pilot Refresher Course
Garmin 530 Course
SkyView Training Course
Seaplane Add-On Rating Course
Seaplane Refresher Course
Multi-Engine Add-On Rating Course
Flight Instructor Refresher Course
Inspection Authorization Training Course
Inspection Authorization Renewal Course
Flight School Security Awareness Course
Safe Pilot Course
Sport Pilot Student Certificate Course
Security-Related Airspace Course
Reduced Vertical Separation Minimums
Online Communication Course
Watching Airplanes Course
Gleim Online Ground School
    U.S. Pilot Certificates and Ratings
    Canadian Certificate Conversion

REVIEWERS AND CONTRIBUTORS

Jamie Beckett, CMEL, CFII, MEI, AGI, A&P, is one of our aviation editors. Mr. Beckett researched questions, wrote and edited answer explanations, and incorporated revisions into the text.

Eric L. Crump, CMEL, CFII, AGI, B.S., Middle Tennessee State University, is one of our aviation editors. Mr. Crump researched questions, wrote and edited answer explanations, and incorporated revisions into the text.

Scott Krogh, CMEL, CFII, MEI, is the Gleim 141 Chief Flight Instructor and one of our aviation editors. Mr. Krogh researched questions, wrote and edited answer explanations, and incorporated revisions into the text.

The CFIs who have worked with us throughout the years to develop and improve our pilot training materials.

The many FAA employees who helped, in person or by telephone, primarily in Gainesville, Orlando, Oklahoma City, and Washington, DC.

The many pilots and student pilots who have provided comments and suggestions about *Sport Pilot FAA Knowledge Test* during the past several decades.

A PERSONAL THANKS

This manual would not have been possible without the extraordinary effort and dedication of Jacob Brunny, Julie Cutlip, Eileen Nickl, Teresa Soard, Justin Stephenson, Joanne Strong, and Candace Van Doren, who typed the entire manuscript and all revisions and drafted and laid out the diagrams and illustrations in this book.

The authors also appreciate the production and editorial assistance of Ellen Buhl, Jessica Felkins, Chris Hawley, Katie Larson, Cary Marcous, Jean Marzullo, Shane Rapp, Drew Sheppard, and Martha Willis.

Finally, we appreciate the encouragement, support, and tolerance of our families throughout this project.

Groundwood Paper and Highlighters – This book is printed on high quality groundwood paper. It is lightweight and easy to recycle. We recommend that you purchase a highlighter specifically designed to be non-bleed-through at your local office supply store.

2014 EDITION
SPORT PILOT

FAA KNOWLEDGE TEST

for the FAA Computer-Based Pilot Knowledge Test

Sport Pilot - General

by

Irvin N. Gleim, Ph.D., CFII

and

Garrett W. Gleim, CFII

ABOUT THE AUTHORS

Irvin N. Gleim earned his private pilot certificate in 1965 from the Institute of Aviation at the University of Illinois, where he subsequently received his Ph.D. He is a commercial pilot and flight instructor (instrument) with multi-engine and seaplane ratings and is a member of the Aircraft Owners and Pilots Association, American Bonanza Society, Civil Air Patrol, Experimental Aircraft Association, National Association of Flight Instructors, and Seaplane Pilots Association. He is the author of flight maneuvers and practical test prep books for the sport, private, instrument, commercial, and flight instructor certificates/ratings and the author of study guides for the sport, private/recreational, instrument, commercial, flight/ground instructor, fundamentals of instructing, airline transport pilot, and flight engineer FAA knowledge tests. Three additional pilot training books are *Pilot Handbook*, *Aviation Weather and Weather Services*, and *FAR/AIM*.

Dr. Gleim has also written articles for professional accounting and business law journals and is the author of widely used review manuals for the CIA (Certified Internal Auditor) exam, the CMA (Certified Management Accountant) exam, the CPA (Certified Public Accountant) exam, and the EA (IRS Enrolled Agent) exam. He is Professor Emeritus, Fisher School of Accounting, University of Florida, and is a CFM, CIA, CMA, and CPA.

Garrett W. Gleim earned his private pilot certificate in 1997 in a Piper Super Cub. He is a commercial pilot (single- and multi-engine), ground instructor (advanced and instrument), and flight instructor (instrument and multi-engine), and he is a member of the Aircraft Owners and Pilots Association and the National Association of Flight Instructors. He is the author of study guides for the sport, private/recreational, instrument, commercial, flight/ground instructor, fundamentals of instructing, and airline transport pilot FAA knowledge tests. He received a Bachelor of Science in Economics from The Wharton School, University of Pennsylvania.

Gleim Publications, Inc.
P.O. Box 12848 · University Station
Gainesville, Florida 32604

(352) 375-0772
(800) 87-GLEIM or (800) 874-5346
Fax: (352) 375-6940

Internet: www.gleim.com
Email: admin@gleim.com

For updates to the first printing of the 2014 edition of
Sport Pilot FAA Knowledge Test

Go To: www.gleim.com/updates

Or: Email update@gleim.com with **SPKT 2014-1** in the subject line. You will receive our current update as a reply.

Updates are available until the next edition is published.

ISSN 1933-4109
ISBN 978-1-58194-400-6

First Printing: July 2013

SOURCES USED IN *SPORT PILOT FAA KNOWLEDGE TEST*

The first lines of our answer explanations contain citations to authoritative sources of the answers. These publications can be obtained from the FAA, the Government Printing Office, and aviation bookstores. These citations are abbreviated as provided below:

A/FD	Airport/Facility Directory	AWS	Aviation Weather Services
AAH	Advanced Avionics Handbook	FAR	Federal Aviation Regulations
AC	Advisory Circular	Fl Comp	Flight Computer
ACL	Aeronautical Chart Legend	IFH	Instrument Flying Handbook
AFH	Airplane Flying Handbook	NTSB	National Transportation Safety Board Regulations
AIM	Aeronautical Information Manual		
AvW	Aviation Weather	PHAK	Pilot's Handbook of Aeronautical Knowledge
AWBH	Aircraft Weight and Balance Handbook		

HELP!!

This 2014 edition is designed specifically for sport pilots. Please send any corrections and suggestions for subsequent editions to the authors, c/o Gleim Publications, Inc. The last two pages in this book have been reserved for you to make comments and suggestions. They can be torn out and mailed to Gleim Publications, Inc.

Two other volumes, **Sport Pilot Flight Maneuvers and Practical Test Prep** and **Pilot Handbook**, are also available. **Sport Pilot Flight Maneuvers and Practical Test Prep** focuses on your flight training and the FAA practical test, just as this book focuses on the FAA knowledge test. **Pilot Handbook** is a complete pilot ground school text in outline format with many diagrams for ease in understanding.

Save time, money, and frustration -- order both books today! Call us, order online, or use the order form on page 327. Please bring Gleim books to the attention of flight instructors, fixed base operators, and others with a potential interest in flying. Wide distribution of these books and increased interest in flying depend on your assistance, good word, etc. Thank you.

NOTE: ANSWER DISCREPANCIES and UPDATES

Our answers have been carefully researched and reviewed. Inevitably, there will be differences with competitors' books and even the FAA. If necessary, we will develop an UPDATE for *Sport Pilot FAA Knowledge Test*. Send an email to update@gleim.com as described above, and visit our website for the latest updates and information on all of our products. Updates for this 2014 edition will be available until the next edition is published. To continue providing our customers with first-rate service, we request that questions about our materials be sent to us via email to aviation@gleim.com. The appropriate staff member will give each question thorough consideration and a prompt response. Questions concerning orders, prices, shipments, or payments will be handled via telephone by our competent and courteous customer service staff.

TABLE OF CONTENTS

NOTE: This book covers everything you need to know to PASS your FAA sport pilot airplane knowledge test. Study Units 1-10 are essential for those learning to fly any category of aircraft. Study Units 11-14 are also essential for those learning to fly airplanes. Those learning to fly other categories of light-sport aircraft (e.g., gliders, rotorcraft, lighter-than-air, powered parachutes, and weight-shift-control) absolutely must obtain additional ground school study materials specific to their LSA category.

The FAA no longer releases the complete database of test questions to the public. Instead, sample questions are released on the Airmen Testing page of the FAA website on a quarterly basis. These questions are similar to the actual test questions, but they are not exact matches.

Gleim utilizes customer feedback and FAA publications to create additional sample questions that closely represent the topical coverage of each FAA knowledge test. In order to do well on the knowledge test, you must study the Gleim outlines in this book, answer all the questions under exam conditions (i.e., without looking at the answers first), and develop an understanding of the topics addressed. You should not simply memorize questions and answers. This will not prepare you for your FAA knowledge test, and it will not help you develop the knowledge you need to safely operate an aircraft.

Always refer to the Gleim update service (www.gleim.com/updates) to ensure you have the latest information that is available. If you see topics covered on your FAA knowledge test that are not contained in this book, please contact us at aviation@gleim.com to report your experience and help us fine-tune our test preparation materials.

Thank you!

PREFACE

The primary purpose of this book is to provide you with the easiest, fastest, and least expensive means of passing the Sport Pilot Airplane FAA knowledge test. The publicly released FAA knowledge test bank does **not** have questions grouped together by topic. We have organized them for you. We have

1. Reproduced all previously released knowledge test questions published by the FAA. We have also included over 250 additional similar test questions, which we believe may appear in some form on your knowledge test.
2. Reordered the questions into logical topics.
3. Organized the testable topics into 14 study units.
4. Explained the answer immediately to the right of each question.
5. Provided an easy-to-study outline of exactly what you need to know (and no more) at the beginning of each study unit.

Accordingly, you can thoroughly prepare for the FAA pilot knowledge test by

1. Studying the brief outlines at the beginning of each study unit.
2. Answering the question on the left side of each page while covering up the answer explanations on the right side of each page.
3. Reading the answer explanation for each question that you answer incorrectly or have difficulty answering.
4. Facilitating this Gleim process with our **FAA Test Prep Online**. Our software allows you to emulate the FAA test (CATS or PSI/LaserGrade). By practicing answering questions on a computer, you will become at ease with the computer testing process and have the confidence to PASS. See pages 17 through 20.
5. Using our **Online Ground School**, which provides you with our outlines, practice problems, and sample tests. This course is easily accessible through the Internet. Also, we give you a money-back guarantee with our **Online Ground School**. If you are unsuccessful, you get your money back! See pages 15 and 16.

Additionally, this book will introduce our entire series of pilot training texts, which use the same presentation method: outlines, illustrations, questions, and answer explanations. For example, **Pilot Handbook** is a textbook of aeronautical knowledge presented in easy-to-use outline format, with many charts, diagrams, figures, etc., included. While this book contains only the material needed to pass the FAA pilot knowledge test, **Pilot Handbook** contains the textbook knowledge required to be a safe and proficient pilot.

Many books create additional work for the user. In contrast, this book and its companion, **Sport Pilot Flight Maneuvers and Practical Test Prep**, facilitate your effort. The outline/illustration format, type styles, and spacing are designed to improve readability. Concepts are often presented as phrases rather than as complete sentences – similar to notes that you would take in a class lecture.

We are confident this book, **FAA Test Prep Online**, and/or **Online Ground School** will facilitate speedy completion of your knowledge test. We also wish you the very best as you complete your sport pilot certificate, in subsequent flying, and in obtaining additional ratings and certificates.

Enjoy Flying Safely!
Irvin N. Gleim
Garrett W. Gleim
July 2013

INTRODUCTION: THE FAA PILOT KNOWLEDGE TEST

The beginning of this Introduction explains how to obtain a sport pilot certificate, and it explains the content and procedures of the Federal Aviation Administration (FAA) knowledge test, including how to take the test at a computer testing center. The remainder of this Introduction discusses and illustrates the Gleim **Online Ground School** and **FAA Test Prep Online**. Achieving a sport pilot certificate is fun. Begin today!

Sport Pilot FAA Knowledge Test is one of five books contained in the Gleim **Sport Pilot Kit**. The other four books are

1. *Sport Pilot Flight Maneuvers and Practical Test Prep*
2. *Sport Pilot Syllabus*
3. *Pilot Handbook*
4. *FAR/AIM*

Sport Pilot Flight Maneuvers and Practical Test Prep presents each flight maneuver you will perform in outline/illustration format so you will know what to expect and what to do before each flight lesson. This book will thoroughly prepare you to complete your FAA practical (flight) test confidently and successfully.

Sport Pilot Syllabus is a step-by-step syllabus of ground and flight training lesson plans for your sport pilot training.

Pilot Handbook is a complete pilot reference book that combines over 100 FAA books and documents, including *AIM*, FARs, ACs, and much more. Aerodynamics, airplane systems, airspace, and navigation are among the topics explained in *Pilot Handbook*. This book, more than any other, will help make you a better and more proficient pilot.

FAR/AIM is an essential part of every pilot's library. The Gleim *FAR/AIM* is an easy-to-read reference book containing all of the Federal Aviation Regulations (FARs) applicable to general aviation flying, plus the full text of the FAA's *Aeronautical Information Manual (AIM)*.

The Gleim *Aviation Weather and Weather Services* is not included in the **Sport Pilot Kit**, but you may want to purchase it if you do not already have it. This book combines all of the information from the FAA's *Aviation Weather* (AC 00-6), *Aviation Weather Services* (AC 00-45), and numerous FAA publications into one easy-to-understand book. It will help you study all aspects of aviation weather and provide you with a single reference book.

WHAT IS A SPORT PILOT CERTIFICATE?

A sport pilot certificate is much like a driver's license. A sport pilot certificate will allow you to fly an airplane and carry a passenger and baggage, although not for compensation or hire. However, operating expenses may be shared with your passenger. The certificate, which is plastic (similar to a driver's license), is sent to you by the FAA upon satisfactory completion of your training program, a pilot knowledge test, and a practical test. A sample sport pilot certificate is reproduced below.

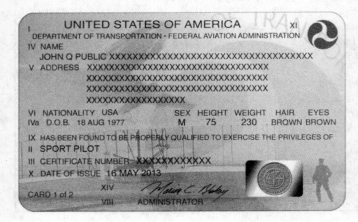 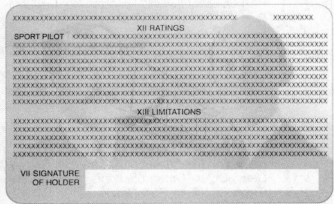

REQUIREMENTS TO OBTAIN A SPORT PILOT CERTIFICATE

1. Be at least 17 years of age (16 years of age to operate a glider or balloon).

2. Be able to read, write, and understand English (certificates with operating limitations may be available for medically related deficiencies).

3. Possess a valid state driver's license or, if required, an FAA medical certificate.

   a. The sport pilot rule states that if an individual's most recent application for an FAA medical certificate has been denied, suspended, or revoked, that person may not use a driver's license as a medical certificate until the denial is cleared from the record.

   b. Additionally, Federal Aviation Regulation 61.53 requires every pilot, from sport pilot to airline transport pilot, to be able to truthfully state before each flight that (s)he is medically fit to operate the aircraft in a safe manner. As pilots, it is our responsibility to ensure that our current medical health in no way jeopardizes the safety of a flight.

   c. Your state driver's license is valid as long as you comply with the laws of your state.

      1) Most states require you to stop driving and notify the state department of motor vehicles if you have a significant change in your health. The more common medical issues that require suspension of driving privileges are

         a) Vision changes
         b) Loss of consciousness
         c) Impairment of judgment
         d) Loss of motor function
         e) Seizures or blackouts

      2) If your license is suspended or revoked due to traffic violations or alcohol/drug-related convictions, you cannot use your state driver's license to establish medical fitness; you would have to possess a third-class medical certificate.

4. Obtain an FAA student pilot certificate. A student pilot certificate can be issued by either an aviation medical examiner (AME) as part of a medical certificate, an aviation safety inspector (ASI), or a designated pilot examiner (DPE).

   a. Your CFI or FBO will be able to recommend the most convenient way of obtaining a student pilot certificate.

   b. Additionally, you may contact your regional FAA Flight Standards District Office (FSDO) for assistance locating AMEs, ASIs, and DPEs in your area, and ask for their contact information. To find the phone numbers of your regional FAA FSDO, visit the FAA's FSDO website at www.faa.gov/about/office_org/field_offices/fsdo.

   c. Contact the AME, ASI, or DPE and schedule an appointment to obtain a student pilot certificate for sport pilot training. Bring the following documents and records to the appointment:

      1) A completed and signed Airman Certificate and/or Rating Application-Sport Pilot (FAA Form 8710-11). The form should be filled out in ink or typewritten.

      2) An acceptable form of photo identification, e.g., a valid driver's license.

5. Receive and log ground training from an authorized instructor or complete a home-study course (such as studying this book, *Sport Pilot Flight Maneuvers and Practical Test Prep*, and **Pilot Handbook** or using the Gleim **Online Ground School**) to learn

   a. *Applicable Federal Aviation Regulations ... that relate to sport pilot privileges, limitations, and flight operations*

   b. *Accident reporting requirements of the National Transportation Safety Board*

   c. *Use of the applicable portions of the Aeronautical Information Manual and FAA ACs (advisory circulars)*

   d. *Use of aeronautical charts for VFR navigation using pilotage, dead reckoning, and navigation systems*

   e. *Recognition of critical weather situations from the ground and in flight, windshear avoidance, and the procurement and use of aeronautical weather reports and forecasts*

   f. *Safe and efficient operation of aircraft, including collision avoidance, and recognition and avoidance of wake turbulence*

   g. *Effects of density altitude on takeoff and climb performance*

   h. *Weight and balance computations*

   i. *Principles of aerodynamics, powerplants, and aircraft systems*

   j. *Stall awareness, spin entry, spins, and spin recovery techniques, as applicable*

   k. *Aeronautical decision making and risk management*

   l. *Preflight action that includes*

      1) *How to obtain information on runway lengths at airports of intended use, data on takeoff and landing distances, weather reports and forecasts, and fuel requirements*

      2) *How to plan for alternatives if the flight cannot be completed or delays are encountered*

6. Pass a knowledge test with a score of 70% or better. All FAA tests are administered at FAA-designated computer testing centers. The sport pilot knowledge test has a 2-hour time limit and consists of 40 multiple-choice questions selected from the questions in the FAA's sport pilot knowledge test bank. The FAA's published sport pilot questions, along with our own similar questions, are reproduced in this book with complete explanations.

7. Accumulate flight experience (FAR 61.313). Use the table on the following pages to determine how much flight experience you will need for the specific type of aircraft you will be applying for.

If you are applying for a sport pilot certificate with...	Then you must log at least...	Which must include at least...
(a) Airplane category and single-engine land or sea class privileges,	(1) 20 hours of flight time, including at least 15 hours of flight training from an authorized instructor in a single-engine airplane and at least 5 hours of solo flight training in the areas of operation listed in Sec. 61.311,	(i) 2 hours of cross-country flight training, (ii) 10 takeoffs and landings to a full stop (with each landing involving a flight in the traffic pattern) at an airport; (iii) One solo cross-country flight of at least 75 nautical miles total distance, with a full-stop landing at a minimum of two points and one segment of the flight consisting of a straight-line distance of at least 25 nautical miles between the takeoff and landing locations, and (iv) 2 hours of flight training with an authorized instructor on those areas of operation specified in Sec. 61.311 in preparation for the practical test within the preceding 2 calendar months from the month of the test.
(b) Glider category privileges, and you have not logged at least 20 hours of flight time in a heavier-than-air aircraft,	(1) 10 hours of flight time in a glider, including 10 flights in a glider receiving flight training from an authorized instructor and at least 2 hours of solo flight training in the areas of operation listed in Sec. 61.311,	(i) Five solo launches and landings, and (ii) At least 3 training flights with an authorized instructor on those areas of operation specified in Sec. 61.311 in preparation for the practical test within the preceding 2 calendar months from the month of the test.
(c) Glider category privileges, and you have logged 20 hours flight time in a heavier-than-air aircraft,	(1) 3 hours of flight time in a glider, including five flights in a glider while receiving flight training from an authorized instructor and at least 1 hour of solo flight training in the areas of operation listed in Sec. 61.311,	(i) Three solo launches and landings, and (ii) At least 3 training flights with an authorized instructor on those areas of operation specified in Sec. 61.311 in preparation for the practical test within the preceding 2 calendar months from the month of the test.
(d) Rotorcraft category and gyroplane class privileges,	(1) 20 hours of flight time, including 15 hours of flight training from an authorized instructor in a gyroplane and at least 5 hours of solo flight training in the areas of operation listed in Sec. 61.311,	(i) 2 hours of cross-country flight training, (ii) 10 takeoffs and landings to a full stop (with each landing involving a flight in the traffic pattern) at an airport, (iii) One solo cross-country flight of at least 50 nautical miles total distance, with a full-stop landing at a minimum of two points, and one segment of the flight consisting of a straight-line distance of at least 25 nautical miles between the takeoff and landing locations, and (iv) 2 hours of flight training with an authorized instructor on those areas of operation specified in Sec. 61.311 in preparation for the practical test within the preceding 2 calendar months from the month of the test.
(e) Lighter-than-air category and airship class privileges,	(1) 20 hours of flight time, including 15 hours of flight training from an authorized instructor in an airship and at least 3 hours performing the duties of pilot in command in an airship with an authorized instructor in the areas of operation listed in Sec. 61.311,	(i) 2 hours of cross-country flight training, (ii) Three takeoffs and landings to a full stop (with each landing involving a flight in the traffic pattern) at an airport, (iii) One cross-country flight of at least 25 nautical miles between the takeoff and landing locations, and (iv) 2 hours of flight training with an authorized instructor on those areas of operation specified in Sec. 61.311 in preparation for the practical test within the preceding 2 calendar months from the month of the test.
(f) Lighter-than-air category and balloon class privileges,	(1) 7 hours of flight time in a balloon, including three flights with an authorized instructor and one flight performing the duties of pilot in command in a balloon with an authorized instructor in the areas of operation listed in Sec. 61.311,	(i) 2 hours of cross-country flight training, and (ii) 1 hours of flight training with an authorized instructor on those areas of operation specified in Sec. 61.311 in preparation for the practical test within the preceding 2 calendar months from the month of the test.

If you are applying for a sport pilot certificate with...	Then you must log at least...	Which must include at least...
(g) Powered parachute category land or sea class privileges,	(1) 12 hours of flight time in a powered parachute, including 10 hours of flight training from an authorized instructor in a powered parachute, and at least 2 hours of solo flight training in the areas of operation listed in Sec. 61.311,	(i) 1 hour of cross-country flight training, (ii) 20 takeoffs and landings to a full stop in a powered parachute with each landing involving flight in the traffic pattern at an airport; (iii) 10 solo takeoffs and landings to a full stop (with each landing involving a flight in the traffic pattern) at an airport, (iv) One solo flight with a landing at a different airport and one segment of the flight consisting of a straight-line distance of at least 10 nautical miles between takeoff and landing locations, and (v) 1 hours of flight training with an authorized instructor on those areas of operation specified in Sec. 61.311 in preparation for the practical test within the preceding 2 calendar months from the month of the test.
(h) Weight-shift-control aircraft category land or sea class privileges,	(1) 20 hours of flight time, including 15 hours of flight training from an authorized instructor in a weight-shift-control aircraft and at least 5 hours of solo flight training in the areas of operation listed in Sec. 61.311,	(i) 2 hours of cross-country flight training; (ii) 10 takeoffs and landings to a full stop (with each landing involving a flight in the traffic pattern) at an airport, (iii) One solo cross-country flight of at least 50 nautical miles total distance, with a full-stop landing at a minimum of two points, and one segment of the flight consisting of a straight-line distance of at least 25 nautical miles between takeoff and landing locations, and (iv) 2 hours of flight training with an authorized instructor on those areas of operation specified in Sec. 61.311 in preparation for the practical test within the preceding 2 calendar months from the month of the test.

8. Receive flight instruction and demonstrate skill (FAR 61.311).

   a. Obtain a logbook sign-off by your CFI on the following areas of operations:

      1) *Preflight preparation*
      2) *Preflight procedures*
      3) *Airport, seaplane base, and gliderport operations, as applicable*
      4) *Takeoffs (or launches), landings, and go-arounds*
      5) *Performance maneuvers and, for gliders, performance speeds*
      6) *Ground reference maneuvers (not applicable to gliders or balloons)*
      7) *Soaring techniques (applicable only to gliders)*
      8) *Navigation*
      9) *Slow flight and stalls (as appropriate)*
      10) *Emergency operations*
      11) *Postflight procedures*

9. Successfully complete a practical (flight) test, which will be given as a final exam by an FAA inspector or designated pilot examiner. The practical test will be conducted as specified in the FAA's Sport Pilot Practical Test Standards (FAA-S-8081-29).

   a. FAA inspectors are FAA employees and do not charge for their services.

   b. FAA-designated pilot examiners are proficient, experienced flight instructors and pilots who are authorized by the FAA to conduct practical tests. They do charge a fee.

   c. The FAA's Sport Pilot Practical Test Standards–Airplane are outlined and reprinted in the Gleim **Sport Pilot Flight Maneuvers and Practical Test Prep** book.

FAA PILOT KNOWLEDGE TEST

1. This book is designed to help you prepare for and pass the Sport Pilot Airplane (SPA) FAA Knowledge Test, which consists of 40 questions and has a time limit of 2 hours.

2. The FAA legends and figures are in a book titled *Computer Testing Supplement for Sport Pilot*, which you will be given to use at the time of your test.

    a. For the purpose of test preparation, all of the FAA legends and figures are reproduced in this book.

3. In an effort to develop better questions, the FAA frequently **pretests** questions on knowledge tests by adding up to five "pretest" questions. The pretest questions will not be graded.

    a. You will NOT know which questions are real and which are pretest, so you must attempt to answer all questions correctly.

    b. When you notice a question NOT covered by Gleim, it might be a pretest question.

        1) We want to know about each pretest question you see.

        2) Please email (aviation@gleim.com) or call (800-874-5346) with your recollection of any possible pretest questions so we may improve our efforts to prepare future pilots.

FAA PILOT KNOWLEDGE TEST QUESTION BANK

In an effort to keep applicants from simply memorizing test questions, the FAA does not currently disclose all the questions you might see on your FAA knowledge test. We encourage you to take the time to fully learn and understand the concepts explained in the knowledge transfer outlines contained in this book. Using this book or other Gleim test preparation material to merely memorize the questions and answers is unwise, unproductive, and will not ensure your success on your FAA knowledge test. Memorization also greatly reduces the amount of information you will actually learn during your study.

The questions and answers provided in this book include all previously released FAA questions in addition to questions developed from current FAA reference materials that closely approximate the types of questions you should see on your knowledge test. We are confident that by studying our knowledge transfer outlines, answering our questions under exam conditions, and not relying on rote memorization, you will be able to successfully pass your FAA knowledge test and begin learning to become a safe and competent pilot.

FAA QUESTIONS WITH TYPOGRAPHICAL ERRORS

Occasionally, FAA test questions contain typographical errors such that there is no correct answer. The FAA test development process involves many steps and people and, as you would expect, glitches occur in the system that are beyond the control of any one person. We indicate "best" rather than correct answers for some questions. Use these best answers for the indicated questions.

Note that the FAA corrects (rewrites) defective questions as they are discovered; these changes are explained in our updates--see page iv. However, problems due to faulty or out-of-date figures printed in the FAA Computer Testing Supplements are expensive to correct. Thus, it is important to carefully study questions that are noted to have a best answer in this book. Even though the best answer may not be completely correct, you should select it when taking your test.

REORGANIZATION OF FAA QUESTIONS

1. In the public FAA knowledge test question bank releases, the questions are **not** grouped together by topic; i.e., they appear to be presented randomly.

    a. We have reorganized and renumbered the questions into study units and subunits.

2. Pages 312 through 318 contain a list of all the questions in FAA learning statement code order, with cross-references to the study units and question numbers in this book.

    a. For example, question 14-1 is assigned the code PLT005, which means it is found in Study Unit 14 as question 1 in this book and is covered under the FAA learning statement, "Calculate aircraft performance - density altitude."

HOW TO PREPARE FOR THE FAA PILOT KNOWLEDGE TEST

1. Begin by carefully reading the rest of this Introduction. You need to have a complete understanding of the examination process prior to initiating your study. This knowledge will make your studying more efficient.

2. After you have spent an hour analyzing this Introduction, set up a study schedule, including a target date for taking your knowledge test.

    a. Do not let the study process drag on and become discouraging; i.e., the quicker the better.

    b. Consider enrolling in an organized ground school course, like the Gleim **Online Ground School**, or one held at your local FBO, community college, etc.

    c. Determine where and when you are going to take your knowledge test.

3. Work through each of Study Units 1 through 14.

    a. All previously released questions in the FAA's sport pilot knowledge test question bank that are applicable to airplanes have been grouped into the following 14 categories, which are the titles of Study Units 1 through 14:

       Study Unit 1: Airports
       Study Unit 2: Airspace
       Study Unit 3: Federal Aviation Regulations – FAR Parts 1 through 71
       Study Unit 4: Federal Aviation Regulations – FAR Parts 91.3 through 91.131
       Study Unit 5: Federal Aviation Regulations – FAR Parts 91.155 through 91.417
                      and NTSB Part 830
       Study Unit 6: Aeromedical Factors and Aeronautical Decision Making (ADM)
       Study Unit 7: Aviation Weather
       Study Unit 8: Weather Services
       Study Unit 9: Sectional Charts and Airspace
       Study Unit 10: Navigation and Preflight Preparation
       Study Unit 11: Airplanes and Aerodynamics
       Study Unit 12: Airplane Instruments
       Study Unit 13: Airplane Engines and Systems
       Study Unit 14: Airplane Performance and Weight and Balance

    b. Within each of the study units listed, questions relating to the same subtopic (e.g., aircraft navigation, stalls, carburetor heat, etc.) are grouped together to facilitate your study program. Each subtopic is called a subunit.

      c.   To the right of each question, we present

         1)   The correct answer

         2)   The appropriate source document for the answer explanation

A/FD	*Airport/Facility Directory*	AWS	*Aviation Weather Services*
AAH	*Advanced Avionics Handbook*	FAR	*Federal Aviation Regulations*
AC	*Advisory Circular*	Fl Comp	*Flight Computer*
ACL	*Aeronautical Chart Legend*	IFH	*Instrument Flying Handbook*
AFH	*Airplane Flying Handbook*	NTSB	*National Transportation Safety Board*
AIM	*Aeronautical Information Manual*		*Regulations*
AvW	*Aviation Weather*	PHAK	*Pilot's Handbook of Aeronautical Knowledge*
AWBH	*Aircraft Weight and Balance Handbook*		

           a)   The codes may refer to an entire document, such as an advisory circular, or to a particular chapter or subsection of a larger document.

               i)   See page 319 for a complete list of abbreviations and acronyms used in this book.

         3)   A comprehensive answer explanation, including

           a)   A discussion of the correct answer or concept

           b)   An explanation of why the other two answer choices are incorrect

4.   Each study unit begins with a list of its subunit titles. The number after each title is the number of questions that cover the information in that subunit. The two numbers following the number of questions are the page numbers on which the outline and the questions for that particular subunit begin, respectively.

5.   Begin by studying the outlines slowly and carefully. The outlines in this part of the book are very brief and have only one purpose: to help you pass the FAA knowledge test.

      a.   **CAUTION:** The **sole purpose** of this book is to expedite your passing the FAA knowledge test for the sport pilot certificate. Accordingly, all extraneous material (i.e., not directly tested on the FAA knowledge test) is omitted, even though much more information and knowledge are necessary to be proficient and fly safely. This additional material is presented in two related Gleim books: *Sport Pilot Flight Maneuvers and Practical Test Prep* and *Pilot Handbook*.

6.   Next, answer the questions under exam conditions. Cover the answer explanations on the right side of each page with a piece of paper while you answer the questions.

      a.   Remember, it is very important to the learning (and understanding) process that you honestly commit yourself to an answer. If you are wrong, your memory will be reinforced by having discovered your error. Therefore, it is crucial to cover up the answer and make an honest attempt to answer the question before reading the answer.

      b.   Study the answer explanation for each question that you answer incorrectly, do not understand, or have difficulty with.

      c.   Use our **Online Ground School** or **FAA Test Prep Online** to ensure that you do not refer to answers before committing to one AND to simulate actual computer testing center exam conditions.

      d.   Go to www.gleim.com/OGS to view our **Online Ground School**. It is a structured course to assist those who have trouble sitting down to books and software.

7.   Note that this test book contains questions grouped by topic. Thus, some questions may appear repetitive, while others may be duplicates or near-duplicates. Accordingly, do not work question after question (i.e., waste time and effort) if you are already conversant with a topic and the type of questions asked.

8. As you move through study units, you may need further explanation or clarification of certain topics. You may wish to obtain and use the following Gleim books described on page 1:

   a. *Sport Pilot Flight Maneuvers and Practical Test Prep*
   b. *Pilot Handbook*
   c. *Aviation Weather and Weather Services*

9. Keep track of your work. As you complete a subunit, grade yourself with an A, B, C, or ? (use a ? if you need help on the subject) next to the subunit title at the front of the respective study unit.

   a. The A, B, C, or ? is your self-evaluation of your comprehension of the material in that subunit and your ability to answer the questions.

      A means a good understanding.
      B means a fair understanding.
      C means a shaky understanding.
      ? means to ask your CFI or others about the material and/or questions, and read the pertinent sections in *Sport Pilot Flight Maneuvers and Practical Test Prep* and/or *Pilot Handbook*.

   b. This procedure will provide you with the ability to quickly see (by looking at the first page of each study unit) how much studying you have done (and how much remains) and how well you have done.

   c. This procedure will also facilitate review. You can spend more time on the subunits that were more difficult for you.

   d. **FAA Test Prep Online** provides you with your historical performance data.

Follow the suggestions given throughout this Introduction and you will have no trouble passing the FAA knowledge test the first time you take it.

With this overview of exam requirements, you are ready to begin the easy-to-study outlines and rearranged questions with answers to build your knowledge and confidence and PASS THE FAA's SPORT PILOT AIRPLANE KNOWLEDGE TEST.

The feedback we receive from users indicates that our materials reduce anxiety, improve FAA test scores, and build knowledge. Studying for each test becomes a useful step toward advanced certificates and ratings.

MULTIPLE-CHOICE QUESTION-ANSWERING TECHNIQUE

Because the sport pilot knowledge test has a set number of questions (40) and a set time limit (2 hours), you can plan your test-taking session to ensure that you leave yourself enough time to answer each question with relative certainty. The following steps will help you move through the knowledge test efficiently and produce better test results.

1. **Budget your time.** We make this point with emphasis. Just as you would fill up your gas tank prior to reaching empty, so too should you finish your exam before time expires.

   a. If you utilize the entire 2-hour time limit, that allows you 3 minutes per question.

   b. If you are adequately prepared for the test, you should finish it within 45-60 minutes.

      1) Use any extra time you have to review questions that you are not sure about, cross-country planning questions with multiple steps and calculations, and similar questions in your exam that may help you answer other questions.

   c. Time yourself when completing study sessions in this book and/or review your time investment reports from the Gleim **FAA Test Prep Online** to track your progress and adherence to the time limit and your own personal time allocation budget.

2. **Answer the questions in consecutive order.**

   a. Do **not** agonize over any one item. Stay within your time budget.

      1) We suggest that you skip cross-country planning questions and other similarly involved computational questions on your first pass through the exam. Come back to them after you have been through the entire test once.

   b. Mark any questions you are unsure of and return to them later as time allows.

      1) Once you initiate test grading, you will no longer be able to review/change any answers.

   c. Never leave a multiple-choice question unanswered. Make your best educated guess in the time allowed.

      1) Your score is based on the number of correct responses. You will not be penalized for guessing incorrectly.

3. **For each multiple-choice question,**

   a. **Try to ignore the answer choices.** Do not allow the answer choices to affect your reading of the question.

      1) If three answer choices are presented, two of them are incorrect. These choices are called **distractors** for good reason. Often, distractors are written to appear correct at first glance until further analysis.

      2) In computational items, the distractors are carefully calculated such that they are the result of making common mistakes. Be careful, and double-check your computations to the extent that time permits.

   b. **Read the question carefully** to determine the precise requirement.

      1) Focusing on what is required enables you to ignore extraneous information, to focus on the relevant facts, and to proceed directly to determining the correct answer.

         a) Be especially careful to note when the requirement is an **exception**; e.g., "Which of the following is **not** a type of hypoxia?"

   c. **Determine the correct answer** before looking at the answer choices.

      1) Mentally note what you believe the correct response is before ever glancing at the available answer choices.

   d. **Read the answer choices carefully.**

      1) Even if the first answer appears to be the correct choice, do **not** skip the remaining answer choices. Questions often require the "best" answer of the choices provided. Thus, each choice requires your consideration.

      2) Treat each answer choice as a true/false question as you analyze it. Is the statement asserted in the answer choice true or false?

   e. **Click on the best answer.**

      1) If you are uncertain, guess intelligently. Improve on your 33% chance of getting the correct answer with blind guessing.

      2) For many multiple-choice questions, at least one answer choice can be eliminated with minimal effort, thereby increasing your educated guess to a 50-50 proposition.

4. After you have been through all the questions in the test, consult the question status list to determine which questions are unanswered and which are marked for review.

   a. Go back to the marked questions and finalize your answer choices.
   b. Verify that all questions have been answered.

5. **If you don't know the answer,**

    a.   Again, guess; but make it an educated guess by selecting the best possible answer.

        1)   Rule out answers that you think are incorrect.

        2)   Speculate on what the FAA is looking for and/or the rationale behind the question.

        3)   Select the best answer or guess between equally appealing answers. Your first guess is usually the most intuitive. If you cannot make an educated guess, re-read the stem and each answer choice and pick the best or most intuitive answer. It's just a guess!

    b.   Avoid lingering on any question for too long. Remember your time budget and the overall test time limit.

SIMULATED FAA PRACTICE TEST

Appendix A, "Sport Pilot Practice Test," beginning on page 291, allows you to practice taking the FAA knowledge test without the answers next to the questions. This test has 40 questions, randomly selected from the questions in our sport pilot knowledge test bank. Topical coverage in this practice test is similar to that of the FAA knowledge test.

It is very important that you answer all 40 questions in one sitting. You should not consult the answers, especially when being referred to figures (charts, tables, etc.) throughout this book where the questions are answered and explained. Analyze your performance based on the answer key that follows the practice test.

Also rely on the Gleim **FAA Test Prep Online** to simulate actual computer testing conditions, including the screen layouts, instructions, etc., for CATS and PSI/LaserGrade.

For more information on the Gleim **FAA Test Prep Online**, see page 17.

AUTHORIZATION TO TAKE THE FAA PILOT KNOWLEDGE TEST

Before taking the sport pilot knowledge test, you must receive an endorsement from an authorized instructor who conducted the ground training or reviewed your home-study in the areas listed in item 5. on page 3, certifying that you are prepared to pass the knowledge test.

For your convenience, a standard authorization form for the sport pilot knowledge test is reproduced on page 325, which can be easily completed, signed by a flight or ground instructor, torn out, and taken to the test site.

Note that if you use the Gleim **FAA Test Prep Online** or **Online Ground School**, the program will generate an authorization signed in facsimile by Dr. Gleim that is accepted at all CATS and PSI/LaserGrade locations.

WHEN TO TAKE THE FAA PILOT KNOWLEDGE TEST

1.   You must be at least 15 years of age to take the sport pilot knowledge test.

2.   You must prepare for the test by successfully completing a ground instruction course, or by using this book as your self-developed home study course.

    a.   See "Authorization to Take the FAA Pilot Knowledge Test" above.

3.   Take the FAA knowledge test within 30 days of beginning your study.

    a.   Get the knowledge test behind you.

4.   Your practical test must follow within 24 months.

    a.   Otherwise, you will have to retake your knowledge test.

WHAT TO TAKE TO THE FAA PILOT KNOWLEDGE TEST

1. The same flight computer that you use to solve the test questions in this book, i.e., one you are familiar with and have used before

2. Navigational plotter

3. A pocket calculator you are familiar with and have used before (no instructional material for the calculator is allowed)

4. Authorization to take the knowledge test (see previous page and page 325)

5. Proper identification that contains your

    a. Photograph
    b. Signature
    c. Date of birth
    d. Actual residential address, if different from your mailing address

NOTE: Paper and pencils are supplied at the examination site.

COMPUTER TESTING CENTERS

The FAA has contracted with two computer testing services to administer FAA knowledge tests. Both of these computer testing services have testing centers throughout the country. To register for the knowledge test, call one of the computer testing services listed below or call one of their testing centers. You can find a location most convenient to you, get information regarding the cost to take the knowledge test, and confirm the time allowed for the test. When you register, you will pay the fee with a credit card. Information about these testing centers and telephone numbers can be found at www.gleim.com/testing_centers.

   CATS   (800) 947-4228   PSI/LaserGrade   (800) 211-2754

COMPUTER TESTING PROCEDURES

When you arrive at the testing center, you will be required to provide positive proof of identification and documentary evidence of your age. The identification must include your photograph, signature, and actual residential address if different from the mailing address. This information may be presented in more than one form of identification. Next, you will sign in on the testing center's daily log. Your signature on the logsheet certifies that, if this is a retest, you meet the applicable requirements (see "Failure on the FAA Pilot Knowledge Test" on page 14) and that you have not passed this test in the past 2 years. Finally, you will present your logbook endorsement or authorization form from your instructor, which authorizes you to take the test. A standard authorization form is provided on page 325 for your use. Both **FAA Test Prep Online** and **Online Ground School** generate an authorization signed in facsimile by Dr. Gleim that is accepted at all CATS and PSI/LaserGrade locations.

Next, you will be taken into the testing room and seated at a computer terminal. A person from the testing center will assist you in logging onto the system, and you will be asked to confirm your personal data (e.g., name, Social Security number, etc.). Then you will be prompted and given an online introduction to the computer testing system, and you will take a sample test. If you have used our **FAA Test Prep Online**, you will be conversant with the computer testing methodology and environment, and you will breeze through the sample test and begin the actual test soon after. You will be allowed 2 hours to complete the actual test, which equates to 3 minutes per question. Confirm the time permitted when you call the testing center to register. When you have completed your test, an Airman Computer Test Report will be printed out, validated (usually with an embossed seal), and given to you by a person from the testing center. Before you leave, you will be required to sign out on the testing center's daily log.

Each testing service has certain idiosyncrasies in its paperwork, scheduling, and telephone procedures as well as in its software. It is for this reason that our **FAA Test Prep Online** emulates both of the FAA-approved computer testing companies.

YOUR FAA PILOT KNOWLEDGE TEST REPORT

1. You will receive your FAA Pilot Knowledge Test Report upon completion of the test. An example test report is reproduced below.

    a. Note that you will receive only one grade as illustrated.
    b. The expiration date is the date by which you must take your FAA practical test.
    c. The report lists the FAA learning statement codes of the questions you missed so you can review the topics you missed prior to your practical test.

Federal Aviation Administration
Airman Computer Test Report

EXAM TITLE: Sport Pilot–Airplane

NAME: Jones David John

ID NUMBER: 123456789   TAKE: 1

DATE: 07/14/13   SCORE: 82   GRADE: Pass

....

Knowledge area codes in which questions were answered incorrectly. See appropriate FAA knowledge test study guide. A code may represent more than one incorrect response.

PLT023 PLT076 PLT334 PLT445

EXPIRATION DATE: 07/31/15

DO NOT LOSE THIS REPORT

....

Authorized instructor's statement (if applicable).

I have given Mr./Ms. _____ additional instruction in each subject area shown to be deficient and consider the applicant competent to pass the test.

Last _____ Initial _____ Cert. No. _____ Type _____

Signature _____

CTD's Embossed Seal

---

2. Use the FAA Listing of Learning Statement Codes on pages 309 through 311 to determine which topics you had difficulty with.

    a. Look them over and review them with your CFI so (s)he can certify that (s)he reviewed the deficient areas and found you competent in them when you take your practical test. Have your CFI sign off your deficiencies on the FAA Pilot Knowledge Test Report.

3. Keep your FAA Pilot Knowledge Test Report in a safe place because you must submit it to the FAA inspector/examiner when you take your practical test.

FAILURE ON THE FAA PILOT KNOWLEDGE TEST

1.   If you fail (score less than 70%) the knowledge test (which is virtually impossible if you follow the Gleim system), you may retake it after your instructor endorses the bottom of your FAA Pilot Knowledge Test Report certifying that you have received the necessary ground training to retake the test.

2.   Upon retaking the test, you will find that the procedure is the same except that you must also submit your FAA Pilot Knowledge Test Report indicating the previous failure to the computer testing center.

3.   Note that the pass rate on the sport pilot knowledge test is about 96%; i.e., less than 1 out of 10 fail the test initially. Reasons for failure include

   a.   Failure to study the material tested and mere memorization of correct answers. (Relevant study material is contained in the outlines at the beginning of Study Units 1 through 14 of this book.)

   b.   Failure to practice working through the questions under test conditions. (All of the previously released FAA questions appear in Study Units 1 through 14 of this book.)

   c.   Poor examination technique, such as misreading questions and not understanding the requirements.

   If this Gleim test book saves you time and frustration in preparing for the FAA sport pilot knowledge test, you should use the Gleim *Sport Pilot Flight Maneuvers and Practical Test Prep* book to prepare for the FAA practical test.

   Just as this book organizes and explains the knowledge needed to pass your FAA knowledge test, *Sport Pilot Flight Maneuvers and Practical Test Prep* will assist you in developing the competence and confidence to pass your FAA practical test.

   Also, flight maneuvers are quickly perfected when you understand exactly what to expect before you get into an airplane to practice the flight maneuvers. You must be ahead of (not behind) your CFI and your airplane. Our flight maneuvers books explain and illustrate all flight maneuvers so the maneuvers and their execution are intuitively appealing to you. Call (800) 874-5346 or visit www.gleim.com/aviation and order your books today!

GLEIM ONLINE GROUND SCHOOL

1. Gleim **Online Ground School (OGS)** course content is based on the Gleim Knowledge Test books, **FAA Test Prep Online**, FAA publications, and Gleim reference books. The delivery system is modeled on the Gleim FAA-approved online **Flight Instructor Refresher Course**.

   a. Online Ground School courses are available for

      1) Private Pilot
      2) Sport Pilot
      3) CFI/CGI
      4) FOI
      5) Instrument Pilot
      6) Commercial Pilot
      7) ATP
      8) Flight Engineer
      9) Canadian Certificate Conversion

   b. OGS courses are airplane-only and have lessons that correspond to the study units in the Gleim FAA Knowledge Test books.

   c. Each course contains study outlines that automatically reference current FAA publications, the appropriate knowledge test questions, FAA figures, and Gleim answer explanations.

   d. OGS is always up to date.

   e. Users achieve very high knowledge test scores and a near-100% pass rate.

   f. **Gleim Online Ground School is the most flexible course available!** Access your OGS personal classroom from any computer with Internet access--24 hours a day, 7 days a week. Your virtual classroom is never closed!

NUMBER	STUDY UNIT	STATUS	SCORE	TIME STARTED	TIME COMPLETED	A/V	OUTLINE	ACTION
1	Airports	Not Started	N/A	N/A	N/A			Start
2	Airspace	Not Started	N/A	N/A	N/A			Start
3	Federal Aviation Regulations - FAR Parts 1 through 71	Not Started	N/A	N/A	N/A			Start
4	Federal Aviation Regulations - FAR 91.3 through 91.131	Not Started	N/A	N/A	N/A			Start
5	Federal Aviation Regulations - FAR 91.155 through 91.417 and NTSB Part 830	Not Started	N/A	N/A	N/A			Start
	Stage Test #1	Not Started	N/A	N/A	N/A	N/A	N/A	
6	Aeromedical Factors and Aeronautical Decision Making (ADM)	Not Started	N/A	N/A	N/A			
7	Aviation Weather	Not Started	N/A	N/A	N/A			
8	Weather Services	Not Started	N/A	N/A	N/A			
9	Sectional Charts and Airspace	Not Started	N/A	N/A	N/A			
10	Navigation and Preflight Preparation	Not Started	N/A	N/A	N/A			
	Stage Test #2	Not Started	N/A	N/A	N/A	N/A	N/A	
11	Airplanes and Aerodynamics	Not Started	N/A	N/A	N/A			
12	Airplane Instruments	Not Started	N/A	N/A	N/A			
13	Airplane Engines and Systems	Not Started	N/A	N/A	N/A			
14	Airplane Performance and Weight and Balance	Not Started	N/A	N/A	N/A			
	Stage Test #3	Not Started	N/A	N/A	N/A	N/A	N/A	
	End-Of-Course Test	Not Started	N/A	N/A	N/A	N/A	N/A	
	Practice Test #1	Not Started	N/A	N/A	N/A	N/A	N/A	
	Practice Test #2	Not Started	N/A	N/A	N/A	N/A	N/A	
	Practice Test #3	Not Started	N/A	N/A	N/A	N/A	N/A	
	Practice Test #4	Not Started	N/A	N/A	N/A	N/A	N/A	
	Practice Test #5	Not Started	N/A	N/A	N/A	N/A	N/A	

g. **Save time and study only the material you need to know!** Gleim **Online Ground School** Certificate Selection will provide you with a customized study plan. You save time because unnecessary questions will be automatically eliminated.

h. **We are truly interactive. We help you focus on any weaker areas.** Answer explanations for wrong choices help you learn from your mistakes.

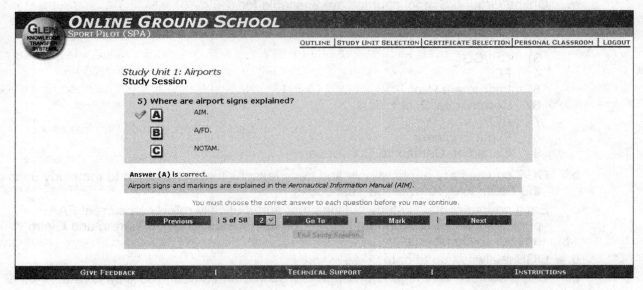

Register for Gleim Online Ground School today:

www.gleim.com/OGS

GLEIM FAA TEST PREP ONLINE

Computer testing is consistent with aviation's use of computers (e.g., DUATS, flight simulators, computerized cockpits, etc.). All FAA knowledge tests are administered by computer.

Computer testing is natural after computer study and computer-assisted instruction is a very efficient and effective method of study. The Gleim **FAA Test Prep Online** is designed to prepare you for computer testing because our software can simulate both CATS and PSI/LaserGrade. We make you comfortable with computer testing!

FAA Test Prep Online contains all of the questions in this book, context-sensitive outline material, and on-screen charts and figures. It allows you to choose either Study Mode or Test Mode.

In Study Mode, the software provides you with an explanation of each answer you choose (correct or incorrect). You design each Study Session:

Topic(s) and/or FAA learning statement codes you wish to cover	Questions marked and/or missed from last session -- test, study, or both
Number of questions	Questions marked and/or missed from all sessions -- test, study, or both
Order of questions -- FAA, Gleim, or random	Questions never seen, answered, or answered correctly
Order of answers to each question -- Gleim or random	

In Test Mode, you decide the format -- CATS or PSI/LaserGrade. When you finish your test, you can and should study the questions missed and access answer explanations. The software emulates the operation of FAA-approved computer testing companies. Thus, you have a complete understanding of how to take an FAA knowledge test and know exactly what to expect before you go to a computer testing center.

Visit www.gleim.com/testing_centers for a listing of all major testing center locations for CATS and PSI/LaserGrade. The Gleim **FAA Test Prep Online** is an all-in-one program designed to help anyone with a computer, Internet access, and an interest in flying pass the FAA knowledge tests.

Study Sessions and Test Sessions

Study Sessions give you immediate feedback on why your answer selection for a particular question is correct or incorrect and allow you to access the context-sensitive outline material that helps to explain concepts related to the question. Choose from several different question sources: all questions available for that library; questions from a certain topic (Gleim study units and subunits); questions that you missed or marked in the last sessions you created; questions that you have never seen, answered, or answered correctly; questions from certain FAA learning statement codes; etc. You can mix up the questions by selecting to randomize the question and/or answer order so that you do not memorize answer letters.

You may then grade your study sessions and track your study progress using the performance analysis charts and graphs. The Performance Analysis information helps you to focus on areas where you need the most improvement, saving you time in the overall study process. You may then want to go back and study questions that you missed in a previous session, or you may want to create a Study Session of questions that you marked in the previous session, and all of these options are made easy with **FAA Test Prep Online**'s Study Sessions.

After studying the outlines and questions in a Study Session, you can further test your skills with a Test Session. These sessions allow you to answer questions under actual testing conditions using one of the simulations of the major testing services. In a Test Session, you will not know which questions you have answered correctly until the session is graded.

Recommended Study Program

1. Start with Study Unit 1 and proceed through study units in chronological order. Follow the three-step process below.

    a. First, carefully study the Gleim Outline.

    b. Second, create a Study Session of all questions in the study unit. Answer and study all questions in the Study Session.

    c. Third, create a Test Session of all questions in the study unit. Answer all questions in the Test Session.

2. After each Study Session and Test Session, create a new Study Session from questions answered incorrectly. This is of critical importance to allow you to learn from your mistakes.

Example Question Screen

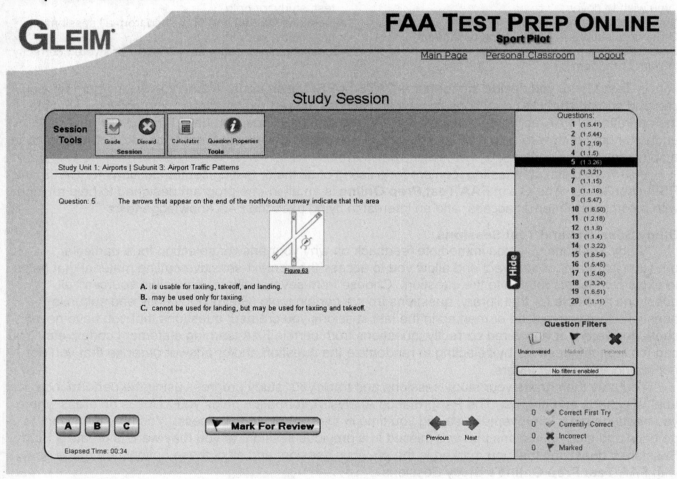

Practice Test

Take an exam in the actual testing environment of either of the major testing centers: CATS or PSI/LaserGrade. **FAA Test Prep Online** simulates the testing formats of these testing centers, making it easy for you to study questions under actual exam conditions. After studying with **FAA Test Prep Online**, you will know exactly what to expect when you go in to take your pilot knowledge test.

On-Screen Charts and Figures

One of the most convenient features of **FAA Test Prep Online** is the easily accessible on-screen charts and figures. Many of the questions refer to drawings, maps, charts, and other pictures that provide information to help answer the question. In **FAA Test Prep Online**, you can pull up any of these figures with the click of a button. You can increase or decrease the size of the images, and you may also use our drawing feature to calculate the true course between two given points (required only on the private pilot knowledge test).

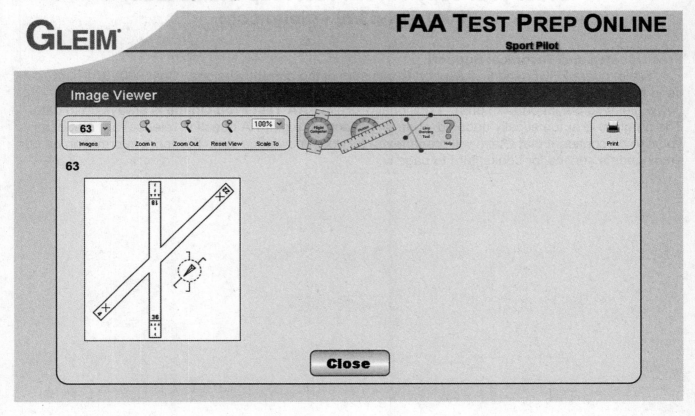

Instructor Sign-Off Sheets

FAA Test Prep Online is capable of generating an instructor sign-off for FAA knowledge tests that require one. This sign-off has been approved by the FAA and can be presented at the computer testing center as authorization to take your test--you do NOT need an additional endorsement from your instructor.

In order to obtain the instructor sign-off sheet for your test, you must first answer all relevant questions in **FAA Test Prep Online** correctly. Then, select "Sign-Off Sheets" under the "Additional Features" area on the Main page. If you have answered all of the required questions, the instructor sign-off sheet will appear for you to print. If you have not yet answered all required questions, a list of the unanswered questions, along with their location, will appear.

Order your copy of FAA Test Prep Online today
(800) 874-5346 • gleim.com

Free Updates and Technical Support

Gleim offers FREE technical support to all users of the current versions. Call (800) 874-5346, send an email to support@gleim.com, or fill out the technical support request form online (www.gleim.com/support/form.php). Additionally, Gleim **FAA Test Prep Online** is always up to date. The program is automatically updated when any changes (e.g., FAA question release) are made, so you can be confident that Gleim will prepare you for your knowledge test. For more information on our email update service for books, turn to page iv.

STUDY UNIT ONE
AIRPORTS

(8 pages of outline)

This study unit contains outlines of major concepts tested, sample test questions and answers regarding airports, and an explanation of each answer. The table of contents above lists each subunit within this study unit, the number of questions pertaining to that particular subunit, and the pages on which the outlines and questions begin, respectively.

CAUTION: Recall that the **sole purpose** of this book is to expedite your passing the FAA pilot knowledge test for the sport pilot certificate. Accordingly, all extraneous material (i.e., topics or regulations not directly tested on the FAA pilot knowledge test) is omitted, even though much more information and knowledge are necessary to fly safely. This additional material is presented in *Pilot Handbook* and *Sport Pilot Flight Maneuvers and Practical Test Prep*, available from Gleim Publications, Inc. See the order form on page 327.

1.1 RUNWAY MARKINGS

1. Airport signs and markings are explained in the *Aeronautical Information Manual (AIM)*.

2. The number at the beginning of each runway indicates its magnetic alignment divided by 10°; e.g., Runway 26 indicates 260° magnetic; Runway 9 indicates 090° magnetic.

3. A displaced threshold is a threshold (marked as a broad solid line across the runway) that is located at a point on the runway other than the designated beginning of the runway. The remainder of the runway, following the displaced threshold, is the landing portion of the runway.

   a. The paved area before the displaced threshold (marked by arrows) is available for taxiing, the landing rollout, and takeoff of aircraft.

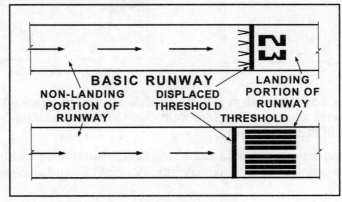

Figure A

4.   Chevrons mark any surface or area extending beyond the usable runway that appears usable but that, due to the nature of its structure, is unusable runway.

   a.   This area is not available for any use other than emergency overrun, not even taxiing.

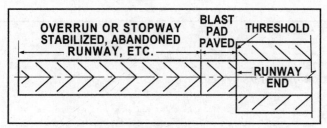

Figure B

5.   Closed runways are marked by an "X" on each runway end that is closed.

6.   **Runway hold position sign** (Figure C below). These signs are located at the holding position on taxiways that intersect a runway and on runways that intersect another runway (if runway is used for land and hold short operations or as a taxiway).

   a.   Runway hold position signs are used to alert pilots of the entrance to the runway, when clear of the runway, and to signal where the aircraft should be held short of the runway.

   b.   Hold position signs have white inscriptions on a red background.

   c.   They are placed adjacent to the **runway holding position markings** (four yellow lines, two solid, and two broken), which are painted on the taxiway or runway and carry out the same functions as hold position signs.

   d.   An aircraft exiting a runway is not clear of the runway until all parts of the aircraft have crossed the applicable holding position marking.

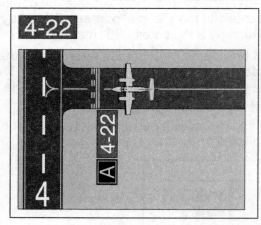

Figure C

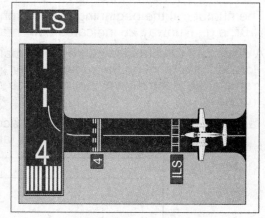

Figure D

7.   **ILS critical area boundary sign** (Figure D above). These signs are visible to aircraft leaving an ILS critical area. They are intended to provide another visual cue as to when the aircraft is clear of the critical area.

   a.   These signs are placed adjacent to the **ILS critical area holding position markings**, which are painted on the taxiway, and consist of a graphic representation of these markings.

8. **Taxiway location sign** (Figure E below). These signs identify the taxiway on which an aircraft is currently located.

    a. Figure E indicates that the aircraft is located on taxiway bravo.

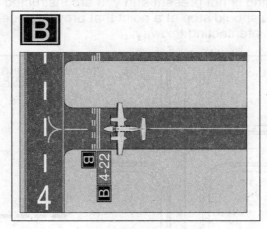

Figure E

9. **Taxiway direction signs** identify the designations of taxiways leading out of an intersection.

    a. An arrow next to each taxiway designation indicates the direction that an aircraft must turn in order to taxi onto that taxiway.

    b. These signs consist of black lettering on a yellow background.

10. **Taxiway ending markers** (Figure F below) feature bold yellow, angled stripes on a black background.

    a. These signs are typically located at the far end of an intersection to indicate that the taxiway does not continue beyond the point where the sign is installed.

Figure F

11. **Runway location sign** (Figure G below). These signs identify the runway on which an aircraft is currently located.

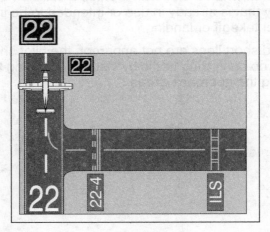

Figure G

12. **Holding position markings for taxiway/taxiway intersections** (Figure H below) consist of one dashed line extending across the width of the taxiway. They are installed on taxiways where Air Traffic Control (ATC) normally holds aircraft short of a taxiway intersection.

   a. When the marking is not present and you are instructed by ATC "hold short of (taxiway)," you should stop at a point that provides adequate clearance from an aircraft on the intersecting taxiway.

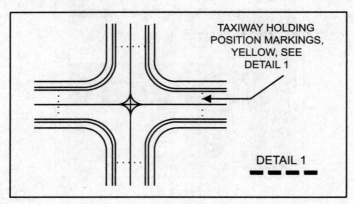

Figure H

13. **Vehicle roadway markings** (Figure I on the next page). These markings are used to define a pathway for vehicle operations in areas that are also intended for aircraft.

   a. Vehicle roadway markings consist of a white solid line to delineate each edge of the roadway and a dashed line to separate lanes within the edges of the roadway.

      1) An alternative to solid edge lines is the use of zipper markings (staggered lines).

14. **Runway incursions** are a special safety interest area with the FAA.

   a. A runway incursion exists when an aircraft, vehicle, person, or object on the ground creates a collision hazard or results in a loss of required separation with an aircraft taking off, intending to take off, landing, or intending to land.

   b. At an airport with an operating control tower, a pilot is considered to have initiated a runway incursion when the aircraft strays beyond a taxiway hold short line without first obtaining a specific clearance to do so from ATC.

      1) A runway incursion does not require that the airplane taxi onto the runway, only that it crosses the hold short line without prior clearance.

   c. At an airport without an operating control tower, a pilot is considered to have initiated a runway incursion when the aircraft creates a collision risk by taxiing too close to or onto a runway that is already in use or intended to be in use by another aircraft, for the purpose of takeoff or landing.

      1) If the hold short lines are not apparent, the pilot should clear the area to verify there is no conflicting traffic by visually scanning the full length of the runway, including the approach areas.

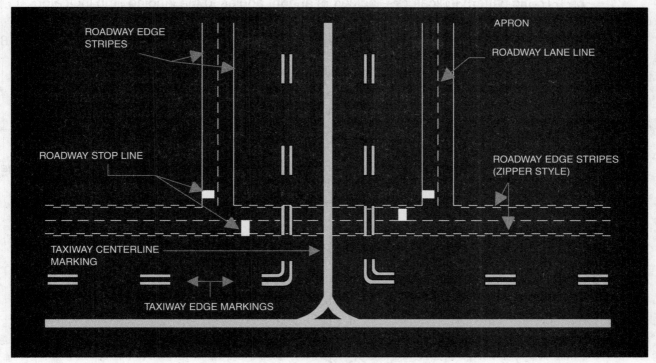

Figure I

1.2 AIRPORT BEACONS

1. Operation of the green and white rotating beacon at an airport located in Class D airspace during the day indicates that the weather is not VFR; i.e.,

    a. The visibility is less than 3 SM or
    b. The ceiling is less than 1,000 ft.

2. A lighted heliport may be identified by a green, yellow, and white rotating beacon.

3. Military airports are indicated by beacons with two white flashes between each green flash.

1.3 AIRPORT TRAFFIC PATTERNS

1. The segmented circle system provides traffic pattern information at airports without operating control towers. It consists of the

    a. Segmented circle – located in a position affording maximum visibility to pilots in the air and on the ground, and providing a centralized point for the other elements of the system
    b. Landing strip indicators – showing the alignment of landing runways (legs sticking out of the segmented circle)

    c. Traffic pattern indicators – indicators at right angles to the landing strip indicator showing the direction of turn from base to final

        1) In the figure below, Runways 22 and 36 use left traffic, while Runways 4 and 18 use right traffic.

        2) The "X" indicates that Runways 4 and 22 are closed.

        3) The area behind the displaced thresholds of Runways 18 and 36 (marked by arrows) can be used for taxiing and takeoff, but not for landing.

    d. Wind direction indicator – a wind cone, wind sock, or wind tee installed near the runways to indicate wind direction

        1) The large end of the wind cone/wind sock points into the wind as does the large end (cross bar) of the wind tree.

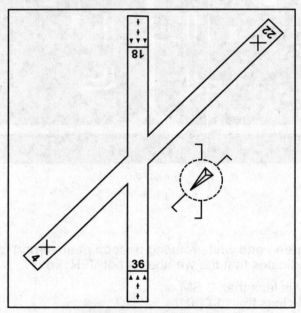

Figure 63 – Airport Diagram

    e. Landing direction indicator – a tetrahedron on a swivel installed when conditions at the airport warrant its use. It is used to indicate the direction of takeoffs and landings. It should be located at the center of a segmented circle and may be lighted for night operations.

        1) The small end points toward the direction in which a takeoff or landing should be made; i.e., the small end points into the wind.

2. If there is no segmented circle installed at the airport, traffic pattern indicators may be installed on or near the end of the runway.

3. Remember, you land

    a. In the same direction as the tip of the tetrahedron is pointing,

    b. As if you were flying out of the large (open) end of the wind cone, or

    c. Toward the cross-bar end of a wind "T" (visualize the "T" as an airplane with no nose, with the top of the "T" being the wings).

4. If you are approaching an airport without an operating control tower,

    a. You must turn to the left when landing unless visual displays advise otherwise.
    b. You must comply with any FAA traffic pattern for that airport when departing.

5. Entries into the traffic pattern while descending create collision hazards and should be avoided. Plan on arriving at the proper traffic pattern altitude prior to entering the traffic pattern.

6. Figure 54 on page 307 shows a segmented circle with wind cone and traffic pattern indicator. The FAA has not released any questions on this figure; however, you may encounter some on your knowledge test. To prepare for such questions, study the explanation with Figure 54 along with this subunit until you are familiar with the interpretation of each element in the figure.

1.4 VISUAL APPROACH SLOPE INDICATORS (VASI)

1. Visual approach slope indicators (VASI) are a system of lights used to provide visual descent information during an approach to landing.

2. The standard VASI consists of a two-barred tier of lights. You are

    a. Below the glide path if both light bars are red; i.e., "red means dead."
    b. On the glide path if the far (on top visually) lights are red and the near (on bottom visually) lights are white.
    c. Above the glide path if both light bars are white.

3. Remember, red over white (i.e., R before W alphabetically) is the desired sequence.

    a. White over red is impossible.

4. A tri-color VASI is a single light unit projecting three colors.

    a. The below glide path indicator is red.
    b. The above glide path indicator is amber.
    c. The on glide path indicator is green.

5. VASI only projects a glide path. It has no bearing on runway alignment.

6. On a precision approach path indicator (PAPI),

    a. Low is four red lights (less than 2.5°).
    b. Slightly low is one white and three reds (2.8°).
    c. On glide path is two whites and two reds (3.0°).
    d. Slightly high is three whites and one red (3.2°).
    e. High is four whites (more than 3.5°).

7. On a pulsating approach slope indicator (a VASI with flashing/pulsating signals),

    a. Low is a pulsating red.
    b. On glide path is a steady white or alternating red/white (depending on model).
    c. High is a pulsating white.

8. Each pilot of an airplane approaching to land on a runway served by a visual approach slope indicator shall maintain an altitude at or above the glide slope until a lower altitude is necessary for landing (FAR 91.129).

1.5 WAKE TURBULENCE

1.   Wingtip vortices (wake turbulence) are only created when airplanes develop lift.

2.   The greatest vortex strength occurs when the generating aircraft is heavy, clean, and slow.

3.   Wingtip vortex turbulence tends to sink into the flight path of airplanes operating below the airplane generating the turbulence.

    a.   Thus, you should fly above the flight path of a larger aircraft rather than below.

    b.   You should also fly upwind rather than downwind of the flight path, since the vortices will drift with the wind.

4.   The most dangerous wind, when taking off or landing behind a heavy aircraft, is the light quartering tailwind. It will push the vortices into your touchdown zone, even if you are executing proper procedures.

1.6 COLLISION AVOIDANCE

1.   A flashing red light on an aircraft is a rotating beacon and may be seen from any angle.

2.   In daylight, the most effective way to scan for other aircraft is to use a series of short, regularly spaced eye movements that bring successive areas of the sky into your central visual field.

    a.   Each movement should not exceed 10°, and each area should be observed for at least 1 second to enable detection.

    b.   Only a very small center area of the eye has the ability to send clear, sharply focused messages to the brain.

3.   To prevent collisions in the traffic pattern, maintain the proper altitude and continually scan the area for traffic.

4.   Any aircraft that appears to have no relative motion with respect to your aircraft and stays in one scan quadrant is likely to be on a collision course.

    a.   If it increases in size, you should take immediate evasive action.

5.   Prior to each maneuver, a pilot should visually scan the entire area for collision avoidance.

    a.   When climbing or descending VFR on an airway, you should execute gentle banks left and right to facilitate scanning for other aircraft.

    b.   Most midair collisions occur on clear days, with good visibilities.

6.   All pilots are responsible for collision avoidance when operating in an alert area.

1.7 GROUND CONTROL

1.   After landing, you should contact ground control only when so instructed by the tower.

2.   A clearance to taxi to the active runway is a clearance to taxi via taxiways to the active runway. You may not cross any runway along your taxi route unless specifically cleared by ATC to do so.

    a.   When cleared to a runway, you are cleared to that runway's runup area but not onto the active runway itself.

    b.   "Line up and wait" is an instruction ATC might issue that clears you to taxi onto the active runway, align yourself with the centerline, and await a clearance to take off. "Line up and wait" does not authorize a takeoff.

3.   In order to increase safety, pilots should state their position on the airport when calling the tower for takeoff from either a runway intersection or the end of the runway.

QUESTIONS AND ANSWER EXPLANATIONS

All of the sport pilot knowledge test questions chosen by the FAA for release as well as additional questions selected by Gleim relating to the material in the previous outlines are reproduced on the following pages. These questions have been organized into the same subunits as the outlines. To the immediate right of each question are the correct answer and answer explanation. You should cover these answers and answer explanations while responding to the questions. Refer to the general discussion in the Introduction on how to take the FAA pilot knowledge test.

Remember that the questions from the FAA pilot knowledge test bank have been reordered by topic and organized into a meaningful sequence. Also, the first line of the answer explanation gives the citation of the authoritative source for the answer.

QUESTIONS
1.1 Runway Markings

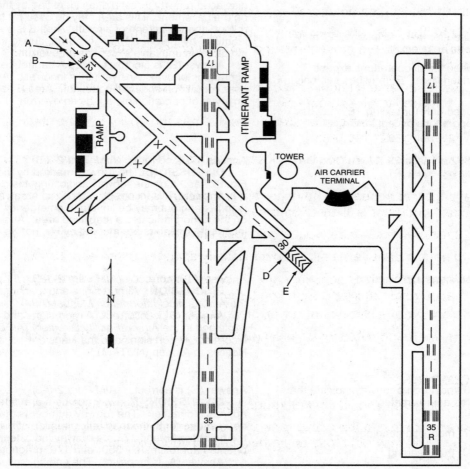

Figure 62. – Airport Diagram.

1. (Refer to Figure 62 above.) That portion of the runway identified by the letter A may be used for

A. landing.

B. taxiing and takeoff.

C. taxiing and landing.

Answer (B) is correct. *(AIM Para 2-3-3)*

DISCUSSION: The portion of the runway identified by the letter A in Fig. 62 is a displaced threshold, as marked by arrows from the beginning of the runway pointing to the displaced threshold, which means it may be used for taxiing or takeoffs but not for landings.

Answer (A) is incorrect. Area A may be used for the landing rollout but not the actual landing. Answer (C) is incorrect. Area A may be used for the landing rollout but not the actual landing.

2. (Refer to Figure 62 on page 29.) According to the airport diagram, which statement is true?

A. Runway 30 is equipped at position E with emergency arresting gear to provide a means of stopping military aircraft.

B. Takeoffs may be started at position A on Runway 12, and the landing portion of this runway begins at position B.

C. The takeoff and landing portion of Runway 12 begins at position B.

Answer (B) is correct. *(AIM Para 2-3-3)*
  DISCUSSION: In Fig. 62, Runway 12 takeoffs may be started at position A, and the landing portion of this runway begins at position B. In this example, a displaced threshold exists at the beginning of Runway 12. The threshold is a heavy line across the runway, designating the beginning portion of a runway usable for landing. The paved area behind the displaced runway threshold is available for taxiing, the landing rollout, and the takeoff of aircraft.
  Answer (A) is incorrect. Arresting cables across the operational area of a runway are indicated by yellow circles 10 ft. in diameter painted across the runway at positions of the arresting cables. Area E has chevron markings, which indicate an overrun area. Answer (C) is incorrect. Only the landing portion of RWY 12 begins at position B. The takeoff may be started in the paved area behind the displaced runway threshold (i.e., position A).

3. (Refer to Figure 62 on page 29.) What is the difference between area A and area E on the airport depicted?

A. "A" may be used for taxi and takeoff; "E" may be used only as an overrun.

B. "A" may be used for all operations except heavy aircraft landings; "E" may be used only as an overrun.

C. "A" may be used only for taxiing; "E" may be used for all operations except landings.

Answer (A) is correct. *(AIM Para 2-3-3)*
  DISCUSSION: Area A in Fig. 62 is the paved area behind a displaced runway threshold, as identified by the arrows painted on the pavement. This area may be used for taxiing, the landing rollout, and the takeoff of aircraft. Area E is a stopway area, as identified by the chevrons. This area, due to the nature of its structure, is unusable except as an overrun.
  Answer (B) is incorrect. Area A cannot be used by any aircraft for landing. Answer (C) is incorrect. Area A can also be used for takeoff and landing rollout. Area E cannot be used for any type of operation except as an overrun.

4. (Refer to Figure 62 on page 29.) Area C on the airport depicted is classified as a

A. stabilized area.

B. multiple heliport.

C. closed runway.

Answer (C) is correct. *(AIM Para 2-3-6)*
  DISCUSSION: The runway marked by the arrow C in Fig. 62 has Xs on the runway, indicating it is closed.
  Answer (A) is incorrect. Stabilized areas are designed to be load bearing but may be limited to emergency use only. Area E on the airport indicates a stabilized area. Answer (B) is incorrect. Heliports are marked by Hs, not Xs.

5. Where are airport signs explained?

A. AIM.

B. A/FD.

C. NOTAM.

Answer (A) is correct. *(AIM Para 2-3-1)*
  DISCUSSION: Airport signs and markings are explained in the *Aeronautical Information Manual (AIM)*.
  Answer (B) is incorrect. Airport signs and markings are not explained in the *Airport/Facility Directory (A/FD)*. Answer (C) is incorrect. Airport signs and markings are not explained in Notices to Airmen (NOTAM).

6. The numbers 35 and 17 on a runway indicate that the runway is oriented approximately

A. 035° and 017° magnetic heading.

B. 350° and 170° true heading.

C. 350° and 170° magnetic heading.

Answer (C) is correct. *(AIM Para 2-3-3)*
  DISCUSSION: Runway numbers are determined from the approach direction. The runway number is the whole number nearest one-tenth the magnetic direction of the centerline. Thus, the numbers 35 and 17 on a runway indicate that the runway is oriented approximately 350° and 170° magnetic heading.
  Answer (A) is incorrect. The ending digit, not a leading zero, is dropped. Answer (B) is incorrect. Runways are numbered based on magnetic heading (not true heading) direction.

7. What is the purpose of the runway hold position sign?

A. Denotes area protected for an aircraft approaching or departing a runway.

B. Denotes runways that intersect other runways.

C. Denotes an entrance to taxiway from a runway.

Answer (B) is correct. *(AIM Para 2-3-8)*
DISCUSSION: Runway hold position signs are mandatory instruction signs that have a red background with a white inscription and are used to denote an entrance to a runway on runways that intersect other runways.
Answer (A) is incorrect. A Runway Approach Area Holding Position Sign, not a Runway Holding Position Sign, denotes the area protected for an aircraft approaching or departing a runway. Answer (C) is incorrect. A Direction Sign, not a Runway Holding Position Sign, denotes the entrance to a taxiway from a runway.

8. What is the purpose for the runway hold position markings on the taxiway?

A. Holds aircraft short of the runway.

B. Allows an aircraft permission onto the runway.

C. Identifies area where aircraft are prohibited.

Answer (A) is correct. *(AIM Para 2-3-5)*
DISCUSSION: Runway holding position markings on taxiways identify the location where you are supposed to stop short of the runway when you do not have an ATC clearance to proceed at an airport with an operating control tower. At an airport without an operating control tower, you must ensure adequate aircraft separation. These markings consist of four yellow lines, two solid and two dashed, spaced 6 inches apart and extending across the width of the taxiway, with the dashed lines nearest the runway. The solid lines are always on the side where the aircraft is to hold.
Answer (B) is incorrect. Runway holding position markings indicate that aircraft should hold short of the runway, not taxi onto it, until a clearance to proceed onto the runway is received. Answer (C) is incorrect. A no entry sign, not a runway hold position marking, identifies an area where aircraft are prohibited.

9. When turning onto a taxiway from another taxiway, the taxiway directional sign indicates

A. direction of takeoff runway.

B. designation and direction of exit taxiway from runway.

C. designation and direction of taxiway leading out of intersection.

Answer (C) is correct. *(AIM Para 2-3-10)*
DISCUSSION: Direction signs consist of black lettering on a yellow background. These signs identify the designations of taxiways leading out of an intersection. An arrow next to each taxiway designation indicates the direction that an aircraft must turn in order to taxi onto that taxiway.
Answer (A) is incorrect. Outbound destination signs, not direction signs, indicate the direction that must be taken out of an intersection in order to follow the preferred taxi route to a runway. Answer (B) is incorrect. The question specifies that you are turning onto a taxiway from another taxiway, not from a runway.

10. The "runway hold position" sign denotes

A. intersecting runways.

B. an entrance to runway from a taxiway.

C. an area protected for an aircraft approaching a runway.

Answer (B) is correct. *(AIM Para 2-3-8)*
DISCUSSION: Runway holding position signs, consisting of white numbering on a red background, are found adjacent to runway holding position markings that are painted on a taxiway or runway. These signs and markings indicate the point at which aircraft are expected to hold short of a runway if an ATC clearance to proceed onto that runway has not been received at an airport with an operating control tower. Runway holding position signs therefore denote the entrance to a runway from a taxiway or from an intersecting runway.
Answer (A) is incorrect. A runway hold position sign is used only to denote an intersecting runway when that runway is used for "Land, Hold Short" operations or as a taxiway. Answer (C) is incorrect. A runway approach area holding position sign, not a runway holding position sign, denotes an area protected for aircraft approaching or departing a runway.

11. Holding position signs have

    A. red inscriptions on white backgrounds.

    B. white inscriptions on red backgrounds.

    C. yellow inscriptions on red background.

Answer (B) is correct. *(AIM Para 2-3-8)*
    DISCUSSION: Holding position signs are mandatory instruction signs that have a white inscription and a red background. They are used to denote an entrance to a runway or critical area. These markings consist of four yellow lines, two solid and two dashed, spaced 6 inches apart and extending across the width of the taxiway, with the dashed lines nearest the runway. The solid lines are always on the side where the aircraft is to hold.
    Answer (A) is incorrect. Holding position signs have white inscriptions with red backgrounds, not red inscriptions with white backgrounds. Answer (C) is incorrect. Holding position signs have white inscriptions, not yellow inscriptions, with red backgrounds.

12. "Runway hold position" markings on the taxiway

    A. identify where aircraft hold short of the runway.

    B. identify areas where aircraft are prohibited.

    C. allows an aircraft permission onto the runway.

Answer (A) is correct. *(AIM Para 2-3-5)*
    DISCUSSION: Runway holding position markings on taxiways identify the location where you are supposed to stop short of the runway when you do not have an ATC clearance to proceed at an airport with an operating control tower. At an airport without an operating control tower, you must ensure adequate aircraft separation. These markings consists of four yellow lines, two solid and two dashed, spaced 6 inches apart and extending across the width of the taxiway, with the dashed lines nearest the runway. The solid lines are always on the side where the aircraft is to hold.
    Answer (B) is incorrect. A no entry sign, not a runway hold position marking, identifies an area where aircraft are prohibited. Answer (C) is incorrect. Runway holding position markings indicate that aircraft should hold short of the runway, not taxi onto it, until a clearance to proceed onto the runway is received.

13. You have just landed at a towered airport and the tower tells you to contact ground control when clear of the runway. You are considered clear of the runway when

    A. all parts of the aircraft have crossed the hold line.

    B. the aircraft cockpit is clear of the hold line.

    C. the tail of the aircraft is clear of the runway edge.

Answer (A) is correct. *(AIM Para 2-3-5)*
    DISCUSSION: An aircraft exiting a runway is not clear of the runway until all parts of the aircraft have crossed the applicable holding position marking.
    Answer (B) is incorrect. All parts of the aircraft, not just the aircraft cockpit, need to have crossed the hold position markings. Answer (C) is incorrect. All parts of the aircraft need to have crossed the hold position markings; having the tail clear of the runway edge will not suffice.

14. (Refer to Figure 72 on page 185.) While clearing an active runway, you are clear of the ILS critical area when you pass which symbol?

    A. Point B.

    B. Point A.

    C. Point D.

Answer (A) is correct. *(AIM Para 2-3-5)*
    DISCUSSION: Point B indicates the Holding Position Marking for Instrument Landing Systems (ILS). Markings for ILS critical areas are designated to protect any ILS transmissions from interference by adjacent ground-based aircraft.
    Answer (B) is incorrect. Point A is a Runway Holding Position sign, not a Holding Position Marking for Instrument Landing System (ILS). Answer (C) is incorrect. Point D is a Runway Holding Position Marking, not a Holding Position Marking for Instrument Landing Systems (ILS).

15. (Refer to Figure 72 on page 185.) Which symbol indicates a taxiway/taxiway intersection hold position marking?

    A. B.

    B. D.

    C. E.

Answer (C) is correct. *(AIM Para 2-3-5)*
    DISCUSSION: Item E is an example of a taxiway/taxiway intersection hold position marking. These markings consist of a single yellow dashed line extending across the width of the taxiway where ATC normally holds an aircraft short of a taxiway intersection.
    Answer (A) is incorrect. Item B is an example of an ILS critical area Holding Position Marking, not of a taxiway/taxiway intersection hold position marking. Answer (B) is incorrect. Item D is an example of a runway holding position marking, not a taxiway/taxiway intersection hold position marking.

16. (Refer to Figure 71 on page 184.) Which sign indicates the runway on which the aircraft is located?

   A. E.

   B. F.

   C. L.

Answer (B) is correct. *(AIM Para 2-3-9)*
   DISCUSSION: Item F is a runway location sign. These signs, which have a yellow inscription with a black background, are used to identify the runway on which the aircraft is located.
   Answer (A) is incorrect. Item E is a taxiway location sign, which is used to identify the taxiway, not runway, on which an aircraft is located. Answer (C) is incorrect. Item L is a runway distance remaining sign and is used to indicate the distance, in thousands of feet, that is remaining on the current runway.

17. (Refer to Figure 72 on page 185.) Which marking indicates a vehicle lane?

   A. A.

   B. C.

   C. E.

Answer (B) is correct. *(AIM Para 2-3-6)*
   DISCUSSION: Marking C is a Vehicle Roadway Marking. It is used when necessary to define a pathway for vehicle operations on or crossing areas that are also intended for aircraft.
   Answer (A) is incorrect. Marking A is a Runway Holding Position sign, not a Vehicle Roadway Marking. Answer (C) is incorrect. Marking E is a Holding Position Marking for Taxiway/Taxiway Intersection, not a Vehicle Roadway Marking.

1.2 Airport Beacons

18. An airport's rotating beacon operated during daylight hours indicates

   A. there are obstructions on the airport.

   B. the ground visibility is less than 3 miles and/or the ceiling is less than 1,000 feet.

   C. the Air Traffic Control tower is not in operation.

Answer (B) is correct. *(AIM Para 2-1-8)*
   DISCUSSION: Operation of the airport beacon during daylight hours often indicates the ground visibility is less than 3 miles and/or the ceiling is less than 1,000 feet. Note that there is no regulatory requirement for daylight operation of an airport's rotating beacon.
   Answer (A) is incorrect. The obstructions near or on airports are usually listed in NOTAMs or the Airport/Facility Directory as appropriate to their hazard. Answer (C) is incorrect. There is no visual signal of tower operation/nonoperation.

19. A lighted heliport may be identified by a

   A. green, yellow, and white rotating beacon.

   B. flashing yellow light.

   C. blue lighted square landing area.

Answer (A) is correct. *(AIM Para 2-1-8)*
   DISCUSSION: A lighted heliport may be identified by a green, yellow, and white rotating beacon.
   Answer (B) is incorrect. A flashing yellow light is sometimes used to help a pilot locate a lighted water airport. It is used in conjunction with the lighted water airport's white and yellow rotating beacon. Answer (C) is incorrect. A lighted heliport may be identified by a green, yellow, and white rotating beacon, not a blue lighted square landing area.

20. A military air station can be identified by a rotating beacon that emits

   A. white and green alternating flashes.

   B. two quick, white flashes between green flashes.

   C. green, yellow, and white flashes.

Answer (B) is correct. *(AIM Para 2-1-8)*
   DISCUSSION: Lighted land airports are distinguished by white and green airport beacons. To further distinguish it as a military airport, there are two quick white flashes between each green.
   Answer (A) is incorrect. White and green alternating flashes designate a lighted civilian land airport. Answer (C) is incorrect. Green, yellow, and white flashes designate a lighted heliport.

1.3   Airport Traffic Patterns

21. (Refer to Figure 64 below.) The segmented circle indicates that the airport traffic is

- A. left-hand for Runway 36 and right-hand for Runway 18.
- B. left-hand for Runway 18 and right-hand for Runway 36.
- C. right-hand for Runway 9 and left-hand for Runway 27.

Answer (A) is correct. *(AIM Para 4-3-3)*
DISCUSSION: A segmented circle (see Fig. 64) is installed at uncontrolled airports to provide traffic pattern information. The landing runway indicators are shown coming out of the segmented circle to show the alignment of landing runways. In Fig. 64 (given the answer choices), the available runways are 18-36 and 9-27.
The traffic pattern indicators are at the end of the landing runway indicators and are angled out at 90°. These indicate the direction of turn from base to final. Thus, the airport traffic is left-hand for Runway 36 and right-hand for Runway 18. It is also left-hand for Runway 9 and right-hand for Runway 27.
Answer (B) is incorrect. Runway 18 is right, not left, and Runway 36 is left, not right. Answer (C) is incorrect. Runway 9 is left, not right, and Runway 27 is right, not left.

22. (Refer to Figure 64 below.) The traffic patterns indicated in the segmented circle have been arranged to avoid flights over an area to the

- A. south of the airport.
- B. north of the airport.
- C. southeast of the airport.

Answer (C) is correct. *(AIM Para 4-3-3)*
DISCUSSION: The traffic patterns indicated in the segmented circle depicted in Fig. 64 have been arranged to avoid flights over an area to the southeast of the airport. All departures from the runways are to the north or west. All approaches to the airport indicate a pattern of arrival from 180° clockwise to 90°, leaving the southeastern quadrant free of flight.
Answer (A) is incorrect. Arrivals on Runway 36 and departures on Runway 18 result in traffic to the south. Answer (B) is incorrect. Runway 9-27 produces traffic to the north in addition to Runway 36 departures and Runway 18 arrivals.

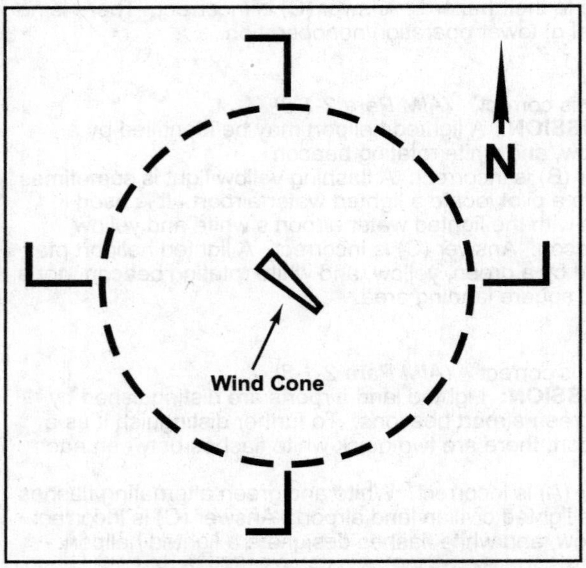

Figure 64. – Airport Landing Indicator.

23. (Refer to Figure 64 above.) The segmented circle indicates that a landing on Runway 26 will be with a

- A. right-quartering headwind.
- B. left-quartering headwind.
- C. right-quartering tailwind.

Answer (A) is correct. *(AIM Para 4-3-3)*
DISCUSSION: The wind cone at the center of the segmented circle depicted in Fig. 64 indicates that a landing on Runway 26 will be with a right-quartering headwind. The large end of the wind cone is pointing to the direction from which the wind is coming, i.e., a northwest headwind on the right quarter of an airplane landing from the east to the west.
Answer (B) is incorrect. A left-quartering headwind would be encountered landing on Runway 35. Answer (C) is incorrect. A right-quartering tailwind would be encountered landing on Runway 17.

24. (Refer to Figure 64 on page 34.) Which runway and traffic pattern should be used as indicated by the wind cone in the segmented circle?

A. Right-hand traffic on Runway 9.

B. Right-hand traffic on Runway 18.

C. Left-hand traffic on Runway 36.

Answer (C) is correct. *(AIM Para 4-3-3)*
    DISCUSSION: The appropriate traffic pattern and runway, given a wind from the northwest (Fig. 64), is left-hand traffic on Runway 36, which would have a quartering headwind.
    Answer (A) is incorrect. Runway 9 uses a left-hand pattern. Also, this would be a tailwind landing. Answer (B) is incorrect. Even though there is right traffic on Runway 18, this would be a tailwind landing.

25. (Refer to Figure 63 below.) If the wind is as shown by the landing direction indicator, the pilot should land on

A. Runway 18 and expect a crosswind from the right.

B. Runway 22 directly into the wind.

C. Runway 36 and expect a crosswind from the right.

Answer (A) is correct. *(AIM Para 4-3-3)*
    DISCUSSION: Given a wind as shown by the landing direction indicator in Fig. 63, the pilot should land to the south on Runway 18 and expect a crosswind from the right. The tetrahedron points to the wind which is from the southwest.
    Answer (B) is incorrect. Runways 4 and 22 are closed, as indicated by the X at each end of the runway. Answer (C) is incorrect. The wind is from the southwest (not the northeast). The landing should be into the wind.

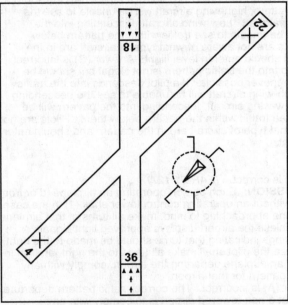

Figure 63. – Airport Diagram.

26. (Refer to Figure 63 above.) The arrows that appear on the end of the north/south runway indicate that the area

A. may be used only for taxiing.

B. is usable for taxiing, takeoff, and landing.

C. cannot be used for landing, but may be used for taxiing and takeoff.

Answer (C) is correct. *(AIM Para 2-3-3)*
    DISCUSSION: The arrows that appear on the end of the north/south runway (displaced thresholds) as shown in Fig. 63 indicate that the area cannot be used for landing but may be used for taxiing, takeoff, and the landing rollout.
    Answer (A) is incorrect. Takeoffs as well as taxiing are permitted. Answer (B) is incorrect. Landings are not permitted on the area before the displaced threshold.

27. (Refer to Figure 63 on page 35.) Select the proper traffic pattern and runway for landing.

    A. Left-hand traffic and Runway 18.

    B. Right-hand traffic and Runway 18.

    C. Left-hand traffic and Runway 22.

Answer (B) is correct. *(AIM Para 4-3-3)*
    DISCUSSION: The tetrahedron indicates wind direction by pointing into the wind. On Fig. 63, Runways 4 and 22 are closed, as indicated by the X at each end of the runway. Accordingly, with the wind from the southwest, the landing should be made on Runway 18. Runway 18 has right-hand traffic, as indicated by the traffic pattern indicator at a 90° angle to the landing runway indicator in the segmented circle.
    Answer (A) is incorrect. Runway 18 uses a right-hand (not left-hand) pattern. Answer (C) is incorrect. The X markings indicate that Runways 4 and 22 are closed.

28. Entries into traffic patterns while descending create specific collision hazards and

    A. should be avoided.

    B. should be used whenever possible.

    C. are illegal.

Answer (A) is correct. *(AIM Para 4-3-3)*
    DISCUSSION: Pilots should avoid entering the traffic pattern while descending to avoid colliding with other aircraft within the traffic pattern. If a pilot descends into the traffic pattern, high-wing aircraft will be unable to see the descending aircraft. Low-wing aircraft descending into the pattern will be unable to see traffic within the pattern below them. Pilots are not aware of what type of aircraft are in the pattern and should enter in level flight.
    Answer (B) is incorrect. Descending into the traffic pattern should be avoided whenever possible. If a pilot descends into the traffic pattern, high-wing aircraft will be unable to see the descending aircraft. Low-wing aircraft descending into the pattern will be unable to see traffic within the pattern below them. Pilots are not aware of what type of aircraft are in the pattern and should enter in level flight. Answer (C) is incorrect. Descending into the traffic pattern is not illegal but should be avoided whenever possible. If a pilot descends into the traffic pattern, high-wing aircraft will be unable to see the descending aircraft. Low-wing aircraft descending into the pattern will be unable to see traffic within the pattern below them. Pilots are not aware of what type of aircraft are in the pattern and should enter in level flight.

29. Which is the correct traffic pattern departure procedure to use at a non-towered airport?

    A. Depart in any direction consistent with safety, after crossing the airport boundary.

    B. Make all turns to the left.

    C. Comply with any FAA traffic pattern established for the airport.

Answer (C) is correct. *(FAR 91.127)*
    DISCUSSION: Each person operating an airplane to or from an airport without an operating control tower shall (1) in the case of an airplane approaching to land, make all turns of that airplane to the left unless the airport displays approved light signals or visual markings indicating that turns should be made to the right, in which case the pilot shall make all turns to the right, and (2) in the case of an airplane departing the airport, comply with any FAA traffic pattern for that airport.
    Answer (A) is incorrect. The correct traffic pattern departure procedure at a non-towered airport is to comply with any FAA-established traffic pattern, not to depart in any direction after crossing the airport boundary. Answer (B) is incorrect. The FAA may establish right- or left-hand traffic patterns, not only left-hand traffic patterns.

30. When approaching to land at an airport in Class G airspace that does not have light signals or other visual markings, an airplane pilot must make

    A. all turns to the left.

    B. all turns to the right.

    C. a straight-in approach.

Answer (A) is correct. *(FAR 91.126)*
    DISCUSSION: When approaching to land at an airport without an operating control tower in Class G airspace, the pilot of an airplane must make all turns to the left, unless otherwise indicated.
    Answer (B) is incorrect. When approaching to land at an airport without an operating control tower in Class G airspace, the pilot should fly a left-hand traffic pattern, unless otherwise indicated by traffic pattern indicators around the segment circle. Additionally, the recommended pattern altitude is 1,000 feet AGL, unless otherwise published. Answer (C) is incorrect. When approaching to land at an airport without an operating control tower in Class G airspace, the pilot should make all turns to the left (unless otherwise indicated), not fly a straight-in approach. Additionally, the recommended pattern altitude is 1,000 feet AGL, unless otherwise published.

1.4 Visual Approach Slope Indicators (VASI)

31. An on glide slope indication from a tri-color VASI is

A. a white light signal.

B. a green light signal.

C. an amber light signal.

Answer (B) is correct. *(AIM Para 2-1-2)*
DISCUSSION: Tri-color visual approach slope indicators normally consist of a single light unit projecting a three-color visual approach path into the final approach area of the runway, upon which the indicator is installed. The below glide path indicator is red. The above glide path indicator is amber. The on glide path indicator is green. This type of indicator has a useful range of approximately 1/2 to 1 mi. in daytime and up to 5 mi. at night.
Answer (A) is incorrect. Tri-color VASI does not emit a white light. Answer (C) is incorrect. Amber indicates above (not on) the glide slope.

32. An above glide slope indication from a tri-color VASI is

A. a white light signal.

B. a green light signal.

C. an amber light signal.

Answer (C) is correct. *(AIM Para 2-1-2)*
DISCUSSION: The tri-color VASI has three lights: amber for above the glide slope, green for on the glide slope, and red for below the glide slope.
Answer (A) is incorrect. Tri-color VASI does not emit a white light. Answer (B) is incorrect. A green light means on (not above) the glide slope.

33. A below glide slope indication from a tri-color VASI is a

A. red light signal.

B. pink light signal.

C. green light signal.

Answer (A) is correct. *(AIM Para 2-1-2)*
DISCUSSION: The tri-color VASI has three lights: amber for above the glide slope, green for on the glide slope, and red for below the glide slope.
Answer (B) is incorrect. A pink light may be seen on a pulsating (not tri-color) VASI when in the area of on, to slightly below, the glide slope. Answer (C) is incorrect. A green light means you are on the glide slope.

34. A below glide slope indication from a pulsating approach slope indicator is a

A. pulsating white light.

B. steady white light.

C. pulsating red light.

Answer (C) is correct. *(AIM Para 2-1-2)*
DISCUSSION: A pulsating VASI indicator normally consists of a single light unit projecting a two-color visual approach path into the final approach area of the runway upon which the indicator is installed. The below glide slope indication is a pulsating red, the above glide slope is pulsating white, and the on glide slope is a steady white light. The useful range of this system is about 4 mi. during the day and up to 10 mi. at night.
Answer (A) is incorrect. A pulsating white light is an above glide slope indication. Answer (B) is incorrect. Steady white is the on glide slope indication.

35. When approaching to land on a runway served by a visual approach slope indicator (VASI), the pilot shall

A. maintain an altitude that captures the glide slope at least 2 miles downwind from the runway threshold.

B. maintain an altitude at or above the glide slope.

C. remain on the glide slope and land between the two-light bar.

Answer (B) is correct. *(FAR 91.129)*
DISCUSSION: An airplane approaching to land on a runway served by a VASI shall maintain an altitude at or above the glide slope until a lower altitude is necessary for a safe landing.
Answer (A) is incorrect. A VASI should not be used for descent until the airplane is visually lined up with the runway. Answer (C) is incorrect. It is unsafe to concentrate on the VASI after nearing the approach end of the runway; i.e., turn your attention to landing the airplane.

36. (Refer to Figure 65 below.) While on final approach to a runway equipped with a standard 2-bar VASI, the lights appear as shown by illustration D. This means that the aircraft is

A. above the glide slope.

B. below the glide slope.

C. on the glide slope.

Answer (B) is correct. *(AIM Para 2-1-2)*
   DISCUSSION: In illustration D of Fig. 65, both rows of lights are red. Thus, the aircraft is below the glide path. Remember, "red means dead."
   Answer (A) is incorrect. If the airplane is above the glide path, the lights would both show white, as indicated by illustration C. Answer (C) is incorrect. If the airplane is on the glide path, the lights would be red over white, as indicated by illustration A.

37. (Refer to Figure 65 below.) VASI lights as shown by illustration C indicate that the airplane is

A. off course to the left.

B. above the glide slope.

C. below the glide slope.

Answer (B) is correct. *(AIM Para 2-1-2)*
   DISCUSSION: In illustration C of Fig. 65, both rows of lights are white, which means the airplane is above the glide path.
   Answer (A) is incorrect. The VASI does not alert a pilot as to runway alignment, but a pilot who is excessively to the left or right may not be able to see the VASI lights at all. Answer (C) is incorrect. If the airplane is below the glide path, both rows of lights would show red, as indicated by illustration D.

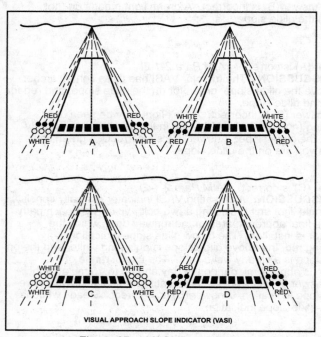

Figure 65. – VASI Illustrations.

38. (Refer to Figure 65 above.) Illustration A indicates that the aircraft is

A. below the glide slope.

B. on the glide slope.

C. above the glide slope.

Answer (B) is correct. *(AIM Para 2-1-2)*
   DISCUSSION: Illustration A indicates that the airplane is on the glide path (glide slope). The basic principle of the VASI is that of color differentiation between red and white. Each light unit projects a beam of light having a white segment in the upper part and a red segment in the lower part of the beam. Thus, to be on the glide slope you need to be on the lower part of the far light (red) and on the upper part of the near light (white).
   Answer (A) is incorrect. If the airplane is below the glide path, both rows of lights will be red, as indicated in D. Answer (C) is incorrect. If the aircraft is above the glide path, both lights will be white, as indicated in C.

39. A slightly high glide slope indication from a precision approach path indicator is

A. four white lights.

B. three white lights and one red light.

C. two white lights and two red lights.

Answer (B) is correct. *(AIM Para 2-1-2)*

DISCUSSION: A precision approach path indicator (PAPI) has a row of four lights, each of which is similar to a VASI in that they emit a red or white light. Above the glide slope (more than 3.5°) is indicated by four white lights, a slightly above glide slope (3.2°) is indicated by three white lights and one red light, on glide slope (3°) is indicated by two white and two red lights, slightly below glide slope (2.8°) is indicated by one white and three red lights, and below (too low) the glide slope (less than 2.5°) is indicated by four red lights.

Answer (A) is incorrect. Four white lights is a high, or more than 3.5°, glide slope indication. Answer (C) is incorrect. Two white and two red lights is an on glide slope (3°) indication.

40. Each pilot of an aircraft approaching to land on a runway served by a visual approach slope indicator (VASI) shall

A. maintain a 3° glide to the runway.

B. maintain an altitude at or above the glide slope.

C. stay high until the runway can be reached in a power-off landing.

Answer (B) is correct. *(FAR 91.129)*

DISCUSSION: When approaching to land on a runway served by a VASI, each pilot of an airplane must fly at or above the VASI glide path until a lower altitude is necessary for a safe landing.

Answer (A) is incorrect. A VASI may be adjusted to provide a glide slope more or less than 3°. Answer (C) is incorrect. Higher than the VASI glide path is not required.

1.5 Wake Turbulence

41. Wingtip vortices are created only when an aircraft is

A. operating at high airspeeds.

B. heavily loaded.

C. developing lift.

Answer (C) is correct. *(AIM Para 7-3-2)*

DISCUSSION: Wingtip vortices are the result of the pressure differential over and under a wing when that wing is producing lift. Wingtip vortices do not develop when an airplane is taxiing, although prop blast or jet thrust turbulence can be experienced near the rear of a large airplane which is taxiing.

Answer (A) is incorrect. The greatest turbulence is produced from an airplane operating at a slow airspeed. Answer (B) is incorrect. Even though a heavily loaded airplane may produce greater turbulence, an airplane does not have to be heavily loaded in order to produce wingtip vortices. Wingtip vortices are produced only when an airplane is developing lift.

42. Wingtip vortices created by large aircraft tend to

A. sink below the aircraft generating turbulence.

B. rise into the traffic pattern.

C. rise into the takeoff or landing path of a crossing runway.

Answer (A) is correct. *(AIM Para 7-3-4)*

DISCUSSION: Wingtip vortices created by large airplanes tend to sink below the airplane generating the turbulence.

Answer (B) is incorrect. Wingtip vortices sink, not rise. Answer (C) is incorrect. Wingtip vortices do not rise or gain altitude, but sink toward the ground. However, they may move horizontally left or right depending on crosswind conditions.

43. When taking off or landing at an airport where heavy aircraft are operating, one should be particularly alert to the hazards of wingtip vortices because this turbulence tends to

A. rise from a crossing runway into the takeoff or landing path.

B. rise into the traffic pattern area surrounding the airport.

C. sink into the flightpath of aircraft operating below the aircraft generating the turbulence.

Answer (C) is correct. *(AIM Para 7-3-4)*

DISCUSSION: When taking off or landing at a busy airport where large, heavy airplanes are operating, you should be particularly alert to the hazards of wingtip vortices because this turbulence tends to sink into the flight paths of airplanes operating below the airplane generating the turbulence. Wingtip vortices are caused by a differential in high and low pressure at the wingtip of an airplane, creating a spiraling effect trailing behind the wingtip, similar to a horizontal tornado.

Answer (A) is incorrect. Wingtip vortices always trail behind an airplane and descend toward the ground. However, they do drift with the wind and will not stay directly behind an airplane if there is a crosswind. Answer (B) is incorrect. Wingtip vortices sink, not rise.

44. The greatest vortex strength occurs when the generating aircraft is

    A. light, dirty, and fast.

    B. heavy, dirty, and fast.

    C. heavy, clean, and slow.

Answer (C) is correct. *(AIM Para 7-3-3)*
    DISCUSSION: Vortices are the greatest when the wingtips are at high angles of attack. This occurs at high gross weight, flaps up, and low airspeed (heavy, clean, and slow).
    Answer (A) is incorrect. Light aircraft produce less vortex turbulence than heavy aircraft. The use of flaps, spoilers, etc. (i.e., dirty), diminishes vortex turbulence. Answer (B) is incorrect. Being dirty and/or fast causes the wingtip to be at a lower angle of attack, presenting less of a danger than when clean and/or slow.

45. What wind condition prolongs the hazards of wake turbulence on a landing runway for the longest period of time?

    A. Direct headwind.

    B. Direct tailwind.

    C. Light quartering tailwind.

Answer (C) is correct. *(AIM Para 7-3-4)*
    DISCUSSION: Light quartering tailwinds require maximum caution because they can move the vortices of preceding aircraft forward into the touchdown zone and hold the upwind vortex on the runway.
    Answer (A) is incorrect. A direct headwind will permit the vortices to move away from each side of the runway. Answer (B) is incorrect. A direct tailwind will permit the vortices to move away from each side of the runway.

46. The wind condition that requires maximum caution when avoiding wake turbulence on landing is a

    A. light, quartering headwind.

    B. light, quartering tailwind.

    C. strong headwind.

Answer (B) is correct. *(AIM Para 7-3-4)*
    DISCUSSION: The most dangerous wind condition when avoiding wake turbulence on landing is a light, quartering tailwind. The tailwind can push the vortices forward which could put it in the touchdown zone of your aircraft even if you used proper procedures and landed beyond the touchdown point of the preceding aircraft. Also the quartering wind may push the upwind vortices to the middle of the runway.
    Answer (A) is incorrect. Headwinds push the vortices out of your touchdown zone if you land beyond the touchdown point of the preceding aircraft. Answer (C) is incorrect. Strong winds help diffuse wake turbulence vortices.

47. When departing behind a heavy aircraft, the pilot should avoid wake turbulence by maneuvering the aircraft

    A. below and downwind from the heavy aircraft.

    B. above and upwind from the heavy aircraft.

    C. below and upwind from the heavy aircraft.

Answer (B) is correct. *(AIM Para 7-3-6)*
    DISCUSSION: The proper procedure for departing behind a large aircraft is to rotate prior to the large aircraft's rotation point then fly above and upwind of the large aircraft. Since vortices sink and drift downwind, this should keep you clear.
    Answer (A) is incorrect. You should remain above and upwind of the heavy aircraft. Answer (C) is incorrect. You should fly above the flight path of the large aircraft to avoid the sinking vortices.

48. When landing behind a large aircraft, the pilot should avoid wake turbulence by staying

    A. above the large aircraft's final approach path and landing beyond the large aircraft's touchdown point.

    B. below the large aircraft's final approach path and landing before the large aircraft's touchdown point.

    C. above the large aircraft's final approach path and landing before the large aircraft's touchdown point.

Answer (A) is correct. *(AIM Para 7-3-6)*
    DISCUSSION: When landing behind a large aircraft, your flight path should be above the other aircraft's flight path since the vortices sink. When the aircraft touches down, the vortices will stop, so you should thus touch down beyond where the large aircraft did.
    Answer (B) is incorrect. Below the flight path, you will fly through the sinking vortices generated by the large aircraft. Answer (C) is incorrect. By landing before the large aircraft's touchdown point, you will have to fly below the preceding aircraft's flight path.

1.6 Collision Avoidance

49. The most effective method of scanning for other aircraft for collision avoidance during daylight hours is to use

    A. regularly spaced concentration on the 3-, 9-, and 12-o'clock positions.

    B. a series of short, regularly spaced eye movements to search each 10-degree sector.

    C. peripheral vision by scanning small sectors and utilizing offcenter viewing.

Answer (B) is correct. *(AC 90-48C)*
    DISCUSSION: The most effective way to scan for other aircraft during daylight hours is to use a series of short, regularly spaced eye movements that bring successive areas of the sky into your central visual field. Each movement should not exceed 10°, and each area should be observed for at least 1 second to enable detection. Only a very small center area of the eye has the ability to send clear, sharply focused messages to the brain. All other areas provide less detail.
    Answer (A) is incorrect. The spacing between the positions should be 10°, not 90°. Answer (C) is incorrect. This is the recommended nighttime scanning procedure.

50. How can you determine if another aircraft is on a collision course with your aircraft?

    A. The other aircraft will always appear to get larger and closer at a rapid rate.

    B. The nose of each aircraft is pointed at the same point in space.

    C. There will be no apparent relative motion between your aircraft and the other aircraft.

Answer (C) is correct. *(AIM Para 8-1-8)*
    DISCUSSION: Any aircraft that appears to have no relative motion and stays in one scan quadrant is likely to be on a collision course. Also, if a target shows no lateral or vertical motion but increases in size, take evasive action.
    Answer (A) is incorrect. Aircraft on collision courses may not always appear to grow larger and/or to close at a rapid rate. Frequently, the degree of proximity cannot be detected. Answer (B) is incorrect. You may not be able to tell exactly in which direction the other airplane is pointed. Even if you could determine the direction of the other airplane, you may not be able to accurately project the flight paths of the two airplanes to determine if they indeed point to the same point in space and will arrive there at the same time (i.e., collide).

51. Most midair collision accidents occur during

    A. clear days.

    B. hazy days.

    C. cloudy nights.

Answer (A) is correct. *(AC 90-48C)*
    DISCUSSION: Most midair collisions occur during clear days, with good visibilities.
    Answer (B) is incorrect. Most midair collisions occur during clear days, not hazy days. Answer (C) is incorrect. Most midair collisions occur during clear days, not cloudy nights.

52. Prior to starting each maneuver, pilots should

    A. check altitude, airspeed, and heading indications.

    B. visually scan the entire area for collision avoidance.

    C. announce their intentions on the nearest CTAF.

Answer (B) is correct. *(AIM Para 4-4-14)*
    DISCUSSION: Prior to each maneuver, a pilot should visually scan the entire area for collision avoidance. Many maneuvers require a clearing turn, which should be used for this purpose.
    Answer (A) is incorrect. Altitude, speed, and heading may not all be critical to every maneuver. Collision avoidance is! Answer (C) is incorrect. CTAF is used for operations at an uncontrolled airport, not for pilots doing maneuvers away from an airport.

53. What is an effective way to prevent a collision hazard in the traffic pattern?

    A. Enter pattern in a descent.

    B. Maintain the proper traffic pattern altitude and continually scan the area.

    C. Rely on radio reports from other aircraft who may be operating in the traffic pattern.

Answer (B) is correct. *(AC 90-48C)*
    DISCUSSION: The most effective way to prevent collisions in the traffic pattern is to maintain the proper altitude and continually scan the area for traffic.
    Answer (A) is incorrect. One should enter the traffic pattern at the traffic pattern altitude, not in a descent, as visibility may be limited during a descent, making detection of traffic difficult. Answer (C) is incorrect. Not all other aircraft in the traffic pattern may be using a radio and/or your frequency.

END OF STUDY UNIT

54. What procedure is recommended when climbing or descending VFR on an airway?

    A. Execute gentle banks, left and right for continuous visual scanning of the airspace.

    B. Advise the nearest FSS of the altitude changes.

    C. Fly away from the centerline of the airway before changing altitude.

Answer (A) is correct. *(AIM Para 4-3-14)*
    DISCUSSION: When climbing (descending) VFR on an airway, you should execute gentle banks left and right to facilitate scanning for other aircraft. Collision avoidance is a constant priority and especially pertinent to climbs and descents on airways where other traffic is expected.
    Answer (B) is incorrect. An FSS provides no en route traffic service. Answer (C) is incorrect. It is not necessary to leave the center of the airway, only to scan for other aircraft.

55. Responsibility for collision avoidance in an alert area rests with

    A. the controlling agency.

    B. all pilots.

    C. Air Traffic Control.

Answer (B) is correct. *(AIM Para 3-4-6)*
    DISCUSSION: Alert areas may contain a high volume of pilot training or other unusual activity. Pilots using the area as well as pilots crossing the area are equally responsible for collision avoidance.
    Answer (A) is incorrect. Pilots are responsible for collision avoidance, not controlling agencies. Answer (C) is incorrect. Pilots are responsible for collision avoidance, not ATC.

1.7 Ground Control

56. After landing at a tower-controlled airport a pilot should contact ground control

    A. when advised by the tower.

    B. prior to turning off the runway.

    C. after reaching a taxiway that leads directly to the parking area.

Answer (A) is correct. *(AC-90-48C)*
    DISCUSSION: After landing at a tower-controlled airport, you should contact ground control on the appropriate frequency only when instructed by the tower.
    Answer (B) is incorrect. A pilot should not change frequencies unless instructed to do so by the tower. Sometimes the tower controller will be handling both tower and ground frequencies. Switching without permission may be confusing to ATC. Answer (C) is incorrect. A pilot should not change frequencies unless instructed to do so by the tower. Sometimes the tower controller will be handling both tower and ground frequencies. Switching without permission may be confusing to ATC.

57. If instructed by ground control to taxi to Runway 9, the pilot may proceed

    A. via taxiways and across runways to, but not onto, Runway 9.

    B. to the next intersecting runway where further clearance is required.

    C. via taxiways and across runways to Runway 9, where an immediate takeoff may be made.

Answer (B) is correct. *(AIM Para 4-3-18)*
    DISCUSSION: A taxi clearance from ATC authorizes the pilot to utilize taxiways along the taxi route, but a specific crossing clearance must be issued for all runways along the route.
    Answer (A) is incorrect. A clearance to taxi to the active runway means a pilot has been given permission to taxi via taxiways to, but not onto, the active runway. ATC must issue a specific clearance to cross any runway along the taxi route. Answer (C) is incorrect. The clearance to taxi to a runway does not permit taxiing onto the active runway.

58. Pilots should state their position on the airport when calling the tower for takeoff

    A. from a runway intersection, during instrument conditions.

    B. from a runway intersection or the end of a runway.

    C. from a runway intersection, only at night.

Answer (B) is correct. *(AIM Para 4-3-10)*
    DISCUSSION: In order to increase safety, pilots should state their position on the airport when calling the tower for takeoff from either a runway intersection or the end of a runway.
    Answer (A) is incorrect. Pilots should state their position on the airport when calling the tower for takeoff in any conditions, not only during instrument conditions. Answer (C) is incorrect. Pilots should state their position on the airport when calling the tower for takeoff in any conditions, not only at night.

END OF STUDY UNIT

STUDY UNIT TWO
AIRSPACE

(4 pages of outline)

This study unit contains outlines of major concepts tested, sample test questions and answers regarding airspace, and an explanation of each answer. The table of contents above lists each subunit within this study unit, the number of questions pertaining to that particular subunit, and the pages on which the outlines and questions begin, respectively.

CAUTION: Recall that the **sole purpose** of this book is to expedite your passing the FAA pilot knowledge test for the sport pilot certificate. Accordingly, all extraneous material (i.e., topics or regulations not directly tested on the FAA pilot knowledge test) is omitted, even though much more information and knowledge are necessary to fly safely. This additional material is presented in *Pilot Handbook* and *Sport Pilot Flight Maneuvers and Practical Test Prep*, available from Gleim Publications, Inc. See the order form on page 327.

2.1 AIRSPACE OVERVIEW

1. Class A lies at and above 18,000 ft. MSL (not relevant to sport pilots).

    a. MSL (mean sea level)
    b. AGL (above ground level)

2. Class B lies from the surface up to 10,000 ft. MSL and approximately 30 miles around large, metropolitan hub airport areas, e.g., Chicago, Orlando, New York, and Los Angeles. Class B airspace requires pilots to receive permission (called a "clearance") to enter and fly, as directed by Air Traffic Control (ATC).

3. Class C lies from the airport elevation up to 4,000 ft. AGL and approximately 10 miles around large, busy airports such as Jacksonville and Daytona Beach (Florida) and Sacramento and Ontario (California). Two-way radio communication is required prior to entering the airspace.

4. Class D lies from the airport elevation up to 2,500 ft. AGL and 4 miles around airports with an operational control tower. Two-way radio communication is required prior to entering the airspace.

5. Class E is controlled from the surface or designated altitude up to the base or underlying base of Class B and C airspace and all airspace 14,500 ft. MSL to 18,000 ft. MSL.

    a. On sectional charts, magenta shading indicates Class E airspace with a lower limit of 700 feet AGL.

6. Class G is uncontrolled and consists of all airspace other than A, B, C, D, and E. Uncontrolled vs. controlled airspace affects minimum VFR flight requirements, e.g., visibility, equipment, and where sport pilots can fly. Sport pilots must have special training and a CFI log book signoff to fly in B, C, and/or D airspace.

2.2 CLASS D AIRSPACE

1. Class D airspace is an area of controlled airspace surrounding an airport with an operating control tower not associated with Class B or Class C airspace areas.

    a. Airspace at an airport with a part-time control tower is classified as Class D airspace only when the control tower is operating. When the tower is not in operation, the Class D airspace becomes Class E airspace, generally.

2. Class D airspace is depicted by a blue segmented (dashed) circle on a sectional chart.

3. When departing a non-tower satellite airport within Class D airspace, you must establish and maintain two-way radio communication with the primary airport's control tower as soon as practicable after departing.

    a. The primary airport is the airport for which the Class D airspace is designated.
    b. A satellite airport is any other airport within the Class D airspace area.

4. Class D airspace is normally the airspace up to 2,500 ft. above the surface of the airport.

2.3 CLASS C AIRSPACE

1. Class C airspace consists of a surface area (formerly called the inner circle) and a shelf area (formerly called the outer circle).

    a. The surface area has a 5-NM radius from the primary airport

        1) Extending from the surface to 4,000 ft. above the airport elevation.
    b. The shelf area is an area from 5 to 10 NM from the primary airport

        1) Extending from 1,200 ft. to 4,000 ft. above the airport elevation.

2. Surrounding the Class C airspace is the outer area. The outer area is not classified as Class C airspace. The normal radius of the outer area of Class C airspace is 20 NM from the primary airport, and ATC provides the same radar services as provided in Class C airspace.

3. The minimum equipment needed to operate in Class C airspace includes

    a. A 4096 code transponder,
    b. Mode C (altitude encoding) capability, and
    c. Two-way radio communication capability.

4. Two-way radio communications with air traffic control (ATC) are required for landing and taking off at all tower-controlled airports, regardless of weather conditions.

5. You must establish and maintain two-way radio communication with ATC prior to entering Class C airspace.

    a. A clearance is not required because "clearance" relates to IFR operations or to the permission required by a pilot prior to entering Class B airspace.

6. When departing from a satellite airport located within Class C airspace and without an operating control tower, you must contact ATC as soon as practicable after takeoff.

2.4 TRANSPONDER CODES

1. Code 1200 is the standard VFR transponder code.
2. The ident feature should not be engaged unless instructed by ATC.

3. Certain special codes should never be engaged (except in an emergency), as they may cause problems at ATC centers:

    a. 7500 is the hijacking code.
    b. 7600 is the lost radio communication code.
    c. 7700 is the general emergency code.
    d. 7777 is the military interceptor code.

2.5 RADIO PHRASEOLOGY

1. When contacting a flight service station, the proper call sign is the name of the FSS followed by "radio" (e.g., McAlester Radio).

2. When contacting an En Route Flight Advisory Service (EFAS), the proper call sign is the name of the Air Route Traffic Control Center facility serving your area followed by "flight watch" (e.g., "Seattle Flight Watch").

3. Civilian aircraft should start their aircraft call sign with the make or model aircraft (e.g., Cessna 44WH or Baron 2DF).

    a. When a make or model is used, the initial November is dropped from the call sign.

4. Pilots should state each digit of the call sign individually (e.g., 6449U = six, four, four, niner, uniform).

5. When calling out altitudes up to but not including 18,000 ft., state the separate digits of the thousands, plus the hundreds, if appropriate (e.g., 4,500 ft. = four thousand five hundred).

NOTE: Unless otherwise noted, the altitudes are MSL.

2.6 ATC TRAFFIC ADVISORIES

1. Radar traffic information services provide pilots with traffic advisories of nearby aircraft.

2. Traffic advisories provide information based on the position of other aircraft from your airplane in terms of clock direction in a no-wind condition (i.e., it is based on your ground track, not heading).

    a. 12 o'clock is straight ahead.
    b. 3 o'clock is directly off your right wing.
    c. 6 o'clock is directly behind you.
    d. 9 o'clock is directly off your left wing.
    e. Other positions are described accordingly, e.g., 2 o'clock, 10 o'clock.

3. Traffic advisories usually also include

    a. Distance away in miles
    b. Direction of flight of other aircraft
    c. Altitude of other aircraft

4. Air Traffic Control will provide radar assistance to any VFR aircraft, as long as they can communicate with the aircraft and see them on radar.

5. ATC uses visual separation to separate aircraft in terminal areas and en route airspace in the NAS.

    a. When pilots accept responsibility to maintain visual separation, they must maintain constant visual surveillance and not pass the other aircraft until it is no longer a factor.
    b. Traffic is no longer a factor when, during departure or en route, the other aircraft turns away or is on a diverging course.

2.7 ATC LIGHT SIGNALS

1. In the absence of radio communications, the tower can communicate with you by light signals.

2. Light signal meanings depend on whether you are on the ground or in the air.

Light Signal	On the Ground	In the Air
Steady Green	Cleared for takeoff	Cleared to land
Flashing Green	Cleared to taxi	Return for landing *(to be followed by steady green at proper time)*
Steady Red	Stop	Give way to other aircraft and continue circling
Flashing Red	Taxi clear of landing area (runway) in use	Airport unsafe -- do not land
Flashing White	Return to starting point on airport	Not applicable
Alternating Red and Green	General warning signal -- exercise extreme caution	General warning signal -- exercise extreme caution

3. Acknowledge light signals in the air by rocking wings in daylight and blinking lights at night.

4. If your radio fails and you wish to land at a tower-controlled airport, remain outside or above the airport's traffic pattern until the direction and flow of traffic has been determined, then join the traffic pattern and maintain visual contact with the tower to receive light signals.

2.8 EMERGENCY LOCATOR TRANSMITTERS (ELTs)

1. ELTs transmit simultaneously on 121.5 and 243.0 MHz.

   a. You can monitor either frequency during flight and before shutdown (after landing) to ensure your ELT has not been activated.

2. Additionally, if faced with an emergency where immediate Air Traffic Control (ATC) assistance is desired and you are not already in contact with ATC, 121.5 MHz is the universally guarded emergency communications frequency.

3. ELTs may only be tested on the ground during the first 5 min. after the hour.

   a. No airborne checks are allowed.

QUESTIONS

2.1 Airspace Overview

1. (Refer to Figure 61 on page 180.) The floor of the Class E airspace over University Airport (0O5) is

A. 1200 feet AGL.

B. the surface.

C. 700 feet AGL.

Answer (C) is correct. *(ACL)*

DISCUSSION: Note the shaded magenta line to the west of University Airport. Class E airspace begins at 700 feet AGL in the region bounded by this line, as indicated in the sectional aeronautical chart legend (Legend 1 on page 171).

Answer (A) is incorrect. Shaded blue lines indicate Class E airspace begins at 1200 feet, while the shaded lines surrounding University Airport are magenta. Answer (B) is incorrect. Class E airspace begins at 700 feet AGL, not at the surface.

2.2 Class D Airspace

2. A blue segmented circle on a Sectional Chart depicts which class airspace?

A. Class B.

B. Class C.

C. Class D.

Answer (C) is correct. *(AIM Para 3-2-5)*

DISCUSSION: A blue segmented circle on a sectional chart depicts Class D airspace.

Answer (A) is incorrect. Class B airspace is depicted on a sectional chart by a solid, not segmented, blue circle. Answer (B) is incorrect. Class C airspace is depicted on a sectional chart by a solid magenta, not a blue segmented, circle.

3. Airspace at an airport with a part-time control tower is classified as Class D airspace only

A. when the prevailing visibility is below 3 statute miles.

B. when the associated control tower is in operation.

C. when the associated Flight Service Station is in operation.

Answer (B) is correct. *(AIM Para 3-2-5)*

DISCUSSION: A Class D airspace area is automatically in effect when and only when the associated part-time control tower is in operation regardless of weather conditions, availability of radar services, or time of day. Airports with part-time operating towers only have a part-time Class D airspace area.

Answer (A) is incorrect. A Class D airspace area is automatically in effect when the tower is in operation, regardless of the weather conditions. Answer (C) is incorrect. A Class D airspace area is in effect when the associated control tower, not FSS, is in operation.

4. What designated airspace associated with an airport becomes inactive when the control tower at that airport is not in operation?

A. Class D, which then becomes Class G.

B. Class D, which becomes Class E.

C. Class D, which then becomes Class C.

Answer (B) is correct. *(AIM Para 3-2-5)*

DISCUSSION: Class D airspace located at airports that have an operating control tower which is not associated with Class B or Class C airspace. Airspace at an airport with a part-time control tower is classified as Class D airspace when the control tower is in operation and as Class E airspace when the control tower is not in operation.

Answer (A) is incorrect. When a part-time control tower is not in operation, the Class D airspace becomes Class E, not Class G, airspace. Answer (C) is incorrect. The primary airport of Class B airspace will have a control tower that operates full-time, not part-time.

5. A non-tower satellite airport, within the same Class D airspace as that designated for the primary airport, requires radio communications to be established and maintained with the

A. satellite airport's UNICOM.

B. associated Flight Service Station.

C. primary airport's control tower.

Answer (C) is correct. *(AIM Para 3-2-5)*

DISCUSSION: Each pilot departing a non-tower satellite airport within Class D airspace must establish and maintain two-way radio communications with the primary airport's control tower as soon as practicable after departing.

Answer (A) is incorrect. When departing a satellite airport without an operating control tower in Class D airspace, you must establish and maintain two-way radio communications with the primary airport's control tower, not the satellite airport's UNICOM. Answer (B) is incorrect. When departing a satellite airport without an operating control tower in Class D airspace, you must establish and maintain two-way radio communications with the primary airport's control tower, not the associated FSS.

6. Class D airspace can be found on a sectional chart by

    A. a solid magenta circle

    B. blue segmented lines

    C. a solid blue circle

Answer (B) is correct. *(AIM Para 3-2-5)*
    DISCUSSION: On a sectional chart, Class D airspace is depicted by blue segmented lines.
    Answer (A) is incorrect. A solid magenta circle on a sectional chart represents Class C, not Class D, airspace. Answer (C) is incorrect. A solid blue circle on a sectional chart represents Class B, not Class D, airspace.

7. When departing a non-tower satellite airport within Class D airspace

    A. you are not required to make radio contact.

    B. you must establish and maintain two-way radio communication with the primary airport's control tower as soon as you have reached cruise altitude.

    C. you must establish and maintain two-way radio communication with the primary airport's control tower as soon as practicable after departing.

Answer (C) is correct. *(AIM Para 3-2-5)*
    DISCUSSION: When departing any airport within Class D airspace, other than the primary airport within the Class D area, you are required to establish and maintain two-way radio communication as soon as practicable after departing.
    Answer (A) is incorrect. You are required to establish and maintain two-way radio communications in Class D airspace; you cannot operate without making radio contact. Answer (B) is incorrect. You must establish and maintain two-way radio communication as soon as practicable after departing, not once you have reached cruise altitude.

2.3 Class C Airspace

8. Unless otherwise authorized, two-way radio communications with Air Traffic Control are required for landings or takeoffs

    A. at all tower controlled airports regardless of weather conditions.

    B. at all tower-controlled airports only when weather conditions are less than VFR.

    C. at all tower-controlled airports within Class D airspace only when weather conditions are less than VFR.

Answer (A) is correct. *(FAR 91.129)*
    DISCUSSION: Two-way radio communications with air traffic control (ATC) are required for landing and taking off at all tower-controlled airports, regardless of weather conditions. However, light signals from the tower may be used during radio failure.
    Answer (B) is incorrect. Radio communication is also required in VFR weather as well as IFR weather at all tower-controlled airports. Answer (C) is incorrect. Radio communication is required in both VFR and IFR weather when landing at or taking off from all tower-controlled airports.

9. The vertical limit of Class C airspace above the primary airport is normally

    A. 1,200 feet AGL.

    B. 3,000 feet AGL.

    C. 4,000 feet AGL.

Answer (C) is correct. *(AIM Para 3-2-4)*
    DISCUSSION: The vertical limit (ceiling) of Class C airspace is normally 4,000 ft. above the primary airport elevation.
    Answer (A) is incorrect. The floor of the Class C airspace shelf area (5 to 10 NM from primary airport) is 1,200 ft. AGL, not the vertical limit. Answer (B) is incorrect. The vertical limit of Class C airspace is normally 4,000 ft. AGL, not 3,000 ft. AGL, above the elevation of the primary airport.

10. The normal radius of the outer area of Class C airspace is

    A. 5 nautical miles.

    B. 15 nautical miles.

    C. 20 nautical miles.

Answer (C) is correct. *(AIM Para 3-2-4)*
    DISCUSSION: Do not confuse the outer area (20 NM radius) with the shelf area (10 NM radius) of Class C airspace. Communication with ATC in the outer area is recommended but not required. Communication with ATC in the shelf area and the inner area of Class C airspace is mandatory.
    Answer (A) is incorrect. The radius of the surface area of the Class C airspace is 5 NM, not the outer area. Answer (B) is incorrect. A dimension not used for any component of Class C airspace is 15 NM.

11. All operations within Class C airspace must be in

    A. accordance with instrument flight rules.

    B. compliance with ATC clearances and instructions.

    C. an aircraft equipped with a 4096-code transponder with Mode C encoding capability.

Answer (C) is correct. *(AIM Para 3-2-4)*
    DISCUSSION: To operate within Class C airspace, an aircraft must be equipped with a 4096-code transponder with Mode C (altitude encoding) capability.
    Answer (A) is incorrect. IFR operations are not required within Class C airspace and there is no minimum pilot certification required; i.e., student pilots may operate within Class C airspace. Answer (B) is incorrect. Clearances are not required to operate within Class C airspace areas; clearances relate to IFR operations.

12. Under what condition may an aircraft operate from a satellite airport within Class C airspace?

A. The pilot must file a flight plan prior to departure.

B. The pilot must monitor ATC until clear of the Class C airspace.

C. The pilot must contact ATC as soon as practicable after takeoff.

Answer (C) is correct. *(AIM Para 3-2-4)*

DISCUSSION: Aircraft departing from a satellite airport within Class C airspace with an operating control tower must establish and maintain two-way radio communication with the control tower and thereafter as instructed by ATC. When departing a satellite airport without an operating control tower, the pilot must contact and maintain two-way radio communication with ATC as soon as practicable after takeoff.

Answer (A) is incorrect. Flight plans are not required in Class C airspace. Answer (B) is incorrect. The pilot must maintain communication with ATC, not just monitor ATC, in Class C airspace.

2.4 Transponder Codes

13. When making routine transponder code changes, pilots should avoid inadvertent selection of which codes?

A. 0700, 1700, 7000

B. 1200, 1500, 7000

C. 7500, 7600, 7700

Answer (C) is correct. *(AIM Para 4-1-19)*

DISCUSSION: Some special codes set aside for emergencies should be avoided during routine VFR flights. They are 7500 for hijacking, 7600 for lost radio communications, and 7700 for a general emergency. Additionally, you should know that code 7777 is reserved for military interceptors.

Answer (A) is incorrect. Any of these may be assigned by ATC. Answer (B) is incorrect. The standard VFR code is 1200.

14. When operating under VFR below 18,000 feet MSL, unless otherwise authorized, what transponder code should be selected?

A. 1200

B. 7600

C. 7700

Answer (A) is correct. *(AIM Para 4-1-19)*

DISCUSSION: The standard VFR transponder code is 1200. Since all flight operations above 18,000 ft. MSL are to be IFR, code 1200 is not used above that height.

Answer (B) is incorrect. The lost radio communications code is 7600. Answer (C) is incorrect. The general emergency code is 7700.

15. When a distress or urgency condition is encountered, the pilot of an aircraft with a coded radar beacon transponder, who desires to alert a ground radar facility, should squawk code

A. 7700

B. 7600

C. 7500

Answer (A) is correct. *(AIM Para 6-2-2)*

DISCUSSION: When a distress or urgency condition is encountered, the pilot of an aircraft equipped with a transponder should squawk code 7700. Code 7700 normally triggers an alarm or special indicator at ground-based radar facilities.

Answer (B) is incorrect. The squawk code 7600 is for two-way communications failure, not a general distress or emergency condition. Answer (C) is incorrect. The squawk code 7500 is for an aircraft hijack situation, not a general distress or emergency condition.

16. Transponder code 1200 should be used

A. during standard VFR operations.

B. during radio failure.

C. only when instructed by ATC.

Answer (A) is correct. *(AIM Para 4-1-19)*

DISCUSSION: Code 1200 is the standard VFR transponder code. Unless otherwise authorized, code 1200 should always be selected.

Answer (B) is incorrect. Pilots should squawk code 7600, not 1200, during radio failure. Answer (C) is incorrect. Code 1200 should be selected during standard VFR operation, not only when instructed by ATC.

17. Pilots should squawk code 7700 during

A. a hijacking.

B. an emergency.

C. flight through an ADIZ.

Answer (B) is correct. *(AIM Para 6-2-2)*

DISCUSSION: Code 7700 should be squawked when experiencing a distress or urgency condition, which includes engine failure.

Answer (A) is incorrect. Code 7500, not 7700, should be squawked for hijacking. Answer (C) is incorrect. Code 7700 should be squawked during an emergency, not for entering an ADIZ. Code 7777 would be required if you had inadvertently entered an ADIZ and were being intercepted by military aircraft.

2.5 Radio Phraseology

18. When flying HAWK N666CB, the proper phraseology for initial contact with McAlester AFSS is

A. "MC ALESTER RADIO, HAWK SIX SIX SIX CHARLIE BRAVO, RECEIVING ARDMORE VORTAC, OVER."

B. "MC ALESTER STATION, HAWK SIX SIX SIX CEE BEE, RECEIVING ARDMORE VORTAC, OVER."

C. "MC ALESTER FLIGHT SERVICE STATION, HAWK NOVEMBER SIX CHARLIE BRAVO, RECEIVING ARDMORE VORTAC, OVER."

Answer (A) is correct. *(AIM Para 4-2-3)*
DISCUSSION: When calling a ground station, pilots should begin with the name of the facility and the type of facility. Any FSS is referred to as "Radio." When the aircraft manufacturer's name or model is stated, the prefix "N" is dropped. When transmitting and receiving on different frequencies, indicate the name of the VOR or frequency on which a reply is expected. Thus, the proper phraseology on initial contact with McAlester AFSS is McAlester Radio, hawk six six six charlie bravo, receiving ardmore VORTAC, over. (NOTE: The word "over" has been dropped from common usage.)
Answer (B) is incorrect. It is McAlester Radio, not station, and CB is charlie bravo, not cee bee. Answer (C) is incorrect. It is radio, not flight service station. November is dropped in favor of hawk; also, it is six, six, six charlie bravo (not six charlie bravo).

19. The correct method of stating 4,500 feet MSL to ATC is

A. "FOUR THOUSAND FIVE HUNDRED."

B. "FOUR POINT FIVE."

C. "FORTY-FIVE HUNDRED FEET MSL."

Answer (A) is correct. *(AIM Para 4-2-9)*
DISCUSSION: The proper phraseology for altitudes up to but not including 18,000 ft. MSL is to state the separate digits of the thousands, plus the hundreds, if appropriate. It would be "four thousand five hundred."
Answer (B) is incorrect. Four point five is slang (not correct) phraseology. Answer (C) is incorrect. The thousand is spoken separately from the hundreds and not together. A stated altitude is understood to be MSL, unless otherwise stated.

20. When flying Cessna N589FF, to make initial contact with Seattle EFAS, your call should begin with

A. "SEATTLE RADIO, CESSNA FIVE EIGHT NINER FOXTROT FOXTROT."

B. "SEATTLE FLIGHT WATCH, CESSNA FIVE EIGHT NINER FOXTROT FOXTROT."

C. "SEATTLE FLIGHT WATCH, CESSNA FIVE EIGHTY NINE EFF EFF."

Answer (B) is correct. *(AIM Para 4-2-6)*
DISCUSSION: When calling an EFAS, the proper call sign is the name of the facility (Seattle), followed by "flight watch"; therefore, it is "Seattle Flight Watch." You then start your aircraft call sign with the make or model aircraft (Cessna), followed by each digit of the call sign (except the "N").
Answer (A) is incorrect. The facility call sign is "Seattle Flight Watch," not "Seattle Radio." Answer (C) is incorrect. Each digit of the aircraft call sign should be spoken individually -- as "Cessna Five Eight Niner Foxtrot Foxtrot," not "Cessna Five Eighty Nine Eff Eff."

21. You would start a call with 'Seattle Flight Watch' when calling

A. a Flight Service Station.

B. a Class D airspace control tower.

C. an En Route Flight Advisory Service (EFAS).

Answer (C) is correct. *(AIM Para 4-2-6)*
DISCUSSION: When calling an En Route Flight Advisory Service (EFAS), the proper call sign is the name of the facility, followed by "Flight Watch" (e.g., "Seattle Flight Watch").
Answer (A) is incorrect. If you were calling a Flight Service Station, you would start with the name of the facility, followed by "RADIO." Answer (B) is incorrect. If you were calling any tower, you would start with the name of the tower followed by "TOWER."

22. If you are advising ATC that your altitude is 1500 feet MSL, you would say

A. FIFTEEN HUNDRED FEET.

B. ONE FIVE ZERO ZERO FEET.

C. ONE THOUSAND FIVE HUNDRED.

Answer (C) is correct. *(AIM Para 4-2-9)*
DISCUSSION: The proper phraseology for altitudes up to but not including 18,000 feet MSL is to state the separate digits of the thousands, plus the hundreds if appropriate. Therefore, 1500 feet is "one thousand five hundred."
Answer (A) is incorrect. Thousands and hundreds should be read individually, without stating "feet," e.g., "one thousand five hundred." Answer (B) is incorrect. You should not state each digit individually; only the thousands and hundreds are stated, e.g., "one thousand five hundred." You do not need to state "feet."

2.6 ATC Traffic Advisories

23. An ATC radar facility issues the following advisory to a pilot flying on a heading of 090°:

"TRAFFIC 3 O'CLOCK, 2 MILES, WESTBOUND..."

Where should the pilot look for this traffic?

A. East.

B. South.

C. West.

Answer (B) is correct. *(AIM Para 4-1-14)*
DISCUSSION: If you receive traffic information service from radar and are told you have traffic at the 3 o'clock position, traffic is in the direction of the right wingtip, or to the south.
Answer (A) is incorrect. East is the 12 o'clock position.
Answer (C) is incorrect. West is the 6 o'clock position.

24. An ATC radar facility issues the following advisory to a pilot flying on a heading of 360°:

"TRAFFIC 10 O'CLOCK, 2 MILES, SOUTHBOUND..."

Where should the pilot look for this traffic?

A. Northwest.

B. Northeast.

C. Southwest.

Answer (A) is correct. *(AIM Para 4-1-14)*
DISCUSSION: The controller is telling you that traffic is at 10 o'clock and 2 mi. The left wingtip is 9 o'clock, and 10 o'clock is 2/3 of the way from the nose of the airplane (12 o'clock) to the left wingtip. Thus, you are looking northwest.
Answer (B) is incorrect. Northeast would be in the 1 to 2 o'clock position. Answer (C) is incorrect. Southwest would be in the 7 to 8 o'clock position.

25. An ATC radar facility issues the following advisory to a pilot during a local flight:

"TRAFFIC 2 O'CLOCK, 5 MILES, NORTHBOUND..."

Where should the pilot look for this traffic?

A. Between directly ahead and 90° to the left.

B. Between directly behind and 90° to the right.

C. Between directly ahead and 90° to the right.

Answer (C) is correct. *(AIM Para 4-1-14)*
DISCUSSION: The right wingtip is 3 o'clock, and the nose is 12 o'clock. A controller report of traffic 2 o'clock, 5 mi., northbound indicates that the traffic is to the right of the airplane's nose, just ahead of the right wingtip.
Answer (A) is incorrect. The area directly ahead to 90° left is the area from 12 o'clock to 9 o'clock. Answer (B) is incorrect. The area directly behind to 90° right is the area from 6 o'clock to 3 o'clock.

26. An ATC radar facility issues the following advisory to a pilot flying north in a calm wind:

"TRAFFIC 9 O'CLOCK, 2 MILES, SOUTHBOUND..."

Where should the pilot look for this traffic?

A. South.

B. North.

C. West.

Answer (C) is correct. *(AIM Para 4-1-14)*
DISCUSSION: Traffic at 9 o'clock is off the left wingtip. The nose of the airplane is 12 o'clock, the left wingtip is 9 o'clock, the tail is 6 o'clock, and the right wingtip is 3 o'clock. With a north heading, the aircraft at 9 o'clock would be west of the pilot.
Answer (A) is incorrect. South would be the 6 o'clock position. Answer (B) is incorrect. North would be the 12 o'clock position.

27. An ATC radar facility issues the following advisory to a pilot flying on a heading of 270°:

"TRAFFIC 3 O'CLOCK, 2 MILES, EASTBOUND..."

Where should the pilot look for this traffic?

A. North.

B. South.

C. West.

Answer (A) is correct. *(AIM Para 4-1-14)*
DISCUSSION: If you receive traffic information service from radar and are told you have traffic at the 3 o'clock position, traffic is in the direction of the right wingtip, or to the north.
Answer (B) is incorrect. South is the 9 o'clock position.
Answer (C) is incorrect. West is the 12 o'clock position.

28. If an ATC radar facility were to advise a pilot flying heading 180, of traffic to the northwest, the call would be

A. "TRAFFIC 4 O'CLOCK, FIVE MILES, SOUTHBOUND."

B. "TRAFFIC 8 O'CLOCK, FIVE MILES, SOUTHBOUND."

C. "TRAFFIC 6 O'CLOCK, FIVE MILES, SOUTHBOUND."

Answer (A) is correct. *(AIM Para 4-1-14)*
DISCUSSION: Traffic to the northwest of an aircraft heading south will be behind and at a bearing between the right wing tip and the tail. The right wing tip is 3 o'clock and the tail is 6 o'clock, so the traffic is at 4 o'clock. You may receive advice of traffic behind you when it is closing and going to pass you.
Answer (B) is incorrect. Traffic at 8 o'clock would be to the northeast, not northwest. Answer (C) is incorrect. Traffic at 6 o'clock would be directly to the north, not the northwest.

29. Radar equipped Air Traffic Control facilities provide radar assistance to VFR aircraft provided the aircraft

A. can communicate with the facility and is within radar range.

B. is on a VFR Flight Plan.

C. is squawking the correct code.

Answer (A) is correct. *(AIM Para 4-1-16)*
DISCUSSION: Air Traffic Control will provide radar assistance to any VFR aircraft, as long as they can communicate with the aircraft and see them on the radar.
Answer (B) is incorrect. Aircraft can receive radar assistance, regardless of whether the aircraft is on a VFR flight plan, provided the aircraft can communicate and is in radar range. Answer (C) is incorrect. An aircraft can receive radar assistance, regardless of the transponder code it is squawking, provided the aircraft can communicate and is in radar range.

30. During departure, when visual separation is employed by Air Traffic Control (ATC), traffic is no longer a factor when

A. the other aircraft turns away or is on a diverging course.

B. visual contact with the other aircraft is lost.

C. the other aircraft is passed.

Answer (A) is correct. *(AIM Para 4-4-13)*
DISCUSSION: ATC uses visual separation to separate aircraft in terminal areas and en route airspace in the NAS. When pilots accept responsibility to maintain visual separation, they must utilize constant visual surveillance and not pass the other aircraft until it is no longer a factor. Traffic is no longer a factor when, during departure or en route, the other aircraft turns away or is on a diverging course.
Answer (B) is incorrect. An aircraft may still be a factor, even if visual contact is lost. Answer (C) is incorrect. Traffic is no longer a factor when the aircraft turns away or is on a diverging course, which may or may not occur after it has been passed.

2.7 ATC Light Signals

31. While on final approach for landing, an alternating green and red light followed by a flashing red light is received from the control tower. Under these circumstances, the pilot should

A. discontinue the approach, fly the same traffic pattern and approach again, and land.

B. exercise extreme caution and abandon the approach, realizing the airport is unsafe for landing.

C. abandon the approach, circle the airport to the right, and expect a flashing white light when the airport is safe for landing.

Answer (B) is correct. *(FAR 91.125)*
DISCUSSION: An alternating red and green light signaled from a control tower means "exercise extreme caution" whether to an airplane on the ground or in the air. The flashing red light received while in the air indicates the airport is not safe and the pilot should not land.
Answer (A) is incorrect. A flashing green (not red) light means to return for a landing. Answer (C) is incorrect. A flashing green (not red) light means to return for a landing, and a flashing white light does not have a meaning to aircraft in flight.

32. A steady green light signal directed from the control tower to an aircraft in flight is a signal that the pilot

A. is cleared to land.

B. should give way to other aircraft and continue circling.

C. should return for landing.

Answer (A) is correct. *(FAR 91.125)*
DISCUSSION: A steady green light signal from the tower to an airplane in flight means cleared to land.
Answer (B) is incorrect. Give way to other aircraft and continue circling is signaled by a steady red light to an airplane in the air. Answer (C) is incorrect. Return for landing is signaled by a flashing green light to an airplane in the air.

33. A steady red light from the tower, for an aircraft on the ground indicates

A. Give way to other aircraft and continue circling.
B. Stop.
C. Taxi clear of the runway in use.

Answer (B) is correct. *(AIM Para 4-3-13)*
DISCUSSION: A steady red light directed to an aircraft on the ground carries the meaning of STOP.
Answer (A) is incorrect. A steady red light directed to an aircraft on the ground means to STOP, not give way to other aircraft and continue circling. Answer (C) is incorrect. A flashing red light, not a steady red light, directed to an aircraft on the ground means taxi clear of the runway in use.

34. A flashing white light signal from the control tower to a taxiing aircraft is an indication to

A. taxi at a faster speed.
B. taxi only on taxiways and not cross runways.
C. return to the starting point on the airport.

Answer (C) is correct. *(FAR 91.125)*
DISCUSSION: A flashing white light given to an aircraft taxiing along the ground means to return to the aircraft's starting point.
Answer (A) is incorrect. There is no light signal that means to taxi at a faster speed. Answer (B) is incorrect. There is no light signal (by itself) that means to taxi only on taxiways and not cross runways.

35. If the control tower uses a light signal to direct a pilot to give way to other aircraft and continue circling, the light will be

A. flashing red.
B. steady red.
C. alternating red and green.

Answer (B) is correct. *(FAR 91.125)*
DISCUSSION: A steady red light signal given to an aircraft in the air means to give way to other aircraft and continue circling.
Answer (A) is incorrect. When in the air, a flashing red light means airport unsafe, do not land. Answer (C) is incorrect. An alternating red and green light always means exercise extreme caution.

36. Which light signal from the control tower clears a pilot to taxi?

A. Flashing green.
B. Steady green.
C. Flashing white.

Answer (A) is correct. *(FAR 91.125)*
DISCUSSION: A flashing green gives the pilot permission to taxi.
Answer (B) is incorrect. A steady green light means cleared to take off if on the ground or to land if in the air. Answer (C) is incorrect. A flashing white light means to return to the starting point on the airport for aircraft only on the ground.

37. An alternating red and green light signal directed from the control tower to an aircraft in flight is a signal to

A. hold position.
B. exercise extreme caution.
C. not land; the airport is unsafe.

Answer (B) is correct. *(FAR 91.125)*
DISCUSSION: A flashing red and green light given anytime means exercise extreme caution.
Answer (A) is incorrect. A steady red when taxiing means hold your position. There is no light signal to tell you to hold your position when in flight, only to give way to other aircraft and continue circling. Answer (C) is incorrect. A flashing red light means do not land, airport unsafe.

38. If the aircraft's radio fails, what is the recommended procedure when landing at a controlled airport?

A. Observe the traffic flow, enter the pattern, and look for a light signal from the tower.
B. Enter a crosswind leg and rock the wings.
C. Flash the landing lights and cycle the landing gear while circling the airport.

Answer (A) is correct. *(AIM Para 4-2-13)*
DISCUSSION: If your radio fails and you wish to land at a tower-controlled airport, remain outside or above the airport's traffic pattern until the direction and flow of traffic has been determined, then join the airport traffic pattern and maintain visual contact with the tower to receive light signals.
Answer (B) is incorrect. Crosswind entry is not required; also, you rock the wings to acknowledge light signals during daylight hours. Answer (C) is incorrect. Flashing the landing light is a method of acknowledging light signals at night, and cycling the landing gear is not an option available to fixed-gear aircraft.

2.8 Emergency Locator Transmitters (ELTs)

39. When activated, an emergency locator transmitter (ELT) transmits on

    A. 118.0 and 118.8 MHz.

    B. 121.5 and 243.0 MHz.

    C. 123.0 and 119.0 MHz.

Answer (B) is correct. *(AIM Para 6-2-5)*
    DISCUSSION: When activated, an emergency locator transmitter (ELT) transmits simultaneously on the international distress frequencies of 121.5 and 243.0 MHz.
    Answer (A) is incorrect. These frequencies are not emergency frequencies. Answer (C) is incorrect. These frequencies are not emergency frequencies.

40. Which procedure is recommended to ensure that the emergency locator transmitter (ELT) has not been activated?

    A. Turn off the aircraft ELT after landing.

    B. Ask the airport tower if they are receiving an ELT signal.

    C. Monitor 121.5 before engine shutdown.

Answer (C) is correct. *(AIM Para 6-2-5)*
    DISCUSSION: To ensure that your ELT has not been activated, you can monitor 121.5 MHz or 243.0 MHz in flight when a receiver is available and prior to engine shut-down at the end of each flight.
    Answer (A) is incorrect. If you turn off the ELT, there is no way of telling whether it has been activated. Answer (B) is incorrect. The tower or ATC should not be bothered by questions about your ELT transmissions. If, however, you do receive signals on 121.5, IMMEDIATELY report it to ATC and/or FSS.

41. If faced with an emergency where Air Traffic Control (ATC) assistance is desired and not already in contact, which frequency can be used to establish communications?

    A. 121.5 MHz.

    B. 122.5 MHz.

    C. 128.725 MHz.

Answer (A) is correct. *(AIM Para 6-3-1)*
    DISCUSSION: The frequency that is guarded for distress and emergency radio communications is 121.5 MHz. If faced with an emergency situation, tune and broadcast on 121.5 your aircraft identification, position, and intentions.
    Answer (B) is incorrect. The frequency that is reserved for emergency broadcasts is 121.5 MHz, not 122.5 MHz. Answer (C) is incorrect. The frequency that is reserved for emergency broadcasts is 121.5 MHz, not 128.725 MHz.

42. Monitoring radio frequency 121.5 MHz before engine shut-down will

    A. indicate to ATC that you have completed your flight safely.

    B. enable you to check that the ELT has not been activated.

    C. ensure that your ELT is operational.

Answer (B) is correct. *(AIM Para 6-2-5)*
    DISCUSSION: By monitoring 121.5 MHz and 243.0 MHz in flight when a receiver is available and prior to engine shutdown at the end of each flight, you can check that your ELT has not inadvertently been activated.
    Answer (A) is incorrect. Monitoring any frequency does not provide any information to ATC. Answer (C) is incorrect. Monitoring the frequency does not indicate anything other than whether or not the ELT is transmitting. Monitoring the frequency will only allow you to check that it is not transmitting.

43. When may an emergency locator transmitter (ELT) be tested?

    A. Anytime.

    B. At 15 and 45 minutes past the hour.

    C. During the first 5 minutes after the hour.

Answer (C) is correct. *(AIM Para 6-2-5)*
    DISCUSSION: Emergency locator transmitters (ELT) may only be tested on the ground during the first 5 min. after the hour. Other times, it is only allowed with prior arrangement with the nearest FAA Control Tower or FSS. No airborne checks are allowed.
    Answer (A) is incorrect. An ELT should only be tested during the first 5 min. after the hour, not anytime. Answer (B) is incorrect. An ELT should only be tested during the first 5 min. after the hour, not at 15 and 45 min. past the hour.

END OF STUDY UNIT

STUDY UNIT THREE
FEDERAL AVIATION REGULATIONS –
FAR PARTS 1 THROUGH 71

(5 pages of outline)

This study unit contains outlines of major concepts tested, sample test questions and answers regarding Federal Aviation Regulations (FAR) Parts 1 through 71, and an explanation of each answer. The table of contents above lists each subunit within this study unit, the number of questions pertaining to that particular subunit, and the pages on which the outlines and questions begin, respectively.

CAUTION: Recall that the **sole purpose** of this book is to expedite your passing the FAA pilot knowledge test for the sport pilot certificate. Accordingly, all extraneous material (i.e., topics or regulations not directly tested on the FAA pilot knowledge test) is omitted, even though much more information and knowledge are necessary to fly safely. This additional material is presented in *Pilot Handbook* and *Sport Pilot Flight Maneuvers and Practical Test Prep*, available from Gleim Publications, Inc. See the order form on page 327.

FAR PART 1

1.1 General Definitions

1. **Light-Sport Aircraft (LSA)** means an aircraft, other than a helicopter or powered-lift that, since its original certification, has continued to meet the following:

   a. A maximum takeoff weight of not more than 1,320 pounds (600 kilograms) for aircraft not intended for operation on water, and 1,430 pounds (650 kilograms) for seaplanes

   b. A maximum airspeed in level flight with maximum continuous power (V_H) of not more than 120 knots CAS

   c. A single reciprocating engine, if powered

   d. A classification as either an Airplane, Gyroplane, Glider, Lighter-than-air, Powered parachute, or Weight-shift-control aircraft

2. **Night** means the time between the end of evening civil twilight and the beginning of morning civil twilight (as published in the *American Air Almanac*), converted to local time.

   a. A sport pilot may not operate an aircraft at night.

3. **Aircraft categories** (for certification of airmen); broad classifications of aircraft.

   a. Airplane   c. Glider
   b. Rotorcraft   d. Lighter-than-air

4. **Airplane classes** (for certification of airmen).

   a. Single-engine land   c. Single-engine sea
   b. Multi-engine land   d. Multi-engine sea

5. **Rotorcraft classes** (for certification of airmen).

   a. Helicopter
   b. Gyrocopter

6. **Lighter-than-air classes** (for certification of airmen).

   a. Airship   c. Hot air balloon
   b. Free balloon   d. Gas balloon

7. Note that the above category and class definitions are for certification of airmen purposes. For certification of aircraft, there are different definitions:

   a. **Category** (for certification of aircraft purposes) is based on intended use or operating limitations.

      1) Transport   5) Restricted
      2) Normal   6) Acrobatic
      3) Utility   7) Provisional
      4) Limited

   b. **Classes** as used for certification of aircraft are the same as, or very similar to, categories for certification of airmen, e.g., airplane, rotorcraft, glider, lighter-than-air.

8. **Air traffic control (ATC) clearance** means an authorization to proceed under specific traffic conditions in controlled airspace.

3.2 FAR PART 21

21.181 Duration of Airworthiness Certificates

1. Airworthiness certificates remain in force as long as maintenance and alteration of the aircraft are performed per FARs.

3.3 FAR PART 39

39.1 Applicability

1. Airworthiness Directives (ADs) are issued under FAR Part 39 by the FAA to require correction of unsafe conditions found in an airplane, an airplane engine, a propeller, or an appliance when such conditions exist and are likely to exist or develop in other products of the same design.

    a. Since ADs are issued under FAR Part 39, they are regulatory and must be complied with, unless a specific exemption is granted.

39.3 General

1. No person may operate a product to which an AD applies except in accordance with the requirements of that AD.

    a. Thus, you may operate an airplane that is not in compliance with an AD, if such operation is allowed by the AD.

3.4 FAR PART 43

43.9 Maintenance Records

1. After preventive maintenance has been performed, the signature, certificate number, kind of certificate held by the person approving the work, the date, and a description of the work must be entered in the aircraft maintenance records.

43 Appendix A. Major Alterations and Repairs and Preventive Maintenance

1. Preventive maintenance means simple or minor preservation operations and the replacement of small standard parts not involving complex assembly operations. Examples include

    a. Replenishing hydraulic fluid and
    b. Servicing landing gear wheel bearings.

3.5 FAR PART 61

61.3 Requirements for Certificates, Ratings, and Authorizations

1. When acting as a pilot in command or as a required pilot flight crewmember, you must have a valid pilot certificate and a current and appropriate medical certificate (or driver's license, if appropriate) in your personal possession or readily accessible in the airplane.

2. You must present your pilot certificate or medical certificate (or driver's license, if appropriate) upon the request of the Administrator of the FAA or his/her representative; the NTSB; or any federal, state, or local law enforcement officer.

61.15 Offenses Involving Alcohol or Drugs

1. A pilot convicted of operating a motor vehicle while either intoxicated by, impaired by, or under the influence of alcohol or a drug is required to provide a written report to the FAA Civil Aviation Security Division (AMC-700) not later than 60 days after the conviction.

2. A pilot convicted for the violation of any federal or state statute relating to the process, manufacture, transportation, distribution, or sale of narcotic drugs is grounds for suspension or revocation of any certificate, rating, or authorization issued under Part 61.

3. A pilot convicted of operating an aircraft as a crewmember under the influence of alcohol or using drugs that affect the person's faculties (acts that are prohibited by Sec. 91.17) is grounds for denial of an application for a certificate, rating, or authorization issued under Part 61 for a period of 1 year after the date of that act.

61.23 Medical Certificates: Requirement and Duration

1. When exercising the privileges of either a sport pilot or student sport pilot certificate in a light-sport aircraft other than a balloon or glider, a person must hold or possess either a valid FAA medical certificate or a current and valid U.S. driver's license.

2. For operations requiring a third-class medical certificate, the certificate will expire at midnight on the last day of the

    a. 60th month (5 years) after the date of examination shown on the certificate, if you have not reached your 40th birthday on or before the date of examination, or

    b. 24th month (2 years) after the date of examination shown on the certificate, if you have reached your 40th birthday on or before the date of examination.

61.56 Flight Review

1. A flight review must have been satisfactorily completed within the previous 24 calendar months to act as pilot in command of an aircraft for which that pilot is rated. A flight review consists of a minimum of 1 hour of flight training by an authorized instructor and 1 hour of ground training.

    a. A proficiency check or flight test for a pilot certificate, rating, or other operating privileges will also satisfy this requirement.

    b. Satisfactory completion of the review or flight test must be endorsed in the pilot's logbook by the reviewer.

2. The expiration of the 24-month period for the flight review falls on the last day of the 24th month after the month of the examination date (i.e., 24 calendar months).

61.57 Recent Flight Experience: Pilot in Command

1. To carry passengers, you must have made three landings and three takeoffs within the preceding 90 days.

    a. All three landings must be made in aircraft of the same category, class, and, if a type rating is required, the same type as the one in which passengers are to be carried.

        1) The categories are airplane, rotorcraft, glider, and lighter-than-air.
        2) The classes are single-engine land, single-engine sea, multi-engine land, and multi-engine sea.

    b. The landings must be to a full stop if the airplane is tailwheel (conventional) rather than nosewheel.

61.60 Change of Address

1. You must notify the FAA Airman Certification Branch in writing of any change in your permanent mailing address.

2. You may not exercise the privileges of your pilot certificate after 30 days from moving unless you make this notification.

61.315 Sport Pilot Privileges and Limitations: Pilot in Command

1. Sport pilots may not act as pilot in command of a light-sport aircraft while carrying more than one passenger.

2. As a sport pilot, you must pay at least half of the operating expenses of a flight. The operating expenses that may be shared with a passenger involve only fuel, oil, airport expenses, or aircraft rental fees.

3. Sport pilots may not operate

    a. For compensation or hire
    b. In furtherance of a business
    c. In Class A airspace

d. In Class B, C, and D airspace or at an airport or through the airspace having an operational control tower without CFI training and logbook endorsement

e. Aircraft in flight to a prospective buyer

f. In a passenger-carrying airlift sponsored by a charitable organization

g. Above 10,000 ft. MSL or 2,000 ft. AGL, whichever is higher

h. Without visual reference to the surface

i. In less than 3 statute miles

j. At night

k. Contrary to any aircraft, flight instructor, or other limitations

l. While towing any object

m. In aircraft with V_H above 87 KCAS (except with CFI training and a logbook endorsement)

n. Outside the United States, unless you have prior authorization from the country in which you seek to operate

o. In aircraft requiring more than one pilot

61.325 Required Endorsements for Class B, C, and D Airspaces

1. A sport pilot must receive and log ground and flight training to operate a light-sport aircraft at an airport in airspace within Class B, C, and D airspace or in other airspace with an airport that has an operational control tower.

    a. The CFI who provides the training must provide the pilot with a logbook endorsement that certifies proficiency in the following aeronautical knowledge areas and areas of operation:

        1) The use of radios, communications, navigation system/facilities, and radar services

        2) Operations at airports with an operating control tower to include three takeoffs and three landings to a full stop, with each landing involving a flight in the traffic pattern at an airport with an operating control tower

        3) Applicable flight rules of FAR Part 91 for operations in Class B, C, and D airspace and air traffic control clearances

3.6 FAR PART 71

71.71 Extent of Federal Airways

1. Federal airways include that Class E airspace

    a. Extending upward from 1,200 ft. AGL to and including 17,999 ft. MSL

    b. Within parallel boundary lines 4 NM each side of the airway's centerline

---

QUESTIONS AND ANSWER EXPLANATIONS

All of the sport pilot knowledge test questions chosen by the FAA for release as well as additional questions selected by Gleim relating to the material in the previous outlines are reproduced on the following pages. These questions have been organized into the same subunits as the outlines. To the immediate right of each question are the correct answer and answer explanation. You should cover these answers and answer explanations while responding to the questions. Refer to the general discussion in the Introduction on how to take the FAA pilot knowledge test.

Remember that the questions from the FAA pilot knowledge test bank have been reordered by topic and organized into a meaningful sequence. Also, the first line of the answer explanation gives the citation of the authoritative source for the answer.

QUESTIONS

3.1 FAR Part 1

1.1 General Definitions

1. Which is a type of Light-Sport Aircraft?

A. Weight-Shift-Control.

B. Multi-engine airplane.

C. A turbo-jet powered homebuilt.

Answer (A) is correct. *(FAR 1.1)*
DISCUSSION: Weight-control aircraft, Powered parachutes, ASEL (1,320 lb. max weight), ASES (1,430 lb. max weight), and Gyroplanes are all examples of Light-Sport Aircraft. LSA are small, simple, low-performance, low-energy aircraft.
Answer (B) is incorrect. Multi-engine aircraft are not examples of Light-Sport Aircraft. Answer (C) is incorrect. Light-Sport Aircraft are limited to reciprocating engines.

2. What is the maximum weight for a Light-Sport Aircraft (not intended for water operations)?

A. 600 pounds.

B. 1320 pounds.

C. 1230 pounds.

Answer (B) is correct. *(FAR 1.1)*
DISCUSSION: The maximum weight for an LSA is 1,320 lb., or 600 kg.
Answer (A) is incorrect. LSA are limited to 1,320 lb., or 600 kg, max weight. Answer (C) is incorrect. LSA are limited to 1,320 lb., or 600 kg, max weight.

3. Which is true for a Light-Sport Aircraft?

A. The maximum speed is 120 knots.

B. The maximum speed is 145 knots.

C. The maximum speed is 100 knots.

Answer (A) is correct. *(FAR 1.1)*
DISCUSSION: LSA are limited to a maximum speed of 120 knots with maximum power in level flight.
Answer (B) is incorrect. LSA are limited to a maximum speed of 120 knots and must have a maximum stall speed of no greater than 45 knots. Answer (C) is incorrect. LSA are limited to a maximum speed of 120 knots and must have a maximum stall speed of no greater than 45 knots.

4. With respect to the certification of airmen, which is a category of aircraft?

A. Gyroplane, helicopter, airship, free balloon.

B. Airplane, rotorcraft, glider, lighter-than-air.

C. Single-engine land and sea, multiengine land and sea.

Answer (B) is correct. *(FAR 1.1)*
DISCUSSION: Category of aircraft, as used with respect to the certification, ratings, privileges, and limitations of airmen, means a broad classification of aircraft. Examples include airplane, rotorcraft, glider, and lighter-than-air.
Answer (A) is incorrect. Gyroplane, helicopter, airship, and free balloon are classes, not categories, used with respect to the certification of airmen. Answer (C) is incorrect. Single-engine land and sea and multiengine land and sea are classes, not categories, used with respect to the certification of airmen.

5. With respect to the certification of airmen, which is a class of aircraft?

A. Airplane, rotorcraft, glider, lighter-than-air.

B. Single-engine land and sea, multiengine land and sea.

C. Lighter-than-air, airship, hot air balloon, gas balloon.

Answer (B) is correct. *(FAR 1.1)*
DISCUSSION: Class of aircraft, as used with respect to the certification, ratings, privileges, and limitations of airmen, means a classification of aircraft within a category having similar operating characteristics. Examples include single-engine, multiengine, land, water, gyroplane, helicopter, airship, and free balloon.
Answer (A) is incorrect. Airplane, rotorcraft, glider, and lighter-than-air are categories, not classes, used with respect to the certification of airmen. Answer (C) is incorrect. Lighter-than-air is a category, not class, of aircraft used with respect to the certification of airmen.

6. The definition of nighttime is

A. sunset to sunrise.

B. 1 hour after sunset to 1 hour before sunrise.

C. the time between the end of evening civil twilight and the beginning of morning civil twilight.

Answer (C) is correct. *(FAR 1.1)*
DISCUSSION: "Night" means the time between the end of evening civil twilight and the beginning of morning civil twilight (as published in the *American Air Almanac*), converted to local time.
Answer (A) is incorrect. "Sunset to sunrise" is the time during which navigation lights must be used. Answer (B) is incorrect. The definition for nighttime recency of experience requirements is 1 hr. after sunset to 1 hr. before sunrise.

7. With respect to the certification of aircraft, which is a category of aircraft?

A. Normal, utility, acrobatic.

B. Airplane, rotorcraft, glider.

C. Landplane, seaplane.

Answer (A) is correct. *(FAR 1.1)*
  DISCUSSION: Category of aircraft, as used with respect to the certification of aircraft, means a grouping of aircraft based upon intended use or operating limitations. Examples include transport, normal, utility, acrobatic, limited, restricted, and provisional.
  Answer (B) is incorrect. Airplane, rotorcraft, and glider are categories of aircraft used with respect to the certification of airmen, not aircraft. Answer (C) is incorrect. Landplane and seaplane are classes, not categories, of aircraft used with respect to the certification of aircraft.

8. With respect to the certification of aircraft, which is a class of aircraft?

A. Airplane, rotorcraft, glider, balloon.

B. Normal, utility, acrobatic, limited.

C. Transport, restricted, provisional.

Answer (A) is correct. *(FAR 1.1)*
  DISCUSSION: Class of aircraft, as used with respect to the certification of aircraft, means a broad grouping of aircraft having similar characteristics of propulsion, flight, or landing. Examples include airplane, rotorcraft, glider, balloon, landplane, and seaplane.
  Answer (B) is incorrect. Normal, utility, acrobatic, and limited are categories, not classes, of aircraft used with respect to the certification of aircraft. Answer (C) is incorrect. Transport, restricted, and provisional are categories, not classes, of aircraft used with respect to the certification of aircraft.

9. If sunset is 2021 and the end of evening civil twilight is 2043, when must a sport pilot terminate the flight?

A. 2021

B. 2043

C. 2121

Answer (B) is correct. *(FAR 1.1, FAR 61.315)*
  DISCUSSION: A sport pilot may not operate an aircraft at night. The FAA defines night (FAR Part 1) as the time between the end of evening civil twilight and the beginning of morning civil twilight, not sunset.
  Answer (A) is incorrect. The FAA defines night (FAR Part 1) as the time between the end of evening civil twilight and the beginning of morning civil twilight, not sunset. Answer (C) is incorrect. The FAA defines night (FAR Part 1) as the time between the end of evening civil twilight and the beginning of morning civil twilight, not 1 hour after sunset.

10. An ATC clearance means an authorization by ATC for an aircraft to proceed under specified conditions within

A. controlled airspace.

B. uncontrolled airspace.

C. published Visual Flight Rules (VFR) routes.

Answer (A) is correct. *(FAR 1.1)*
  DISCUSSION: An ATC clearance is an authorization by ATC for an aircraft to proceed under the specified conditions of the clearance within controlled airspace.
  Answer (B) is incorrect. ATC clearances can only be issued for flight into controlled airspace. Answer (C) is incorrect. ATC clearances may apply when flying on published Visual Flight Rules routes, Instrument Flight Rules routes, or both.

3.2 FAR Part 21

21.181 Duration of Airworthiness Certificates

11. How long does the Airworthiness Certificate of an aircraft remain valid?

A. As long as the aircraft has a current Registration Certificate.

B. Indefinitely, unless the aircraft suffers major damage.

C. As long as the aircraft is maintained and operated as required by Federal Aviation Regulations.

Answer (C) is correct. *(FAR 21.181)*
  DISCUSSION: The airworthiness certificate of an airplane remains valid as long as the airplane is in an airworthy condition, i.e., operated and maintained as required by the FARs.
  Answer (A) is incorrect. The registration certificate is the document evidencing ownership. A changed registration has no effect on the airworthiness certificate. Answer (B) is incorrect. The airplane must be maintained and operated according to the FARs, not indefinitely. Even if the aircraft suffers major damage, as long as all required repairs are made, the Airworthiness Certificate remains valid.

3.3 FAR Part 39

39.1 Applicability

12. What should an owner or operator know about Airworthiness Directives (AD's)?

    A. For informational purposes only.

    B. They are mandatory.

    C. They are voluntary.

Answer (B) is correct. *(FAR 39.3)*

    DISCUSSION: Airworthiness Directives (ADs) are issued under FAR Part 39 by the FAA to require correction of unsafe conditions found in an airplane, an airplane engine, a propeller, or an appliance when such conditions exist and are likely to exist or develop in other products of the same design. Since ADs are issued under FAR Part 39, they are regulatory and must be complied with, unless a specific exemption is granted.

    Answer (A) is incorrect. ADs outline required maintenance; they are not for informational purposes only. Answer (C) is incorrect. ADs are mandatory, not voluntary.

39.3 General

13. May a pilot operate an aircraft that is not in compliance with an Airworthiness Directive (AD)?

    A. Yes, under VFR conditions only.

    B. Yes, AD's are only voluntary.

    C. Yes, if allowed by the AD.

Answer (C) is correct. *(FAR 39.3)*

    DISCUSSION: An AD is used to notify aircraft owners and other interested persons of unsafe conditions and prescribe the conditions under which the product (e.g., an aircraft) may continue to be operated. An AD may be one of an emergency nature requiring immediate compliance upon receipt or one of a less urgent nature requiring compliance within a relatively longer period of time. You may operate an airplane that is not in compliance with an AD, if such operation is allowed by the AD.

    Answer (A) is incorrect. An AD, not the operating conditions, may allow an aircraft to be operated before compliance with the AD. Answer (B) is incorrect. ADs are mandatory, not voluntary.

3.4 FAR Part 43

43.9 Maintenance Records

14. Preventive maintenance has been performed on an aircraft. What paperwork is required?

    A. A full, detailed description of the work done must be entered in the airframe logbook.

    B. Only the date, name, and signature of the person who performed the work must be entered in the aircraft maintenance records.

    C. The signature, certificate number, and kind of certificate held by the person approving the work and a description of the work must be entered in the aircraft maintenance records.

Answer (C) is correct. *(FAR 43.9)*

    DISCUSSION: After preventive maintenance has been performed, the signature, certificate number, and kind of certificate held by the person approving the work and a description of the work must be entered in the aircraft maintenance records.

    Answer (A) is incorrect. The signature, certificate number, and kind of certificate, in addition to the description of work performed, must be entered into the maintenance records. Answer (B) is incorrect. A description of the work completed, the date completed, name, signature, certificate number, and kind of certificate held by the person approving the work (if different than the person who did the work) must be entered in the maintenance records.

Part 43 Appendix A. Major Alterations and Repairs and Preventive Maintenance

15. Which operation would be described as preventive maintenance?

    A. Servicing landing gear wheel bearings.

    B. Alteration of main seat support brackets.

    C. Engine adjustments to allow automotive gas to be used.

Answer (A) is correct. *(Appendix A to Part 43)*

    DISCUSSION: Appendix A to Part 43 provides a list of work that is considered preventive maintenance. Preventive maintenance means simple or minor preservation operations and the replacement of small standard parts not involving complex assembly operations. Servicing landing gear wheel bearings, such as cleaning and greasing, is considered preventive maintenance.

    Answer (B) is incorrect. The alteration of main seat support brackets is considered an airframe major repair, not preventive maintenance. Answer (C) is incorrect. Engine adjustments to allow automotive gas to be used is considered a powerplant major alteration, not preventive maintenance.

16. Which operation would be described as preventive maintenance?

A. Repair of landing gear brace struts.

B. Replenishing hydraulic fluid.

C. Repair of portions of skin sheets by making additional seams.

Answer (B) is correct. *(Appendix A to Part 43)*
DISCUSSION: Appendix A to Part 43 provides a list of work that is considered preventive maintenance. Preventive maintenance means simple or minor preservation operations and the replacement of small standard parts not involving complex assembly operations. An example of preventive maintenance is replenishing hydraulic fluid.
Answer (A) is incorrect. The repair of landing gear brace struts is considered an airframe major repair, not preventive maintenance. Answer (C) is incorrect. The repair of portions of skin sheets by making additional seams is considered an airframe major repair, not preventive maintenance.

3.5 FAR Part 61

61.3 Requirements for Certificates, Ratings, and Authorizations

17. When must a current pilot certificate be in the pilot's personal possession or readily accessible in the aircraft?

A. When acting as a crew chief during launch and recovery.

B. Only when passengers are carried.

C. Anytime when acting as pilot in command or as a required crewmember.

Answer (C) is correct. *(FAR 61.3)*
DISCUSSION: Current and appropriate pilot and medical certificates (or driver's license, if appropriate) must be in your personal possession or readily accessible in the aircraft when you act as pilot in command (PIC) or as a required pilot flight crewmember.
Answer (A) is incorrect. A current pilot certificate must be in your personal possession when acting as a PIC or as a required crewmember of an aircraft, not when acting as a crew chief during launch and recovery of an airship. Answer (B) is incorrect. Anytime you fly as PIC or as a required crewmember, you must have a current pilot certificate in your personal possession regardless of whether passengers are carried or not.

18. What document(s) must be in your personal possession or readily accessible in the aircraft while operating as pilot in command of an aircraft?

A. Certificates showing accomplishment of a checkout in the aircraft and a current biennial flight review.

B. A pilot certificate with an endorsement showing accomplishment of an annual flight review and a pilot logbook showing recency of experience.

C. An appropriate pilot certificate and an appropriate current medical certificate (or driver's license if appropriate) if required.

Answer (C) is correct. *(FAR 61.3)*
DISCUSSION: Current and appropriate pilot and medical certificates (or driver's license, if appropriate) must be in your personal possession or readily accessible in the aircraft when you act as pilot in command (PIC) or as a required pilot flight crewmember.
Answer (A) is incorrect. Flight reviews and checkouts in aircraft are documented in your logbook rather than on separate certificates and need not be in your personal possession. Answer (B) is incorrect. The endorsement after satisfactorily completing a flight review is made in your logbook, not on your pilot certificate. You are not required to have your pilot logbook in your personal possession while acting as pilot in command.

19. Each person who holds a pilot certificate, a U.S. driver's license, or a medical certificate shall present it for inspection upon the request of the Administrator, the National Transportation Safety Board, or any

A. representative of an airport.

B. person in a position of authority.

C. federal, state, or local law enforcement officer.

Answer (C) is correct. *(FAR 61.3)*
DISCUSSION: Each person who holds a pilot certificate, flight instructor certificate, medical certificate, authorization, or license required by the FARs shall present it for inspection upon the request of the Administrator (of the FAA), an authorized representative of the National Transportation Safety Board, or any federal, state, or local law enforcement officer.
Answer (A) is incorrect. A representative of an airport, such as a spokesman, does not necessarily have the authority to inspect certificates. Answer (B) is incorrect. Not just any person with any kind of authority, such as a foreman, can inspect a pilot certificate or medical certificate.

61.15 Offenses Involving Alcohol or Drugs

20. A pilot convicted of operating a motor vehicle while either intoxicated by, impaired by, or under the influence of alcohol or a drug is required to provide a

A. written report to the FAA Civil Aeromedical Institute (CAMI) within 60 days after the motor vehicle action.

B. written report to the FAA Civil Aviation Security Division (AMC-700) not later than 60 days after the conviction.

C. notification of the conviction to an FAA Aviation Medical Examiner (AME) not later than 60 days after the conviction.

Answer (B) is correct. *(FAR 61.15)*
DISCUSSION: A pilot convicted of operating a motor vehicle while either intoxicated by, impaired by, or under the influence of alcohol or a drug is required to provide a written report to the FAA Civil Aviation Security Division (AMC-700) not later than 60 days after the conviction.
Answer (A) is incorrect. A pilot convicted of operating a motor vehicle while either intoxicated by, impaired by, or under the influence of alcohol or a drug is required to provide a written report to the FAA Civil Aviation Security Division, not the FAA Civil Aeromedical Institute (CAMI), within 60 days after the motor vehicle action. Answer (C) is incorrect. A pilot convicted of operating a motor vehicle while either intoxicated by, impaired by, or under the influence of alcohol or a drug is required to provide a written report to the FAA Civil Aviation Security Division, not notify an AME, not later than 60 days after the conviction.

21. A pilot convicted for the violation of any Federal or State statute relating to the process, manufacture, transportation, distribution, or sale of narcotic drugs is grounds for

A. a written report to be filed with the FAA Civil Aviation Security Division (AMC-700) not later than 60 days after the conviction.

B. notification of this conviction to the FAA Civil Aeromedical Institute (CAMI) within 60 days after the conviction.

C. suspension or revocation or any certificate, rating, or authorization issued under 14 CFR part 61.

Answer (C) is correct. *(FAR 61.15)*
DISCUSSION: A pilot convicted for the violation of any federal or state statute relating to the process, manufacture, transportation, distribution, or sale of narcotic drugs is grounds for suspension or revocation of any certificate, rating, or authorization issued under 14 CFR part 61.
Answer (A) is incorrect. A written report must be filed with the FAA Civil Aviation Security Division not later than 60 days after a pilot is convicted of a motor vehicle offense involving alcohol or drugs, not for a conviction for the violation of any federal or state statute relating to the process, manufacture, transportation, distribution, or sale of narcotic drugs. Answer (B) is incorrect. A pilot convicted for the violation of any federal or state statute relating to the process, manufacture, transportation, distribution, or sale of narcotic drugs is grounds for suspension or revocation or any certificate, rating, or authorization issued under 14 CFR part 61. The pilot is not required to notify CAMI of the conviction.

22. A pilot convicted of operating an aircraft under the influence of alcohol, or using drugs that affect the person's faculties, is grounds for a

A. denial of an application for an FAA certificate, rating, or authorization issued under 14 CFR part 61.

B. written notification to the FAA Civil Aeromedical Institute (CAMI) within 60 days after the conviction.

C. written report to be filed with the FAA Civil Aviation Security Division (AMC-700) not later than 60 days after the conviction.

Answer (A) is correct. *(FAR 91.17)*
DISCUSSION: A pilot convicted of operating an aircraft under the influence of alcohol, or using drugs that affect that person's faculties, is grounds for denial of an application for an FAA certificate, rating, or authorization issued under 14 CFR part 61.
Answer (B) is incorrect. A pilot convicted of operating an aircraft under the influence of alcohol, or using drugs that affect the person's faculties, is grounds for denial for an application for an FAA certificate or rating. The pilot is not required to notify CAMI of the conviction. Answer (C) is incorrect. A written report must be filed with the FAA Civil Aviation Security Division (AMC-700) not later than 60 days after a pilot convicted of operating a motor vehicle while either intoxicated by, impaired by, or under the influence of alcohol or a drug.

61.23 Medical Certificates: Requirement and Duration

23. For sport pilot operations, a Second-Class Medical Certificate issued to a 42-year-old pilot on July 15, this year, will expire at midnight on

A. July 15, 2 years later.

B. July 31, 1 year later.

C. July 31, 2 years later.

Answer (C) is correct. *(FAR 61.23)*
DISCUSSION: For sport pilot operations, a second-class medical certificate will expire at the end of the last day of the month, 2 years after it was issued, for pilots 40 years old or older on the date of the medical examination. For sport pilot operations, a second-class medical certificate issued to a 42-year-old pilot on July 15 will be valid until midnight on July 31, 2 years later.
Answer (A) is incorrect. A medical certificate expires on the last day of the month. Thus, a medical certificate issued on July 15 will expire on July 31, not July 15. Answer (B) is incorrect. A second-class medical certificate is valid for 1 year for operations requiring a commercial pilot certificate.

24. A Third-Class Medical Certificate is issued to a 36-year-old pilot on August 10, this year. To exercise the privileges of a Sport Pilot Certificate, the medical certificate will be valid until midnight on

A. August 10, 2 years later.

B. August 31, 5 years later.

C. August 31, 2 years later.

Answer (B) is correct. *(FAR 61.23)*

DISCUSSION: A pilot may exercise the privileges of a sport pilot certificate under a third-class medical certificate until it expires at the end of the last day of the month 5 years after it was issued, for pilots less than 40 years old on the date of the medical examination. A third-class medical certificate issued to a 36-year-old pilot on Aug. 10 will be valid until midnight on Aug. 31, 5 years later.

Answer (A) is incorrect. Medical certificates expire at the last day of the month. Thus, a medical certificate issued on Aug. 10 will expire on Aug. 31, not Aug. 10. Additionally, since the pilot is less than 40 years old, the third-class medical certificate is valid for 5 years, not 2 years. Answer (C) is incorrect. A pilot may exercise the privileges of a sport pilot certificate under a third-class medical certificate until it expires at the end of the last day of the month 2 years later if the pilot was 40 years old or older, not less than 40 years old, on the date of the medical examination.

25. A Third-Class Medical Certificate is issued to a 51-year-old pilot on May 3, this year. To exercise the privileges of a Sport Pilot Certificate, the medical certificate will be valid until midnight on

A. May 3, 1 year later.

B. May 31, 1 year later.

C. May 31, 2 years later.

Answer (C) is correct. *(FAR 61.23)*

DISCUSSION: A pilot may exercise the privileges of a sport pilot certificate under a third-class medical certificate until it expires at the end of the last day of the month 2 years after it was issued, for pilots 40 years old or older on the date of the medical examination. A third-class medical certificate issued to a 51-year-old pilot on May 3 will be valid until midnight on May 31, 2 years later.

Answer (A) is incorrect. Medical certificates expire on the last day of the month. Thus, a medical certificate issued on May 3 will expire on May 31, not May 3. Additionally, a third-class medical certificate is valid for 2 years, not 1 year, if the pilot is over 40 years old. Answer (B) is incorrect. A pilot may exercise the privileges of a sport pilot certificate under a third-class medical certificate until it expires at the end of the last day of the month, 2 years, not 1 year, later if the pilot was 40 years old or older on the date of the examination.

26. For sport pilot operations, a First-Class Medical Certificate issued to a 23-year-old pilot on October 21, this year, will expire at midnight on

A. October 21, 2 years later.

B. October 31, next year.

C. October 31, 5 years later.

Answer (C) is correct. *(FAR 61.23)*

DISCUSSION: For sport pilot operations, a first-class medical certificate will expire at the end of the last day of the month, 5 years after it was issued, for pilots less than 40 years old on the date of the medical examination. For sport pilot operations, a first-class medical certificate issued to a 23-year-old pilot on Oct. 21 will be valid until midnight on Oct. 31, 5 years later.

Answer (A) is incorrect. A medical certificate expires on the last day of the month. Thus, a medical certificate issued on Oct. 21 will expire on Oct. 31, not Oct. 21. Additionally, for sport pilot operations, the medical certificate is valid for 5 years, not 2 years, for a pilot less than 40 years old on the date of the medical examination. Answer (B) is incorrect. A first-class medical certificate is valid for 1 year for operations requiring a commercial pilot certificate.

27. A Third-Class Medical Certificate was issued to a 19-year-old pilot on August 10, this year. To exercise the privileges of a recreational or sport pilot certificate, the medical certificate will expire at midnight on

A. August 10, 2 years later.

B. August 31, 5 years later.

C. August 31, 2 years later.

Answer (B) is correct. *(FAR 61.23)*

DISCUSSION: A pilot may exercise the privileges of a recreational or sport pilot certificate under a third-class medical certificate until it expires at the end of the last day of the month 5 years after it was issued, for pilots less than 40 years old at the time of the medical examination. A third-class medical certificate issued to a 19-year-old pilot on Aug. 10 will expire at midnight on Aug. 31, 5 years later.

Answer (A) is incorrect. Medical certificates expire at the end of the month. A medical certificate issued on Aug. 10 will expire at midnight on Aug. 31, not Aug. 10. Answer (C) is incorrect. A pilot may exercise the privileges of a recreational or sport pilot certificate under a third-class medical certificate until it expires at the end of the last day of the month 2 years later if the pilot was 40 years old or older, not less than 40 years old, on the date of the medical examination.

61.56 Flight Review

28. To act as pilot in command of an aircraft carrying passengers, a pilot must show by logbook endorsement the satisfactory completion of a flight review or completion of a pilot proficiency check within the preceding

A. 6 calendar months.

B. 12 calendar months.

C. 24 calendar months.

Answer (C) is correct. *(FAR 61.56)*
DISCUSSION: To act as pilot in command of an aircraft (whether carrying passengers or not), a pilot must show by logbook endorsement the satisfactory completion of a flight review or completion of a pilot proficiency check within the preceding 24 calendar months.
Answer (A) is incorrect. A pilot must have satisfactorily completed a flight review or completion of a pilot proficiency check within the preceding 24 (not 6) calendar months. Answer (B) is incorrect. A pilot must have satisfactorily completed a flight review or completion of a pilot proficiency check within the preceding 24 (not 12) calendar months.

61.57 Recent Flight Experience: Pilot in Command

29. To act as pilot in command of an aircraft carrying passengers, the pilot must have made at least three takeoffs and three landings in an aircraft of the same category, class, and if a type rating is required, of the same type, within the preceding

A. 90 days.

B. 12 calendar months.

C. 24 calendar months.

Answer (A) is correct. *(FAR 61.57)*
DISCUSSION: To act as pilot in command of an airplane with passengers aboard, you must have made at least three takeoffs and three landings (to a full stop if in a tailwheel airplane) in an airplane of the same category, class, and, if a type rating is required, of the same type within the preceding 90 days. Category refers to airplane, rotorcraft, etc.; class refers to single- or multi-engine, land or sea.
Answer (B) is incorrect. A flight review, not recency experience, is required every 24, not 12, calendar months. Answer (C) is incorrect. A flight review, not recency experience, is normally required of all pilots every 24 months.

30. To act as pilot in command of an aircraft carrying passengers, the pilot must have made three takeoffs and three landings within the preceding 90 days in an aircraft of the same

A. make and model.

B. category and class, but not type.

C. category, class, and type, if a type rating is required.

Answer (C) is correct. *(FAR 61.57)*
DISCUSSION: No one may act as pilot in command of an airplane carrying passengers unless within the preceding 90 days (s)he has made three takeoffs and three landings as sole manipulator of the controls in an aircraft of the same category and class and, if a type rating is required, the same type. If the aircraft is a tailwheel airplane, the landings must have been to a full stop.
Answer (A) is incorrect. It must be the same category and class (not make and model) and, if a type rating is required, the same type. Answer (B) is incorrect. It must be the same type aircraft if a type rating is required for that aircraft.

31. The takeoffs and landings required to meet the recency of experience requirements for carrying passengers in a tailwheel airplane

A. may be touch and go or full stop.

B. must be touch and go.

C. must be to a full stop.

Answer (C) is correct. *(FAR 61.57)*
DISCUSSION: To comply with recency requirements for carrying passengers in a tailwheel airplane, one must have made three takeoffs and landings to a full stop within the past 90 days.
Answer (A) is incorrect. In a tailwheel airplane, the takeoffs and landings must be to a full stop only, not touch and go. Answer (B) is incorrect. In a tailwheel airplane, the takeoffs and landings must be to a full stop, not touch and go.

61.60 Change of Address

32. If a certificated pilot changes permanent mailing address and fails to notify the FAA Airmen Certification Branch of the new address, the pilot is entitled to exercise the privileges of the pilot certificate for a period of only

    A. 30 days after the date of the move.

    B. 60 days after the date of the move.

    C. 90 days after the date of the move.

Answer (A) is correct. *(FAR 61.60)*

DISCUSSION: If you have changed your permanent mailing address, you may not exercise the privileges of your pilot certificate after 30 days from the date of the address change unless you have notified the FAA of the change. You are required to notify the Airmen Certification Branch at P.O. Box 25082, Oklahoma City, OK 73125. You may also use the airmen services system on the FAA website.

NOTE: While you must notify the FAA if your address changes, you are not required to carry a certificate that shows your current address. The FAA will not issue a new certificate upon receipt of your new address unless you send a written request and $2 to the address shown above.

Answer (B) is incorrect. If you change your permanent mailing address, you may exercise the privileges of your pilot certificate for a period of only 30 (not 60) days after the date you move unless you notify the FAA in writing of the change. Answer (C) is incorrect. If you change your permanent mailing address, you may exercise the privileges of your pilot certificate for a period of only 30 (not 90) days after the date you move unless you notify the FAA in writing of the change.

61.315 Sport Pilot Privileges and Limitations: Pilot in Command

33. How many passengers is a sport pilot allowed to carry on board?

    A. One.

    B. Two.

    C. Three.

Answer (A) is correct. *(FAR 61.315[c])*

DISCUSSION: As a sport pilot, you may not act as a pilot in command of a light-sport aircraft while carrying more than one passenger.

Answer (B) is incorrect. As a sport pilot, you are not permitted to carry any more than one passenger. Answer (C) is incorrect. As a sport pilot, you are not permitted to carry any more than one passenger.

34. According to regulations pertaining to privileges and limitations, a sport pilot may

    A. be paid for the operating expenses of a flight if at least three takeoffs and three landings were made by the pilot within the preceding 90 days.

    B. not pay less than half of the share of the operating expenses of a flight with passengers provided the expenses involve only fuel, oil, airport expenditures, or rental fees.

    C. not be paid in any manner for the operating expenses of a flight.

Answer (B) is correct. *(FAR 61.315)*

DISCUSSION: A sport pilot may not pay less than an equal (pro rata) share of the operating expenses of a flight with passengers. These expenses may involve only fuel, oil, airport expenditures (e.g., landing fees, tie-down fees, etc.), or rental fees.

Answer (A) is incorrect. A sport pilot may be paid for the operating expenses of a flight in connection with any business or employment if the flight is only incidental to that business or employment and no passengers or property are carried for compensation or hire, not if the pilot has made three takeoffs and landings in the preceding 90 days. Answer (C) is incorrect. A sport pilot may equally share the operating expenses of a flight with his/her passengers.

35. As a sport pilot, you may carry no more than

    A. one passenger.

    B. two passengers.

    C. three passengers.

Answer (A) is correct. *(FAR 61.315)*

DISCUSSION: Sport pilots may not act in command of a light-sport aircraft while carrying more than one passenger.

Answer (B) is incorrect. Sport pilots may not act as pilot in command of a light-sport aircraft while carrying more than one, not two, passengers. Answer (C) is incorrect. Sport pilots may not act as pilot in command of a light-sport aircraft while carrying more than one, not three, passengers.

36. The highest altitude at which sport pilots may operate is

    A. 7,500 ft. MSL, or 2,000 ft. AGL, whichever is higher.

    B. 10,000 ft. MSL, or 2,000 ft. AGL, whichever is higher.

    C. 9,000 ft. MSL, or 2,000 ft. AGL, whichever is higher.

Answer (B) is correct. *(FAR 61.315)*

DISCUSSION: Sport pilots are restricted to operating within a number of limitations, including not above 10,000 ft. MSL or 2,000 ft. AGL, whichever is higher.

Answer (A) is incorrect. Sport pilots may fly over 7,500 ft. MSL. They are restricted to flying at altitudes of 10,000 ft. MSL or 2,000 ft. AGL, whichever is higher. Answer (C) is incorrect. Sport pilots may fly over 9,000 ft. MSL. They are restricted to flying at altitudes of 10,000 ft. MSL or 2,000 ft. AGL, whichever is higher.

61.325 Required Endorsements for Class B, C, and D Airspaces

37. Which is true regarding flight operations to a satellite airport, without an operating tower, within Class C airspace?

A. Prior to entering that airspace, a sport pilot must contact the FSS.

B. Prior to entering that airspace, a sport pilot must contact the primary airport tower.

C. Prior to entering that airspace, a sport pilot must receive the appropriate logbook endorsement.

Answer (C) is correct. *(FAR 61.325)*
DISCUSSION: A sport pilot must receive and log ground and flight training to operate a light-sport aircraft at an airport or in airspace within Class B, C, and D airspace, or in another airspace with an airport that has an operational control tower. Therefore, a sport pilot must receive the appropriate logbook endorsement prior to entering Class C airspace.
Answer (A) is incorrect. FSS does not have authority to control Class C airspace. Only ATC has this authority. Answer (B) is incorrect. The sport pilot, after (s)he has received the appropriate logbook endorsement, should contact ATC and establish two-way radio communications prior to entering Class C airspace.

38. In order to operate a light-sport aircraft at an airport within, or in airspace within, Class B, C, and D airspace, a sport pilot

A. does not have to meet any additional requirements.

B. must receive ground training on operations within Class B, C, and D airspace.

C. must receive and log ground and flight training on operations within Class B, C, and D airspace.

Answer (C) is correct. *(FAR 61.325)*
DISCUSSION: A sport pilot must receive and log ground and flight training to operate a light-sport aircraft at an airport or in airspace within Class B, C, and D airspace, or in other airspace with an airport that has an operational control tower.
Answer (A) is incorrect. Sport pilots do have to meet the additional requirements of receiving and logging ground and flight training on operations within Class B, C, and D airspace. Answer (B) is incorrect. Sport pilots must not only receive ground training on operations within Class B, C, and D airspace but must also receive and log flight training in operations within Class B, C, and D airspace.

3.6 FAR Part 71

71.71 Extent of Federal Airways

39. The width of a Federal Airway from either side of the centerline is

A. 4 nautical miles.

B. 6 nautical miles.

C. 8 nautical miles.

Answer (A) is correct. *(FAR 71.71)*
DISCUSSION: The width of a Federal Airway from either side of the centerline is 4 NM.
Answer (B) is incorrect. The width of a Federal Airway from either side of the centerline is 4 NM, not 6 NM. Answer (C) is incorrect. The width of a Federal Airway from either side of the centerline is 4 NM, not 8 NM.

40. Unless otherwise specified, Federal Airways include that Class E airspace extending upward from

A. 700 feet above the surface, up to and including 17,999 feet MSL.

B. 1,200 feet above the surface, up to and including 17,999 feet MSL.

C. the surface, up to and including 18,000 feet MSL.

Answer (B) is correct. *(FAR 71.71)*
DISCUSSION: Unless otherwise specified, Federal Airways include that Class E airspace extending from 1,200 ft. above the surface, up to and including 17,999 ft.
Answer (A) is incorrect. Federal Airways extend from 1,200 (not 700) ft. above the surface, up to and including 17,999 ft. MSL. Answer (C) is incorrect. Federal Airways extend from 1,200 ft. above the surface, up to and including 17,999 ft. MSL, not 18,000 ft. MSL. The airspace that extends upward from 18,000 ft. MSL is Class A airspace.

END OF STUDY UNIT

STUDY UNIT FOUR
FEDERAL AVIATION REGULATIONS – FAR PARTS 91.3 THROUGH 91.131

(4 pages of outline)

This study unit contains outlines of major concepts tested, sample test questions and answers regarding Federal Aviation Regulations (FAR) 91.3 through 91.131, and an explanation of each answer. The table of contents above lists each subunit within this study unit, the number of questions pertaining to that particular subunit, and the pages on which the outlines and questions begin, respectively.

CAUTION: Recall that the **sole purpose** of this book is to expedite your passing the FAA pilot knowledge test for the sport pilot certificate. Accordingly, all extraneous material (i.e., topics or regulations not directly tested on the FAA pilot knowledge test) is omitted, even though much more information and knowledge are necessary to fly safely. This additional material is presented in *Pilot Handbook* and *Sport Pilot Flight Maneuvers and Practical Test Prep*, available from Gleim Publications, Inc. See the order form on page 327.

4.1 FAR 91.3

91.3 Responsibility and Authority of the Pilot in Command

1. In emergencies, a pilot may deviate from the FARs to the extent needed to maintain the safety of the airplane and passengers.

2. The pilot in command of an aircraft is directly responsible for, and is the final authority as to, the operation of that aircraft.

3. A written report of any deviations from FARs should be filed with the FAA upon request.

4.2 FAR 91.7 THROUGH 91.9

91.7 Civil Aircraft Airworthiness

1. The pilot in command is responsible for determining that the airplane is airworthy prior to every flight.

    a. The pilot in command shall discontinue the flight when unairworthy conditions (whether electrical, mechanical, or structural) occur.

91.9 Civil Aircraft Flight Manual, Marking, and Placard Requirements

1. The airworthiness certificate, the FAA registration certificate, and the aircraft flight manual or operating limitations must be aboard.

2. The operating limitations of an airplane may be found in the current FAA-approved flight manual, approved manual material, markings, and placards, or any combination thereof.

4.3 FAR 91.15 THROUGH 91.107

91.15 Dropping Objects

1. No pilot in command of a civil aircraft may allow any object to be dropped from that aircraft in flight that creates a hazard to persons or property.

    a. However, this section does not prohibit the dropping of any object if reasonable precautions are taken to avoid injury or damage to persons or property.

91.17 Alcohol or Drugs

1. No person may act as a crewmember of a civil airplane while having .04 percent by weight or more alcohol in the blood or if any alcoholic beverages have been consumed within the preceding 8 hours.

2. No person may act as a crewmember of a civil airplane if using any drug that affects the person's faculties in any way contrary to safety.

3. Operating or attempting to operate an aircraft as a crewmember while under the influence of drugs or alcohol is grounds for the denial of an application for a certificate, rating, or authorization issued under 14 CFR Part 91.

4. Pilots may not allow a person who is obviously intoxicated or under the influence of drugs to be carried in a civil airplane.

    a. An exception is if the person is a medical patient under proper care or in an emergency.

91.103 Preflight Action

1. Pilots are required to familiarize themselves with all available information concerning the flight prior to every flight and specifically to determine an alternate course of action if the flight cannot be completed as planned.

    a. For any flight, pilots must be familiar with runway lengths at airports of intended use and the airplane's takeoff and landing requirements.

91.105 Flight Crewmembers at Stations

1. During takeoff and landing, and while en route, each required flight crewmember shall keep his/her safety belt fastened while at his/her station.

    a. If shoulder harnesses are available, they must be used for takeoff and landing.

91.107 Use of Safety Belts, Shoulder Harnesses, and Child Restraint Systems

1. Pilots must ensure that each occupant is briefed on how to use the safety belts and, if installed, shoulder harnesses.

2. Pilots must notify all occupants to fasten their safety belts before taxiing, taking off, or landing.

3. All passengers of airplanes must wear their safety belts during taxi, takeoffs, and landings.

    a. Sport parachutists may use the floor of the aircraft as a seat (but still must use safety belts).

4.4 FAR 91.111 THROUGH 91.121

91.111 Operating near Other Aircraft

1. No person may operate an aircraft in formation flight except by prior arrangement with the pilot in command of each aircraft in the formation.

91.113 Right-of-Way Rules: Except Water Operations

1. Aircraft in distress have the right-of-way over all other aircraft.

2. When two aircraft are approaching head on or nearly so, the pilot of each aircraft should turn to his/her right, regardless of category.

3. When two aircraft of different categories are converging, the right-of-way depends upon who has the least maneuverability. Thus, the right-of-way belongs to

    a. Balloons over
    b. Gliders over
    c. Airships over
    d. Airplanes or rotorcraft

4. When aircraft of the same category are converging at approximately the same altitude, except head on or nearly so, the aircraft to the other's right has the right-of-way.

    a. If an airplane of the same category as yours is approaching from your right side, it has the right-of-way.

5. When two or more aircraft are approaching an airport for the purpose of landing, the aircraft at the lower altitude has the right-of-way.

    a. This rule shall not be abused by cutting in front of or overtaking another aircraft.

6. An aircraft towing or refueling another aircraft has the right-of-way over all engine-driven aircraft.

91.115 Right-of-Way Rules: Water Operations

1. When aircraft or an aircraft and a vessel are on crossing courses, the aircraft or vessel to the other's right has the right-of-way.

91.119 Minimum Safe Altitudes: General

1. Over congested areas (cities, towns, settlements, or open-air assemblies), a pilot must maintain an altitude of 1,000 ft. above the highest obstacle within a horizontal radius of 2,000 ft. of the airplane.

2. The minimum altitude over other than congested areas is 500 ft. AGL.

    a. Over open water or sparsely populated areas, an airplane may not be operated closer than 500 ft. to any person, vessel, vehicle, or structure.

3. Altitude in all areas must be sufficient to permit an emergency landing without undue hazard to persons or property on the surface if a power unit fails.

91.121 Altimeter Settings

1. Prior to takeoff, the altimeter should be set to the current local altimeter setting.

    a. If the current local altimeter setting is not available, use the departure airport elevation.

4.5 FAR 91.123 THROUGH 91.131

91.123 Compliance with ATC Clearances and Instructions

1. You must not deviate from an ATC clearance unless you receive an amended clearance, if there is an emergency, or in response to a traffic collision avoidance system resolution advisory.

2. If you receive priority from ATC in an emergency, you must, upon request, file a detailed report within 48 hr. to the chief of that ATC facility even if no rule has been violated.

91.126 Operating on or in the Vicinity of an Airport in Class G Airspace

1. When approaching to land at an airport without an operating control tower in Class G airspace, each pilot of an airplane must make all turns of that airplane to the left unless the airport displays approved light signals or visual markings indicating that turns should be made to the right.

91.130 Operations in Class C Airspace

1. Pilots must not operate an aircraft in Class C airspace unless two-way radio communications have been established with ATC.

    a. Prior to entering Class C airspace, contact approach control on the appropriate frequency.

    b. Unless otherwise authorized by the ATC facility having jurisdiction over the Class C airspace, no person may operate an aircraft in a Class C airspace area unless the aircraft is equipped with an operating transponder and automatic altitude reporting equipment (Mode C).

91.131 Operations in Class B Airspace

1. No person may operate an aircraft in a Class B airspace area unless the aircraft is equipped with an operating transponder and automatic altitude reporting equipment (Mode C).

2. For operations in Class B airspace, the operator must receive an ATC clearance from the ATC facility having jurisdiction for the area before operating an aircraft in that area.

QUESTIONS AND ANSWER EXPLANATIONS

All of the sport pilot knowledge test questions chosen by the FAA for release as well as additional questions selected by Gleim relating to the material in the previous outlines are reproduced on the following pages. These questions have been organized into the same subunits as the outlines. To the immediate right of each question are the correct answer and answer explanation. You should cover these answers and answer explanations while responding to the questions. Refer to the general discussion in the Introduction on how to take the FAA pilot knowledge test.

Remember that the questions from the FAA pilot knowledge test bank have been reordered by topic and organized into a meaningful sequence. Also, the first line of the answer explanation gives the citation of the authoritative source for the answer.

QUESTIONS

4.1 FAR 91.3

91.3 Responsibility and Authority of the Pilot in Command

1. The final authority as to the operation of an aircraft is the

  A. Federal Aviation Administration.

  B. pilot in command.

  C. aircraft manufacturer.

Answer (B) is correct. *(FAR 91.3)*
DISCUSSION: The final authority as to the operation of an aircraft is the pilot in command.
Answer (A) is incorrect. The final authority as to the operation of an aircraft is the pilot in command, not the FAA. Answer (C) is incorrect. The final authority as to the operation of an aircraft is the pilot in command, not the aircraft manufacturer.

2. When must a pilot who deviates from a regulation during an emergency send a written report of that deviation to the Administrator?

  A. Within 7 days.

  B. Within 10 days.

  C. Upon request.

Answer (C) is correct. *(FAR 91.3)*
DISCUSSION: A pilot who deviates from a regulation during an emergency must send a written report of that deviation to the Administrator of the FAA only upon request.
Answer (A) is incorrect. A written report of a deviation from a regulation during an emergency must be sent to the Administrator upon request, not within 7 days. Answer (B) is incorrect. A written report of a deviation from a regulation during an emergency must be sent to the Administrator upon request, not within 10 days.

3. When would a pilot be required to submit a detailed report of an emergency which caused the pilot to deviate from an ATC clearance?

  A. When requested by ATC.

  B. Immediately.

  C. Within 7 days.

Answer (A) is correct. *(FAR 91.3)*
DISCUSSION: A pilot who deviates from a regulation during an emergency must send a written report of that deviation to the Administrator of the FAA only upon request.
Answer (B) is incorrect. A written report of a deviation from a regulation during an emergency must be sent to the Administrator upon request, not immediately. Answer (C) is incorrect. A written report of a deviation from a regulation during an emergency must be sent to the Administrator upon request, not within 7 days.

4. If an in-flight emergency requires immediate action, the pilot in command may

  A. deviate from any rule of 14 CFR 91 to the extent required to meet the emergency, but must submit a written report to the Administrator within 24 hours.

  B. deviate from any rule of 14 CFR 91 to the extent required to meet that emergency.

  C. not deviate from any rule of 14 CFR 91 unless prior to the deviation approval is granted by the Administrator.

Answer (B) is correct. *(FAR 91.3)*
DISCUSSION: In an in-flight emergency requiring immediate action, the pilot in command may deviate from any rule of 14 CFR 91 to the extent required to meet that emergency. A written report of the deviation must be sent to the Administrator of the FAA only if requested.
Answer (A) is incorrect. A written report must be sent to the Administrator of the FAA only upon request. Answer (C) is incorrect. The pilot in command may deviate from any rule of 14 CFR 91 to the extent required to meet that emergency without the approval of the Administrator of the FAA.

4.2   FAR 91.7 through 91.9

91.7   Civil Aircraft Airworthiness

5.   Who is responsible for determining if an aircraft is in condition for safe flight?

    A.   A certificated aircraft mechanic.

    B.   The pilot in command.

    C.   The owner or operator.

Answer (B) is correct.   *(FAR 91.7)*
DISCUSSION: The pilot in command of an aircraft is directly responsible for, and is the final authority for, determining whether the airplane is in condition for safe flight.
Answer (A) is incorrect. The pilot in command (not a certificated aircraft mechanic) is responsible for determining if an aircraft is in condition for safe flight. Answer (C) is incorrect. The pilot in command (not the owner or operator) is responsible for determining if an aircraft is in condition for safe flight.

91.9   Civil Aircraft Flight Manual, Marking, and Placard Requirements

6.   Where may an aircraft's operating limitations be found?

    A.   On the Airworthiness Certificate.

    B.   In the current, FAA-approved flight manual, approved manual material, markings, and placards, or any combination thereof.

    C.   In the aircraft airframe and engine logbooks.

Answer (B) is correct.   *(FAR 91.9)*
DISCUSSION: An aircraft's operating limitations may be found in the current FAA-approved flight manual, approved manual material, markings, and placards, or any combination thereof.
Answer (A) is incorrect. The airworthiness certificate only indicates the airplane was in an airworthy condition when delivered from the factory, not its operating limitations. Answer (C) is incorrect. The airframe and engine logbooks contain the airplane's maintenance record, not its operating limitations.

4.3   FAR 91.15 through 91.107

91.15   Dropping Objects

7.   Under what conditions may objects be dropped from an aircraft?

    A.   Only in an emergency.

    B.   If precautions are taken to avoid injury or damage to persons or property on the surface.

    C.   If prior permission is received from the Federal Aviation Administration.

Answer (B) is correct.   *(FAR 91.15)*
DISCUSSION: No pilot in command of a civil aircraft may allow any object to be dropped from that aircraft in flight that creates a hazard to persons or property. However, this section does not prohibit the dropping of any object if reasonable precautions are taken to avoid injury or damage to persons or property.
Answer (A) is incorrect. Objects may be dropped from an aircraft if precautions are taken to avoid injury or damage to persons or property on the surface, not only in an emergency. Answer (C) is incorrect. Objects may be dropped from an aircraft if precautions are taken to avoid injury or damage to persons or property on the surface. Prior permission from the FAA is not required.

91.17   Alcohol or Drugs

8.   No person may act or attempt to act as a crewmember of a civil aircraft with

    A.   .008 percent by weight or more alcohol in the blood.

    B.   .004 percent by weight or more alcohol in the blood.

    C.   .04 percent by weight or more alcohol in the blood.

Answer (C) is correct.   *(FAR 91.17)*
DISCUSSION: No person may act or attempt to act as a crewmember of a civil aircraft while having a .04% by weight or more alcohol in the blood.
Answer (A) is incorrect. No person may act or attempt to act as a crewmember of a civil aircraft with .04% (not .008%) by weight or more alcohol in the blood. Answer (B) is incorrect. No person may act or attempt to act as a crewmember of a civil aircraft with .04% (not .004%) by weight or more alcohol in the blood.

9.   A person may not act as a crewmember of a civil aircraft if alcoholic beverages have been consumed by that person within the preceding

    A.   8 hours.

    B.   12 hours.

    C.   24 hours.

Answer (A) is correct.   *(FAR 91.17)*
DISCUSSION: No person may act as a crewmember of a civil aircraft if alcoholic beverages have been consumed by that person within the preceding 8 hr.
Answer (B) is incorrect. No person may act as a crewmember of a civil aircraft within 8 (not 12) hr. after the consumption of any alcoholic beverage. Answer (C) is incorrect. No person may act as a crewmember of a civil aircraft within 8 (not 24) hr. after the consumption of any alcoholic beverage.

91.103 Preflight Action

10. Preflight action, as required for all flights away from the vicinity of an airport, shall include

  A. the designation of an alternate airport.

  B. a study of arrival procedures at airports of intended use.

  C. an alternate course of action if the flight cannot be completed as planned.

Answer (C) is correct. *(FAR 91.103)*
 DISCUSSION: Preflight actions for flights not in the vicinity of an airport include checking weather reports and forecasts, fuel requirements, alternatives available if the planned flight cannot be completed, and any known traffic delays.
 Answer (A) is incorrect. Preflight action, as required for all flights away from the vicinity of an airport, shall include an alternate course of action if the flight cannot be completed as planned, not just the designation of an alternate airport. Answer (B) is incorrect. Preflight action, as required for all flights away from the vicinity of an airport, shall include an alternate course of action if the flight cannot be completed as planned, not simply a study of arrival procedures at airports of intended use.

11. In addition to other preflight actions for a VFR flight away from the vicinity of the departure airport, regulations specifically require the pilot in command to

  A. review traffic control light signal procedures.

  B. check the accuracy of the navigation equipment and the emergency locator transmitter (ELT).

  C. determine runway lengths at airports of intended use and the aircraft's takeoff and landing distance data.

Answer (C) is correct. *(FAR 91.103)*
 DISCUSSION: Preflight actions for a VFR flight away from the vicinity of the departure airport specifically require the pilot in command to determine runway lengths at airports of intended use and the aircraft's takeoff and landing distance data.
 Answer (A) is incorrect. Preflight actions for a VFR flight away from the vicinity of an airport require the pilot in command to determine runway lengths at airports of intended use and takeoff and landing distance data, not a review of traffic control light signal procedures. Answer (B) is incorrect. Preflight actions for a VFR flight away from the vicinity of an airport require the pilot in command to determine runway lengths at airports of intended use and takeoff and landing distance data, not a check of navigation equipment accuracy and the ELT.

12. Which preflight action is specifically required of the pilot prior to each flight?

  A. Check the aircraft logbooks for appropriate entries.

  B. Become familiar with all available information concerning the flight.

  C. Review wake turbulence avoidance procedures.

Answer (B) is correct. *(FAR 91.103)*
 DISCUSSION: Each pilot in command will, before beginning a flight, become familiar with all available information concerning that flight.
 Answer (A) is incorrect. During preflight action, the pilot is required to become familiar with all available information concerning the flight, not just to check the aircraft logbook for appropriate entries. Answer (C) is incorrect. During preflight action, the pilot is required to become familiar with all available information concerning the flight, not simply review wake turbulence avoidance procedures.

91.105 Flight Crewmembers at Stations

13. Flight crewmembers are required to keep their safety belts and shoulder harnesses fastened during

  A. takeoffs and landings.

  B. all flight conditions.

  C. flight in turbulent air.

Answer (A) is correct. *(FAR 91.105)*
 DISCUSSION: During takeoff and landing and while en route, each required flight crewmember shall keep his/her safety belt fastened while at the crewmember station. If shoulder harnesses are available, they must be used by crewmembers during takeoff and landing.
 Answer (B) is incorrect. Flight crewmembers are required to keep their shoulder harnesses fastened only during takeoffs and landings, not during all flight conditions. Answer (C) is incorrect. Flight crewmembers are required to keep their shoulder harnesses fastened only during takeoffs and landings, not during flight in turbulent air.

14. Which best describes the flight conditions under which pilots are specifically required to keep their safety belts and shoulder harnesses fastened?

A. Safety belts during takeoff and landing; shoulder harnesses during takeoff and landing.

B. Safety belts during takeoff and landing; shoulder harnesses during takeoff and landing and while en route.

C. Safety belts during takeoff and landing and while en route; shoulder harnesses during takeoff and landing.

Answer (C) is correct. *(FAR 91.105)*
DISCUSSION: During takeoff and landing and while en route, each pilot shall keep his/her safety belt fastened while at the crewmember station. If shoulder harnesses are available, they must be used by crewmembers during takeoff and landing.
Answer (A) is incorrect. Safety belts must be worn while en route. Answer (B) is incorrect. Safety belts (not shoulder harnesses) are required to be fastened while en route.

91.107 Use of Safety Belts, Shoulder Harnesses, and Child Restraint Systems

15. With respect to passengers, what obligation, if any, does a pilot in command have concerning the use of safety belts?

A. The pilot in command must instruct the passengers to keep their safety belts fastened for the entire flight.

B. The pilot in command must brief the passengers on the use of safety belts and notify them to fasten their safety belts during taxi, takeoff, and landing.

C. The pilot in command has no obligation in regard to passengers' use of safety belts.

Answer (B) is correct. *(FAR 91.107)*
DISCUSSION: The pilot in command is required to brief the passengers on the use of safety belts and notify them to fasten their safety belts during taxi, takeoff, and landing.
Answer (A) is incorrect. The pilot in command is only required to notify the passengers to fasten their safety belts during taxi, takeoff, and landing, not during the entire flight. Answer (C) is incorrect. The pilot in command has the obligation both to instruct passengers on the use of safety belts and to require their use during taxi, takeoffs, and landings.

16. Safety belts are required to be properly secured about which persons in an aircraft and when?

A. Pilots only, during takeoffs and landings.

B. Passengers, during taxi, takeoffs, and landings.

C. Each person on board the aircraft during the entire flight.

Answer (B) is correct. *(FAR 91.107)*
DISCUSSION: Regulations require that safety belts in an airplane be properly secured about all passengers during taxi, takeoffs, and landings.
Answer (A) is incorrect. Regulations require passengers as well as crewmembers to wear safety belts during takeoffs and landings. Answer (C) is incorrect. Although it is a good procedure, safety belts are required only for passengers during taxi, takeoffs, and landings.

17. With certain exceptions, safety belts are required to be secured about passengers during

A. taxi, takeoffs, and landings.

B. all flight conditions.

C. flight in turbulent air.

Answer (A) is correct. *(FAR 91.107)*
DISCUSSION: During the taxi, takeoff, and landing of U.S. registered civil aircraft, each person on board that aircraft must occupy a seat or berth with a safety belt and shoulder harness, if installed, properly secured about him/her. However, a person who has not reached his/her second birthday may be held by an adult who is occupying a seat or berth, and a person on board for the purpose of engaging in sport parachuting may use the floor of the aircraft as a seat (but is still required to use approved safety belts for takeoff).
Answer (B) is incorrect. Safety belts are required to be secured about passengers only during taxi, takeoffs, and landings, not during all flight conditions. Answer (C) is incorrect. Safety belts are required to be secured about passengers during taxi, takeoffs, and landings, not during flight in turbulent air.

18. The Pilot in Command is responsible for ensuring that each person on board applicable U.S. Registered aircraft is briefed and instructed on

    A. how and where to fasten and unfasten their seatbelt and shoulder harness.

    B. adjusting their seats.

    C. where the exits are.

Answer (A) is correct. *(FAR 91.107)*
    DISCUSSION: The pilot in command is required to brief the passengers of the use of safety belts and notify them to fasten their safety belts during taxi, takeoff, and landing.
    Answer (B) is incorrect. There is not a requirement for the pilot in command to ensure that each person on board applicable U.S. registered aircraft is briefed and instructed on adjusting seat positions. Answer (C) is incorrect. The pilot in command is not required to ensure that each person on board applicable U.S. registered aircraft is briefed and instructed on where the exits are.

19. The pilot in command is responsible for ensuring that each person on board applicable U.S. Registered aircraft is briefed and instructed on

    A. how and when to fasten and unfasten their seat belt and shoulder harness.

    B. adjusting their seats.

    C. operating the fire extinguisher.

Answer (A) is correct. *(FAR 91.107)*
    DISCUSSION: The pilot in command is required to brief the passengers on the use of safety belts and notify them to fasten their safety belts during taxi, takeoff, and landing.
    Answer (B) is incorrect. The pilot in command is required to brief each person on board on the use of safety belts, not on seat adjustments. Answer (C) is incorrect. The pilot in command is not required to brief each person on board on fire extinguisher use, only on seatbelt use.

4.4 FAR 91.111 through 91.121

91.111 Operating near Other Aircraft

20. No person may operate an aircraft in formation flight

    A. over a densely populated area.

    B. in Class D airspace.

    C. except by prior arrangement with the pilot in command of each aircraft.

Answer (C) is correct. *(FAR 91.111)*
    DISCUSSION: No person may operate in formation flight except by arrangement with the pilot in command of each aircraft in formation.
    Answer (A) is incorrect. No person may operate an aircraft in formation flight except by prior arrangement with the pilot in command of each aircraft. There are no restrictions about formation flights over a densely populated area. Answer (B) is incorrect. No person may operate an aircraft in formation flight except by prior arrangement with the pilot in command of each aircraft. There are no restrictions about formation flight in Class D airspace.

91.113 Right-of-Way Rules: Except Water Operations

21. An airplane and an airship are converging. If the airship is left of the airplane's position, which aircraft has the right-of-way?

    A. The airship.

    B. The airplane.

    C. Each pilot should alter course to the right.

Answer (A) is correct. *(FAR 91.113)*
    DISCUSSION: When aircraft of different categories are converging, the less maneuverable aircraft has the right-of-way. Thus, the airship has the right-of-way in this question.
    Answer (B) is incorrect. When converging, the airship has the right-of-way over an airplane or rotorcraft. Answer (C) is incorrect. Each pilot would alter course to the right if the airship and airplane were approaching head-on, or nearly so, not converging.

22. When two or more aircraft are approaching an airport for the purpose of landing, the right-of-way belongs to the aircraft

    A. that has the other to its right.

    B. that is the least maneuverable.

    C. at the lower altitude, but it shall not take advantage of this rule to cut in front of or to overtake another.

Answer (C) is correct. *(FAR 91.113)*
    DISCUSSION: When two or more aircraft are approaching an airport for the purpose of landing, the aircraft at the lower altitude has the right-of-way, but it shall not take advantage of this rule to cut in front of or to overtake another aircraft.
    Answer (A) is incorrect. When two or more aircraft are approaching an airport for the purpose of landing, the right-of-way belongs to the aircraft at the lower altitude, not the aircraft that has the other to the right. Answer (B) is incorrect. When two or more aircraft are approaching an airport for the purpose of landing, the right-of-way belongs to the aircraft at the lower altitude, not the aircraft that is the least maneuverable.

23. Which aircraft has the right-of-way over the other aircraft listed?

A. Glider.

B. Airship.

C. Aircraft refueling other aircraft.

Answer (A) is correct. *(FAR 91.113)*
DISCUSSION: If aircraft of different categories are converging, the right-of-way depends upon who has the least maneuverability. A glider has right-of-way over an airship, airplane or rotorcraft.
Answer (B) is incorrect. An airship has the right-of-way over an airplane or rotorcraft, not a glider. Answer (C) is incorrect. Aircraft refueling other aircraft have right-of-way over all engine-driven aircraft. A glider has no engine.

24. What action should the pilots of a glider and an airplane take if on a head-on collision course?

A. The airplane pilot should give way to the left.

B. The glider pilot should give way to the right.

C. Both pilots should give way to the right.

Answer (C) is correct. *(FAR 91.113)*
DISCUSSION: When aircraft are approaching head-on, or nearly so (regardless of category), each aircraft shall alter course to the right.
Answer (A) is incorrect. The glider has the right-of-way unless the two aircraft are approaching head-on, in which case both pilots should give way by turning to the right. Answer (B) is incorrect. Both pilots of a glider and an airplane should give way to the right, not only the glider pilot.

25. What action is required when two aircraft of the same category converge, but not head-on?

A. The faster aircraft shall give way.

B. The aircraft on the left shall give way.

C. Each aircraft shall give way to the right.

Answer (B) is correct. *(FAR 91.113)*
DISCUSSION: When two aircraft of the same category converge (but not head-on), the aircraft to the other's right has the right-of-way. Thus, an airplane on the left gives way to the airplane on the right.
Answer (A) is incorrect. When two aircraft of the same category converge (but not head-on), the aircraft on the left (not the faster aircraft) shall give way. Answer (C) is incorrect. The required action when two aircraft are approaching head-on or nearly so is for each aircraft to give way to the right.

26. Which aircraft has the right-of-way over the other aircraft listed?

A. Airship.

B. Aircraft towing other aircraft.

C. Gyroplane.

Answer (B) is correct. *(FAR 91.113)*
DISCUSSION: An aircraft towing or refueling another aircraft has the right-of-way over all engine-driven aircraft. An airship is an engine-driven, lighter-than-air aircraft that can be steered.
Answer (A) is incorrect. An airship has the right-of-way over an airplane or rotorcraft, but not an aircraft towing other aircraft. Answer (C) is incorrect. A gyroplane (which is a rotorcraft) must give way to both an airship and aircraft towing other aircraft.

27. Which aircraft has the right-of-way over all other air traffic?

A. A balloon.

B. An aircraft in distress.

C. An aircraft on final approach to land.

Answer (B) is correct. *(FAR 91.113)*
DISCUSSION: An aircraft in distress has the right-of-way over all other aircraft.
Answer (A) is incorrect. An aircraft in distress (not a balloon) has the right-of-way over all other air traffic. Answer (C) is incorrect. An aircraft in distress (not an aircraft on final approach to land) has the right-of-way over all other air traffic.

91.115 Right-of-Way Rules: Water Operations

28. A seaplane and a motorboat are on crossing courses. If the motorboat is to the left of the seaplane, which has the right-of-way?

A. The motorboat.

B. The seaplane.

C. Both should alter course to the right.

Answer (B) is correct. *(FAR 91.115)*
DISCUSSION: When aircraft, or an aircraft and a vessel (e.g., a motorboat), are on crossing courses, the aircraft or vessel to the other's right has the right-of-way. Since the seaplane is to the motorboat's right, the seaplane has the right-of-way.
Answer (A) is incorrect. On crossing courses, the aircraft or vessel to the other's right has the right-of-way. Since the seaplane is to the right of the motorboat, the seaplane (not the motorboat) has the right-of-way. Answer (C) is incorrect. Both would alter course to the right only if they were approaching head-on or nearly so.

91.119 Minimum Safe Altitudes: General

29. Except when necessary for takeoff or landing, an aircraft may not be operated closer than what distance from any person, vessel, vehicle, or structure?

A. 500 feet.

B. 700 feet.

C. 1,000 feet.

Answer (A) is correct. *(FAR 91.119)*
DISCUSSION: Over other than congested areas, an altitude of 500 ft. above the surface is required. Over open water and sparsely populated areas, a distance of 500 ft. from any person, vessel, vehicle, or structure must be maintained.
Answer (B) is incorrect. An aircraft may not be operated closer than 500 (not 700) ft. from any person, vessel, vehicle, or structure. Answer (C) is incorrect. An aircraft may not be operated closer than 500 (not 1,000) ft. from any person, vessel, vehicle, or structure.

30. Except when necessary for takeoff or landing, what is the minimum safe altitude for a pilot to operate an aircraft anywhere?

A. An altitude allowing, if a power unit fails, an emergency landing without undue hazard to persons or property on the surface.

B. An altitude of 500 feet above the surface and no closer than 500 feet to any person, vessel, vehicle, or structure.

C. An altitude of 500 feet above the highest obstacle within a horizontal radius of 1,000 feet.

Answer (A) is correct. *(FAR 91.119)*
DISCUSSION: Except when necessary for takeoff or landing, no person may operate an aircraft anywhere below an altitude allowing, if a power unit fails, an emergency landing without undue hazard to persons or property on the surface.
Answer (B) is incorrect. An altitude of 500 ft. above the surface is the minimum safe altitude over other than congested areas and no closer than 500 ft. to any person, vessel, vehicle, or structure is the minimum safe altitude over open water or sparsely populated areas. Answer (C) is incorrect. The minimum safe altitude anywhere is an altitude that allows an emergency landing to be made without undue hazards to persons or property on the surface, not 500 ft. above the highest obstacle within a horizontal radius of 1,000 ft.

31. Except when necessary for takeoff or landing, what is the minimum safe altitude required for a pilot to operate an aircraft over congested areas?

A. An altitude of 1,000 feet above any person, vessel, vehicle, or structure.

B. An altitude of 500 feet above the highest obstacle within a horizontal radius of 1,000 feet of the aircraft.

C. An altitude of 1,000 feet above the highest obstacle within a horizontal radius of 2,000 feet of the aircraft.

Answer (C) is correct. *(FAR 91.119)*
DISCUSSION: When operating an aircraft over any congested area of a city, town, or settlement, or over an open-air assembly of persons, a pilot must remain at an altitude of 1,000 ft. above the highest obstacle within a horizontal radius of 2,000 ft. of the aircraft.
Answer (A) is incorrect. The minimum safe altitude to operate an aircraft over a congested area is an altitude of 1,000 ft. above the highest obstacle (not above any person, vessel, vehicle, or structure) within a horizontal distance of 2,000 ft. Answer (B) is incorrect. The minimum safe altitude to operate an aircraft over a congested area is an altitude of 1,000 (not 500) ft. above the highest obstacle within a horizontal radius of 2,000 (not 1,000) ft. of the aircraft.

32. Except when necessary for takeoff or landing, what is the minimum safe altitude required for a pilot to operate an aircraft over other than a congested area?

A. An altitude allowing, if a power unit fails, an emergency landing without undue hazard to persons or property on the surface.

B. An altitude of 500 feet AGL, except over open water or a sparsely populated area, which requires 500 feet from any person, vessel, vehicle, or structure.

C. An altitude of 500 feet above the highest obstacle within a horizontal radius of 1,000 feet.

Answer (B) is correct. *(FAR 91.119)*
DISCUSSION: Over other than congested areas, an altitude of 500 ft. above the surface is required. Over open water and sparsely populated areas, a distance of 500 ft. from any person, vessel, vehicle, or structure must be maintained.
Answer (A) is incorrect. An altitude allowing, if a power unit fails, an emergency landing without undue hazard to persons or property on the surface is the general minimum safe altitude for anywhere, not specifically for operation over other than a congested area. Answer (C) is incorrect. The minimum safe altitude over other than a congested area is an altitude of 500 ft. AGL (not above the highest obstacle within a horizontal radius of 1,000 ft.), except over open water or a sparsely populated area, which requires 500 ft. from any person, vessel, vehicle, or structure.

91.121 Altimeter Settings

33. Prior to takeoff, the altimeter should be set to which altitude or altimeter setting?

A. The current local altimeter setting, if available, or the departure airport elevation.

B. The corrected density altitude of the departure airport.

C. The corrected pressure altitude for the departure airport.

Answer (A) is correct. *(FAR 91.121)*
DISCUSSION: Prior to takeoff, the altimeter should be set to either the local altimeter setting or the departure airport elevation.
Answer (B) is incorrect. Density altitude is pressure altitude corrected for nonstandard temperature variations and is determined from flight computers or graphs, not an altimeter. Answer (C) is incorrect. Pressure altitude is only used at or above 18,000 ft. MSL.

34. If an altimeter setting is not available before flight, to which altitude should the pilot adjust the altimeter?

A. The elevation of the nearest airport corrected to mean sea level.

B. The elevation of the departure area.

C. Pressure altitude corrected for nonstandard temperature.

Answer (B) is correct. *(FAR 91.121)*
DISCUSSION: When the local altimeter setting is not available at takeoff, the pilot should adjust the altimeter to the elevation of the departure area.
Answer (A) is incorrect. Airport elevation is always expressed in true altitude, or feet above MSL. Answer (C) is incorrect. Pressure altitude adjusted for nonstandard temperature is density altitude, not true altitude.

4.5 FAR 91.123 through 91.131

91.123 Compliance with ATC Clearances and Instructions

35. When an ATC clearance has been obtained, no pilot in command may deviate from that clearance unless that pilot obtains an amended clearance. The one exception to this regulation is

A. when the clearance states, "at pilot's discretion."

B. an emergency.

C. if the clearance contains a restriction.

Answer (B) is correct. *(FAR 91.123)*
DISCUSSION: When an ATC clearance has been obtained, no pilot in command may deviate from that clearance, except in an emergency, unless an amended clearance is obtained.
Answer (A) is incorrect. The words "at the pilot's discretion" are part of an ATC clearance, so this is not an exception. Answer (C) is incorrect. Any restriction is still part of the clearance, so this is not an exception.

36. What action, if any, is appropriate if the pilot deviates from an ATC instruction during an emergency and is given priority?

A. Take no special action since you are pilot in command.

B. File a detailed report within 48 hours to the chief of the appropriate ATC facility, if requested.

C. File a report to the FAA Administrator, as soon as possible.

Answer (B) is correct. *(FAR 91.123)*
DISCUSSION: Each pilot in command who is given priority by ATC in an emergency shall, if requested by ATC, submit a detailed report within 48 hr. to the manager of that ATC facility.
Answer (A) is incorrect. As pilot in command you must file a detailed report within 48 hr. to the chief of the appropriate ATC facility, if requested. Answer (C) is incorrect. A detailed report must be filed to the chief of the appropriate ATC facility (not the FAA Administrator) if requested (not as soon as possible).

91.126 Operating on or in the Vicinity of an Airport in Class G Airspace

37. When approaching to land at an airport, without an operating control tower, in Class G airspace, the pilot should

    A. enter and fly a traffic pattern at 800 feet AGL.

    B. make all turns to the left, unless otherwise indicated.

    C. fly a left-hand traffic pattern at 800 feet AGL.

Answer (B) is correct. *(FAR 91.126)*
DISCUSSION: When approaching to land at an airport without an operating control tower in Class G airspace, each pilot of an airplane must make all turns of that airplane to the left unless the airport displays approved light signals or visual markings indicating that turns should be made to the right.
Answer (A) is incorrect. A normal traffic pattern would be flown at 1,000 feet AGL, not 800 feet. Answer (C) is incorrect. Although the traffic pattern is flown to the left, the altitude should be 1,000 feet AGL.

91.130 Operations in Class C Airspace

38. Which initial action should a pilot take prior to entering Class C airspace?

    A. Contact approach control on the appropriate frequency.

    B. Contact the tower and request permission to enter.

    C. Contact the Flight Service Station (FSS) for traffic advisories.

Answer (A) is correct. *(FAR 91.130)*
DISCUSSION: No person may operate an aircraft in Class C airspace unless two-way radio communication is established with the ATC facility having jurisdiction over the airspace prior to entering that area.
Answer (B) is incorrect. The pilot must contact ATC, i.e., approach control, before entering Class C airspace. Answer (C) is incorrect. A FSS is not ATC and does not control Class C airspace.

91.131 Operations in Class B Airspace

39. Which is true regarding flight operations in Class B airspace?

    A. The pilot in command must hold at least a private pilot certificate with an instrument rating.

    B. The pilot in command must hold at least a student pilot certificate.

    C. The aircraft must be equipped with an ATC transponder and altitude reporting equipment.

Answer (C) is correct. *(FAR 91.131)*
DISCUSSION: No person may operate an aircraft in a Class B airspace area unless the aircraft is equipped with an applicable operating transponder and automatic altitude reporting equipment (Mode C).
Answer (A) is incorrect. No person may take off or land aircraft at an airport within Class B airspace or operate an aircraft within Class B airspace unless they are at least a private pilot or, if a student pilot or sport pilot, they have the appropriate logbook endorsement required by FAR 61.95 or 61.325. Answer (B) is incorrect. No person may take off or land aircraft at an airport within Class B airspace or operate an aircraft within Class B airspace unless (s)he is at least a private pilot or, if a student pilot or sport pilot, (s)he has the appropriate logbook endorsement required by FAR 61.95 or 61.325.

40. Which is true regarding flight operations in Class B airspace?

    A. The pilot must receive an ATC clearance before operating an aircraft in that area.

    B. Flight under VFR is not authorized unless the pilot in command is instrument rated.

    C. Solo student pilot operations are not authorized.

Answer (A) is correct. *(FAR 91.131)*
DISCUSSION: For operations in Class (B) airspace, the operator must receive an ATC clearance from the ATC facility having jurisdiction for the area before operating an aircraft in that area.
Answer (B) is incorrect. VFR operations are authorized as long as the operator receives an ATC clearance and all aircraft equipment requirements are met. Answer (C) is incorrect. Student pilot operations are authorized as long as the pilot receives the proper logbook endorsement from an authorized instructor.

END OF STUDY UNIT

82

STUDY UNIT FIVE
FEDERAL AVIATION REGULATIONS –
FAR PARTS 91.155 THROUGH 91.417
AND NTSB PART 830

(4 pages of outline)

This study unit contains outlines of major concepts tested, sample test questions and answers regarding Federal Aviation Regulations (FAR) 91.155 through 91.417 and NTSB Part 830, and an explanation of each answer. The table of contents above lists each subunit within this study unit, the number of questions pertaining to that particular subunit, and the pages on which the outlines and questions begin, respectively.

CAUTION: Recall that the **sole purpose** of this book is to expedite your passing the FAA pilot knowledge test for the sport pilot certificate. Accordingly, all extraneous material (i.e., topics or regulations not directly tested on the FAA pilot knowledge test) is omitted, even though much more information and knowledge are necessary to fly safely. This additional material is presented in *Pilot Handbook* and *Sport Pilot Flight Maneuvers and Practical Test Prep*, available from Gleim Publications, Inc. See the order form on page 327.

5.1 FAR 91.155 THROUGH 91.159

91.155 Basic VFR Weather Minimums

1. Minimum flight visibility for sport pilots is 3 SM.

2. Pilots must maintain 500 ft. below, 1,000 ft. above, and 2,000 ft. horizontally from clouds. Memory aid: 500 is less and below; 1,000 is more and above.

   a. **Exceptions:** Pilots need only remain "clear of clouds" in Class B airspace AND when below 1,200 ft. AGL in Class G airspace.

3. Also note that 61.315 precludes sport pilots from

   a. Flying above 10,000 ft. MSL or 2,000 ft. AGL, whichever is higher, and
   b. Flying without visual reference to the surface.

4. Sport rules on minimums are easy; ignore all the other complicated rules and exceptions.

91.159 VFR Cruising Altitude or Flight Level

1. Specified altitudes are required for VFR cruising flight at more than 3,000 ft. AGL and below 18,000 ft. MSL.

   a. The altitude prescribed is based upon the magnetic course (not magnetic heading).
   b. The altitude is prescribed in ft. above mean sea level (MSL).
   c. Use an odd thousand-foot MSL altitude plus 500 ft. for magnetic courses of 0° to 179°, e.g., 3,500, 5,500, 7,500 ft.
   d. Use an even thousand-foot MSL altitude plus 500 ft. for magnetic courses of 180° to 359°, e.g., 4,500, 6,500, or 8,500 ft.
   e. As a memory aid, the "e" in "even" does not indicate east; i.e, on east headings of 0° through 179°, use odd rather than even.

      1) "East is odd; west is even odder."

5.2 FAR 91.203 THROUGH 91.319

91.203 Civil Aircraft: Certifications Required

1. The aircraft's airworthiness certificate, registration certificate, and operating limitations must be aboard an aircraft during flight.

91.207 Emergency Locator Transmitters

1. ELT batteries must be replaced (or recharged, if rechargeable) after 1 cumulative hr. of use or after 50% of their useful life expires.

91.209 Aircraft Lights

1. If an aircraft is equipped with an anticollision light system, the anticollision lights must be lighted during all operations of that aircraft.

91.303 Aerobatic Flight

1. Aerobatic flight includes all intentional maneuvers that

   a. Are not necessary for normal flight and
   b. Involve an abrupt change in the aircraft's attitude or abnormal acceleration.

2.   Aerobatic flight is prohibited

    a.   When visibility is less than 3 SM;

    b.   When altitude is less than 1,500 ft. above the ground;

    c.   Within the lateral boundaries of the surface areas of Class B, Class C, Class D, or Class E airspace designated for an airport;

    d.   Within 4 NM of the centerline of any federal airway; or

    e.   Over any congested area or over an open-air assembly of people.

91.307 Parachutes and Parachuting

1.   With certain exceptions, each occupant of an aircraft must wear an approved parachute during any intentional maneuver exceeding

    a.   60° bank or

    b.   A nose-up or nose-down attitude of 30°.

2.   Parachutes that are available for emergency use must be packed within a specific time period, based on the materials from which they are constructed.

    a.   Parachutes that include a canopy, shrouds, and harness that are composed exclusively of nylon, rayon, or other similar synthetic fibers must have been repacked by a certificated and appropriately rated parachute rigger within the preceding 180 days.

    b.   Parachutes that include any part that is composed of silk, pongee, or other natural fiber or materials must be repacked by a certificated and appropriately rated parachute rigger within the preceding 60 days.

91.313 Restricted Category Civil Aircraft: Operating Limitations

1.   Restricted category civil aircraft may not normally be operated

    a.   Over densely populated areas,

    b.   In congested airways, or

    c.   Near a busy airport where passenger transport is conducted.

91.319 Aircraft Having Experimental Certificates: Operating Limitations

1.   No person may operate an aircraft that has an experimental or restricted certificate over a densely populated area or in a congested airway unless authorized by the FAA.

5.3 FAR 91.403 THROUGH 91.417

91.403 General

1.   The owner or operator of an aircraft is primarily responsible for maintaining that aircraft in an airworthy condition and for complying with all Airworthiness Directives (ADs).

2.   An operator is a person who uses, or causes to use or authorizes to use, an aircraft for the purpose of air navigation, including the piloting of an aircraft, with or without the right of legal control (i.e., owner, lessee, or otherwise).

    a.   Thus, the pilot in command is also responsible for ensuring that the aircraft is maintained in an airworthy condition and that there is compliance with all ADs.

91.405 Maintenance Required

1.   Each owner or operator of an aircraft shall ensure that maintenance personnel make the appropriate entries in the aircraft maintenance records indicating the aircraft has been approved for return to service.

91.407 Operation after Maintenance, Preventive Maintenance, Rebuilding, or Alteration

1. When aircraft alterations or repairs change the flight characteristics, the aircraft must be test flown and approved for return to service prior to carrying passengers.

91.409 Inspections

1. Annual inspections expire on the last day of the 12th calendar month after the previous annual inspection.

91.417 Maintenance Records

1. An airplane may not be flown unless it has been given an annual inspection within the preceding 12 calendar months.

    a. The annual inspection expires after 1 year on the last day of the month of issuance.

2. The completion of the annual inspection and the airplane's return to service should be appropriately documented in the airplane maintenance records.

    a. The documentation should include the current status of airworthiness directives and the method of compliance.

3. The airworthiness of an airplane can be determined by a preflight inspection and a review of the maintenance records.

5.4 NTSB PART 830

830.5 Immediate Notification

1. Even when no injuries occur to occupants, an airplane accident resulting in substantial damage must be reported to the nearest National Transportation Safety Board (NTSB) field office immediately.

    a. Substantial damage does not include damage to the landing gear, wheels, or tires.

2. The following incidents must also be reported immediately to the NTSB:

    a. Inability of any required crewmember to perform normal flight duties because of in-flight injury or illness
    b. In-flight fire
    c. Flight control system malfunction or failure
    d. An overdue airplane that is believed to be involved in an accident
    e. An airplane collision in flight
    f. Turbine (jet) engine failures

830.10 Preservation of Aircraft Wreckage, Mail, Cargo, and Records

1. Prior to the time the Board or its authorized representative takes custody of aircraft wreckage, mail, or cargo, such wreckage, mail, or cargo may not be disturbed or moved except to

    a. Remove persons injured or trapped,
    b. Protect the wreckage from further damage, or
    c. Protect the public from injury.

830.15 Reports and Statements to Be Filed

1. The operator of an aircraft shall file a report on Board Form 6120.1/2 within 10 days after an accident.

    a. A report must be filed within 7 days if an overdue aircraft is still missing.

2. A report on an incident for which immediate notification is required (830.5) shall be filed only when requested by an authorized representative of the Board.

QUESTIONS AND ANSWER EXPLANATIONS

All of the sport pilot knowledge test questions chosen by the FAA for release as well as additional questions selected by Gleim relating to the material in the previous outlines are reproduced on the following pages. These questions have been organized into the same subunits as the outlines. To the immediate right of each question are the correct answer and answer explanation. You should cover these answers and answer explanations while responding to the questions. Refer to the general discussion in the Introduction on how to take the FAA pilot knowledge test.

Remember that the questions from the FAA pilot knowledge test bank have been reordered by topic and organized into a meaningful sequence. Also, the first line of the answer explanation gives the citation of the authoritative source for the answer.

QUESTIONS

5.1 FAR 91.155 through 91.159

91.155 Basic VFR Weather Minimums

1. VFR flight in controlled airspace above 1,200 feet AGL and below 10,000 feet MSL requires a minimum visibility and vertical cloud clearance of

  A. 3 miles, and 500 feet below or 1,000 feet above the clouds in controlled airspace.

  B. 5 miles, and 1,000 feet below or 1,000 feet above the clouds at all altitudes.

  C. 5 miles, and 1,000 feet below or 1,000 feet above the clouds only in Class A airspace.

Answer (A) is correct. *(FAR 91.155)*
DISCUSSION: Controlled airspace is the generic term for Class A, B, C, D, or E airspace. Only in Class C, D, or below 10,000 ft. MSL in Class E airspace are the minimum flight visibility and vertical distance from cloud for VFR flight required to be 3 SM, and 500 ft. below or 1,000 ft. above the clouds.
NOTE: AGL altitudes are not used in controlled airspace. In Class E airspace, the visibility and distance from clouds are given for (1) below 10,000 ft. MSL and (2) at or above 10,000 ft. MSL.
Answer (B) is incorrect. Five SM and 1,000 ft. above and below the clouds is the minimum visibility and vertical cloud clearance in Class E airspace at altitudes at or above, not below, 10,000 ft. MSL. Answer (C) is incorrect. VFR flight in Class A airspace is prohibited.

2. Basic day visual flight rules (VFR) minimum flight visibility for Class E airspace less than 10,000 feet mean sea level (MSL) is

  A. 2,000 feet horizontal.

  B. 3 statute miles.

  C. 3 nautical miles.

Answer (B) is correct. *(FAR 91.155)*
DISCUSSION: Basic VFR minimum flight visibility for Class E airspace less than 10,000 feet MSL is 3 statute miles.
Answer (A) is incorrect. The VFR minimum flight visibility for Class E airspace less than 10,000 feet MSL is 3 statute miles, not 2,000 feet horizontal. Answer (C) is incorrect. The VFR minimum flight visibility for Class E airspace less than 10,000 feet MSL is 3 statute, not nautical, miles.

3. Sport pilot minimum flight visibility for Class E airspace less than 10,000 feet mean sea level (MSL) is

  A. 2,000 feet horizontal.

  B. 3 statute miles.

  C. 3 nautical miles.

Answer (B) is correct. *(FAR 91.155)*
DISCUSSION: The minimum flight visibility for VFR flight operations in Class E airspace less than 10,000 ft. MSL is 3 SM. Sport pilots have a minimum visibility requirement of 3 statute miles in all airspace. Additionally, they must have visual reference to the surface.
Answer (A) is incorrect. A distance from cloud restriction, not a visibility restriction, is 2,000 feet horizontal. Answer (C) is incorrect. The flight visibility restriction is designated in statute miles, not nautical miles.

4. The minimum distance from clouds required for VFR operations on an airway below 10,000 feet MSL is

   A. remain clear of clouds.

   B. 500 feet below, 1,000 feet above, and 2,000 feet horizontally.

   C. 500 feet above, 1,000 feet below, and 2,000 feet horizontally.

Answer (B) is correct. *(FAR 91.155)*
   DISCUSSION: An airway includes that Class E airspace extending upward from 1,200 ft. AGL to but not including 18,000 ft. MSL. The minimum distance from clouds below 10,000 ft. MSL in Class E airspace is 500 ft. below, 1,000 ft. above, and 2,000 ft. horizontally.
   Answer (A) is incorrect. Clear of clouds is the minimum distance from clouds required in Class B, not Class E, airspace. Answer (C) is incorrect. The minimum distance from clouds required for VFR operations in Class E airspace below 10,000 ft. MSL is 500 ft. below, not above; 1,000 ft. above, not below; and 2,000 ft. horizontally.

5. What minimum visibility and clearance from clouds are required for VFR operations in Class G airspace at 700 feet AGL or below during daylight hours?

   A. 1 mile visibility and clear of clouds.

   B. 1 mile visibility, 500 feet below, 1,000 feet above, and 2,000 feet horizontal clearance from clouds.

   C. 3 miles visibility and clear of clouds.

Answer (C) is correct. *(FAR 91.155, FAR 61.315)*
   DISCUSSION: Sport pilots have a 3-statute-mile visibility requirement in ALL airspace. The other answers relate to other pilot certifications.
   Answer (A) is incorrect. One mile visibility and clear of clouds relates to other pilot certifications. Answer (B) is incorrect. One mile visibility, 500 feet below, 1,000 feet above, and 2,000 feet horizontal clearance from clouds relates to other pilot certifications.

6. The basic VFR weather minimums for operating an aircraft within Class D airspace are

   A. 500-foot ceiling and 1 mile visibility.

   B. 1,000-foot ceiling and 3 miles visibility.

   C. clear of clouds and 2 miles visibility.

Answer (B) is correct. *(FAR 91.155)*
   DISCUSSION: The basic VFR weather minimums for operating an aircraft within Class D airspace are 1,000-ft. ceiling and 3-SM visibility.
   Answer (A) is incorrect. The basic VFR weather minimums for operating an aircraft in Class D airspace are a 1,000-ft., not 500-ft., ceiling and 3, not 1, SM visibility. Answer (C) is incorrect. The basic VFR weather minimums for operating an aircraft in Class D airspace are a 1,000-ft. ceiling, not clear of clouds, and 3, not 2, SM visibility.

7. What minimum flight visibility is required for VFR flight operations on an airway below 10,000 feet MSL?

   A. 1 mile.

   B. 3 miles.

   C. 4 miles.

Answer (B) is correct. *(FAR 91.155)*
   DISCUSSION: An airway includes that Class E airspace extending upward from 1,200 ft. AGL to but not including 18,000 ft. MSL. The minimum flight visibility for VFR flight operations in Class E airspace less than 10,000 ft. MSL is 3 SM.
   Answer (A) is incorrect. One SM is the minimum daytime visibility for a VFR flight below 10,000 ft. MSL in Class G, not Class E, airspace for pilots other than sport pilots. Answer (C) is incorrect. The minimum flight visibility for VFR flight operations in Class E airspace below 10,000 ft. MSL is 3 SM, not 4 SM.

8. During operations within Class E airspace at altitudes of less than 1,200 feet AGL, the minimum horizontal distance from clouds requirement for VFR flight is

   A. 1,000 feet.

   B. 1,500 feet.

   C. 2,000 feet.

Answer (C) is correct. *(FAR 91.155)*
   DISCUSSION: Controlled airspace is the generic term for Class A, B, C, D, or E airspace. Only in Class C, D, or below 10,000 ft. MSL in Class E airspace is the minimum horizontal distance from clouds for VFR flight required to be 2,000 ft. NOTE: AGL altitudes are not used in controlled airspace. In Class E airspace, the visibility and distance from clouds are given for (1) below 10,000 ft. MSL and (2) at or above 10,000 ft. MSL.
   Answer (A) is incorrect. The minimum vertical, not horizontal, distance above the clouds in Class E airspace below 10,000 ft. MSL is 1,000 ft. Answer (B) is incorrect. The minimum horizontal distance is 2,000 ft., not 1,500 ft.

91.159 VFR Cruising Altitude or Flight Level

9. Which VFR cruising altitude is acceptable for a flight on a Victor Airway with a magnetic course of 175°? The terrain is less than 1,000 feet.

    A. 4,500 feet.

    B. 5,000 feet.

    C. 5,500 feet.

Answer (C) is correct. *(FAR 91.159)*
DISCUSSION: When operating a VFR flight above 3,000 ft. AGL on a magnetic course of 0° through 179°, fly any odd thousand-ft. MSL altitude plus 500 ft. Thus, on a magnetic course of 175°, an appropriate VFR cruising altitude is 5,500 ft.
Answer (A) is incorrect. An acceptable VFR cruising altitude would be 4,500 ft. if you were on a magnetic course of 180° to 359°, not 175°. Answer (B) is incorrect. On a magnetic course of 175°, the acceptable VFR cruising altitude is an odd thousand plus 500 ft. (5,500 ft., not 5,000 ft.).

10. Which cruising altitude is appropriate for a VFR flight on a magnetic course of 135°?

    A. Even thousand.

    B. Even thousand plus 500 feet.

    C. Odd thousand plus 500 feet.

Answer (C) is correct. *(FAR 91.159)*
DISCUSSION: When operating a VFR flight above 3,000 ft. AGL on a magnetic course of 0° through 179°, fly any odd thousand-ft. MSL altitude plus 500 ft. Thus, on a magnetic course of 135°, an appropriate VFR cruising altitude is an odd thousand plus 500 ft.
Answer (A) is incorrect. A VFR flight on a magnetic course of 135° will use an odd (not even) thousand plus 500 ft. altitude. Answer (B) is incorrect. A VFR flight on a magnetic course of 135° will use an odd (not even) thousand plus 500 ft. altitude.

11. Which VFR cruising altitude is appropriate when flying above 3,000 feet AGL on a magnetic course of 185°?

    A. 4,000 feet.

    B. 4,500 feet.

    C. 5,000 feet.

Answer (B) is correct. *(FAR 91.159)*
DISCUSSION: When operating a VFR flight above 3,000 ft. AGL on a magnetic course of 180° through 359°, fly any even thousand-ft. MSL altitude, plus 500 ft. Thus, on a magnetic course of 185°, an appropriate VFR cruising altitude is 4,500 ft.
Answer (A) is incorrect. On a magnetic course of 185°, the appropriate VFR cruising altitude is an even thousand-ft. plus 500 ft. altitude (4,500 ft., not 4,000 ft.). Answer (C) is incorrect. On a magnetic course of 185°, the appropriate VFR cruising altitude is an even (not odd) thousand-ft. plus 500 ft. (4,500 ft., not 5,000 ft.).

12. Each person operating an aircraft at a VFR cruising altitude shall maintain an odd-thousand plus 500-foot altitude while on a

    A. magnetic heading of 0° through 179°.

    B. magnetic course of 0° through 179°.

    C. true course of 0° through 179°.

Answer (B) is correct. *(FAR 91.159)*
DISCUSSION: When operating above 3,000 ft. AGL but less than 18,000 ft. MSL on a magnetic course of 0° to 179°, fly at an odd thousand-ft. MSL altitude plus 500 ft.
Answer (A) is incorrect. A magnetic heading includes wind correction, and VFR cruising altitudes are based on magnetic course, i.e., without wind correction. Answer (C) is incorrect. True course does not include an adjustment for magnetic variation.

5.2 FAR 91.203 through 91.319

91.203 Civil Aircraft: Certifications Required

13. In addition to a valid Airworthiness Certificate, what documents or records must be aboard an aircraft during flight?

    A. Aircraft engine and airframe logbooks, and owner's manual.

    B. Radio operator's permit, and repair and alteration forms.

    C. Operating limitations and Registration Certificate.

Answer (C) is correct. *(FAR 91.203 and 91.9)*
DISCUSSION: FAR 91.203 requires both an Airworthiness Certificate and a Registration Certificate to be aboard aircraft during flight. FAR 91.9 requires that operating limitations be available in the aircraft in an approved Airplane Flight Manual, approved manual material, markings, and placards, or any combination thereof.
Answer (A) is incorrect. The airframe and engine logbooks are usually maintained and stored on the ground. Answer (B) is incorrect. Repair and alteration forms are handled in the maintenance shop. Also, the Radio Operator's permit, although carried by the pilot, is an FCC requirement. A pilot may still fly without it as long as (s)he does not use any radio equipment that transmits a signal (e.g., communication, DME, or transponder).

91.207 Emergency Locator Transmitters

14. When must batteries in an emergency locator transmitter (ELT) be replaced or recharged, if rechargeable?

    A. After any inadvertent activation of the ELT.

    B. When the ELT has been in use for more than 1 cumulative hour.

    C. When the ELT can no longer be heard over the airplane's communication radio receiver.

Answer (B) is correct. *(FAR 91.207)*
    DISCUSSION: ELT batteries must be replaced or recharged (if rechargeable) when the transmitter has been in use for more than 1 cumulative hr. or when 50% of their useful life (or useful life of charge) has expired.
    Answer (A) is incorrect. The batteries in an ELT must be replaced (or recharged, if rechargeable) only after the transmitter has been used for more than 1 cumulative hr. Answer (C) is incorrect. ELT batteries are replaced (or recharged, if rechargeable) based on use or useful life.

15. When are non-rechargeable batteries of an emergency locator transmitter (ELT) required to be replaced?

    A. Every 24 months.

    B. When 50 percent of their useful life expires.

    C. At the time of each 100-hour or annual inspection.

Answer (B) is correct. *(FAR 91.207)*
    DISCUSSION: Non-rechargeable batteries of an ELT must be replaced when 50% of their useful life expires or after the transmitter has been in use for more than 1 cumulative hr.
    Answer (A) is incorrect. Every 24 months is the requirement for the transponder to be tested and inspected. Answer (C) is incorrect. Non-rechargeable ELT batteries are replaced when 50% of their useful life expires or after 1 cumulative hr. of use, not necessarily at the time of each 100-hr. or annual inspection.

16. When must the battery in an emergency locator transmitter (ELT) be replaced (or recharged if the battery is rechargeable)?

    A. After one-half the battery's useful life.

    B. During each annual and 100-hour inspection.

    C. Every 24 calendar months.

Answer (A) is correct. *(FAR 91.207)*
    DISCUSSION: Emergency locator transmitter (ELT) batteries must be replaced or recharged after 50% of their useful life has expired or when the transmitter has been in use for more than 1 cumulative hr.
    Answer (B) is incorrect. ELT batteries must be replaced (or recharged) after one-half the battery's useful life has expired. Answer (C) is incorrect. A transponder (not an ELT battery) must be tested and inspected every 24 calendar months.

91.209 Aircraft Lights

17. Pilots must operate the anti-collision lights

    A. at night or in inclement weather.

    B. at night or when the visibility is less than three miles and while flying in Class B airspace.

    C. day and night, except when the pilot-in-command determines that they constitute a hazard to safety.

Answer (C) is correct. *(FAR 91.209)*
    DISCUSSION: Anticollision lights, if the aircraft is equipped, must be operated day and night, except when the pilot in command determines that they constitute a hazard to safety.
    Answer (A) is incorrect. Anticollision lights must be operated in all conditions, not just at night or in inclement weather. Answer (B) is incorrect. Anticollision lights must be operated in all conditions, not just at night or while flying in Class B airspace.

91.303 Aerobatic Flight

18. In which class of airspace is acrobatic flight prohibited?

    A. Class E airspace not designated for Federal Airways above 1,500 feet AGL.

    B. Class E airspace below 1,500 feet AGL.

    C. Class G airspace above 1,500 feet AGL.

Answer (B) is correct. *(FAR 91.303)*
    DISCUSSION: No person may operate an aircraft in acrobatic flight below an altitude of 1,500 ft. AGL.
    Answer (A) is incorrect. Acrobatic flight is prohibited in Class E airspace within 4 NM of the centerline of a Federal Airway, not in all Class E airspace. Answer (C) is incorrect. Acrobatic flight is only prohibited below 1,500 ft. AGL.

19. No person may operate an aircraft in acrobatic flight when the flight visibility is less than

    A. 3 miles.

    B. 5 miles.

    C. 7 miles.

Answer (A) is correct. *(FAR 91.303)*
    DISCUSSION: No person may operate an aircraft in acrobatic flight when the flight visibility is less than 3 SM.
    Answer (B) is incorrect. The minimum flight visibility for acrobatic flight is 3 SM, not 5 SM. Answer (C) is incorrect. The minimum flight visibility for acrobatic flight is 3 SM, not 7 SM.

20. What is the lowest altitude permitted for acrobatic flight?

A. 1,000 feet AGL.

B. 1,500 feet AGL.

C. 2,000 feet AGL.

Answer (B) is correct. *(FAR 91.303)*
DISCUSSION: No person may operate an aircraft in acrobatic flight below 1,500 ft. AGL.
Answer (A) is incorrect. The lowest altitude permitted for acrobatic flight is 1,500 ft. AGL, not 1,000 ft. AGL. Answer (C) is incorrect. The lowest altitude permitted for acrobatic flight is 1,500 ft. AGL, not 2,000 ft. AGL.

21. No person may operate an aircraft in acrobatic flight when

A. flight visibility is less than 5 miles.

B. over any congested area of a city, town, or settlement.

C. less than 2,500 feet AGL.

Answer (B) is correct. *(FAR 91.303)*
DISCUSSION: No person may operate an aircraft in acrobatic flight over any congested area of a city, town, or settlement.
Answer (A) is incorrect. The flight visibility limitation for acrobatic flight is 3 SM, not 5 SM. Answer (C) is incorrect. The minimum altitude for acrobatic flight is 1,500 ft. AGL, not 2,500 ft. AGL.

91.307 Parachutes and Parachuting

22. With certain exceptions, when must each occupant of an aircraft wear an approved parachute?

A. When a door is removed from the aircraft to facilitate parachute jumpers.

B. When intentionally pitching the nose of the aircraft up or down 30° or more.

C. When intentionally banking in excess of 30°.

Answer (B) is correct. *(FAR 91.307)*
DISCUSSION: Unless each occupant of an airplane is wearing an approved parachute, no pilot carrying any other person (other than a crewmember) may execute any intentional maneuver that exceeds a bank of 60° or a nose-up or nose-down attitude of 30° relative to the horizon.
Answer (A) is incorrect. Pilots of airplanes that are carrying parachute jumpers are not required to use a parachute. Answer (C) is incorrect. A parachute is required when an intentional bank that exceeds 60°, not 30°, is to be made.

23. A parachute composed of nylon, rayon, or other synthetic fibers must have been packed by a certificated and appropriately rated parachute rigger within the preceding

A. 60 days.

B. 90 days.

C. 180 days.

Answer (C) is correct. *(FAR 91.307)*
DISCUSSION: No pilot of a civil aircraft may allow a parachute that is available for emergency use to be carried in that aircraft unless it is an approved type and, if a chair type, it has been packed by a certificated and appropriately rated parachute rigger within the preceding 180 days, if synthetic fibers are used in its design.
Answer (A) is incorrect. A parachute composed of nylon, rayon, or other synthetic fibers must have been packed by a certificated and appropriately rated parachute rigger within the preceding 180 days, not 60 days. A parachute constructed with natural fibers must be repacked every 60 days. Answer (B) is incorrect. A parachute composed of nylon, rayon, or other synthetic fibers must have been packed by a certificated and appropriately rated parachute rigger within the preceding 180 days, not 90 days.

24. An approved parachute constructed of natural fibers may be carried in an aircraft for emergency use if it has been packed by an appropriately rated parachute rigger within the preceding

A. 60 days.

B. 120 days.

C. 180 days.

Answer (A) is correct. *(FAR 91.307)*
DISCUSSION: No pilot of a civil aircraft may allow a parachute that is available for emergency use to be carried in that aircraft unless it is an approved type and has been packed by a certificated and appropriately rated parachute rigger within the preceding 60 days if natural fibers are used in its design.
Answer (B) is incorrect. A parachute constructed of natural fibers must have been packed by an appropriately rated parachute rigger within the preceding 60 (not 120) days. Answer (C) is incorrect. A parachute constructed of natural fibers must have been packed by an appropriately rated parachute rigger within the preceding 60 (not 180) days. A parachute constructed from synthetic fibers must be repacked every 180 days.

91.313 Restricted Category Civil Aircraft: Operating Limitations

25. Which is normally prohibited when operating a restricted category civil aircraft?

    A. Flight under instrument flight rules.

    B. Flight over a densely populated area.

    C. Flight within Class D airspace.

Answer (B) is correct. *(FAR 91.313)*
    DISCUSSION: Normally, no person may operate a restricted category civil aircraft over a densely populated area.
    Answer (A) is incorrect. Flight over a densely populated area, not IFR flight, is normally prohibited when operating a restricted category civil aircraft. Answer (C) is incorrect. Flight over a densely populated area, not within Class D airspace, is normally prohibited when operating a restricted category civil aircraft.

91.319 Aircraft Having Experimental Certificates: Operating Limitations

26. Unless otherwise specifically authorized, no person may operate an aircraft that has an experimental certificate

    A. beneath the floor of Class B airspace.

    B. over a densely populated area or in a congested airway.

    C. from the primary airport within Class D airspace.

Answer (B) is correct. *(FAR 91.319)*
    DISCUSSION: Unless otherwise specifically authorized, no person may operate an aircraft that has an experimental certificate over a densely populated area or along a congested airway.
    Answer (A) is incorrect. Normally, no person may operate an aircraft that has an experimental certificate along a congested airway, not beneath the floor of Class B airspace. Answer (C) is incorrect. A person can operate an aircraft that has an experimental certificate from the primary airport within Class D airspace as long as ATC is notified of the experimental nature of the aircraft.

5.3 FAR 91.403 through 91.417

91.403 General

27. The responsibility for ensuring that an aircraft is maintained in an airworthy condition is primarily that of the

    A. pilot in command.

    B. owner or operator.

    C. mechanic who performs the work.

Answer (B) is correct. *(FAR 91.403)*
    DISCUSSION: The owner or operator of an aircraft is primarily responsible for maintaining that aircraft in an airworthy condition. The term "operator" includes the pilot in command.
    Answer (A) is incorrect. The owner or operator, not only the pilot in command, of an aircraft is responsible for ensuring the airworthiness of the aircraft. Answer (C) is incorrect. Although a mechanic will perform inspections and maintenance, the primary responsibility for an aircraft's airworthiness lies with its owner or operator.

28. Who is responsible for ensuring Airworthiness Directives (AD's) are complied with?

    A. Owner or operator.

    B. Repair station.

    C. Mechanic with inspection authorization (IA).

Answer (A) is correct. *(FAR 91.403)*
    DISCUSSION: Airworthiness Directives (ADs) are regulatory and must be complied with, unless a specific exemption is granted. It is the responsibility of the owner or operator to ensure compliance with all pertinent ADs, including those ADs that require recurrent or continuing action.
    Answer (B) is incorrect. The owner or operator, not a repair station, is responsible for ensuring ADs are complied with. Answer (C) is incorrect. The owner or operator, not a mechanic with inspection authorization, is responsible for ensuring ADs are complied with.

91.405 Maintenance Required

29. The responsibility for ensuring that maintenance personnel make the appropriate entries in the aircraft maintenance records indicating the aircraft has been approved for return to service lies with the

    A. owner or operator.

    B. pilot in command.

    C. mechanic who performed the work.

Answer (A) is correct. *(FAR 91.405)*
    DISCUSSION: Each owner or operator of an aircraft shall ensure that maintenance personnel make the appropriate entries in the aircraft maintenance records indicating the aircraft has been approved for return to service.
    Answer (B) is incorrect. The owner or operator, not only the pilot in command, is responsible for ensuring that maintenance personnel make the proper entries in the aircraft's maintenance records. Answer (C) is incorrect. The owner or operator, not the mechanic who performed the work, is responsible for ensuring that proper entries are made in the aircraft's maintenance records.

30. Who is responsible for ensuring appropriate entries are made in maintenance records indicating the aircraft has been approved for return to service?

A. Owner or operator.

B. Certified mechanic.

C. Repair station.

Answer (A) is correct. *(FAR 91.405)*
DISCUSSION: It is the responsibility of the owner or operator of an aircraft to ensure that appropriate entries are made in maintenance records by maintenance personnel indicating the aircraft has been approved for return to service.
Answer (B) is incorrect. The certified mechanic performing the work must make the entries, but it is the responsibility of the owner or operator to ensure that the entries have been made. Answer (C) is incorrect. It is the responsibility of the owner or operator, not a repair station, to ensure appropriate entries have been made.

91.407 Operation after Maintenance, Preventive Maintenance, Rebuilding, or Alteration

31. If an alteration or repair substantially affects an aircraft's operation in flight, that aircraft must be test flown by an appropriately-rated pilot and approved for return to service prior to being operated

A. by any sport pilot.

B. with passengers aboard.

C. for compensation or hire.

Answer (B) is correct. *(FAR 91.407)*
DISCUSSION: If an alteration or repair has been made that substantially affects the airplane's flight characteristics, the airplane must be test flown and approved for return to service by an appropriately rated pilot prior to being operated with passengers aboard. The test pilot must be at least a sport pilot and appropriately rated for the airplane being tested, must make an operational check of the alteration or repair made, and must log the flight in the aircraft records.
Answer (A) is incorrect. If an alteration or repair substantially affects an aircraft's operation in flight, a sport pilot may only test fly that airplane if (s)he is appropriately rated to fly that airplane. Answer (C) is incorrect. After any alteration or repair that substantially affects an aircraft's operation in flight, that aircraft must be test flown and approved for return to service prior to being operated with any passengers aboard, not for compensation or hire.

91.409 Inspections

32. An aircraft's annual inspection was performed on July 12, this year. The next annual inspection will be due no later than

A. July 1, next year.

B. July 13, next year.

C. July 31, next year.

Answer (C) is correct. *(FAR 91.409)*
DISCUSSION: Annual inspections expire on the last day of the 12th calendar month after the previous annual inspection. If an annual inspection is performed on July 12 of this year, it will expire at midnight on July 31 next year.
Answer (A) is incorrect. Annual inspections are due on the last day of the month. Thus, if an annual inspection is performed July 12 this year, the next annual inspection is due July 31 (not July 1) next year. Answer (B) is incorrect. Annual inspections are due on the last day of the month. Thus, if an annual inspection is performed July 12 this year, the next annual inspection is due July 31 (not July 13) next year.

91.417 Maintenance Records

33. Completion of an annual inspection and the return of the aircraft to service should always be indicated by

A. the relicensing date on the Registration Certificate.

B. an appropriate notation in the aircraft maintenance records.

C. an inspection sticker placed on the instrument panel that lists the annual inspection completion date.

Answer (B) is correct. *(FAR 91.417)*
DISCUSSION: Completion of an annual inspection and the return of the aircraft to service should always be indicated by an appropriate notation in the aircraft's maintenance records.
Answer (A) is incorrect. The registration certificate shows ownership, not completion of an annual inspection. Answer (C) is incorrect. Maintenance information is found in the airplane logbooks, not on inspection stickers.

34. To determine the expiration date of the last annual aircraft inspection, a person should refer to the

A. Airworthiness Certificate.

B. Registration Certificate.

C. aircraft maintenance records.

Answer (C) is correct. *(FAR 91.417)*
DISCUSSION: After maintenance inspections have been completed, maintenance personnel should make the appropriate entries in the aircraft maintenance records or logbooks. This is where the date of the last annual inspection can be found.
Answer (A) is incorrect. To determine the expiration date of the last annual inspection, a person should refer to the aircraft maintenance records, not the Airworthiness Certificate. Answer (B) is incorrect. To determine the expiration date of the last annual inspection, a person should refer to the aircraft maintenance records, not the Registration Certificate.

35. Which records or documents shall the owner or operator of an aircraft keep to show compliance with an applicable Airworthiness Directive?

A. Aircraft maintenance records.

B. Airworthiness Certificate and *Pilot's Operating Handbook*.

C. Airworthiness and Registration Certificates.

Answer (A) is correct. *(FAR 91.417)*
DISCUSSION: Aircraft maintenance records must show the current status of applicable airworthiness directives (ADs) including, for each, the method of compliance, the AD number, and revision date. If the AD involves recurring action, the records must show the time and date when the next action is required.
Answer (B) is incorrect. Compliance with an AD is found in aircraft maintenance records, not the Airworthiness Certificate and Pilot's Operating Handbook. Answer (C) is incorrect. Compliance with an AD is found in aircraft maintenance records, not in the Airworthiness and Registration Certificates.

36. The airworthiness of an aircraft can be determined by a preflight inspection and a

A. statement from the owner or operator that the aircraft is airworthy.

B. log book endorsement from a flight instructor.

C. review of the maintenance records.

Answer (C) is correct. *(FAR 91.417)*
DISCUSSION: As pilot in command, you are responsible for determining whether your aircraft is in condition for safe flight. Only by conducting a preflight inspection and a review of the maintenance records can you determine whether all required maintenance has been performed and, thus, whether the aircraft is airworthy.
Answer (A) is incorrect. A statement from the owner or operator that the aircraft is airworthy does not ensure that all required maintenance has been performed. Answer (B) is incorrect. A log book endorsement from a flight instructor does not give any assurance that the aircraft has received required maintenance, and it is not required for determining airworthiness.

5.4 NTSB Part 830

830.5 Immediate Notification

37. If an aircraft is involved in an accident which results in substantial damage to the aircraft, the nearest NTSB field office should be notified

A. immediately.

B. within 48 hours.

C. within 7 days.

Answer (A) is correct. *(NTSB 830.5)*
DISCUSSION: The NTSB must be notified immediately and by the most expeditious means possible when an aircraft accident or any of various listed incidents occurs or when an aircraft is overdue and is believed to have been in an accident.
Answer (B) is incorrect. An aircraft involved in an accident must be reported immediately (not within 48 hr.) to the NTSB office. Answer (C) is incorrect. An aircraft accident must be reported immediately (not within 7 days) to the nearest NTSB office.

38. Which incident requires an immediate notification be made to the nearest NTSB field office?

A. An overdue aircraft that is believed to be involved in an accident.

B. An in-flight radio communications failure.

C. An in-flight generator or alternator failure.

Answer (A) is correct. *(NTSB 830.5)*
DISCUSSION: The NTSB must be notified immediately and by the most expeditious means possible when an aircraft is overdue and is believed to have been involved in an accident.
Answer (B) is incorrect. An in-flight radio communications failure does not require notification to the NTSB at any time. Answer (C) is incorrect. An in-flight generator or alternator failure does not require notification to the NTSB at any time.

39. Which incident would necessitate an immediate notification to the nearest NTSB field office?

A. An in-flight generator/alternator failure.

B. An in-flight fire.

C. An in-flight loss of VOR receiver capability.

Answer (B) is correct. *(NTSB 830.5)*
DISCUSSION: The NTSB must be notified immediately and by the most expeditious means possible when an aircraft accident or any of various listed incidents occurs or when an aircraft is overdue and believed to have been in an accident. The following are considered incidents:

1. Flight control system malfunction or failure;
2. Inability of any required flight crewmember to perform normal flight duties as a result of injury or illness;
3. Failure of structural components of a turbine engine, excluding compressor and turbine blades and vanes;
4. In-flight fire; or
5. Aircraft collision in flight.

Answer (A) is incorrect. An in-flight generator/alternator failure does not require immediate notification. Answer (C) is incorrect. An in-flight loss of VOR receiver capability does not require any type of notification to the NTSB.

40. Which incident requires an immediate notification to the nearest NTSB field office?

A. A forced landing due to engine failure.

B. Landing gear damage, due to a hard landing.

C. Flight control system malfunction or failure.

Answer (C) is correct. *(NTSB 830.5)*
DISCUSSION: The NTSB must be notified immediately and by the most expeditious means possible when an aircraft accident or any of various listed incidents occurs or when an aircraft is overdue and believed to have been in an accident. The following are considered incidents:

1. Flight control system malfunction or failure;
2. Inability of any required flight crewmember to perform normal flight duties as a result of injury or illness;
3. Failure of structural components of a turbine engine, excluding compressor and turbine blades and vanes;
4. In-flight fire; or
5. Aircraft collision in flight.

Answer (A) is incorrect. Only failure of structural components of a turbine engine (not a forced landing due to engine failure) must be reported immediately to the nearest NTSB office. Answer (B) is incorrect. Landing gear damage due to a hard landing is not considered an incident that requires immediate notification to the NTSB.

830.10 Preservation of Aircraft Wreckage, Mail, Cargo, and Records

41. May aircraft wreckage be moved prior to the time the NTSB takes custody?

A. Yes, but only if moved by a federal, state, or local law enforcement officer.

B. Yes, but only to protect the wreckage from further damage.

C. No, it may not be moved under any circumstances.

Answer (B) is correct. *(NTSB 830.10)*
DISCUSSION: Prior to the time the Board or its authorized representative takes custody of aircraft wreckage, mail, or cargo, such wreckage, mail, or cargo may not be disturbed or moved except to the extent necessary to

1. Remove persons injured or trapped,
2. Protect the wreckage from further damage, or
3. Protect the public from injury.

Answer (A) is incorrect. Aircraft wreckage can only be moved to protect the wreckage from further damage, protect the public from injury, or remove persons injured or trapped, not by any federal, state, or local law enforcement officer. Answer (C) is incorrect. Aircraft wreckage may be moved in certain circumstances, such as to remove persons injured or trapped, protect the wreckage from further damage, or protect the public from injury.

830.15 Reports and Statements to Be Filed

42. The operator of an aircraft that has been involved in an accident is required to file an accident report within how many days?

    A. 5

    B. 7

    C. 10

Answer (C) is correct. *(NTSB 830.15)*
    DISCUSSION: The operator of an aircraft shall file a report on NTSB Form 6120.1/2 within 10 days after an accident, or after 7 days if an overdue aircraft is still missing. A report on an incident for which notification is required shall be filed only as required.
    Answer (A) is incorrect. NTSB Form 6120.1/2 is required within 10 (not 5) days after an accident. Answer (B) is incorrect. NTSB Form 6120.1/2 is required within 10 (not 7) days after an accident.

43. The operator of an aircraft that has been involved in an incident is required to submit a report to the nearest field office of the NTSB

    A. within 7 days.

    B. within 10 days.

    C. when requested.

Answer (C) is correct. *(NTSB 830.15)*
    DISCUSSION: The operator of an aircraft shall file a report on NTSB Form 6120.1/2 only when requested. A report is required within 10 days of an accident or after 7 days if an overdue aircraft is still missing.
    Answer (A) is incorrect. The time allowed to file a written report on an overdue aircraft that is still missing is 7 days; an incident requires a report only when requested. Answer (B) is incorrect. A report must be filed within 10 days of an accident; an incident requires a report only when requested.

44. How many days after an accident is a report required to be filed with the nearest NTSB field office?

    A. 2

    B. 7

    C. 10

Answer (C) is correct. *(NTSB 830.15)*
    DISCUSSION: The operator of an aircraft shall file a report within 10 days after an accident.
    Answer (A) is incorrect. A report is required within 10 days, not 2 days, after an accident. Answer (B) is incorrect. A report is required after 7 days if an overdue aircraft is still missing, not after an accident.

45. While taxiing on the parking ramp, the landing gear, wheel, and tire are damaged by striking ground equipment. What action would be required to comply with NTSB Part 830?

    A. A report must be filed with the nearest FAA field office within 7 days.

    B. An immediate notification must be filed by the operator of the aircraft with the nearest NTSB field office.

    C. No notification or report is required.

Answer (C) is correct. *(NTSB 830.15)*
    DISCUSSION: An aircraft accident is an occurrence associated with the operation of an aircraft that takes place between the time any person boards the aircraft with the intention of flight and all such persons have disembarked, and in which any person suffers death or serious injury, or in which the aircraft receives substantial damage. Damage to landing gear, wheels, and tires are not considered substantial damage.
    However, damage to property, other than aircraft, estimated to exceed $25,000 for repair does require immediate notification. For the purposes of this question, assume that the ground equipment requires less than $25,000 in repair.
    Answer (A) is incorrect. When an accident occurs, the pilot in command must notify the nearest NTSB field office, not the FAA field office. Answer (B) is incorrect. Damage to landing gear, wheels, and tires is not considered substantial damage and therefore does not necessitate notification to the nearest NTSB field office.

END OF STUDY UNIT

STUDY UNIT SIX
AEROMEDICAL FACTORS AND
AERONAUTICAL DECISION MAKING (ADM)

(5 pages of outline)

This study unit contains outlines of major concepts tested, sample test questions and answers regarding aeromedical factors and aeronautical decision making (ADM), and an explanation of each answer. The table of contents above lists each subunit within this study unit, the number of questions pertaining to that particular subunit, and the pages on which the outlines and questions begin, respectively.

CAUTION: Recall that the **sole purpose** of this book is to expedite your passing the FAA pilot knowledge test for the sport pilot certificate. Accordingly, all extraneous material (i.e., topics or regulations not directly tested on the FAA pilot knowledge test) is omitted, even though much more information and knowledge are necessary to fly safely. This additional material is presented in *Pilot Handbook* and *Sport Pilot Flight Maneuvers and Practical Test Prep*, available from Gleim Publications, Inc. See the order form on page 327.

6.1 HYPOXIA

1. Hypoxia is oxygen deficiency in the bloodstream and may cause lack of clear thinking, fatigue, euphoria, and, shortly thereafter, unconsciousness.

2. The following are four types of hypoxia based on their causes:

    a. **Hypoxic hypoxia** is a result of insufficient oxygen available to the body as a whole.

        1) EXAMPLE: Reduction of partial pressure at high altitude, a blocked airway, or drowning

    b. **Hypemic hypoxia** occurs when the blood is not able to take up and transport a sufficient amount of oxygen to the cells in the body. The result is oxygen deficiency in the blood rather than a lack of inhaled oxygen.

        1) EXAMPLE: Carbon monoxide poisoning

    c. **Stagnant hypoxia** results when oxygen-rich blood in the lungs is not moving.

        1) EXAMPLE: Shock, reduced circulation due to extreme cold, or pulling excessive Gs in flight

    d. **Histotoxic hypoxia** is the inability of cells to effectively use oxygen.

        1) EXAMPLE: Impairment due to alcohol and drugs

3. Symptoms of hypoxia include an initial feeling of euphoria but lead to more serious concerns such as headache, decreased reaction time, visual impairment, and eventual unconsciousness.

4. The correct response to counteracting feelings of hypoxia is to lower altitude or use supplemental oxygen.

6.2 HYPERVENTILATION

1. Hyperventilation occurs when an excessive amount of air is breathed out of the lungs, e.g., when one becomes excited or undergoes stress, tension, fear, or anxiety.

   a. This results in an excessive amount of carbon dioxide passed out of the body and too much oxygen retained.

   b. The symptoms are lightheadedness, suffocation, drowsiness, tingling in the extremities, etc.

2. Overcome hyperventilation symptoms by slowing the breathing rate, breathing into a bag, or talking aloud.

6.3 ALCOHOL

1. Alcohol is a central nervous system depressant and interferes with the brain's ability to use oxygen. Judgment and decision-making abilities are adversely affected by even small amounts of alcohol.

2. Altitude multiplies the effects of alcohol on the brain; at higher altitudes, alcohol from two drinks may have the same effect as three or four drinks at lower altitudes.

3. 14 CFR 91.17 requires that blood alcohol level be less than 0.04 percent and that 8 hours pass between consuming alcohol and piloting an aircraft.

6.4 SPATIAL DISORIENTATION

1. Spatial disorientation, e.g., not knowing whether you are going up, down, or turning, is a state of temporary confusion resulting from misleading information being sent to the brain by various sensory organs.

2. If you lose outside visual references and become disoriented, you are experiencing spatial disorientation. This occurs when you rely on the sensations of muscles and the inner ear to tell you what the airplane's attitude is.

   a. This might occur during a night flight, in clouds, or in dust.

   b. Examples of spatial disorientation in flight could include the following:

      1) **Graveyard spiral.** An observed loss of altitude during a coordinated constant-rate turn that has ceased stimulating the motion-sensing system can create the illusion of being in a descent with the wings level. The disoriented pilot will pull back on the controls, tightening the spiral and increasing the loss of altitude.

      2) **False horizon.** Sloping cloud formations, an obscured horizon, and certain geometric patterns of ground lights can create the illusion of not being correctly aligned with the true horizon. Without reference to instruments, a pilot may place the airplane in a dangerous attitude based on incorrect visual cues.

3. Ways to overcome the effects of spatial disorientation include relying on the airplane instruments, avoiding sudden head movements, and ensuring that outside visual references are fixed points on the surface.

6.5 DEHYDRATION

1. **Dehydration** is the excessive loss of water from the body, as from illness or fluid deprivation.

   a. This fluid loss can occur in any environment; causes include hot cockpits and flight lines, high humidity, diuretic drinks (e.g., coffee, tea, colas), as well as improper attire.

2.   Some common signs and symptoms of dehydration include headache, fatigue, cramps, sleepiness, dizziness, severe hydration, lethargy, and coma.

   a.   Heat exhaustion often accompanies dehydration. Below are the three stages of heat exhaustion, along with accompanying signs and symptoms.

      1)   Heat stress (body temp: 99.5°-100° F) – reduces performance, decision-making ability, alertness, and visual capabilities

      2)   Heat exhaustion (body temp: 101°-105° F) – causes fatigue, nausea/vomiting, cramps, rapid breathing, and fainting

      3)   Heat stroke (body temp: >105° F) – causes body's heat control mechanism to stop working, mental confusion, disorientation, and coma

3.   To help prevent dehydration and heat exhaustion, you should drink 2 to 4 quarts of water every 24 hours. Or, follow the generally prescribed eight-glasses-a-day rule.

   a.   Because each individual is physiologically different, this is only to be used as a guide. Your daily fluid intake should be varied to meet your individual needs depending on work conditions, environment, and individual physiology.

   b.   Other useful tips on avoiding heat exhaustion are limiting your daily intake of caffeine and alcohol (both are diuretics), properly acclimating to major weather and/or climate changes, and planning ahead by carrying sufficient fluids and choosing appropriate attire for the forecast conditions.

6.6 VISION

1.   Scanning for traffic is best accomplished by bringing small portions of the sky into the central field of vision slowly and in succession.

2.   Haze can create the illusion of traffic or terrain being farther away than they actually are.

3.   Visual illusions may affect a pilot's ability to properly judge a landing.

   a.   Rain on a windscreen can create the illusion of greater height from the runway.

   b.   Haze can create the illusion of greater distance from the runway.

   c.   Landing errors from these illusions can be overcome by knowledge and anticipation of the illusions.

6.7 CARBON MONOXIDE

1.   Blurred (hazy) thinking, uneasiness, dizziness, and tightness across the forehead are early symptoms of carbon monoxide poisoning. They are followed by a headache and, with large accumulations of carbon monoxide, a loss of muscle power.

2.   Increases in altitude increase susceptibility to carbon monoxide poisoning because of decreased oxygen availability.

6.8 AERONAUTICAL DECISION MAKING (ADM)

1.   **Aeronautical decision making (ADM)** is a systematic approach to the mental process used by pilots to consistently determine the best course of action in response to a given set of circumstances.

2.   **Risk management** is the part of the decision-making process that relies on situational awareness, problem recognition, and good judgment to reduce risks associated with flight.

3. A **Poor Judgment (PJ) Chain** is a series of mistakes that may lead to an accident or incident, also often called an **Error Chain**.

   a. Two basic principles generally associated with the creation of a PJ chain are

      1) One bad decision often leads to another.

      2) As a string of bad decisions grows, it reduces the number of subsequent alternatives for continued safe flight.

   b. ADM is intended to break the PJ chain before it can cause an accident or incident.

4. The Decide Model

   a. A good tool to use in making good aeronautical decisions is the **DECIDE** Model shown below.

      1) **D**etect. The decision maker detects the fact that change has occurred.

      2) **E**stimate. The decision maker estimates the need to counter or react to the change.

      3) **C**hoose. The decision maker chooses a desirable outcome (in terms of success) for the flight.

      4) **I**dentify. The decision maker identifies actions that could successfully control the change.

      5) **D**o. The decision maker takes the necessary action.

      6) **E**valuate. The decision maker evaluates the effect(s) of his/her action countering the change.

   b. The six elements of the Decide Model represent a continuous-loop decision process that can be used to assist a pilot in the decision-making process when (s)he is faced with a change in a situation that requires a judgment.

      1) This Decide Model is primarily focused on the intellectual component but can have an impact on the motivational component of judgment as well.

      2) If a pilot practices the Decide Model in all decision making, its use can become very natural and result in better decisions being made under all types of situations.

5. Most pilots have fallen prey to dangerous tendencies or behavioral problems at some time. Scud running, continuing visual flight into instrument conditions, neglecting checklists, and showing the "right stuff" are four examples of these dangerous tendencies or behavioral problems that must be identified and eliminated.

   a. In scud running, a pilot pushes his/her capabilities and the airplane to the limits by trying to maintain visual contact with the terrain while trying to avoid contact with it during low visibility and ceilings.

   b. Continuing visual flight into instrument conditions often leads to spatial disorientation or collision with the ground or obstacles.

   c. Neglect of checklists is an example of a pilot's unjustified reliance on his/her short- and long-term memory for repetitive tasks.

      1) To avoid missing important steps, you should always use the appropriate checklists whenever they are available. Consistent adherence to approved checklists is a sign of a disciplined and competent pilot.

   d. The drive to demonstrate the "right stuff" can have an adverse effect on safety and can impose an unrealistic assessment of piloting skills under stressful conditions.

   e. Getting behind the aircraft means allowing events or the situation to control your actions rather than the other way around. This dangerous tendency is characterized by a constant state of surprise at what happens next. An extreme case of getting behind the aircraft can result in loss of positional or situation awareness, which results in not knowing your location, being unable to recognize deteriorating circumstances, and/or misjudging the rate of deterioration.

      f.   Because of these pitfalls, pilots who become apprehensive for their safety for any reason should request assistance immediately. A variety of resources are available in the form of radio, radar vectors, other aircraft, and direction finding stations, all of which are a radio call away.

6.   ADM addresses five hazardous attitudes that contribute to poor pilot judgment.

      a.   Recognition of hazardous attitudes (thoughts) is the first step in neutralizing them in the ADM process.

      b.   When you recognize a hazardous attitude, you should label it as hazardous and then correct it by stating the corresponding antidote, as shown below.

Hazardous Attitude	Antidote
Antiauthority: *Don't tell me!*	Follow the rules. They are usually right.
Impulsivity: *Do something quickly!*	Not so fast. Think first.
Invulnerability: *It won't happen to me.*	It could happen to me.
Macho: *I can do it.*	Taking chances is foolish.
Resignation: *What's the use?*	I'm not helpless. I can make a difference.

7.   You are responsible for determining whether or not you are fit to fly for a particular flight.

      a.   FAR 61.23 prohibits a person from exercising the privileges of a sport pilot certificate while knowing of or having reason to know of any medical or health condition that would make that person unable to operate a light-sport aircraft in a safe manner.

      b.   A sport pilot may not act as pilot in command if that person knows or has reason to know of any medical condition that would make that person unable to operate a light-sport aircraft in a safe manner.

          1)   If advice is needed concerning possible flight with an illness, a pilot should contact an Aviation Medical Examiner.

8.   Human error is the one common factor that affects most preventable accidents.

      a.   A pilot who is involved in an accident usually knows what went wrong and was aware of the possible hazards when (s)he was making the decision that led to the wrong course of action.

      b.   For example, fuel starvation accidents are generally the result of the conscious human error of ignoring minimum fuel reserve requirements because of overconfidence, disregard of applicable regulations, or simple lack of flight planning.

6.9 EAR BLOCK

You may also see a question on the following, especially the last sentence:

1.   As the aircraft cabin pressure decreases during ascent, the expanding air in the middle ear pushes the eustachian tube open and, by escaping down it to the nasal passages, equalizes in pressure with the cabin pressure. During descent, the pilot must periodically open the eustachian tube to equalize pressure. This can be accomplished by swallowing, yawning, tensing muscles in the throat, or, if these do not work, by a combination of closing the mouth, pinching the nose closed, and attempting to blow through the nostrils.

QUESTIONS AND ANSWER EXPLANATIONS

All of the sport pilot knowledge test questions chosen by the FAA for release as well as additional questions selected by Gleim relating to the material in the previous outlines are reproduced on the following pages. These questions have been organized into the same subunits as the outlines. To the immediate right of each question are the correct answer and answer explanations. You should cover these answers and answer explanations while responding to the questions. Refer to the general discussion in the Introduction on how to take the FAA pilot knowledge test.

Remember that the questions from the FAA pilot knowledge test bank have been reordered by topic and organized into a meaningful sequence. Also, the first line of the answer explanation gives the citation of the authoritative source for the answer.

QUESTIONS

6.1 Hypoxia

1. Which statement best defines hypoxia?

A. A state of oxygen deficiency in the body.

B. An abnormal increase in the volume of air breathed.

C. A condition of gas bubble formation around the joints or muscles.

Answer (A) is correct. *(AIM Para 8-1-2)*
DISCUSSION: Hypoxia is oxygen deficiency in the bloodstream and may cause lack of clear thinking, fatigue, euphoria and, shortly thereafter, unconsciousness.
Answer (B) is incorrect. It describes a cause of hyperventilation. Answer (C) is incorrect. It describes decompression sickness after scuba diving.

2. Which is not a type of hypoxia?

A. Histotoxic.

B. Hypoxic.

C. Hypertoxic.

Answer (C) is correct. *(PHAK Chap 16)*
DISCUSSION: There is no such thing as hypertoxic hypoxia. The four types of hypoxia are histotoxic, hypoxic, hypemic, and stagnant hypoxia.
Answer (A) is incorrect. The four types of hypoxia are histotoxic, hypoxic, hypemic, and stagnant hypoxia. Answer (B) is incorrect. The four types of hypoxia are histotoxic, hypoxic, hypemic, and stagnant hypoxia.

3. Which of the following is a correct response to counteract the feelings of hypoxia in flight?

A. Promptly descend altitude.

B. Increase cabin air flow.

C. Avoid sudden inhalations.

Answer (A) is correct. *(PHAK Chap 16)*
DISCUSSION: The correct response to counteract feelings of hypoxia is to lower altitude or use supplemental oxygen if the aircraft is so equipped.
Answer (B) is incorrect. Increasing the amount of air flowing inside an aircraft will not help counteract hypoxia. Because of the reduction of partial pressure at higher altitudes, there is less oxygen in the air to draw from. Answer (C) is incorrect. Breathing deeply or suddenly will not counteract feelings of hypoxia.

6.2 Hyperventilation

4. Which would most likely result in hyperventilation?

A. Emotional tension, anxiety, or fear.

B. The excessive consumption of alcohol.

C. An extremely slow rate of breathing and insufficient oxygen.

Answer (A) is correct. *(AIM Para 8-1-3)*
DISCUSSION: Hyperventilation usually occurs when one becomes excited or undergoes stress, which results in an increase in one's rate of breathing.
Answer (B) is incorrect. Hyperventilation is usually caused by some type of stress, not by alcohol. Answer (C) is incorrect. The opposite is true: Hyperventilation is an extremely fast rate of breathing and an intake of excessive oxygen.

5. As hyperventilation progresses a pilot can experience

    A. decreased breathing rate and depth.

    B. heightened awareness and feeling of well-being.

    C. symptoms of suffocation and drowsiness.

Answer (C) is correct. *(AIM Para 8-1-3)*
    DISCUSSION: Hyperventilation is an abnormal increase in breathing, which can occur subconsciously when a stressful situation is encountered. It can cause lightheadedness, drowsiness, suffocation, tingling in the extremities, and coolness.
    Answer (A) is incorrect. Hyperventilation is an increase, not a decrease, of the breathing rate and depth. Answer (B) is incorrect. Heightened awareness and euphoria are potential symptoms of hypoxia, not hyperventilation.

6. To overcome the symptoms of hyperventilation, a pilot should

    A. swallow or yawn.

    B. slow the breathing rate.

    C. increase the breathing rate.

Answer (B) is correct. *(AIM Para 8-1-3)*
    DISCUSSION: A pilot should be able to overcome the symptoms of hyperventilation by slowing the breathing rate or breathing into a bag.
    Answer (A) is incorrect. Swallowing or yawning helps to equalize ear pressures, not overcome hyperventilation. Answer (C) is incorrect. Increasing the breathing rate aggravates hyperventilation.

7. A pilot should be able to overcome the symptoms or avoid future occurrences of hyperventilation by

    A. closely monitoring the flight instruments to control the airplane.

    B. slowing the breathing rate, breathing into a bag, or talking aloud.

    C. increasing the breathing rate in order to increase lung ventilation.

Answer (B) is correct. *(AIM Para 8-1-3)*
    DISCUSSION: To recover from hyperventilation, the pilot should slow the breathing rate, breathe into a bag, or talk aloud.
    Answer (A) is incorrect. Closely monitoring the flight instruments is used to overcome vertigo (spatial disorientation). Answer (C) is incorrect. Increased breathing aggravates hyperventilation.

6.3 Alcohol

8. Which is true regarding the presence of alcohol within the human body?

    A. A small amount of alcohol increases vision acuity.

    B. An increase in altitude decreases the adverse effect of alcohol.

    C. Judgment and decision-making abilities can be adversely affected by even small amounts of alcohol.

Answer (C) is correct. *(AIM Para 8-1-1)*
    DISCUSSION: As little as 1 ounce of liquor, 12 ounces of beer, or 4 ounces (one glass) of wine can impair flying skills, with the alcohol consumed in these drinks being detectable in the breath and blood for at least 3 hr.
    Answer (A) is incorrect. Any amount of alcohol decreases, not increases, virtually all mental and physical activities. Answer (B) is incorrect. Increases in altitude increase, not decrease, the adverse effects of alcohol.

9. According to current regulations, how many hours must elapse between consuming alcohol and piloting an aircraft?

    A. 4 hours.

    B. 8 hours.

    C. 16 hours.

Answer (B) is correct. *(PHAK Chap 16)*
    DISCUSSION: According to 14 CFR 91.17, 8 hours must pass between consuming alcohol and flying an aircraft.
    Answer (A) is incorrect. Regulations require that 8 hours, not 4, must pass between consuming alcohol and flying an aircraft. Answer (C) is incorrect. While considerable amounts of alcohol may remain in the body for over 16 hours, and it is good to be cautious about flying too soon after drinking, the regulations state that only 8 hours must elapse between consuming alcohol and flying.

10. Which of the following statements concerning the combination of alcohol and altitude is true?

    A. Judgment and decision-making abilities will only be affected at altitudes greater than 2,000 ft. MSL.

    B. Altitude multiplies the effects of alcohol.

    C. Increases in altitude do not change how alcohol affects individuals.

Answer (B) is correct. *(PHAK Chap 16)*
    DISCUSSION: Altitude multiplies the effects of alcohol on the brain; at higher altitudes, alcohol from two drinks may have the same effect as three or four drinks at lower altitudes.
    Answer (A) is incorrect. An increase in altitude, no matter how small, can multiply the effects of alcohol on the body. Answer (C) is incorrect. Increasing altitude multiplies the effects alcohol will have on the body.

6.4   Spatial Disorientation

11. A state of temporary confusion resulting from misleading information being sent to the brain by various sensory organs is defined as

    A. spatial disorientation.

    B. hyperventilation.

    C. hypoxia.

Answer (A) is correct.   *(AIM Para 8-1-5)*
    DISCUSSION: A state of temporary confusion resulting from misleading information being sent to the brain by various sensory organs is defined as vertigo (spatial disorientation). Put simply, the pilot cannot determine his/her relationship to the earth's horizon.
    Answer (B) is incorrect. Hyperventilation causes excessive oxygen and/or a decrease in carbon dioxide in the bloodstream. Answer (C) is incorrect. Hypoxia occurs when there is insufficient oxygen in the bloodstream.

12. How may a pilot overcome spatial disorientation?

    A. By relying on his flight instruments.

    B. By decreasing the amount of time spent looking inside.

    C. By relying on all outside visual references.

Answer (A) is correct.   *(PHAK Chap 16)*
    DISCUSSION: Ways to overcome the effects of spatial disorientation include relying on the airplane instruments, avoiding sudden head movements, and ensuring that outside visual references are fixed points on the surface.
    Answer (B) is incorrect. Decreasing the amount of time spent looking inside is not a remedy for overcoming spatial disorientation. Answer (C) is incorrect. Not all visual references can be relied on, as some may be moving. A pilot must ensure that any outside visual references are fixed points on the surface.

13. Which of the following flight conditions would indicate a pilot is experiencing spatial disorientation?

    A. Steep turn.

    B. Graveyard spiral.

    C. Turns around a point.

Answer (B) is correct.   *(PHAK Chap 16)*
    DISCUSSION: A graveyard spiral is an example of a pilot being adversely affected by spatial disorientation.
    Answer (A) is incorrect. Steep turns are common maneuvers performed during training and do not indicate that a pilot is experiencing spatial disorientation. Answer (C) is incorrect. Turns around a point are maneuvers performed during training and do not indicate that a pilot is experiencing spatial disorientation.

6.5   Dehydration

14. As a pilot, flying for long periods in hot summer temperatures increases the susceptibility of dehydration since the

    A. dry air at altitude tends to increase the rate of water loss from the body.

    B. moist air at altitude helps retain the body's moisture.

    C. temperature decreases with altitude.

Answer (A) is correct.   *(PHAK Chap 16)*
    DISCUSSION: Flying for long periods in hot summer temperatures or at high altitudes increases the susceptibility to dehydration since the dry air at altitude tends to increase the rate of water loss from the body.
    Answer (B) is incorrect. The air at altitude is not moist; it is dry, and it does not help to retain the body's moisture.
    Answer (C) is incorrect. The general decrease in temperature with altitude does not affect the rate of dehydration.

15. What is a sign of heat stress?

    A. Coma.

    B. Rapid breathing.

    C. Reduced alertness.

Answer (C) is correct.   *(PHAK Chap 16)*
    DISCUSSION: Heat stress, the first stage in heat exhaustion, reduces performance, decision-making ability, alertness, and visual capabilities.
    Answer (A) is incorrect. A coma is a sign of heat stroke, the last stage of heat exhaustion. Answer (B) is incorrect. Rapid breathing occurs during heat exhaustion, not heat stress.

6.6 Vision

16. To scan properly for traffic, a pilot should

    A. slowly sweep the field of vision from one side to the other at intervals.

    B. concentrate on any peripheral movement detected.

    C. use a series of short, regularly spaced eye movements that bring successive areas of the sky into the central visual field.

Answer (C) is correct. *(AIM Para 8-1-6)*
    DISCUSSION: The most effective way to scan for other aircraft during the day is to use a series of short, regularly spaced eye movements that bring successive areas of the sky into your central vision. Each movement should not exceed 10°, and each area should be observed for at least 1 sec. to facilitate detection.
    Answer (A) is incorrect. You must concentrate on different segments systematically. Answer (B) is incorrect. Peripheral movement will not be detected easily, especially under adverse conditions such as haze.

17. Which technique should a pilot use to scan for traffic to the right and left during straight-and-level flight?

    A. Systematically focus on different segments of the sky for short intervals.

    B. Concentrate on relative movement detected in the peripheral vision area.

    C. Continuous sweeping of the windshield from right to left.

Answer (A) is correct. *(AIM Para 8-1-6)*
    DISCUSSION: Due to the fact that eyes can focus only on a narrow viewing area, effective scanning is accomplished with a series of short, regularly spaced eye movements that bring successive areas of the sky into the central vision field.
    Answer (B) is incorrect. It concerns scanning for traffic at night. Answer (C) is incorrect. You must continually scan successive, small portions of the sky. The eyes can focus only on a narrow viewing area and require at least 1 sec. to detect a faraway object.

18. What effect does haze have on the ability to see traffic or terrain features during flight?

    A. Haze causes the eyes to focus at infinity.

    B. The eyes tend to overwork in haze and do not detect relative movement easily.

    C. All traffic or terrain features appear to be farther away than their actual distance.

Answer (C) is correct. *(AIM Para 8-1-5)*
    DISCUSSION: Atmospheric haze can create the illusion of being at a greater distance from traffic or terrain than you actually are. This is especially prevalent on landings.
    Answer (A) is incorrect. In haze, the eyes focus at a comfortable distance, which may be only 10 to 30 ft. outside of the cockpit. Answer (B) is incorrect. In haze, the eyes relax and tend to stare outside without focusing or looking for common visual cues.

19. Haze creates which of the following atmospheric illusions?

    A. Being at a greater distance from the runway.

    B. Being at a closer distance from the runway.

    C. Haze creates no atmospheric illusions.

Answer (A) is correct. *(AIM Para 8-1-5)*
    DISCUSSION: Rain on a windscreen can create the illusion of greater height from the runway, and haze can create the illusion of greater distance from the runway; landing errors from these illusions can be overcome by knowledge and anticipation of the illusions.
    Answer (B) is incorrect. Haze creates the illusion of being further from, not closer to, the runway. Answer (C) is incorrect. Haze creates the illusion of being at a greater distance from the runway.

6.7 Carbon Monoxide

20. Large accumulations of carbon monoxide in the human body result in

    A. tightness across the forehead.

    B. loss of muscular power.

    C. an increased sense of well-being.

Answer (B) is correct. *(AC 20-32B)*
    DISCUSSION: Carbon monoxide reduces the ability of the blood to carry oxygen. Large accumulations result in loss of muscular power.
    Answer (A) is incorrect. It describes an early symptom, not the effect of large accumulations. Answer (C) is incorrect. Euphoria is a result of the lack of sufficient oxygen, not specifically an accumulation of carbon monoxide.

21. Susceptibility to carbon monoxide poisoning increases as

    A. altitude increases.

    B. altitude decreases.

    C. air pressure increases.

Answer (A) is correct. *(AC 20-32B)*
    DISCUSSION: Carbon monoxide poisoning results in an oxygen deficiency. Since there is less oxygen available at higher altitudes, carbon monoxide poisoning can occur with lesser amounts of carbon monoxide as altitude increases.
    Answer (B) is incorrect. There is more available oxygen at lower altitudes. Answer (C) is incorrect. There is more available oxygen at higher air pressures.

6.8 Aeronautical Decision Making (ADM)

22. Aeronautical Decision Making (ADM) is a

A. systematic approach to the mental process used by pilots to consistently determine the best course of action for a given set of circumstances.

B. decision making process which relies on good judgment to reduce risks associated with each flight.

C. mental process of analyzing all information in a particular situation and making a timely decision on what action to take.

Answer (A) is correct. *(AC 60-22)*
DISCUSSION: ADM is a systematic approach to the mental process used by pilots to consistently determine the best course of action in response to a given set of circumstances.
Answer (B) is incorrect. Risk management, not ADM, is the part of the decision-making process that relies on situational awareness, problem recognition, and good judgment to reduce risks associated with each flight. Answer (C) is incorrect. Judgment, not ADM, is the mental process of recognizing and analyzing all pertinent information in a particular situation, rationally evaluating alternative actions in response to it, and making a timely decision on which action to take.

23. Risk management, as part of the Aeronautical Decision Making (ADM) process, relies on which features to reduce the risks associated with each flight?

A. The mental process of analyzing all information in a particular situation and making a timely decision on what action to take.

B. Application of stress management and risk element procedures.

C. Situational awareness, problem recognition, and good judgment.

Answer (C) is correct. *(AC 60-22)*
DISCUSSION: Risk management is the part of the ADM process that relies on situational awareness, problem recognition, and good judgment to reduce risks associated with each flight.
Answer (A) is incorrect. Judgment, not risk management, is the mental process of recognizing and analyzing all pertinent information in a particular situation, rationally evaluating alternative actions in response to it, and making a timely decision on what action to take. Answer (B) is incorrect. Risk management relies on situational awareness, problem recognition, and good judgment, not the application of stress management and risk element procedures, to reduce the risks associated with each flight.

24. A series of judgmental errors that can lead to a human factors-related accident is sometimes referred to as the

A. error chain.

B. course of action.

C. DECIDE model.

Answer (A) is correct. *(PHAK Chap 17)*
DISCUSSION: Error chain is a term used to describe the series of judgmental errors that can lead to a human factors-related accident. Breaking one link in the chain is normally all that is necessary to change the outcome of events.
Answer (B) is incorrect. The error chain, not the course of action, is the series of judgmental errors that can lead to an accident. Answer (C) is incorrect. The error chain, not the DECIDE model, is the series of judgmental errors that can lead to an accident.

25. Which of the following is the first step of the DECIDE Model for effective risk management and Aeronautical Decision Making (ADM)?

A. Detect.

B. Identify.

C. Evaluate.

Answer (A) is correct. *(AC 60-22)*
DISCUSSION: The DECIDE Model, comprised of a six-step process, is intended to provide you with a logical way of approaching decision making. The six steps (in order) are detect, estimate, choose, identify, do, and evaluate.
Answer (B) is incorrect. Identify is the fourth step, not the first step, in the DECIDE Model. Answer (C) is incorrect. Evaluate is the final step, not the first step, in the DECIDE Model.

26. What is it often called when a pilot pushes his or her capabilities and the aircraft's limits by trying to maintain visual contact with the terrain in low visibility and ceiling?

A. Scud running.

B. Mindset.

C. Peer pressure.

Answer (A) is correct. *(AC 60-22)*
DISCUSSION: Scud running refers to a pilot pushing his/her capabilities and the aircraft's limits by trying to maintain visual contact with the terrain while flying with a low visibility or ceiling. Scud running is a dangerous (and often illegal) practice that may lead to a mishap. This dangerous tendency must be identified and eliminated.
Answer (B) is incorrect. Mindset may produce an inability to recognize and cope with changes in the situation requiring actions different from those anticipated or planned. Answer (C) is incorrect. Peer pressure may produce poor decision making based upon an emotional response to peers rather than an objective evaluation of a situation.

27. Which is the final step of the DECIDE Model for Decision Making and Aeronautical Decision Making (ADM)?

A. Eliminate.

B. Estimate.

C. Evaluate.

Answer (C) is correct. *(AC 60-22)*
DISCUSSION: The DECIDE Model, comprised of a six-step process, is intended to provide you with a logical way of approaching decision making. The six steps (in order) are detect, estimate, choose, identify, do, and evaluate.
Answer (A) is incorrect. Eliminate is not a step in the DECIDE Model. Answer (B) is incorrect. Estimate is the second step, not the final step, in the DECIDE Model.

28. What often leads to spatial disorientation or collision with ground/obstacles when flying under Visual Flight Rules (VFR)?

A. Continual flight into instrument conditions.

B. Getting behind the aircraft.

C. Duck-under syndrome.

Answer (A) is correct. *(AC 60-22)*
DISCUSSION: Continuing VFR flight into instrument conditions often leads to spatial disorientation or collision with ground/obstacles due to the loss of outside visual references. It is even more dangerous if the pilot is not instrument qualified or current.
Answer (B) is incorrect. Getting behind the aircraft results in allowing events or the situation to control your actions rather than the other way around. Answer (C) is incorrect. Duck-under syndrome is the tendency to descend below minimums during an approach based on the belief that there is always a fudge factor built in; it occurs during IFR, not VFR, flight.

29. What is one of the neglected items when a pilot relies on short and long term memory for repetitive tasks?

A. Checklists.

B. Situational awareness.

C. Flying outside the envelope.

Answer (A) is correct. *(AC 60-22)*
DISCUSSION: Neglect of checklists, flight planning, preflight inspections, etc., indicate a pilot's unjustified reliance on his/her short- and long-term memory for repetitive flying tasks.
Answer (B) is incorrect. Situational awareness suffers when a pilot gets behind the airplane, which results in an inability to recognize deteriorating circumstances and/or misjudgment on the rate of deterioration. Answer (C) is incorrect. Flying outside the envelope occurs when the pilot believes (often in error) that the aircraft's high-performance capability meets the demands imposed by the pilot's (often overestimated) flying skills.

30. To avoid missing important steps, always use the

A. appropriate checklists.

B. placarded airspeeds.

C. airworthiness certificate.

Answer (A) is correct. *(PHAK Chap 8)*
DISCUSSION: To avoid missing important steps, you should always use the appropriate checklists whenever they are available. Consistent adherence to approved checklists is a sign of a disciplined and competent pilot.
Answer (B) is incorrect. Placards contain information on the operation of the aircraft, but in order to avoid missing important steps, you should always use checklists. Answer (C) is incorrect. The airworthiness certificate is required to be in the plane, but in order to avoid missing important steps, you should always use checklists.

31. Consistent adherence to approved checklists is a sign of a

A. disciplined and competent pilot.

B. pilot who lacks the required knowledge.

C. low-time pilot.

Answer (A) is correct. *(PHAK Chap 8)*
DISCUSSION: The consistent adherence to approved checklists is a sign of a disciplined and competent pilot. Checklists exist as a resource to assist in the management of the flight and the operation of the aircraft.
Answer (B) is incorrect. The consistent adherence to checklists is a sign of a disciplined and competent pilot, not a pilot who lacks knowledge. Answer (C) is incorrect. All pilots, not just low-time pilots, must strive to consistently use and adhere to checklists.

32. A pilot who relies on short and long term memory for repetitive tasks often neglects

A. flying outside the envelope.

B. checklists.

C. situational awareness.

Answer (B) is correct. *(AC 60-22)*
DISCUSSION: Neglect of checklists, flight planning, preflight inspections, etc., indicate a pilot's unjustified reliance on his/her short- and long-term memory for repetitive flying tasks.
Answer (A) is incorrect. Flying outside the envelope occurs when the pilot believes (often in error) that the aircraft's high-performance capability meets the demands imposed by the pilot's (often overestimated) flying skills. Answer (C) is incorrect. Situational awareness suffers when a pilot gets behind the airplane, which results in an inability to recognize deteriorating circumstances and/or misjudgment on the rate of deterioration.

33. The basic drive for a pilot to demonstrate the "right stuff" can have an adverse effect on safety, by

   A. a total disregard for any alternative course of action.

   B. generating tendencies that lead to practices that are dangerous, often illegal, and may lead to a mishap.

   C. allowing events, or the situation, to control his or her actions.

Answer (B) is correct. *(AC 60-22)*
DISCUSSION: The basic drive to demonstrate the "right stuff" can have an adverse effect on safety and can impose an unrealistic assessment of piloting skills under stressful conditions. These tendencies ultimately may lead to practices that are dangerous and often illegal and may result in a mishap.
   Answer (A) is incorrect. "Get-there-itis," not a basic drive to demonstrate the "right stuff," has an adverse effect on safety when a pilot totally disregards any alternative course of action. Answer (C) is incorrect. Getting behind the aircraft, not a basic drive to demonstrate the "right stuff," has an adverse effect on safety by allowing events or the situation to control the pilot's actions.

34. An extreme case of a pilot getting behind the aircraft can lead to the operational pitfall of

   A. loss of situational awareness.

   B. loss of workload.

   C. internal stress.

Answer (A) is correct. *(PHAK Chap 17)*
DISCUSSION: In extreme cases when a pilot gets behind the aircraft, a loss of situational or positional awareness may result.
   Answer (B) is incorrect. When a pilot gets behind the aircraft, a loss of situational awareness can be the potential result, not loss of workload. Answer (C) is incorrect. When a pilot gets behind the aircraft, a loss of situational awareness can be the potential result, not internal stress.

35. Pilots who become apprehensive for their safety for any reason should

   A. request assistance immediately.

   B. reduce their situational awareness.

   C. change their mindset.

Answer (A) is correct. *(AIM Para 6-1-2)*
DISCUSSION: Pilots who become apprehensive for their safety for any reason should request assistance immediately. Ready and willing help is available in the form of radio, radar, other aircraft, and/or direction finding stations, all of which are a radio call away.
   Answer (B) is incorrect. Requesting assistance, not reducing situational awareness, is the best way to overcome the apprehension for safety. Answer (C) is incorrect. Requesting assistance, not changing one's mindset, is the best way to overcome the apprehension for safety.

36. What is the first step in neutralizing a hazardous attitude in the ADM process?

   A. Dealing with improper judgment.

   B. Recognition of hazardous thoughts.

   C. Recognition of invulnerability in the situation.

Answer (B) is correct. *(AC 60-22)*
DISCUSSION: The first step in neutralizing hazardous attitudes is recognizing hazardous thoughts. When a pilot recognizes a hazardous thought, (s)he then should correct it by stating the corresponding antidote.
   Answer (A) is incorrect. Recognizing hazardous thoughts, not dealing with improper judgment, is the first step in neutralizing hazardous attitudes. Answer (C) is incorrect. Recognizing hazardous thoughts, not the invulnerability in the situation, is the first step in neutralizing hazardous attitudes.

37. What are some of the hazardous attitudes dealt with in Aeronautical Decision Making (ADM)?

   A. Antiauthority (don't tell me), impulsivity (do something quickly without thinking), macho (I can do it).

   B. Risk management, stress management, and risk elements.

   C. Poor decision making, situational awareness, and judgment.

Answer (A) is correct. *(AC 60-22)*
DISCUSSION: ADM addresses five hazardous attitudes: antiauthority ("Don't tell me"), impulsivity ("Do something quickly without thinking"), invulnerability ("It won't happen to me"), macho ("I can do it"), and resignation ("What's the use?").
   Answer (B) is incorrect. Risk management, stress management, and risk elements are all part of the ADM process, not hazardous attitudes dealt with in ADM. Answer (C) is incorrect. Situational awareness and judgment are part of the mental process in ADM to prevent or stop poor judgment, not hazardous attitudes in ADM.

38. When a pilot recognizes a hazardous thought, he or she should then correct it by stating the corresponding antidote. Which of the following is the antidote for antiauthority?

   A. Not so fast. Think first.

   B. It could happen to me.

   C. Follow the rules. They are usually right.

Answer (C) is correct. *(AC 60-22)*
DISCUSSION: When you recognize a hazardous thought, you should then correct it by stating the corresponding antidote. The antidote for an antiauthority ("Do not tell me") attitude is "Follow the rules. They are usually right."
   Answer (A) is incorrect. "Not so fast. Think first" is the antidote for the impulsivity, not the antiauthority, attitude. Answer (B) is incorrect. "It could happen to me" is the antidote for the invulnerability ("It will not happen to me"), not the antiauthority, attitude.

39. What is the antidote when a pilot has a hazardous attitude, such as antiauthority?

    A. Rules do not apply in this situation.

    B. I know what I am doing.

    C. Follow the rules.

Answer (C) is correct. *(AC 60-22)*
    DISCUSSION: When you recognize a hazardous thought, you should correct it by stating the corresponding antidote. The antidote for the antiauthority ("Do not tell me!") hazardous attitude is "Follow the rules. They are usually right."
    Answer (A) is incorrect. "Rules do not apply in this situation" is an example of the antiauthority hazardous attitude, not its antidote. Answer (B) is incorrect. "I know what I'm doing" is an example of the macho hazardous attitude, not an antidote to the antiauthority attitude.

40. What is the antidote when a pilot has a hazardous attitude, such as impulsivity?

    A. It could happen to me.

    B. Do it quickly to get it over with.

    C. Not so fast. Think first.

Answer (C) is correct. *(AC 60-22)*
    DISCUSSION: When you recognize a hazardous thought, you should correct it by stating the corresponding antidote. The antidote for the impulsivity ("Do something quickly!") hazardous attitude is "Not so fast. Think first."
    Answer (A) is incorrect. "It could happen to me" is the antidote for the invulnerability, not impulsivity, hazardous attitude. Answer (B) is incorrect. "Do it quickly and get it over with" is an example of the impulsivity hazardous attitude, not its antidote.

41. What is the antidote when a pilot has the hazardous attitude of invulnerability?

    A. It will not happen to me.

    B. It cannot be that bad.

    C. It could happen to me.

Answer (C) is correct. *(AC 60-22)*
    DISCUSSION: When you recognize a hazardous thought, you should correct it by stating the corresponding antidote. The antidote for the invulnerability ("It will not happen to me") hazardous attitude is "It could happen to me."
    Answer (A) is incorrect. "It will not happen to me" is an example of the invulnerability hazardous attitude, not its antidote. Answer (B) is incorrect. "It cannot be that bad" is an example of the invulnerability hazardous attitude, not its antidote.

42. What is the antidote when a pilot has a hazardous attitude, such as macho?

    A. I can do it.

    B. Taking chances is foolish.

    C. Nothing will happen.

Answer (B) is correct. *(AC 60-22)*
    DISCUSSION: When you recognize a hazardous thought, you should correct it by stating the corresponding antidote. The antidote for the macho ("I can do it") hazardous attitude is "Taking chances is foolish."
    Answer (A) is incorrect. "I can do it" is an example of the macho hazardous attitude, not its antidote. Answer (C) is incorrect. "Nothing will happen" is an example of the invulnerability hazardous attitude, not an antidote to the macho attitude.

43. What is the antidote when a pilot has a hazardous attitude, such as resignation?

    A. What is the use.

    B. Someone else is responsible.

    C. I am not helpless.

Answer (C) is correct. *(AC 60-22)*
    DISCUSSION: When you recognize a hazardous thought, you should correct it by stating the corresponding antidote. The antidote for the resignation ("What is the use?") hazardous attitude is "I am not helpless. I can make a difference."
    Answer (A) is incorrect. "What is the use?" is an example of the resignation hazardous attitude, not its antidote. Answer (B) is incorrect. "Someone else is responsible" is an example of the resignation hazardous attitude, not its antidote.

44. A pilot feels that accidents never happen to him. He recognizes this as a hazardous attitude. To counter this old attitude he should have a new attitude that

    A. whatever will happen will happen.

    B. it could happen to him.

    C. he knows what to do.

Answer (B) is correct. *(AC 60-22)*
    DISCUSSION: Pilots can be vulnerable to various hazardous attitudes. Each attitude has an antidote to help overcome it. The antidote to the hazardous attitude referred to as invulnerability ("It won't happen to me") is "It could happen to me."
    Answer (A) is incorrect. It refers to the hazardous attitude resignation, which can be countered with the antidote "I'm not helpless. I can make a difference." Answer (C) is incorrect. It refers to the response to resignation, not to invulnerability.

45. Who is responsible for determining whether a pilot is fit to fly for a particular flight, even though the pilot holds a current and valid U.S. driver's license?

A. The FAA.

B. The medical examiner.

C. The pilot.

Answer (C) is correct. *(AC 60-22)*
DISCUSSION: A number of factors, from lack of sleep to an illness, can reduce a pilot's fitness to make a particular flight. It is the responsibility of the pilot to determine whether (s)he is fit to make a particular flight, even though (s)he holds a current medical certificate. Additionally, FAR 61.53 prohibits a pilot who possesses a current medical certificate from acting as pilot in command, or in any other capacity as a required pilot flight crewmember, while the pilot has a known medical condition or an aggravation of a known medical condition that would make the pilot unable to meet the standards for a medical certificate.
Answer (A) is incorrect. The pilot, not the FAA, is responsible for determining whether (s)he is fit for a particular flight. Answer (B) is incorrect. The pilot, not the medical examiner, is responsible for determining whether (s)he is fit for a particular flight.

46. If advice is needed concerning possible flight with an illness, a pilot should contact

A. an Aviation Medical Examiner.

B. their family doctor.

C. the nearest hospital.

Answer (A) is correct. *(AIM 8-1-1)*
DISCUSSION: Aviation Medical Examiners are physicians with a special interest in aviation safety and training in aviation medicine.
Answer (B) is incorrect. The family doctor, if not an Aviation Medical Examiner, may not have the correct advice concerning flying. Answer (C) is incorrect. The nearest hospital may not have an Aviation Medical Examiner on staff.

47. What is the one common factor which affects most preventable accidents?

A. Structural failure.

B. Mechanical malfunction.

C. Human error.

Answer (C) is correct. *(AC 60-22)*
DISCUSSION: Most preventable accidents, such as fuel starvation or exhaustion, VFR flight into IFR conditions leading to disorientation, and flight into known icing, have one common factor: human error. Pilots who are involved in accidents usually know what went wrong. In the interest of expediency, cost savings, or other often irrelevant factors, the wrong course of action (decision) was chosen.
Answer (A) is incorrect. Most preventable accidents have human error, not structural failure, as a common factor. Answer (B) is incorrect. Most preventable accidents have human error, not mechanical malfunction, as a common factor.

48. Ignoring minimum fuel reserve requirements is generally the result of overconfidence, disregarding applicable regulations, or

A. lack of flight planning.

B. impulsivity.

C. physical stress.

Answer (A) is correct. *(PHAK Chap 17)*
DISCUSSION: Ignoring minimum fuel reserve requirements is generally the result of overconfidence, disregard of the regulations, or lack of flight planning.
Answer (B) is incorrect. Impulsivity is the hazardous attitude that says do something, anything, quickly, not the reason for ignoring minimum fuel reserves. Answer (C) is incorrect. Lack of flight planning, not physical stress, is the last reason for ignoring fuel reserve minimums.

49. What should a pilot do when recognizing a thought as hazardous?

A. Correct this hazardous thought by making a thorough risk assessment.

B. Label the thought as hazardous and then correct that thought by stating the corresponding antidote.

C. Avoid allowing this hazardous thought to develop.

Answer (B) is correct. *(AC 60-22)*
DISCUSSION: When you recognize a hazardous thought, you should label it as hazardous and then correct the attitude by stating the corresponding antidote. Antidotes should be memorized for each of the hazardous attitudes so that they automatically come to mind when needed.
Answer (A) is incorrect. When you recognize a hazardous thought, you should label it as hazardous and then correct the attitude by stating the corresponding antidote, not by making a thorough risk assessment. Answer (C) is incorrect. While you do not want the hazardous thought to develop, the way to avoid this is to recognize and label the thought as hazardous and then correct it by stating the corresponding antidote.

END OF STUDY UNIT

STUDY UNIT SEVEN
AVIATION WEATHER

(5 pages of outline)

This study unit contains outlines of major concepts tested, sample test questions and answers regarding aviation weather, and an explanation of each answer. The table of contents above lists each subunit within this study unit, the number of questions pertaining to that particular subunit, and the pages on which the outlines and questions begin, respectively.

CAUTION: Recall that the **sole purpose** of this book is to expedite your passing the FAA pilot knowledge test for the sport pilot certificate. Accordingly, all extraneous material (i.e., topics or regulations not directly tested on the FAA pilot knowledge test) is omitted, even though much more information and knowledge are necessary to fly safely. This additional material is presented in *Pilot Handbook* and *Sport Pilot Flight Maneuvers and Practical Test Prep*, available from Gleim Publications, Inc. See the order form on page 327.

7.1 CAUSES OF WEATHER

1. Every physical process of weather is accompanied by, or is the result of, heat exchanges.

2. Unequal heating of the Earth's surface causes differences in pressure and altimeter settings.

3. The Coriolis force deflects winds to the right in the Northern Hemisphere. It is caused by the Earth's rotation.

   a. The deflections caused by Coriolis force are less at the surface due to the slower wind speed.

   b. The wind speed is slower at the surface due to friction between wind and the Earth's surface.

7.2 CONVECTIVE CURRENTS

1. Sea breezes are caused by cool and more dense air moving inland off the water. Once inland over the warmer land, the air heats up and rises. Currents push the air over the water where it cools and descends, starting the process over again.

2. The development of thermals depends upon solar heating.

7.3 FRONTS

1. A front is the zone of transition (boundary) between two air masses of different density, e.g., the area separating a high-pressure system and a low-pressure system.

    a. A high-pressure area is an area of descending air. A low-pressure area is an area of rising air.

2. There is always a change in wind when flying across a front.

3. The most easily recognizable change when crossing a front is the change in temperature.

7.4 THUNDERSTORMS

1. Thunderstorms have three phases in their life cycle:

    a. Cumulus: The building stage of a thunderstorm when there are continuous updrafts

    b. Mature: The time of greatest intensity when there are both updrafts and downdrafts (causing severe wind shear and turbulence)

        1) The commencing of rain on the Earth's surface indicates the beginning of the mature stage of a thunderstorm.

    c. Dissipating: When there are only downdrafts; i.e., the storm is raining itself out

2. Thunderstorms are produced by cumulonimbus clouds. They form when there is

    a. Sufficient water vapor,

    b. An unstable lapse rate, and

    c. An initial upward boost to start the process.

3. Thunderstorms produce wind shear turbulence, a hazardous and invisible phenomenon particularly for airplanes landing and taking off.

    a. Hazardous wind shear near the ground can also be present during periods of strong temperature inversion.

4. The most severe thunderstorm conditions (heavy hail, destructive winds, tornadoes, etc.) are generally associated with squall line thunderstorms.

    a. A squall line is a nonfrontal, narrow band of thunderstorms usually ahead of a cold front.

5. A thunderstorm, by definition, has lightning because that is what causes thunder.

6. Embedded thunderstorms are obscured (i.e., pilots cannot see them) because they occur in very cloudy conditions.

7.5 ICING

1. Structural icing requires two conditions:

    a. Flight through visible moisture and

    b. The temperature at freezing or below.

2. Freezing rain usually causes the greatest accumulation of structural ice.

3. Ice pellets are caused when rain droplets freeze at a higher altitude, i.e., freezing rain exists above.

7.6 MOUNTAIN WAVE

1. Lenticular clouds are almond- or lens-shaped clouds usually found on the leeward side of a mountain range.

    a. They may contain winds of 50 kt. or more.
    b. They appear stationary as the wind blows through them.

2. Expect mountain wave turbulence when the air is stable and winds of 40 kt. or greater blow across a mountain or ridge.

    a. Underneath each wave crest is a rotary circulation called a rotor. Turbulence is most frequent and most severe in and below the rotor clouds.

7.7 WIND SHEAR

1. Wind shear can occur at any altitude and be horizontal and/or vertical, i.e., whenever adjacent air is flowing in different directions or speeds.

2. Expect wind shear in a temperature inversion whenever wind speed at 2,000 to 4,000 ft. AGL is 25 kt. or more.

3. Hazardous wind shear may be expected in areas of low-level temperature inversions, frontal zones, and clear air turbulence.

7.8 TEMPERATURE/DEW POINT AND FOG

1. When the air temperature is within 5° of the dew point and the spread is decreasing, you should expect fog and/or low clouds.

    a. Dew point is the temperature at which the air will have 100% humidity, i.e., be saturated.
    b. Thus, air temperature determines how much water vapor can be held by the air.
    c. Frost forms when both the collecting surface is below the dew point of the adjacent air and the dew point is below freezing. Frost is the direct sublimation of water vapor to ice crystals.

2. Water vapor becomes visible as it condenses into clouds, fog, or dew.

3. Evaporation is the conversion of liquid to water vapor.

4. Sublimation is the conversion of solids (e.g., ice) to water vapor or water vapor to solids (e.g., frost).

5. Radiation fog (shallow fog) is most likely to occur when there is a clear sky, little or no wind, and a small temperature/dew point spread.

6. Advection fog forms as a result of moist air condensing as it moves over a cooler surface.

7. Upslope fog results from warm, moist air being cooled as it is forced up sloping terrain.

8. Precipitation-induced fog occurs when warm rain or drizzle falls through cool air and evaporation from the precipitation saturates the cool air and forms fog.

    a. Precipitation-induced fog is usually associated with fronts.
    b. Because of this, it is in the proximity of icing, turbulence, and thunderstorms.

9. Steam fog forms in winter when cold, dry air passes from land areas over comparatively warm ocean waters. It is composed entirely of water droplets that often freeze quickly.

    a. Low-level turbulence can occur and icing can become hazardous in steam fog.

7.9 CLOUDS

1. Clouds are divided into four families based on their height:
    a. High clouds
    b. Middle clouds
    c. Low clouds
    d. Clouds with extensive vertical development

2. The greatest turbulence is in cumulonimbus clouds.

3. Towering cumulus are early stages of cumulonimbus; they usually indicate convective turbulence.

4. Lifting action, unstable air, and moisture are the ingredients for the formation of cumulonimbus clouds.

5. Nimbus means rain cloud.

6. When air rises in a convective current, it cools at the rate of 5.4°F/1,000 ft., and its dew point decreases 1°F/1,000 ft. The temperature and dew point then are converging at 4.4°F/1,000 ft.

    a. Since clouds form when the temperature/dew point spread is 0°, we can use this to estimate the bases of cumulus clouds.
    b. The surface temperature/dew point spread divided by 4.4°F equals the bases of cumulus clouds in thousands of feet above ground level (AGL).
    c. EXAMPLE: A surface dew point of 56°F and a surface temperature of 69°F results in an estimate of cumulus cloud bases at 3,000 ft. AGL: 69°F − 56°F = 13°F temperature/dew point spread; 13°F/4.4°F = approximately 3,000 ft. AGL.

7.10 STABILITY OF AIR MASSES

1. Stable air characteristics
    a. Stratiform clouds
    b. Smooth air
    c. Fair-to-poor visibility in haze and smoke
    d. Continuous precipitation

2. Unstable air characteristics
    a. Cumuliform clouds
    b. Turbulent air
    c. Good visibility
    d. Showery precipitation

3. When air is warmed from below, it rises and causes instability.
    a. Generally, during the propagation of thermals, the net upward displacement of air equals the net downward displacement. Faster rising thermals only cover a small percentage of the total convective area, while slower downdrafts predominate.

4. The lapse rate is the decrease in temperature with increase in altitude. As the lapse rate increases (i.e., air cools more with increases in altitude), air is more unstable.
    a. The lapse rate can be used to determine the stability of air masses.

5. Moist, stable air moving up a mountain slope produces stratus type clouds as it cools.

6. Turbulence and clouds with extensive vertical development result when unstable air rises.

7. Steady precipitation preceding a front is usually an indication of a warm front, which results from warm air being cooled from the bottom by colder air.
    a. This results in stable air with stratiform clouds and little or no turbulence.

7.11 TEMPERATURE INVERSIONS

1. Normally, temperature decreases as altitude increases. A temperature inversion occurs when temperature increases as altitude increases.

2. Temperature inversions usually result in a stable layer of air.

3. A temperature inversion often develops near the ground on clear, cool nights when the wind is light.

   a. It is caused by terrestrial radiation.

4. Smooth air with restricted visibility is usually found beneath a low-level temperature inversion.

QUESTIONS AND ANSWER EXPLANATIONS

All of the sport pilot knowledge questions chosen by the FAA for release as well as additional questions selected by Gleim relating to the material in the previous outlines are reproduced on the following pages. These questions have been organized into the same subunits as the outlines. To the immediate right of each question are the correct answer and answer explanations. You should cover these answers and answer explanations while responding to the questions. Refer to the general discussion in the Introduction on how to take the FAA pilot knowledge test.

Remember that the questions from the FAA pilot knowledge test bank have been reordered by topic and organized into a meaningful sequence. Also, the first line of the answer explanation gives the citation of the authoritative source for the answer.

QUESTIONS

7.1 Causes of Weather

1. Every physical process of weather is accompanied by, or is the result of, a

A. movement of air.

B. pressure differential.

C. heat exchange.

Answer (C) is correct. *(AvW Chap 2)*
DISCUSSION: Every physical process of weather is accompanied by, or is the result of, a heat exchange. A heat differential (difference between the temperatures of two air masses) causes a differential in pressure, which in turn causes movement of air. Heat exchanges occur constantly, e.g., melting, cooling, updrafts, downdrafts, wind, etc.
Answer (A) is incorrect. Movement of air is a result of heat exchange. Answer (B) is incorrect. Pressure differential is a result of heat exchange.

2. What causes variations in altimeter settings between weather reporting points?

A. Unequal heating of the Earth's surface.

B. Variation of terrain elevation.

C. Coriolis force.

Answer (A) is correct. *(AvW Chap 3)*
DISCUSSION: Unequal heating of the Earth's surface causes differences in air pressure, which is reflected in differences in altimeter settings between weather reporting points.
Answer (B) is incorrect. Variations in altimeter settings between stations is a result of unequal heating of the Earth's surface, not variations of terrain elevations. Answer (C) is incorrect. Variations in altimeter settings between stations is a result of unequal heating of the Earth's surface, not the Coriolis force.

3. The wind at 5,000 feet AGL is southwesterly while the surface wind is southerly. This difference in direction is primarily due to

A. stronger pressure gradient at higher altitudes.

B. friction between the wind and the surface.

C. stronger Coriolis force at the surface.

Answer (B) is correct. *(AvW Chap 4)*
DISCUSSION: Winds aloft at 5,000 ft. are largely affected by Coriolis force, which deflects wind to the right, in the Northern Hemisphere. But at the surface, the winds will be more southerly (they were southwesterly aloft) because Coriolis force has less effect at the surface where the wind speed is slower. The wind speed is slower at the surface due to the friction between the wind and the surface.
Answer (A) is incorrect. Pressure gradient is a force that causes wind, not the reason for wind direction differences. Answer (C) is incorrect. The Coriolis force at the surface is weaker (not stronger) with slower wind speed.

7.2   Convective Currents

4. Convective circulation patterns associated with sea breezes are caused by

    A. warm, dense air moving inland from over the water.

    B. water absorbing and radiating heat faster than the land.

    C. cool, dense air moving inland from over the water.

Answer (C) is correct.   *(AvW Chap 4)*
DISCUSSION: Sea breezes are caused by cool and more dense air moving inland off the water. Once over the warmer land, the air heats up and rises. Thus the cooler, more dense air from the sea forces the warmer air up. Currents push the hot air over the water where it cools and descends, starting the cycle over again. This process is caused by land heating faster than water.
Answer (A) is incorrect. The air over the water is cooler (not warmer). Answer (B) is incorrect. Water absorbs and radiates heat slower (not faster) than land.

5. The development of thermals depends upon

    A. a counterclockwise circulation of air.

    B. temperature inversions.

    C. solar heating.

Answer (C) is correct.   *(AvW Chap 16)*
DISCUSSION: Thermals are updrafts in small-scale convective currents. Convective currents are caused by uneven heating of the earth's surface. Solar heating is the means of heating the earth's surface.
Answer (A) is incorrect. A counterclockwise circulation describes an area of low pressure in the Northern Hemisphere. Answer (B) is incorrect. A temperature inversion is an increase in temperature with height, which hinders the development of thermals.

7.3   Fronts

6. The boundary between two different air masses is referred to as a

    A. frontolysis.

    B. frontogenesis.

    C. front.

Answer (C) is correct.   *(AvW Chap 8)*
DISCUSSION: A front is a surface, interface, or transition zone of discontinuity between two adjacent air masses of different densities. It is the boundary between two different air masses.
Answer (A) is incorrect. Frontolysis is the dissipation of a front. Answer (B) is incorrect. Frontogenesis is the initial formation of a front or frontal zone.

7. Which is true with respect to a high- or low-pressure system?

    A. A high-pressure area or ridge is an area of rising air.

    B. A low-pressure area or trough is an area of descending air.

    C. A high-pressure area or a ridge is an area of descending air.

Answer (C) is correct.   *(AvW Chap 8)*
DISCUSSION: High-pressure air descends because it is heavier than low-pressure air. Ridge refers to an elongated area of high pressure.
Answer (A) is incorrect. High-pressure air descends, not rises. Answer (B) is incorrect. Low-pressure air rises, not descends.

8. One weather phenomenon which will always occur when flying across a front is a change in the

    A. wind direction.

    B. type of precipitation.

    C. stability of the air mass.

Answer (A) is correct.   *(AvW Chap 8)*
DISCUSSION: The definition of a front is the zone of transition between two air masses of different air pressure or density, e.g., the area separating high- and low-pressure systems. Due to the difference in changes in pressure systems, there will be a change in wind.
Answer (B) is incorrect. Frequently, precipitation will exist or not exist for both sides of the front: rain showers before and after or no precipitation before or after a dry front. Answer (C) is incorrect. Fronts separate air masses with different pressures, not stabilities, e.g., both air masses could be either stable or unstable.

9. One of the most easily recognized discontinuities across a front is

A. a change in temperature.

B. an increase in cloud coverage.

C. an increase in relative humidity.

Answer (A) is correct. *(AvW Chap 8)*
DISCUSSION: Of the many changes which take place across a front, the most easily recognized is the change in temperature. When flying through a front, you will notice a significant change in temperature, especially at low altitudes.
Answer (B) is incorrect. Although cloud formations may indicate a frontal system, they may not be present or easily recognized across the front. Answer (C) is incorrect. Precipitation is not always associated with a front.

7.4 Thunderstorms

10. If there is thunderstorm activity in the vicinity of an airport at which you plan to land, which hazardous atmospheric phenomenon might be expected on the landing approach?

A. Precipitation static.

B. Wind-shear turbulence.

C. Steady rain.

Answer (B) is correct. *(AvW Chap 11)*
DISCUSSION: The most hazardous atmospheric phenomenon near thunderstorms is wind shear turbulence.
Answer (A) is incorrect. Precipitation static is a steady, high level of noise in radio receivers that is caused by intense corona discharges from sharp metallic points and edges of flying aircraft. This discharge may be seen at night and is also called St. Elmo's fire. Answer (C) is incorrect. Thunderstorms are usually associated with unstable air, which would produce rain showers (not steady rain).

11. A nonfrontal, narrow band of active thunderstorms that often develop ahead of a cold front is known as a

A. prefrontal system.

B. squall line.

C. dry line.

Answer (B) is correct. *(AvW Chap 11)*
DISCUSSION: A nonfrontal, narrow band of active thunderstorms that often develop ahead of a cold front is known as a squall line.
Answer (A) is incorrect. A prefrontal system is a term that has no meaning. Answer (C) is incorrect. A dry line is a front that seldom has any significant air mass contrast, except for moisture.

12. What conditions are necessary for the formation of thunderstorms?

A. High humidity, lifting force, and unstable conditions.

B. High humidity, high temperature, and cumulus clouds.

C. Lifting force, moist air, and extensive cloud cover.

Answer (A) is correct. *(AvW Chap 11)*
DISCUSSION: Thunderstorms form when there is sufficient water vapor, an unstable lapse rate, and an initial upward boost (lifting) to start the storm process.
Answer (B) is incorrect. A high temperature is not required for the formation of thunderstorms. Answer (C) is incorrect. Extensive cloud cover is not necessary for the formation of thunderstorms.

13. During the life cycle of a thunderstorm, which stage is characterized predominately by downdrafts?

A. Cumulus.

B. Dissipating.

C. Mature.

Answer (B) is correct. *(AvW Chap 11)*
DISCUSSION: Thunderstorms have three life cycles: cumulus, mature, and dissipating. It is in the dissipating stage that the storm is characterized by downdrafts as the storm rains itself out.
Answer (A) is incorrect. Cumulus is the building stage when there are updrafts. Answer (C) is incorrect. The mature stage is when there are both updrafts and downdrafts, which create dangerous wind shears.

14. Thunderstorms reach their greatest intensity during the

A. mature stage.

B. downdraft stage.

C. cumulus stage.

Answer (A) is correct. *(AvW Chap 11)*
DISCUSSION: Thunderstorms reach their greatest intensity during the mature stage, where updrafts and downdrafts cause a high level of wind shear.
Answer (B) is incorrect. The downdraft stage is known as the dissipating stage, which is when the thunderstorm rains itself out. Answer (C) is incorrect. The cumulus stage is characterized by continuous updrafts and is not the most intense stage of a thunderstorm.

15. What feature is normally associated with the cumulus stage of a thunderstorm?

A. Roll cloud.

B. Continuous updraft.

C. Frequent lightning.

Answer (B) is correct. *(AvW Chap 11)*
    DISCUSSION: The cumulus stage of a thunderstorm has continuous updrafts which build the storm. The water droplets are carried up until they become too heavy. Once they begin falling and creating downdrafts, the storm changes from the cumulus to the mature stage.
    Answer (A) is incorrect. The roll cloud is the cloud on the ground that is formed by the downrushing cold air pushing out from underneath the bottom of the thunderstorm. Answer (C) is incorrect. Frequent lightning is associated with the mature stage where there is a considerable amount of wind shear and static electricity.

16. Which weather phenomenon signals the beginning of the mature stage of a thunderstorm?

A. The appearance of an anvil top.

B. Precipitation beginning to fall.

C. Maximum growth rate of the clouds.

Answer (B) is correct. *(AvW Chap 11)*
    DISCUSSION: The mature stage of a thunderstorm begins when rain begins falling. This means that the downdrafts are occurring sufficiently to carry water all the way through the thunderstorm.
    Answer (A) is incorrect. The appearance of an anvil top normally occurs during the dissipating stage when the upper winds blow the top of the cloud downwind. Answer (C) is incorrect. The maximum growth rate of clouds is later in the mature stage and does not necessarily mark the start of the mature stage.

17. Thunderstorms which generally produce the most intense hazard to aircraft are

A. squall line thunderstorms.

B. steady-state thunderstorms.

C. warm front thunderstorms.

Answer (A) is correct. *(AvW Chap 11)*
    DISCUSSION: A squall line is a nonfrontal, narrow band of active thunderstorms. It often contains severe, steady-state thunderstorms and presents the single most intense weather hazard to airplanes.
    Answer (B) is incorrect. Steady-state thunderstorms are normally associated with weather systems and often form into squall lines. Answer (C) is incorrect. Squall line (not warm front) thunderstorms generally produce the most intense hazard to aircraft.

18. Which weather phenomenon is always associated with a thunderstorm?

A. Lightning.

B. Heavy rain.

C. Hail.

Answer (A) is correct. *(AvW Chap 11)*
    DISCUSSION: A thunderstorm, by definition, has lightning, because lightning causes the thunder.
    Answer (B) is incorrect. While heavy rain showers usually occur, hail may occur instead. Answer (C) is incorrect. Hail is produced only when the lifting action extends above the freezing level and the supercooled water begins to freeze.

7.5 Icing

19. One in-flight condition necessary for structural icing to form is

A. small temperature/dewpoint spread.

B. stratiform clouds.

C. visible moisture.

Answer (C) is correct. *(AvW Chap 10)*
    DISCUSSION: Two conditions are necessary for structural icing while in flight. First, the airplane must be flying through visible moisture, such as rain or cloud droplets. Second, the temperature at the point where the moisture strikes the airplane must be freezing or below.
    Answer (A) is incorrect. The temperature dew point spread is not a factor in icing as it is in the formation of fog or clouds. Answer (B) is incorrect. No special cloud formation is necessary for icing as long as visible moisture is present.

20. In which environment is aircraft structural ice most likely to have the highest accumulation rate?

A. Cumulus clouds with below freezing temperatures.

B. Freezing drizzle.

C. Freezing rain.

Answer (C) is correct. *(AvW Chap 10)*
    DISCUSSION: Freezing rain usually causes the highest accumulation rate of structural icing because of the nature of the supercooled water striking the airplane.
    Answer (A) is incorrect. While icing potential is great in cumulus clouds with below-freezing temperatures, the highest accumulation rate is in an area with large, supercooled water drops (i.e., freezing rain). Answer (B) is incorrect. Freezing drizzle will not build up ice as quickly as freezing rain will.

21. The presence of ice pellets at the surface is evidence that there

A. are thunderstorms in the area.

B. has been cold frontal passage.

C. is a temperature inversion with freezing rain at a higher altitude.

Answer (C) is correct. *(AvW Chap 5)*
    DISCUSSION: Rain falling through colder air may freeze during its descent, falling as ice pellets. Ice pellets always indicate freezing rain at a higher altitude.
    Answer (A) is incorrect. Ice pellets form when rain freezes during its descent, which may or may not be as a result of a thunderstorm. Answer (B) is incorrect. Ice pellets only indicate that rain is freezing at a higher altitude, not that a cold front has passed through an area.

7.6 Mountain Wave

22. An almond or lens-shaped cloud which appears stationary, but which may contain winds of 50 knots or more, is referred to as

A. an inactive frontal cloud.

B. a funnel cloud.

C. a lenticular cloud.

Answer (C) is correct. *(AvW Chap 9)*
    DISCUSSION: Lenticular clouds are lens-shaped clouds that indicate the crests of standing mountain waves. They form in the updraft and dissipate in the downdraft, so they do not move as the wind blows through them. Lenticular clouds may contain winds of 50 kt. or more and are extremely dangerous.
    Answer (A) is incorrect. Frontal clouds usually do not contain winds of 50 kt. or more, and if they do, they do not appear stationary. Answer (B) is incorrect. A funnel cloud is not stationary.

23. Crests of standing mountain waves may be marked by stationary, lens-shaped clouds known as

A. mammatocumulus clouds.

B. standing lenticular clouds.

C. roll clouds.

Answer (B) is correct. *(AvW Chap 9)*
    DISCUSSION: Lens-shaped clouds, which indicate crests of standing mountain waves, are called standing lenticular clouds. They form in the updraft and dissipate in the downdraft so that they do not move as the wind blows through them.
    Answer (A) is incorrect. Cumulonimbus mamma clouds (also mammatocumulus) are cumulonimbus clouds with pods or circular domes on the bottom that indicate severe turbulence. Answer (C) is incorrect. Roll clouds are low-level, turbulent areas in the shear zone between the plow wind surrounding the outrushing air from a thunderstorm and the surrounding air.

24. Possible mountain wave turbulence could be anticipated when winds of 40 knots or greater blow

A. across a mountain ridge, and the air is stable.

B. down a mountain valley, and the air is unstable.

C. parallel to a mountain peak, and the air is stable.

Answer (A) is correct. *(AvW Chap 9)*
    DISCUSSION: Always anticipate possible mountain wave turbulence when the air is stable and winds of 40 kt. or greater blow across a mountain or ridge.
    Answer (B) is incorrect. The wind must blow across the mountain or ridge before it flows down a valley. The air must also be stable. If the air is unstable and produces convective turbulence, it will rise and disrupt the "wave." Answer (C) is incorrect. Anytime the winds are 40 kt. or more and blowing across (not parallel) to the mountains, you should anticipate mountain wave turbulence.

25. One of the most dangerous features of mountain waves is the turbulent area in and

A. below rotor clouds.

B. above rotor clouds.

C. below lenticular clouds.

Answer (A) is correct. *(AWS Chap 9)*
DISCUSSION: When stable air flows across a mountain range, large waves occur downwind from the mountains. Underneath each wave crest is a rotary circulation called a rotor. Turbulence is most frequent and most severe in and below the rotor clouds.
Answer (B) is incorrect. The turbulent area of a mountain wave is in and below (not above) the rotor clouds. Answer (C) is incorrect. The most turbulent area of a mountain wave is in and below the rotor (not lenticular) clouds.

7.7 Wind Shear

26. Where does wind shear occur?

A. Only at higher altitudes.

B. Only at lower altitudes.

C. At all altitudes, in all directions.

Answer (C) is correct. *(AvW Chap 9)*
DISCUSSION: Wind shear is the eddies between two wind currents of differing velocities, direction, or both. Wind shear may be associated with either a wind shift or a wind speed gradient at any level in the atmosphere.
Answer (A) is incorrect. A wind shear may occur at any (not only higher) altitudes. Answer (B) is incorrect. A wind shear may occur at any (not only lower) altitudes.

27. A pilot can expect a wind-shear zone in a temperature inversion whenever the windspeed at 2,000 to 4,000 feet above the surface is at least

A. 10 knots.

B. 15 knots.

C. 25 knots.

Answer (C) is correct. *(AvW Chap 9)*
DISCUSSION: When taking off or landing in calm wind under clear skies within a few hours before or after sunset, prepare for a temperature inversion near the ground. You can be relatively certain of a shear zone in the inversion if you know the wind is 25 kt. or more at 2,000 to 4,000 ft. Allow a margin of airspeed above normal climb or approach speed to alleviate the danger of stall in the event of turbulence or sudden change in wind velocity.
Answer (A) is incorrect. A wind shear zone can be expected in a temperature inversion at 2,000 to 4,000 ft. AGL if the wind speed is at least 25 (not 10) kt. Answer (B) is incorrect. A wind shear zone can be expected in a temperature inversion at 2,000 to 4,000 ft. AGL if the wind speed is at least 25 (not 15) kt.

28. When may hazardous wind shear be expected?

A. When stable air crosses a mountain barrier where it tends to flow in layers forming lenticular clouds.

B. In areas of low-level temperature inversion, frontal zones, and clear air turbulence.

C. Following frontal passage when stratocumulus clouds form indicating mechanical mixing.

Answer (B) is correct. *(AvW Chap 9)*
DISCUSSION: Wind shear is the abrupt rate of change of wind velocity (direction and/or speed) per unit of distance and is normally expressed as vertical or horizontal wind shear. Hazardous wind shear may be expected in areas of low-level temperature inversion, frontal zones, and clear air turbulence.
Answer (A) is incorrect. A mountain wave forms when stable air crosses a mountain barrier where it tends to flow in layers forming lenticular clouds. Turbulence, not wind shear, is expected in this area. Answer (C) is incorrect. Mechanical turbulence (not wind shear) may be expected following frontal passage when clouds form, indicating mechanical mixing.

29. If a temperature inversion is encountered immediately after takeoff or during an approach to a landing, a potential hazard exists due to

A. wind shear.

B. strong surface winds.

C. strong convective currents.

Answer (A) is correct. *(AvW Chap 9)*
DISCUSSION: A wind shear develops in a zone between cold, calm air covered by warm air with a strong wind. This often occurs during a temperature inversion.
Answer (B) is incorrect. Strong surface winds by themselves do not create the potential hazard that wind shear does. Answer (C) is incorrect. Temperature inversion precludes (not generates) strong convective currents.

7.8 Temperature/Dew Point and Fog

30. If the temperature/dewpoint spread is small and decreasing, and the temperature is 62°F, what type weather is most likely to develop?

   A. Freezing precipitation.

   B. Thunderstorms.

   C. Fog or low clouds.

Answer (C) is correct. *(AvW Chap 5)*
   DISCUSSION: The difference between the air temperature and dew point is the temperature/dew point spread. As the temperature/dew point spread decreases, fog or low clouds tend to develop.
   Answer (A) is incorrect. There cannot be freezing precipitation if the temperature is 62°F. Answer (B) is incorrect. Thunderstorms have to do with unstable lapse rates, not temperature/dew point spreads.

31. What is meant by the term "dewpoint"?

   A. The temperature at which condensation and evaporation are equal.

   B. The temperature at which dew will always form.

   C. The temperature to which air must be cooled to become saturated.

Answer (C) is correct. *(AvW Chap 5)*
   DISCUSSION: Dew point is the temperature to which air must be cooled to become saturated, or have 100% humidity.
   Answer (A) is incorrect. Evaporation is the change from water to water vapor and is not directly related to the dew point. Answer (B) is incorrect. Dew forms only when heat radiates from an object whose temperature lowers below the dew point of the adjacent air.

32. The amount of water vapor which air can hold depends on the

   A. dewpoint.

   B. air temperature.

   C. stability of the air.

Answer (B) is correct. *(AvW Chap 5)*
   DISCUSSION: Air temperature largely determines how much water vapor can be held by the air. Warm air can hold more water vapor than cool air.
   Answer (A) is incorrect. Dew point is the temperature at which air must be cooled to become saturated by the water vapor already present in the air. Answer (C) is incorrect. Air stability is the state of the atmosphere at which vertical distribution of temperature is such that air particles will resist displacement from their initial level.

33. What are the processes by which moisture is added to unsaturated air?

   A. Evaporation and sublimation.

   B. Heating and condensation.

   C. Supersaturation and evaporation.

Answer (A) is correct. *(AvW Chap 5)*
   DISCUSSION: Evaporation is the process of converting a liquid to water vapor, and sublimation is the process of converting ice to water vapor.
   Answer (B) is incorrect. Heating alone does not add moisture. Condensation is the change of water vapor to liquid water. Answer (C) is incorrect. Supersaturation is a nonsense term in this context.

34. Which conditions result in the formation of frost?

   A. The temperature of the collecting surface is at or below freezing when small droplets of moisture fall on the surface.

   B. The temperature of the collecting surface is at or below the dewpoint of the adjacent air and the dewpoint is below freezing.

   C. The temperature of the surrounding air is at or below freezing when small drops of moisture fall on the collecting surface.

Answer (B) is correct. *(AvW Chap 5)*
   DISCUSSION: Frost forms when both the collecting surface is below the dew point of the adjacent air and the dew point is below freezing. Frost is the direct sublimation of water vapor to ice crystals.
   Answer (A) is incorrect. If small droplets of water fall on the collecting surface which is at or below freezing, ice (not frost) will form. Answer (C) is incorrect. If small droplets of water fall while the surrounding air is at or below freezing, ice (not frost) will form.

35. Clouds, fog, or dew will always form when

   A. water vapor condenses.

   B. water vapor is present.

   C. relative humidity reaches 100 percent.

Answer (A) is correct. *(AvW Chap 5)*
   DISCUSSION: As water vapor condenses, it becomes visible as clouds, fog, or dew.
   Answer (B) is incorrect. Water vapor is usually present but does not form clouds, fog, or dew without condensation. Answer (C) is incorrect. Even at 100% humidity, water vapor may not condense, e.g., sufficient condensation nuclei may not be present.

36. Low-level turbulence can occur and icing can become hazardous in which type of fog?

A. Rain-induced fog.

B. Upslope fog.

C. Steam fog.

Answer (C) is correct. *(AvW Chap 14)*

DISCUSSION: Steam fog forms in winter when cold, dry air passes from land areas over comparatively warm ocean waters. It is composed entirely of water droplets that often freeze quickly. Low-level turbulence can occur, and icing can become hazardous.

Answer (A) is incorrect. Precipitation- (rain-) induced fog is formed when relatively warm rain or drizzle falls through cool air, and evaporation from the precipitation saturates the cool air and forms fog. While the hazards of turbulence and icing may occur in the proximity of rain-induced fog, these hazards occur as a result of the steam fog formation process. Answer (B) is incorrect. Upslope fog forms when moist, stable air is cooled as it moves up sloping terrain.

37. In which situation is advection fog most likely to form?

A. A warm, moist air mass on the windward side of mountains.

B. An air mass moving inland from the coast in winter.

C. A light breeze blowing colder air out to sea.

Answer (B) is correct. *(AvW Chap 12)*

DISCUSSION: Advection fog forms when moist air moves over colder ground or water. It is most common in coastal areas.

Answer (A) is incorrect. A warm, moist air mass on the windward side of mountains produces rain or upslope fog as it blows upward and cools. Answer (C) is incorrect. A light breeze blowing colder air out to sea causes steam fog.

38. What situation is most conducive to the formation of radiation fog?

A. Warm, moist air over low, flatland areas on clear, calm nights.

B. Moist, tropical air moving over cold, offshore water.

C. The movement of cold air over much warmer water.

Answer (A) is correct. *(AvW Chap 12)*

DISCUSSION: Radiation fog is shallow fog of which ground fog is one form. It occurs under conditions of clear skies, little or no wind, and a small temperature/dew point spread. The fog forms almost exclusively at night or near dawn as a result of terrestrial radiation cooling the ground and the ground cooling the air on contact with it.

Answer (B) is incorrect. Moist, tropical air moving over cold, offshore water causes advection fog, not radiation fog. Answer (C) is incorrect. Movement of cold, dry air over much warmer water results in steam fog.

39. What types of fog depend upon wind in order to exist?

A. Radiation fog and ice fog.

B. Steam fog and ground fog.

C. Advection fog and upslope fog.

Answer (C) is correct. *(AvW Chap 12)*

DISCUSSION: Advection fog forms when moist air moves over colder ground or water. It is most common in coastal areas. Upslope fog forms when wind blows moist air upward over rising terrain and the air cools below its dew point. Both advection fog and upslope fog require wind to move air masses.

Answer (A) is incorrect. No wind is required for the formation of either radiation or ice fog. Answer (B) is incorrect. No wind is required for the formation of ground (radiation) fog.

7.9 Clouds

40. Clouds are divided into four families according to their

A. outward shape.

B. height range.

C. composition.

Answer (B) is correct. *(AvW Chap 7)*

DISCUSSION: The four families of clouds are high clouds, middle clouds, low clouds, and clouds with extensive vertical development. Thus, they are based upon their height range.

Answer (A) is incorrect. Clouds are divided by their height range, not outward shape. Answer (C) is incorrect. Clouds are divided by their height range, not by their composition.

41. The suffix "nimbus," used in naming clouds, means

A. a cloud with extensive vertical development.

B. a rain cloud.

C. a middle cloud containing ice pellets.

Answer (B) is correct. *(AvW Chap 7)*

DISCUSSION: The suffix nimbus or the prefix nimbo means a rain cloud.

Answer (A) is incorrect. Clouds with extensive vertical development are called either towering cumulus or cumulonimbus. Answer (C) is incorrect. A middle cloud has the prefix alto.

42. The conditions necessary for the formation of cumulonimbus clouds are a lifting action and

    A. unstable air containing an excess of condensation nuclei.

    B. unstable, moist air.

    C. either stable or unstable air.

Answer (B) is correct. *(AvW Chap 9)*
    DISCUSSION: Unstable, moist air in addition to a lifting action, i.e., convective activity, is needed to form cumulonimbus clouds.
    Answer (A) is incorrect. There must be moisture available to produce the clouds and rain, i.e., in a hot, dry dust storm, there would be no thunderstorm. Answer (C) is incorrect. The air must be unstable or there will be no lifting action.

43. What clouds have the greatest turbulence?

    A. Towering cumulus.

    B. Cumulonimbus.

    C. Nimbostratus.

Answer (B) is correct. *(AvW Chap 7)*
    DISCUSSION: The greatest turbulence occurs in cumulonimbus clouds, which are thunderstorm clouds.
    Answer (A) is incorrect. Towering cumulus are an earlier stage of cumulonimbus clouds. Answer (C) is incorrect. Nimbostratus is a gray or dark, massive cloud layer diffused by continuous rain or ice pellets. It is a middle cloud with very little turbulence but may pose serious icing problems.

44. Which cloud types would indicate convective turbulence?

    A. Cirrus clouds.

    B. Nimbostratus clouds.

    C. Towering cumulus clouds.

Answer (C) is correct. *(AvW Chap 7)*
    DISCUSSION: Towering cumulus clouds are an early stage of cumulonimbus clouds, or thunderstorms, which are based on convective turbulence, i.e., an unstable lapse rate.
    Answer (A) is incorrect. Cirrus clouds are high, thin, featherlike ice crystal clouds in patches and narrow bands that are not based on any convective activity. Answer (B) is incorrect. Nimbostratus are gray or dark, massive clouds diffused by continuous rain or ice pellets with very little turbulence.

45. At approximately what altitude above the surface would the pilot expect the base of cumuliform clouds if the surface air temperature is 82°F and the dewpoint is 38°F?

    A. 9,000 feet AGL.

    B. 10,000 feet AGL.

    C. 11,000 feet AGL.

Answer (B) is correct. *(AvW Chap 6)*
    DISCUSSION: The height of cumuliform cloud bases can be estimated using surface temperature/dew point spread. Unsaturated air in a convective current cools at about 5.4°F/1,000 ft., and dew point decreases about 1°F/1,000 ft. In a convective current, temperature and dew point converge at about 4.4°F/1,000 ft. Thus, if the temperature/dew point spread is 44° (82° − 38°), divide 44 by 4.4 to obtain 10,000 ft. AGL.
    Answer (A) is incorrect. The approximate height of the base of cumuliform clouds is 9,000 ft. AGL if the temperature/dew point spread is 40°F. Answer (C) is incorrect. The approximate height of the base of cumuliform clouds is 11,000 ft. AGL if the temperature/dew point spread is 48°F.

46. What is the approximate base of the cumulus clouds if the surface air temperature at 1,000 feet MSL is 70°F and the dewpoint is 48°F?

    A. 4,000 feet MSL.

    B. 5,000 feet MSL.

    C. 6,000 feet MSL.

Answer (C) is correct. *(AvW Chap 6)*
    DISCUSSION: The height of cumuliform cloud bases can be estimated using surface temperature/dew point spread. Unsaturated air in a convective current cools at about 5.4°F/1,000 ft., and dew point decreases about 1°F/1,000 ft. In a convective current, temperature and dew point converge at about 4.4°F/1,000 ft. Thus, if the temperature and dew point are 70°F and 48°F, respectively, at 1,000 ft. MSL, there would be a 22° spread which, divided by the lapse rate of 4.4, is approximately 5,000 ft. AGL, or 6,000 ft. MSL (5,000 + 1,000).
    Answer (A) is incorrect. The approximate base of the cumulus clouds is 4,000 ft. MSL if the temperature at 1,000 ft. MSL is 61°F, not 70°F. Answer (B) is incorrect. The approximate base of the cumulus clouds is 5,000 ft. AGL, not MSL.

7.10 Stability of Air Masses

47. Which is a characteristic of stable air?

A. Stratiform clouds.

B. Unlimited visibility.

C. Cumulus clouds.

Answer (A) is correct. *(AvW Chap 8)*
 DISCUSSION: Characteristics of a stable air mass include stratiform clouds, continuous precipitation, smooth air, and fair to poor visibility in haze and smoke.
 Answer (B) is incorrect. Restricted, not unlimited, visibility is an indication of stable air. Answer (C) is incorrect. Fair weather cumulus clouds indicate unstable conditions, not stable conditions.

48. Moist, stable air flowing upslope can be expected to

A. produce stratus type clouds.

B. cause showers and thunderstorms.

C. develop convective turbulence.

Answer (A) is correct. *(AvW Chap 6)*
 DISCUSSION: Moist, stable air flowing upslope can be expected to produce stratus type clouds as the air cools adiabatically as it moves up sloping terrain.
 Answer (B) is incorrect. Showers and thunderstorms are characteristics of unstable (not stable) air. Answer (C) is incorrect. Convective turbulence is a characteristic of unstable (not stable) air.

49. If an unstable air mass is forced upward, what type clouds can be expected?

A. Stratus clouds with little vertical development.

B. Stratus clouds with considerable associated turbulence.

C. Clouds with considerable vertical development and associated turbulence.

Answer (C) is correct. *(AvW Chap 6)*
 DISCUSSION: When unstable air is lifted, it usually results in considerable vertical development and associated turbulence, i.e., convective activity.
 Answer (A) is incorrect. Stable rather than unstable air creates stratus clouds with little vertical development. Answer (B) is incorrect. Stratus (layer-type) clouds usually have little turbulence unless they are lenticular clouds created by mountain waves or other high-altitude clouds associated with high winds near or in the jet stream.

50. Which is generally true when comparing the rate of vertical motion of updrafts with that of downdrafts associated with thermals?

A. Updrafts and downdrafts move vertically at the same rate.

B. Downdrafts have a slower rate of vertical motion than do updrafts.

C. Updrafts have a slower rate of vertical motion than do downdrafts.

Answer (B) is correct. *(AvW Chap 16)*
 DISCUSSION: During the propagation of thermals, the net upward displacement of air must equal the net downward displacement. Faster rising thermals generally cover a small percentage of convective area, while slower downdrafts predominate over the remaining great portion.
 Answer (A) is incorrect. Thermals are much less prevalent than downdrafts in the convective area, and therefore must rise at a faster rate to equal out the net displacement of air. Answer (C) is incorrect. Thermals are much less prevalent than downdrafts in the convective area, and therefore must rise at a faster rate to equal out the net displacement of air.

51. What are characteristics of unstable air?

A. Turbulence and good surface visibility.

B. Turbulence and poor surface visibility.

C. Nimbostratus clouds and good surface visibility.

Answer (A) is correct. *(AvW Chap 8)*
 DISCUSSION: Characteristics of an unstable air mass include cumuliform clouds, showery precipitation, turbulence, and good visibility, except in blowing obstructions.
 Answer (B) is incorrect. Poor surface visibility is a characteristic of stable (not unstable) air. Answer (C) is incorrect. Stratus clouds are characteristic of stable (not unstable) air.

52. A stable air mass is most likely to have which characteristic?

A. Showery precipitation.

B. Turbulent air.

C. Smooth air.

Answer (C) is correct. *(AvW Chap 8)*
 DISCUSSION: Characteristics of a stable air mass include stratiform clouds and fog, continuous precipitation, smooth air, and fair to poor visibility in haze and smoke.
 Answer (A) is incorrect. Showery precipitation is a characteristic of an unstable (not stable) air mass. Answer (B) is incorrect. Turbulent air is a characteristic of an unstable (not stable) air mass.

53. Steady precipitation preceding a front is an indication of

A. stratiform clouds with moderate turbulence.

B. cumuliform clouds with little or no turbulence.

C. stratiform clouds with little or no turbulence.

Answer (C) is correct. *(AvW Chap 8)*
 DISCUSSION: Steady precipitation preceding a front is usually an indication of a warm front, which results from warm air being cooled from the bottom by colder air. This results in stratiform clouds with little or no turbulence.
 Answer (A) is incorrect. Stratiform clouds usually are not turbulent. Answer (B) is incorrect. Cumuliform clouds have showery rather than steady precipitation.

54. What are characteristics of a moist, unstable air mass?

A. Cumuliform clouds and showery precipitation.

B. Poor visibility and smooth air.

C. Stratiform clouds and showery precipitation.

Answer (A) is correct. *(AvW Chap 8)*
 DISCUSSION: Characteristics of an unstable air mass include cumuliform clouds, showery precipitation, turbulence, and good visibility, except in blowing obstructions.
 Answer (B) is incorrect. Poor visibility and smooth air are characteristics of stable (not unstable) air. Answer (C) is incorrect. Stratiform clouds and continuous precipitation are characteristics of stable (not unstable) air.

55. What measurement can be used to determine the stability of the atmosphere?

A. Atmospheric pressure.

B. Actual lapse rate.

C. Surface temperature.

Answer (B) is correct. *(AvW Chap 6)*
 DISCUSSION: The stability of the atmosphere is determined by vertical movements of air. Warm air rises when the air above is cooler. The actual lapse rate, which is the decrease of temperature with altitude, is therefore a measure of stability.
 Answer (A) is incorrect. Atmospheric pressure is the pressure exerted by the atmosphere as a consequence of gravitational attraction exerted upon the "column" of air lying directly above the point in question. It cannot be used to determine stability. Answer (C) is incorrect. While the surface temperature may have some effect on temperature changes and air movements, it is the actual lapse rate that determines the stability of the atmosphere.

56. What would decrease the stability of an air mass?

A. Warming from below.

B. Cooling from below.

C. Decrease in water vapor.

Answer (A) is correct. *(AvW Chap 6)*
 DISCUSSION: When air is warmed from below, even though cooling adiabatically, it remains warmer than the surrounding air. The colder, more dense surrounding air forces the warmer air upward and an unstable condition develops.
 Answer (B) is incorrect. Cooling from below means the surrounding air is warmer, which would increase (not decrease) the stability of an air mass. Answer (C) is incorrect. As water vapor in air decreases, the air mass tends to increase (not decrease) stability.

7.11 Temperature Inversions

57. What feature is associated with a temperature inversion?

A. A stable layer of air.

B. An unstable layer of air.

C. Chinook winds on mountain slopes.

Answer (A) is correct. *(AvW Chap 6)*
 DISCUSSION: A temperature inversion is associated with an increase in temperature with height, a reversal of normal decrease in temperature with height. Thus, any warm air rises to where it is the same temperature and forms a stable layer of air.
 Answer (B) is incorrect. Instability is a result of rising air remaining warmer than the surrounding air aloft, which would not occur with a temperature inversion. Answer (C) is incorrect. A Chinook wind is a warm, dry downslope wind blowing down the eastern slopes of the Rocky Mountains over the adjacent plains in the U.S. and Canada.

58. The most frequent type of ground or surface-based temperature inversion is that which is produced by

A. terrestrial radiation on a clear, relatively still night.

B. warm air being lifted rapidly aloft in the vicinity of mountainous terrain.

C. the movement of colder air under warm air, or the movement of warm air over cold air.

Answer (A) is correct.   *(AvW Chap 2)*
DISCUSSION: An inversion often develops near the ground on clear, cool nights when wind is light. The ground loses heat and cools the air near the ground while the temperature a few hundred feet above changes very little. Thus, temperature increases in height, which is an inversion.
Answer (B) is incorrect. Warm air being lifted rapidly aloft in the vicinity of mountainous terrain describes convective activity. Answer (C) is incorrect. The movement of colder air under warm air, which causes an inversion, is caused by a cold front, not terrestrial radiation (warm air moving over cold air is a warm front).

59. A temperature inversion would most likely result in which weather condition?

A. Clouds with extensive vertical development above an inversion aloft.

B. Good visibility in the lower levels of the atmosphere and poor visibility above an inversion aloft.

C. An increase in temperature as altitude is increased.

Answer (C) is correct.   *(AvW Chap 2)*
DISCUSSION: By definition, a temperature inversion is a situation in which the temperature increases as altitude increases. The normal situation is that the temperature decreases as altitude increases.
Answer (A) is incorrect. Vertical development does not occur in an inversion situation because the warm air cannot rise when the air above is warmer. Answer (B) is incorrect. The inversion traps dust, smoke, and other nuclei beneath the inversion, which reduces visibility.

60. Which weather conditions should be expected beneath a low-level temperature inversion layer when the relative humidity is high?

A. Smooth air, poor visibility, fog, haze, or low clouds.

B. Light wind shear, poor visibility, haze, and light rain.

C. Turbulent air, poor visibility, fog, low stratus type clouds, and showery precipitation.

Answer (A) is correct.   *(AvW Chap 12)*
DISCUSSION: Beneath temperature inversions, there is usually smooth air because there is little vertical movement due to the inversion. There is also poor visibility due to fog, haze, and low clouds (when there is high relative humidity).
Answer (B) is incorrect. Wind shears usually do not occur below a low-level temperature inversion. They occur at or just above the inversion. Answer (C) is incorrect. Turbulent air and showery precipitation are not present with low-level temperature inversions.

END OF STUDY UNIT

STUDY UNIT EIGHT
WEATHER SERVICES

(9 pages of outline)

This study unit contains outlines of major concepts tested, sample test questions and answers regarding weather services, and an explanation of each answer. The table of contents above lists each subunit within this study unit, the number of questions pertaining to that particular subunit, and the pages on which the outlines and questions begin, respectively.

CAUTION: Recall that the **sole purpose** of this book is to expedite your passing the FAA pilot knowledge test for the sport pilot certificate. Accordingly, all extraneous material (i.e., topics or regulations not directly tested on the FAA pilot knowledge test) is omitted, even though much more information and knowledge are necessary to fly safely. This additional material is presented in *Pilot Handbook* and *Sport Pilot Flight Maneuvers and Practical Test Prep*, available from Gleim Publications, Inc. See the order form on page 327.

8.1 WEATHER BRIEFINGS

1. When requesting a telephone weather briefing, you should identify

   a. Yourself as a pilot
   b. Your intended route
   c. Your intended destination
   d. Whether you are flying VFR or IFR
   e. The type of aircraft you are flying
   f. Your proposed departure time and time en route

2. A standard briefing should be obtained before every flight. This briefing will provide all the necessary information for a safe flight.

3. An outlook briefing is provided when it is 6 or more hours before proposed departure time.

4. An abbreviated briefing will be provided when the user requests information to

   a. Supplement mass disseminated data,
   b. Update a previous briefing, or
   c. Be limited to specific information.

8.2 AVIATION ROUTINE WEATHER REPORT (METAR)

1. Aviation routine weather reports (METARs) are actual weather observations at the time indicated on the report. There are two types of reports.

   a. METAR is a routine weather report.
   b. SPECI is a nonroutine weather report.

2. Following the type of report are the elements listed below:

   a. The four-letter ICAO station identifier.

      1) In the contiguous 48 states, the three-letter domestic identifier is prefixed with a "K."

   b. Date and time of report. It is appended with a "Z" to denote Coordinated Universal Time (UTC).

   c. Modifier (if required).

   d. Wind. Wind is reported as a five-digit group (six digits if the wind speed is greater than 99 kt.). It is appended with the abbreviation KT to denote the use of knots for wind speed.

      1) If the wind is gusty, it is reported as a "G" after the speed, followed by the highest gust reported.

      2) EXAMPLE: **11012G18KT** means wind from 110° true at 12 kt. with gusts to 18 kt.

   e. Visibility. Prevailing visibility is reported in statute miles with "SM" appended to it.

      1) EXAMPLE: **1 1/2SM** means visibility 1 1/2 SM.

   f. Sky conditions.

      1) The ceiling is the lowest broken or overcast layer or vertical visibility into an obscuration.

      2) Cloud bases are reported with three digits in hundreds of feet AGL.

         a) EXAMPLE: **OVC007** means overcast cloud layer at 700 ft. AGL.

   g. Temperature/dew point. They are reported in a two-digit form in whole degrees Celsius separated by a solidus, "/."

   h. Altimeter.

   i. Remarks (RMK).

      1) EXAMPLE: **RAB35** means rain began at 35 min. past the hour.

3. EXAMPLE: METAR KAUS 301651Z 12008KT 4SM -RA HZ BKN010 OVC023 21/17 A3005 RMK RAB25

   a. **METAR** is a routine weather observation.
   b. **KAUS** is Austin, TX.
   c. **301651Z** means the observation was taken on the 30th day at 1651 UTC (or Z).
   d. **12008KT** means the wind is from 120° true at 8 kt.
   e. **4SM** means the visibility is 4 statute miles.
   f. **-RA HZ** means light rain and haze.
   g. **BKN010 OVC023** means ceiling 1,000 ft. broken, 2,300 ft. overcast.
   h. **21/17** means the temperature is 21°C and the dew point is 17°C.
   i. **A3005** means the altimeter setting is 30.05 in. of Hg.
   j. **RMK RAB25** means remarks: rain began at 25 min. past the hour, i.e., 1625 UTC.

4.   Figure 3 on page 297 includes some sample METARs. The FAA has not released any questions on this figure; however, you may encounter some on your knowledge test. To prepare for such questions, study the explanations with Figure 3 along with this subunit until you are familiar with the interpretation of each element in the figure.

8.3 SIGMETs AND AIRMETs

1.   SIGMETs and AIRMETs are issued to notify pilots en route of the possibility of encountering hazardous flying conditions.

2.   SIGMET advisories include weather phenomena that are potentially hazardous to all aircraft.

    a.   Convective SIGMETs include

        1)   Tornadoes
        2)   Lines of thunderstorms
        3)   Embedded thunderstorms
        4)   Thunderstorm areas greater than or equal to thunderstorm intensity level 4 with an area coverage of 40% or more
        5)   Hail greater than or equal to 3/4 in. in diameter

    b.   SIGMETs include

        1)   Severe or extreme turbulence or clear air turbulence (CAT) not associated with thunderstorms
        2)   Severe icing not associated with thunderstorms
        3)   Duststorms, sandstorms, or volcanic ash lowering visibility to less than 3 SM
        4)   Volcanic eruption

3.   AIRMETs are advisories of significant weather phenomena, but of lower intensities than SIGMETs, and are intended to notify all pilots of

    a.   Moderate icing
    b.   Moderate turbulence
    c.   Visibility less than 3 SM or ceilings less than 1,000 ft.
    d.   Sustained winds of 30 kt. or more at the surface
    e.   Extensive mountain obscurement

8.4 PILOT WEATHER REPORT (PIREP)

1. No observation is more timely or needed than the one you make from the cockpit.

2. PIREPs are transmitted in a format illustrated below.

UUA/UA	Type of report: URGENT (UUA) - Any PIREP that contains any of the following weather phenomena: tornadoes, funnel clouds, or waterspouts; severe or extreme turbulence, including clear air turbulence (CAT); severe icing; hail; low-level wind shear (LLWS) (pilot reports air speed fluctuations of 10 knots or more within 2,000 feet of the surface); any other weather phenomena reported that are considered by the controller to be hazardous, or potentially hazardous, to flight operations. ROUTINE (UA) - Any PIREP that contains weather phenomena not listed above, including low-level wind shear reports with air speed fluctuations of less than 10 knots.
/OV	Location: Use VHF NAVAID(s) or an airport using the three- or four-letter location identifier. Position can be over a site, at some location relative to a site, or along a route. Ex: /OV KABC; /OV KABC090025; /OV KABC045020-DEF; /OV KABC-KDEF
/TM	Time: Four digits in UTC. Ex: /TM 0915
/FL	Altitude/Flight level: Three digits for hundreds of feet with no space between FL and altitude. If not known, use UNKN. Ex: /FL095; /FL310; /FLUNKN
/TP	Aircraft type: Four digits maximum; if not known, use UNKN. Ex: /TP L329; /TP B737; /TP UNKN
/SK	Sky cover: Describes cloud amount, height of cloud bases, and height of cloud tops. If unknown, use UNKN. Ex: /SK SCT040-TOP080; /SK BKNUNKN-TOP075; /SK BKN-OVC050-TOPUNKN; /SK OVCUNKN-TOP085
/WX	Flight visibility and weather: Report flight visibility (FV) first and use standard METAR weather symbols. Intensity (– for light, no qualifier for moderate, and + for heavy) shall be coded for all precipitation types except ice crystals and hail. Ex: /WX FV05SM – RA; /WX FV01 SN BR; /WX RA
/TA	Temperature (Celsius): If below zero, prefix with an "M." Temperature should also be reported if icing is reported. Ex: /TA 15; /TA M06
/WV	Wind: Direction from which the wind is blowing coded in tens of degrees using three digits. Directions of less than 100 degrees shall be preceded by a zero. The wind speed shall be entered as a two- or three-digit group immediately following the direction, coded in whole knots using the hundreds, tens, and units digits. Ex: /WV 27045KT; /WV 280110KT
/TB	Turbulence: Use standard contractions for intensity and type (CAT or CHOP when appropriate). Include altitude only if different from FL. Ex: /TB EXTRM; /TB OCNL LGT-MDT BLO 090; /TB MOD-SEV CHOP 080-110
/IC	Icing: Describe using standard intensity and type contractions. Include altitude only if different from FL. Ex: /IC LGT-MDT RIME; /IC SEV CLR 028-045
/RM	Remarks: Use free form to clarify the report, putting hazardous elements first. Ex: /RM LLWS –15 KT SFC-030 DURGC RY 22 JFK

3. All heights are given as MSL. To determine AGL, subtract the field height from the given height.

4. Turbulence is reported as

   a. Light = LGT
   b. Moderate = MDT
   c. Severe = SVR

5. Icing is reported as

   a. Clear = CLR
   b. Rime = RIME

6. Cloud layers are reported with heights for bases, tops, and layer type if available. "No entry" means that information was not given.

   a. EXAMPLE: SK 024 BKN 032/042 BKN-OVC decoded means a broken layer 2,400 ft. MSL to 3,200 ft. MSL. A second layer is broken to overcast starting at 4,200 ft. MSL.

7. Wind direction and velocity are given as a five- or six-digit code (e.g., /**WV 27045** means 270° at 45 kt.).

8. Air temperature is expressed in degrees Celsius (°C).

8.5 AVIATION AREA FORECAST

1. Aviation area forecasts (FA) are forecasts of visual meteorological conditions (VMC), clouds, and general weather conditions for several states and/or portions of states. They can be used to interpolate conditions at airports that have no terminal forecasts. FAs are issued three times a day and consist of

   a. A 12-hr. forecast
   b. An additional 6-hr. categorical outlook

2. FA weather format. An example is presented on page 142 for questions 30 through 33 on page 143. It is presented in abbreviations. You will see this same FA utilizing abbreviations on your pilot knowledge test.

3. There are four sections in an FA:

   a. Communication and product header section
   b. Precautionary statements section
   c. Synopsis section (for the purposes of the test, this section is not considered a forecast)
   d. VFR clouds/weather section (VFR CLDS/WX); this section is referred to as the forecast section

      1) Included in the VFR CLDS/WX section is a categorical outlook that is valid for an additional 6 hours. For the purposes of the test, the categorical outlook is not considered a forecast.

4. In order to get a complete weather picture, including icing, turbulence, and IFR conditions, an FA must be supplemented by In-Flight Aviation Weather Advisories (AIRMETs Zulu, Tango, and Sierra).

   a. A pilot should refer to the In-Flight Aviation Weather Advisories to determine the freezing level and areas of probable icing aloft.

8.6 TERMINAL AERODROME FORECAST (TAF)

1. Terminal aerodrome forecasts (TAFs) are weather forecasts for selected airports throughout the country.

2. The elements of a TAF are listed below:

    a. Type of report.

        1) **TAF** is a routine forecast.
        2) **TAF AMD** is an amended forecast.

    b. ICAO station identifier.

    c. Date and time the forecast is actually prepared.

    d. Valid period of the forecast.

    e. Forecast meteorological conditions. This is the body of the forecast and includes the following:

        1) Wind
        2) Visibility
        3) Weather
        4) Sky condition

            a) Cumulonimbus clouds (CB) are the only cloud type forecast in TAFs.

3. EXAMPLE:

    TAF
    KBRO 300545Z 300606 VRB04KT 3SM SCT040 OVC150 TEMPO 2124 SHRA
    FM0200 10010KT P6SM OVC020 BECMG0306 NSW BKN020=

    a. **TAF** is a routine forecast.

    b. **KBRO** is Brownsville, TX.

    c. **300545Z** means the forecast was prepared on the 30th day at 0545 UTC.

    d. **300606** means the forecast is valid from the 30th day at 0600 UTC until 0600 UTC the following day.

    e. **VRB04KT 3SM SCT040 OVC150 TEMPO 2124 SHRA** means the forecast from 0600 until 0200 UTC is wind variable in direction at 4 kt., visibility 3 SM, scattered cloud layer at 4,000 ft., ceiling 15,000 ft. overcast, with occasional rain showers between 2100 and 2400 UTC.

    f. **FM0200 10010KT P6SM OVC020 BECMG0306 NSW BKN020=** means the forecast from 0200 until 0300 is wind 100° true at 10 kt., visibility greater than 6 SM, ceiling 2,000 ft. overcast then becoming no significant weather, ceiling 2,000 ft. broken between 0300 to 0600 UTC.

        1) Note that, since the becoming group (BECMG) did not forecast wind and visibility, they are the same as the previous forecast group, i.e., wind 100° true at 10 kt., visibility greater than 6 SM.

8.7 WEATHER DEPICTION CHARTS

1. A weather depiction chart is an outline of the United States depicting sky conditions at the time stated on the chart based on METAR reports.

   a. Reporting stations are marked with a little circle.

      1) If the sky is clear, the circle is open; if overcast, the circle is solid; if scattered, the circle is 1/4 solid; if broken, the circle is 3/4 solid. If the sky is obscured, there is an "X" in the circle.

      2) The height of clouds is expressed in hundreds of feet above ground level, e.g., 120 means 12,000 ft. AGL.

2. Areas with ceilings below 1,000 ft. and/or visibility less than 3 SM, i.e., below VFR, are bracketed with solid black contour lines and are shaded.

   a. Visibility is indicated next to the circle; e.g., 2 stands for 2-SM visibility.

      1) If the visibility is greater than 6 SM, it is not reported.

   b. Areas of marginal VFR with ceilings of 1,000 to 3,000 ft. and/or visibility at 3 to 5 SM are bracketed by solid black contour lines and are unshaded.

   c. Ceilings greater than 3,000 ft. and visibility greater than 5 SM are not indicated by contour lines on weather depiction charts.

3. Station models and significant weather are indicated by the following symbols:

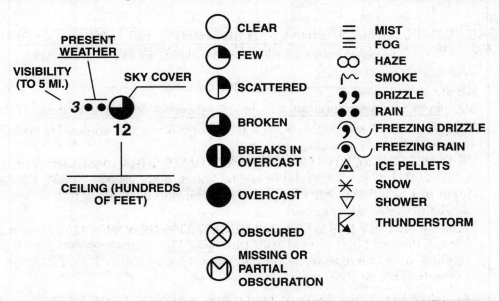

4. The weather depiction chart quickly shows pilots where weather conditions reported are above or below VFR minimums.

5. The weather depiction chart displays recent positions of frontal systems and indicates the type of front by symbols.

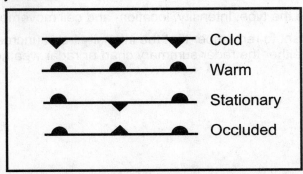

6.   Figures 10 and 11 on page 299 show some weather depiction chart symbols. The FAA has not released any questions on these figures; however, you may encounter some on your knowledge test. To prepare for such questions, study the explanations with Figures 10 and 11 along with this subunit until you are familiar with the interpretation of each element in the figures.

8.8 RADAR SUMMARY CHARTS AND RADAR WEATHER REPORTS

1.   Radar summary charts graphically display a collection of radar reports concerning the type, intensity, and movement of precipitation, e.g., squall lines, specific thunderstorm cells, and other areas of hazardous precipitation.

   a.   Lines and cells of hazardous thunderstorms can be seen on radar summary charts and are not shown on other weather charts.

2.   The symbols below are used on radar summary charts.

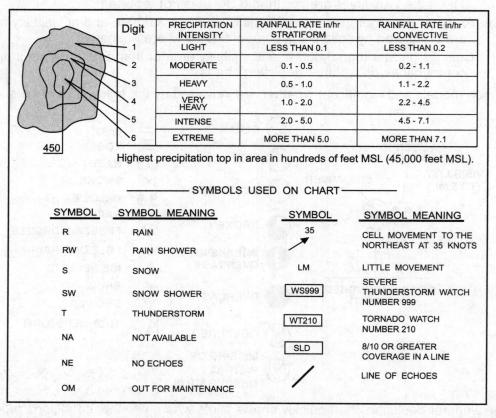

Digit	PRECIPITATION INTENSITY	RAINFALL RATE in/hr STRATIFORM	RAINFALL RATE in/hr CONVECTIVE
1	LIGHT	LESS THAN 0.1	LESS THAN 0.2
2	MODERATE	0.1 - 0.5	0.2 - 1.1
3	HEAVY	0.5 - 1.0	1.1 - 2.2
4	VERY HEAVY	1.0 - 2.0	2.2 - 4.5
5	INTENSE	2.0 - 5.0	4.5 - 7.1
6	EXTREME	MORE THAN 5.0	MORE THAN 7.1

Highest precipitation top in area in hundreds of feet MSL (45,000 feet MSL).

——————— SYMBOLS USED ON CHART ———————

SYMBOL	SYMBOL MEANING	SYMBOL	SYMBOL MEANING
R	RAIN	35 ↗	CELL MOVEMENT TO THE NORTHEAST AT 35 KNOTS
RW	RAIN SHOWER		
S	SNOW	LM	LITTLE MOVEMENT
SW	SNOW SHOWER	WS999	SEVERE THUNDERSTORM WATCH NUMBER 999
T	THUNDERSTORM	WT210	TORNADO WATCH NUMBER 210
NA	NOT AVAILABLE	SLD	8/10 OR GREATER COVERAGE IN A LINE
NE	NO ECHOES	/	LINE OF ECHOES
OM	OUT FOR MAINTENANCE		

3.   Severe weather watch areas are enclosed by a heavy dashed line, usually in the form of a rectangular box.

4.   Radar weather reports are textual reports of weather radar observations.

   a.   They include the type, intensity, location, and cell movement of precipitation.

5.   Finally, it is important to remember that the intensity trend (increasing or weakening) is no longer coded on either the radar summary chart or radar weather report (SD/ROB).

8.9 EN ROUTE FLIGHT ADVISORY SERVICE (EFAS)

1. En Route Flight Advisory Service (EFAS) provides weather advisories on 122.0 MHz below FL 180. It is called Flight Watch.

   a. Generally, service is available from 6 a.m. to 10 p.m. local time.

   b. EFAS provides information regarding actual weather and thunderstorm activity along a proposed route.

2. It is designed to be a continual exchange of information on winds, turbulence, visibility, icing, etc., between pilots and weather briefers.

8.10 WIND AND TEMPERATURE ALOFT FORECASTS (FB)

1. Forecast winds and temperatures are provided at specified altitudes for specific locations in the United States.

2. A four-digit group (used when temperatures are not forecast) shows wind direction with reference to **true** north and the wind speed in **knots**.

   a. The first two digits indicate the wind direction after a zero is added.

   b. The next two digits indicate the wind speed.

   c. No temperature is forecast for the 3,000-ft. level or for a level within 2,500 ft. AGL of the station.

3. A six-digit group includes the forecast temperature aloft.

   a. The last two digits indicate the temperature in degrees Celsius.

   b. Plus or minus is indicated before the temperature, except at higher altitudes (above 24,000 ft. MSL) where it is always below freezing.

4. When the wind speed is less than 5 kt., the forecast is coded 9900, which means that the wind is light and variable.

5. When the wind speed is over 100 kt., the forecaster adds 50 to the direction and subtracts 100 from the speed. To decode, you must reverse the process. For example, 730649 = 230° (73 − 50) at 106 kt. (100 + 06) and −49° (above 24,000 ft.).

6. An example forecast is provided on page 151 for questions 59 through 63.

QUESTIONS AND ANSWER EXPLANATIONS

All of the sport pilot knowledge test questions chosen by the FAA for release as well as additional questions selected by Gleim relating to the material in the previous outlines are reproduced on the following pages. These questions have been organized into the same subunits as the outlines. To the immediate right of each question are the correct answer and answer explanation. You should cover these answers and answer explanations while responding to the questions. Refer to the general discussion in the Introduction on how to take the FAA pilot knowledge test.

Remember that the questions from the FAA pilot knowledge test bank have been reordered by topic and organized into a meaningful sequence. Also, the first line of the answer explanation gives the citation of the authoritative source for the answer.

QUESTIONS

8.1 Weather Briefings

1. To get a complete weather briefing for the planned flight, the pilot should request

    A. a general briefing.

    B. an abbreviated briefing.

    C. a standard briefing.

Answer (C) is correct. *(AWS Sect 1)*
    DISCUSSION: To get a complete briefing before a planned flight, the pilot should request a standard briefing. This will include all pertinent information needed for a safe flight.
    Answer (A) is incorrect. A general briefing is not standard terminology for any type of weather briefing. Answer (B) is incorrect. An abbreviated briefing is only provided as a supplement to mass disseminated data or a previous briefing, or it is to be limited to specific information.

2. Which type weather briefing should a pilot request, when departing within the hour, if no preliminary weather information has been received?

    A. Outlook briefing.

    B. Abbreviated briefing.

    C. Standard briefing.

Answer (C) is correct. *(AWS Sect 1)*
    DISCUSSION: A pilot should request a standard briefing anytime (s)he is planning a flight and has not received a previous briefing or has not received preliminary information through mass dissemination media (e.g., TWEB, PATWAS, etc.).
    Answer (A) is incorrect. Outlook briefings are for flights 6 hr. or more in the future. Answer (B) is incorrect. Abbreviated briefings are to update previous briefings, supplement other data, or answer a specific inquiry.

3. Which type of weather briefing should a pilot request to supplement mass disseminated data?

    A. An outlook briefing.

    B. A supplemental briefing.

    C. An abbreviated briefing.

Answer (C) is correct. *(AWS Sect 1)*
    DISCUSSION: An abbreviated briefing will be provided when the user requests information to supplement mass disseminated data, update a previous briefing, or answer a specific inquiry.
    Answer (A) is incorrect. An outlook briefing should be requested if the proposed departure time is 6 hr. or more in the future. Answer (B) is incorrect. A supplemental briefing is not a standard type of briefing.

4. A weather briefing that is provided when the information requested is 6 or more hours in advance of the proposed departure time is

    A. an outlook briefing.

    B. a forecast briefing.

    C. a prognostic briefing.

Answer (A) is correct. *(AWS Sect 1)*
    DISCUSSION: An outlook briefing is given when the briefing is 6 or more hours before the proposed departure time.
    Answer (B) is incorrect. A forecast briefing is not a type of weather briefing. Answer (C) is incorrect. A prognostic briefing is not a type of weather briefing.

5. What should pilots state initially when telephoning a weather briefing facility for preflight weather information?

    A. Tell the number of occupants on board.

    B. State their total flight time.

    C. Identify themselves as pilots.

Answer (C) is correct. *(AWS Sect 1)*
    DISCUSSION: When telephoning for a weather briefing, you should identify yourself as a pilot so the person can give you an aviation-oriented briefing. Many nonpilots call weather briefing facilities to get the weather for other activities.
    Answer (A) is incorrect. The number of occupants on board is information needed for a flight plan, not for a weather briefing. Answer (B) is incorrect. Total flight time is a question asked by insurance companies, not information needed for a weather briefing.

6. What should pilots state initially when telephoning a weather briefing facility for preflight weather information?

    A. The intended route of flight radio frequencies.

    B. The intended route of flight and destination.

    C. The address of the pilot in command.

Answer (B) is correct. *(AWS Sect 1)*
    DISCUSSION: By telling the briefer your intended route and destination, the briefer will be able to provide you a more relevant briefing.
    Answer (A) is incorrect. The radio frequencies to be used are the pilot's preflight responsibility, not the weather briefer's. Answer (C) is incorrect. The address of the pilot in command is information needed for a flight plan, not for a weather briefing.

7. When telephoning a weather briefing facility for preflight weather information, pilots should state

    A. the aircraft identification or the pilot's name.

    B. true airspeed.

    C. fuel on board.

Answer (A) is correct. *(AWS Sect 1)*
    DISCUSSION: When requesting a briefing, you should provide the briefer with the following information: VFR or IFR, aircraft identification or the pilot's name, aircraft type, departure point, route of flight, destination, altitude, estimated time of departure, and time en route or estimated time of arrival.
    Answer (B) is incorrect. True airspeed is information provided on a flight plan. Answer (C) is incorrect. Fuel on board is information provided on a flight plan.

8. When telephoning a weather briefing facility for preflight weather information, pilots should state

    A. the full name and address of the formation commander.

    B. that they possess a current pilot certificate.

    C. whether they intend to fly VFR only.

Answer (C) is correct. *(AWS Sect 1)*
    DISCUSSION: When telephoning for a weather briefing, you should identify yourself as a pilot and state the route, destination, type of airplane, and whether you intend to fly VFR or IFR to permit the weather briefer to give you the most complete briefing.
    Answer (A) is incorrect. The full name and address of the formation commander is information provided on a flight plan. Answer (B) is incorrect. You should state that you are a pilot, not that you possess a current pilot certificate.

9. To update a previous weather briefing, a pilot should request

    A. an abbreviated briefing.

    B. a standard briefing.

    C. an outlook briefing.

Answer (A) is correct. *(AWS Sect 1)*
    DISCUSSION: An abbreviated briefing will be provided when the user requests information (1) to supplement mass disseminated data, (2) to update a previous briefing, or (3) to be limited to specific information.
    Answer (B) is incorrect. A standard briefing is a complete preflight briefing to include all (not update) information pertinent to a safe flight. Answer (C) is incorrect. An outlook briefing is for a flight at least 6 hr. in the future.

10. When requesting weather information for the following morning, a pilot should request

    A. an outlook briefing.

    B. a standard briefing.

    C. an abbreviated briefing.

Answer (A) is correct. *(AWS Sect 1)*
    DISCUSSION: An outlook briefing should be requested when the briefing is 6 or more hr. in advance of the proposed departure.
    Answer (B) is incorrect. A standard briefing should be requested if the proposed departure time is less than 6 hr. in the future and you have not received a previous briefing or have received information through mass dissemination media. Answer (C) is incorrect. An abbreviated briefing is requested to supplement mass disseminated data, to update a previous briefing, or to be limited to specific information.

8.2 Aviation Routine Weather Report (METAR)

11. For aviation purposes, ceiling is defined as the height above the Earth's surface of the

    A. lowest reported obscuration and the highest layer of clouds reported as overcast.

    B. lowest broken or overcast layer or vertical visibility into an obscuration.

    C. lowest layer of clouds reported as scattered, broken, or thin.

Answer (B) is correct. *(AWS Sect 3)*
    DISCUSSION: A ceiling layer is not designated in the METAR code. For aviation purposes, the ceiling is the lowest broken or overcast layer or vertical visibility into an obscuration.
    Answer (A) is incorrect. A ceiling is the lowest, not highest, broken or overcast layer or the vertical visibility into an obscuration, not the lowest obscuration. Answer (C) is incorrect. A ceiling is the lowest broken or overcast, not scattered, layer. Also, there is no provision for reporting thin layers in the METAR code.

12. (Refer to Figure 53 below.) What are the current conditions depicted for Chicago Midway Airport (KMDW)?

A.   Sky 700 feet overcast, visibility 1-1/2 SM, rain.

B.   Sky 7000 feet overcast, visibility 1-1/2 SM, heavy rain.

C.   Sky 700 feet overcast, visibility 11, occasionally 2 SM, with rain.

Answer (A) is correct.   *(AWS Sect 3)*
   DISCUSSION: At KMDW a special METAR (SPECI) was taken at 1856Z and reported wind 320° at 5 kt., visibility 1-1/2 SM in moderate rain, overcast clouds at 700 ft., temperature 17°C, dew point 16°C, altimeter 29.80 in. Hg, remarks follow, rain began at 35 min. past the hour.
   Answer (B) is incorrect. The intensity of the rain is moderate, not heavy. Heavy rain would be coded +RA. Answer (C) is incorrect. Visibility is 1-1/2 SM, not 11 SM with an occasional 2 SM.

METAR KINK 121845Z 11012G18KT 15SM SKC 25/17 A3000

METAR KBOI 121854Z 13004KT 30SM SCT150 17/6 A3015

METAR KLAX 121852Z 25004KT 6SM BR SCT007 SCT250 16/15 A2991

SPECI KMDW 121856Z 32005KT 1 1/2SM RA OVC007 17/16 A2980 RMK RAB35

SPECI KJFK 121853Z 18004KT 1/2SM FG R04/2200 OVC005 20/18 A3006

Figure 53. – Aviation Routine Weather Reports (METAR).

---

13. (Refer to Figure 53 above.) Which of the reporting stations have VFR weather?

A.   All.

B.   KINK, KBOI, and KJFK.

C.   KINK, KBOI, and KLAX.

Answer (C) is correct.   *(AWS Sect 3)*
   DISCUSSION: KINK is reporting visibility of 15 SM and sky clear (15SM SKC); KBOI is reporting visibility of 30 SM and a scattered cloud layer base at 15,000 ft. (30SM SCT150); and KLAX is reporting visibility of 6 SM in mist (fog) with a scattered cloud layer at 700 ft. and another one at 25,000 ft. (6SM BR SCT007 SCT250). All of these conditions are above VFR weather minimums of a 1,000-ft. ceiling and/or a 3-SM visibility.
   Answer (A) is incorrect. KMDW is reporting a visibility of 1-1/2 SM in rain and a ceiling of 700 ft. overcast (1 1/2SM RA OVC007), and KJFK is reporting a visibility of 1/2 SM in fog and a ceiling of 500 ft. overcast (1/2SM FG OVC005). Both of these are below VFR weather minimums of a 1,000-ft. ceiling and/or a 3-SM visibility. Answer (B) is incorrect. KJFK is reporting a visibility of 1/2 SM in fog and a ceiling of 500 ft. overcast (1/2SM FG OVC005), which is below the VFR weather minimums of a 1,000-ft. ceiling and/or a 3-SM visibility.

14. (Refer to Figure 53 above.) The wind direction and velocity at KJFK is from

A.   180° true at 4 knots.

B.   180° magnetic at 4 knots.

C.   040° true at 18 knots.

Answer (A) is correct.   *(AWS Sect 3)*
   DISCUSSION: The wind group at KJFK is coded as 18004KT. The first three digits are the direction the wind is blowing from referenced to true north. The next two digits are the speed in knots. Thus, the wind direction and speed at KJFK are 180° true at 4 kt.
   Answer (B) is incorrect. Wind direction is referenced to true, not magnetic, north. Answer (C) is incorrect. The wind direction is 180° true, not 040° true, at 4 kt., not 18 kt.

15. (Refer to Figure 53 above.) What are the wind conditions at Wink, Texas (KINK)?

A.   Calm.

B.   110° at 12 knots, gusts 18 knots.

C.   111° at 2 knots, gusts 18 knots.

Answer (B) is correct.   *(AWS Sect 3)*
   DISCUSSION: The wind group at KINK is coded as 11012G18KT. The first three digits are the direction the wind is blowing from referenced to true north. The next two digits are the wind speed in knots. If the wind is gusty, it is reported as a "G" after the speed followed by the highest (or peak) gust reported. Thus, the wind conditions at KINK are 110° true at 12 kt., peak gust at 18 kt.
   Answer (A) is incorrect. A calm wind would be reported as 00000KT, not 11012G18KT. Answer (C) is incorrect. The wind conditions at KINK are 110°, not 111°, at 12 kt., not 2 kt.

16. (Refer to Figure 53 on page 138.) The remarks section for KMDW has RAB35 listed. This entry means

    A. blowing mist has reduced the visibility to 1-1/2 SM.

    B. rain began at 1835Z.

    C. the barometer has risen .35" Hg.

Answer (B) is correct. *(AWS Sect 3)*
    DISCUSSION: In the remarks (RMK) section for KMDW, RAB35 means that rain began at 35 min. past the hour. Since the report was taken at 1856Z, rain began at 35 min. past the hour, or 1835Z.
    Answer (A) is incorrect. RAB35 means that rain began at 35 min. past the hour, not that blowing mist has reduced the visibility to 1-1/2 SM. Answer (C) is incorrect. RAB35 means that rain began at 35 min. past the hour, not that the barometer has risen .35 in. Hg.

8.3 SIGMETs and AIRMETs

17. SIGMETs are issued as a warning of weather conditions hazardous to which aircraft?

    A. Small aircraft only.

    B. Large aircraft only.

    C. All aircraft.

Answer (C) is correct. *(AWS Sect 6)*
    DISCUSSION: SIGMETs (significant meteorological information) warn of weather considered potentially hazardous to all aircraft. SIGMET advisories cover severe and extreme turbulence; severe icing; and widespread duststorms, sandstorms, or volcanic ash that reduce visibility to less than 3 SM.
    Answer (A) is incorrect. SIGMETs apply to all aircraft, not just to small aircraft. Answer (B) is incorrect. SIGMETs apply to all aircraft, not just to large aircraft.

18. AIRMETs are advisories of significant weather phenomena but of lower intensities than SIGMETs and are intended for dissemination to

    A. only IFR pilots.

    B. all pilots.

    C. only VFR pilots.

Answer (B) is correct. *(AWS Sect 6)*
    DISCUSSION: AIRMETs are advisories of significant weather phenomena that describe conditions at intensities lower than those requiring the issuance of SIGMETs. They are intended for dissemination to all pilots.
    Answer (A) is incorrect. AIRMETs are intended for dissemination to all pilots, not just IFR pilots. Answer (C) is incorrect. AIRMETs are intended for dissemination to all pilots, not just VFR pilots.

19. What information is contained in a CONVECTIVE SIGMET?

    A. Tornadoes, embedded thunderstorms, and hail 3/4 inch or greater in diameter.

    B. Severe icing, severe turbulence, or widespread dust storms lowering visibility to less than 3 miles.

    C. Surface winds greater than 40 knots or thunderstorms equal to or greater than video integrator processor (VIP) level 4.

Answer (A) is correct. *(AWS Sect 6)*
    DISCUSSION: Convective SIGMETs are issued for tornadoes, lines of thunderstorms, embedded thunderstorms of any intensity level, areas of thunderstorms greater than or equal to VIP level 4 with an area coverage of 40% or more, and hail 3/4 in. or greater.
    Answer (B) is incorrect. A SIGMET, not a convective SIGMET, is issued for severe icing, severe turbulence, or widespread duststorms lowering visibility to less than 3 SM. Answer (C) is incorrect. A severe thunderstorm having surface winds of 50 kt. or greater, not 40 kt., will be contained in a convective SIGMET.

20. What is indicated when a current CONVECTIVE SIGMET forecasts thunderstorms?

    A. Moderate thunderstorms covering 30 percent of the area.

    B. Moderate or severe turbulence.

    C. Thunderstorms obscured by massive cloud layers.

Answer (C) is correct. *(AWS Sect 6)*
    DISCUSSION: Convective SIGMETs are issued for tornadoes, lines of thunderstorms, embedded (i.e., obscured by massive cloud layers) thunderstorms of any intensity level, areas of thunderstorms greater than or equal to VIP level 4 with an area coverage of 40% or more, and hail 3/4 in. or greater.
    Answer (A) is incorrect. Thunderstorms would be very strong (VIP level 4) or greater, not moderate, and cover 40%, not 30%, of the area for a convective SIGMET. Answer (B) is incorrect. A convective SIGMET that is issued for thunderstorms implies severe or greater, not moderate, turbulence.

8.4 Pilot Weather Report (PIREP)

21. (Refer to Figure 4 below.) If the terrain elevation is 1,295 feet MSL, what is the height above ground level of the base of the ceiling?

    A. 505 feet AGL.

    B. 1,295 feet AGL.

    C. 6,586 feet AGL.

Answer (A) is correct. *(AWS Sect 3)*
DISCUSSION: Refer to the PIREP (identified by the letters UA) in Fig. 4. The base of the ceiling is reported in the sky cover (SK) section. The first layer is considered a ceiling (i.e., broken), and the base is 1,800 ft. MSL. The height above ground of the broken base is 505 ft. AGL (1,800 – 1,295).
Answer (B) is incorrect. The terrain elevation is 1,295 ft. MSL (not AGL). Answer (C) is incorrect. The ceiling base is 505 ft. (not 6,586 ft.) AGL.

22. (Refer to Figure 4 below.) The base and tops of the overcast layer reported by a pilot are

    A. 1,800 feet MSL and 5,500 feet MSL.

    B. 5,500 feet AGL and 7,200 feet MSL.

    C. 7,200 feet MSL and 8,900 feet MSL.

Answer (C) is correct. *(AWS Sect 3)*
DISCUSSION: Refer to the PIREP (identified by the letters UA) in Fig. 4. The base and tops of the overcast layer are reported in the sky conditions (identified by the letters SK). This pilot has reported the base of the overcast layer at 7,200 ft. and the top of the overcast layer at 8,900 ft. (072 OVC 089). All altitudes are stated in MSL unless otherwise noted. Thus, the base and top of the overcast layer are reported as 7,200 ft. MSL and 8,900 ft. MSL, respectively.
Answer (A) is incorrect. The base and top of the broken (BKN), not overcast (OVC), layer are 1,800 ft. MSL and 5,500 ft. MSL. Answer (B) is incorrect. The top of the broken (BKN) layer, not the base of the overcast (OVC) layer, is 5,500 ft. MSL (not AGL).

23. (Refer to Figure 4 below.) The wind and temperature at 12,000 feet MSL as reported by a pilot are

    A. 080° at 21 knots and –7°C.

    B. 090° at 21 MPH and –9°F.

    C. 090° at 21 knots and –9°C.

Answer (A) is correct. *(AWS Sect 3)*
DISCUSSION: Refer to the PIREP (identified by the letters UA) in Fig. 4. The wind is reported in the section identified by the letters WV and is presented in five or six digits. The temperature is reported in the section identified by the letters TA in °C, and if below 0°C, prefixed with an "M." The wind is reported as 080° at 21 kt. with a temperature of –7°C.
Answer (B) is incorrect. Speed is given in kt., not MPH. Temperature is given in degrees Celsius (not Fahrenheit) and is reported as –7, not –9. Answer (C) is incorrect. The wind is reported as being from 080°, not 090°, and the temperature is reported as –7°C, not –9°C.

24. (Refer to Figure 4 below.) The intensity of the turbulence reported at a specific altitude is

    A. moderate at 5,500 feet and at 7,200 feet.

    B. moderate from 5,500 feet to 7,200 feet.

    C. light from 5,500 feet to 7,200 feet.

Answer (C) is correct. *(AWS Sect 3)*
DISCUSSION: Refer to the PIREP (identified by the letters UA) in Fig. 4. The turbulence is reported in the section identified by the letters TB. In the PIREP, the turbulence is reported as light from 5,500 ft. to 7,200 ft. (TB LGT 055-072).
Answer (A) is incorrect. Turbulence is reported from 5,500 to 7,200 ft. MSL, not only at 5,500 ft. and 7,200 ft. Answer (B) is incorrect. Rime ice (not turbulence) is reported as light to moderate from 7,200 to 8,900 ft. MSL (not 5,500 to 7,200 ft. MSL).

UA/OV KOKC-KTUL/TM 1800/FL120/TP BE90//SK BKN018-TOP055/OVC072-
TOP089/CLR ABV/TA M7/WV 08021/TB LGT 055-072/IC LGT-MOD RIME 072-089

Figure 4. – Pilot Weather Report.

25. (Refer to Figure 4 above.) The intensity and type of icing reported by a pilot is

    A. light to moderate.

    B. light to moderate clear.

    C. light to moderate rime.

Answer (C) is correct. *(AWS Sect 3)*
DISCUSSION: Refer to the PIREP (identified by the letters UA) in Fig. 4. The icing conditions are reported following the letters IC. In this report, icing is reported as light to moderate rime (LGT-MDT RIME) between 7,200 to 8,900 ft. MSL (072-089).
Answer (A) is incorrect. The question asks not only for the intensity of the icing (light to moderate) but also the type, which is rime (RIME) ice. Answer (B) is incorrect. The type is rime (not clear) ice.

8.5 Aviation Area Forecast

26. To best determine general forecast weather conditions over several states, the pilot should refer to

    A. Aviation Area Forecasts.

    B. Weather Depiction Charts.

    C. Satellite Maps.

Answer (A) is correct. *(AWS Sect 7)*
    DISCUSSION: An aviation area forecast is a prediction of general weather conditions over an area consisting of several states or portions of states. It is used to obtain expected en route weather conditions and also to provide an insight to weather conditions that might be expected at airports where weather reports or forecasts are not issued.
    Answer (B) is incorrect. Weather depiction charts are compiled from METAR reports of observed, not forecast, areas. Answer (C) is incorrect. Satellite pictures (maps) are observed pictures used to determine the presence and types of clouds, not forecast conditions.

27. To determine the freezing level and areas of probable icing aloft, the pilot should refer to the

    A. Inflight Aviation Weather Advisories.

    B. Weather Depiction Chart.

    C. Area Forecast.

Answer (A) is correct. *(AWS Sect 7)*
    DISCUSSION: To determine the freezing level and areas of probable icing aloft, you should refer to the In-Flight Aviation Weather Advisories (AIRMET Zulu for icing and freezing level; AIRMET Tango for turbulence, strong winds/low-level wind shear; and AIRMET Sierra for IFR conditions and mountain obscuration). In-Flight Aviation Weather Advisories supplement the area forecast.
    Answer (B) is incorrect. The Weather Depiction Chart does not include any icing information. Answer (C) is incorrect. The Area Forecast alone contains no icing information; it must be supplemented by In-Flight Aviation Weather Advisories.

28. The section of the Area Forecast entitled "VFR CLDS/WX" contains a general description of

    A. cloudiness and weather significant to flight operations broken down by states or other geographical areas.

    B. forecast sky cover, cloud tops, visibility, and obstructions to vision along specific routes.

    C. weather advisories still in effect at the time of issue.

Answer (A) is correct. *(AWS Sect 7)*
    DISCUSSION: The VFR CLDS/WX is the clouds and weather plus categorical outlook section, which contains a summary of cloudiness and weather significant to VFR flight operations broken down by states or other geographical areas.
    Answer (B) is incorrect. A summary of forecast sky cover, cloud tops, visibility, and obstructions to vision along specific routes is contained in a TWEB route forecast. Answer (C) is incorrect. AIRMETs and SIGMETs are listed in in-flight weather advisories, not an FA.

29. From which primary source should information be obtained regarding expected weather at the estimated time of arrival if your destination has no Terminal Forecast?

    A. Low-Level Prognostic Chart.

    B. Weather Depiction Chart.

    C. Area Forecast.

Answer (C) is correct. *(AWS Sect 7)*
    DISCUSSION: An area forecast (FA) is a forecast of general weather conditions over an area the size of several states. It is used to determine forecast en route weather and to interpolate conditions at airports that do not have a TAF issued.
    Answer (A) is incorrect. A Low-Level Prognostic Chart forecasts weather conditions expected to exist 12 hr. and 24 hr. in the future for the entire U.S. Answer (B) is incorrect. A Weather Depiction Chart is a national map prepared from METAR reports that give a broad overview of observed weather conditions as of the time on the chart. It is not a forecast.

```
BOSC FA 241845
SYNOPSIS AND VFR CLDS/WX
SYNOPSIS VALID UNTIL 251300
CLDS/WX VALID UNTIL 250700...OTLK VALID 250700-251300
ME NH VT MA RI CT NY LO NJ PA OH LE WV MD DC DE VA AND CSTL WTRS

SEE AIRMET SIERRA FOR IFR CONDS AND MTN OBSCN.
TS IMPLY SEV OR GTR TURB SEV ICE LLWS AND IFR CONDS.
NON MSL HGTS DENOTED BY AGL OR CIG.

SYNOPSIS...19Z CDFNT ALG A 160NE ACK-ENE LN...CONTG AS A QSTNRY
FNT ALG AN END-50SW MSS LN. BY 13Z...CDFNT ALG A 140ESE ACK-HTO
LN...CONTG AS A QSTNRY FNT ALG A HTO-SYR-YYZ LN. TROF ACRS CNTRL
PA INTO NRN VA.  ...REYNOLDS...

OH LE
NRN HLF OH LE...SCT-BKN025 OVC045. CLDS LYRD 150. SCT SHRA. WDLY
     SCT TSRA. CB TOPS FL350. 23-01Z OVC020-030.  VIS 3SM BR. OCNL -
     RA. OTLK...IFR CIG BR FG.
SWRN QTR OH...BKN050-060 TOPS 100. OTLK...MVFR BR.
SERN QTR OH...SCT-BKN040 BKN070 TOPS 120. WDLY SCT -TSRA. 00Z
     SCT-BKN030 OVC050. WDLY SCT -TSRA. CB TOPS FL350. OTLK...VFR
     SHRA.

CHIC FA 241945
SYNOPSIS AND VFR CLDS/WX
SYNOPSIS VALID UNTIL 251400
CLDS/WX VALID UNTIL 250800...OTLK VALID 250800-251400
ND SD NE KS MN IA MO WI LM LS MI LH IL IN KY

SEE AIRMET SIERRA FOR IFR CONDS AND MTN OBSCN.
TS IMPLY SEV OR GTR TURB SEV ICE LLWS AND IFR CONDS.
NON MSL HGTS DENOTED BY AGL OR CIG.

SYNOPSIS...LOW PRES AREA 20Z CNTRD OVR SERN WI FCST MOV NEWD INTO
LH BY 12Z AND WKN. LOW PRES FCST DEEPEN OVR ERN CO DURG PD AND
MOV NR WRN KS BORDER BY 14Z. DVLPG CDFNT WL MOV EWD INTO S CNTRL
NE-CNTRL KS BY 14Z  ..SMITH..

UPR MI LS
WRN PTNS...AGL SCT030 SCT-BKN050. TOPS 080. 02-05Z BECMG CIG
     OVC010 VIS 3-5SM BR. OTLK...IFR CIG BR.
ERN PTNS...CIG BKN020 OVC040. OCNL VIS 3-5SM -RA BR. TOPS FL200.
     23Z CIG OVC010 VIS 3-5SM -RA BR. OTLK...IFR CIG BR.

LWR MI LM LH
CNTRL/NRN PTNS...CIG OVC010 VIS 3-5SM -RA BR. TOPS FL200.
     OTLK...IFR CIG BR.

SRN THIRD...CIG OVC015-025. SCT -SHRA. TOPS 150. 00-02Z BECMG CIG
     OVC010 VIS 3-5SM BR. TOPS 060. OTLK...IFR CIG BR.

IN
NRN HALF...CIG BKN035 BKN080. TOPS FL200. SCT -SHRA. 00Z CIG
     BKN-SCT040 BKN-SCT080. TOPS 120. 06Z AGL SCT-BKN030. TOPS 080.
     OCNL VIS 3-5SM BR. OTLK...MVFR CIG BR.
SRN HALF...AGL SCT050 SCT-BKN100. TOPS 120. 07Z AGL SCT 030
     SCT 100. OTLK...VFR.
```

Figure 6. – Aviation Area Forecast (FA).

30. (Refer to Figure 6 on page 142.) The Chicago FA forecast section is valid until the twenty-fifth at

A. 1945Z.

B. 0800Z.

C. 1400Z.

Answer (B) is correct. *(AWS Sect 7)*
    DISCUSSION: The Chicago area forecast (FA) is the second of two FAs depicted in Fig. 6. There is a note in the communication and product header section that says "CLDS/WX VALID UNTIL 250800," which means that the VFR clouds and weather section of the FA (the forecast section) is valid until 0800Z on the 25th.
    Answer (A) is incorrect. The note "CHIC FA 241945" in the communication and product header section means that the FA was issued at 1945Z on the 24th, not that it is valid until 1945Z on the 25th. Answer (C) is incorrect. The synopsis and categorical outlook (which are not considered to be forecasts), not the forecast section, are valid until 1400Z on the 25th, as indicated by the notes "SYNOPSIS VALID UNTIL 251400" and "OTLK VALID 250800-251400."

31. (Refer to Figure 6 on page 142.) What sky condition and visibility are forecast for upper Michigan in the eastern portions after 2300Z?

A. Ceiling 100 feet overcast and 3 to 5 statute miles visibility.

B. Ceiling 1,000 feet overcast and 3 to 5 nautical miles visibility.

C. Ceiling 1,000 feet overcast and 3 to 5 statute miles visibility.

Answer (C) is correct. *(AWS Sect 7)*
    DISCUSSION: The Chicago area forecast (FA) is the second of two FAs depicted in Fig. 6. It contains an entry labeled "UPR MI LS," meaning "upper Michigan and Lake Superior." Under this heading is a section labeled "ERN PTNS," meaning "eastern portions." The entry "23Z CIG OVC010 VIS 3-5SM -RA BR" means that from 2300Z, the forecast weather is an overcast ceiling at 1,000 ft. AGL, with 3 to 5 statute miles visibility in light rain and mist.
    Answer (A) is incorrect. The ceiling is forecast to be overcast at 1,000 ft., not 100 ft., which would be coded as "OVC001." Answer (B) is incorrect. Visibilities are always given in statute, not nautical, miles.

32. (Refer to Figure 6 on page 142.) What is the outlook for the southern half of Indiana after 0700Z?

A. VFR.

B. Scattered clouds at 3,000 feet AGL.

C. Scattered clouds at 10,000 feet.

Answer (A) is correct. *(AWS Sect 7)*
    DISCUSSION: The question asks for the outlook for the southern half of Indiana after 0700Z. Indiana (IN) is covered by the Chicago area forecast (FA), which is the second of two FAs depicted in Fig. 6. There is a heading under "IN" labeled "SRN HALF," meaning "southern half." Under this heading is an entry, "OTLK...VFR," meaning that the categorical outlook is for VFR conditions. Note in the communication and product header section that there is a note, "OTLK VALID 250800-251400," meaning that the categorical outlook is valid from 0800Z to 1400Z on the 25th. Therefore, the outlook does not become valid until 1 hour after 0700Z. You should still select "VFR" as the answer for this question because it specifically asks for the outlook after 0700Z, not at 0700Z; 0800Z is after 0700Z.
    Answer (B) is incorrect. Scattered clouds at 3,000 ft. AGL is a forecast sky condition from 0700Z to 0800Z (when the VFR CLDS/WX section becomes invalid); it is not an outlook, which would simply indicate whether VFR, MVFR, or IFR conditions are expected. Answer (C) is incorrect. Scattered clouds at 10,000 ft. is a forecast sky condition from 0700Z to 0800Z (when the VFR CLDS/WX section becomes invalid); it is not an outlook, which would simply indicate whether VFR, MVFR, or IFR conditions are expected.

33. (Refer to Figure 6 on page 142.) What sky condition and type obstructions to vision are forecast for upper Michigan in the western portions from 0200Z until 0500Z?

A. Ceiling becoming 1,000 feet overcast with visibility 3 to 5 statute miles in mist.

B. Ceiling becoming 100 feet overcast with visibility 3 to 5 statute miles in mist.

C. Ceiling becoming 1,000 feet overcast with visibility 3 to 5 nautical miles in mist.

Answer (A) is correct. *(AWS Sect 7)*
    DISCUSSION: The Chicago area forecast (FA) is the second of two FAs depicted in Fig. 6. It contains an entry labeled "UPR MI LS," meaning "upper Michigan and Lake Superior." Under this heading is a section labeled "WRN PTNS," meaning "western portions." The entry "02-05Z BECMG CIG OVC 010 VIS 3-5SM BR" means that, between 0200Z and 0500Z, the weather conditions are forecast to become an overcast ceiling at 1,000 ft., with 3-5 statute miles visibility in mist.
    Answer (B) is incorrect. The ceiling is forecast to become overcast at 1,000 ft., not 100 ft., which would be coded as "OVC001." Answer (C) is incorrect. Visibilities are always given in statute, not nautical, miles.

8.6 Terminal Aerodrome Forecast (TAF)

```
TAF

KMEM    121720Z 121818 20012KT 5SM HZ BKN030 PROB40 2022 1SM TSRA OVC008CB
        FM2200 33015G20KT P6SM BKN015 OVC025 PROB40 2202 3SM SHRA
        FM0200 35012KT OVC008 PROB40 0205 2SM -RASN BECMG 0608 02008KT BKN012
         BECMG 1012 00000KT 3SM BR SKC TEMPO 1214 1/2SM FG
        FM1600 VRB06KT P6SM SKC=


KOKC    051130Z 051212 14008KT 5SM BR BKN030 TEMPO 1316 1 1/2SM BR
        FM1600 18010KT P6SM SKC BECMG 2224 20013G20KT 4SM SHRA OVC020
        PROB40 0006 2SM TSRA OVC008CB BECMG 0608 21015KT P6SM SCT040=
```

Figure 5. – Terminal Aerodrome Forecasts (TAF).

34. (Refer to Figure 5 above.) In the TAF for KMEM, what does "SHRA" stand for?

A. Rain showers.

B. A shift in wind direction is expected.

C. A significant change in precipitation is possible.

Answer (A) is correct. *(AWS Sect 7)*
   DISCUSSION: SHRA is a coded group of forecast weather. SH is a descriptor that means showers. RA is a type of precipitation that means rain. Thus, SHRA means rain showers.
   Answer (B) is incorrect. SHRA means rain showers, not that a shift in wind direction is expected. A change in wind direction would be reflected by a forecast wind. Answer (C) is incorrect. SHRA means rain showers, not that a significant change in precipitation is possible.

35. (Refer to Figure 5 above.) During the time period from 0600Z to 0800Z, what visibility is forecast for KOKC?

A. Greater than 6 statute miles.

B. Possibly 6 statute miles.

C. Not forecasted.

Answer (A) is correct. *(AWS Sect 7)*
   DISCUSSION: At KOKC, between 0600Z and 0800Z, conditions are forecast to become wind 210 at 15 kt., visibility greater than 6 SM (P6SM), scattered clouds at 4,000 ft. with conditions continuing until the end of the forecast (1200Z).
   Answer (B) is incorrect. Between 0600Z and 0800Z, the visibility is forecast to be greater than, not possibly, 6 SM. Answer (C) is incorrect. Between 0600Z and 0800Z, the visibility is forecast to be greater than 6 statute miles (P6SM).

36. (Refer to Figure 5 above.) In the TAF from KOKC, the clear sky becomes

A. overcast at 2,000 feet during the forecast period between 2200Z and 2400Z.

B. overcast at 200 feet with a 40% probability of becoming overcast at 600 feet during the forecast period between 2200Z and 2400Z.

C. overcast at 200 feet with the probability of becoming overcast at 400 feet during the forecast period between 2200Z and 2400Z.

Answer (A) is correct. *(AWS Sect 7)*
   DISCUSSION: In the TAF for KOKC, from 2200Z to 2400Z, the conditions are forecast to gradually become wind 200° at 13 kt. with gusts to 20 kt., visibility 4 SM in moderate rain showers, overcast clouds at 2,000 ft. Between the hours of 0000Z and 0600Z, a chance (40%) exists of visibility 2 SM in thunderstorm with moderate rain, and 800 ft. overcast, cumulonimbus clouds.
   Answer (B) is incorrect. Between 2200Z and 2400Z, the coded sky condition of OVC020 means overcast clouds at 2,000 ft., not 200 ft. Answer (C) is incorrect. Between 2200Z and 2400Z, the coded sky condition of OVC020 means overcast clouds at 2,000 ft., not 200 ft.

37. (Refer to Figure 5 above.) What is the valid period for the TAF for KMEM?

A. 1200Z to 1200Z.

B. 1200Z to 1800Z.

C. 1800Z to 1800Z.

Answer (C) is correct. *(AWS Sect 7)*
   DISCUSSION: The valid period of a TAF follows the four-letter location identifier and the six-digit issuance date/time. The valid period group is a two-digit date followed by the two-digit beginning hour and the two-digit ending hour. The valid period of the TAF for KMEM is 121818, which means the forecast is valid from the 12th day at 1800Z until the 13th at 1800Z.
   Answer (A) is incorrect. The valid period of the TAF for KOKC, not KMEM, is from 1200Z to 1200Z. Answer (B) is incorrect. The valid period of the TAF for KMEM is from the 12th day, not 1200Z, at 1800Z until the 13th at 1800Z.

38. (Refer to Figure 5 on page 144.) Between 1000Z and 1200Z the visibility at KMEM is forecast to be?

    A. 1/2 statute mile.

    B. 3 statute miles.

    C. 6 statute miles.

Answer (B) is correct. *(AWS Sect 7)*
    DISCUSSION: Between 1000Z and 1200Z, the conditions at KMEM are forecast to gradually become wind calm, visibility 3 SM in mist, sky clear with temporary (occasional) visibility 1/2 SM in fog between 1200Z and 1400Z. Conditions are expected to continue until 1600Z.
    Answer (A) is incorrect. Between the hours of 1200Z and 1400Z, not between 1000Z and 1200Z, the forecast is for temporary (occasional) visibility of 1/2 SM in fog. Answer (C) is incorrect. Between 1000Z and 1200Z, the forecast visibility for KMEM is 3 SM, not 6 SM.

39. (Refer to Figure 5 on page 144.) What is the forecast wind for KMEM from 1600Z until the end of the forecast?

    A. No significant wind.

    B. Variable in direction at 6 knots.

    C. Variable in direction at 4 knots.

Answer (B) is correct. *(AWS Sect 7)*
    DISCUSSION: The forecast for KMEM from 1600Z until the end of the forecast (1800Z) is wind direction variable at 6 kt. (VRB06KT), visibility greater than 6 SM, and sky clear.
    Answer (A) is incorrect. The wind is forecast to be variable in direction at 6 kt. Answer (C) is incorrect. The wind is forecast to be variable in direction at 6 kt., not 4 kt. KMEM of 020° at 8 kt. is for 0600Z until 0800Z, not from 1600Z until the end of the forecast.

40. (Refer to Figure 5 on page 144.) In the TAF from KOKC, the "FM (FROM) Group" is forecast for the hours from 1600Z to 2200Z with the wind from

    A. 160° at 10 knots.

    B. 180° at 10 knots.

    C. 180° at 10 knots, becoming 200° at 13 knots.

Answer (B) is correct. *(AWS Sect 7)*
    DISCUSSION: The **FM** group states that, from 1600Z until 2200Z (time of next change group), the forecast wind is 180° at 10 kt.
    Answer (A) is incorrect. The wind is from 180°, not 160°, at 10 kt. Answer (C) is incorrect. The **BECMG** (becoming) group is a change group and is not part of the **FM** forecast group. The wind will gradually become 200° at 13 kt. with gusts to 20 kt. between 2200Z and 2400Z.

41. (Refer to Figure 5 on page 144.) The only cloud type forecast in TAF reports is

    A. Nimbostratus.

    B. Cumulonimbus.

    C. Scattered cumulus.

Answer (B) is correct. *(AWS Sect 7)*
    DISCUSSION: Cumulonimbus clouds are the only cloud type forecast in TAFs. If cumulonimbus clouds are expected at the airport, the contraction **CB** is appended to the cloud layer, which represents the base of the cumulonimbus cloud(s).
    Answer (A) is incorrect. The only cloud type forecast in TAFs is cumulonimbus, not nimbostratus, clouds. Answer (C) is incorrect. The only cloud type forecast in TAFs is cumulonimbus, not scattered cumulus, clouds.

8.7 Weather Depiction Charts

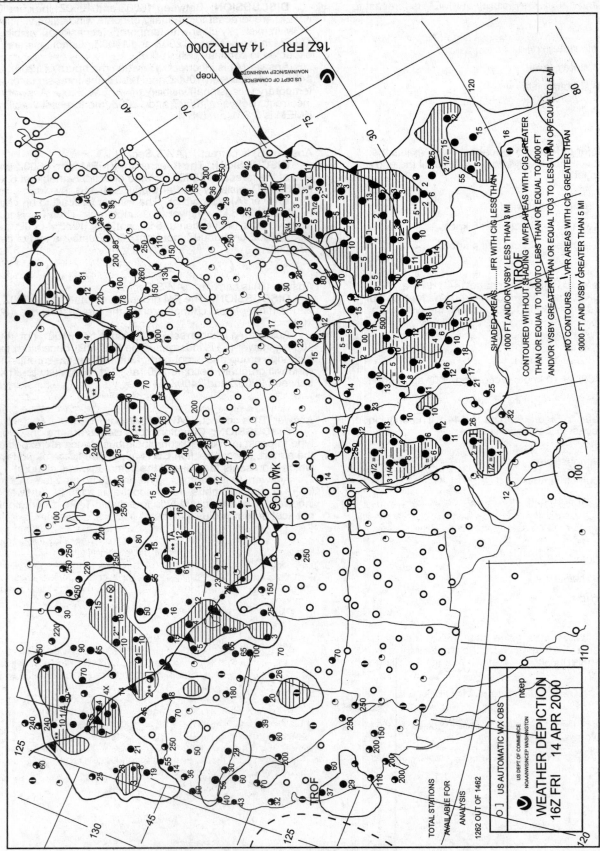

Figure 12. – Weather Depiction Chart.

42. (Refer to Figure 12 on page 146.) Of what value is the Weather Depiction Chart to the pilot?

A. For determining general weather conditions on which to base flight planning.

B. For a forecast of cloud coverage, visibilities, and frontal activity.

C. For determining frontal trends and air mass characteristics.

Answer (A) is correct. *(AWS Sect 5)*
 DISCUSSION: The weather depiction chart is prepared from surface aviation weather reports giving a quick picture of weather conditions as of the time stated on the chart. Thus, it presents general weather conditions on which to base flight planning.
 Answer (B) is incorrect. A significant weather prognostic chart can provide a forecast of cloud coverage, visibilities, and frontal activity. A weather depiction chart shows actual, not forecast, conditions. Answer (C) is incorrect. A composite moisture stability chart would be used to determine the characteristics of an air mass.

43. (Refer to Figure 12 on page 146.) The IFR weather in northern Texas is due to

A. intermittent rain.

B. low ceilings.

C. dust devils.

Answer (B) is correct. *(AWS Sect 5)*
 DISCUSSION: Refer to the Weather Depiction Chart in Fig. 12. The shaded area around northern Texas and central Oklahoma indicates that IFR conditions exist. The symbols "3=⚇" and "3=⚉" mean that the visibility is 3 SM in fog (3=) and the sky is overcast at 600 ft. (⚇) to 800 ft. (⚉) AGL. Thus, low ceilings between 600-800 ft. are the source of IFR weather conditions.
 Answer (A) is incorrect. A solid round dot (•) indicates intermittent rain. Answer (C) is incorrect. The symbol ⚡ indicates dust devils, which are small vigorous whirlwinds, usually of short duration, made visible by dust, sand, or debris picked up from the ground.

44. (Refer to Figure 12 on page 146.) What weather phenomenon is causing IFR conditions in central Oklahoma?

A. Low visibility only.

B. Low ceilings and visibility.

C. Heavy rain showers.

Answer (B) is correct. *(AWS Sect 5)*
 DISCUSSION: Refer to the Weather Depiction Chart in Fig. 12. In central Oklahoma, the IFR conditions are caused by low ceilings and visibility. In the shaded area over central Oklahoma and northern Texas, there are six darkened circles with numbers ranging from one to eight below them, signifying overcast skies with ceilings at 100 to 800 ft. The circles also have numbers ranging from 1/2 to 3-1/4 beside them, signifying visibilities between 3/4 and 3 statute miles. The IFR conditions are therefore due to low ceilings and visibility.
 Answer (A) is incorrect. There are also low ceilings in the area from 100 to 800 ft. Answer (C) is incorrect. Heavy rain showers are shown by the symbol ▼.

45. (Refer to Figure 12 on page 146.) What is the status of the front that extends from Nebraska through the upper peninsula of Michigan?

A. Cold.

B. Stationary.

C. Warm.

Answer (A) is correct. *(AWS Sect 5)*
 DISCUSSION: Refer to the Weather Depiction Chart in Fig. 12. The front that extends from Nebraska through the upper peninsula of Michigan is a cold front, as shown by the pointed scallops on the southern side of the frontal line.
 Answer (B) is incorrect. A stationary front has pointed scallops on one side of the frontal line and rounded scallops on the other. Answer (C) is incorrect. A warm front has rounded scallops, not pointed scallops.

46. (Refer to Figure 12 on page 146.) According to the Weather Depiction Chart, the weather for a flight from southern Michigan to north Indiana is ceilings

A. 1,000 to 3,000 feet and/or visibility 3 to 5 miles.

B. less than 1,000 feet and/or visibility less than 3 miles.

C. greater than 3,000 feet and visibility greater than 5 miles.

Answer (C) is correct. *(AWS Sect 5)*
 DISCUSSION: Refer to the Weather Depiction Chart in Fig. 12. The weather from southern Michigan to north Indiana is shown by the lack of shading or contours to have ceilings greater than 3,000 ft. and visibilities greater than 5 miles.
 Answer (A) is incorrect. On Weather Depiction Charts, 1,000-to 3,000-foot ceilings and/or visibilities between 3 and 5 statute miles (MVFR conditions) are indicated by an unshaded area surrounded by a contour. Answer (B) is incorrect. Ceilings less than 1,000 ft. and/or visibilities less than 3 statute miles (IFR conditions) are indicated on Weather Depiction Charts by a shaded area surrounded by a contour.

47. (Refer to Figure 12 on page 146.) The marginal weather in central Kentucky is due to low

A. ceiling.

B. ceiling and visibility.

C. visibility.

Answer (A) is correct. *(AWS Sect 5)*
DISCUSSION: Refer to the Weather Depiction Chart in Fig. 12. The MVFR weather in central Kentucky is indicated by the contour line without shading. The station symbol indicates an overcast ceiling at 3,000 ft. MVFR is ceiling 1,000 ft. to 3,000 ft. and/or visibility 3 to 5 SM. Thus, the marginal weather is due to a low ceiling.
Answer (B) is incorrect. The marginal weather is caused by low ceilings only. Answer (C) is incorrect. The visibility is greater than 6 SM (indicated by the lack of a report). Therefore, the visibility is not a cause of the marginal conditions.

8.8 Radar Summary Charts and Radar Weather Reports

48. (Refer to Figure 13 on page 149.) (Refer to Area B.) What is the top for precipitation of the radar return?

A. 24,000 feet AGL.

B. 2,400 feet MSL.

C. 24,000 feet MSL.

Answer (C) is correct. *(AWS Sect 5)*
DISCUSSION: Refer to the Radar Summary Chart in Fig. 13. The radar return at B (northern Nevada) has a "240" with a line under it. This means the maximum top of the precipitation is 24,000 ft. MSL.
Answer (A) is incorrect. The height of precipitation returns is given in MSL, not AGL. Answer (B) is incorrect. The height of precipitation returns is given in hundreds, not tens, of feet MSL. The figure "240" means 24,000, not 2,400.

49. What does the heavy dashed line that forms a large rectangular box on a radar summary chart refer to?

A. Areas of heavy rain.

B. Severe weather watch area.

C. Areas of hail 1/4 inch in diameter.

Answer (B) is correct. *(AWS Sect 5)*
DISCUSSION: On a Radar Summary Chart, severe weather watch areas are outlined by heavy dashed lines.
Answer (A) is incorrect. Areas of heavy rain would be labeled with "R" for rain and "+" for heavy or increasing in intensity. Answer (C) is incorrect. Hail is denoted by a box with "hail" printed inside (HAIL).

50. (Refer to Figure 13 on page 149.) (Refer to area B.) What type of weather is occurring in the radar return?

A. Continuous rain.

B. Light to moderate rain.

C. Rain showers increasing in intensity.

Answer (B) is correct. *(AWS Sect 5)*
DISCUSSION: The intensity and type of the precipitation are indicated by the contour lines and symbols adjacent to the precipitation areas depicted on the radar summary chart. Next to area B, the intensity of the precipitation is light to moderate (single contour line), and the type is rain (R).
Answer (A) is incorrect. The term "continuous rain" applies to prognostic charts, not radar summary charts. Answer (C) is incorrect. The type of precipitation is rain (R), not showers (RW). Also, the intensity trend (increasing or weakening) is no longer coded on either the radar summary chart or the radar weather report (SD).

51. (Refer to Figure 13 on page 149.) (Refer to area D.) What is the direction and speed of movement of the cell?

A. North at 17 knots.

B. South at 17 knots.

C. North at 17 MPH.

Answer (A) is correct. *(AWS Sect 5)*
DISCUSSION: Refer to the Radar Summary Chart in Fig. 13. The radar return at D (Virginia) has an arrow pointing north with "17" at the point. The movement is thus north at 17 kt.
Answer (B) is incorrect. The arrow above the cell at point D points north, not south. This arrow indicates the direction of the cell's movement. Answer (C) is incorrect. The speed of cell movement is given in knots, not MPH.

52. (Refer to Figure 13 on page 149.) (Refer to area E.) The top of the precipitation of the cell is

A. 16,000 feet AGL.

B. 25,000 feet MSL.

C. 16,000 feet MSL.

Answer (C) is correct. *(AWS Sect 5)*
DISCUSSION: Refer to the Radar Summary Chart in Fig. 13. The cell 1/2 in. below point E (Virginia/North Carolina) has a "160" with a line under it. This means the maximum top of the precipitation is 16,000 ft. MSL.
Answer (A) is incorrect. The height of precipitation returns is given in MSL, not AGL. Answer (B) is incorrect. The "250" with a line under it (indicating 25,000 ft. MSL) extends from the large cell covering Florida, Alabama, and Georgia. This cell is associated with area G, not area E.

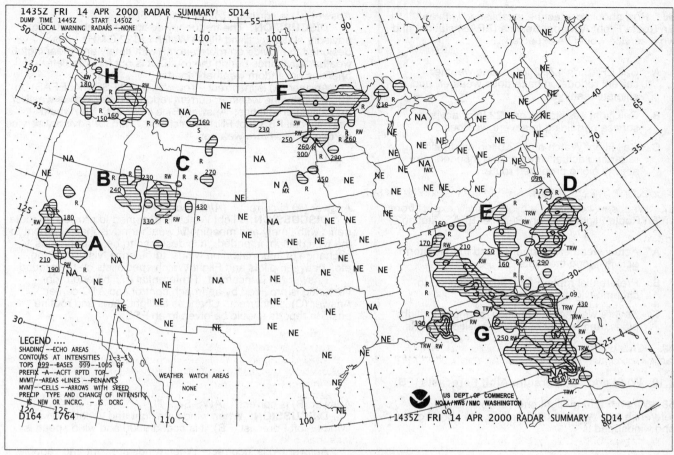

Figure 13. – Radar Summary Chart.

53. What information is provided by the Radar Summary Chart that is not shown on other weather charts?

A. Lines and cells of hazardous thunderstorms.

B. Ceilings and precipitation between reporting stations.

C. Types of clouds between reporting stations.

Answer (A) is correct. *(AWS Sect 5)*
DISCUSSION: The Radar Summary Charts show lines of thunderstorms and hazardous cells that are not shown on other weather charts.
Answer (B) is incorrect. Weather radar primarily detects particles of precipitation size within a cloud or falling from a cloud; it does not detect clouds and fog. Thus, it cannot determine ceilings. Answer (C) is incorrect. The Radar Summary Chart can provide the type of precipitation (not clouds) between reporting stations.

54. Radar weather reports are of special interest to pilots because they indicate

A. large areas of low ceilings and fog.

B. location of precipitation along with type, intensity, and cell movement of precipitation.

C. location of precipitation along with type, intensity, and trend.

Answer (B) is correct. *(AWS Sect 3)*
DISCUSSION: Radar weather reports are of special interest to pilots because they report the location of precipitation along with type, intensity, and cell movement.
Answer (A) is incorrect. Weather radar cannot detect clouds or fog, only precipitation size particles. Answer (C) is incorrect. Radar weather reports no longer include trend information.

8.9 En Route Flight Advisory Service (EFAS)

55. Below FL180, en route weather advisories should be obtained from an FSS on

A. 122.0 MHz.

B. 122.1 MHz.

C. 123.6 MHz.

Answer (A) is correct. *(AIM Para 7-1-5)*
DISCUSSION: Below FL 180, to receive weather advisories along your route, you should contact Flight Watch on 122.0 MHz.
Answer (B) is incorrect. The pilot-to-FSS frequency used on duplex remote communication facilities is 122.1 MHz.
Answer (C) is incorrect. The common FSS frequency for airport advisory service is 123.6 MHz.

56. How should contact be established with an En Route Flight Advisory Service (EFAS) station, and what service would be expected?

A. Call EFAS on 122.2 for routine weather, current reports on hazardous weather, and altimeter settings.

B. Call flight assistance on 122.5 for advisory service pertaining to severe weather.

C. Call Flight Watch on 122.0 for information regarding actual weather and thunderstorm activity along proposed route.

Answer (C) is correct. *(AIM Para 7-1-5)*
DISCUSSION: The frequency designed for en route flight advisory stations calling Flight Watch is 122.0 MHz. It is designed to provide en route aircraft with timely and meaningful weather advisories during the route. It is not for complete briefings or random weather reports.
    Answer (A) is incorrect. You would call FSS (not EFAS) on 122.2 for routine weather, current reports on hazardous weather, and altimeter settings. Answer (B) is incorrect. You would possibly call FSS (not Flight Watch) on 122.5 for advisory service pertaining to severe weather.

57. What service should a pilot normally expect from an En Route Flight Advisory Service (EFAS) station?

A. Actual weather information and thunderstorm activity along the route.

B. Preferential routing and radar vectoring to circumnavigate severe weather.

C. Severe weather information, changes to flight plans, and receipt of routine position reports.

Answer (A) is correct. *(AIM Para 7-1-5)*
DISCUSSION: Flight Watch is designed to provide en route traffic with timely and meaningful weather advisories pertinent to the type of flight intended. It is designed to be a continuous exchange of information on winds, turbulence, visibility, icing, etc., between pilots and Flight Watch specialists on the ground.
    Answer (B) is incorrect. Preferential routing and radar vectoring is provided by approach control and ATC center. Answer (C) is incorrect. Changes to flight plans and routine position reports should be given to an FSS.

8.10 Wind and Temperature Aloft Forecasts (FB)

58. When the term "light and variable" is used in reference to a Winds Aloft Forecast, the coded group and windspeed is

A. 0000 and less than 7 knots.

B. 9900 and less than 5 knots.

C. 9999 and less than 10 knots.

Answer (B) is correct. *(AWS Sect 7)*
DISCUSSION: When winds are light and variable on a Winds Aloft Forecast (FB), it is coded 9900 and wind speed is less than 5 kt.
    Answer (A) is incorrect. When winds are light and variable, it is coded 9900 (not 0000), and the wind speed is less than 5 (not 7) kt. Answer (C) is incorrect. When winds are light and variable, it is coded 9900 (not 9999), and the wind speed is less than 5 (not 10) kt.

59. (Refer to Figure 7 on page 151.) What wind is forecast for STL at 9,000 feet?

A. 230° magnetic at 25 knots.

B. 230° true at 32 knots.

C. 230° true at 25 knots.

Answer (B) is correct. *(AWS Sect 7)*
DISCUSSION: Refer to the FB forecast in Fig. 7. Locate STL on the left side of the chart and move right to the 9,000-ft. column. The coded wind forecast (first four digits) is 2332. Thus, the forecast wind is 230° true at 32 kt.
    Answer (A) is incorrect. Wind direction is forecast in true (not magnetic) direction. Wind forecast of 230° true at 25 kt. is for STL at 6,000 ft., not 9,000 ft. Answer (C) is incorrect. The wind forecast for STL at 6,000 ft., not 9,000 ft, is 230° at 25 kt.

60. (Refer to Figure 7 on page 151.) What wind is forecast for STL at 12,000 feet?

A. 230° true at 39 knots.

B. 230° true at 56 knots.

C. 230° magnetic at 56 knots.

Answer (A) is correct. *(AWS Sect 7)*
DISCUSSION: Refer to the FB forecast in Fig. 7. Locate STL and move right to the 12,000-ft. column. The wind forecast (first four digits) is coded as 2339, which means the wind is 230° true at 39 kt.
    Answer (B) is incorrect. The forecast wind direction and speed for 18,000 ft., not 12,000 ft, is 230° true at 56 kt. Answer (C) is incorrect. The first two digits are direction referenced to true (not magnetic) north. Thus, 2356 is 230° true (not magnetic) at 56 kt., which is the forecast wind direction and speed for 18,000 ft., not 12,000 ft.

```
FD WBC 151745
DATA BASED ON 151200Z
VALID 1600Z FOR USE 1800-0300Z.  TEMPS NEG ABV 24000
```

FT	3000	6000	9000	12000	18000	24000	30000	34000	39000
ALS			2420	2635–08	2535–18	2444–30	245945	246755	246862
AMA		2714	2725+00	2625–04	2531–15	2542–27	265842	256352	256762
DEN			2321–04	2532–08	2434–19	2441–31	235347	236056	236262
HLC		1707–01	2113–03	2219–07	2330–17	2435–30	244145	244854	245561
MKC	0507	2006+03	2215–01	2322–06	2338–17	2348–29	236143	237252	238160
STL	2113	2325+07	2332+02	2339–04	2356–16	2373–27	239440	730649	731960

Figure 7. – Winds and Temperatures Aloft Forecast (FB).

61. (Refer to Figure 7 above.) Determine the wind and temperature aloft forecast for DEN at 9,000 feet.

A.   230° magnetic at 53 knots, temperature 47°C.

B.   230° true at 53 knots, temperature –47°C.

C.   230° true at 21 knots, temperature –4°C.

Answer (C) is correct. *(AWS Sect 7)*
   DISCUSSION: Refer to the FB forecast in Fig. 7. Locate DEN on the left side of the chart and move to the right to the 9,000-ft. column. The wind and temperature forecast is coded as 2321-04. The forecast is decoded as 230° true at 21 kt., temperature –4°C.
   Answer (A) is incorrect. The 23 means 230° true (not magnetic), and the temperature is –4°C, not 47°C. Answer (B) is incorrect. The temperature is –4°C, not –47°C, which is the temperature for DEN at 30,000 ft., not 9,000 ft.

62. (Refer to Figure 7 above.) What wind is forecast for STL at 12,000 feet?

A.   230° magnetic at 39 knots.

B.   230° true at 39 knots.

C.   230° true at 106 knots.

Answer (B) is correct. *(AWS Sect 7)*
   DISCUSSION: Refer to the FB forecast in Fig. 7. Locate STL on the left side of the chart, and move to the right to the 12,000 ft. column. The wind forecast (first four digits) is coded as 2339. The forecast is decoded as 230° true at 39 kt.
   Answer (A) is incorrect. The wind is from 230° true, not magnetic. Answer (C) is incorrect. The forecast wind speed and direction for 34,000 ft., not 12,000 ft. (coded as 7306), is 230° true at 106 kt.

63. (Refer to Figure 7 above.) Determine the wind and temperature aloft forecast for MKC at 6,000 ft.

A.   050° true at 7 knots, temperature missing.

B.   200° magnetic at 6 knots, temperature +3°C.

C.   200° true at 6 knots, temperature +3°C.

Answer (C) is correct. *(AWS Sect 7)*
   DISCUSSION: Refer to the FB forecast in Fig. 7. Locate MKC on the left side of the chart and move to the right to the 6,000-ft. column. The wind and temperature forecast is coded as 2006+03, which translates as the forecast wind at 200° true at 6 kt. and a temperature of 3°C.
   Answer (A) is incorrect. The forecast for MKC at 3,000 ft., not 6,000 ft, is 050° true at 7 kt. with no forecast temperature. Answer (B) is incorrect. Wind direction is given in true degrees, not magnetic degrees.

64. What values are used for Winds Aloft Forecasts?

A.   Magnetic direction and knots.

B.   Magnetic direction and miles per hour.

C.   True direction and knots.

Answer (C) is correct. *(AWS Sect 7)*
   DISCUSSION: For Winds Aloft Forecasts, the wind direction is given in true direction, and the wind speed is in knots.
   Answer (A) is incorrect. ATC (not Winds Aloft Forecasts) will provide winds in magnetic direction and kt. Answer (B) is incorrect. Winds Aloft Forecast will provide winds based on true (not magnetic) direction and speed in kt. (not MPH).

END OF STUDY UNIT

STUDY UNIT NINE
SECTIONAL CHARTS AND AIRSPACE

(5 pages of outline)

This study unit contains outlines of major concepts tested, sample test questions and answers regarding sectional charts and airspace, and an explanation of each answer. The table of contents above lists each subunit within this study unit, the number of questions pertaining to that particular subunit, and the pages on which the outlines and questions begin, respectively.

Many of the questions in this study unit ask about the sectional (aeronautical) charts, which appear as Legend 1 and as Figures 44 through 46, 56 through 61, 66, 69, 70, and 73. The acronym ACL is the question source code used to refer to this aeronautical chart legend. To produce the legend and these charts economically, we have put them on pages 171 through 186, along with other color figures referred to in this book. As you will need to turn to these pages frequently, mark them with "dog ears"; i.e., fold their corners or paper-clip them. Also, the first subunit, "Airspace and Altitudes," is long (40 questions) and covers a number of diverse topics regarding interpretation of sectional charts. Be prepared.

CAUTION: Recall that the **sole purpose** of this book is to expedite your passing the FAA pilot knowledge test for the sport pilot certificate. Accordingly, all extraneous material (i.e., topics or regulations not directly tested on the FAA pilot knowledge test) is omitted, even though much more information and knowledge are necessary to fly safely. This additional material is presented in the *Pilot Handbook* and *Sport Pilot Flight Maneuvers and Practical Test Prep*, available from Gleim Publications, Inc. See the order form on page 327.

9.1 AIRSPACE AND ALTITUDES

1. Class G airspace is all navigable airspace that is not classified as Class A, Class B, Class C, Class D, or Class E airspace.

2. Class E airspace is controlled airspace that is not defined as Class A, Class B, Class C, or Class D.

    a. The lower limits of Class E airspace are specified by markings on terminal and sectional charts.

    1) The surface in areas marked by segmented (dashed) magenta lines.
    2) 700 ft. AGL in areas marked by shaded magenta lines.
    3) 1,200 ft. AGL in areas marked by shaded blue lines.
    4) 1,200 ft. AGL in areas defined as Federal Airways. Blue lines between VOR facilities labeled with the letter "V" followed by numbers, e.g., V-120.
    5) A specific altitude depicted in En Route Domestic Areas denoted by blue "zipper" marks.

    b. If not defined, the floor of Class E airspace begins at 14,500 ft. MSL or 1,500 ft. AGL, whichever is higher.

    c. Class E airspace extends up to, but does not include, 18,000 ft. MSL.

Cloud Clearance and Visibility Required for VFR

Airspace	Flight Visibility	Distance from Clouds
Class A	Not Applicable	Not applicable
Class B	3 SM	Clear of Clouds
Class C	3 SM	500 ft. below 1,000 ft. above 2,000 ft. horiz.
Class D	3 SM	500 ft. below 1,000 ft. above 2,000 ft. horiz.
Class E		
Less than 10,000 ft. MSL	3 SM	500 ft. below 1,000 ft. above 2,000 ft. horiz.
At or above 10,000 ft. MSL	5 SM	1,000 ft. below 1,000 ft. above 1 SM horiz.

Airspace	Flight Visibility	Distance from Clouds
Class G:		
1,200 ft. or less above the surface (regardless of MSL altitude)		
Day	1 SM	Clear of clouds
Night	3 SM	500 ft. below 1,000 ft. above 2,000 ft. horiz.
More than 1,200 ft. above the surface but less than 10,000 ft. MSL		
Day	1 SM	500 ft. below 1,000 ft. above 2,000 ft. horiz.
Night	3 SM	500 ft. below 1,000 ft. above 2,000 ft. horiz.
More than 1,200 ft. above the surface and at or above 10,000 ft. MSL	5 SM	1,000 ft. below 1,000 ft. above 1 SM horiz.

3. Class D airspace is an area of controlled airspace surrounding an airport with an operating control tower. It is not associated with Class B or Class C airspace areas.

    a. Class D airspace is depicted by a segmented (dashed) blue line on sectional charts.

    b. The height of the Class D airspace is shown in a broken box and is expressed in hundreds of feet MSL.

        1) EXAMPLE: [29] means the height of the Class D airspace is 2,900 ft. MSL.

4. Class C airspace areas are depicted by solid magenta lines on sectional charts.

    a. The surface area (formerly called the inner circle) of Class C airspace, the area within 5 NM from the primary airport, begins at the surface and goes up to 4,000 ft. above the airport. The shelf area (formerly called the outer circle) of a Class C airspace area, the area from 5 NM to 10 NM from the primary airport, begins at about 1,200 ft. AGL and extends to the same altitude as the surface area.

    b. The vertical limits are indicated on the chart within each circle and are expressed in hundreds of feet MSL. The top limit is shown above a straight line and the bottom limit beneath the line.

        1) EXAMPLE: See Fig. 69 on page 182. At the bottom right (area 3) is the Savannah Class C airspace.

            a) $\frac{41}{SFC}$ in the surface area means Class C airspace extends from the surface (SFC) to 4,100 ft. MSL.

            b) $\frac{41}{13}$ in the shelf area means Class C airspace extends from 1,300 ft. MSL to 4,100 ft. MSL.

    c.   The minimum equipment needed to operate in Class C or Class B airspace includes

        1)   A 4096-code transponder
        2)   Mode C (altitude encoding) capability
        3)   Two-way radio communication capability

    d.   You must establish and maintain two-way radio communication with ATC prior to entering Class C airspace.

5.   When overlapping airspace designations apply to the same airspace, the more restrictive designation applies. Remember that Class A airspace is the most restrictive, and Class G is the least restrictive.

    a.   EXAMPLE: The primary airport of a Class D airspace area underlies Class B airspace. The ceiling of the Class D airspace is 3,100 ft. MSL, and the floor of the Class B airspace is 3,000 ft. MSL. Since Class B is more restrictive than Class D, the overlapping airspace between 3,000 ft. and 3,100 ft. MSL is considered to be Class B airspace.

6.   Special use airspace includes prohibited, restricted, warning, military operations, alert, national security, and controlled firing areas.

    a.   **Restricted areas** denote the existence of unusual, often invisible, hazards to aircraft, such as military firing, aerial gunnery, or guided missiles.

    b.   **Warning areas** contain activity that may be hazardous to nonparticipating aircraft, e.g., aerial gunnery, guided missiles, etc.

        1)   Warning areas extend from 3 NM outward from the U.S. coast.
        2)   A warning area may be located over domestic air, international waters, or both.

    c.   **Military operations areas (MOAs)** denote areas of military training activities.

        1)   Pilots should contact any FSS within 100 NM to determine the MOA hours of operation.
        2)   If it is active, the pilot should contact the controlling agency prior to entering the MOA for traffic advisories because of high-density military training.
        3)   When operating in an MOA, exercise extreme caution when military activity is being conducted.

    d.   **Temporary Flight Restrictions** denote areas of restricted or prohibited flight privileges, usually set in place to protect persons (i.e., public figures) or property on the ground.

7.   **Military training routes (MTR)** are established below 10,000 ft. MSL for operations at speeds in excess of 250 kt.

    a.   IR means the routes are made in accordance with IFRs.

        1)   VR means the routes are made in accordance with VFRs.

    b.   MTRs that include one or more segments above 1,500 ft. AGL are identified by a three-digit number.

        1)   MTRs with no segment above 1,500 ft. AGL are identified by a four-digit number.

8.   Information about parachute jumping areas and glider operations is contained in the *Airport/Facility Directory (A/FD)*. Parachute jumping areas are marked on sectional charts with a parachute symbol.

9.   Over national wildlife refuges, pilots are requested to maintain a minimum altitude of 2,000 ft. AGL.

10. Airport data on sectional charts include the following information:

    a. The name of the airport.

    b. The elevation of the airport, followed by the length of the longest hard-surfaced runway. An L between the altitude and length indicates lighting.

        1) EXAMPLE: 1008 L 70 means 1,008 ft. MSL airport elevation, L is for lighting sunset to sunrise, and the length of the longest hard-surfaced runway is 7,000 ft.

        2) If the L has an asterisk beside it, airport lighting limitations exist, and you should refer to the *A/FD* for information.

    c. The UNICOM frequency if one has been assigned (e.g., 122.8) is shown after or underneath the runway length.

    d. At controlled airports, the tower frequency is usually under the airport name and above the runway information. It is preceded by CT.

        1) If not a federal control tower, NFCT precedes the CT frequency.

    e. A small, star-shaped symbol immediately above the airport symbol indicates a rotating beacon from sunset to sunrise.

    f. The notation "NO SVFR" above the airport name means that fixed-wing special VFR operations are prohibited.

11. Obstructions on sectional charts

    a. Obstructions of a height less than 1,000 ft. AGL have the symbol Λ.

        1) A group of such obstructions has the symbol $\mathbb{M}$.

    b. Obstructions of a height of 1,000 ft. or more AGL have the symbol λ.

        1) A group of such obstructions has the symbol $\mathbb{M}$.

    c. Obstructions with high-intensity lights have arrows, or lightning bolts, projecting from the top of the obstruction symbol.

    d. The actual height of the top of obstructions is listed near the obstruction by two numbers: one in bold print over another in light print with parentheses around it.

        1) The bold number is the elevation of the top of the obstruction in feet above MSL.

        2) The light number in parentheses is the height of the obstruction in feet AGL.

        3) The elevation (MSL) at the base of the obstruction equals the bold figure minus the light figure.

            a) Use this computation to compute terrain elevation.

            b) Terrain elevation is also given in the airport identifier for each airport and by the contour lines and color shading on the chart.

    e. You must maintain at least 1,000 ft. above obstructions in congested areas and 500 ft. above obstructions in other areas.

    f. All tower structures should be avoided horizontally by at least 2,000 ft. to ensure clearance of any supporting guy wires, which can be difficult to see.

12. Navigational facilities are depicted on sectional charts with various symbols depending on type and services available. These symbols are shown in Legend 1 on page 171.

    a. A VORTAC is depicted as a hexagon with a dot in the center and a small solid rectangle attached to three of the six sides.

    b. A VOR/DME is depicted as a hexagon within a square.

    c. A VOR is depicted as a hexagon with a dot in the center.

9.2 IDENTIFYING LANDMARKS

1. On aeronautical charts, magenta (red) flags denote prominent landmarks that may be used as visual reporting checkpoints for VFR traffic when contacting ATC.

2. The word "CAUTION" on aeronautical charts usually has an accompanying explanation of the hazard.

3. Airports with a rotating beacon will have a star at the top of the airport symbol on sectional charts.

4. Airports attended during normal business hours that have fuel service are indicated on airport symbols by the presence of small solid squares at the top and bottom and on both sides (9 o'clock and 3 o'clock) of the airport symbol.

9.3 RADIO FREQUENCIES

1. At airports without operating control towers, you should use the Common Traffic Advisory Frequency (CTAF), marked with a letter C in the airport data on the sectional chart.

   a. The control tower (CT) frequency is usually used for CTAF when the control tower is closed.

   b. At airports without control towers but with FSS at the airport, the FSS airport advisory frequency is usually the CTAF.

   c. At airports without a tower or FSS, the UNICOM frequency is the CTAF.

   d. At airports without a tower, FSS, or UNICOM, the CTAF is MULTICOM, i.e., 122.9.

   e. Inbound and outbound traffic should communicate position and monitor CTAF within a 10-NM radius of the airport and give position reports when in the traffic pattern. Additionally, outbound pilots should begin self-announce procedures before taxiing and again before taking the active runway.

   f. At airports with operating control towers the UNICOM frequency listed on the sectional chart and *A/FD* can be used to request services, such as fuel, phone calls, and catering.

2. Flight Watch is the common term for En Route Flight Advisory Service (EFAS). It specifically provides en route aircraft with current weather along their route of flight.

   a. Flight Watch is available throughout the country on 122.0 between 5,000 ft. MSL and 18,000 ft. MSL.

   b. The name of the nearest Flight Watch facility is sometimes indicated in communications boxes.

3. Hazardous Inflight Weather Advisory Service (HIWAS) is available from navigation facilities that have a small square inside the lower right corner of the navigation aid identifier box.

9.4 LONGITUDE AND LATITUDE

1. The location of an airport can be determined by the intersection of lines of latitude and longitude.

   a. Lines of latitude are parallel to the equator, and those north of the equator are numbered from 0° to 90° north latitude.

   b. Lines of longitude extend from the north pole to the south pole. The prime meridian (which passes through Greenwich, England) marks 0° longitude. The prime meridian and the 180° line of longitude on the opposite side of the globe separate the Eastern and Western hemispheres.

2. The lines of latitude and longitude are printed on aeronautical charts (e.g., sectional) with each degree subdivided into 60 equal segments called minutes, i.e., 1/2° is 30' (the min. symbol is " ' ").

QUESTIONS AND ANSWER EXPLANATIONS

All of the sport pilot knowledge test questions chosen by the FAA for release as well as additional questions selected by Gleim relating to the material in the previous outlines are reproduced on the following pages. These questions have been organized into the same subunits as the outlines. To the immediate right of each question are the correct answer and answer explanation. You should cover these answers and answer explanations while responding to the questions. Refer to the general discussion in the Introduction on how to take the FAA pilot knowledge test.

Remember that the questions from the FAA pilot knowledge test bank have been reordered by topic and organized into a meaningful sequence. Also, the first line of the answer explanation gives the citation of the authoritative source for the answer.

QUESTIONS

9.1 Airspace and Altitudes

1. (Refer to Figure 59 on page 178.) (Refer to area 2.) What hazards to aircraft may exist in areas such as Devils Lake East MOA?

    A. Unusual, often invisible, hazards to aircraft such as artillery firing, aerial gunnery, or guided missiles.

    B. Military training activities that necessitate acrobatic or abrupt flight maneuvers.

    C. High volume of pilot training or an unusual type of aerial activity.

Answer (B) is correct. *(AIM Para 3-4-5)*
    DISCUSSION: Military Operations Areas (MOAs) such as Devils Lake East in Fig. 59 consist of defined lateral and vertical limits that are designated for the purpose of separating military training activities from IFR traffic. Most training activities necessitate acrobatic or abrupt flight maneuvers. Therefore, the likelihood of a collision is increased inside an MOA. VFR traffic is permitted, but extra vigilance should be exercised in seeing and avoiding military aircraft.
    Answer (A) is incorrect. Unusual, often invisible, hazards to aircraft, such as artillery firing, aerial gunnery, or guided missiles, are characteristic of restricted areas, not MOAs. Answer (C) is incorrect. A high volume of pilot training or an unusual type of aerial activity is characteristic of alert areas, not MOAs.

2. (Refer to Figure 59 on page 178.) (Refer to area 3.) When flying over Arrowwood National Wildlife Refuge, a pilot should fly no lower than

    A. 2,000 feet AGL.

    B. 2,500 feet AGL.

    C. 3,000 feet AGL.

Answer (A) is correct. *(AIM Para 7-4-6)*
    DISCUSSION: See Fig. 59, area 3. All aircraft are requested to maintain a minimum altitude of 2,000 ft. above the surface of a national wildlife refuge except if forced to land by emergency, landing at a designated site, or on official government business.
    Answer (B) is incorrect. This flight altitude has no significance to wildlife refuges. Answer (C) is incorrect. This flight altitude has no significance to wildlife refuges.

3. (Refer to Figure 59 on page 178.) (Refer to area 1.) Identify the airspace over Lowe Airport.

    A. Class G airspace -- surface up to but not including 1,200 feet AGL; Class E airspace -- 1,200 feet AGL up to but not including 18,000 feet MSL.

    B. Class G airspace -- surface up to but not including 18,000 feet MSL.

    C. Class G airspace -- surface up to but not including 700 feet MSL; Class E airspace -- 700 feet to 14,500 feet MSL.

Answer (A) is correct. *(ACL)*
    DISCUSSION: The requirement is the type of airspace above Lowe Airport, which is located 2 inches left of 1 on Fig. 59. Because there is no blue shading depicted on the chart, Class E airspace is understood to begin at 1,200 ft. AGL unless otherwise indicated. There are no airspace symbols surrounding Lowe Airport, so Class G airspace exists from the surface to 1,200 ft. AGL, and Class E airspace exists from 1,200 ft. AGL up to, but not including, 18,000 ft. MSL.
    Answer (B) is incorrect. The Class G airspace above Lowe Airport ends at 1,200 ft. AGL (the beginning of Class E airspace), not 18,000 ft. MSL. Answer (C) is incorrect. Class G airspace above Lowe Airport extends to 1,200 ft. AGL, indicated by the lack of any airspace symbols surrounding the airport (without which, Class G airspace is understood to begin at 1,200 ft. AGL). Class G airspace up to 700 ft. AGL (not MSL) would be indicated by magenta shading surrounding Lowe Airport. Additionally, Class E airspace above Lowe Airport extends to 18,000 ft. MSL, not 14,500 ft. MSL.

4. (Refer to Figure 59 on page 178.) The floor of Class E airspace over the Jamestown airport is

A. 700 feet AGL.

B. 1,200 feet AGL.

C. 1,200 feet MSL.

Answer (A) is correct. *(ACL)*
DISCUSSION: The magenta-shaded ring around the Jamestown airport indicates that Class E airspace descends to 700 ft. AGL. Below 700 ft. AGL is Class G airspace.
Answer (B) is incorrect. Class E airspace with a floor of 1,200 ft. AGL is depicted with a blue-shaded ring, not a magenta-shaded one, as is the case around the Jamestown airport. Answer (C) is incorrect. Class E airspace with a floor of 1,200 ft. AGL, not MSL, is depicted with a blue-shaded ring, not a magenta-shaded one, as is the case around the Jamestown airport.

5. (Refer to Figure 66 on page 181.) (Refer to area 3.) The base of that portion of Class E airspace designated as a Federal Airway over Magee Airport is

A. 1,200 feet AGL.

B. 700 feet MSL.

C. 7,500 feet MSL.

Answer (A) is correct. *(ACL)*
DISCUSSION: Magee Airport is northwest of area 3 on Fig. 66. The floor of a Class E airspace designated as an airway is 1,200 ft. AGL unless otherwise indicated.
Answer (B) is incorrect. The base of the airway in Class E airspace is 1,200 ft. AGL unless otherwise indicated. Answer (C) is incorrect. Class E airspace designated as an airway begins at 1,200 ft. AGL, not at 7,500 ft. MSL.

6. What action should a pilot take when operating under VFR in a Military Operations Area (MOA)?

A. Obtain a clearance from the controlling agency prior to entering the MOA.

B. Operate only on the airways that transverse the MOA.

C. Exercise extreme caution when military activity is being conducted.

Answer (C) is correct. *(AIM Para 3-4-5)*
DISCUSSION: Military operations areas consist of airspace established for separating military training activities from IFR traffic. VFR traffic should exercise extreme caution when flying within an MOA. Information regarding MOA activity can be obtained from flight service stations (FSSs) within 100 mi. of the MOA.
Answer (A) is incorrect. A clearance is not required to enter an MOA. Answer (B) is incorrect. VFR flights may fly anywhere in the MOA.

7. Pilots flying over a national wildlife refuge are requested to fly no lower than

A. 1,000 feet AGL.

B. 2,000 feet AGL.

C. 3,000 feet AGL.

Answer (B) is correct. *(AIM Para 7-4-6)*
DISCUSSION: The Fish and Wildlife Service requests that pilots maintain a minimum altitude of 2,000 ft. above the terrain of national wildlife refuge areas.
Answer (A) is incorrect. The required distance above obstructions over congested areas is 1,000 ft. AGL. Answer (C) is incorrect. This flight altitude has no significance to wildlife refuges.

8. (Refer to Figure 56 on page 175.) (Refer to area 4.) What hazards to aircraft may exist in restricted areas such as R-5302B?

A. Unusual, often invisible, hazards such as aerial gunnery or guided missiles.

B. High volume of pilot training or an unusual type of aerial activity.

C. Military training activities that necessitate acrobatic or abrupt flight maneuvers.

Answer (A) is correct. *(AIM Para 3-4-4)*
DISCUSSION: The question asks what may exist in restricted areas such as R-5302B (Fig. 56). Restricted areas denote the existence of unusual, often invisible, hazards to aircraft, such as military firing, aerial gunnery, or guided missiles.
Answer (B) is incorrect. A high volume of pilot training or an unusual type of aerial activity describes an alert area, not a restricted area. Answer (C) is incorrect. Military training activities that necessitate acrobatic or abrupt flight maneuvers are characteristic of MOAs, not restricted areas.

9. (Refer to Figure 66 on page 181.) (Refer to area 3.) The vertical limits of that portion of Class E airspace designated as a Federal Airway over Magee Airport are

A. 1,200 feet AGL to 17,999 feet MSL.

B. 700 feet MSL to 12,500 feet MSL.

C. 7,500 feet MSL to 17,999 feet MSL.

Answer (A) is correct. *(ACL)*
DISCUSSION: Magee Airport on Fig. 66 is northwest of 3. The question asks for the vertical limits of the Class E airspace over the airport. Class E airspace areas extend upwards but do not include 18,000 ft. MSL (base of Class A airspace). The floor of a Class E airspace designated as an airway is 1,200 ft. AGL unless otherwise indicated.
Answer (B) is incorrect. This airway begins at 1,200 ft. AGL and extends upward to 17,999 ft. MSL, not 12,500 ft. MSL. Answer (C) is incorrect. Class E airspace designated as a Federal Airway begins at 1,200 ft. AGL, not 7,500 ft. MSL, unless otherwise indicated.

10. (Refer to Figure 66 on page 181 and Legend 1 on page 171.) (Refer to area 2.) For information about the parachute jumping and glider operations at Silverwood Airport, refer to

    A. notes on the border of the chart.

    B. the Airport/Facility Directory.

    C. the Notices to Airmen (NOTAM) publication.

Answer (B) is correct. *(ACL)*
    DISCUSSION: The miniature parachute near the Silverwood Airport (at 2 on Fig. 66) indicates a parachute jumping area. In Legend 1, the symbol for a parachute jumping area instructs you to see the *Airport/Facility Directory (A/FD)* for more information. The *A/FD* will also have information on the glider operations at Silverwood Airport.
    Answer (A) is incorrect. The sectional chart legend identifies symbols only. Answer (C) is incorrect. NOTAMs are issued only for hazards to flight.

11. Inbound to an airport with no tower in operation but with a Flight Service Station (FSS) open, a pilot should communicate with the FSS on the common traffic advisory frequency (CTAF)

    A. 20 miles out.

    B. 10 miles out.

    C. 5 miles out.

Answer (B) is correct. *(AIM Para 4-1-9)*
    DISCUSSION: Inbound aircraft should initiate contact when approximately 10 miles from the airport. The pilot should state the aircraft identification and type, altitude, location relative to the airport, and intentions (landing, over-fly, etc.)
    Answer (A) is incorrect. Pilots of inbound aircraft should initiate contact with the FSS on the CTAF when 10 miles out, not 20 miles out. Answer (C) is incorrect. Pilots of inbound aircraft should initiate contact with the FSS on the CTAF when 10 miles out, not 5 miles out.

12. When outbound from an airport with a UNICOM station on the published common traffic advisory frequency (CTAF) and there is no tower or Flight Service Station (FSS), the pilot should contact UNICOM or use self-announce procedures on CTAF before

    A. engine start.

    B. taxiing and before taxiing on the runway.

    C. the preflight inspection.

Answer (B) is correct. *(AIM Para 4-1-9)*
    DISCUSSION: When outbound from an airport with a UNICOM station on the CTAF, you should begin self-announce procedures before taxiing and again before taxiing on the runway.
    Answer (A) is incorrect. You should not begin self-announce procedures before the engine is started. Answer (C) is incorrect. You should not begin self-announce procedures before the preflight inspection.

13. When outbound from an airport without a UNICOM station, a tower, or a Flight Service Station (FSS), the pilot should self-announce on frequency

    A. 122.7

    B. 122.9

    C. 122.8

Answer (B) is correct. *(AIM Para 4-1-9)*
    DISCUSSION: When outbound from an airport without a UNICOM station, a tower, or an FSS, the pilot should self-announce on the MULTICOM frequency of 122.9 before taxiing and again before taxiing onto the runway.
    Answer (A) is incorrect. The frequency of 122.7 is one of the most common UNICOM frequencies, not a MULTICOM frequency. Answer (C) is incorrect. The frequency of 122.8 is also one of the most common UNICOM frequencies, not a MULTICOM frequency.

14. (Refer to Figure 61 on page 180.) (Refer to point 6.) Mosier Airport is

    A. an airport restricted to use by private and recreational pilots.

    B. a restricted military stage field within restricted airspace.

    C. a nonpublic-use airport.

Answer (C) is correct. *(ACL)*
    DISCUSSION: Mosier Airport (west of 6) is a private, i.e., nonpublic-use, airport as indicated by the term "(Pvt)" after the airport name. Private airports that are shown on the sectional charts have an emergency or landmark value.
    Answer (A) is incorrect. The airport symbol with the letter "R" in the center means it is a nonpublic-use airport, not that only private and recreational pilots may use the airport. Answer (B) is incorrect. Military airfields are labeled as AFB, NAS, AAF, NAAS, NAF, MCAS, or DND.

15. Guy wires, which support antenna towers, can extend horizontally; therefore, the towers should be avoided horizontally by at least

    A. 2,000 feet horizontally.

    B. 300 feet horizontally.

    C. 1,000 feet horizontally.

Answer (A) is correct. *(AIM Para 7-5-3)*
    DISCUSSION: Many antenna towers are supported by guy wires, which are very difficult to see in good weather and can be invisible at dusk or during periods of reduced visibility. These wires can extend about 1,500 feet horizontally from the structure; therefore, all tower structures should be avoided horizontally by at least 2,000 feet.
    Answer (B) is incorrect. You should avoid antenna towers by at least 2,000, not 300, feet horizontally. Answer (C) is incorrect. You should avoid antenna towers by at least 2,000, not 1,000, feet horizontally.

16. (Refer to Figure 56 on page 175.) (Refer to area 1.) The Nalf Fentress (NFE) airport is in what type of airspace?

A. Class C

B. Class E

C. Class G

Answer (B) is correct. *(ACL)*

DISCUSSION: Nalf Fentress (NFE) airport is circled by a dashed magenta line. This dashed magenta line represents Class E airspace for Nalf Fentress airport.

Answer (A) is incorrect. Class C airspace is represented by a thick, solid magenta line, not a dashed magenta line, surrounding an airport. Answer (C) is incorrect. Class G airspace is not illustrated by a colored circle around the airport. If an airport is located in Class G airspace, there will be no colored circle surrounding the airport.

17. (Refer to Figure 70 on page 183.) (Refer to point 1.) What minimum altitude is required to avoid the Livermore Airport (LVK) Class D airspace?

A. 2,503 feet MSL.

B. 2,901 feet MSL.

C. 3,297 feet MSL.

Answer (B) is correct. *(ACL)*

DISCUSSION: The Class D airspace (as denoted by the blue segmented circle) overlying Livermore Airport has an upper limit of 2,900 ft. MSL (as depicted by the "29" within the broken box next to the airport symbol). Thus, the minimum altitude required to avoid the Class D airspace is 2,901 ft. MSL.

Answer (A) is incorrect. The minimum altitude to avoid the Livermore Class D airspace is 2,901 ft. MSL, not 2,503 ft. MSL. Answer (C) is incorrect. The minimum altitude to avoid the Livermore Class D airspace is 2,901 ft. MSL, not 3,297 ft. MSL.

18. The purpose of Military Training Routes, charted as VFR Military Training Routes (VR) and IFR Military Training Routes (IR) on sectional charts, is to ensure the greatest practical level of safety for all flight operations and to allow the military to conduct

A. low altitude, high-speed training.

B. radar instrument training.

C. air-to-air refueling training.

Answer (A) is correct. *(AIM Para 3-5-2)*

DISCUSSION: Military Training Routes (MTRs) are developed by the FAA and Department of Defense for use by the military for the purpose of conducting low-altitude, high-speed training.

Answer (B) is incorrect. MTRs are developed for the purpose of military low-altitude, high-speed training, not radar instrument training. Answer (C) is incorrect. MTRs are developed for the purpose of military low-altitude, high-speed training, not air-to-air refueling training.

19. Who is responsible for collision avoidance in a Military Operations Area (MOA)?

A. Each pilot.

B. ATC controllers.

C. Military controllers.

Answer (A) is correct. *(AIM Para 3-4-5)*

DISCUSSION: Each pilot operating VFR within a Military Operations Area (MOA) should exercise extreme caution while flying within the MOA and maintain an enhanced vigilance in their collision avoidance, scanning for other traffic, and maintaining situational awareness.

Answer (B) is incorrect. Each pilot, not the ATC controllers, is responsible for collision avoidance while operating within an MOA. Answer (C) is incorrect. Each pilot, not the military controllers, is responsible for collision avoidance while operating within an MOA.

20. (Refer to Figure 57 on page 176.) (Refer to area 2.) The floor of Class B airspace at Addison Airport is

A. at the surface.

B. 3,000 feet MSL.

C. 3,100 feet MSL.

Answer (B) is correct. *(ACL and FAR 71.9)*

DISCUSSION: Addison Airport (Fig. 57, area 2) has a segmented blue circle around it depicting Class D airspace. Addison Airport also underlies Class B airspace as depicted by solid blue lines. The altitudes of the Class B airspace are shown as $\frac{110}{30}$ to the east of the airport. The bottom number denotes the floor of the Class B airspace to be 3,000 ft. MSL.

Answer (A) is incorrect. The floor of Class D, not Class B, airspace is at the surface. Answer (C) is incorrect. This altitude is not a defined limit of any airspace over Addison airport.

21. (Refer to Figure 57 on page 176.) (Refer to area 4.) The floor of Class B airspace overlying Hicks Airport (T67) north-northwest of Fort Worth Meacham Field is

A. at the surface.

B. 3,200 feet MSL.

C. 4,000 feet MSL.

Answer (C) is correct. *(ACL)*

DISCUSSION: Hicks Airport (T67) on Fig. 57 is northeast of 4. Class B airspace is depicted by a solid blue line, as shown just west of the airport. Follow the blue line toward the bottom of the chart until you find a number over a number in blue, $\frac{110}{40}$. The bottom number denotes the floor of the Class B airspace as 4,000 ft. MSL.

Answer (A) is incorrect. The floor of the Class B airspace would be at the surface if SFC, not 40, were below the 100, as depicted just south of Dallas-Ft. Worth International Airport. Answer (B) is incorrect. The upper limit of the Class D airspace for the Ft. Worth/Meacham Airport is 3,200 ft., not the floor of Class B airspace overlying Hicks Airport.

22. (Refer to Figure 69 on page 182.) (Refer to area 3.) What is the floor of the Savannah Class C airspace at the shelf area (outer circle)?

A. 1,200 feet AGL.

B. 1,300 feet MSL.

C. 1,700 feet MSL.

Answer (B) is correct. *(ACL)*

DISCUSSION: Class C airspace consists of a surface area and a shelf area. The floor of the shelf area is 1,200 ft. above the airport elevation. The Savannah Class C airspace (Fig. 69, area 3) is depicted by solid magenta circles. For each circle, there is a number over a number or SFC. The numbers are in hundreds of feet MSL. The lower number represents the floor of the airspace. Thus, the floor of the shelf area of the Class C airspace is 1,300 ft. MSL (41/13).

Answer (A) is incorrect. The floor of the outer circle of Class C airspace does not vary with the ground elevation. The FAA specifies a fixed MSL altitude, rounded to the nearest 100 ft., which is about 1,200 ft. above the airport elevation. Answer (C) is incorrect. The maximum elevation figure (MEF) of the quadrant encompassing Savannah Class C airspace is 1,700 ft., not the floor of the shelf area.

23. (Refer to Figure 57 on page 176.) (Refer to area 7.) The airspace overlying McKinney (TKI) is controlled from the surface to

A. 700 feet AGL.

B. 2,900 feet MSL.

C. 2,500 feet MSL.

Answer (B) is correct. *(ACL)*

DISCUSSION: The airspace overlying McKinney airport (TKI) (Fig. 57, northeast of 7) is Class D airspace as denoted by the segmented blue lines. The upper limit is depicted in a broken box in hundreds of feet MSL to the left of the airport symbol. The box contains the number "29," meaning that the vertical limit of the Class D airspace is 2,900 ft. MSL.

Answer (A) is incorrect. Normally, the vertical limit of uncontrolled, not controlled, airspace in the vicinity of non-towered airports with an authorized instrument approach is 700 ft. AGL. Answer (C) is incorrect. Normally, the upper limit of Class D airspace is 2,500 ft. AGL, not MSL. This is not the case here, where the upper limit is somewhat lower, at about 2,300 ft. AGL [2,900 ft. MSL – 586 ft. AGL (field elevation) = 2,314 ft. AGL].

24. (Refer to Figure 59 on page 178.) (Refer to area 6.) The airspace overlying and within 5 miles of Barnes County Airport is

A. Class D airspace from the surface to the floor of the overlying Class E airspace.

B. Class E airspace from the surface to 1,200 feet MSL.

C. Class G airspace from the surface to 700 feet AGL.

Answer (C) is correct. *(ACL)*

DISCUSSION: The requirement is the type of airspace overlying and within 5 SM from Barnes County Airport (Fig. 59). Note at 6 that Barnes County Airport is in the lower right and is surrounded by a shaded magenta (reddish) band, which means the floor of the controlled airspace is 700 ft. Thus, Class G airspace extends from the surface to 700 ft. AGL.

Answer (A) is incorrect. Class D airspace requires a control tower. The Barnes County Airport does not have a control tower, since the airport identifier is magenta, not blue. Answer (B) is incorrect. An airport located in Class E airspace would be marked by dashed magenta lines such as the ones surrounding Jamestown Airport to the left. Barnes has no such lines.

25. (Refer to Figure 59 on page 178.) (Refer to area 2.) The visibility and cloud clearance requirements to operate VFR during daylight hours over the town of Cooperstown between 1,200 feet AGL and 10,000 feet MSL are

  A. 1 mile and clear of clouds.

  B. 1 mile and 1,000 feet above, 500 feet below, and 2,000 feet horizontally from clouds.

  C. 3 miles and 1,000 feet above, 500 feet below, and 2,000 feet horizontally from clouds.

Answer (C) is correct. *(FAR 91.155)*
    DISCUSSION: The airspace over the town of Cooperstown (Fig. 59, north of 2) is Class G airspace up to 700 ft. AGL and Class E airspace from 700 ft. AGL up to, but not including, 18,000 ft. MSL (indicated by the magenta shading). Therefore, the visibility and cloud clearance requirements for daylight VFR operation over the town of Cooperstown between 1,200 ft. AGL and 10,000 ft. MSL are 3 miles and 1,000 ft. above, 500 ft. below, and 2,000 ft. horizontally.
    Answer (A) is incorrect. One mile and clear of clouds are the visibility and cloud clearance requirements for daylight VFR operation over the town of Cooperstown up to, but not above, 700 ft. AGL (i.e., the visibility and cloud clearance requirements for Class G airspace below 1,200 ft. AGL). Answer (B) is incorrect. One mile and a distance from clouds of 1,000 ft. above, 500 ft. below, and 2,000 ft. horizontally are the visibility and cloud clearance requirements for daylight VFR operations at or above 1,200 ft. AGL, but below 10,000 ft. MSL, in Class G airspace. The airspace above Cooperstown is Class E above 700 ft. AGL.

26. (Refer to Figure 56 on page 175.) (Refer to area 2.) The elevation of the Chesapeake Regional Airport is

  A. 20 feet.

  B. 36 feet.

  C. 360 feet.

Answer (A) is correct. *(ACL)*
    DISCUSSION: The requirement is the elevation of the Chesapeake Regional Airport (Fig. 56). East of 2, note that the second line of the airport identifier for Chesapeake Regional reads "20 L 55 123.05." The first number, in bold type, is the altitude of the airport above MSL. It is followed by the L for lighted runway(s), 55 for the length of the longest runway (5,500 ft.), and the CTAF frequency (123.05).
    Answer (B) is incorrect. The elevation of anything near Chesapeake airport is not listed as 36 ft. Answer (C) is incorrect. The height above ground of the group obstructions approximately 6 NM southeast of Chesapeake airport is 360 ft., not the elevation of the airport.

27. (Refer to Figure 66 on page 181.) (Refer to area 1.) The visibility and cloud clearance requirements for a sport pilot to operate over Sandpoint Airport at less than 700 feet AGL are

  A. 3 miles and clear of clouds.

  B. 3 miles and 1,000 feet above, 500 feet below, and 2,000 feet horizontally from each cloud.

  C. 1 mile and 1,000 feet above, 500 feet below, and 2,000 feet horizontally from each cloud.

Answer (A) is correct. *(FAR 61.315 and 91.155)*
    DISCUSSION: Sandpoint Airport is about 1 in. above the number 1 in Fig. 66. The airspace around Sandpoint Airport is Class G from the surface to 2,827 ft. MSL (700 ft. AGL). For a sport pilot to operate over Sandpoint Airport at less than 700 ft. AGL, the visibility and cloud clearance requirements are 3 SM and clear of clouds. Note: Sport pilots may not act as pilot-in-command with a flight visibility of less than 3 miles.
    Answer (B) is incorrect. The cloud clearance of 1,000 ft. above, 500 ft. below, and 2,000 ft. horizontally is the requirement in Class G airspace above 1,200 ft. AGL, not less than 700 ft. AGL. Answer (C) is incorrect. A sport pilot must have a visibility of, at minimum, 3 SM, not 1 SM. Cloud clearance of 1,000 ft. above, 500 ft. below, and 2,000 ft. horizontally is the requirement in Class G airspace above 1,200 ft. AGL, not less than 700 ft. AGL.

28. (Refer to Figure 69 on page 182.) (Refer to area 3.) What is the height of the lighted obstacle approximately 6 nautical miles southwest of Savannah International?

  A. 1,500 feet MSL.

  B. 1,531 feet AGL.

  C. 1,549 feet MSL.

Answer (C) is correct. *(ACL)*
    DISCUSSION: On Fig. 69, find the lighted obstacle noted by its proximity to Savannah International by being outside the surface area of the Class C airspace, which has a 5-NM radius. It is indicated with the obstacle symbol with arrows or lightning flashes extending from the tip. According to the numbers to the northeast of the symbol, the height of the obstacle is 1,549 ft. MSL, or 1,534 ft. AGL.
    Answer (A) is incorrect. The unlighted tower 8 NM, not 6 NM, southwest of the airport has a height of 1,500 ft. MSL. Answer (B) is incorrect. An unlighted tower 9 NM, not 6 NM, southwest of the airport has a height of 1,531 ft. AGL.

29. (Refer to Figure 60 on page 179.) (Refer to area 1.) What minimum altitude is necessary to vertically clear the obstacle on the northeast side of Airpark East Airport by 500 feet?

    A. 1,010 feet MSL.

    B. 1,273 feet MSL.

    C. 1,283 feet MSL.

Answer (B) is correct. *(ACL and FAR 91.119)*
    DISCUSSION: Find Airpark East, which is near 1 in Fig. 60. Remember to locate the actual airport symbol, not just the name of the airport. It is 1 in. southwest of 1. The elevation of the top of the obstacle on the northeast side of the airport is marked in bold as 773 ft. MSL. Minimum altitude to clear the 773-ft. obstacle by 500 ft. is 1,273 ft. MSL.
    Answer (A) is incorrect. The airport elevation, not the obstacle, is 510 ft. Answer (C) is incorrect. An AGL altitude of a tower 1 in. west of Caddo Mills Airport appears as 283.

30. (Refer to Figure 60 on page 179.) (Refer to area 2.) What minimum altitude is necessary to vertically clear the obstacle on the southeast side of Winnsboro Airport by 500 feet?

    A. 823 feet MSL.

    B. 1,013 feet MSL.

    C. 1,403 feet MSL.

Answer (C) is correct. *(ACL)*
    DISCUSSION: The first step is to find the obstacle on the southeast side of Winnsboro Airport on Fig. 60, near 2. The elevation numbers to the right of the obstruction symbol indicate that its top is 903 ft. MSL, or a height of 323 ft. AGL. Thus, the clearance altitude is 1,403 ft. MSL (903 ft. MSL + 500 ft. of clearance).
    Answer (A) is incorrect. Since the obstacle height is 323 ft. AGL (number in parentheses), the minimum altitude to clear the obstacle by 500 ft. is 823 ft. AGL, not 823 ft. MSL. Answer (B) is incorrect. This amount represents the altitude at 500 ft. above the airport elevation (513 ft. MSL), not 500 ft. above the top of the obstacle height of 903 ft.

31. (Refer to Figure 57 on page 176.) (Refer to area 4.) The airspace directly overlying Fort Worth Meacham is

    A. Class B airspace to 10,000 feet MSL.

    B. Class C airspace to 5,000 feet MSL.

    C. Class D airspace to 3,200 feet MSL.

Answer (C) is correct. *(ACL)*
    DISCUSSION: The airspace overlying Fort Worth Meacham (Fig. 57, southeast of 4) is Class D airspace as denoted by the segmented blue lines. The upper limit is depicted in a broken box in hundreds of feet MSL northeast of the airport. Thus, the Class D airspace extends from the surface to 3,200 ft. MSL.
    Answer (A) is incorrect. Class D, not Class B, airspace extends from the surface of Ft. Worth Meacham. Class B airspace overlies the airport from 4,000 ft. MSL to 10,000 ft. MSL. Answer (B) is incorrect. Class D, not Class C, airspace directly overlies Ft. Worth Meacham from the surface to 3,200 ft. MSL, not 5,000 ft. MSL.

32. What minimum radio equipment is required for operation within Class C airspace?

    A. Two-way radio communications equipment and a 4096-code transponder.

    B. Two-way radio communications equipment, a 4096-code transponder, and DME.

    C. Two-way radio communications equipment, a 4096-code transponder, and an encoding altimeter.

Answer (C) is correct. *(AIM Para 3-2-4)*
    DISCUSSION: To operate within Class C airspace, the aircraft must have

1. Two-way radio communications equipment,
2. A 4096-code transponder, and
3. An encoding altimeter.

    Answer (A) is incorrect. An encoding altimeter (Mode C) is required in Class C airspace. Answer (B) is incorrect. DME is not required in Class C airspace.

33. What minimum radio equipment is required for VFR operation within Class B airspace?

    A. Two-way radio communications equipment and a 4096-code transponder.

    B. Two-way radio communications equipment, a 4096-code transponder, and an encoding altimeter.

    C. Two-way radio communications equipment, a 4096-code transponder, an encoding altimeter, and a VOR or TACAN receiver.

Answer (B) is correct. *(AIM Para 3-2-3)*
    DISCUSSION: To operate within Class B airspace, the aircraft must have

1. Two-way radio communications equipment,
2. A 4096-code transponder, and
3. An encoding altimeter.

    Answer (A) is incorrect. An encoding altimeter (Mode C) is also required in Class B airspace. Answer (C) is incorrect. A VOR or TACAN receiver is required for IFR, not VFR, operation within Class B airspace.

34. (Refer to Figure 57 on page 176.) (Refer to area 8.) What minimum altitude is required to fly over the Cedar Hill TV towers in the congested area south of NAS Dallas?

A. 2,555 feet MSL.

B. 3,449 feet MSL.

C. 3,349 feet MSL.

Answer (B) is correct. *(FAR 91.119)*
DISCUSSION: The Cedar Hill TV towers (Fig. 57, west of 8) have an elevation of 2,449 ft. MSL. The minimum safe altitude over a congested area is 1,000 ft. above the highest obstacle within a horizontal radius of 2,000 ft. of the aircraft. Thus, to vertically clear the towers, the minimum altitude is 3,449 ft. MSL (2,449 + 1,000).
Answer (A) is incorrect. The minimum height to fly over the shortest, not the tallest, of the obstructions in the group is 2,555 ft. AGL, not 2,555 ft. MSL. Answer (C) is incorrect. This altitude is only 900 ft., not 1,000 ft., above the tallest structure.

35. (Refer to Figure 58 on page 177.) The terrain elevation of the light tan area between Minot (area 1) and Audubon Lake (area 2) varies from

A. sea level to 2,000 feet MSL.

B. 2,000 feet to 2,500 feet MSL.

C. 2,000 feet to 2,700 feet MSL.

Answer (B) is correct. *(ACL)*
DISCUSSION: The requirement is the terrain elevation in the tan area between 1 and 2 in Fig. 58. The tan area indicates terrain between 2,000 ft. and 3,000 ft. The elevation contours on sectionals vary by 500 ft. increments. The 2,000-ft. contour line is located where the color changes from light green to light tan. Since there is no other contour line in the light tan area, the terrain elevation is between 2,000 ft. and 2,500 ft. MSL. Also, Poleschook Airport (halfway between 1 and 2) indicates an elevation above MSL of 2,245.
Answer (A) is incorrect. The light tan area indicates terrain elevation from 2,000 ft. to 3,000 ft. MSL, not from sea level to 2,000 ft. MSL. Answer (C) is incorrect. Elevation contours vary by 500 ft., not 700 ft.

36. Which is true regarding flight operations to a satellite airport, without an operating control tower, within Class C airspace area?

A. Prior to entering that airspace, a pilot must contact the FSS.

B. Prior to entering that airspace, a pilot must contact the tower.

C. Prior to entering that airspace, a pilot must establish and maintain communication with the ATC serving facility.

Answer (C) is correct. *(FAR 91.130)*
DISCUSSION: Prior to entering Class C airspace, a pilot must establish and maintain two-way radio communications with the ATC facility providing air traffic services.
Answer (A) is incorrect. Contacting FSS does not satisfy the two-way communications requirement of Class C airspace. Answer (B) is incorrect. The question states that the satellite airport does not have an operating control tower.

37. (Refer to Figure 60 on page 179.) The floor of the Class E airspace over the town of Commerce is

A. 1,200 feet MSL.

B. 700 feet AGL.

C. 1,200 feet AGL.

Answer (B) is correct. *(ACL)*
DISCUSSION: The Class E airspace over the town of Commerce is depicted by a shaded magenta ring. This indicates that the airspace is Class E airspace, with lower limits beginning at 700 ft. AGL.
Answer (A) is incorrect. A blue shaded ring, not a magenta shaded ring, depicts Class E airspace with lower limits at 1,200 ft. MSL. Answer (C) is incorrect. A blue shaded ring, not a magenta shaded ring, depicts Class E airspace with lower limits at 1,200 ft. AGL.

38. Which is true concerning the blue and magenta colors used to depict airports on Sectional Aeronautical Charts?

A. Airports with control towers underlying Class A, B, and C airspace are shown in blue. Class D and E airspace are shown in magenta.

B. Airports with control towers underlying Class C, D, and E airspace are shown in magenta.

C. Airports with control towers underlying Class B, C, D, and E airspace are shown in blue.

Answer (C) is correct. *(ACL)*
DISCUSSION: On sectional charts, airports with control towers underlying Class B, C, D, E, or G airspace are shown in blue. Airports with no control towers are shown in magenta.
Answer (A) is incorrect. There are no airports in Class A airspace. Airports with control towers are shown in blue, all others in magenta. Answer (B) is incorrect. Airports with control towers are shown in blue, not magenta.

39. Which is true concerning the colors used to depict airports on Sectional Aeronautical Charts?

A. Airports with control towers underlying Class D and E airspace are magenta.

B. Airports with control towers are shown in magenta.

C. Airports with control towers are shown in blue.

Answer (C) is correct. *(ACL)*
   DISCUSSION: Airports having control towers are shown in blue as indicated on the chart legend.
   Answer (A) is incorrect. Airports with control towers underlying Class D and E airspace are blue. Answer (B) is incorrect. Airports other than those with control towers are shown in magenta.

40. One of the purposes for issuing a Temporary Flight Restriction (TFR) is to

A. announce parachute jump areas.

B. protect public figures.

C. identify airport advisory areas.

Answer (B) is correct. *(AIM Para 3-5-3)*
   DISCUSSION: One of the purposes for issuing Temporary Flight Restrictions (TFRs) is to protect public figures, e.g., the president or the vice president.
   Answer (A) is incorrect. TFRs are not issued for the purpose of announcing parachute jump areas. Answer (C) is incorrect. TFRs do not identify airport advisory areas.

9.2 Identifying Landmarks

41. (Refer to Figure 56 on page 175.) (Refer to area 2.) The flag symbol at Lake Drummond represents a

A. compulsory reporting point for Norfolk Class C airspace.

B. compulsory reporting point for Hampton Roads Airport.

C. visual checkpoint used to identify position for initial callup to Norfolk Approach Control.

Answer (C) is correct. *(ACL)*
   DISCUSSION: The magenta (reddish) flag (Fig. 56, north of 2) at Lake Drummond signifies that the lake is a visual checkpoint that can be used to identify the position for initial callup to the Norfolk approach control.
   Answer (A) is incorrect. Compulsory reporting points are on IFR, not sectional, charts. They are used on IFR flights. Answer (B) is incorrect. Compulsory reporting points are on IFR, not sectional, charts. They are used on IFR flights.

42. (Refer to Figure 56 on page 175.) (Refer to area 5.) The CAUTION box denotes what hazard to aircraft?

A. Unmarked blimp hangars at 300 feet MSL.

B. Unmarked balloon on cable to 3,000 feet AGL.

C. Unmarked balloon on cable to 3,000 feet MSL.

Answer (C) is correct. *(ACL)*
   DISCUSSION: On Fig. 56, northwest of 5, find "CAUTION: UNMARKED BALLOON ON CABLE TO 3,000 MSL." This is self-explanatory.
   Answer (A) is incorrect. The box clearly says that there is an unmarked balloon, not blimp hangars, to 3,000 ft. MSL, not 300 ft. MSL. Answer (B) is incorrect. The balloon extends to 3,000 ft. MSL, not AGL.

43. (Refer to Figure 58 on page 177.) Which public use airports depicted are indicated as having fuel?

A. Minot Int'l (area 1) and Mercer County Regional Airport (area 3).

B. Minot Int'l (area 1) and Garrison (area 2).

C. Mercer County Regional Airport (area 3) and Garrison (area 2).

Answer (A) is correct. *(ACL)*
   DISCUSSION: On Fig. 58, the requirement is to identify the airports having fuel available. Airports having fuel available are designated by small squares extending from the top, bottom, and both sides of the airport symbol. Only Minot (area 1) and Mercer County Regional Airport (area 3) have such symbols.
   Answer (B) is incorrect. Garrison (2 inches left of 2) does not indicate that fuel is available. Answer (C) is incorrect. Garrison (2 inches left of 2) does not indicate that fuel is available.

44. (Refer to Figure 69 on page 182.) (Refer to areas 2 and 3.) The flag symbols at Statesboro Bullock County Airport, Claxton-Evans County Airport, and Ridgeland Airport are

A. outer boundaries of Savannah Class C airspace.

B. airports with special traffic patterns.

C. visual checkpoints to identify position for initial callup prior to entering Savannah Class C airspace.

Answer (C) is correct. *(ACL)*
    DISCUSSION: On Fig. 69, note the flag symbols at Claxton-Evans County Airport (1 in. to the left of 2), at Statesboro Bullock County Airport (2 in. above 2), and at Ridgeland Airport (2 in. above 3). These airports are visual checkpoints to identify position for initial callup prior to entering the Savannah Class C airspace.
    Answer (A) is incorrect. They do not indicate outer boundaries of the Class C airspace. The flags are outside the Class C airspace area, the boundaries of which are marked by solid magenta lines. Answer (B) is incorrect. Airports with special traffic patterns are noted in the *Airport/Facility Directory* and also by markings at the airport around the wind sock or tetrahedron.

9.3 Radio Frequencies

45. (Refer to Figure 58 on page 177.) On what frequency can a pilot receive Hazardous Inflight Weather Advisory Service (HIWAS) in the vicinity of area 1?

A. 117.1 MHz.

B. 118.0 MHz.

C. 122.0 MHz.

Answer (A) is correct. *(ACL)*
    DISCUSSION: On Fig. 58, 1 is on the upper left and the Minot VORTAC information box is 1 in. below 1. Availability of Hazardous Inflight Weather Advisory Service (HIWAS) will be indicated by a circle that contains an "H," found in the upper right corner of a navigation frequency box. Note that the Minot VORTAC information box has such a symbol. Accordingly, a HIWAS can be obtained on the VOR frequency of 117.1.
    Answer (B) is incorrect. "Ch 118" in the Minot VORTAC information box refers to the TACAN channel (the military equivalent of VOR/DME). Answer (C) is incorrect. The universal frequency for Flight Watch is 122.0.

46. (Refer to Figure 59 on page 178.) (Refer to area 2.) What is the recommended communication procedure when inbound to land at Cooperstown Airport?

A. Broadcast intentions when 10 miles out on the CTAF/MULTICOM frequency, 122.9 MHz.

B. Contact UNICOM when 10 miles out on 122.8 MHz.

C. Circle the airport in a left turn prior to entering traffic.

Answer (A) is correct. *(AIM Para 4-1-9)*
    DISCUSSION: Find Cooperstown Airport, which is at the top of Fig. 59, just north of 2. You should broadcast your intentions when 10 NM out on the CTAF/MULTICOM frequency, 122.9 MHz.
    Answer (B) is incorrect. There is no UNICOM indicated at Cooperstown, and the CTAF is 122.9, not 122.8. Answer (C) is incorrect. A left turn is not a communication procedure.

47. (Refer to Figure 59 on page 178.) (Refer to area 6.) What is the CTAF/UNICOM frequency at Barnes County Airport?

A. 122.0 MHz.

B. 122.8 MHz.

C. 123.6 MHz.

Answer (B) is correct. *(ACL)*
    DISCUSSION: In Fig. 59, Barnes County Airport is 1 in. below 6. The CTAF at Barnes County Airport is marked as the UNICOM frequency for the airport, i.e., 122.8.
    Answer (A) is incorrect. Flight Watch is 122.0. Answer (C) is incorrect. An FSS frequency is 123.6.

48. (Refer to Figure 66 on page 181 and Figure 67 on page 168.) (Refer to area 2 in Figure 66.) What is the correct UNICOM frequency to be used at Coeur D'Alene?

A. 135.075 MHz.

B. 122.1/108.8 MHz.

C. 122.8 MHz.

Answer (C) is correct. *(ACL)*
    DISCUSSION: The correct UNICOM frequency to be used at Coeur D'Alene Airport is 122.8 MHz. It is given in Fig. 66, after "L74" in the airport information on the sectional chart. Radio frequencies are also given in Fig. 67, the *Airport/Facility Directory (A/FD)*, under "Communications."
    Answer (A) is incorrect. The AWOS frequency for Coeur D'Alene Airport is 135.075. Answer (B) is incorrect. The COE VOR/DME frequency is 108.8, not the UNICOM, and 122.1 is not a frequency associated with Coeur D'Alene Airport.

49. (Refer to Figure 67 below, and Figure 66 on page 181.) (Refer to area 2 in Figure 66.) At Coeur D'Alene, which frequency should be used as a Common Traffic Advisory Frequency (CTAF) to monitor airport traffic?

A. 122.05 MHz.

B. 135.075 MHz.

C. 122.8 MHz.

Answer (C) is correct. *(A/FD)*

DISCUSSION: Fig. 67 is the *A/FD* excerpt for Coeur D'Alene Air Terminal. Look for the section titled Communications. On that same line, it states that the CTAF (and UNICOM) frequency is 122.8. The CTAF can also be found in the airport information on the sectional chart.

Answer (A) is incorrect. This is the remote communication outlet (RCO) frequency to contact Boise FSS in the vicinity of Coeur D'Alene, not the CTAF. Answer (B) is incorrect. The AWOS frequency is 135.075, not the CTAF.

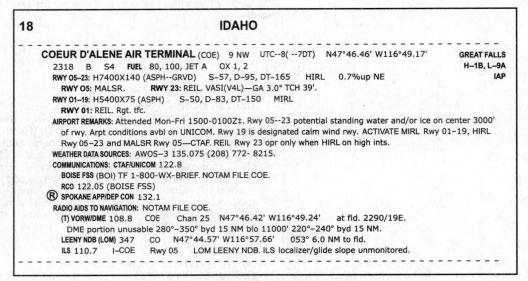

Figure 67. – Airport/Facility Directory Excerpt.

50. (Refer to Figure 67 above, and Figure 66 on page 181.) (Refer to area 2 in Figure 66.) At Coeur D'Alene, which frequency should be used as a Common Traffic Advisory Frequency (CTAF) to self-announce position and intentions?

A. 122.05 MHz.

B. 122.1/108.8 MHz.

C. 122.8 MHz.

Answer (C) is correct. *(A/FD)*

DISCUSSION: Fig. 67 is the *A/FD* excerpt for Coeur D'Alene Air Terminal. Look for the section titled Communications. On that same line, it states the CTAF (and UNICOM) frequency is 122.8.

Answer (A) is incorrect. This is the remote communications outlet (RCO) frequency to contact Boise FSS in the vicinity of Coeur D'Alene, not the CTAF. Answer (B) is incorrect. The COE VOR/DME frequency is 108.8, not the CTAF.

51. (Refer to Figure 56 on page 175.) (Refer to area 3.) What is the recommended communications procedure for a landing at Currituck County Airport?

A. Transmit intentions on 122.9 MHz when 10 miles out and give position reports in the traffic pattern.

B. Contact Elizabeth City FSS for airport advisory service.

C. Contact New Bern FSS for area traffic information.

Answer (A) is correct. *(AIM Para 4-1-9)*

DISCUSSION: Find the symbol for Currituck County Airport, 1/2 in. northeast of 3 in Fig. 56. Incoming flights should use MULTICOM, 122.9, as the CTAF, because it is marked with a C. The recommended procedure is to report 10 NM out and then give position reports in the airport traffic pattern.

Answer (B) is incorrect. There is no Elizabeth City FSS. Elizabeth City is serviced by the Raleigh FSS, as indicated by "Raleigh" just below the identifier box for Elizabeth City VOR. Answer (C) is incorrect. The controlling FSS is Raleigh, not New Bern, and Raleigh FSS does not monitor 122.9, which is marked as the CTAF at Currituck County Airport.

52. (Refer to Figure 58 on page 177.) (Refer to area 2.) The CTAF/MULTICOM frequency for Garrison Airport is

A. 122.8 MHz.

B. 122.9 MHz.

C. 123.0 MHz.

Answer (B) is correct. *(ACL)*
DISCUSSION: The CTAF for Garrison Municipal Airport (2 inches left of 2 in Fig. 58) is 122.9, because that frequency is marked with a C.
Answer (A) is incorrect. There is no indication of 122.8 at Garrison. Answer (C) is incorrect. There is no indication of 123.0 at Garrison.

53. (Refer to Figure 57 on page 176.) (Refer to area 3.) If Redbird Tower is not in operation, which frequency should be used as a Common Traffic Advisory Frequency (CTAF) to monitor airport traffic?

A. 120.3 MHz.

B. 122.95 MHz.

C. 126.35 MHz.

Answer (A) is correct. *(ACL)*
DISCUSSION: In Fig. 57, find the Redbird Airport just above 3. When the Redbird tower is not in operation, the CTAF is 120.3 because that frequency is marked with a C.
Answer (B) is incorrect. The UNICOM frequency is 122.95. Answer (C) is incorrect. The ATIS frequency is 126.35.

54. (Refer to Figure 59 on page 178.) (Refer to area 4.) The CTAF/UNICOM frequency at Jamestown Airport is

A. 122.0 MHz.

B. 123.0 MHz.

C. 123.6 MHz.

Answer (B) is correct. *(ACL)*
DISCUSSION: The UNICOM frequency is printed in bold italics in the airport identifier. At Jamestown it is 123.0 MHz. The C next to it indicates it as the CTAF.
Answer (A) is incorrect. The Flight Watch frequency is 122.0, not UNICOM. Answer (C) is incorrect. An FSS frequency is 123.6, not UNICOM.

9.4 Longitude and Latitude

55. (Refer to Figure 56 on page 175.) (Refer to area 3.) Determine the approximate latitude and longitude of Currituck County Airport.

A. 36°24'N – 76°01'W.

B. 36°48'N – 76°01'W.

C. 47°24'N – 75°58'W.

Answer (A) is correct. *(PHAK Chap 15)*
DISCUSSION: On Fig. 56, find the Currituck County Airport, which is northeast of area 3. Note that the airport symbol is just to the west of 76° longitude (find 76° just north of Virginia Beach). There are 60 min. between the 76° and 77° lines of longitude, with each tick mark depicting 1 min. The airport is one tick to the west of the 76° line, or 76°01'W.
The latitude is below the 30-min. latitude line across the center of the chart. See the numbered latitude line at the top (37°) of the chart. Since each tick mark represents 1 min. of latitude, and the airport is approximately six ticks south of the 36°30'N latitude, the airport is at 36°24'N latitude. Thus, Currituck County Airport is located at approximately 36°24'N – 76°01'W.
Answer (B) is incorrect. Currituck County Airport is south of the 36°30'N (not 37°00'N) line of latitude. Answer (C) is incorrect. Currituck County Airport is west (not east) of the 76°W line of longitude and 47°24'N is 11°N of the airport.

56. (Refer to Figure 58 on page 177.) (Refer to area 3.) Which airport is located at approximately 47°21'N latitude and 101°01'W longitude?

A. Underwood.

B. Evenson.

C. Washburn.

Answer (C) is correct. *(PHAK Chap 15)*
DISCUSSION: See Fig. 58. Find the 48° line of latitude (2/3 up the page). Start at the 47°30' line of latitude (the line below the 48° line) and count down nine ticks to the 47°21' mark and draw a horizontal line on the chart. Next find the 101° line of longitude and go left one tick and draw a vertical line. The closest airport is Washburn.
Answer (A) is incorrect. Underwood is a city (not an airport) northwest of Washburn by about 1 in. Answer (B) is incorrect. Evenson is north of the 47°36' latitude line.

57. (Refer to Figure 58 on page 177.) (Refer to area 2.) Which airport is located at approximately 47°39'30"N latitude and 100°53'00"W longitude?

A. Linrud.

B. Crooked Lake.

C. Johnson.

Answer (B) is correct.   *(PHAK Chap 15)*
    DISCUSSION: On Fig. 58, you are asked to locate an airport at 47°39'30"N latitude and 100°53'W longitude. Note that the 101° longitude line runs down the middle of the page. Accordingly, the airport you are seeking is 7 min. to the east of that line.
    Each crossline is 1 min. on the latitude and longitude lines. The 48° latitude line is approximately two-thirds of the way up the chart. The 47°30N latitude line is about one-fourth of the way up. One-third up from 47°30' to 48° latitude would be 47°39'. At this spot is Crooked Lake Airport.
    Answer (A) is incorrect. Linrud is north of the 48° latitude line. Answer (C) is incorrect. Both Johnson airports are south of 47°30' latitude line.

58. (Refer to Figure 66 on page 181.) (Refer to area 3.) Determine the approximate latitude and longitude of Shoshone County Airport.

A. 47°02'N – 116°11'W.

B. 47°33'N – 116°11'W.

C. 47°32'N – 116°41'W.

Answer (B) is correct.   *(PHAK Chap 15)*
    DISCUSSION: See Fig. 66, just below 3. Shoshone County Airport is just west of the 116° line of longitude (find 116° in the 8,000 MSL northwest of Shoshone). There are 60 min. between the 116° line and the 117° line. These are depicted in 1-min. ticks. Shoshone is 11 ticks or 11 min. past the 116° line.
    Note that the 48° line of latitude is labeled. Find 48° just northeast of the 116°. The latitude and longitude lines are presented each 30 min. Since lines of latitude are also divided into 1-min. ticks, the airport is three ticks above the 47°30' line, or 47°33'. The correct latitude and longitude is thus 47°33'N – 116°11'W.
    Answer (A) is incorrect. Shoshone Airport is just north of the 47°30' line of latitude (not 47°00'). Answer (C) is incorrect. Shoshone Airport is 11 ticks past the 116°00' line of longitude (not 116°30').

59. (Refer to Figure 59 on page 178.) (Refer to area 2.) What is the approximate latitude and longitude of Cooperstown Airport?

A. 47°25'N – 98°06'W.

B. 47°25'N – 99°54'W.

C. 47°55'N – 98°06'W.

Answer (A) is correct.   *(PHAK Chap 15)*
    DISCUSSION: First locate the Cooperstown Airport on Fig. 59. It is just above 2, middle right of chart. Note that it is to the left (west) of the 98° line of longitude. The line of longitude on the left side of the chart is 99°. Thus, the longitude is a little bit more than 98°, but not near 99°.
    With respect to latitude, note that Cooperstown Airport is just below a line of latitude that is not marked in terms of degrees. However, the next line of latitude below is 47° (see the left side of the chart, northwest of the Jamestown Airport). As with longitude, there are two lines of latitude for every degree of latitude; i.e., each line is 30 min. Thus, latitude of the Cooperstown Airport is almost 47°30', but not quite. Accordingly, Cooperstown Airport's latitude is 47°25'N and longitude is 98°06'W.
    Answer (B) is incorrect. Cooperstown is just west of the 98° line of longitude (not just east of 99°). Answer (C) is incorrect. Cooperstown is just south of the 47°30' line of latitude (not the 48°00' line).

END OF STUDY UNIT

Legend 1. – Sectional Aeronautical Chart.

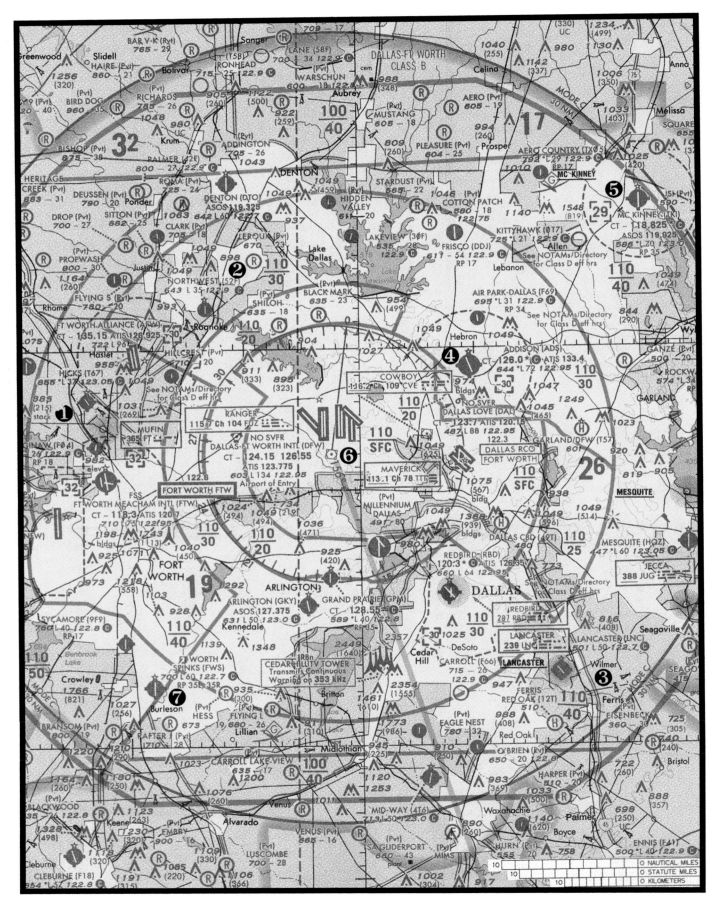

Figure 44. – Sectional Chart Excerpt.

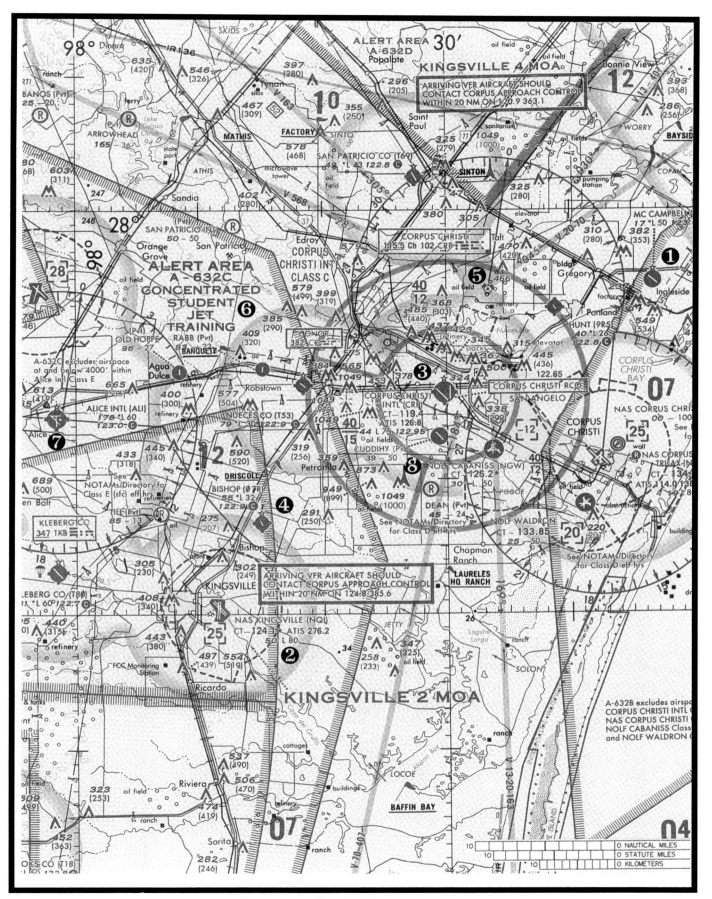

Figure 45. – Sectional Chart Excerpt.

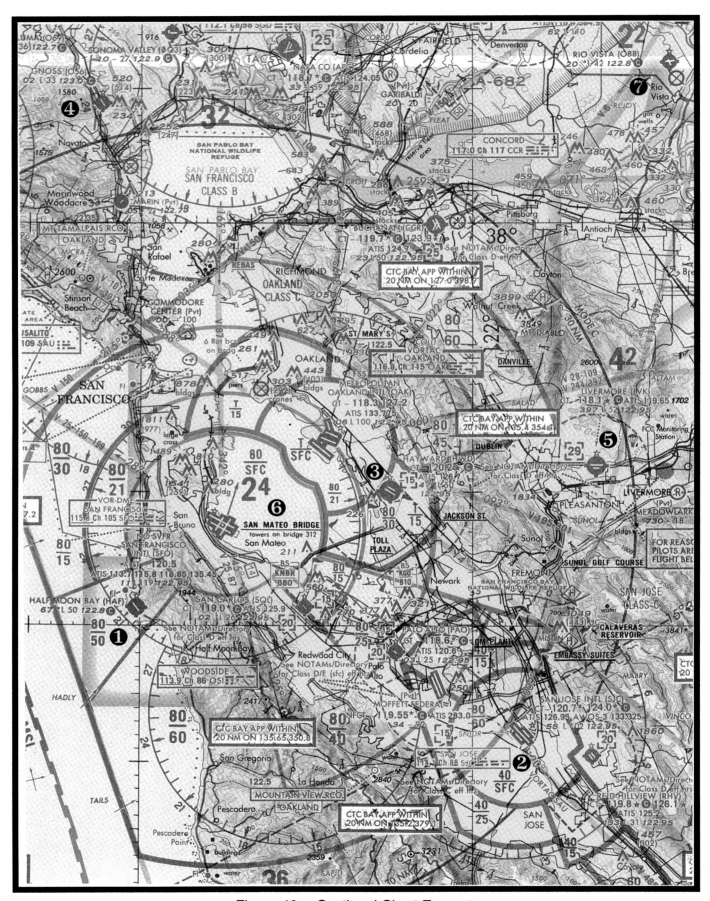

Figure 46. – Sectional Chart Excerpt.

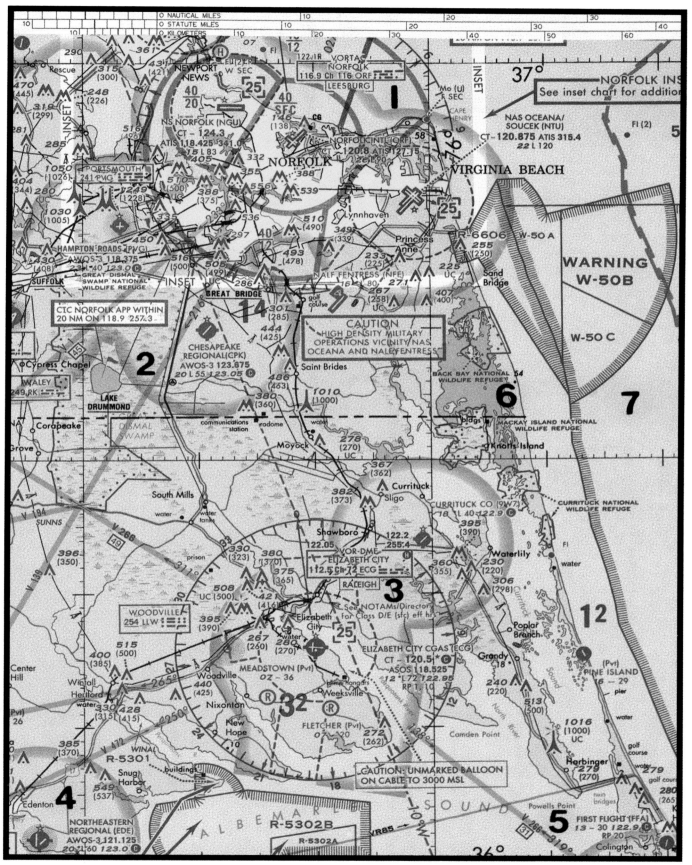

Figure 56. – Sectional Chart Excerpt.

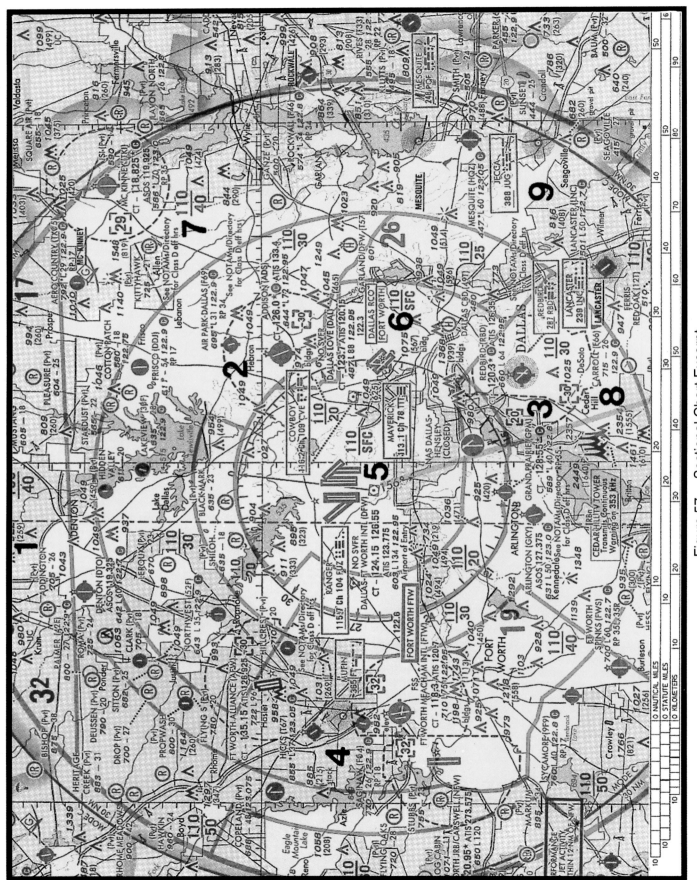

Figure 57. – Sectional Chart Excerpt.

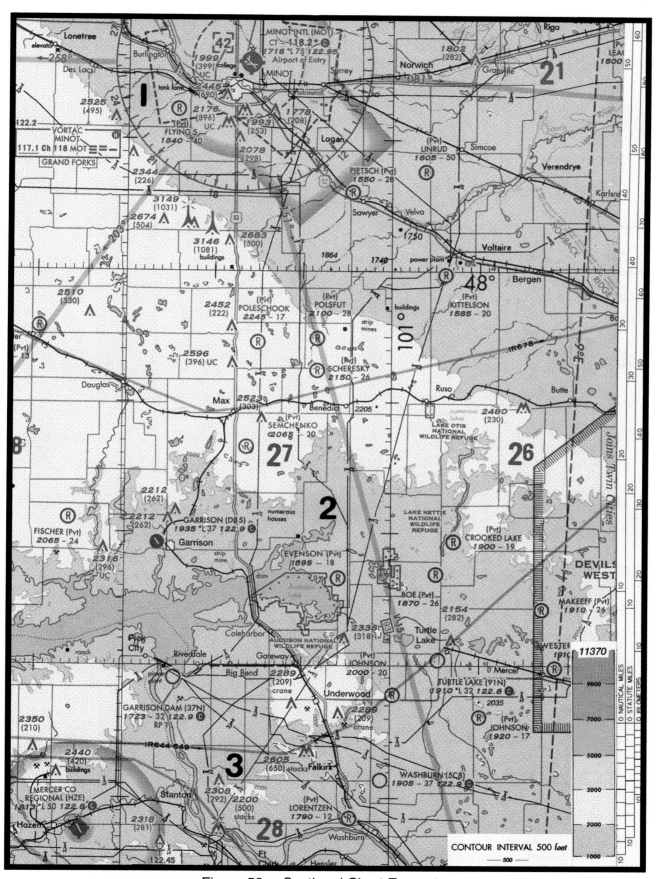

Figure 58. – Sectional Chart Excerpt.

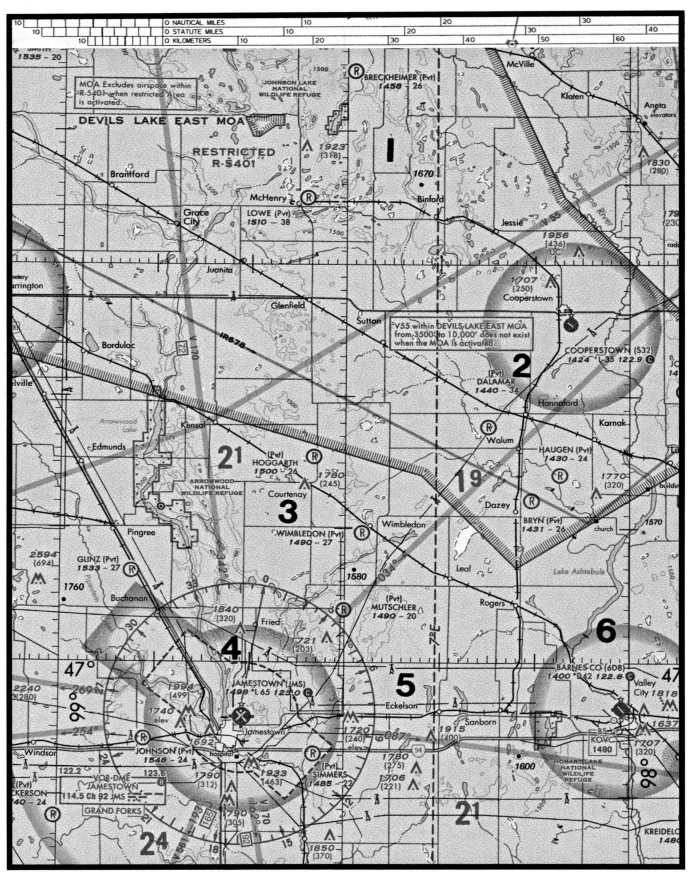

Figure 59. – Sectional Chart Excerpt.

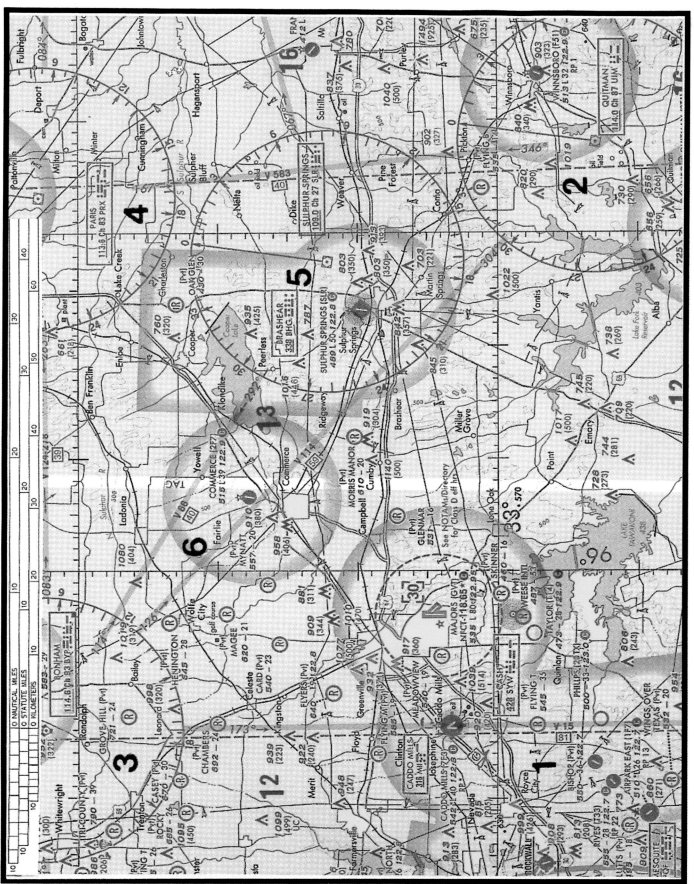

Figure 60. – Sectional Chart Excerpt.

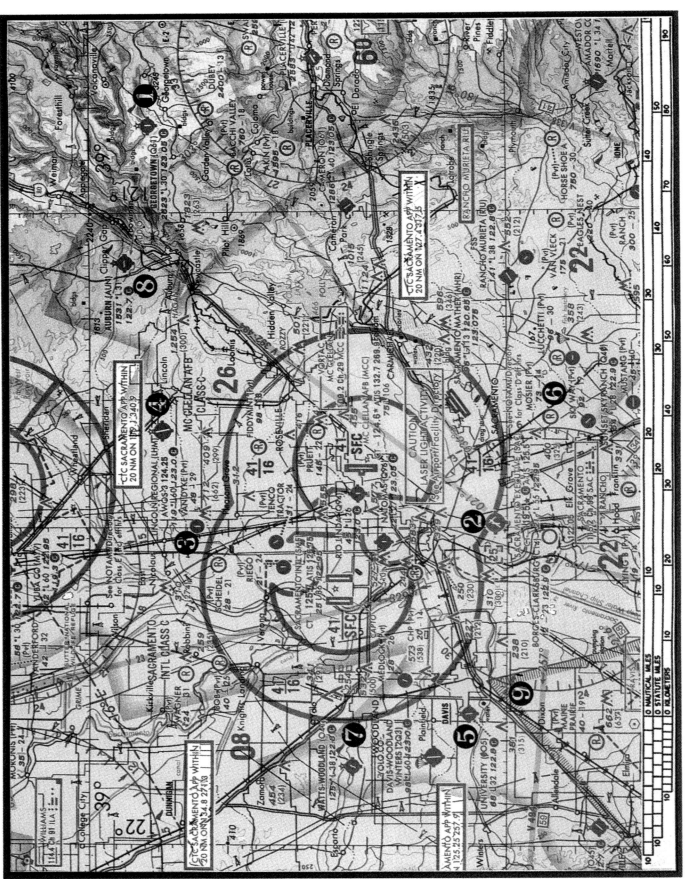

Figure 61. – Sectional Chart Excerpt.

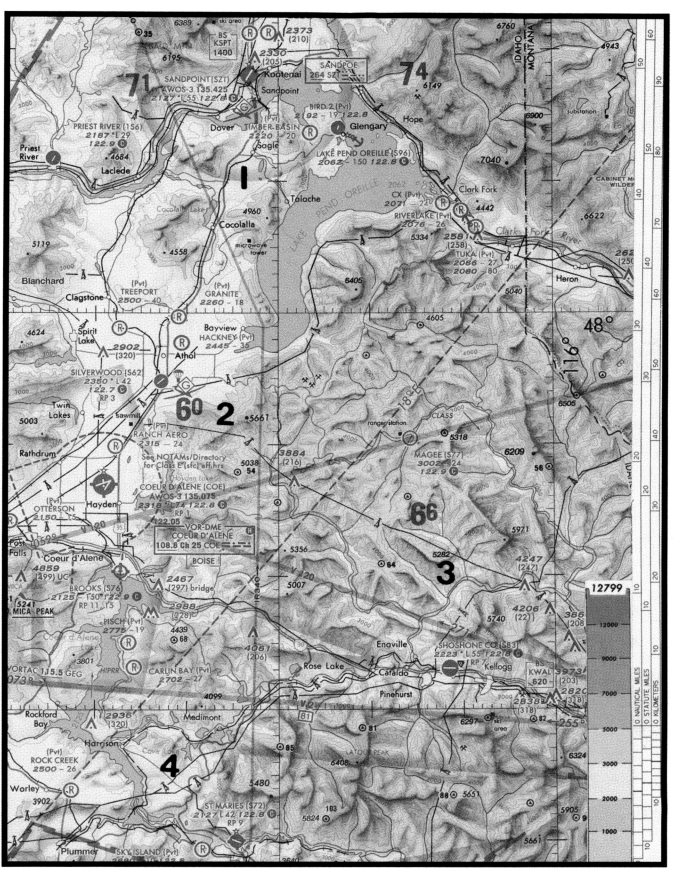

Figure 66. – Sectional Chart Excerpt.

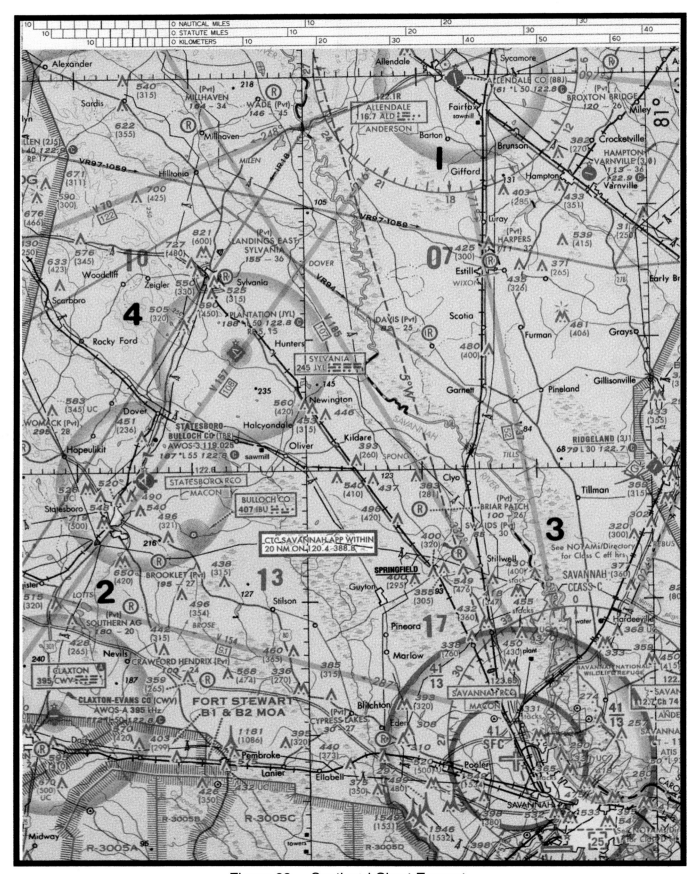

Figure 69. – Sectional Chart Excerpt.

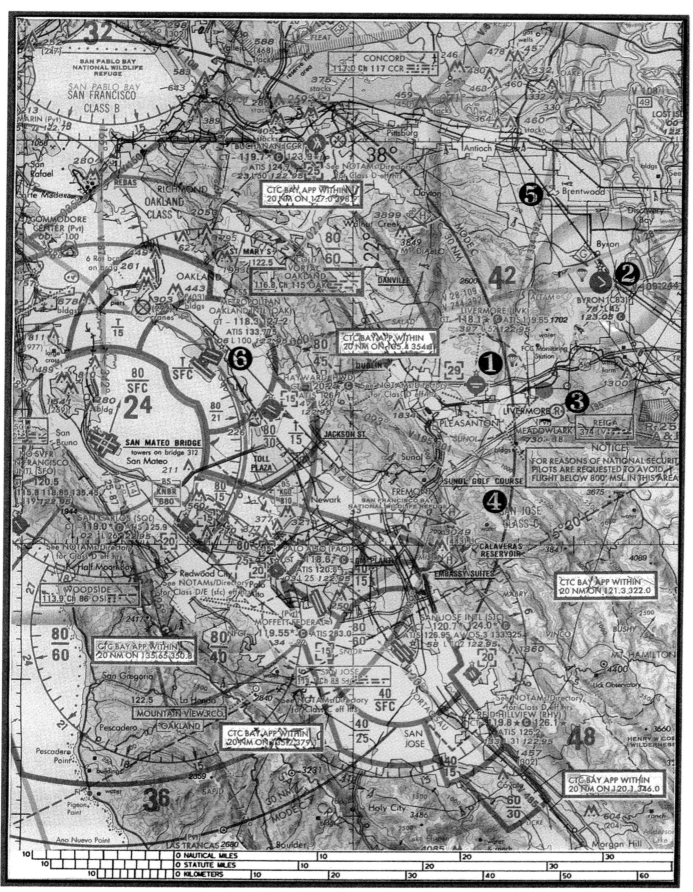

Figure 70. – Sectional Chart Excerpt.

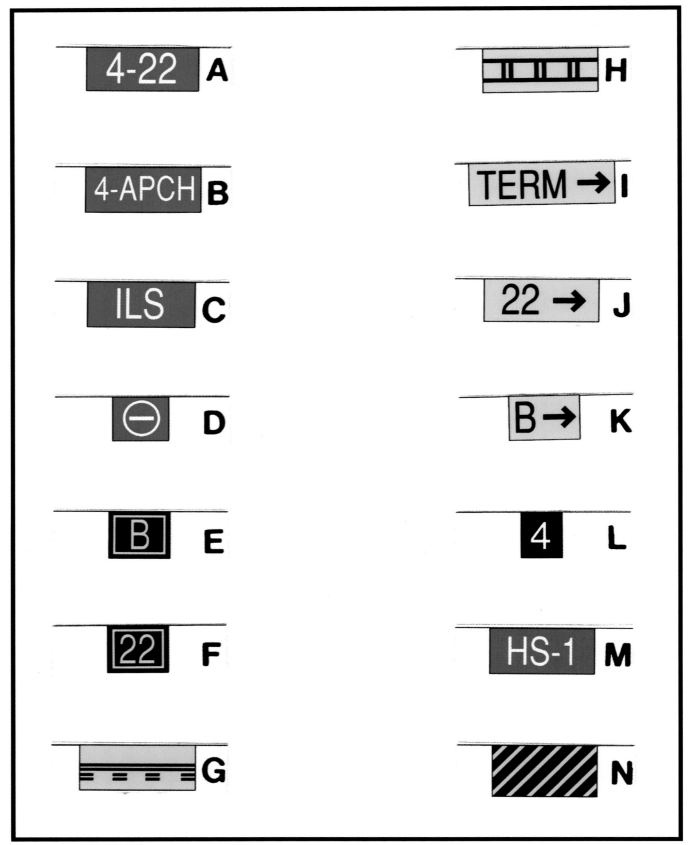

Figure 71. – U.S. Airport Signs.

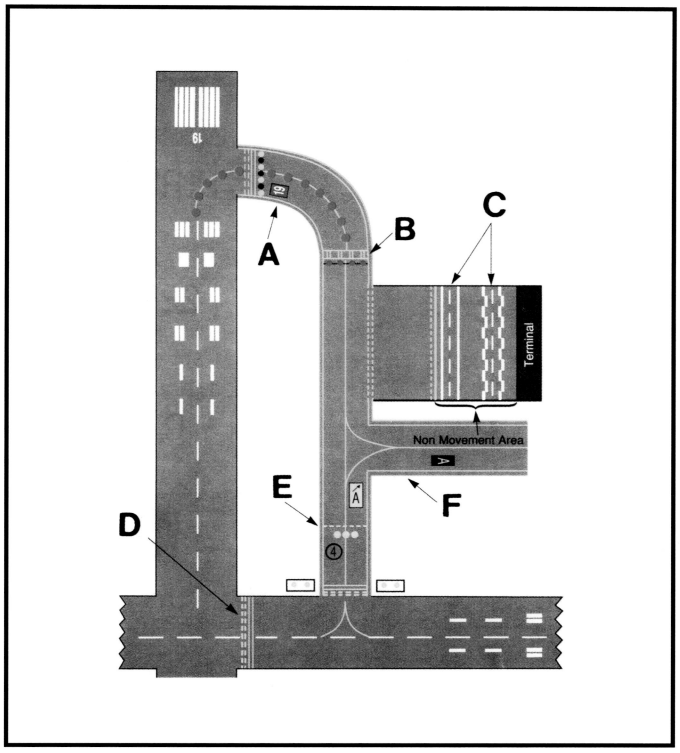

Figure 72. – Airport Markings.

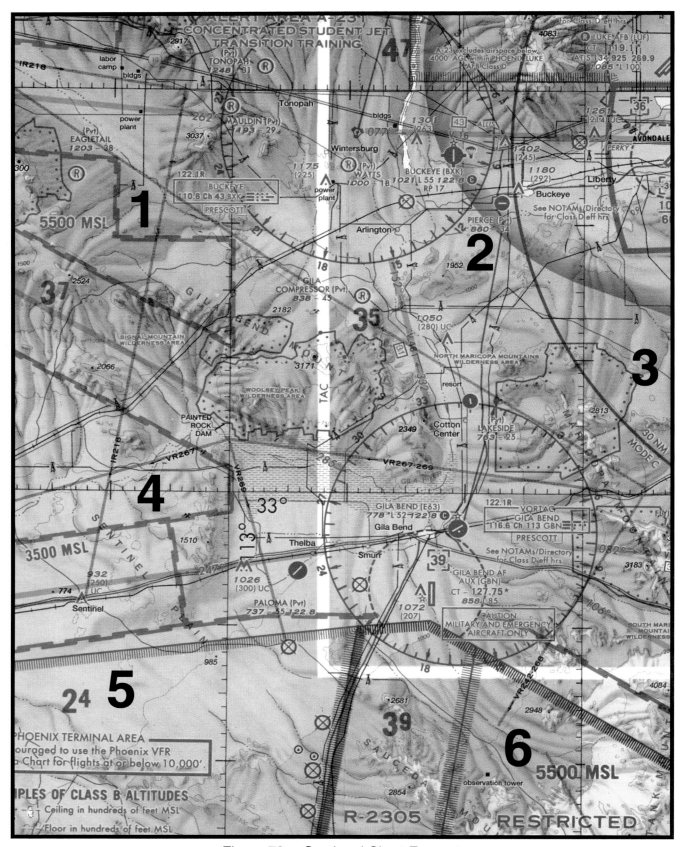

Figure 73. – Sectional Chart Excerpt.

STUDY UNIT TEN
NAVIGATION AND PREFLIGHT PREPARATION

(11 pages of outline)

This study unit contains outlines of major concepts tested, sample test questions and answers regarding navigation and preflight preparation, and an explanation of each answer. The table of contents above lists each subunit within this study unit, the number of questions pertaining to that particular subunit, and the pages on which the outlines and questions begin, respectively.

CAUTION: Recall that the **sole purpose** of this book is to expedite your passing the FAA pilot knowledge test for the sport pilot certificate. Accordingly, all extraneous material (i.e., topics or regulations not directly tested on the FAA pilot knowledge test) is omitted, even though much more information and knowledge are necessary to fly safely. This additional material is presented in the *Pilot Handbook* and *Sport Pilot Flight Maneuvers and Practical Test Prep*, available from Gleim Publications, Inc. See the order form on page 327.

10.1 DENSITY ALTITUDE

1. Density altitude is a measurement of the density of the air expressed in terms of altitude.

   a. Air density varies inversely with altitude; i.e., air is very dense at low altitudes and less dense at high altitudes.

   b. Temperature, humidity, and barometric pressure also affect air density.

      1) A scale of air density to altitude has been established using a standard temperature and pressure for each altitude. At sea level, standard is 15°C and 29.92" Hg.

      2) When temperature and pressure are not at standard (which is almost always), density altitude will not be the same as true altitude.

2. You are required to know how barometric pressure, temperature, and humidity affect density altitude. Visualize the following:

   a. As barometric pressure increases, the air becomes more compressed and compact. This is an increase in density. Air density is higher if the pressure is high, so the density altitude is said to be lower.

      1) Density altitude is increased by a decrease in pressure.
      2) Density altitude is decreased by an increase in pressure.

   b. As temperature increases, the air expands and therefore becomes less dense. This decrease in density means a higher density altitude. Remember, air is normally less dense at higher altitudes.

      1) Density altitude is increased by an increase in temperature.
      2) Density altitude is decreased by a decrease in temperature.

    c.   As relative humidity increases, the air becomes less dense. A given volume of moist air weighs less than the same volume of dry air. This decrease in density means a higher density altitude.

        1)   Density altitude is increased by an increase in humidity.

        2)   Density altitude is decreased by a decrease in humidity.

3.   Said another way, density altitude varies directly with temperature and humidity, and inversely with barometric pressure:

    a.   Cold, dry air and higher barometric pressure = low density altitude.

    b.   Hot, humid air and lower barometric pressure = high density altitude.

4.   Pressure altitude is based on standard temperature. Therefore, density altitude will exceed pressure altitude if the temperature is above standard.

5.   The primary reason for computing density altitude is to determine airplane performance.

    a.   High density altitude reduces an airplane's overall performance.

    b.   For example, climb performance is less and takeoff distance is longer.

    c.   Propellers have less efficiency because there is less air for the propeller to grip.

    d.   However, the same indicated airspeed is used for takeoffs and landings regardless of altitude or air density because the airspeed indicator is also directly affected by air density.

10.2 PREFLIGHT PREPARATION

1.   Normally you will have at least one and perhaps more days to plan a cross-country flight. Once you know where you are going, you can start your initial planning.

    a.   You should follow the weather so that you have a general understanding of the location and movement of pressure systems and fronts.

        1)   Weather information is normally gathered by watching various weather programs on television, utilizing DUATS, checking weather resources on the Internet, or contacting an Automated Flight Service Station (AFSS).

        2)   This background knowledge will help you understand the weather briefing you will receive on the day of your flight.

    b.   As part of your weather analysis, you should also obtain pertinent Notices to Airmen (NOTAMs) for your departure and destination as well as your route of flight.

        1)   The NOTAM system disseminates time-critical aeronautical information that either is of a temporary nature or is not sufficiently known in advance to permit publication on aeronautical charts or in other operational publications.

            a)   NOTAM information is aeronautical information that could affect your decision to make a flight.

        2)   NOTAMs are grouped into four types:

            a)   **NOTAM (D)** includes information such as airport or primary runway closures; changes in the status of navigational aids, ILSs, and radar service availability; and other information essential to planned en route, terminal, or landing operations. Also included is information on airport taxiways, aprons, ramp areas, and associated lighting.

            b)   **FDC NOTAMs** are issued by the Flight Data Center and contain regulatory information such as amendments to published instrument approach charts and other current aeronautical charts.

c) **Pointer NOTAMs** reduce total NOTAM volume by pointing to other NOTAMs (D) and FDC NOTAMs rather than duplicating potentially unnecessary information for an airport or NAVAID. They allow pilots to reference NOTAMs that might not be listed under a given airport or NAVAID identifier.

d) **Military NOTAMs** reference military airports and NAVAIDs and are rarely of any interest to civilian pilots.

3) The ***Notices to Airmen Publication (NTAP)*** is issued every 28 days and is an integral part of the NOTAM system. Once a NOTAM is published in the NTAP, the NOTAM is not provided during pilot weather briefings unless specifically requested.

a) The *NTAP* contains NOTAMs (D) that are expected to remain in effect for an extended period and FDC NOTAMs that are current at the time of publication.

c. Obtain the appropriate charts and other navigation publications (i.e., *A/FD, NTAP*) that you will need for your cross-country flight.

1) Be sure that you use only current charts and publications since revisions in aeronautical information occur constantly.

a) These revisions may include changes in radio frequencies, new obstructions, temporary or permanent closing of runways and airports, and other temporary or permanent hazards to flight.

d. Draw a course line from the center of your departure airport to the center of your destination airport on your sectional chart.

1) If your route is direct, it will consist of a single straight line between the airports.

2) If your route is not direct, it will consist of two or more straight line segments.

3) Make sure the course line is dark enough to read easily but light enough not to obscure any chart information.

4) If a fuel stop is required, show the airport as an intermediate stop or as the first leg of your flight.

e. Once you have your course line(s) drawn, survey where your flight will be taking you.

1) Look for available alternate airports en route.

2) Look at the type of terrain and obstructions, e.g., mountains, swamps, or large bodies of water, that would have an impact if an off-airport landing became necessary.

a) Mentally prepare for any type of emergency situation and the action to be taken during your flight.

3) By knowing the highest terrain and obstructions, you will know the minimum safe altitude to meet the requirements of FAR Part 91.

4) You should check the course and areas on either side of your planned route to determine if any type of airspace along your route should concern you (e.g., restricted, prohibited, etc.) or if any airspace has special operational requirements (e.g., Class B, C, or D airspace).

5) After you have looked at all of these aspects, you may choose an alternate route that offers fewer hazards and more safety options than your initial choice.

f.   There is no set rule for selecting a landmark as a checkpoint. Every locality has its own peculiarities.

    1)   The general rule to follow is never to place complete reliance on any single landmark.

    2)   You should have a checkpoint within 5 NM of your departure airport that you could fly over to put you on your desired course.

g.   The course measured on a sectional chart by reference to a meridian is known as the true course (TC). Use your plotter to determine the TC, the total distance of your flight, and the distance between each checkpoint.

    1)   Place the small hole in the center of the protractor section over a meridian (line of longitude), and then align either the bottom or upper edge of the plotter with your course line, as shown below.

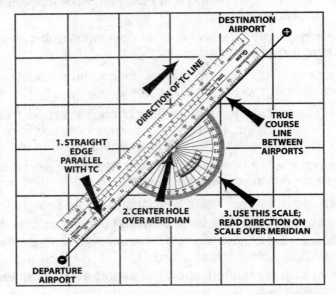

    a)   In the illustration above, the TC, which is read on the scale over the meridian, is 043°. Ensure that you use the proper scale for your direction of flight.

    b)   Meridians are not parallel lines. They converge at the poles. Therefore, course measurements should be made near the midpoint of each segment.

    2)   If your course is nearly north or south and does not cross a meridian, place the hole of your plotter over a parallel (line of latitude), and use the inner scale as shown on page 191.

    3)   Once you determine the TC, we suggest that you determine the magnetic variation along your route and apply that to the TC to determine the magnetic course (MC).

        a)   Determine the magnetic variation by locating the nearest isogonic line on the sectional chart.

            i)   Isogonic lines are depicted as dashed magenta-colored lines on the sectional chart and are labeled with the number of degrees of variation east (E) or west (W), e.g., 3°W.

            ii) $MC = TC \genfrac{}{}{0pt}{}{+W}{-E} Var.$

h.   Next, measure the total distance of the course, as well as the distance between checkpoints.

1)   Use the nautical mile scale at the bottom of the plotter.

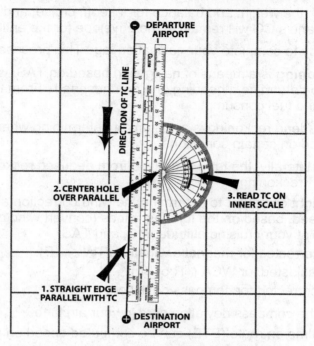

i.   Complete as much as you can of your navigation log.

1)   Fill in the checkpoints you have selected.
2)   If you are using VORs, fill in the frequency and the Morse code identifier.

2.   On the day of your flight, you should obtain a weather briefing that, among many other important items, will include forecast winds and temperatures aloft. You will use this information to complete your flight planning log.

3.   Ensure that you maintain an altitude appropriate for obstacle or terrain clearance and the FARs.

a.   FAR 91.119 requires the following minimum altitudes, except during takeoffs and landings:

1)   If an engine fails, an altitude allowing an emergency landing without undue hazards to persons or property on the ground
2)   Over any congested area of a city, town, or settlement, or over any open-air assembly of persons, an altitude 1,000 ft. above the highest obstacle within a horizontal radius of 2,000 ft. of the airplane
3)   Over other than congested areas, an altitude of 500 ft. AGL, except

a)   No closer than 500 ft. to any person, vessel, vehicle, or structure when over open water or sparsely populated areas

b.   You are requested to maintain a minimum altitude of 2,000 ft. AGL over the following:

1)   National parks, monuments, seashores, lakeshores, recreation areas, and scenic riverways administered by the National Park Service
2)   National wildlife refuges, big game refuges, and wildlife ranges administered by the U.S. Fish and Wildlife Service
3)   Wilderness and primitive areas administered by the U.S. Forest Service

4. Use the performance charts in your POH to determine takeoff distance, cruise performance (i.e., TAS and fuel consumption), and landing distance.

    a. An associated task is to calculate the weight and balance for your airplane.

        1) Check the weight and balance for takeoff, cruise, and landing to ensure the airplane's CG will remain in the envelope for the entire flight.

5. Now you are ready to complete your navigation log. This process is called dead reckoning.

    a. **Dead reckoning** is a means of navigation based on TAS, wind direction and velocity, and MC to determine a heading and groundspeed. From this you can determine time en route and fuel consumption.

        1) Thus, dead reckoning is a system of determining where the airplane should be, based on certain conditions.

            a) Literally, the term is derived from deduced reckoning, i.e., ded., or "dead," reckoning.

    b. Use your flight computer to determine the wind correction angle (WCA) and estimated groundspeed, based on the forecast winds (convert wind direction from true to magnetic) at your cruising altitude, MC, and TAS.

    c. MC is TC corrected for magnetic variation (+W or –E).

    d. MH is MC adjusted for WCA (+R or –L).

    e. CH is MH corrected for compass deviation.

        1) See the compass deviation card in your airplane.

    f. Estimated time en route (ETE) can be computed based on groundspeed and distance.

        1) During your flight, to calculate the distance flown in a given amount of time, multiply the time by the ground speed.

    g. Estimated fuel consumption is computed based on fuel flow and ETE.

        1) VFR fuel requirements. FARs require that there be sufficient fuel (based on forecast wind and weather conditions) to fly to the intended destination at normal cruise speed AND

            a) Be able to continue on for 30 min. in daytime.

6. On the day of your flight, you should

    a. Obtain a complete weather briefing. Based on the information you receive, you may

        1) Be able to proceed with the flight as planned;

        2) Need to adjust your route of flight, plan different alternate airports, or plan extra fuel stops; or

        3) Cancel the flight altogether.

    b. Complete a navigation log.

        1) Note the availability of Flight Service Stations (FSS) along your route of flight. In the event you get lost, Flight Service can provide you with assistance.

    c. Be sure to have your pilot and medical certificate or driver's license in your possession.

        1) A student pilot is also required to carry his/her logbook.

    d. Thoroughly preflight your airplane, and make sure that it is appropriately fueled and that all equipment is operational.

    e. Complete a weight-and-balance computation.

7.   Prior to flight, a briefing should be conducted that includes the procedure for the exchange of the flight controls. A positive three-step process is a proven procedure and strongly recommended.

   a.   When exchanging the flight controls from the instructor to the student, the instructor initially states, "You have the flight controls." The student acknowledges by saying, "I have the flight controls." The instructor again says, "You have the flight controls."

   b.   The procedure is reversed for exchanging the flight controls from the student to the instructor.

10.3 WEIGHT AND BALANCE

1.   Weight-and-balance calculation must be reviewed prior to each flight. On local training flights without baggage and even with full fuel, weight and balance should not be a problem. On cross-country flights, weight and balance data warrant more attention.

2.   Overloading an aircraft causes reduced climb rates, excessive structural loads, and shortened cruise range. Operation in excess of the maximum weight or outside CG limits is prohibited and extremely dangerous.

3.   Use the airplane's certified weight and balance information (normally located in the POH) to calculate the weight and balance.

   a.   Make sure you are within maximum weight and CG limits.

   b.   Weight-and-balance calculations are covered in Study Unit 14 – "Airplane Performance and Weight and Balance."

4.   Excessive weight will have adverse effects on an airplane's performance in most respects

   a.   With more weight, the airplane requires more lift, resulting in additional drag and therefore using more fuel.

   b.   In an emergency, the reduced performance becomes more critical and the safety margin is reduced.

10.4 NAVIGATION

1.   The following are two major types of navigation applicable to sport pilots:

   a.   **Pilotage** is the navigation of your airplane using your sectional chart to fly from one visible landmark to another.

      1)   Pilotage becomes difficult in areas without prominent landmarks or under conditions of low visibility.

      2)   During your flight, you will use pilotage in conjunction with dead reckoning to verify your calculations and keep track of your position.

      3)   You will be tested on your pilotage skills in the sport pilot practical test.

   b.   **Dead reckoning** is the navigation of your airplane by means of computations based on true airspeed, course, heading, wind direction and speed, groundspeed, and elapsed time.

      1)   During your flight, you will keep track of your actual compass heading and the time.

         a)   You will mark down the time over every checkpoint. Then you can compare your estimated groundspeed to actual groundspeed and revise your estimated fuel (used and remaining).

         b)   From this you can determine the actual wind conditions, groundspeed, time en route, and fuel consumption.

         c)   Thus, you can deduce your time of arrival at your next checkpoint and the amount of fuel that will be used.

2)   A good knowledge of the principles of dead reckoning will assist you in determining your position after having become disoriented or confused.

a)   By using information from the part of the flight already completed, it is possible to restrict your search for identifiable landmarks to a limited area to verify calculations and to locate yourself.

3)   Correcting true course (TC) for wind direction and velocity produces true heading (TH).

2.   Roads that are well traveled or those most apparent when viewed from the air will be shown on sectional charts.

10.5 GLOBAL POSITIONING SYSTEM (GPS) NAVIGATION

1.   The Global Positioning System (GPS) is a satellite-based radio navigation system.

2.   GPS is composed of a constellation of 24 satellites.

a.   The GPS constellation is designed so that at least five satellites are always observable by a user anywhere on earth.

3.   The GPS receiver needs at least four satellites to yield a three-dimensional position (latitude, longitude, and altitude) and time solution.

a.   The GPS receiver computes navigational data, such as distance and bearing to a waypoint (e.g., an airport), groundspeed, etc., by using the airplane's known latitude/longitude (position) and referencing it to a database built into the receiver.

4.   Navigating by GPS must be integrated with other forms of electronic navigation as well as pilotage and dead reckoning.

a.   VFR pilots should never rely solely on one system of navigation.

10.6 DETERMINING WIND DIRECTION AND SPEED

1.   An important aspect of flying is the effect wind can have on your flight path. The speed and direction of the winds aloft affect both the speed and direction in which the aircraft moves over the earth's surface.

a.   For example, if a flight is made on a course to the east and the wind is blowing from the northeast, the airplane must be headed somewhat to the north in order to counteract the wind drift.

2.   You can determine the actual winds aloft at your cruising altitude. To do so you need to know the following:

a.   True course (actual path of travel)
b.   True heading
c.   Groundspeed
d.   TAS

3.   EXAMPLE: Determine the winds aloft given a TAS of 98 kt., a true course of 095°, a true heading of 105°, and a groundspeed of 85 kt.

a.   Rotate the plotting transparency so the true course (095°) is under the True Index.
b.   Move the sliding card so the grommet is over the groundspeed (85 kt.) speed arc.
c.   Determine the WCA by locating the true heading on the compass rose, and directly above determine the WCA on the correction scale. In this example, the true heading of 105° is opposite 10° on the correction scale and to the right of the True Index.
d.   Locate the TAS (98 kt.) speed arc and move right to the 10° wind correction line and mark a wind dot at that location.
e.   Rotate the plotting transparency so the wind dot is on the center line above the grommet and move the sliding card so the grommet is over the 100-kt. speed arc.

f.   Wind direction is read under the True Index, and the wind speed is the number of units above the grommet.

1)   In this example, the wind direction is 150° true, and the wind speed is 20 kt.

4.   Find wind direction, wind speed, and wind correction angle (WCA).

5.   Use your flight computer to solve these practice problems (answers are located below).

	Wind Direction	Wind Speed	TC	TAS	WCA	TH	Ground-speed
a.	___°	__ kt.	130°	150 kt.	___	142°	147 kt.
b.	___°	__ kt.	100°	110 kt.	~15	085°	80 kt.

6.   Answers to practice problems:

	Wind Direction	Wind Speed	WCA
a.	220°	31 kt.	12°R
b.	53°	39 kt.	15°L

10.7   VFR FLIGHT PLAN

1.   A VFR flight plan is a form (see Figure 152 on page 204) that contains 17 blocks of information. Only the following blocks are tested on the sport pilot knowledge test:

a.   Block 7: "Cruising Altitude." Use only your initial requested altitude on your VFR flight plan.

b.   Block 9: "Destination (Name of airport and city)" should include the airport or place at which you plan to make your last landing for this flight.

1)   Unless you plan a stopover of more than 1 hr. elsewhere en route

c.   Block 12: "Fuel on Board" (in hours and minutes) requires the amount of usable fuel in the airplane at the time of departure, expressed in hours of flying time.

2.   You should close your flight plan with the nearest FSS or, if one is not available, you may request any ATC facility to relay your cancelation to the FSS.

a.   Control towers (and ground control) do not automatically close VFR or DVFR flight plans since they do not know if a particular VFR aircraft is on a flight plan.

10.8   PREFLIGHT INSPECTION

1.   During the preflight inspection, the pilot in command is responsible for determining that the airplane is safe for flight.

2.   The owner or operator is responsible for maintaining the airplane in an airworthy condition.

3.   For the first flight of the day, the preflight inspection should be accomplished by a thorough and systematic means recommended by the manufacturer.

10.9   FAA ADVISORY CIRCULARS

1.   The FAA issues advisory circulars to provide a systematic means for the issuance of nonregulatory materials of interest to the aviation public.

2.   The circulars are issued in a numbered system of general subject matter areas to correspond with the subject areas in Federal Aviation Regulations (e.g., 60 Airmen, 70 Airspace, 90 Air Traffic Control and General Operation).

3. FAA advisory circulars are available from the FAA and the U.S. Government Printing Office.

   a. All Advisory Circulars can be viewed from the FAA's website at www.faa.gov, under the Regulations and Policies link.

   b. An *Advisory Circular Checklist* (AC 00-2) is available by writing the U.S. Department of Transportation, Subsequent Distribution Office, SVC-121.23, Ardmore East Business Center, 3341 Q 75th Ave., Landover, MD 20785. Fax requests can be sent to (301) 386-5394.

4. Time-critical information on airports and changes that affect the national airspace system are provided by Notices to Airmen (NOTAMs).

   a. Flight Data Center (FDC) NOTAMs are issued by the National Flight Data Center and contain regulatory information, such as Temporary Flight Restrictions, etc.

   b. NOTAM-Ls (Local NOTAMs) include only items of a local nature. NOTAM-L information must be specifically requested from the FSS that has responsibility for the airport concerned.

5. The FAA publication that provides the aviation community with basic flight information and Air Traffic Control procedures for use in the National Airspace System is the *Aeronautical Information Manual (AIM).*

10.10 *AIRPORT/FACILITY DIRECTORY*

1. *Airport/Facility Directories (A/FDs)* are published by the U.S. Department of Commerce every 56 days for each of seven geographical districts of the United States.

   a. *A/FDs* provide information on services available, runways, special conditions at the airport, communications, navigation aids, etc.

2. The airport name comes first.

3. The third item on the first line is the number of miles and direction of the airport from the city.

   a. EXAMPLE: **4 NW** means 4 NM northwest of the city.

4. Right-turn traffic is indicated by "Rgt tfc" following a runway number.

5. When a control tower is not in operation, the CTAF frequency (found in the section titled **Communications**) should be used for traffic advisories.

6. Initial communication should be with Approach Control if available where you are landing. The frequency is listed following "APP/DEP CON."

   a. It may be different for approaches from different headings.
   b. It may be operational only for certain hours of the day.

7. In class C airspace, VFR aircraft are provided the following radar services:

   a. Sequencing to the primary Class C airport
   b. Approved separation between IFR and VFR aircraft
   c. Basic radar services, including safety alerts, limited vectoring, and traffic advisories

8. A sample *A/FD* legend is reproduced on the following page.

9. Figure 55 on page 308 shows an excerpt from an *A/FD*. The FAA has not released any questions on this figure; however, you may encounter some on your knowledge test. To prepare for such questions, study Figure 55 along with this subunit until you are familiar with the interpretation of each element in the figure.

2 　　　　　　　　　DIRECTORY LEGEND

SAMPLE

　① 　　　③ ④ 　⑤ 　　　　⑥ 　　　　　　　　　　⑦

CITY NAME
　AIRPORT NAME(ORL)　4 E　UTC-5(-4DT)　N28° 32.72'　W81° 21.17'　　　　**JACKSONVILLE**
　200　B　S4　**FUEL** 100.JET A　OX 1, 2, 3　TPA--1000(800)　AOE　ARFF Index A　Not insp.　**COPTER**
　　　　　　　　　　　　　　　　　　　　　　　　　　　　　　　　　　H--4G, L--19C
　⑨ ⑩ ⑪ 　　⑫ 　　　⑬ 　　⑭ 　　　　⑮ ⑯ 　　⑰ 　　　　**IAP**
　　　　　　　　　　　　　　　　　　　　　　　　　　　　　　　　　　　⑧

⑱→　**RWY 07-25:** H6000X150 (ASPH-PFC)　S--90, D--160, DT--300--PCN 80 R/B/W/T　　HIRL　CL　0.4% up E
　　RWY 07: ALSF1. Trees.　　　**RWY 25:** REIL. Rgt tfc.
　　RWY 13-31: H4620X100 (ASPH)　　HIRL
　　RWY 13: SAVASI(S2L)--GA 3.3°　TCH 89'. Pole.　　　　**RWY 31:** PAPI(P2L)--GA 3.1°　TCH 36'. Tree. Rgt tfc.
　　RUNWAY DECLARED DISTANCE INFORMATION
　　RWY 07:　TORA-6000　　TODA-6700　　ASDA-5700　　LDA-5500
　　RWY 25:　TORA-6000　　TODA-6000　　ASDA-6000　　LDA-5700
⑲→　**AIRPORT REMARKS:** Special Air Traffic Rules--Part 93, see Regulatory Notices. Attended 1200-0300Z‡. Parachute
　　Jumping. CAUTION cattle and deer on arpt. Acft. 100,000 lbs. or over ctc Director of Aviation for approval
　　305--894-9831. Fee for all airline charters, travel clubs and certain revenue producing acft. Flight Notification
　　Service (ADCUS) available.
⑳→　**WEATHER DATA SOURCES:** AWOS-1 120.3 (202) 426-8000. LLWAS.
㉑→　**COMMUNICATONS: ATIS** 127.25　**UNICOM** 122.95
　　NAME FSS (ORL) on arpt. 123.65 122.65 122.2. TF 1-899-WX-BRIEF, NOTAM FILE ORL.　　　　　　←　　②
　Ⓡ **NAME APP/DEP CON** 128.35 (1200-0400Z‡)
　　TOWER 118.7　**GND CON** 121.7　　**CLNC DEL** 125.55　　**PRE TAXI CLNC** 125.5
㉒→　**AIRSPACE: CLASS B** See VFR Terminal Area Chart.
㉓→　**RADIO AIDS TO NAVIGATION:** NOTAM FILE MCO. VHF/DF ctc. FSS.
　　(H) ABVORTAC 112.2　MCO　Chan 59　N28° 32.55'　W81° 20.12'　at fld.　　1110/8E.
　　　TWEB avbl 1300-0100Z‡. VOR unusable 050°--060° beyond 15 NM below 5000'.
　　HERNY NDB (LOM) 221　OR　N28° 30.40'　W81° 26.05'　　067°　5.4 NM to fld.
　　ILS 109.9　I-ORL　Rwy 07,　LOM HERNY NDB.
　　ASR/PAR (1200--0400Z‡)
㉔→　**COMM/NAVAID REMARKS:** Emerg frequency 121.5 not available at tower.

　　• •
　　HELIPAD H1: H100x75 (ASPH)
　　HELIPAD H2: H60x60 (ASPH)　　　　　　　　　　　　　　　　　　　　　　↗
　　HELIPORT REMARKS: Helipad H2 lctd on general aviation side and H2 lctd on air carrier side of arpt.　① ↙
　　• •
　　187　　TPA 1000(813)
　　WATERWAY 13-31: 5000x300 (WATER)
　　SEAPLANE REMARKS: Birds roosting and feeding areas along river banks. Seaplanes operating adjacent to NE side of
　　arpt not visible from twr and are required to ctc twr.

D AIRPORT NAME (MCO)　6 SE　UTC-5(-4DT)　N28°25.88'　W81°19.48'　　　**JACKSONVILLE**
　96　B　**FUEL** 100.JET A, MOGAS　LRA　　　　　　　　　　　　　　　　　　**H--4G, L--19C**
　RWY 18R-36L: H12004x300 (CONC-GRVD)　S--100, D--200, DT--400　　HIRL　　　　**IAP**
　　RWY 18R: ALSF1. REIL. Rgt tfc.　0.3% up　　**RWY 36L:** ALSF1.　0.4% down
　RWY 18R-36R: H12004x200 (ASPH)　S--165, D--200, DT--400　　HIRL
　　RWY 18L: LDIN. ALSF1. TDZL REIL. VASI(V4L)--GA 3.5°　TCH 36',Thld dsplcd 300'. Trees. Rgt tfc. Arresting device.
　AIRPORT REMARKS: Attended 1200.0300Z‡, ACTIVATE HIRL Rwy 18L-36R---CTAF.
　COMMUNICATONS: CTAF 124.3　**ATIS** 127.75　**UNICOM** 122.8
　NAME FSS (MCO) TF 1-800-WX-BRIEF. LC894-0869. NOTAM FILE MCO.
　NAME RCO 122.4 112.2T 122.1R (NAME FSS)
　Ⓡ **APP CON** 124.8 (337°-179°)　　120.1 (180°-336°)　　**DEP CON** 120.15
　　TOWER 124.3 NFCT (1200-0400Z‡)　　**GND CON** 121.85　　**CLNC DEL** 134.7
　AIRSPACE: CLASS D svc 1200--0400Z‡ other times CLASS E.
　RADIO AIDS TO NAVIGATION: NOTAM FILE MCO.
　　(H) VORTAC 112.2　MCO　Chan 59　N28° 32.55'　W81° 20.12'　173°　5.7 NM to fld. 1110/8E.　**HIWAS.**
　　MLS　Chan 514　Rwy 36R

All Bearings and Radials are Magnetic unless otherwise specified.
All mileages are nautical unless otherwise noted.
All times are UTC except as noted.
The horizontal reference datum of this publication is North American Datum of 1983 (NAD83), which for charting purposes
is considered equivalent to World Geodetic System 1984 (WGS 84).

Legend 2. -- Airport/Facility Directory.

QUESTIONS

10.1 Density Altitude

1. What are the standard temperature and pressure values for sea level?

A. 15°C and 29.92" Hg.

B. 59°C and 1013.2 millibars.

C. 59°F and 29.92 millibars.

Answer (A) is correct. *(AvW Chap 3)*
DISCUSSION: The standard temperature and pressure values for sea level are 15°C and 29.92" Hg. This is equivalent to 59°F and 1013.2 millibars of mercury.
Answer (B) is incorrect. Standard temperature is 59°F (not 59°C). Answer (C) is incorrect. Standard pressure is 29.92" Hg (not 29.92 millibars).

2. What is density altitude?

A. The height above the standard datum plane.

B. The pressure altitude corrected for nonstandard temperature.

C. The altitude read directly from the altimeter.

Answer (B) is correct. *(PHAK Chap 10)*
DISCUSSION: Density altitude is the pressure altitude corrected for nonstandard temperature.
Answer (A) is incorrect. It defines pressure altitude. Answer (C) is incorrect. It is indicated altitude.

3. Density altitude, and its effect on landing performance, is defined by

A. pressure altitude and ambient temperature.

B. headwind and landing weight.

C. humidity and braking friction forces.

Answer (A) is correct. *(PHAK Chap 10)*
DISCUSSION: Density altitude is defined as pressure altitude adjusted for nonstandard temperature. An increase in density altitude will increase the landing speed of an aircraft. The aircraft will land at the same indicated airspeed as at sea level, but, because of the reduced density, the true airspeed (TAS) will be greater.
Answer (B) is incorrect. Headwind and landing weight have no effect on density altitude. Answer (C) is incorrect. While humidity can affect density altitude, braking friction forces have no effect on density altitude.

4. What effect, if any, does high humidity have on aircraft performance?

A. It increases performance.

B. It decreases performance.

C. It has no effect on performance.

Answer (B) is correct. *(PHAK Chap 3)*
DISCUSSION: As the air becomes more humid, it becomes less dense. This is because a given volume of moist air weighs less than the same volume of dry air. Less dense air reduces aircraft performance.
Answer (A) is incorrect. High humidity reduces (not increases) performance. Answer (C) is incorrect. The three factors that affect aircraft performance are pressure, temperature, and humidity.

5. Which factor would tend to increase the density altitude at a given airport?

A. An increase in barometric pressure.

B. An increase in ambient temperature.

C. A decrease in relative humidity.

Answer (B) is correct. *(AvW Chap 3)*
DISCUSSION: When air temperature increases, density altitude increases because, at a higher temperature, the air is less dense.
Answer (A) is incorrect. Density altitude decreases as barometric pressure increases. Answer (C) is incorrect. Density altitude decreases as relative humidity decreases.

6. What effect does high density altitude, as compared to low density altitude, have on propeller efficiency and why?

    A. Efficiency is increased due to less friction on the propeller blades.

    B. Efficiency is reduced because the propeller exerts less force at high density altitudes than at low density altitudes.

    C. Efficiency is reduced due to the increased force of the propeller in the thinner air.

Answer (B) is correct. *(AvW Chap 3)*
    DISCUSSION: The propeller produces thrust in proportion to the mass of air being accelerated through the rotating propeller. If the air is less dense, the propeller efficiency is decreased. Remember, higher density altitude refers to less dense air.
    Answer (A) is incorrect. There is decreased, not increased, efficiency. Answer (C) is incorrect. The propeller exerts less (not more) force on the air when the air is thinner, i.e., at higher density altitudes.

7. What effect does high density altitude have on aircraft performance?

    A. It increases engine performance.

    B. It reduces climb performance.

    C. It increases takeoff performance.

Answer (B) is correct. *(PHAK Chap 10)*
    DISCUSSION: High density altitude reduces all aspects of an airplane's performance, including takeoff and climb performance.
    Answer (A) is incorrect. Engine performance is decreased (not increased). Answer (C) is incorrect. Takeoff runway length is increased, i.e., reduces takeoff performance.

8. Which combination of atmospheric conditions will reduce aircraft takeoff and climb performance?

    A. Low temperature, low relative humidity, and low density altitude.

    B. High temperature, low relative humidity, and low density altitude.

    C. High temperature, high relative humidity, and high density altitude.

Answer (C) is correct. *(PHAK Chap 10)*
    DISCUSSION: Takeoff and climb performance are reduced by high density altitude. High density altitude is a result of high temperatures and high relative humidity.
    Answer (A) is incorrect. Low temperature, low relative humidity, and low density altitude all improve airplane performance. Answer (B) is incorrect. Low relative humidity and low density altitude both improve airplane performance.

9. If the outside air temperature (OAT) at a given altitude is warmer than standard, the density altitude is

    A. equal to pressure altitude.

    B. lower than pressure altitude.

    C. higher than pressure altitude.

Answer (C) is correct. *(PHAK Chap 10)*
    DISCUSSION: When temperature increases, the air expands and therefore becomes less dense. This decrease in density means a higher density altitude. Pressure altitude is based on standard temperature. Thus, density altitude exceeds pressure altitude when the temperature is warmer than standard.
    Answer (A) is incorrect. Density altitude equals pressure altitude only when temperature is standard. Answer (B) is incorrect. Density altitude is lower than pressure altitude when the temperature is below standard.

10.2 Preflight Preparation

10. When NOTAMs are published in the Notices to Airmen Publication (NTAP), they are

    A. Still a part of a standard weather briefing.

    B. Only available in a standard weather briefing if the pilot requests published NOTAMs.

    C. Canceled and are no longer valid.

Answer (B) is correct. *(AIM Para 5-1-3)*
    DISCUSSION: Once a NOTAM is published in the NTAP, the NOTAM is not provided during pilot weather briefings unless specifically requested.
    Answer (A) is incorrect. Published NOTAMs are only available in a pilot weather briefing if the pilot makes a specific request for them. NOTAMs that have not been published are a part of a standard weather briefing. Answer (C) is incorrect. A published NOTAM remains in effect until its expiration date or until an additional NOTAM is issued to cancel it.

11. What information is contained in the Notices to Airmen Publication (NTAP)?

    A. Current NOTAM (D) and FDC NOTAMs.

    B. Military NOTAMs only.

    C. Current NOTAM (D), FDC NOTAMs, and military NOTAMs.

Answer (A) is correct. *(AIM Para 5-1-3)*
    DISCUSSION: The *NTAP* contains NOTAMs (D) that are expected to remain in effect for an extended period and FDC NOTAMs that are current at the time of publication.
    Answer (B) is incorrect. Military NOTAMs are not published in the *NTAP*. Answer (C) is incorrect. While current NOTAMs (D) and FDC NOTAMs are published in the *NTAP*, military NOTAMs are not.

12. The course measured on a sectional chart by reference to a meridian is known as the

    A. true course.

    B. magnetic course.

    C. true heading.

Answer (A) is correct. *(PHAK Chap 15)*
    DISCUSSION: True course can be determined by using lines of meridian.
    Answer (B) is incorrect. Magnetic course is true course, corrected magnetic variation. Answer (C) is incorrect. True heading is the true course corrected for wind.

13. True course measurements on a Sectional Aeronautical Chart should be made at a meridian near the midpoint of the course because the

    A. values of isogonic lines change from point to point.

    B. angles formed by isogonic lines and lines of latitude vary from point to point.

    C. angles formed by lines of longitude and the course line vary from point to point.

Answer (C) is correct. *(PHAK Chap 15)*
    DISCUSSION: Because meridians (lines of longitude) converge toward the poles, the angles formed by meridians and the course line may vary from point to point. Thus, course measurement should be taken at a meridian near the midpoint of the course rather than at the departure point.
    Answer (A) is incorrect. Isogonic lines are used to calculate magnetic (not true) course. Answer (B) is incorrect. Isogonic lines are used to calculate magnetic (not true) course.

14. To find the distance flown in a given time, multiply time by

    A. ground speed.

    B. indicated airspeed.

    C. equivalent airspeed.

Answer (A) is correct. *(PHAK Chap 15)*
    DISCUSSION: To find the distance flown in a given amount of time, multiply groundspeed by time. To calculate the distance flown in 1 hour 30 minutes at a groundspeed of 150 knots, multiply 1.5 × 150, or 225 nautical miles.
    Answer (B) is incorrect. Your indicated airspeed is not the actual speed the aircraft is traveling over the ground. It is the airspeed the aircraft is traveling through the air. Answer (C) is incorrect. Equivalent airspeed is airspeed corrected for installation position, or instrument error, and for adiabatic compressible flow for the particular altitude.

15. If an aircraft is consuming 3 gallons of fuel per hour at a cruising altitude of 500 feet and the groundspeed is 45 mph, how much fuel is required to travel 75 SM?

    A. 6 gallons.

    B. 5 gallons.

    C. 3 gallons.

Answer (B) is correct. *(PHAK Chap 15)*
    DISCUSSION: In order to determine the quantity of fuel required, you must first determine the time in flight. To do this, divide travel distance by the groundspeed: 75 ÷ 45 = 1.67 hours. Then multiply the time in flight by the stated fuel consumption rate: 1.67 hours × 3 gallons per hour = 5 gallons.
    Answer (A) is incorrect. Fuel required to travel a distance of 90 SM, not 75 SM, would be 6 gallons. Answer (C) is incorrect. Fuel required to travel a distance of 45 SM, not 75 SM, would be 3 gallons.

16. What information can a pilot receive from a Flight Service Station (FSS)?

    A. Assistance when lost.

    B. Taxi instructions.

    C. Airport fuel prices.

Answer (A) is correct. *(AIM Para 4-1-3)*
    DISCUSSION: A Flight Service Station can provide assistance to lost aircraft. The sectional aeronautical chart shows direct and remote communication outlets where these facilities can be reached. Make note of FSS frequencies when you plan flights outside of your local area to make it easier for you to contact Flight Service if necessary.
    Answer (B) is incorrect. Only Air Traffic Control can issue taxi instructions. Answer (C) is incorrect. Flight Service does not have access to airport fuel pricing information.

17. The positive three-step process in the exchange of flight controls between pilots includes these verbal steps: (1) You have the flight controls, (2) I have the flight controls, and (3)

    A. You have the flight controls.

    B. I have the aircraft.

    C. I have the flight controls.

Answer (A) is correct. *(AIH Chap 8)*
    DISCUSSION: In the exchange of flight controls, the three-step process is completed with the following verbal commands: (1) You have the flight controls, (2) I have the flight controls, and (3) You have the flight controls.
    Answer (B) is incorrect. The command "I have the aircraft" is an incorrect second command. Answer (C) is incorrect. The command "I have the flight controls" is the second, not third and last, command.

10.3 Weight and Balance

18. Problems caused by overloading an aircraft include

    A. reduced climb rate, excessive structural loads, and shortened cruising range.

    B. increased service ceiling, increased angle of climb, and increased cruising speed.

    C. slower takeoff speed, increased maneuverability, and shorter takeoff roll.

Answer (A) is correct. *(PHAK Chap 4)*
    DISCUSSION: Overloading an aircraft will result in a reduced climb rate, excessive structural loads, and shortened cruise range. The excessive weight forces the aircraft to produce a greater amount of lift to sustain flight. This results in a lower climb rate, more structural strain due to an increase in load factor, and also an increase in drag due to the higher angle of attack of the wing, thus reducing range.
    Answer (B) is incorrect. Increased service ceiling, increased angle of climb, and increased cruising speed would be the result of lowering the weight of the aircraft, not overloading the aircraft. Answer (C) is incorrect. Slower takeoff speed, increased maneuverability, and shorter takeoff roll would be the result of lowering the weight of the aircraft, not overloading the aircraft.

19. The efficiency of an aircraft and the safety margin available if an emergency condition should arise is

    A. reduced by insufficient weight.

    B. reduced by excessive weight.

    C. not affected by weight.

Answer (B) is correct. *(PHAK Chap 9)*
    DISCUSSION: Excessive weight will have adverse effects on an airplane's performance in most respects. With more weight, the airplane requires more lift, resulting in additional drag and therefore using more fuel. In an emergency, the reduced performance becomes more critical and the safety margin is reduced.
    Answer (A) is incorrect. Insufficient weight will result in better performance, with less lift required, less drag, and therefore less fuel. Performance is likely to be better, providing more safety margin in case of an emergency. Answer (C) is incorrect. Weight substantially affects aircraft efficiency and flight performance, therefore affecting safety margin.

10.4 Navigation

20. During VFR navigation without radio instruments, heading and groundspeed, as calculated by dead reckoning, should be constantly monitored and corrected by

    A. pilotage as observed from checkpoints.

    B. the wind triangle.

    C. wet compass and the groundspeed indicator.

Answer (A) is correct. *(PHAK Chap 15)*
    DISCUSSION: The heading and groundspeed calculated prior to the flight are constantly monitored and updated by pilotage as observed from checkpoints. Pilotage is navigation by reference to landmarks or checkpoints.
    Answer (B) is incorrect. A wind triangle is used to determine the distance an aircraft will cover in 1 hour in relation to wind correction. Answer (C) is incorrect. A "groundspeed indicator" (e.g., GPS, loran) is not used in dead reckoning calculations.

21. Heading and groundspeed are calculated using dead reckoning procedures. In flight, they are constantly monitored and corrected by

    A. pilotage as observed from checkpoints.

    B. the wind triangle.

    C. the wet compass and the groundspeed indicator.

Answer (A) is correct. *(PHAK Chap 15)*
    DISCUSSION: The heading and groundspeed calculated prior to the flight are constantly monitored and updated by pilotage as observed from checkpoints. Pilotage is navigation by reference to landmarks or checkpoints.
    Answer (B) is incorrect. A wind triangle is used to determine the distance an aircraft will cover in 1 hour in relation to wind correction. Answer (C) is incorrect. A "groundspeed indicator" (e.g., GPS, loran) is not used in dead reckoning calculations.

22. For cross-country flights over land, navigation without radio instruments is usually accomplished using dead reckoning and

A. pilotage.
B. the wind triangle.
C. compass heading.

Answer (A) is correct. *(PHAK Chap 15)*
    DISCUSSION: For cross-country flights over land, navigation should be accomplished using dead reckoning (navigation calculations done prior to flight) and pilotage (navigation by reference to checkpoints or landmarks).
    Answer (B) is incorrect. A wind triangle is used to determine the distance an aircraft will cover in 1 hour in relation to wind correction. Answer (C) is incorrect. Compass heading is not the primary way of navigation when flying VFR. Compass heading is used to provide a general direction of flight between checkpoints and the destination.

23. If you are on a cross country flight and have corrected for the wind direction, you are following

A. General course that you want.
B. Magnetic heading.
C. True heading.

Answer (C) is the best answer. *(PHAK Chap 15)*
    DISCUSSION: True heading is true course corrected for wind direction. Headings or courses are flown with reference to a magnetic compass and are thus flown on magnetic headings. So while this answer is the best choice for this question, flying on a true heading is not a proper navigation procedure.
    Answer (A) is incorrect. General course is not something used in flying. On a cross-country flight, when you have corrected for wind, you are following magnetic heading. Answer (B) is incorrect. Magnetic heading is your plotted course corrected for wind direction and magnetic variation. While this answer could be correct, the question states that you have corrected for wind direction only.

24. (Refer to Figure 58 on page 177.) The elevation at Garrison airport (Area 2) is

A. 122.9
B. 37
C. 1935

Answer (C) is correct. *(ACL)*
    DISCUSSION: On sectional charts, the line below an airport's name lists its elevation, then its runway length (in hundreds of feet), and finally, where available, its CTAF or UNICOM frequency.
    Answer (A) is incorrect. The airport's CTAF frequency, not its elevation, is 122.9. Answer (B) is incorrect. It refers to the runway length, 3700 feet, not its elevation.

25. Roads shown on the Sectional Charts are

A. all roads with two or more lanes.
B. primarily well traveled roads or those most apparent when viewed from the air.
C. only paved roads.

Answer (B) is correct. *(PHAK Chap 15)*
    DISCUSSION: Sectional charts are designed to show features that can be used in the air for navigation. Roads that are well traveled or those most apparent when viewed from the air will be shown on sectional charts.
    Answer (A) is incorrect. Roads with two or more lanes may not always be shown on a sectional chart if they are not well traveled or easily visible from the air. Answer (C) is incorrect. Unpaved roads may also be shown on a sectional chart if they are well traveled or easily apparent when viewed from the air.

10.5 Global Positioning System (GPS) Navigation

26. How many satellites make up the Global Positioning System (GPS)?

A. 25
B. 22
C. 24

Answer (C) is correct. *(AIM Para 1-1-19)*
    DISCUSSION: The Global Positioning System (GPS) is composed of a constellation of 24 satellites that broadcast signals decoded by a receiver in order to determine a three-dimensional position.
    Answer (A) is incorrect. The GPS is composed of 24, not 25, satellites. Answer (B) is incorrect. The GPS is composed of 24, not 22, satellites.

27. What is the minimum number of Global Positioning System (GPS) satellites that are observable by a user anywhere on earth?

A. 6
B. 5
C. 4

Answer (B) is correct. *(AIM Para 1-1-19)*
    DISCUSSION: The Global Positioning System is composed of 24 satellites, at least five of which are observable at any given time anywhere on earth.
    Answer (A) is incorrect. At least five, not six, satellites are visible anywhere on earth. Answer (C) is incorrect. At least five, not four, satellites are visible anywhere on earth.

28. How many Global Positioning System (GPS) satellites are required to yield a three dimensional position (latitude, longitude, and altitude) and time solution?

    A. 5

    B. 6

    C. 4

Answer (C) is correct. *(AIM Para 1-1-19)*
    DISCUSSION: GPS satellites broadcast radio signals that are decoded by a receiver in order to triangulate a three-dimensional position by calculating distances based on the amount of time it takes the radio signals to reach the receiver. At least four GPS satellites are required to yield a three-dimensional position (latitude, longitude, and altitude) and time solution.
    Answer (A) is incorrect. Four, not five, satellites are required for a three-dimensional position and time solution. Answer (B) is incorrect. Four, not six, satellites are required for a three-dimensional position and time solution.

29. Which of the following is a true statement about the Global Positioning System?

    A. It is ground based.

    B. It is satellite based.

    C. It is antenna based.

Answer (B) is correct. *(PHAK Chap 15)*
    DISCUSSION: The Global Positioning System (GPS) is a satellite-based radio navigation system.
    Answer (A) is incorrect. GPS is satellite based, not ground based. Answer (C) is incorrect. GPS is satellite based, not antenna based.

10.6 Determining Wind Direction and Speed

30. Motion of the air affects the speed with which aircraft move

    A. over the earth's surface.

    B. south of east to counteract drift.

    C. north to counteract torque.

Answer (A) is correct. *(PHAK Chap 15)*
    DISCUSSION: The motion of the air affects the speed at which an aircraft moves over the surface of the earth (i.e., groundspeed).
    Answer (B) is incorrect. The motion of the air does not affect the aircraft's airspeed or movement through the air. An aircraft's airspeed will remain constant no matter the direction or velocity of the wind. Answer (C) is incorrect. The motion of the air affects ground speed, not the rate of turn of an aircraft.

31. If a flight is to be made on a course to the east, with a wind blowing from northeast, the aircraft must be headed

    A. somewhat to the north of east to counteract drift.

    B. south of east to counteract drift.

    C. north to counteract torque.

Answer (A) is correct. *(PHAK Chap 15)*
    DISCUSSION: If the air is blowing from the northeast (i.e., to the southwest), the aircraft must be pointed somewhat to the northeast to maintain an easterly track.
    Answer (B) is incorrect. If the wind is from the northeast, the aircraft will drift to the south when flying east. Thus, by flying a southeasterly heading, you would be increasing your drift to the south and would no longer maintain an easterly track.
Answer (C) is incorrect. Torque is not related to wind and drift. Torque is produced by the engine of the aircraft.

32. GIVEN:

True Course	050
True Heading	040
True Airspeed	75 kt.
Groundspeed	65 kt.

Determine the wind direction and speed.

    A. 105 degrees and 16 knots.

    B. 355 degrees and 16 knots.

    C. 355 degrees and 10 knots.

Answer (B) is correct. *(PHAK Chap 15)*
    DISCUSSION: Using your Gleim flight computer, rotate the plotting transparency so the true course (050) is under the true index. Move the sliding card so the grommet is over the groundspeed (65 kt.) speed arc. The magnetic heading (040) is to the left and below the 10° correction line (WCA). Locate the intersection of the TAS (75 kt.) speed arc and the 10° wind correction line and mark a wind dot at that location. Rotate the plotting transparency clockwise so the wind dot is on the center line above the grommet. Wind direction is read under the true index, and the wind speed is the number of units above the grommet.
    Answer (A) is incorrect. You must place the wind dot on the same side as the true heading. In this case, 40° is to the left, not the right. Thus, the wind dot must be on the left. Answer (C) is incorrect. The grommet should be positioned over the 65 kt. wind speed arc, and the wind dot should be located at approximately the 81 kt. position. This indicates a 16 kt. wind.

10.7 VFR Flight Plan

				Form Approved: OMB No. 2120-0026	

U.S. DEPARTMENT OF TRANSPORTATION FEDERAL AVIATION ADMINISTRATION	(FAA USE ONLY)	☐ PILOT BRIEFING ☐ VNR	TIME STARTED	SPECIALIST INITIALS
FLIGHT PLAN		☐ STOPOVER		

1 TYPE	2 AIRCRAFT IDENTIFICATION	3 AIRCRAFT TYPE/ SPECIAL EQUIPMENT	4 TRUE AIRSPEED	5 DEPARTURE POINT	6 DEPARTURE TIME		7 CRUISING ALTITUDE
VFR					PROPOSED (Z)	ACTUAL (Z)	
IFR							
DVFR			KTS				

8 ROUTE OF FLIGHT

9 DESTINATION (Name of airport and city)	10 EST. TIME ROUTE		11 REMARKS
	HOURS	MINUTES	

12 FUEL ON BOARD		13 ALTERNATE AIRPORT(S)	14 PILOT'S NAME, ADDRESS & TELEPHONE NUMBER & AIRCRAFT HOME BASE	15 NUMBER ABOARD
HOURS	MINUTES			
			17 DESTINATION CONTACT/TELEPHONE (OPTIONAL)	

16 COLOR OF AIRCRAFT	CIVIL AIRCRAFT PILOTS. FAR Part 91 requires you file an IFR flight plan to operate under instrument flight rules in controlled airspace. Failure to file could result in a civil penalty not to exceed $1,000 for each violaton (Section 901 of the Federal Aviation Act of 1958, as amended). Filing of a VFR flight plan is recommended as a good operating practice. See also Part 99 for requirements concerning DVFR flight plans.

FAA Form 7233-1 (8-82)   **CLOSE VFR FLIGHT PLAN WITH _____ FSS ON ARRIVAL**

Figure 152. – Flight Plan Form.

33. (Refer to Figure 152 above.) If more than one cruising altitude is intended, which should be entered in block 7 of the flight plan?

A. Initial cruising altitude.

B. Highest cruising altitude.

C. Lowest cruising altitude.

Answer (A) is correct. *(AIM Para 5-1-4)*
DISCUSSION: Use only your initial requested altitude on your VFR flight plan to assist briefers in providing weather and wind information.
Answer (B) is incorrect. The initial, not highest, altitude should be filed on your VFR flight plan. Answer (C) is incorrect. The initial, not lowest, altitude should be filed on your VFR flight plan.

34. (Refer to Figure 152 above.) What information should be entered in block 12 for a VFR day flight?

A. The estimated time en route plus 30 minutes.

B. The estimated time en route plus 45 minutes.

C. The amount of usable fuel on board expressed in time.

Answer (C) is correct. *(AIM Para 5-1-4)*
DISCUSSION: Block 12 of the flight plan requires the amount of usable fuel in the airplane at the time of departure. It should be expressed in hours and minutes of flying time.
Answer (A) is incorrect. It states the VFR fuel requirement for day flight. Answer (B) is incorrect. It states the VFR fuel requirement for night flight.

35. (Refer to Figure 152 above.) What information should be entered in block 9 for a VFR day flight?

A. The name of the airport of first intended landing.

B. The name of destination airport if no stopover for more than 1 hour is anticipated.

C. The name of the airport where the aircraft is based.

Answer (B) is correct. *(AIM Para 5-1-4)*
DISCUSSION: In block 9 of the flight plan form in Fig. 152, enter the name of the airport of last intended landing for that flight, as long as no stopover exceeds 1 hr.
Answer (A) is incorrect. The first intended landing, i.e., the end of the first leg of the flight, is included in the route of flight (block 8). Answer (C) is incorrect. The name of the airport where the airplane is based is entered in block 14.

36. How should a VFR flight plan be closed at the completion of the flight at a controlled airport?

A. The tower will automatically close the flight plan when the aircraft turns off the runway.

B. The pilot must close the flight plan with the nearest FSS or other FAA facility upon landing.

C. The tower will relay the instructions to the nearest FSS when the aircraft contacts the tower for landing.

Answer (B) is correct. *(AIM Para 5-1-13)*
DISCUSSION: A pilot is responsible for ensuring that the VFR or DVFR flight plan is canceled (FAR 91.153). You should close your flight plan with the nearest FSS or, if one is not available, you may request any ATC facility to relay your cancellation to the FSS.
Answer (A) is incorrect. The tower will automatically close an IFR (not VFR) flight plan. Answer (C) is incorrect. The tower will relay to the nearest FSS only if requested.

10.8 Preflight Inspection

37. During the preflight inspection, who is responsible for determining the aircraft as safe for flight?

A. The pilot in command.

B. The owner or operator.

C. The certificated mechanic who performed the annual inspection.

Answer (A) is correct. *(FAR 91.7)*
DISCUSSION: During the preflight inspection, the pilot in command is responsible for determining whether the airplane is in condition for safe flight.
Answer (B) is incorrect. The owner or operator is responsible for maintaining the airplane in an airworthy condition, not for determining whether the airplane is safe for flight during the preflight inspection. Answer (C) is incorrect. The pilot in command, not the mechanic who performed the annual inspection, is responsible for determining whether the airplane is safe for flight.

38. Who is primarily responsible for maintaining an aircraft in airworthy condition?

A. Pilot-in-command.

B. Owner or operator.

C. Mechanic.

Answer (B) is correct. *(PHAK Chap 8)*
DISCUSSION: The owner or operator of an airplane is primarily responsible for maintaining an airplane in an airworthy condition, including compliance with all applicable Airworthiness Directives (ADs).
Answer (A) is incorrect. The pilot in command is responsible for determining that the airplane is in airworthy condition, not for maintaining the airplane. Answer (C) is incorrect. The owner or operator, not a mechanic, is responsible for maintaining an airplane in an airworthy condition.

39. How should an aircraft preflight inspection be accomplished for the first flight of the day?

A. Quick walk around with a check of gas and oil.

B. Thorough and systematic means recommended by the manufacturer.

C. Any sequence as determined by the pilot-in-command.

Answer (B) is correct. *(PHAK Chap 8)*
DISCUSSION: For the first flight of the day, the preflight inspection should be accomplished by a thorough and systematic means recommended by the manufacturer.
Answer (A) is incorrect. A quick walk around with a check of gas and oil may be adequate if it is not the first flight of the day in that airplane. Answer (C) is incorrect. A preflight inspection should be done in the sequence recommended by the manufacturer in the POH, not in any sequence determined by the pilot in command.

10.9 FAA Advisory Circulars

40. FAA advisory circulars (some free, others at cost) are available to all pilots and are obtained by

A. distribution from the nearest FAA district office.

B. ordering those desired from the Government Printing Office.

C. subscribing to the *Federal Register*.

Answer (B) is correct. *(AC 00-2.15)*
DISCUSSION: FAA Advisory Circulars are issued with the purpose of informing the public of nonregulatory material of interest. Free advisory circulars can be ordered from the FAA, while those at cost can be ordered from the Government Printing Office.
Answer (A) is incorrect. FAA offices have their own copies but none for distribution to the public. Answer (C) is incorrect. The *Federal Register* contains Notices of Proposed Rulemaking (NPRM) and final rules. It is a federal government publication.

41. FAA advisory circulars containing subject matter specifically related to Air Traffic Control and General Operations are issued under which subject number?

A. 60

B. 70

C. 90

Answer (C) is correct. *(AC 00-2.15)*
DISCUSSION: FAA advisory circulars are numbered based on the numbering system used in the FARs:

    60 Airmen
    70 Airspace
    90 Air Traffic Control and General Operation

    Answer (A) is incorrect. This number refers to Airmen, not Air Traffic Control. Answer (B) is incorrect. This number refers to Airspace, not Air Traffic Control.

42. FAA advisory circulars containing subject matter specifically related to Airmen are issued under which subject number?

A. 60

B. 70

C. 90

Answer (A) is correct. *(AC 00-2.15)*
DISCUSSION: FAA advisory circulars are numbered based on the numbering system used in the FARs:

    60 Airmen
    70 Airspace
    90 Air Traffic Control and General Operation

    Answer (B) is incorrect. This number relates to Airspace, not Airmen. Answer (C) is incorrect. This number relates to Air Traffic Control and General Operation (not Airmen).

43. FAA advisory circulars containing subject matter specifically related to Airspace are issued under which subject number?

A. 60

B. 70

C. 90

Answer (B) is correct. *(AC 00-2.15)*
DISCUSSION: FAA advisory circulars are numbered based on the numbering system used in the FARs:

    60 Airmen
    70 Airspace
    90 Air Traffic Control and General Operation

    Answer (A) is incorrect. This number relates to Airmen, not Airspace. Answer (C) is incorrect. This number relates to Air Traffic Control and General Operation, not Airspace.

44. Some Advisory Circulars (ACs) are available free of charge while the remaining ACs must be purchased. All aviation safety ACs may be obtained by following the procedures in the AC Checklist (AC 00-2) or by

A. referring to the FAA Internet home page and following the links to ACs.

B. contacting the local airport Fixed Base Operator and requesting the desired AC.

C. reading the ACs in the Aeronautical Information Manual (AIM).

Answer (A) is correct. *(AC 00-2.15)*
DISCUSSION: You can locate all the advisory circulars on the FAA's homepage at faa.gov, under the Regulations and Policies link.
    Answer (B) is incorrect. Fixed Based Operators (FBO) may have access to some but not all the advisory circulars. Answer (C) is incorrect. The *AIM* does not contain advisory circulars. The *AIM* contains general information published by the FAA pertaining to various items related to basic flight and ATC procedures in the United States.

45. Unless incorporated into a regulation by reference, Advisory Circulars (ACs) are issued to inform the public of nonregulatory material

A. and are not binding.

B. but are binding.

C. and self-cancel after 1 year.

Answer (A) is correct. *(AC 00-2.15)*
DISCUSSION: The FAA issues advisory circulars (ACs) to provide a systematic means for issuing nonregulatory material of interest to the aviation public. Unless incorporated into a regulation by reference, the contents of the AC are not binding.
    Answer (B) is incorrect. Advisory circulars are not binding, unless incorporated into a regulation by reference. They are issued for informational purposes to the general aviation public. Answer (C) is incorrect. Advisory circulars do not self-cancel after 1 year. Advisory circulars are current until the FAA publishes updates, revisions, cancelations, or new publications.

46. Time-critical information on airports and changes that affect the national airspace system are provided by

    A. Notices to Airmen (NOTAMs).

    B. the Airport/Facilities Directory (A/FD).

    C. Advisory Circulars (ACs).

Answer (A) is correct. *(PHAK Chap 13)*
    DISCUSSION: The National Notice to Airmen (NOTAM) system disseminates time-critical information that can affect airports and the national airspace system. NOTAM information is that aeronautical information that could affect the decision to make a flight.
    Answer (B) is incorrect. The *Airport/Facilities Directory* does not issue time-critical information. *A/FDs* are only published every 8 weeks and contain information on specific airports in one of seven geographical areas throughout the United States. Answer (C) is incorrect. Advisory Circulars are issued by the FAA to provide a systematic means for issuing nonregulatory material of interest to the aviation public. Unless incorporated into a regulation by reference, the contents of an AC are not binding.

47. Flight Data Center (FDC) NOTAMs are issued by the National Flight Data Center and contain regulatory information, such as

    A. temporary flight restrictions.

    B. markings and signs used at airports.

    C. standard communication.

Answer (A) is correct. *(PHAK Chap 13)*
    DISCUSSION: NOTAMs issued by the Flight Data Center (FDC) are regulatory in nature and include such information as amendments to published IAPs and other current aeronautical charts. It also advertises temporary flight restrictions caused by such things as natural disasters or large-scale public events that may generate a congestion of air traffic over a site.
    Answer (B) is incorrect. The markings and signs used at airports are not issued in FDC NOTAMs. Airport markings and signs are published in the *Aeronautical Information Manual (AIM)*. Answer (C) is incorrect. Standard communication procedures are not issued in FDC NOTAMs. Standard communication procedures are published in the *Aeronautical Information Manual (AIM)*.

48. NOTAM-Ls (Local NOTAMs) include items of a local nature. NOTAM-Ls are maintained at each Flight Service Station (FSS) for facilities in their area only. NOTAM-L information for other FSS areas must be specifically requested from the FSS

    A. that has responsibility for the airport concerned.

    B. with which the pilot communicates.

    C. where the flight plan is filed.

Answer (A) is correct. *(PHAK Chap 13)*
    DISCUSSION: NOTAM-L information for other FSS areas must be specifically requested directly from the FSS that has responsibility for the airport concerned.
    Answer (B) is incorrect. The FSS the pilot communicates with may not be the FSS that has responsibility over the airport for which the NOTAM-L was requested. A pilot must contact the controlling FSS to receive information on a specific airport in that FSS's area. Answer (C) is incorrect. The FSS controlling the destination airport may not be the FSS governing the airport the pilot is concerned with. The pilot must contact the FSS that has responsibility for the airport concerned.

49. The Federal Aviation Administration publication that provides the aviation community with basic flight information and Air Traffic Control procedures for use in the National Airspace System of the United States is the

    A. Aeronautical Information Manual (AIM).

    B. Airport/Facility Directory (A/FD).

    C. Advisory Circular Checklist (AC 00-2).

Answer (A) is correct. *(AIM)*
    DISCUSSION: The *Aeronautical Information Manual (AIM)* is published by the FAA to provide information concerning basic flight information and Air Traffic Control procedures for use in the National Airspace System of the United States.
    Answer (B) is incorrect. The *Airport/Facility Directory (A/FD)* is a Civil Flight Information Publication published and distributed every 8 weeks by the National Aeronautical Charting Office (NACO), a division of the FAA. Answer (C) is incorrect. The AC 00-2 is used to order a free comprehensive list of the advisory circulars.

10.10 *Airport/Facility Directory*

50. (Refer to Figure 153 on page 209.) When approaching Lincoln Municipal from the west at noon for the purpose of landing, initial communications should be with

A. Lincoln Approach Control on 124.0 MHz.

B. Minneapolis Center on 128.75 MHz.

C. Lincoln Tower on 118.5 MHz.

Answer (A) is correct. *(A/FD)*
DISCUSSION: Fig. 153 contains the *A/FD* excerpt for Lincoln Municipal. Locate the section titled Airspace and note that Lincoln Municipal is located in Class C airspace. The Class C airspace is in effect from 0530-0030 local time (1130-0630Z). You should contact approach control (app con) during that time before entering. Move up three lines to App/Dep Con and note that aircraft arriving from the west of Lincoln (i.e., 170° – 349°) at noon should initially contact Lincoln Approach Control on 124.0.
Answer (B) is incorrect. You would contact Minneapolis Center for basic radar services (i.e., flight following, assistance, etc.) between 0030 and 0530 local time, not at noon. Answer (C) is incorrect. When approaching Lincoln Municipal at noon, your initial contact should be with approach control, not the tower.

51. (Refer to Figure 153 on page 209.) Traffic patterns in effect at Lincoln Municipal are

A. to the right on Runway 17L and Runway 35L; to the left on Runway 17R and Runway 35R.

B. to the left on Runway 17L and Runway 35L; to the right on Runway 17R and Runway 35R.

C. to the right on Runways 14 - 32.

Answer (B) is correct. *(A/FD)*
DISCUSSION: Fig. 153 contains the *A/FD* excerpt for Lincoln Municipal. For this question, you need to locate the runway end data elements, i.e., Rwy 17R, Rwy 35L, Rwy 14, Rwy 32, Rwy 17L, and Rwy 35R. Traffic patterns are to the left unless right traffic is noted by the contraction Rgt tfc. The only runways with right traffic are Rwy 17R and Rwy 35R.
Answer (A) is incorrect. Traffic patterns are to the left, not right, for Rwy 17L and Rwy 35L. Traffic patterns are to the right, not left, on Rwy 17R and Rwy 35R. Answer (C) is incorrect. The traffic pattern for Rwy 14 and Rwy 32 is to the left, not right.

52. (Refer to Figure 153 on page 209.) Where is Loup City Municipal located with relation to the city?

A. Northeast approximately 3 miles.

B. Northwest approximately 1 mile.

C. East approximately 10 miles.

Answer (B) is correct. *(A/FD)*
DISCUSSION: Fig. 153 contains the *A/FD* excerpt for Loup City Municipal. On the first line, the third item listed, 1 NW, means that Loup City Municipal is located approximately 1 NM northwest of the city.
Answer (A) is incorrect. (NE03) is the airport identifier, not an indication that the airport is 3 NM northeast of the city. Answer (C) is incorrect. The airport is approximately 1 NM northwest, not 10 NM east, of the city.

53. (Refer to Figure 153 on page 209.) What is the recommended communications procedure for landing at Lincoln Municipal during the hours when the tower is not in operation?

A. Monitor airport traffic and announce your position and intentions on 118.5 MHz.

B. Contact UNICOM on 122.95 MHz for traffic advisories.

C. Monitor ATIS for airport conditions, then announce your position on 122.95 MHz.

Answer (A) is correct. *(A/FD)*
DISCUSSION: When the Lincoln Municipal tower is closed, you should monitor airport traffic and announce your position and intentions on the CTAF. Fig. 153 contains the *A/FD* excerpt for Lincoln Municipal. Locate the section titled Communications and note that on that same line the CTAF frequency is 118.5.
Answer (B) is incorrect. When the tower is not in operation, you should monitor other traffic and announce your position and intentions on the specified CTAF. At Lincoln Municipal, the CTAF is the tower frequency of 118.5, not the UNICOM frequency of 122.95. Answer (C) is incorrect. When the tower is not in operation, you should monitor other traffic and announce your position and intentions on the specified CTAF. At Lincoln Municipal, the CTAF is the tower frequency of 118.5, not the UNICOM frequency of 122.95.

54. For a complete listing of information provided in an Airport/Facility Directory (A/FD) and how the information may be decoded, refer to the

A. "Directory Legend Sample" located in the front of each A/FD.

B. Aeronautical Information Manual (AIM).

C. legend on sectional, VFR terminal area, and world aeronautical charts.

Answer (A) is correct. *(PHAK Chap 13)*
DISCUSSION: The "Directory Legend Sample" located in the front of each *A/FD* contains a complete listing of the information located within the *A/FD* and also provides information on how to decode the information located within the *A/FD*.
Answer (B) is incorrect. The *Aeronautical Information Manual (AIM)* only provides a brief description of an *A/FD* and what information the *A/FD* provides. Answer (C) is incorrect. The information located in the legend of sectional, VFR terminal area, and world aeronautical charts only pertains to those particular charts and the information they contain.

---

180   **NEBRASKA**

LINCOLN MUNI   (LNK)   4 NW   UTC–6(–5DT)   N40°51.05' W98°45.55'   **OMAHA**
    1218   B   S4   **FUEL** 100LL. JET A   TPA—2218(1000)   ARFF Index B   H—1E, 3F, 4F, L —11B
    RWY 17R–35L: **H12901X200** (ASPH–CONC–GRVD)   S--100. D--200. DT--400   HIRL   IAP
      RWY 17R: MALSR. VASI(V4L)—GA 3.0° TCH 55'. Rgt tfc.   0.4% down.
      RWY 35L: MALSR. VASI(V4L)—GA 3.0° TCH 55'.
    RWY 14–32: H8620X150 (ASPH--CONC--GRVD)   S--80. D--170. DT--280   MIRL
      RWY 14: REIL. VASI(V4L)—GA 3.0° TCH 48'.
      RWY 32: VASI(V4L)—GA 3.0° TCH 53'. Thld dsplcd 431'. Pole.   0.3% up.
    RWY 17L–35R: H5400X100 (ASPH--CONC--AFSC)   S--49. D--60   HIRL   0.8% up N
      RWY 17L: PAPI(P4L)—GA 3.0° TCH 33'.   RWY 35R: PAPI(P4L)—GA 3.0° TCH 40'. Pole. Rgt tfc.
    AIRPORT REMARKS: Attended continuously. Birds in vicinity of arpt. Twy D clsd between taxiways S and H indef. For
      MALSR Rwy 17R and Rwy 35L ctc twr. When twr clsd MALSR Rwy 17R and Rwy 35L preset on med ints. and REIL
      Rwy 14 left on when wind favor. NOTE: See Land and Hold Short Operations Section.
    WEATHER DATA SOURCES: ASOS (402) 474--9214. LLWAS
    COMMUNICATIONS: CTAF 118.5   ATIS 118.05   UNICOM 122.95
      COLUMBUS FSS (OLU) TF 1--800--WX--BRIEF. NOTAM FILE LNK.
      RCO 122.65 (COLUMBUS FSS)
    Ⓡ APP/DEP CON 124.0 (170°--349°) 124.8 (350°--169°) (1130--0630Z‡)
    Ⓡ MINNEAPOLIS CENTER APP/DEP CON 128.75 (0630--1130Z‡)
      TOWER 118.5 125.7 (1130--0630Z‡)   GND CON 121.9   CLNC DEL 120.7
    AIRSPACE: CLASS C svc 1130--0630Z‡ ctc APP CON other times CLASS E.
    RADIO AIDS TO NAVIGATION: NOTAM FILE LNK. VHF/DF ctc FSS.
      (H) VORTACW 116.1   LNK   Chan 108   N40°55.43' W 96°44.52'   181° 4.5 NM to fld. 1370/9E
      POTTS NDB (MHW/LOM) 385   LN   N40°44.83' W 96°45.75'   355° 6.2 NM to fld. Unmonitored when twr clsd.
      ILS 111.1   I--OCZ   Rwy 17R.   MM and OM unmonitored
      ILS 109.9   I--LNK   Rwy 35L.   LOM POTTS NDB. MM unmonitored. LOM unmonitored when twr clsd.
    COMM/NAVAID REMARKS: Emerg frequency 121.5 not available at tower.

LOUP CITY MUNI   (NEØ3)   1 NW   UTC --6(--5DT)   N41° 17.42' W 98° 59.44'   **OMAHA**
    2070   B   **FUEL** 100LL   L-11B
    RWY 15–33: H3200X50 (ASPH)   S--8   LIRL
      RWY 33: Trees.
    RWY 04--22: 2100X100 (TURF)
      RWY 04: Tree.   RWY 22: Road.
    AIRPORT REMARKS: Unattended. For svc call 308–745–0328/1244/0664
    COMMUNICATIONS: CTAF 122.9
      COLUMBUS FSS (OLU) TF 1–800–WX–BRIEF. NOTAM FILE OLU.
    RADIO AIDS TO NAVIGATION: NOTAM FILE OLU.
      WOLBACH (H) VORTAC 114.8   OBH   Chan 95   N41° 22.54' W 98° 21.22'   253° 29.3 NM to fld. 2010/7E.

MARTIN FLD   (See SO SIOUX CITY)

MC COOK MUNI   (MCK)   2E   UTC --6(--5DT)   N40° 12.36' W 100°35.51'   **OMAHA**
    2579   B   S4   **FUEL** 100LL. JET A   ARFF Index Ltd.   H--20. L--11A
    RWY 12–30: H5999X100 (CONC)   S--30. D--38   MIRL   0.6% up NW   IAP
      RWY 12: MALS. VASI(V4L)—GA 3.0° TCH 33'. Tree.   RWY 30: REIL. VASI(V4L)—GA 3.0° TCH 42'.
    RWY 03--21: H3999X75 (CONC)   S--30. D--38   MIRL
      RWY 03: VASI(V2L)—GA 3.0° TCH 26'. Rgt tfc.   RWY 21: VASI(V2L)—GA 3.0° TCH 26'.
    RWY 17--35: 1350X200 (TURF)
    AIRPORT REMARKS: Attended daylight hours. Parachute Jumping. Deer on and in vicinity of arpt. Numerous
      waterfowl/migratory birds invof arpt. Arpt closed to air carrier operations with more than 30 passengers except
      24 hour PPR, call arpt manager 308--345--2022. Avoid McCook State (abandoned) arpt 7miles NW on the MCK
      VOR/DME 313° radial at 8.3 DME. ACTIVATE VASI Rwys 12 and 30 and MALS Rwy 12 —CTAF.
    COMMUNICATIONS: CTAF/UNICOM 122.8
      COLUMBUS FSS (OLU) TF 1--800--WX--BRIEF. NOTAM FILE MCK.
      RCO 122.6 (COLUMBUS FSS)
      DENVER CENTER APP/DEP CON 132.7
    AIRSPACE: CLASS E svc effective 1100--0500Z‡ except holidays other times CLASS G.
    RADIO AIDS TO NAVIGATION: NOTAM FILE MCK.
      (H) VORW/DME 115.3   MCK   Chan 100   N40° 12.23' W 100°35.65'   at fld. 2570/8E.

Figure 153. – Airport/Facility Directory Excerpt.

55. The most comprehensive information on a given airport is provided by

    A. the Airport/Facility Directory (A/FD).

    B. Notices to Airmen (NOTAMs).

    C. world aeronautical charts (WACs).

Answer (A) is correct. *(PHAK Chap 13)*
    DISCUSSION: The *Airport/Facility Directory (A/FD)* is a Civil Flight Information Publication concerning airport information. It is published and distributed every 8 weeks by the National Aeronautical Charting Office (NACO), a division of the FAA.
    Answer (B) is incorrect. Notices to Airmen (NOTAMs) are time-critical aeronautical information publications that either are of a temporary nature or are not sufficiently known in advance to permit publication on aeronautical charts or in other operational publications. Answer (C) is incorrect. World aeronautical charts are similar to sectional charts except that they cover a larger area on a smaller scale; these charts are generally published annually.

56. The Airport/Facility Directory (A/FD) will generally have the latest information pertaining to airport elevation, runway facilities, and control tower frequencies. If there are differences, it should be used in preference to the information

    A. on the sectional chart.

    B. in the Pilot's Handbook of Aeronautical Knowledge.

    C. in the Aeronautical Information Manual (AIM).

Answer (A) is correct. *(AIM Para 9-1-4)*
    DISCUSSION: The *Airport Facility Directory (A/FD)* generally contains the latest information pertaining to airport information, runway facilities, and control tower frequencies. The *A/FD* also provides a means for pilots to update sectional charts between edition dates; the *A/FD* is published every 56 days while sectional charts are generally revised every 6 months.
    Answer (B) is incorrect. The *Pilot's Handbook of Aeronautical Knowledge* contains information pertaining to various topics in aviation. It does not contain updated information on specific airports. Answer (C) is incorrect. The *Aeronautical Information Manual* contains general information published by the FAA pertaining to various items related to basic flight and ATC procedures in the United States.

END OF STUDY UNIT

STUDY UNIT ELEVEN
AIRPLANES AND AERODYNAMICS

(7 pages of outline)

This study unit contains outlines of major concepts tested, sample test questions and answers regarding airplanes and aerodynamics, and an explanation of each answer. The table of contents above lists each subunit within this study unit, the number of questions pertaining to that particular subunit, and the pages on which the outlines and questions begin, respectively.

CAUTION: Recall that the **sole purpose** of this book is to expedite your passing the FAA pilot knowledge test for the sport pilot certificate. Accordingly, all extraneous material (i.e., topics or regulations not directly tested on the FAA pilot knowledge test) is omitted, even though much more information and knowledge are necessary to fly safely. This additional material is presented in the *Pilot Handbook* and *Sport Pilot Flight Maneuvers and Practical Test Prep*, available from Gleim Publications, Inc. See the order form on page 327.

11.1 FLIGHT CONTROLS

1. The three primary flight controls of an airplane are the ailerons, the elevator (or stabilator), and the rudder.

   a. Movement of any of these primary flight control surfaces changes the airflow and pressure distribution over and around the airfoil.

      1) These changes affect the lift and drag produced and allow a pilot to control the aircraft about its three axes of rotation.

   b. **Ailerons** are control surfaces attached to each wing that move in the opposite direction from one another to control roll about the longitudinal axis.

      1) EXAMPLE: Moving the yoke or stick to the right causes the right aileron to deflect upward, resulting in decreased lift on the right wing. The left aileron moves in the opposite direction and increases the lift on the left wing. Thus, the increased lift on the left wing and and the decreased lift on the right wing causes the airplane to roll to the right.

   c. The **elevator**, which changes the pitch about the lateral axis, is the primary control device for changing the pitch attitude of an airplane. It is usually located on the fixed horizontal stabilizer on the tail of the airplane.

      1) EXAMPLE: Pulling back on the yoke or stick deflects the trailing edge of the elevator up. This position creates a downward aerodynamic force, causing the tail of the aircraft to move down and the nose to pitch up.

      2) A **stabilator** is a one-piece horizontal stabilizer and elevator that pivots from a central hinge point.

        3)   A **canard** is similar to the horizontal stabilizer but is located in front of the main wings. An elevator is attached to the trailing edge of the canard to control pitch.

            a)   The canard, however, actually creates lift and holds the nose up rather than the aft-tail design that prevents the nose from rotating downward.

    d.   The **rudder** controls movement of the aircraft about its vertical axis.

        1)   When deflecting the rudder into the airflow, a horizontal force is exerted in the opposite direction. This motion is called yaw.

        2)   Rudder effectiveness increases with speed because there is more airflow over the surface of the control device.

2.   Secondary flight controls may consist of wing flaps, leading edge devices, spoilers, and trim systems.

    a.   **Flaps** are attached to the trailing edge of the wing and are used during approach and landing to increase wing lift. This allows an increase in the angle of descent without increasing airspeed.

        1)   The most common flap used on general aviation aircraft today is the slotted flap.

        2)   When the slotted flap is lowered, high-pressure air from the lower surface of the wing is ducted to the upper surface of the flap, delaying airflow separation.

    b.   **Spoilers** are high-drag devices deployed from the wings to reduce lift and increase drag. They are found on gliders and some high-speed aircraft.

    c.   **Trim systems** are used to relieve the pilot of the need to maintain constant back pressure on the flight controls. They include trim tabs, antiservo tabs, and ground adjustable tabs.

        1)   Trim tabs are attached to the trailing edge of the elevator.

            a)   EXAMPLE: If the trim tab is set to the full nose-up position, the tab moves full down. This causes the tail of the airplane to pitch down and the nose to pitch up.

11.2 AERODYNAMIC FORCES

1.   The four aerodynamic forces acting on an airplane during flight are

    a.   Lift – the upward-acting force
    b.   Weight – the downward-acting force
    c.   Thrust – the forward-acting force
    d.   Drag – the rearward-acting force

2.   These forces are at equilibrium when the airplane is in unaccelerated flight:

$$\text{Lift} = \text{Weight}$$
$$\text{Thrust} = \text{Drag}$$

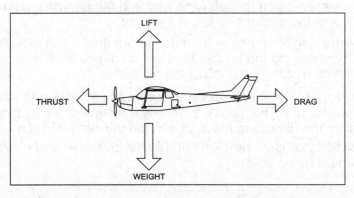

3. Induced drag is a type of drag that results from and is a byproduct of lift. Induced drag is the result of the differential air pressures above and below the wing attempting to equalize near and around the wing tips. Therefore, as the angle of attack increases, so does the induced drag.

11.3 ANGLE OF ATTACK

1. The angle of attack is the angle between the wing chord line and the direction of the relative wind.

    a. The wing chord line is an imaginary straight line from the leading edge to the trailing edge of the wing.

    b. The relative wind is the direction of airflow relative to the wing when the wing is moving through the air.

2. The angle of attack at which a wing stalls remains constant regardless of weight, airplane loading, etc.

11.4 FUNDAMENTALS OF FLIGHT

1. The four fundamentals involved in maneuvering an aircraft are

    a. Straight-and-level flight
    b. Turns
    c. Climbs
    d. Descents

11.5 STALLS AND SPINS

1. An airplane can be stalled at any airspeed in any flight attitude. A stall results whenever the critical angle of attack is exceeded.

    a. An airfoil will always stall at the same angle of attack, regardless of gross weight and center of gravity position.

2. An airplane in a given configuration will stall at the same indicated airspeed regardless of altitude because the airspeed indicator is directly related to air density.

3. An airplane spins when one wing is less stalled than the other wing.

    a. To enter a spin, an airplane must always be stalled first.

11.6 FROST

1. Frost forms when the temperature of the collecting surface is at or below the dew point of the adjacent air and the dew point is below freezing.

    a. The water vapor sublimates directly as ice crystals on the wing surface.

2. Frost on wings disrupts the smooth airflow over the airfoil by causing early airflow separation from the wing. This

    a. Decreases lift,
    b. Causes friction, and
    c. Increases drag.

3. Frost may make it difficult or impossible for an airplane to take off.

4. Frost should be removed before attempting to take off.

11.7 GROUND EFFECT

1.   Ground effect is the result of the interference of the ground (or water) surface with the airflow patterns about an airplane.

2.   The vertical component of the airflow around the wing is restricted, which alters the wing's upwash, downwash, and wingtip vortices.

3.   The reduction of the wingtip vortices alters the spanwise lift distribution and reduces the induced angle of attack and induced drag.

     a.   Thus, the wing will require a lower angle of attack in ground effect to produce the same lift coefficient or, if a constant angle of attack is maintained, an increase in the lift coefficient will result.

4.   An airplane is affected by ground effect when it is within the length of the airplane's wingspan above the ground. The ground effect is most often recognized when the airplane is less than one-half the wingspan's length above the ground.

5.   Ground effect may cause an airplane to float on landings or permit it to become airborne with insufficient airspeed to stay in flight above the area of ground effect.

     a.   An airplane may settle back to the surface abruptly after flying through the ground effect if the pilot has not attained recommended takeoff airspeed.

11.8 AIRPLANE TURN

1.   The horizontal component of lift makes an airplane turn.

     a.   To attain this horizontal component of lift, the pilot coordinates rudder, aileron, and elevator.

2.   The rudder on an airplane controls the yaw, i.e., rotation about the vertical axis, but does not cause the airplane to turn.

11.9 AIRPLANE STABILITY

1.   An inherently stable airplane returns to its original condition (position or attitude) after being disturbed. It requires less effort to control.

2.   The location of the center of gravity (CG) with respect to the center of lift determines the longitudinal stability of an airplane.

3.   Airplanes (except a T-tail) normally pitch down when power is reduced (and the controls are not adjusted) because the downwash on the elevators from the propeller slipstream is reduced and elevator effectiveness is reduced. This allows the nose to drop.

4.   When the CG in an airplane is located at or rear of the aft CG limit, the airplane

     a.   Develops an inability to recover from stall conditions and
     b.   Becomes less stable at all airspeeds.

11.10 TORQUE AND P-FACTOR

1.   Torque effect (left-turning tendency) is greatest at low airspeed, high angles of attack, and high power, e.g., on takeoff.

2.   P-factor (asymmetric propeller loading) causes the airplane to yaw to the left when at high angles of attack because the descending right side of the propeller (as seen from the rear) has a higher angle of attack (than the upward-moving blade on the left side) and provides more thrust.

11.11 LOAD FACTOR

1. Load factor refers to the additional weight carried by the wings due to the airplane's weight plus the centrifugal force.

    a. The amount of excess load that can be imposed on an airplane's wings varies directly with the airplane's speed and the excess lift available.

        1) At low speeds, very little excess lift is available, so very little excess load can be imposed.

        2) At high speeds, the wings' lifting capacity is so great that the load factor can quickly exceed safety limits.

    b. An increased load factor will result in an airplane stalling at a higher airspeed.

    c. As bank angle increases, the load factor increases. The wings not only have to carry the airplane's weight, but the centrifugal force as well.

2. On the exam, a load factor chart is given with the amount of bank on the horizontal axis (along the bottom of the graph) and the load factor on the vertical axis (up the left side of the graph). Additionally, a table that provides the load factor corresponding to specific bank angles is found on the left side of the chart. Use this table to answer load factor questions.

    a. Compute the load factor by multiplying the airplane's weight by the load factor that corresponds to the given angle of bank. For example, the wings of a 2,000-lb. airplane in a 60° bank must support 4,000 lb. (2,000 × 2.000).

    b. Example load factor chart:

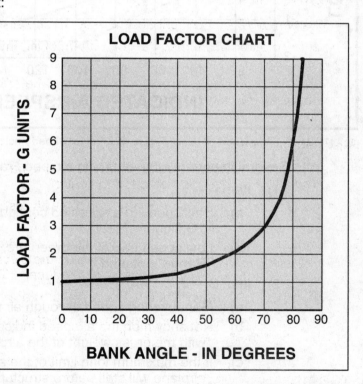

ANGLE of BANK ϕ	LOAD FACTOR n
0°	1.0
10°	1.015
30°	1.154
45°	1.414
60°	2.000
70°	2.923
80°	5.747
85°	11.473
90°	∞

3. Load factor (or G units) is a multiple of the regular weight or, alternatively, a multiple of the force of gravity.

    a. Straight-and-level flight has a load factor at 1.0. (Verify on the chart above.)

    b. A 60° level bank has a load factor of 2.0. Due to centrifugal force, the wings must hold up twice the amount of weight.

    c. A 50° level bank has a load factor of about 1.5.

4.   The effect of load factor on both the stalling speed and the structural limits of the airplane are illustrated in the Velocity-Gravity, or V-G, Diagram.

a.   The V-G diagram, also referred to as a Velocity-Load Factor Chart, is a graph that depicts velocity, or airspeed, on the horizontal axis and various gravities, or load factors, on the vertical axis.

b.   A sample V-G diagram is shown below.

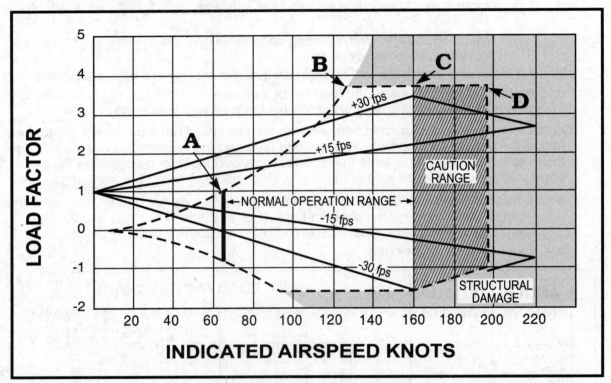

Figure 17.–Velocity/Load Factor Chart.

c.   Several important airspeeds and airspeed ranges are depicted on this graph.

1)   Item A -- V_{S1}

a)   Stall speed in a specified configuration (flaps and gear up, throttle closed, 1G flight)

b)   Low speed end of the green arc, as indicated by the "Normal Operating Range" notation

2)   Item B -- V_A

a)   Maneuvering speed or rough air penetration speed.

b)   Not shown on the airspeed indicator because it changes proportionately with the gross weight of the airplane.

c)   If the maximum load limit of the airplane is exceeded **below** this speed, the airplane will stall before structural damage occurs.

d)   If the maximum load limit of the airplane is exceeded **above** this speed, the airplane will be subject to structural damage and/or failure.

e)   When flying in rough, turbulent air, slow to a speed at or below maneuvering speed to avoid possibly damaging the airplane.

3) Item C -- V_{NO}

    a) Maximum structural cruising speed or maximum normal operating speed.

    b) The low-speed end of the yellow arc, as indicated by the "Caution Range" notation.

    c) You should not exceed this airspeed except in completely smooth air.

4) Item D -- V_{NE}

    a) Never-exceed speed.

    b) The red line on the airspeed indicator.

    c) Above this speed, even in smooth air, the structural limits of the airplane will be exceeded, and structural damage and/or structural failure may occur.

5) The dashed curve that runs from point A to point B is the stall curve.

    a) At any speed and load factor combination to the left of this curve, the airplane will stall.

6) The dashed line from B to D is the positive limit load factor.

    a) Any additional loading encountered beyond this point may result in structural damage.

QUESTIONS AND ANSWER EXPLANATIONS

All of the sport pilot knowledge test questions chosen by the FAA for release as well as additional questions selected by Gleim relating to the material in the previous outlines are reproduced on the following pages. These questions have been organized into the same subunits as the outlines. To the immediate right of each question are the correct answer and answer explanation. You should cover these answers and answer explanations while responding to the questions. Refer to the general discussion in the Introduction on how to take the FAA pilot knowledge test.

Remember that the questions from the FAA pilot knowledge test bank have been reordered by topic and organized into a meaningful sequence. Also, the first line of the answer explanation gives the citation of the authoritative source for the answer.

QUESTIONS
11.1 Flight Controls

1. What is one purpose of wing flaps?

A. To enable the pilot to make steeper approaches to a landing without increasing the airspeed.

B. To relieve the pilot of maintaining continuous pressure on the controls.

C. To decrease wing area to vary the lift.

Answer (A) is correct. *(PHAK Chap 5)*
DISCUSSION: Extending the flaps increases the wing camber and the angle of attack of the wing. This increases wing lift and induced drag, which enables the pilot to make steeper approaches to a landing without an increase in airspeed.
Answer (B) is incorrect. Trim tabs (not wing flaps) help relieve control pressures. Answer (C) is incorrect. Wing area usually remains the same, except for certain specialized flaps that increase (not decrease) the wing area.

2. One of the main functions of flaps during approach and landing is to

A. decrease the angle of descent without increasing the airspeed.

B. permit a touchdown at a higher indicated airspeed.

C. increase the angle of descent without increasing the airspeed.

Answer (C) is correct. *(PHAK Chap 5)*
DISCUSSION: Extending the flaps increases the wing camber and the angle of attack of the wing. This increases wing lift and induced drag, which enables the pilot to increase the angle of descent without increasing the airspeed.
Answer (A) is incorrect. Extending the flaps increases lift and induced drag, which enables the pilot to increase (not decrease) the angle of descent without increasing the airspeed. Answer (B) is incorrect. Flaps increase lift at slow airspeed, which permits touchdown at a lower (not higher) indicated airspeed.

3. What is the purpose of the rudder on an airplane?

   A. To control yaw.

   B. To control overbanking tendency.

   C. To control roll.

Answer (A) is correct. *(PHAK Chap 5)*
   DISCUSSION: The rudder is used to control yaw, which is rotation about the airplane's vertical axis.
   Answer (B) is incorrect. The ailerons (not the rudder) control overbanking. Overbanking tendency refers to the outside wing traveling significantly faster than the inside wing in a steep turn and generating incremental lift to raise the outside wing higher unless corrected by aileron pressure. Answer (C) is incorrect. Roll is movement about the longitudinal axis and is controlled by ailerons.

4. Which is not a primary flight control surface?

   A. Flaps.

   B. Stabilator.

   C. Ailerons.

Answer (A) is correct. *(PHAK Chap 5)*
   DISCUSSION: The three primary flight controls of an airplane are the ailerons, the elevator (or stabilator), and the rudder.
   Answer (B) is incorrect. The stabilator, or elevator, is a primary flight control surface. Answer (C) is incorrect. Ailerons are a primary flight control surface.

5. The elevator controls movement around which axis?

   A. Longitudinal.

   B. Lateral.

   C. Vertical.

Answer (B) is correct. *(PHAK Chap 5)*
   DISCUSSION: The elevator is the primary control device for changing the pitch attitude of an airplane, changing the pitch about the lateral axis.
   Answer (A) is incorrect. Ailerons are control surfaces attached to each wing that move in the opposite direction from one another to control roll about the longitudinal axis.
Answer (C) is incorrect. The rudder controls movement of the aircraft about its vertical axis.

6. Which statement is true concerning primary flight controls?

   A. The effectiveness of each control surface increases with speed because there is more flow over them.

   B. Only when all three primary flight controls move in sequence do the airflow and pressure distribution change over and around the airfoil.

   C. Primary flight controls include ailerons, rudder, elevator, and trim systems.

Answer (A) is correct. *(PHAK Chap 5)*
   DISCUSSION: Rudder, aileron, and elevator effectiveness increase with speed because there is more airflow over the surface of the control device.
   Answer (B) is incorrect. Movement of any primary flight control surfaces changes the airflow and pressure distribution over and around the airfoil. Answer (C) is incorrect. The primary flight controls do not include trim systems; these are considered secondary flight controls.

7. Which of the following is true concerning flaps?

   A. Flaps are attached to the leading edge of the wing and are used to increase wing lift.

   B. Flaps allow an increase in the angle of descent without increasing airspeed.

   C. Flaps are high drag devices deployed from the wings to reduce lift.

Answer (B) is correct. *(PHAK Chap 5)*
   DISCUSSION: Flaps are attached to the trailing edge of the wing and are used during approach and landing to increase wing lift. This allows an increase in the angle of descent without increasing airspeed.
   Answer (A) is incorrect. Flaps are attached to the trailing edge, not the leading edge, of the wing. Answer (C) is incorrect. Spoilers, not flaps, are high-drag devices deployed from the wings to reduce lift and increase drag.

8. Trim systems are designed to do what?

   A. They relieve the pilot of the need to maintain constant back pressure on the flight controls.

   B. They are used during approach and landing to increase wing lift.

   C. They move in the opposite direction from one another to control roll.

Answer (A) is correct. *(PHAK Chap 5)*
   DISCUSSION: Trim systems are used to relieve the pilot of the need to maintain constant back pressure on the flight controls. They include trim tabs, antiservo tabs, and ground adjustable tabs.
   Answer (B) is incorrect. Flaps, not trim systems, are used during approach and landing to increase lift. This allows an increase in the angle of descent without increasing airspeed. Answer (C) is incorrect. Ailerons are control surfaces attached to each wing that move in the opposite direction from one another to control roll about the longitudinal axis.

9. Which device is a secondary flight control?

A. Spoilers.

B. Ailerons.

C. Stabilators.

Answer (A) is correct. *(PHAK Chap 5)*
DISCUSSION: Spoilers are high-drag devices that assist an aircraft in slowing down and losing altitude without gaining extra speed. They are common on gliders and some high-speed aircraft.
Answer (B) is incorrect. Ailerons control the roll of the aircraft and are a primary flight control surface. Answer (C) is incorrect. Stabilators function as both a horizontal stabilizer and an elevator, which makes them a primary control surface.

11.2 Aerodynamic Forces

10. The four forces acting on an airplane in flight are

A. lift, weight, thrust, and drag.

B. lift, weight, gravity, and thrust.

C. lift, gravity, power, and friction.

Answer (A) is correct. *(PHAK Chap 4)*
DISCUSSION: Lift is produced by the wings and opposes weight, which is the result of gravity. Thrust is produced by the engine/propeller and opposes drag, which is the resistance of the air as the airplane moves through it.
Answer (B) is incorrect. Gravity reacts with the airplane's mass, thus producing weight which opposes lift. Answer (C) is incorrect. Gravity results in weight, power produces thrust, and friction is a cause of drag. Power, gravity, velocity, and friction are not aerodynamic forces in themselves.

11. When are the four forces that act on an airplane in equilibrium?

A. During unaccelerated flight.

B. When the aircraft is accelerating.

C. When the aircraft is at rest on the ground.

Answer (A) is correct. *(PHAK Chap 4)*
DISCUSSION: The four forces (lift, weight, thrust, and drag) that act on an airplane are in equilibrium during unaccelerated flight.
Answer (B) is incorrect. Thrust must exceed drag in order for the airplane to accelerate. Answer (C) is incorrect. When the airplane is at rest on the ground, there are no aerodynamic forces acting on it other than weight (gravity).

12. What is the relationship of lift, drag, thrust, and weight when the airplane is in straight-and-level flight?

A. Lift equals weight and thrust equals drag.

B. Lift, drag, and weight equal thrust.

C. Lift and weight equal thrust and drag.

Answer (A) is correct. *(PHAK Chap 4)*
DISCUSSION: When the airplane is in straight-and-level flight (assuming no change of airspeed), it is not accelerating, and therefore lift equals weight and thrust equals drag.
Answer (B) is incorrect. Lift equals weight and drag equals thrust. Answer (C) is incorrect. Lift and weight are equal and thrust and drag are equal, but the four are not equal to each other.

13. Induced drag is a byproduct of lift and will

A. decrease in direct proportion to increases in angle of attack.

B. increase in direct proportion to decreases in angle of attack.

C. increase in direct proportion to increases in angle of attack.

Answer (C) is correct. *(PHAK Chap 4)*
DISCUSSION: Induced drag is a direct result and byproduct of lift (the result of the differential air pressures above and below the wing attempting to equalize near and around the wingtips). As the angle of attack (and therefore lift) increases, induced drag increases proportionally.
Answer (A) is incorrect. Induced drag will increase, not decrease, in proportion to increases in angle of attack. Answer (B) is incorrect. Induced drag will decrease, not increase, in proportion to decreases in angle of attack.

11.3 Angle of Attack

14. The term "angle of attack" is defined as the angle

A. between the wing chord line and the relative wind.

B. between the airplane's climb angle and the horizon.

C. formed by the longitudinal axis of the airplane and the chord line of the wing.

Answer (A) is correct. *(PHAK Chap 3)*
DISCUSSION: The angle of attack is the angle between the wing chord line and the direction of the relative wind. The wing chord line is a straight line from the leading edge to the trailing edge of the wing. The relative wind is the direction of airflow relative to the wing when the wing is moving through the air.
Answer (B) is incorrect. The angle between the airplane's climb angle and the horizon does not describe any term. Answer (C) is incorrect. The angle formed by the longitudinal axis of the airplane and the chord line of the wing is the angle of incidence (not attack).

15. Angle of attack is defined as the angle between the chord line of an airfoil and the

A. direction of the relative wind.

B. pitch angle of an airfoil.

C. rotor plane of rotation.

Answer (A) is correct. *(PHAK Chap 3)*
DISCUSSION: The angle of attack is the angle between the wing chord line and the direction of the relative wind. The wing chord line is a straight line from the leading edge to the trailing edge of the wing. The relative wind is the direction of airflow relative to the wing when the wing is moving through the air.
Answer (B) is incorrect. Pitch is used in conjunction with the aircraft or longitudinal axis, not the chord line of the airfoil. Answer (C) is incorrect. Rotor plane of rotation deals with helicopters, not fixed-wing aircraft.

16. (Refer to Figure 101 below.) The acute angle A is the angle of

A. incidence.

B. attack.

C. dihedral.

Answer (B) is correct. *(PHAK Chap 3)*
DISCUSSION: The angle between the relative wind and the wing chord line is the angle of attack. The wing chord line is a straight line from the leading edge to the trailing edge of the wing.
Answer (A) is incorrect. The angle of incidence is the acute angle formed by the chord line of the wing and the longitudinal axis of the airplane. Answer (C) is incorrect. The dihedral is the angle at which the wings are slanted upward from the wing root to the wingtip.

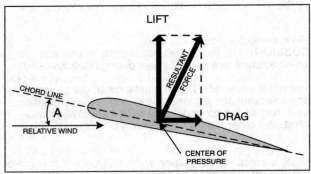

Figure 101. – Lift Vector.

17. The angle of attack at which an airplane wing stalls will

A. increase if the CG is moved forward.

B. change with an increase in gross weight.

C. remain the same regardless of gross weight.

Answer (C) is correct. *(PHAK Chap 4)*
DISCUSSION: A given airplane wing will always stall at the same angle of attack regardless of airspeed, weight, load factor, or density altitude. Each wing has a particular angle of attack (the critical angle of attack) at which the airflow separates from the upper surface of the wing and the stall occurs.
Answer (A) is incorrect. A change in CG will not change the wing's critical angle of attack. Answer (B) is incorrect. The critical angle of attack does not change when gross weight changes.

11.4 Fundamentals of Flight

18. Name the four fundamentals involved in maneuvering an aircraft.

A. Power, pitch, bank, and trim.

B. Thrust, lift, turns, and glides.

C. Straight-and-level flight, turns, climbs, and descents.

Answer (C) is correct. *(PHAK Chap 4)*
DISCUSSION: The four fundamentals involved in maneuvering an aircraft are straight-and-level flight, turns, climbs, and descents.
Answer (A) is incorrect. Power, pitch, bank, and trim are adjustments pilots can make, not the four fundamentals involved in maneuvering an aircraft. Answer (B) is incorrect. This is a mix of some maneuvers (turning and gliding), one of the four main forces involved in flight (thrust), and an aerodynamic force (lift).

11.5 Stalls and Spins

19. As altitude increases, the indicated airspeed at which a given airplane stalls in a particular configuration will

A. decrease as the true airspeed decreases.

B. decrease as the true airspeed increases.

C. remain the same regardless of altitude.

Answer (C) is correct. *(AC 61-67C)*

DISCUSSION: All the performance factors of an airplane are dependent upon air density. As air density decreases, the airplane stalls at a higher true airspeed. However, you cannot detect the effect of high density altitude on your airspeed indicator. Accordingly, an airplane will stall in a particular configuration at the same indicated airspeed regardless of altitude.

Answer (A) is incorrect. True airspeed increases, not decreases, with increased altitude, and indicated airspeed at which an airplane stalls remains the same (not decreases). Answer (B) is incorrect. The indicated airspeed of the stall does not change with increased altitude.

20. In what flight condition must an aircraft be placed in order to spin?

A. Partially stalled with one wing low.

B. In a steep diving spiral.

C. Stalled.

Answer (C) is correct. *(AC 61-67C)*

DISCUSSION: In order to enter a spin, an airplane must always first be stalled. Thereafter, the spin is caused when one wing becomes less stalled than the other wing.

Answer (A) is incorrect. The aircraft must first be fully stalled. Answer (B) is incorrect. A steep diving spiral has a relatively low angle of attack and thus does not produce a stall.

21. The angle of attack at which an airfoil stalls will

A. increase if the CG is moved forward.

B. remain the same regardless of gross weight.

C. change with an increase in gross weight.

Answer (B) is correct. *(PHAK Chap 3)*

DISCUSSION: The direct cause of every stall is an excessive angle of attack. Each airplane has a particular angle of attack where the airflow separates from the upper surface of the wing and the stall occurs. This is the critical angle of attack. While an airplane may stall at different airspeeds, it will always stall at the same angle of attack regardless of airspeed, weight, load factor, or density altitude.

Answer (A) is incorrect. A given airplane will always stall at the same angle of attack. Each airplane has a particular angle of attack where the airflow separates from the upper surface of the wing and the stall occurs. This is the critical angle of attack. Answer (C) is incorrect. A given airplane will always stall at the same angle of attack regardless of airspeed, weight, load factor, or density altitude.

22. The direct cause of every stall is excessive

A. angle of attack.

B. density altitude.

C. upward vertical velocity.

Answer (A) is correct. *(PHAK Chap 3)*

DISCUSSION: Excessive angle of attack is the only factor that will cause a stall. When the critical angle of attack is exceeded, airflow over the wing is no longer sufficient to create enough lift to maintain level flight and the airfoil will stall, regardless of any other factors.

Answer (B) is incorrect. Density altitude will not cause a stall; exceeding the critical angle of attack is the direct cause of every stall. Answer (C) is incorrect. Upward vertical velocity is not the direct cause of every stall. An excessive angle of attack (beyond the critical angle of attack) is the direct cause of every stall.

23. During a spin to the left, which wing(s) is/are stalled?

A. Both wings are stalled.

B. Neither wing is stalled.

C. Only the left wing is stalled.

Answer (A) is correct. *(AC 61-67C)*

DISCUSSION: In order to enter a spin, an airplane must always first be stalled. Thereafter, the spin is caused when one wing is less stalled than the other wing. In a spin to the left, the right wing is less stalled than the left wing.

Answer (B) is incorrect. Both wings must be at least partially stalled through the spin. Answer (C) is incorrect. Both wings are stalled; the right wing is simply less stalled than the left.

11.6   Frost

24. How will frost on the wings of an airplane affect takeoff performance?

    A. Frost will disrupt the smooth flow of air over the wing, adversely affecting its lifting capability.

    B. Frost will change the camber of the wing, increasing its lifting capability.

    C. Frost will cause the airplane to become airborne with a higher angle of attack, decreasing the stall speed.

Answer (A) is correct.   *(PHAK Chap 11)*
DISCUSSION: Frost does not change the basic aerodynamic shape of the wing, but the roughness of its surface spoils the smooth flow of air, thus causing an increase in drag and an early airflow separation over the wing, resulting in a loss of lift.
    Answer (B) is incorrect. Frost will decrease (not increase) lift during takeoff and has no effect on the wing camber. Answer (C) is incorrect. A layer of frost on an airplane will increase drag, which increases (not decreases) the stall speed.

25. Why is frost considered hazardous to flight?

    A. Frost changes the basic aerodynamic shape of the airfoils, thereby decreasing lift.

    B. Frost slows the airflow over the airfoils, thereby increasing control effectiveness.

    C. Frost spoils the smooth flow of air over the wings, thereby decreasing lifting capability.

Answer (C) is correct.   *(AvW Chap 10)*
DISCUSSION: Frost does not change the basic aerodynamic shape of the wing, but the roughness of its surface spoils the smooth flow of air, thus causing an increase in drag and an early airflow separation over the wing, resulting in a loss of lift.
    Answer (A) is incorrect. Frost is thin and does not change the basic aerodynamic shape of the airfoil. Answer (B) is incorrect. The smooth flow of air over the airfoil is affected, not control effectiveness.

26. How does frost affect the lifting surfaces of an airplane on takeoff?

    A. Frost may prevent the airplane from becoming airborne at normal takeoff speed.

    B. Frost will change the camber of the wing, increasing lift during takeoff.

    C. Frost may cause the airplane to become airborne with a lower angle of attack at a lower indicated airspeed.

Answer (A) is correct.   *(AvW Chap 10)*
DISCUSSION: Frost that is not removed from the surface of an airplane prior to takeoff may make it difficult to get the airplane airborne at normal takeoff speed. The frost disrupts the airflow over the wing, which increases drag.
    Answer (B) is incorrect. The smoothness of the wing, not its curvature, is affected and lift is decreased (not increased). Answer (C) is incorrect. Ground effect (not frost) may cause an airplane to become airborne with a lower angle of attack at a lower indicated airspeed.

11.7   Ground Effect

27. What is ground effect?

    A. The result of the interference of the surface of the Earth with the airflow patterns about an airplane.

    B. The result of an alteration in airflow patterns increasing induced drag about the wings of an airplane.

    C. The result of the disruption of the airflow patterns about the wings of an airplane to the point where the wings will no longer support the airplane in flight.

Answer (A) is correct.   *(PHAK Chap 4)*
DISCUSSION: Ground effect is due to the interference of the ground (or water) surface with the airflow patterns about the airplane in flight. As the wing encounters ground effect, there is a reduction in the upwash, downwash, and the wingtip vortices. The result is a reduction in induced drag. Thus, for a given angle of attack, the wing will produce more lift in ground effect than it does out of ground effect.
    Answer (B) is incorrect. The result of the alteration in airflow patterns about the wing decreases, not increases, the induced drag. Answer (C) is incorrect. The disruption of the airflow patterns about the wing decreases induced drag, which causes an increase, not decrease, in lift at a given angle of attack.

28. Floating caused by the phenomenon of ground effect will be most realized during an approach to land when at

    A. less than the length of the wingspan above the surface.

    B. twice the length of the wingspan above the surface.

    C. a higher-than-normal angle of attack.

Answer (A) is correct.   *(PHAK Chap 4)*
DISCUSSION: Ground effect is most usually recognized when the airplane is within one-half of the length of its wingspan above the surface. It may extend as high as a full wingspan length above the surface. Due to an alteration of the airflow about the wings, induced drag decreases, which reduces the thrust required at low airspeeds. Thus, any excess speed during the landing flare may result in considerable floating.
    Answer (B) is incorrect. Ground effect generally extends up to only one wingspan length, not two. Answer (C) is incorrect. Floating will occur with excess airspeed, which results in a lower-than-normal, not higher-than-normal, angle of attack.

29. What must a pilot be aware of as a result of ground effect?

    A. Wingtip vortices increase creating wake turbulence problems for arriving and departing aircraft.

    B. Induced drag decreases; therefore, any excess speed at the point of flare may cause considerable floating.

    C. A full stall landing will require less up elevator deflection than would a full stall when done free of ground effect.

Answer (B) is correct. *(PHAK Chap 4)*
    DISCUSSION: Ground effect reduces the upwash, downwash, and vortices caused by the wings, resulting in a decrease in induced drag. Thus, thrust required at low airspeeds will be reduced, and any excess speed at the point of flare may cause considerable floating.
    Answer (A) is incorrect. Wingtip vortices are decreased, not increased. Answer (C) is incorrect. A full stall landing will require more, not less, up elevator deflection since the wing will require a lower angle of attack in ground effect to produce the same amount of lift.

30. Ground effect is most likely to result in which problem?

    A. Settling to the surface abruptly during landing.

    B. Becoming airborne before reaching recommended takeoff speed.

    C. Inability to get airborne even though airspeed is sufficient for normal takeoff needs.

Answer (B) is correct. *(PHAK Chap 4)*
    DISCUSSION: Due to the reduction of induced drag in ground effect, the airplane may seem capable of becoming airborne well below the recommended takeoff speed. However, as the airplane rises out of ground effect (a height greater than the wingspan) with a deficiency of speed, the increase in induced drag may result in very marginal initial climb performance. In extreme cases, the airplane may become airborne initially, with a deficiency of airspeed, only to settle back on the runway when attempting to fly out of the ground effect area.
    Answer (A) is incorrect. The airplane will experience a little extra lift on landing due to the reduction in induced drag, causing it to float rather than settle abruptly. Answer (C) is incorrect. Ground effect would not hamper the airplane from becoming airborne if the airspeed were sufficient for normal takeoff. Ground effect may allow the airplane to become airborne before reaching the recommended takeoff speed.

11.8 Airplane Turn

31. What force makes an airplane turn?

    A. The horizontal component of lift.

    B. The vertical component of lift.

    C. Centrifugal force.

Answer (A) is correct. *(AFH Chap 3)*
    DISCUSSION: When the wings of an airplane are not level, the lift is not entirely vertical and tends to pull the airplane toward the direction of the lower wing. An airplane is turned when the pilot coordinates rudder, aileron, and elevator to bank in order to attain a horizontal component of lift.
    Answer (B) is incorrect. The vertical component of lift opposes weight and controls vertical, not horizontal, movement. Answer (C) is incorrect. The horizontal component of lift opposes centrifugal force, which acts toward the outside of the turn.

11.9 Airplane Stability

32. An airplane said to be inherently stable will

    A. be difficult to stall.

    B. require less effort to control.

    C. not spin.

Answer (B) is correct. *(PHAK Chap 4)*
    DISCUSSION: An inherently stable airplane will usually return to the original condition of flight (except when in a bank) if disturbed by a force such as air turbulence. Thus, an inherently stable airplane will require less effort to control than an inherently unstable one.
    Answer (A) is incorrect. Stability of an airplane has an effect on stall characteristic, not on the difficulty level of entering a stall. Answer (C) is incorrect. An inherently stable aircraft will spin.

33. What determines the longitudinal stability of an airplane?

A. The location of the CG with respect to the center of lift.

B. The effectiveness of the horizontal stabilizer, rudder, and rudder trim tab.

C. The relationship of thrust and lift to weight and drag.

Answer (A) is correct.   *(PHAK Chap 4)*
DISCUSSION: The location of the center of gravity with respect to the center of lift determines, to a great extent, the longitudinal stability of the airplane. Positive stability is attained by having the center of lift behind the center of gravity. Then the tail provides negative lift, creating a downward tail force, which counteracts the nose's tendency to pitch down.
Answer (B) is incorrect. The rudder and rudder trim tab control the yaw, not the pitch. Answer (C) is incorrect. The relationship of thrust and lift to weight and drag affects speed and altitude, not longitudinal stability.

34. An airplane has been loaded in such a manner that the CG is located aft of the aft CG limit. One undesirable flight characteristic a pilot might experience with this airplane would be

A. a longer takeoff run.

B. difficulty in recovering from a stalled condition.

C. stalling at higher-than-normal airspeed.

Answer (B) is correct.   *(PHAK Chap 4)*
DISCUSSION: The recovery from a stall in any airplane becomes progressively more difficult as its center of gravity moves backward. Generally, airplanes become less controllable, especially at slow flight speeds, as the center of gravity is moved backward.
Answer (A) is incorrect. An airplane with an aft CG has less drag, resulting in a shorter, not longer, takeoff run. Answer (C) is incorrect. An airplane with an aft CG flies at a lower angle of attack, resulting in a lower, not higher, stall speed.

35. What causes an airplane (except a T-tail) to pitch nosedown when power is reduced and controls are not adjusted?

A. The CG shifts forward when thrust and drag are reduced.

B. The downwash on the elevators from the propeller slipstream is reduced and elevator effectiveness is reduced.

C. When thrust is reduced to less than weight, lift is also reduced and the wings can no longer support the weight.

Answer (B) is correct.   *(PHAK Chap 4)*
DISCUSSION: The relative wind on the tail is the result of the airplane's movement through the air and the propeller slipstream. When that slipstream is reduced, the horizontal stabilizer (except a T-tail) will produce less negative lift and the nose will pitch down.
Answer (A) is incorrect. The CG is not affected by changes in thrust or drag. Answer (C) is incorrect. Thrust and weight have no relationship to each other.

36. Loading an airplane to the most aft CG will cause the airplane to be

A. less stable at all speeds.

B. less stable at slow speeds, but more stable at high speeds.

C. less stable at high speeds, but more stable at low speeds.

Answer (A) is correct.   *(PHAK Chap 4)*
DISCUSSION: Airplanes become less stable at all speeds as the center of gravity is moved backward. The rearward center of gravity limit is determined largely by considerations of stability.

11.10 Torque and P-Factor

37. In what flight condition is torque effect the greatest in a single-engine airplane?

A. Low airspeed, high power, high angle of attack.

B. Low airspeed, low power, low angle of attack.

C. High airspeed, high power, high angle of attack.

Answer (A) is correct.   *(PHAK Chap 4)*
DISCUSSION: The effect of torque increases in direct proportion to engine power and inversely to airspeed. Thus, at low airspeeds, high angles of attack, and high power settings, torque is the greatest.
Answer (B) is incorrect. Torque effect is the greatest at high (not low) power settings, and high (not low) angle of attack. Answer (C) is incorrect. Torque effect is the greatest at low (not high) airspeeds.

38. The left turning tendency of an airplane caused by P-factor is the result of the

  A. clockwise rotation of the engine and the propeller turning the airplane counterclockwise.

  B. propeller blade descending on the right, producing more thrust than the ascending blade on the left.

  C. gyroscopic forces applied to the rotating propeller blades acting 90° in advance of the point the force was applied.

Answer (B) is correct. *(PHAK Chap 4)*
DISCUSSION: Asymmetric propeller loading (P-factor) occurs when the airplane is flown at a high angle of attack. The downward-moving blade on the right side of the propeller (as seen from the rear) has a higher angle of attack, which creates higher thrust than the upward moving blade on the left. Thus, the airplane yaws around the vertical axis to the left.
    Answer (A) is incorrect. Torque reaction (not P-factor) is a result of the clockwise rotation of the engine and the propeller turning the airplane counterclockwise. Answer (C) is incorrect. Gyroscopic precession (not P-factor) is a result of the gyroscopic forces applied to the rotating propeller blades acting 90° in advance of the point the force was applied.

39. When does P-factor cause the airplane to yaw to the left?

  A. When at low angles of attack.

  B. When at high angles of attack.

  C. When at high airspeeds.

Answer (B) is correct. *(PHAK Chap 4)*
DISCUSSION: P-factor or asymmetric propeller loading occurs when an airplane is flown at a high angle of attack because the downward-moving blade on the right side of the propeller (as seen from the rear) has a higher angle of attack, which creates higher thrust than the upward-moving blade on the left. Thus, the airplane yaws around the vertical axis to the left.
    Answer (A) is incorrect. At low angles of attack, both sides of the propeller have similar angles of attack and "pull" the airplane straight ahead. Answer (C) is incorrect. At high speeds, an airplane is not at a high angle of attack.

11.11 Load Factor

40. The amount of excess load that can be imposed on the wing of an airplane depends upon the

  A. position of the CG.

  B. speed of the airplane.

  C. abruptness at which the load is applied.

Answer (B) is correct. *(PHAK Chap 4)*
DISCUSSION: The amount of excess load that can be imposed on the wing depends upon how fast the airplane is flying. At low speeds, the maximum available lifting force of the wing is only slightly greater than the amount necessary to support the weight of the airplane. Thus, any excess load would simply cause the airplane to stall. At high speeds, the lifting capacity of the wing is so great (as a result of the greater flow of air over the wings) that a sudden movement of the elevator controls (strong gust of wind) may increase the load factor beyond safe limits. This is why maximum speeds are established by airplane manufacturers.
    Answer (A) is incorrect. The position of the CG affects the stability of the airplane but not the total load the wings can support. Answer (C) is incorrect. It is the amount of load, not the abruptness of the load, that is limited. However, the abruptness of the maneuver can affect the amount of the load.

41. Which basic flight maneuver increases the load factor on an airplane as compared to straight-and-level flight?

  A. Climbs.

  B. Turns.

  C. Stalls.

Answer (B) is correct. *(PHAK Chap 4)*
DISCUSSION: Turns increase the load factor because the lift from the wings is used to pull the airplane around a corner as well as to offset the force of gravity. The wings must carry the airplane's weight plus offset centrifugal force during the turn. For example, a 60° bank results in a load factor of 2; i.e., the wings must support twice the weight they do in level flight.
    Answer (A) is incorrect. The wings only have to carry the weight of the airplane once the airplane is established in a climb. Answer (C) is incorrect. In a stall, the wings are not producing lift.

42. During an approach to a stall, an increased load factor will cause the airplane to

  A. stall at a higher airspeed.

  B. have a tendency to spin.

  C. be more difficult to control.

Answer (A) is correct. *(PHAK Chap 4)*
DISCUSSION: The greater the load (whether from gross weight or from centrifugal force), the more lift is required. Therefore, an airplane will stall at higher airspeeds when the load and/or load factor is increased.
    Answer (B) is incorrect. An airplane's tendency to spin is not related to an increase in load factors. Answer (C) is incorrect. An airplane's stability (not load factor) determines its controllability.

43. (Refer to Figure 102 below.) If an airplane weighs 2,300 pounds, what approximate weight would the airplane structure be required to support during a 60° banked turn while maintaining altitude?

A. 2,300 pounds.

B. 3,400 pounds.

C. 4,600 pounds.

Answer (C) is correct. *(PHAK Chap 4)*
DISCUSSION: Note on Fig. 102 that at a 60° bank angle the load factor is 2. Thus, a 2,300-lb. airplane in a 60° bank would require its wings to support 4,600 lb. (2,300 × 2).
Answer (A) is incorrect. A 1,150-lb. airplane would be required to support a 2,300-lb. load in a 60° banked turn. Answer (B) is incorrect. A 1,700-lb. airplane would be required to support a 3,400-lb. load in a 60° banked turn.

44. (Refer to Figure 102 below.) If an airplane weighs 3,300 pounds, what approximate weight would the airplane structure be required to support during a 30° banked turn while maintaining altitude?

A. 1,200 pounds.

B. 3,100 pounds.

C. 3,960 pounds.

Answer (C) is correct. *(PHAK Chap 4)*
DISCUSSION: Look on the left side of the chart in Fig. 102 to see that at a 30° bank angle the load factor is 1.154. Thus, a 3,300-lb. airplane in a 30° bank would require its wings to support 3,808.2 lb. (3,300 × 1.154). The answer choice closest to this value is 3,960 pounds.
Answer (A) is incorrect. A 1,000-lb. airplane would be required to support a 1,200-lb. load in a 30° banked turn. Answer (B) is incorrect. A 2,583-lb. airplane would be required to support a 3,100-lb. load in a 30° banked turn.

45. (Refer to Figure 102 below.) If an airplane weighs 4,500 pounds, what approximate weight would the airplane structure be required to support during a 45° banked turn while maintaining altitude?

A. 4,500 pounds.

B. 6,750 pounds.

C. 7,200 pounds.

Answer (B) is correct. *(PHAK Chap 4)*
DISCUSSION: Look on the left side of the chart under 45° and note that the load factor curve is 1.414. Thus, a 4,500-lb. airplane in a 45° bank would require its wings to support 6,363 lb. (4,500 × 1.414). This answer is closest to this value.
Answer (A) is incorrect. A 3,000-lb. airplane would be required to support a 4,500-lb. load in a 45° banked turn. Answer (C) is incorrect. A 4,800-lb. airplane would be required to support a 7,200-lb. load in a 45° banked turn.

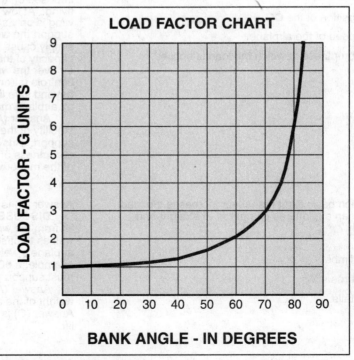

ANGLE of BANK ϕ	LOAD FACTOR n
0°	1.0
10°	1.015
30°	1.154
45°	1.414
60°	2.000
70°	2.923
80°	5.747
85°	11.473
90°	∞

Figure 102. – Load Factor Chart.

46. (Refer to Figure 17 below.) What speed is represented by point A?

A. V_{NO}.

B. V_{NE}.

C. V_{S1}.

Answer (C) is correct. *(PHAK Chap 4)*

DISCUSSION: Point A is the low-speed end of the the green arc, which is V_{S1} – stall speed in a specified configuration (flaps and gear up, throttle closed, 1G flight).

Answer (A) is incorrect. V_{NO} is the normal operating speed and is represented by point C. Answer (B) is incorrect. V_{NE} is the never-exceed speed and is represented by point D.

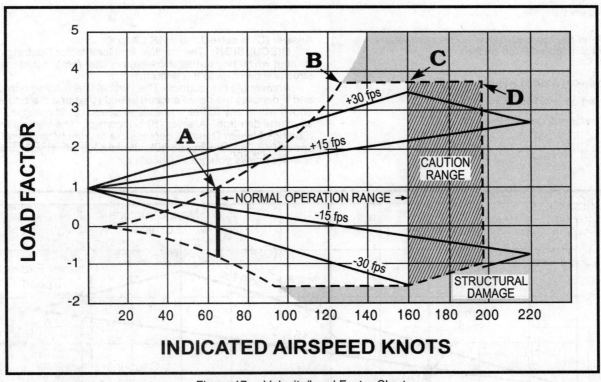

Figure 17. – Velocity/Load Factor Chart.

47. (Refer to Figure 17 above.) What speed is represented by point B?

A. V_A.

B. V_G.

C. V_Y.

Answer (A) is correct. *(PHAK Chap 4)*

DISCUSSION: Point B represents the maneuvering speed, or rough air penetration speed, of the airplane, which is V_A.

Answer (B) is incorrect. V_G represents best glide speed and is not represented on a V-G diagram. Answer (C) is incorrect. V_Y represents the best rate of climb and is not represented on a V-G diagram.

48. (Refer to Figure 17 above.) If you are flying at 120 knots indicated airspeed and encounter a sudden 4G downdraft, what will be the effect on the airplane?

A. The airplane will be overstressed and possibly damaged.

B. The airplane will stall before structural damage is caused.

C. The airplane will experience an engine failure due to instantaneous fuel exhaustion.

Answer (B) is correct. *(PHAK Chap 4)*

DISCUSSION: Because you are flying below the maneuvering speed of the airplane, a load factor that exceeds the design limits of the airplane will result in a stall before structural damage occurs.

Answer (A) is incorrect. You are flying below the maneuvering speed of the airplane. Thus, the airplane will stall before structural damage occurs. Answer (C) is incorrect. An instantaneous, non-sustained downdraft will not cause fuel exhaustion.

49. (Refer to Figure 17 on page 227.) What is represented by the dashed curve running between point A and point B?

A. The stall curve.

B. The lift curve.

C. The change in maneuvering speed versus load factor.

Answer (A) is correct. *(PHAK Chap 4)*
   DISCUSSION: The stall curve illustrates the airspeed and load factor combinations that will result in a stall. Any combinations to the left of the curve will cause a wing stall.
   Answer (B) is incorrect. The lift curve is not depicted on a V-G diagram. Answer (C) is incorrect. Maneuvering speed does not change with load factor but rather with gross weight.

50. (Refer to Figure 68 below.) The positive limit load factor is represented by the

A. vertical dashed line from E to F.

B. vertical solid line from D to G.

C. horizontal dashed line from C to E.

Answer (C) is correct. *(PHAK Chap 4)*
   DISCUSSION: The positive limit load factor illustrates the point at which any further increases in load factor could result in structural damage to the aircraft.
   Answer (A) is incorrect. The vertical line running between E and F denotes the never exceed speed (V_{NE}) and the boundary above which any further increase in speed could result in structural damage. Answer (B) is incorrect. The vertical line running between D and G denotes the maximum structural cruise speed (V_{NO}) and the speed boundary above which you should not operate unless you are in smooth air.

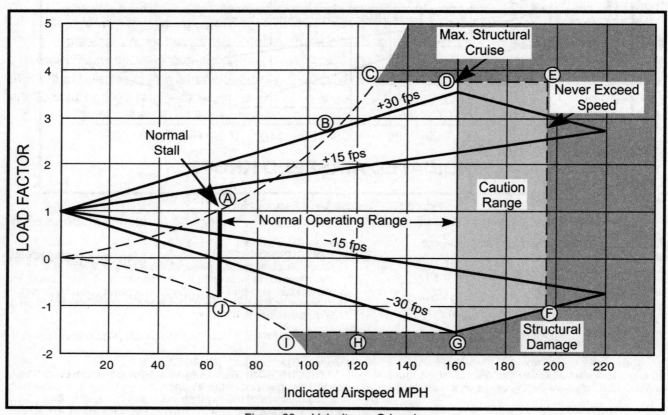

Figure 68. – Velocity vs. G-Loads.

END OF STUDY UNIT

STUDY UNIT TWELVE
AIRPLANE INSTRUMENTS

(5 pages of outline)

This study unit contains outlines of major concepts tested, sample test questions and answers regarding airplane instruments, and an explanation of each answer. The table of contents above lists each subunit within this study unit, the number of questions pertaining to that particular subunit, and the pages on which the outlines and questions begin, respectively.

CAUTION: Recall that the **sole purpose** of this book is to expedite your passing the FAA pilot knowledge test for the sport pilot certificate. Accordingly, all extraneous material (i.e., topics or regulations not directly tested on the FAA pilot knowledge test) is omitted, even though much more information and knowledge are necessary to fly safely. This additional material is presented in the *Pilot Handbook* and *Sport Pilot Flight Maneuvers and Practical Test Prep*, available from Gleim Publications, Inc. See the order form on page 327.

12.1 MAGNETIC COMPASS

1. Prior to flight, make sure that the compass is full of fluid.

2. During turns, the compass should swing freely and indicate known headings.

3. On the ground, runways as well as taxiways have known headings and thus can be used to check the accuracy of the compass.

4. During flight, magnetic compasses can be considered accurate only during straight-and-level flight at constant airspeed.

5. The difference between direction indicated by a magnetic compass not installed in an airplane and one installed in an airplane is called deviation.

   a. Magnetic fields produced by metals and electrical accessories in an airplane disturb the compass needles.

6. In the Northern Hemisphere, acceleration/deceleration error occurs when on an east or west heading. Remember ANDS: Accelerate North, Decelerate South.

   a. A magnetic compass will indicate a turn toward the north during acceleration when on an east or west heading.

   b. A magnetic compass will indicate a turn toward the south during deceleration when on an east or west heading.

   c. Acceleration/deceleration error does not occur when on a north or south heading.

7.   In the Northern Hemisphere, compass turning error occurs when turning from a north or south heading.

    a.   A magnetic compass will lag (and, at the start of a turn, indicate a turn in the opposite direction) when turning from a north heading.

        1)   If turning to the east (right), the compass will initially indicate a turn to the west and then lag behind the actual heading until your airplane is headed east (at which point there is no error).

        2)   If turning to the west (left), the compass will initially indicate a turn to the east and then lag behind the actual heading until your airplane is headed west (at which point there is no error).

    b.   A magnetic compass will lead or precede the turn when turning from a south heading.

    c.   Turning errors do not occur when turning from an east or west heading.

8.   These errors diminish as the acceleration/deceleration or turns are completed.

UNOS (Understood North, Overstood South)

12.2 PITOT-STATIC SYSTEM

1.   The pitot-static system is a source of pressure for the

    a.   Altimeter
    b.   Vertical-speed indicator
    c.   Airspeed indicator

2.   The pitot tube provides impact (or ram) pressure for the airspeed indicator only.

3.   When the pitot tube and the outside static vents or just the static vents are clogged, all three instruments mentioned above will provide inaccurate readings.

    a.   If only the pitot tube is clogged, only the airspeed indicator will be inoperative.

12.3 AIRSPEED INDICATOR

1.   Airspeed indicators have several color-coded markings (see Figure 104 on page 236).

    a.   The white arc is the full flap operating range.

        1)   The lower limit is the power-off stalling speed with wing flaps and landing gear in the landing position (V_{S0}).

        2)   The upper limit is the maximum full flaps-extended speed (V_{FE}).

    b.   The green arc is the normal operating range.

        1)   The lower limit is the power-off stalling speed in a specified configuration (V_{S1}). This is normally wing flaps up and landing gear retracted.

        2)   The upper limit is the maximum structural cruising speed (V_{NO}) for normal operation.

    c.   The yellow arc is airspeed, which is safe in smooth air only.

        1)   It is known as the caution range.

    d.   The red radial line is the speed that should never be exceeded (V_{NE}).

        1)   This is the maximum speed at which the airplane may be operated in smooth air (or under any circumstances).

2.   The most important airspeed limitation, which is **not** color-coded, is the maneuvering speed (V_A).

    a.   The maneuvering speed is the maximum speed at which full deflection of aircraft controls can be made without causing structural damage.

    b.   It is usually the maximum speed for flight in turbulent air.

12.4 ALTIMETER

1. Altimeters have three hands (e.g., as a clock has the hour, minute, and second hands; see Figure 103 on page 238).

2. The three hands on the altimeter are the

    a. 10,000-ft. interval (short needle)
    b. 1,000-ft. interval (medium needle)
    c. 100-ft. interval (long needle)

3. Altimeters are numbered 0-9.

4. To read an altimeter,

    a. First, determine whether the short needle points between 0 and 1 (1-10,000), 1 and 2 (10,000-20,000), or 2 and 3 (20,000-30,000).
    b. Second, determine whether the medium needle is between 0 and 1 (0-1,000), 1 and 2 (1,000-2,000), etc.
    c. Third, determine at which number the long needle is pointing, e.g., 1 for 100 ft., 2 for 200 ft., etc.

12.5 TYPES OF ALTITUDE

1. Absolute altitude is the altitude above the surface, i.e., AGL.

2. True altitude is the actual distance above mean sea level, i.e., MSL. It is not susceptible to variation with atmospheric conditions.

3. Density altitude is pressure altitude corrected for nonstandard temperatures.

4. Pressure altitude is the height above the standard datum plane of 29.92 in. of mercury. Thus, it is the indicated altitude when the altimeter setting is adjusted to 29.92 in. of mercury (also written 29.92" Hg).

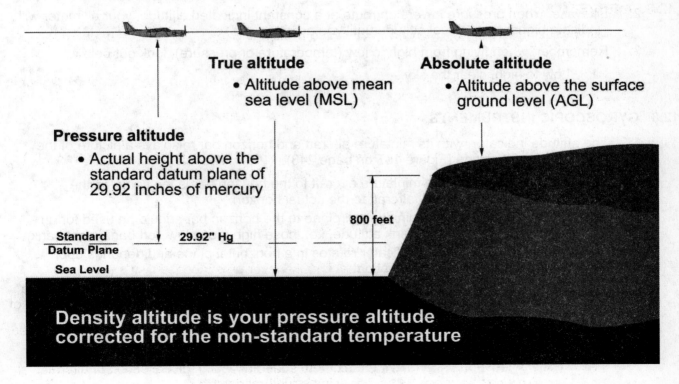

5. Pressure altitude and density altitude are the same at standard temperature.

6. Indicated altitude is the same as true altitude when standard conditions exist and the altimeter is calibrated properly.

7. Pressure altitude and true altitude are the same when standard atmospheric conditions (29.92" Hg and 15°C at sea level) exist.

8. When the altimeter is adjusted on the ground so that indicated altitude equals true altitude at airport elevation, the altimeter setting is that for your location, i.e., approximately the setting you would get from the control tower.

12.6 SETTING THE ALTIMETER

1. The indicated altitude on the altimeter increases when you change the altimeter setting to a higher pressure and decreases when you change the setting to a lower pressure.

   a. This is opposite to the altimeter's reaction due to changes in air pressure.

2. The indicated altitude will change at a rate of approximately 1,000 ft. for 1 in. of pressure change in the altimeter setting.

   a. EXAMPLE: When changing the altimeter setting from 29.15" to 29.85", there is a 0.70" change in pressure (29.85" – 29.15"). The indicated altitude would increase (due to a higher altimeter setting) by 700 ft. (0.70" × 1,000).

12.7 ALTIMETER ERRORS

1. Since altimeter readings are adjusted for changes in barometric pressure but not for temperature changes, an airplane will be at lower than indicated altitude when flying in colder than standard temperature air when maintaining a constant indicated altitude.

   a. On warm days, the altimeter indicates lower than actual altitude.

2. Likewise, when pressure lowers en route at a constant indicated altitude, your altimeter will indicate higher than actual altitude until you adjust it.

3. Remember, when flying from high to low (temperature or pressure), look out below.

   a. Low to high, clear the sky.

12.8 GYROSCOPIC INSTRUMENTS

1. The attitude indicator, with its miniature aircraft and horizon bar, displays a picture of the attitude of the airplane (Figure 107 on page 243).

   a. The relationship of the miniature aircraft to the horizon bar is the same as the relationship of the real aircraft to the actual horizon.

   b. The relationship of the miniature airplane to the horizon bar should be used for an indication of pitch and bank attitude, i.e., nose high, nose low, left bank, right bank.

   c. The gyro in the attitude indicator rotates in a horizontal plane and depends upon rigidity in space for its operation.

   d. An adjustment knob is provided with which the pilot may move the miniature airplane up or down to align the miniature airplane with the horizon bar to suit the pilot's line of vision.

2. The turn coordinator shows the roll and yaw movement of the airplane (Figure 105 on page 243).

    a. It displays a miniature airplane which moves proportionally to the roll rate of the airplane. When the bank is held constant, the turn coordinator indicates the rate of turn.

    b. The ball indicates whether the angle of bank is coordinated with the rate of turn.

3. The heading indicator is a gyro instrument which depends on the principle of rigidity in space for its operation (Figure 106 on page 243).

    a. Due to gyro precession, it must be periodically realigned with a magnetic compass.

12.9 GLASS COCKPITS

1. Glass cockpits, or systems of advanced avionics, are replacing the older round-dial gauges common in many training aircraft.

    a. These systems vary widely but generally provide flight information such as flight progress, engine monitoring, navigation, terrain, traffic, and weather.

    b. These systems are designed to decrease pilot workload, enhance situational awareness, and increase the safety margin.

2. A **primary flight display** (PFD) integrates all flight instruments critical to safe flight in one screen.

    a. Some PFDs incorporate or overlay navigation instruments on top of primary flight instruments.

        1) EXAMPLE: An ILS or VOR may be integrated with the heading indicator.

3. A **multi-function display** (MFD) not only shows primary instrumentation but can combine information from multiple systems on one page or screen.

    a. Moving maps provide a pictorial view of the aircraft's location, route, airspace, and nearby geographical features.

    NOTE: A moving map should not be used as the primary navigation instrument; it should be a supplement, not a substitute, in the navigational process.

    b. Onboard weather systems, including radar, may provide real-time weather.

    c. Other information that could be included on MFDs include terrain and traffic avoidance, checklists, and fuel management systems.

4. Care should be taken that reliance on glass cockpits does not negate safety. A regular scan, both visually outside and on backup gauges inside, should be combined with other means of navigation and checklists to ensure safe flight.

QUESTIONS AND ANSWER EXPLANATIONS

All of the sport pilot knowledge test questions chosen by the FAA for release as well as additional questions selected by Gleim relating to the material in the previous outlines are reproduced on the following pages. These questions have been organized into the same subunits as the outlines. To the immediate right of each question are the correct answer and answer explanation. You should cover these answers and answer explanations while responding to the questions. Refer to the general discussion in the Introduction on how to take the FAA pilot knowledge test.

Remember that the questions from the FAA pilot knowledge test bank have been reordered by topic and organized into a meaningful sequence. Also, the first line of the answer explanation gives the citation of the authoritative source for the answer.

QUESTIONS

12.1 Magnetic Compass

1. Accuracy of the compass can be checked by comparing the compass reading with

    A. the compass deviation card.

    B. isogonic lines.

    C. known runway headings.

Answer (C) is correct. *(PHAK Chap 7)*
    DISCUSSION: Prior to flight, make sure that the compass is full of fluid. Then, during turns, the compass should swing freely and indicate known headings. On the ground, runways as well as taxiways have known headings and thus can be used to check the accuracy of the compass.
    Answer (A) is incorrect. There is no such item as a compass deviation card. There is a compass correction card that shows corrections to compass headings for metal and electrical accessories within the airplane. Answer (B) is incorrect. Isogonic lines are lines that connect points of equal variation. They will not show the accuracy of the compass.

2. In the Northern Hemisphere, a magnetic compass will normally indicate a turn toward the north if

    A. a right turn is entered from an east heading.

    B. a left turn is entered from a west heading.

    C. an aircraft is accelerated while on an east or west heading.

Answer (C) is correct. *(PHAK Chap 7)*
    DISCUSSION: In the Northern Hemisphere, a magnetic compass will normally indicate a turn toward the north if an airplane is accelerated while on an east or west heading.
    Answer (A) is incorrect. There is no compass turning error on turns from an east heading. Answer (B) is incorrect. There is no compass turning error on turns from a west heading.

3. During flight, when are the indications of a magnetic compass accurate?

    A. Only in straight-and-level unaccelerated flight.

    B. As long as the airspeed is constant.

    C. During turns if the bank does not exceed 18°.

Answer (A) is correct. *(PHAK Chap 7)*
    DISCUSSION: During flight, the magnetic compass indications can be considered accurate only when in straight-and-level, unaccelerated flight. During acceleration, deceleration, or turns, the compass card will dip and cause false readings.
    Answer (B) is incorrect. Even with a constant airspeed, the magnetic compass may not be accurate during a turn. Answer (C) is incorrect. Due to the compass card dip, the compass may not be accurate even during shallow turns.

4. Deviation in a magnetic compass is caused by the

    A. presence of flaws in the permanent magnets of the compass.

    B. difference in the location between true north and magnetic north.

    C. magnetic fields within the aircraft distorting the lines of magnetic force.

Answer (C) is correct. *(PHAK Chap 7)*
    DISCUSSION: Magnetic fields produced by metals and electrical accessories in the airplane disturb the compass needle and produce errors. These errors are referred to as compass deviation.
    Answer (A) is incorrect. A properly functioning magnetic compass is still subject to deviation. Answer (B) is incorrect. The difference in the location between true and magnetic north refers to magnetic variation, not deviation.

5. In the Northern Hemisphere, if an aircraft is accelerated or decelerated, the magnetic compass will normally indicate

    A. a turn momentarily.

    B. correctly when on a north or south heading.

    C. a turn toward the south.

Answer (B) is correct. *(PHAK Chap 7)*
    DISCUSSION: Acceleration and deceleration errors on magnetic compasses do not occur when on a north or south heading in the Northern Hemisphere. They occur on east and west headings.
    Answer (A) is incorrect. Acceleration and deceleration errors occur only on easterly and westerly headings. Answer (C) is incorrect. A turn to the north is indicated upon acceleration, and a turn to the south is indicated on deceleration when on east or west headings.

6. In the Northern Hemisphere, a magnetic compass will normally indicate initially a turn toward the west if

    A. a left turn is entered from a north heading.

    B. a right turn is entered from a north heading.

    C. an aircraft is accelerated while on a north heading.

Answer (B) is correct. *(PHAK Chap 7)*
    DISCUSSION: Due to the northerly turn error in the Northern Hemisphere, a magnetic compass will initially indicate a turn toward the west if a right (east) turn is entered from a north heading.
    Answer (A) is incorrect. If a left (west) turn were made from a north heading, the compass would initially indicate a turn toward the east. Answer (C) is incorrect. Acceleration/deceleration error does not occur on a north heading.

7. In the Northern Hemisphere, the magnetic compass will normally indicate a turn toward the south when

    A. a left turn is entered from an east heading.

    B. a right turn is entered from a west heading.

    C. the aircraft is decelerated while on a west heading.

Answer (C) is correct. *(PHAK Chap 7)*
    DISCUSSION: In the Northern Hemisphere, a magnetic compass will normally indicate a turn toward the south if an airplane is decelerated while on an east or west heading.
    Answer (A) is incorrect. Turning errors do not occur from an east heading. Answer (B) is incorrect. Turning errors do not occur from a west heading.

8. In the Northern Hemisphere, a magnetic compass will normally indicate initially a turn toward the east if

    A. an aircraft is decelerated while on a south heading.

    B. an aircraft is accelerated while on a north heading.

    C. a left turn is entered from a north heading.

Answer (C) is correct. *(PHAK Chap 7)*
    DISCUSSION: In the Northern Hemisphere, a magnetic compass normally initially indicates a turn toward the east if a left (west) turn is entered from a north heading.
    Answer (A) is incorrect. Acceleration/deceleration errors do not occur while on a south heading, only on an east or west heading. Answer (B) is incorrect. Acceleration/deceleration errors do not occur while on a north heading, only on an east or west heading.

12.2 Pitot-Static System

9. The pitot system provides impact pressure for which instrument?

    A. Altimeter.

    B. Vertical-speed indicator.

    C. Airspeed indicator.

Answer (C) is correct. *(PHAK Chap 7)*
    DISCUSSION: The pitot system provides impact pressure, or ram pressure, for only the airspeed indicator.
    Answer (A) is incorrect. The altimeter operates off the static (not pitot) system. Answer (B) is incorrect. The vertical-speed indicator operates off the static (not pitot) system.

10. Which instrument will become inoperative if the pitot tube becomes clogged?

    A. Altimeter.

    B. Vertical speed.

    C. Airspeed.

Answer (C) is correct. *(PHAK Chap 7)*
    DISCUSSION: The pitot-static system is a source of pressure for the altimeter, vertical-speed indicator, and airspeed indicator. The pitot tube is connected directly to the airspeed indicator and provides impact pressure for it alone. Thus, if the pitot tube becomes clogged, only the airspeed indicator will become inoperative.
    Answer (A) is incorrect. The altimeter operates off the static system and is not affected by a clogged pitot tube. Answer (B) is incorrect. The vertical speed indicator operates off the static system and is not affected by a clogged pitot tube.

11. If the pitot tube and outside static vents become clogged, which instruments would be affected?

    A. The altimeter, airspeed indicator, and turn-and-slip indicator.

    B. The altimeter, airspeed indicator, and vertical speed indicator.

    C. The altimeter, attitude indicator, and turn-and-slip indicator.

Answer (B) is correct. *(PHAK Chap 7)*
    DISCUSSION: The pitot-static system is a source of air pressure for the operation of the altimeter, airspeed indicator, and vertical speed indicator. Thus, if the pitot and outside static vents become clogged, all of these instruments will be affected.
    Answer (A) is incorrect. The turn-and-slip indicator is a gyroscopic instrument and does not operate on the pitot-static system. Answer (C) is incorrect. The attitude indicator and turn-and-slip indicator are both gyroscopic instruments and do not operate on the pitot-static system.

12. Which instrument(s) will become inoperative if the static vents become clogged?

    A. Airspeed only.

    B. Altimeter only.

    C. Airspeed, altimeter, and vertical speed.

Answer (C) is correct. *(PHAK Chap 7)*
    DISCUSSION: The pitot-static system is a source of air pressure for the operation of the airspeed indicator, altimeter, and vertical speed indicator. Thus, if the static vents become clogged, all three instruments will become inoperative.
    Answer (A) is incorrect. Not only will the airspeed indicator become inoperative, but also the altimeter and vertical speed indicator. Answer (B) is incorrect. Not only will the altimeter become inoperative, but also the airspeed and vertical speed indicators.

12.3 Airspeed Indicator

13. What does the red line on an airspeed indicator represent?

A. Maneuvering speed.

B. Turbulent or rough-air speed.

C. Never-exceed speed.

Answer (C) is correct. *(PHAK Chap 7)*
DISCUSSION: The red line on an airspeed indicator indicates the maximum speed at which the airplane can be operated in smooth air, which should never be exceeded intentionally. This speed is known as the never-exceed speed.
Answer (A) is incorrect. Maneuvering speed is not indicated on the airspeed indicator. Answer (B) is incorrect. Turbulent or rough-air speed is not indicated on the airspeed indicator.

14. What is an important airspeed limitation that is not color-coded on airspeed indicators?

A. Never-exceed speed.

B. Maximum structural cruising speed.

C. Maneuvering speed.

Answer (C) is correct. *(PHAK Chap 7)*
DISCUSSION: The maneuvering speed of an airplane is an important airspeed limitation not color-coded on the airspeed indicator. It is found in the airplane manual (Pilot's Operating Handbook) or placarded in the cockpit. Maneuvering speed is the maximum speed at which full deflection of the airplane controls can be made without incurring structural damage. Maneuvering speed or less should be held in turbulent air to prevent structural damage due to excessive loads.
Answer (A) is incorrect. The never-exceed speed is indicated on the airspeed indicator by a red radial line. Answer (B) is incorrect. The maximum structural cruising speed is indicated by the upper limit of the green arc on the airspeed indicator.

15. (Refer to Figure 104 on page 237.) What is the caution range of the airplane?

A. 0 to 60 MPH.

B. 100 to 165 MPH.

C. 165 to 208 MPH.

Answer (C) is correct. *(PHAK Chap 7)*
DISCUSSION: The caution range is indicated by the yellow arc on the airspeed indicator. Operation within this range is safe only in smooth air. The airspeed indicator in Fig. 104 indicates the caution range from 165 to 208 MPH.
Answer (A) is incorrect. Stall speed is more than 0 to 60 MPH. Answer (B) is incorrect. The normal operating airspeed range from maximum flap extension speed to maximum structural cruising speed is 100 to 165 MPH.

16. (Refer to Figure 104 on page 237.) The maximum speed at which the airplane can be operated in smooth air is

A. 100 MPH.

B. 165 MPH.

C. 208 MPH.

Answer (C) is correct. *(PHAK Chap 7)*
DISCUSSION: The maximum speed at which the airplane can be operated in smooth air is indicated by the red radial line. The airspeed indicator in Fig. 104 indicates the red line is at 208 MPH.
Answer (A) is incorrect. The maximum flaps-extended speed is 100 MPH, the upper limit of the white arc. Answer (B) is incorrect. The maximum structural cruising speed is 165 MPH, the upper limit of the green arc.

17. (Refer to Figure 104 on page 237.) What is the full flap operating range for the airplane?

A. 60 to 100 MPH.

B. 60 to 208 MPH.

C. 65 to 165 MPH.

Answer (A) is correct. *(PHAK Chap 7)*
DISCUSSION: The full flap operating range is indicated by the white arc on the airspeed indicator. The airspeed indicator in Fig. 104 indicates the full flap operating range is from 60 to 100 MPH.
Answer (B) is incorrect. The entire operating range of this airplane is 60 to 208 MPH. Answer (C) is incorrect. The normal operating range for this airplane (green arc) is 65 to 165 MPH.

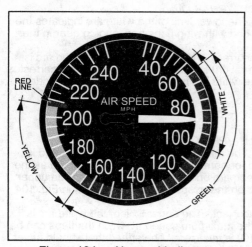

Figure 104. – Airspeed Indicator.

18. (Refer to Figure 104 above.) Which color identifies the never-exceed speed?

A. Lower limit of the yellow arc.

B. Upper limit of the white arc.

C. The red radial line.

Answer (C) is correct. *(PHAK Chap 7)*
  DISCUSSION: The never-exceed speed is indicated by a red line and is found at the upper limit of the yellow arc. Operating above this speed may result in structural damage.
  Answer (A) is incorrect. The lower limit of the yellow arc is the beginning of the caution range. Answer (B) is incorrect. The upper limit of the white arc is the maximum speed at which flaps may be extended.

19. (Refer to Figure 104 above.) Which color identifies the power-off stalling speed in a specified configuration?

A. Upper limit of the green arc.

B. Upper limit of the white arc.

C. Lower limit of the green arc.

Answer (C) is correct. *(PHAK Chap 7)*
  DISCUSSION: The lower airspeed limit of the green arc indicates the power-off stalling speed in a specified configuration. "Specified configuration" refers to flaps up and landing gear retracted.
  Answer (A) is incorrect. The upper limit of the green arc is the maximum structural cruising speed. Answer (B) is incorrect. The upper airspeed limit of the white arc is the maximum flaps-extended speed. Structural damage to the flaps could occur if the flaps are extended above this airspeed.

20. (Refer to Figure 104 above.) What is the maximum flaps-extended speed?

A. 65 MPH.

B. 100 MPH.

C. 165 MPH.

Answer (B) is correct. *(PHAK Chap 7)*
  DISCUSSION: The maximum flaps-extended speed is indicated by the upper limit of the white arc. This is the highest airspeed at which a pilot should extend full flaps. At higher airspeeds, severe strain or structural failure could result. The upper limit of the white arc on the airspeed indicator shown in Fig. 104 indicates 100 MPH.
  Answer (A) is incorrect. The lower limit of the green arc is 65 MPH, which is the power-off stall speed in a specified configuration. Answer (C) is incorrect. The upper limit of the green arc is 165 MPH, which is the maximum structural cruising speed.

21. (Refer to Figure 104 above.) Which color identifies the normal flap operating range?

A. The lower limit of the white arc to the upper limit of the green arc.

B. The green arc.

C. The white arc.

Answer (C) is correct. *(PHAK Chap 7)*
  DISCUSSION: The normal flap operating range is indicated by the white arc. The power-off stall speed with flaps extended is at the lower limit of the arc, and the maximum speed at which flaps can be extended without damage to them is the upper limit of the arc.
  Answer (A) is incorrect. The upper limit of the green arc well exceeds the upper limit of the white arc, which is the maximum flap extended speed. Answer (B) is incorrect. The green arc represents the normal operating range.

22. (Refer to Figure 104 on page 237.) Which color identifies the power-off stalling speed with wing flaps and landing gear in the landing configuration?

A. Upper limit of the green arc.

B. Upper limit of the white arc.

C. Lower limit of the white arc.

Answer (C) is correct. *(PHAK Chap 7)*
   DISCUSSION: The lower limit of the white arc indicates the power-off stalling speed with wing flaps and landing gear in the landing position.
   Answer (A) is incorrect. The upper limit of the green arc is the maximum structural cruising speed. Answer (B) is incorrect. The upper limit of the white arc is the maximum flaps-extended speed.

23. (Refer to Figure 104 on page 237.) What is the maximum structural cruising speed?

A. 100 MPH.

B. 165 MPH.

C. 208 MPH.

Answer (B) is correct. *(PHAK Chap 7)*
   DISCUSSION: The maximum structural cruising speed is the maximum speed for normal operation and is indicated as the upper limit of the green arc on an airspeed indicator. The upper limit of the green arc on the airspeed indicator shown in Fig. 104 indicates 165 MPH.
   Answer (A) is incorrect. The upper limit of the white arc is 100 MPH, which is the maximum speed at which the flaps can be extended. Answer (C) is incorrect. The speed that should never be exceeded is 208 MPH. Beyond this speed, structural damage to the airplane may occur.

12.4 Altimeter

24. (Refer to Figure 103 below.) Altimeter 2 indicates

A. 1,500 feet.

B. 4,500 feet.

C. 14,500 feet.

Answer (C) is correct. *(PHAK Chap 7)*
   DISCUSSION: Altimeter 2 indicates 14,500 ft. because the shortest needle is between the 1 and the 2, indicating about 15,000 ft.; the middle needle is between 4 and 5, indicating 4,500 ft.; and the long needle is on 5, indicating 500 ft., i.e., 14,500 ft.
   Answer (A) is incorrect. For 1,500 ft., the middle needle would have to be between 1 and 2, and the shortest needle between 0 and 1. Answer (B) is incorrect. For 4,500 ft., the shortest needle would have to be between 0 and 1.

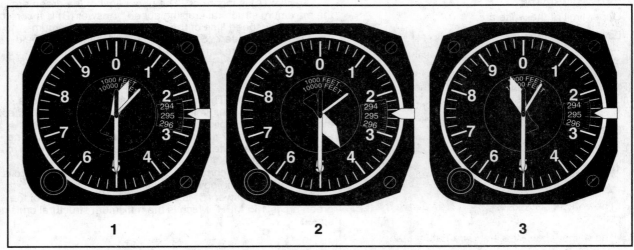

Figure 103. – Altimeter.

25. (Refer to Figure 103 on page 238.) Altimeter 1 indicates

A. 500 feet.

B. 1,500 feet.

C. 10,500 feet.

Answer (C) is correct. *(PHAK Chap 7)*

DISCUSSION: The altimeter has three needles. The short needle indicates 10,000-ft. intervals, the middle-length needle indicates 1,000-ft. intervals, and the long needle indicates 100-ft. intervals. In altimeter 1, the shortest needle is on 1, which indicates about 10,000 ft. The middle-length needle indicates half-way between zero and 1, which is 500 ft. This is confirmed by the longest needle on 5, indicating 500 ft., i.e., 10,500 ft.

Answer (A) is incorrect. If it were indicating just 500 ft., the short and medium needles would have to be on or near zero. Answer (B) is incorrect. If it were 1,500 ft., the shortest needle would be near zero and the middle needle would be between the 1 and the 2.

26. (Refer to Figure 103 on page 238.) Altimeter 3 indicates

A. 9,500 feet.

B. 10,950 feet.

C. 15,940 feet.

Answer (A) is correct. *(PHAK Chap 7)*

DISCUSSION: Altimeter 3 indicates 9,500 ft. because the shortest needle is near 1 (i.e., about 10,000 ft.); the middle needle is between 9 and the 0, indicating between 9,000 and 10,000 ft.; and the long needle is on 5, indicating 500 ft.

Answer (B) is incorrect. For 10,950 ft., the middle needle would have to be near the 1 and the long needle would have to be between the 9 and 0. Answer (C) is incorrect. For 15,940 ft., the short needle would have to be between 1 and 2, the middle needle near the 6, and the large needle between the 9 and 0.

27. (Refer to Figure 103 on page 238.) Which altimeter(s) indicate(s) more than 10,000 feet?

A. 1, 2, and 3.

B. 1 and 2 only.

C. 1 only.

Answer (B) is correct. *(PHAK Chap 7)*

DISCUSSION: Altimeters 1 and 2 indicate over 10,000 ft. because 1 indicates 10,500 ft. and 2 indicates 14,500 ft. The short needle on 3 points just below 1, i.e., below 10,000 ft.

Answer (A) is incorrect. Altimeter 3 is indicating 9,500 ft., which is less than 10,000 ft. Answer (C) is incorrect. Altimeter 2 is indicating 14,500 ft., which is also more than 10,000 ft.

12.5 Types of Altitude

28. What is absolute altitude?

A. The altitude read directly from the altimeter.

B. The vertical distance of the aircraft above the surface.

C. The height above the standard datum plane.

Answer (B) is correct. *(PHAK Chap 7)*

DISCUSSION: Absolute altitude is altitude above the surface, i.e., AGL.

Answer (A) is incorrect. It is indicated altitude. Answer (C) is incorrect. It is pressure altitude.

29. What is true altitude?

A. The vertical distance of the aircraft above sea level.

B. The vertical distance of the aircraft above the surface.

C. The height above the standard datum plane.

Answer (A) is correct. *(PHAK Chap 7)*

DISCUSSION: True altitude is the actual altitude above mean sea level, i.e., MSL.

Answer (B) is incorrect. It represents absolute altitude. Answer (C) is incorrect. It is pressure altitude.

30. What is density altitude?

A. The height above the standard datum plane.

B. The pressure altitude corrected for nonstandard temperature.

C. The altitude read directly from the altimeter.

Answer (B) is correct. *(PHAK Chap 10)*

DISCUSSION: Density altitude is the pressure altitude corrected for nonstandard temperature.

Answer (A) is incorrect. It defines pressure altitude. Answer (C) is incorrect. It is indicated altitude.

31. Under what condition is pressure altitude and density altitude the same value?

    A. At sea level, when the temperature is 0°F.

    B. When the altimeter has no installation error.

    C. At standard temperature.

Answer (C) is correct. *(PHAK Chap 7)*
    DISCUSSION: Pressure altitude and density altitude are the same when temperature is standard.
    Answer (A) is incorrect. Standard temperature at sea level is 59°F, not 0°F. Answer (B) is incorrect. Installation error refers to pitot tubes and airspeed, not altimeter and altitude.

32. Under what condition is indicated altitude the same as true altitude?

    A. If the altimeter has no mechanical error.

    B. When at sea level under standard conditions.

    C. When at 18,000 feet MSL with the altimeter set at 29.92.

Answer (B) is correct. *(PHAK Chap 7)*
    DISCUSSION: Indicated altitude (what you read on your altimeter) approximates the true altitude (distance above mean sea level) when standard conditions exist and your altimeter is properly calibrated.
    Answer (A) is incorrect. The indicated altitude must be adjusted for nonstandard temperature for true altitude. Answer (C) is incorrect. The altimeter reads pressure altitude when set to 29.92" Hg., and that is only true altitude under standard conditions.

33. Under which condition will pressure altitude be equal to true altitude?

    A. When the atmospheric pressure is 29.92" Hg.

    B. When standard atmospheric conditions exist.

    C. When indicated altitude is equal to the pressure altitude.

Answer (B) is correct. *(AvW Chap 6)*
    DISCUSSION: Pressure altitude equals true altitude when standard atmospheric conditions (29.92" Hg and 15°C at sea level) exist.
    Answer (A) is incorrect. Standard temperature must also exist. Answer (C) is incorrect. Indicated altitude does not necessarily relate to true or pressure altitudes.

34. What is pressure altitude?

    A. The indicated altitude corrected for position and installation error.

    B. The altitude indicated when the barometric pressure scale is set to 29.92.

    C. The indicated altitude corrected for nonstandard temperature and pressure.

Answer (B) is correct. *(PHAK Chap 7)*
    DISCUSSION: Pressure altitude is the airplane's height above the standard datum plane of 29.92" Hg. If the altimeter is set to 29.92" Hg, the indicated altitude is the pressure altitude.
    Answer (A) is incorrect. "Corrected for position and installation error" is used to define calibrated airspeed, not a type of altitude. Answer (C) is incorrect. It describes density altitude.

35. Altimeter setting is the value to which the barometric pressure scale of the altimeter is set so the altimeter indicates

    A. calibrated altitude at field elevation.

    B. absolute altitude at field elevation.

    C. true altitude at field elevation.

Answer (C) is correct. *(PHAK Chap 7)*
    DISCUSSION: Altimeter setting is the value to which the scale of the pressure altimeter is set so that the altimeter indicates true altitude at field elevation.
    Answer (A) is incorrect. "Calibrated" refers to airspeed and airspeed indicators, not altitude and altimeters. Answer (B) is incorrect. Absolute altitude is the altitude above the surface, not above MSL.

12.6 Setting the Altimeter

36. If it is necessary to set the altimeter from 29.15 to 29.85, what change occurs?

    A. 70-foot increase in indicated altitude.

    B. 70-foot increase in density altitude.

    C. 700-foot increase in indicated altitude.

Answer (C) is correct. *(PHAK Chap 7)*
    DISCUSSION: When increasing the altimeter setting from 29.15" to 29.85", the indicated altitude increases by 700 ft. The altimeter-indicated altitude moves in the same direction as the altimeter setting and changes about 1,000 ft. for every change of 1" Hg in the altimeter setting.
    Answer (A) is incorrect. A .7" Hg change in pressure is equal to 700 ft., not 70 ft., of altitude. Answer (B) is incorrect. Density altitude is not affected by changing the altimeter setting.

37. If a pilot changes the altimeter setting from 30.11 to 29.96, what is the approximate change in indication?

    A. Altimeter will indicate .15" Hg higher.

    B. Altimeter will indicate 150 feet higher.

    C. Altimeter will indicate 150 feet lower.

Answer (C) is correct. *(PHAK Chap 7)*
    DISCUSSION: Atmospheric pressure decreases approximately 1" of mercury for every 1,000 ft. of altitude gained. As an altimeter setting is changed, the change in altitude indication changes the same way (i.e., approximately 1,000 ft. for every 1" change in altimeter setting) and in the same direction (i.e., lowering the altimeter setting lowers the altitude reading). Thus, changing from 30.11" to 29.96" is a decrease of .15" Hg., or 150 ft. (.15 × 1,000 ft.) lower.
    Answer (A) is incorrect. The altimeter indicates feet, not inches of mercury. Answer (B) is incorrect. The altimeter will show 150 ft. lower, not higher.

12.7 Altimeter Errors

38. If a flight is made from an area of low pressure into an area of high pressure without the altimeter setting being adjusted, the altimeter will indicate

    A. the actual altitude above sea level.

    B. higher than the actual altitude above sea level.

    C. lower than the actual altitude above sea level.

Answer (C) is correct. *(AvW Chap 3)*
    DISCUSSION: When an altimeter setting is at a lower value than the correct setting, the altimeter is indicating less than it should and thus would be showing lower than the actual altitude above sea level.
    Answer (A) is incorrect. The altimeter will show actual altitude only when it is set correctly. Answer (B) is incorrect. The increase in pressure causes the altimeter to read lower, not higher, than actual altitude.

39. If a flight is made from an area of high pressure into an area of lower pressure without the altimeter setting being adjusted, the altimeter will indicate

    A. lower than the actual altitude above sea level.

    B. higher than the actual altitude above sea level.

    C. the actual altitude above sea level.

Answer (B) is correct. *(AvW Chap 3)*
    DISCUSSION: When flying from higher pressure to lower pressure without adjusting your altimeter, the altimeter will indicate a higher than actual altitude. As you adjust an altimeter barometric setting lower, the altimeter indicates lower.
    Answer (A) is incorrect. The decrease in pressure causes the altimeter to read higher, not lower, than actual altitude. Answer (C) is incorrect. The altimeter will show actual altitude only when it is set correctly.

40. Which condition would cause the altimeter to indicate a lower altitude than true altitude?

    A. Air temperature lower than standard.

    B. Atmospheric pressure lower than standard.

    C. Air temperature warmer than standard.

Answer (C) is correct. *(AvW Chap 3)*
    DISCUSSION: In air that is warmer than standard temperature, the airplane will be higher than the altimeter indicates. Said another way, the altimeter will indicate a lower altitude than actually flown.
    Answer (A) is incorrect. When flying in air that is colder than standard temperature, the airplane will be lower than the altimeter indicates ("high to low, look out below"). Answer (B) is incorrect. The altimeter setting corrects the altimeter for nonstandard pressure.

41. Under what condition will true altitude be lower than indicated altitude?

    A. In colder than standard air temperature.

    B. In warmer than standard air temperature.

    C. When density altitude is higher than indicated altitude.

Answer (A) is correct. *(AvW Chap 3)*
    DISCUSSION: The airplane will be lower than the altimeter indicates when flying in air that is colder than standard temperature. Remember that altimeter readings are adjusted for changes in barometric pressure but not for changes in temperature. When one flies from warmer to cold air and keeps a constant indicated altitude at a constant altimeter setting, the plane has actually descended.
    Answer (B) is incorrect. The altimeter indicates lower than actual altitude in warmer than standard temperature. Answer (C) is incorrect. A higher density altitude is usually the result of warmer, not colder, than standard temperature.

42. How do variations in temperature affect the altimeter?

A. Pressure levels are raised on warm days and the indicated altitude is lower than true altitude.

B. Higher temperatures expand the pressure levels and the indicated altitude is higher than true altitude.

C. Lower temperatures lower the pressure levels and the indicated altitude is lower than true altitude.

Answer (A) is correct. *(PHAK Chap 7)*
  DISCUSSION: On warm days, the atmospheric pressure levels are higher than on cold days. Your altimeter will indicate a lower than true altitude. Remember, "low to high, clear the sky."
  Answer (B) is incorrect. Expanding (or raising) the pressure levels will cause indicated altitude to be lower (not higher) than true altitude. Answer (C) is incorrect. Lower pressure levels will cause indicated altitude to be higher (not lower) than true altitude.

12.8 Gyroscopic Instruments

43. (Refer to Figure 107 on page 243.) The proper adjustment to make on the attitude indicator during level flight is to align the

A. horizon bar to the level-flight indication.

B. horizon bar to the miniature airplane.

C. miniature airplane to the horizon bar.

Answer (C) is correct. *(PHAK Chap 7)*
  DISCUSSION: The horizon bar (marked as B) on Fig. 107 represents the true horizon. This bar is fixed to the gyro and remains on a horizontal plane as the airplane is pitched or banked about its lateral or longitudinal axis, indicating the attitude of the airplane relative to the true horizon. An adjustment knob is provided, with which the pilot may move the miniature airplane (marked as C) up or down to align the miniature airplane with the horizontal bar to suit the pilot's line of vision.
  Answer (A) is incorrect. Aligning the miniature airplane to the horizon bar provides a level-flight indication. Answer (B) is incorrect. The miniature airplane is adjustable, not the horizon bar.

44. (Refer to Figure 107 on page 243.) How should a pilot determine the direction of bank from an attitude indicator such as the one illustrated?

A. By the direction of deflection of the banking scale (A).

B. By the direction of deflection of the horizon bar (B).

C. By the relationship of the miniature airplane (C) to the deflected horizon bar (B).

Answer (C) is correct. *(PHAK Chap 7)*
  DISCUSSION: The direction of bank on the attitude indicator (AI) is indicated by the relationship of the miniature airplane to the deflecting horizon bar. The miniature airplane's relative position to the horizon indicates its attitude: nose high, nose low, left bank, right bank. As you look at the attitude indicator, you see your airplane as it is positioned with respect to the actual horizon. The attitude indicator in Fig. 107 indicates a level right turn.
  Answer (A) is incorrect. The banking scale (marked as A) may move in the opposite direction, which is confusing. Answer (B) is incorrect. The horizon bar (marked as B) moves in the direction opposite the turn.

45. (Refer to Figure 105 on page 243.) A turn coordinator provides an indication of the

A. movement of the aircraft about the yaw and roll axes.

B. angle of bank up to but not exceeding 30°.

C. attitude of the aircraft with reference to the longitudinal axis.

Answer (A) is correct. *(PHAK Chap 7)*
  DISCUSSION: There really are no yaw and roll axes; i.e., an airplane yaws about its vertical axis and rolls about its longitudinal axis. However, this is the best answer since the turn coordinator does indicate the roll and yaw movement of the airplane. The movement of the miniature airplane is proportional to the roll rate of the airplane. When the roll rate is reduced to zero (i.e., when the bank is held constant), the instrument provides an indication of the rate of turn.
  Answer (B) is incorrect. The turn coordinator shows the rate of turn rather than angle of bank. Answer (C) is incorrect. The turn coordinator does not show the attitude of the airplane (as does the attitude indicator); it shows the rate of the roll and turn.

46. (Refer to Figures 105, 106, and 107 below.) To receive accurate indications during flight from a heading indicator, the instrument must be

A. set prior to flight on a known heading.

B. calibrated on a compass rose at regular intervals.

C. periodically realigned with the magnetic compass as the gyro precesses.

Answer (C) is correct. *(PHAK Chap 7)*

DISCUSSION: Due to gyroscopic precession, directional gyros must be periodically realigned with a magnetic compass. Friction is the major cause of its drifting from the correct heading.

Answer (A) is incorrect. The instrument must be periodically reset, not just set initially. Answer (B) is incorrect. There is no calibration of the heading indicator; rather, it is reset.

Figure 105. – Turn Coordinator.

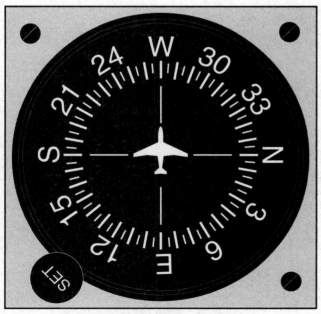

Figure 106. – Heading Indicator.

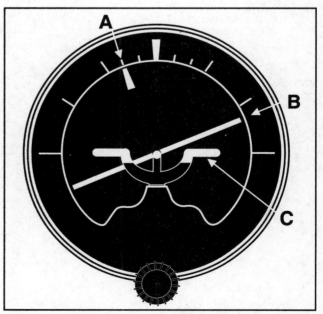

Figure 107. – Attitude Indicator.

12.9 Glass Cockpits

47. What is a benefit of flying with a glass cockpit?

A. There is no longer a need to carry paper charts in flight.

B. Situational awareness is increased.

C. Terrain avoidance is guaranteed.

Answer (B) is correct. *(AAH Chap 5)*
   DISCUSSION: Glass cockpits are designed to decrease pilot workload, enhance situational awareness, and increase the safety margin.
   Answer (A) is incorrect. Pilots should still have current information and backup electronic navigation to enhance safety. Answer (C) is incorrect. Terrain avoidance is not guaranteed solely by means of relying on advanced avionics.

48. What steps must be taken when flying with glass cockpits to ensure safe flight?

A. Use the moving map for primary means of navigation, use the MFD to check engine systems and weather, back up with supplementary forms of information.

B. Regularly scan each item on the PFD, confirm on the MFD.

C. Regularly scan both inside and outside, use all appropriate checklists, and cross-check with other forms of information.

Answer (C) is correct. *(AAH Chap 5)*
   DISCUSSION: A regular scan, both visually outside and inside on backup gauges, should be combined with other means of navigation and checklists to ensure safe flight.
   Answer (A) is incorrect. The moving map should not be the sole means of navigation. Moving maps should be used as a supplement, not as a replacement. Answer (B) is incorrect. While you should scan both the PFD and MFD, more is needed to ensure a safe flight, such as visually scanning outside and confirming indications from other sources.

END OF STUDY UNIT

STUDY UNIT THIRTEEN
AIRPLANE ENGINES AND SYSTEMS

(4 pages of outline)

This study unit contains outlines of major concepts tested, sample test questions and answers regarding airplane engines and systems, and an explanation of each answer. The table of contents above lists each subunit within this study unit, the number of questions pertaining to that particular subunit, and the pages on which the outlines and questions begin, respectively.

CAUTION: Recall that the **sole purpose** of this book is to expedite your passing the FAA pilot knowledge test for the sport pilot certificate. Accordingly, all extraneous material (i.e., topics or regulations not directly tested on the FAA pilot knowledge test) is omitted, even though much more information and knowledge are necessary to fly safely. This additional material is presented in the *Pilot Handbook* and *Sport Pilot Flight Maneuvers and Practical Test Prep*, available from Gleim Publications, Inc. See the order form on page 327.

13.1 ELECTRICAL SYSTEMS

1. Most aircraft have either a 14- or 28-volt direct current electrical system.

2. Engine-driven alternators (or generators) supply electrical current to the electrical system and maintain an electrical charge on the battery.

   a. The alternator voltage output should be slightly higher than the battery voltage to keep the battery charged.

      1) EXAMPLE: A 14-volt alternator system would keep a positive charge on a 12-volt battery.

3. The electrical system is turned on by the master switch, providing electrical current to all electrical systems except the ignition system.

   a. Lights, radios, and electric fuel pumps are examples of equipment that commonly use the electrical system.

4. An ammeter shows if the alternator is producing an adequate supply of electrical power and indicates whether the battery is receiving an electrical charge.

   a. A positive indication on the ammeter shows the rate of charge on the battery, while a negative indication means more current is being drawn from the battery than is being replaced.

5. A battery and alternator failure during flight inevitably results in avionics equipment failure due to the lack of electricity.

13.2 LUBRICATION SYSTEM

1. Most 4-cycle engines utilize a forced lubrication system.

    a. Due to the size and complexity of 4-cycle engines, a forced lubrication system, often including an engine-driven oil pump, is typically employed.

       1) The oil system lubricates engine parts as well as plays a role in engine cooling.

13.3 ENGINE TEMPERATURE

1. Excessively high engine temperature either in the air or on the ground will cause loss of power, excessive oil consumption, and excessive wear on the internal engine.

2. Aircraft engines are cooled by airflow, circulated coolant, or some combination of both.

    a. Air-cooled engines rely on direct airflow of the engine's cylinders to dissipate collected heat. Cooling fins increase the surface area of the cylinder to allow for better cooling.

    b. Liquid-cooled engines rely on an air-cooled radiator, fluid lines, coolant, and an engine-driven coolant pump to remove heat from engine components.

3. Engine oil and cylinder head temperatures can exceed their normal operating range because of (among other causes)

    a. Operating with too much power
    b. Climbing too steeply (i.e., at too low an airspeed) in hot weather
    c. Using fuel that has a lower-than-specified octane rating
    d. Operating with too lean a mixture
    e. The oil level being too low

4. Excessively high engine temperatures can be reduced by reversing any of the previous situations, i.e., reducing power, climbing less steeply (increasing airspeed), using higher octane fuel, enriching the mixture, etc.

13.4 ENGINE IGNITION SYSTEMS

1. One purpose of the dual-ignition system is to provide for improved engine performance.

    a. The other is increased safety due to system redundancy.

13.5 CARBURETOR ICING

1. Carburetor-equipped engines are more susceptible to icing than fuel-injected engines.

    a. The operating principle of float-type carburetors is the difference in air pressure between the venturi throat and the air inlet. According to Bernoulli's principle, as air flows through the venturi tube, the pressure will decrease, and a low pressure area is created.

    b. Fuel-injected engines do not have a carburetor.

2. The first indication of carburetor ice on airplanes with fixed-pitch propellers and float-type carburetors is a loss of RPM.

3. Carburetor ice is likely to form when outside air temperature is between 20°F and 70°F and there is visible moisture or high humidity.

4. When carburetor heat is applied to eliminate carburetor ice in an airplane equipped with a fixed-pitch propeller, there will be a further decrease in RPM (due to the less dense hot air entering the engine) followed by a gradual increase in RPM as the ice melts.

13.6 CARBURETOR HEAT

1. Carburetor heat enriches the fuel/air mixture

   a. Because warm air is less dense than cold air.

   b. When the air density decreases (because the air is warm), the fuel/air mixture (ratio) becomes richer since there is less air for the same amount of fuel.

2. Applying carburetor heat decreases engine output and increases operating temperature.

13.7 FUEL/AIR MIXTURE

1. At higher altitudes, the fuel/air mixture must be leaned to decrease the fuel flow in order to compensate for the decreased air density, i.e., to keep the fuel/air mixture constant.

   a. If you descend from high altitudes to lower altitudes without enriching the mixture, the mixture will become leaner because the air is denser at lower altitudes.

2. If you are running up your engine at a high-altitude airport, you may eliminate engine roughness by leaning the mixture, particularly if the engine runs even worse with carburetor heat since warm air further enriches the mixture.

13.8 ABNORMAL COMBUSTION

1. Detonation occurs when the fuel/air mixture explodes instead of burning evenly.

2. Detonation is usually caused by using a lower-than-specified grade (octane) of aviation fuel or by excessive engine temperature.

   a. This causes many engine problems, including excessive wear and higher than normal operating temperatures.

3. Lower the nose slightly if you suspect that an engine (with a fixed-pitch propeller) is detonating during climbout after takeoff. This will increase cooling and decrease the engine's workload.

4. Pre-ignition is the uncontrolled firing of the fuel/air charge in advance of the normal spark ignition.

13.9 AVIATION FUEL PRACTICES

1. Use of the next-higher-than-specified (octane) grade of fuel is better than using the next-lower-than-specified grade of fuel. This will prevent the possibility of detonation, exceeding the normal limits for cylinder head or oil temperature gauges, or running the engine too hot.

2. Filling the fuel tanks at the end of the day prevents moisture condensation by eliminating the airspace in the tanks.

3. In an airplane equipped with fuel pumps, the auxiliary electric fuel pump is used in the event the engine-driven fuel pump fails.

4. Fuel should be drained from the fuel strainer quick drain and from each fuel tank sump into a transparent container, and then be checked for dirt and water.

   a. When the fuel strainer is being drained, water in the tank may not appear until all the fuel has been drained from the lines leading to the tank.

13.10 MISCELLANEOUS AIRSPEED QUESTIONS

1. When turbulence is encountered, the airplane's airspeed should be reduced to maneuvering speed (V_A).

    a. The pilot should attempt to maintain a level flight attitude.

    b. Constant altitude and constant airspeed are usually impossible and result in additional control pressure, which adds stress to the airplane.

2. In the event of a power failure after becoming airborne, the most important thing to do is to immediately establish and maintain the best glide airspeed.

    a. Do not maintain altitude at the expense of airspeed or a stall/spin will result.

13.11 TAXIING TECHNIQUE

1. When taxiing in strong quartering headwinds, the aileron should be up on the side from which the wind is blowing.

    a. The elevator should be in the neutral position for tricycle-geared airplanes.

    b. The elevator should be in the up position for tailwheel airplanes.

2. When taxiing during strong quartering tailwinds, the aileron should be down on the side from which the wind is blowing.

    a. The elevator should be in the down position (for both tricycle and tailwheel airplanes).

3. When taxiing high-wing, nosewheel-equipped airplanes, the most critical wind condition is a quartering tailwind.

13.12 STARTING THE ENGINE

1. After the engine starts, the throttle should be adjusted for proper RPM and the engine gauges, especially the oil pressure, checked.

2. When starting an airplane engine by hand, it is extremely important that a competent pilot be at the controls in the cockpit.

QUESTIONS AND ANSWER EXPLANATIONS

All of the sport pilot knowledge test questions chosen by the FAA for release as well as additional questions selected by Gleim relating to the material in the previous outlines are reproduced on the following pages. These questions have been organized into the same subunits as the outlines. To the immediate right of each question are the correct answer and answer explanation. You should cover these answers and answer explanations while responding to the questions. Refer to the general discussion in the Introduction on how to take the FAA pilot knowledge test.

Remember that the questions from the FAA pilot knowledge test bank have been reordered by topic and organized into a meaningful sequence. Also, the first line of the answer explanation gives the citation of the authoritative source for the answer.

QUESTIONS

13.1 Electrical Systems

1. An electrical system failure (battery and alternator) occurs in a magneto equipped aircraft during flight. In this situation, you would

    A. probably experience engine failure due to the loss of the engine-driven fuel pump and also experience failure of the radio equipment, lights, and all instruments that require alternating current.

    B. probably experience failure of the engine ignition system, fuel gauges, aircraft lighting system, and avionics equipment.

    C. experience avionics equipment failure.

Answer (C) is correct. *(PHAK Chap 6)*
    DISCUSSION: A battery and alternator failure during flight inevitably results in avionics equipment failure due to the lack of electricity.
    Answer (A) is incorrect. Engine-driven fuel pumps are mechanical and not dependent upon electricity. Answer (B) is incorrect. The engine ignition systems are based on magnetos, which generate their own electricity to operate the spark plugs.

2. A positive indication on an ammeter

    A. indicates the aircraft's battery will soon lose its charge.

    B. shows the rate of charge on the battery.

    C. means more current is being drawn from the battery than is being replaced.

Answer (B) is correct. *(PHAK Chap 6)*
    DISCUSSION: A positive indication on the ammeter shows the rate of charge on the battery.
    Answer (A) is incorrect. A battery will not lose its charge while being charged, which is what a positive indication on an ammeter indicates. Answer (C) is incorrect. A negative indication on an ammeter means more current is being drawn from the battery than is being replaced.

3. To keep a battery charged, the alternator voltage output should be

    A. less than the battery voltage.

    B. equal to the battery voltage.

    C. higher than the battery voltage.

Answer (C) is correct. *(PHAK Chap 6)*
    DISCUSSION: The alternator voltage output should be slightly higher than the battery voltage to keep the battery charged. For example, a 14-volt alternator system would keep a positive charge on a 12-volt battery.
    Answer (A) is incorrect. If the alternator voltage output were less than the battery voltage, the battery would quickly lose its charge. Answer (B) is incorrect. If there were no difference in voltage, the battery would not have or keep a full charge.

4. Which of the following is a true statement concerning electrical systems?

    A. The master switch provides current to the electrical system.

    B. The airspeed indicator is driven by the electrical system.

    C. Lights and radios use the electrical system for power.

Answer (C) is correct. *(PHAK Chap 6)*
    DISCUSSION: Lights, radios, and electrical fuel pumps are examples of equipment that commonly use the electrical system.
    Answer (A) is incorrect. The master switch provides electrical current to all electrical systems except the ignition system. Answer (B) is incorrect. The airspeed indicator operates on the pitot-static system, not the electrical system.

13.2 Lubrication System

5. Many 4-cycle engines utilize what type of lubrication system?

    A. Forced.

    B. Gravity.

    C. Fuel/oil mixture.

Answer (A) is correct. *(PHAK Chap 6)*
    DISCUSSION: Due to the size and complexity of 4-cycle engines, a forced lubrication system, often including an engine-driven pump, is typically employed.
    Answer (B) is incorrect. Many 4-cycle engines utilize a gravity feed system to sling oil from the crankshaft into the engine case. However, engine oil is still forced into the crankshaft using an engine-driven pump. Gravity-fed systems feature an oil sump on top of the crank case, which is not common in 4-cycle engines, due mainly to the size of the engine block. Answer (C) is incorrect. A fuel/oil mixture lubrication system is common in 2-cycle, not 4-cycle, engines.

13.3 Engine Temperature

6. Air cooled engines dissipate heat

A. through cooling fins on the cylinder and head.

B. by air flowing through the radiator fins.

C. through the cylinder head temperature probe.

Answer (A) is correct. *(PHAK Chap 6)*
  DISCUSSION: Air cooled engines rely on direct airflow over the engine cylinders to dissipate heat. The addition of cooling fins increases the surface area of the cylinder to allow for better cooling.
  Answer (B) is incorrect. An air cooled engine does not employ a radiator. Radiators are found on liquid cooled engines. Answer (C) is incorrect. The cylinder head temperature (CHT) probe measures the temperature of the cylinder head, but it does not offer any help in cooling the cylinder.

7. Coolant in a liquid cooled engine is normally circulated by

A. capillary attraction.

B. an electric pump.

C. an engine driven pump.

Answer (C) is correct. *(PHAK Chap 6)*
  DISCUSSION: A liquid cooled engine relies on an engine-driven pump similar to the oil pump to circulate coolant through the system.
  Answer (A) is incorrect. While an effective circulation method, capillary attraction does not provide the rate of flow required to dissipate the heat produced by a liquid cooled engine. Answer (B) is incorrect. Because engine cooling is a required function at all times during engine operation, a coolant pump is driven by the engine itself, rather than by an auxiliary electric pump.

8. An abnormally high engine oil temperature indication may be caused by

A. the oil level being too low.

B. operating with a too high viscosity oil.

C. operating with an excessively rich mixture.

Answer (A) is correct. *(PHAK Chap 6)*
  DISCUSSION: Operating with an excessively low oil level prevents the oil from being cooled adequately; i.e., an inadequate supply of oil will not be able to transfer engine heat to the engine's oil cooler (similar to a car engine's water radiator). Insufficient oil may also damage an engine from excessive friction within the cylinders and on other metal-to-metal contact parts.
  Answer (B) is incorrect. The higher the viscosity, the better the lubricating and cooling capability of the oil. Answer (C) is incorrect. A rich fuel/air mixture usually decreases (not increases) engine temperature.

9. Excessively high engine temperatures will

A. cause damage to heat-conducting hoses and warping of the cylinder cooling fins.

B. cause loss of power, excessive oil consumption, and possible permanent internal engine damage.

C. not appreciably affect an aircraft engine.

Answer (B) is correct. *(PHAK Chap 6)*
  DISCUSSION: Excessively high engine temperatures will result in loss of power, excessive oil consumption, and possible permanent internal engine damage.
  Answer (A) is incorrect. Excessively high engine temperatures may cause internal engine damage, but external damage is less likely. Answer (C) is incorrect. An excessively high engine temperature can cause a loss of performance and possibly internal engine damage.

10. For internal cooling, air cooled engines are especially dependent on

A. a properly functioning thermostat.

B. air flowing over the exhaust manifold.

C. the circulation of lubricating oil.

Answer (C) is correct. *(PHAK Chap 6)*
  DISCUSSION: An engine accomplishes much of its cooling by the flow of oil through the lubrication system. The lubrication system aids in cooling by reducing friction and absorbing heat from internal engine parts. Many airplane engines use an oil cooler, a small radiator device that will cool the oil before it is recirculated through the engine.
  Answer (A) is incorrect. Airplanes with air-cooled engines do not use thermostats. Answer (B) is incorrect. Air flowing over the exhaust manifold would have little effect on internal engine parts cooling.

11. If the engine oil temperature and cylinder head temperature gauges have exceeded their normal operating range, the pilot may have been operating with

    A. the mixture set too rich.

    B. higher-than-normal oil pressure.

    C. too much power and with the mixture set too lean.

Answer (C) is correct. *(PHAK Chap 6)*
    DISCUSSION: If the engine oil temperature and cylinder head temperature gauges exceed their normal operating range, it is possible that the power setting is too high and the fuel/air mixture is set excessively lean. These conditions may cause engine overheating.
    Answer (A) is incorrect. A rich mixture setting normally causes lower (not higher-than-normal) engine temperature. Answer (B) is incorrect. A higher-than-normal oil pressure does not normally increase the engine temperature.

12. What action can a pilot take to aid in cooling an engine that is overheating during a climb?

    A. Reduce rate of climb and increase airspeed.

    B. Reduce climb speed and increase RPM.

    C. Increase climb speed and increase RPM.

Answer (A) is correct. *(PHAK Chap 6)*
    DISCUSSION: If an airplane is overheating during a climb, the engine temperature will be decreased if the airspeed is increased. Airspeed will increase if the rate of climb is reduced.
    Answer (B) is incorrect. Reducing airspeed hinders cooling, and increasing RPM will further increase engine temperature. Answer (C) is incorrect. Increasing RPM will increase (not decrease) engine temperature.

13. What is one procedure to aid in cooling an engine that is overheating?

    A. Enrich the fuel mixture.

    B. Increase the RPM.

    C. Reduce the airspeed.

Answer (A) is correct. *(PHAK Chap 6)*
    DISCUSSION: Enriched fuel mixtures have a cooling effect on an engine.
    Answer (B) is incorrect. Increasing the RPM increases the engine's internal heat. Answer (C) is incorrect. Reducing the airspeed decreases the airflow needed for cooling, thus increasing the engine's temperature.

13.4 Engine Ignition Systems

14. One purpose of the dual ignition system on an aircraft engine is to provide for

    A. improved engine performance.

    B. uniform heat distribution.

    C. balanced cylinder head pressure.

Answer (A) is correct. *(PHAK Chap 6)*
    DISCUSSION: Most airplane engines are equipped with dual ignition systems, which have two magnetos to supply the electrical current to two spark plugs for each combustion chamber. The main advantages of the dual system are increased safety and improved burning and combustion of the mixture, which results in improved performance.
    Answer (B) is incorrect. The heat distribution within a cylinder is usually not uniform, even with dual ignition. Answer (C) is incorrect. Balanced cylinder-head pressure is a nonsense phrase.

15. One purpose of the dual ignition system on a two-cycle engine is to provide for

    A. system redundancy in the ignition system.

    B. uniform heat distribution.

    C. balanced cylinder head pressure.

Answer (A) is correct. *(PHAK Chap 6)*
    DISCUSSION: A dual ignition system provides increased reliability through redundancy and improves the combustion of the fuel/air mixture, resulting in slightly higher performance.
    Answer (B) is incorrect. A dual ignition system provides more even combustion, but not necessarily uniform heat distribution. Answer (C) is incorrect. Dual ignition systems do not ensure balanced cylinder head pressure.

13.5 Carburetor Icing

16. With regard to carburetor ice, float-type carburetor systems in comparison to fuel injection systems are generally considered to be

    A. more susceptible to icing.

    B. equally susceptible to icing.

    C. susceptible to icing only when visible moisture is present.

Answer (A) is correct. *(PHAK Chap 6)*
    DISCUSSION: Float-type carburetor systems are generally more susceptible to icing than fuel-injected engines. When there is visible moisture or high humidity and the temperature is between 20°F and 70°F, icing is possible, particularly at low power settings.
    Answer (B) is incorrect. Fuel injection systems are less susceptible to internal icing than carburetor systems, although air intake icing is equally possible in both systems. Answer (C) is incorrect. Carburetor icing may occur in high humidity with no visible moisture.

17. The operating principle of float-type carburetors is based on the

    A. automatic metering of air at the venturi as the aircraft gains altitude.

    B. difference in air pressure at the venturi throat and the air inlet.

    C. increase in air velocity in the throat of a venturi causing an increase in air pressure.

Answer (B) is correct. *(PHAK Chap 6)*
    DISCUSSION: In a float-type carburetor, air flows into the carburetor and through a venturi tube (a narrow throat in the carburetor). As the air flows more rapidly through the venturi, a low pressure area is created, which draws the fuel from a main fuel jet located at the throat of the carburetor and into the airstream where it is mixed with flowing air. It is called a float-type carburetor in that a ready supply of gasoline is kept in the float bowl by a float, which activates a fuel inlet valve.
    Answer (A) is incorrect. The metering at the venturi is fuel, not air, and this is done manually with a mixture control. Answer (C) is incorrect. The increase in air velocity in the throat of a venturi causes a decrease (not increase) in air pressure (which draws the gas from the main fuel jet into the low-pressure air).

18. According to Bernoulli's principle, as air passes through a venturi tube the pressure will

    A. Increase.

    B. Decrease.

    C. Remain the same.

Answer (B) is correct. *(PHAK Chap 3)*
    DISCUSSION: Bernoulli stated that an increase in the speed or flow of a fluid (or air) would cause a decrease in pressure. When air flows through a venturi tube, a low-pressure area is created.
    Answer (A) is incorrect. An increase in speed or flow of a fluid (or air) will cause a decrease, not an increase, in pressure. Answer (C) is incorrect. An increase in the speed or flow of a fluid (or air) will cause a decrease in pressure. When air flows through a venturi tube, a low-pressure area is created.

19. If an aircraft is equipped with a fixed-pitch propeller and a float-type carburetor, the first indication of carburetor ice would most likely be

    A. a drop in oil temperature and cylinder head temperature.

    B. engine roughness.

    C. loss of RPM.

Answer (C) is correct. *(PHAK Chap 6)*
    DISCUSSION: In an airplane equipped with a fixed-pitch propeller and float-type carburetor, the first indication of carburetor ice would be a loss in RPM.
    Answer (A) is incorrect. A carburetor icing condition does not cause a drop in oil temperature or cylinder head temperature. Answer (B) is incorrect. A loss in engine RPM should be evident before engine roughness became noticeable.

20. The presence of carburetor ice in an aircraft equipped with a fixed-pitch propeller can be verified by applying carburetor heat and noting

    A. an increase in RPM and then a gradual decrease in RPM.

    B. a decrease in RPM and then a constant RPM indication.

    C. a decrease in RPM and then a gradual increase in RPM.

Answer (C) is correct. *(PHAK Chap 6)*
    DISCUSSION: The presence of carburetor ice in an airplane equipped with a fixed-pitch propeller can be verified by applying carburetor heat and noting a decrease in RPM and then a gradual increase. The decrease in RPM as heat is applied is caused by less dense hot air entering the engine and reducing power output. Also, if ice is present, melting water entering the engine may also cause a loss in performance. As the carburetor ice melts, however, the RPM gradually increases until it stabilizes when the ice is completely removed.
    Answer (A) is incorrect. The warm air decreases engine power output and RPM. Ice melting further decreases RPM and then RPM increases slightly after the ice melts. Answer (B) is incorrect. After the ice melts, the RPM will increase gradually (not remain constant).

21. Which condition is most favorable to the development of carburetor icing?

A. Any temperature below freezing and a relative humidity of less than 50 percent.

B. Temperature between 32°F and 50°F and low humidity.

C. Temperature between 20°F and 70°F and high humidity.

Answer (C) is correct. *(PHAK Chap 6)*
DISCUSSION: When the temperature is between 20°F and 70°F with visible moisture or high humidity, one should be on the alert for carburetor ice. During low or closed throttle settings, an engine is particularly susceptible to carburetor icing.
Answer (A) is incorrect. Icing is possible at temperatures up to 70°F and only in high humidity or visible moisture. Answer (B) is incorrect. Low humidity will generally preclude icing and the correct temperature range is 20°F to 70°F.

22. The possibility of carburetor icing exists even when the ambient air temperature is as

A. high as 70°F and the relative humidity is high.

B. high as 95°F and there is visible moisture.

C. low as 0°F and the relative humidity is high.

Answer (A) is correct. *(PHAK Chap 6)*
DISCUSSION: When the temperature is between 20°F and 70°F with visible moisture or high humidity, one should be on the alert for carburetor ice. During low or closed throttle settings, an engine is particularly susceptible to carburetor icing.
Answer (B) is incorrect. Icing is usually not a problem above 70°F. Answer (C) is incorrect. Icing is usually not a problem below 20°F.

23. Carburetor ice

A. occurs mostly as a function of temperature.

B. can only form when the outside air temperature is near freezing with high relative humidity.

C. is more likely to form when outside air temperatures are below 70°F and relative humidity is above 80%.

Answer (C) is correct. *(PHAK Chap 6)*
DISCUSSION: Carburetor ice may form at any temperature but is most likely to occur at temperatures at or below 70°F with the relative humidity at or above 80%.
Answer (A) is incorrect. Carburetor ice is not a function of air temperature alone. The relative humidity must also be considered. Answer (B) is incorrect. Due to the venturi effect of the carburetor causing the intake air to cool the air, temperature does not need to be at or near freezing for carburetor ice to occur. While carburetor ice is most likely to occur at temperatures at or below freezing, it is possible for carburetor ice to occur at even higher temperatures.

13.6 Carburetor Heat

24. Generally speaking, the use of carburetor heat tends to

A. decrease engine performance.

B. increase engine performance.

C. have no effect on engine performance.

Answer (A) is correct. *(PHAK Chap 6)*
DISCUSSION: Use of carburetor heat tends to decrease the engine performance and also to increase the operating temperature. Warmer air is less dense, and engine performance decreases with density. Thus, carburetor heat should not be used when full power is required (as during takeoff) or during normal engine operation except as a check for the presence or removal of carburetor ice.
Answer (B) is incorrect. Carburetor heat decreases (not increases) engine performance. Answer (C) is incorrect. Carburetor heat does have an effect on performance.

25. Applying carburetor heat will

A. result in more air going through the carburetor.

B. enrich the fuel/air mixture.

C. not affect the fuel/air mixture.

Answer (B) is correct. *(PHAK Chap 6)*
DISCUSSION: Applying carburetor heat will enrich the fuel/air mixture. Warm air is less dense than cold air, hence the application of heat increases the fuel-to-air ratio.
Answer (A) is incorrect. Applying carburetor heat will not result in more air going into the carburetor. Answer (C) is incorrect. Applying carburetor heat will enrich the fuel/air mixture.

26. What change occurs in the fuel/air mixture when carburetor heat is applied?

A. A decrease in RPM results from the lean mixture.

B. The fuel/air mixture becomes richer.

C. The fuel/air mixture becomes leaner.

Answer (B) is correct. *(PHAK Chap 6)*
DISCUSSION: When carburetor heat is applied, hot air is introduced into the carburetor. Hot air is less dense than cold air; therefore, the decrease in air density with a constant amount of fuel makes a richer mixture.
Answer (A) is incorrect. A drop in RPM as carburetor heat is applied is due to the less dense air and melting ice, not a lean mixture. Answer (C) is incorrect. When carburetor heat is applied, the fuel/air mixture becomes richer, not leaner.

13.7 Fuel/Air Mixture

27. During the run-up at a high-elevation airport, a pilot notes a slight engine roughness that is not affected by the magneto check but grows worse during the carburetor heat check. Under these circumstances, what would be the most logical initial action?

   A. Check the results obtained with a leaner setting of the mixture.

   B. Taxi back to the flight line for a maintenance check.

   C. Reduce manifold pressure to control detonation.

Answer (A) is correct. *(PHAK Chap 6)*
DISCUSSION: If, during a run-up at a high-elevation airport, you notice a slight roughness that is not affected by a magneto check but grows worse during the carburetor heat check, you should check the results obtained with a leaner setting of the mixture control. At a high-elevation field, the air is less dense and the application of carburetor heat increases the already too rich fuel-to-air mixture. By leaning the mixture during the run-up, the condition should improve.
Answer (B) is incorrect. This mixture condition is normal at a high-elevation field. However, if a satisfactory run-up cannot be obtained after leaning the mixture, the pilot should taxi back to the flight line for a maintenance check. Answer (C) is incorrect. The question describes a symptom of an excessively rich mixture, not detonation.

28. The basic purpose of adjusting the fuel/air mixture at altitude is to

   A. decrease the amount of fuel in the mixture in order to compensate for increased air density.

   B. decrease the fuel flow in order to compensate for decreased air density.

   C. increase the amount of fuel in the mixture to compensate for the decrease in pressure and density of the air.

Answer (B) is correct. *(PHAK Chap 6)*
DISCUSSION: At higher altitudes, the air density is decreased. Thus, the mixture control must be adjusted to decrease the fuel flow in order to maintain a constant fuel/air ratio.
Answer (A) is incorrect. Air density decreases (not increases) at altitude. Answer (C) is incorrect. The mixture is decreased (not increased) in order to compensate for decreased air density.

29. While cruising at 9,500 feet MSL, the fuel/air mixture is properly adjusted. What will occur if a descent to 4,500 feet MSL is made without readjusting the mixture?

   A. The fuel/air mixture may become excessively lean.

   B. There will be more fuel in the cylinders than is needed for normal combustion, and the excess fuel will absorb heat and cool the engine.

   C. The excessively rich mixture will create higher cylinder head temperatures and may cause detonation.

Answer (A) is correct. *(PHAK Chap 6)*
DISCUSSION: At 9,500 ft., the mixture control is adjusted to provide the proper fuel/air ratio. As the airplane descends, the density of the air increases, and there will be less fuel to air in the ratio, causing a leaner running engine. This excessively lean mixture will create higher cylinder temperature and may cause detonation.
Answer (B) is incorrect. As air becomes more dense during the descent, there will be less (not more) fuel in the cylinders than is needed. Answer (C) is incorrect. The mixture will be excessively lean (not rich). Also, a rich mixture would create lower (not higher) cylinder head temperatures.

13.8 Abnormal Combustion

30. Detonation occurs in a reciprocating aircraft engine when

   A. the spark plugs are fouled or shorted out or the wiring is defective.

   B. hot spots in the combustion chamber ignite the fuel/air mixture in advance of normal ignition.

   C. the unburned charge in the cylinders explodes instead of burning normally.

Answer (C) is correct. *(PHAK Chap 6)*
DISCUSSION: Detonation occurs when the fuel/air mixture in the cylinders explodes instead of burning normally. This more rapid force slams the piston down instead of pushing it.
Answer (A) is incorrect. If the spark plugs are "fouled" or the wiring is defective, the cylinders would not be firing; i.e., there would be no combustion. Answer (B) is incorrect. Hot spots in the combustion chamber igniting the fuel/air mixture in advance of normal ignition is pre-ignition.

31. Detonation may occur at high-power settings when

    A. the fuel mixture ignites instantaneously instead of burning progressively and evenly.

    B. an excessively rich fuel mixture causes an explosive gain in power.

    C. the fuel mixture is ignited too early by hot carbon deposits in the cylinder.

Answer (A) is correct. *(PHAK Chap 6)*
    DISCUSSION: Detonation occurs when the fuel/air mixture in the cylinders explodes instead of burning progressively and evenly. This more rapid force slams the piston down instead of pushing it.
    Answer (B) is incorrect. An excessively rich fuel mixture lowers the temperature inside the cylinder, thus inhibiting the complete combustion of the fuel and producing an appreciable lack of power. Answer (C) is incorrect. Hot carbon deposits in the combustion chamber igniting the fuel/air mixture too early or in advance of normal ignition is termed pre-ignition.

32. If a pilot suspects that the engine (with a fixed-pitch propeller) is detonating during climb-out after takeoff, the initial corrective action to take would be to

    A. lean the mixture.

    B. lower the nose slightly to increase airspeed.

    C. apply carburetor heat.

Answer (B) is correct. *(PHAK Chap 6)*
    DISCUSSION: If you suspect engine detonation during climb-out after takeoff, you would normally decrease the pitch to increase airspeed (more cooling) and decrease the load on the engine. Detonation is usually caused by a poor grade of fuel or an excessive engine temperature.
    Answer (A) is incorrect. Leaning the mixture will increase engine temperature and increase detonation. Answer (C) is incorrect. While carburetor heat will increase the fuel-to-air ratio, hot air flowing into the carburetor will not lower engine temperature. Also, the less dense air will decrease the engine power for climb-out.

33. If the grade of fuel used in an aircraft engine is lower than specified for the engine, it will most likely cause

    A. a mixture of fuel and air that is not uniform in all cylinders.

    B. lower cylinder head temperatures.

    C. detonation.

Answer (C) is correct. *(PHAK Chap 6)*
    DISCUSSION: If the grade of fuel used in an airplane engine is lower than specified for the engine, it will probably cause detonation. Lower grades of fuel ignite at lower temperatures. A higher temperature engine (which should use a higher grade of fuel) may cause lower grade fuel to explode (detonate) rather than burn evenly.
    Answer (A) is incorrect. The carburetor meters the lower-grade fuel quantity in the same manner as a higher grade of fuel. Answer (B) is incorrect. A lower grade of fuel will cause higher (not lower) cylinder head temperatures.

34. The uncontrolled firing of the fuel/air charge in advance of normal spark ignition is known as

    A. combustion.

    B. preignition.

    C. detonation.

Answer (B) is correct. *(PHAK Chap 6)*
    DISCUSSION: Preignition is the ignition of the fuel prior to normal ignition or ignition before the electrical arcing occurs at the spark plug. Preignition may be caused by excessively hot exhaust valves, carbon particles, or spark plugs and electrodes heated to an incandescent, or glowing, state. These hot spots are usually caused by high temperatures encountered during detonation. A significant difference between preignition and detonation is that, if the conditions for detonation exist in one cylinder, they usually exist in all cylinders, but preignition often takes place in only one or two cylinders.
    Answer (A) is incorrect. Combustion is the normal process that takes place inside the cylinders. Answer (C) is incorrect. Detonation is an uncontrolled, explosive ignition of the fuel/air mixture within the cylinder's combustion chamber caused by a combination of excessively high temperature and pressure in the cylinder.

13.9 Aviation Fuel Practices

35. What type fuel can be substituted for an aircraft if the recommended octane is not available?

    A. The next higher octane aviation gas.

    B. The next lower octane aviation gas.

    C. Unleaded automotive gas of the same octane rating.

Answer (A) is correct. *(PHAK Chap 6)*
    DISCUSSION: If the recommended octane is not available for an airplane, the next higher octane aviation gas should be used.
    Answer (B) is incorrect. If the grade of fuel used in an airplane engine is lower than specified for the engine, it will probably cause detonation. Answer (C) is incorrect. Except for very special situations, only aviation gas should be used.

36. Which would most likely cause the cylinder head temperature and engine oil temperature gauges to exceed their normal operating ranges?

    A. Using fuel that has a lower-than-specified fuel rating.

    B. Using fuel that has a higher-than-specified fuel rating.

    C. Operating with higher-than-normal oil pressure.

Answer (A) is correct. *(PHAK Chap 6)*
    DISCUSSION: Use of fuel with lower-than-specified fuel ratings, e.g., 80 octane instead of 100, can cause many problems, including higher operating temperatures, detonation, etc.
    Answer (B) is incorrect. Higher octane fuels usually result in lower cylinder head temperatures. Answer (C) is incorrect. Higher-than-normal oil pressure provides better lubrication and cooling (although too high an oil pressure can break parts, lines, etc.).

37. Filling the fuel tanks after the last flight of the day is considered a good operating procedure because this will

    A. force any existing water to the top of the tank away from the fuel lines to the engine.

    B. prevent expansion of the fuel by eliminating airspace in the tanks.

    C. prevent moisture condensation by eliminating airspace in the tanks.

Answer (C) is correct. *(PHAK Chap 6)*
    DISCUSSION: Filling the fuel tanks after the last flight of the day is considered good operating practice because it prevents moisture condensation by eliminating airspace in the tanks. Humid air may result in condensation at night when the airplane cools.
    Answer (A) is incorrect. Water is heavier than fuel and will always settle to the bottom of the tank. Answer (B) is incorrect. Filling the fuel tank will not prevent expansion of the fuel.

38. On aircraft equipped with fuel pumps, when is the auxiliary electric driven pump used?

    A. All the time to aid the engine-driven fuel pump.

    B. In the event engine-driven fuel pump fails.

    C. Constantly except in starting the engine.

Answer (B) is correct. *(PHAK Chap 6)*
    DISCUSSION: In a fuel pump system, two fuel pumps are used on most airplanes. The main fuel pump is engine-driven, and an auxiliary electric-driven pump is provided for use in the event the engine pump fails.
    Answer (A) is incorrect. An auxiliary fuel pump is a backup system to the engine-driven fuel pump; it is not intended to aid the engine-driven fuel pump. Answer (C) is incorrect. The auxiliary electric fuel pump is normally used in starting the engine.

39. To properly purge water from the fuel system of an aircraft equipped with fuel tank sumps and a fuel strainer quick drain, it is necessary to drain fuel from the

    A. fuel strainer drain.

    B. lowest point in the fuel system.

    C. fuel strainer drain and the fuel tank sumps.

Answer (C) is correct. *(PHAK Chap 6)*
    DISCUSSION: Fuel should be drained from the fuel strainer quick drain and from each fuel tank sump into a transparent container. It should then be checked for dirt and water.
    Answer (A) is incorrect. It is important to check fuel from the fuel strainer drain and also from each fuel tank sump.
Answer (B) is incorrect. Fuel should be drained from each fuel sump and the fuel strainer, not the lowest point in the fuel system. The lowest point in the fuel system may not account for water or dirt currently in the fuel lines.

13.10 Miscellaneous Airspeed Questions

40. Upon encountering severe turbulence, which flight condition should the pilot attempt to maintain?

A. Constant altitude and airspeed.

B. Constant angle of attack.

C. Level flight attitude.

Answer (C) is correct. *(AC 00-24B)*
DISCUSSION: Attempting to hold altitude and airspeed in severe turbulence can lead to overstressing the airplane. Rather, you should set power to what normally will maintain V_A and simply attempt to maintain a level flight attitude.
Answer (A) is incorrect. Maintaining a constant altitude will require additional control movements, adding stress to the airplane. Answer (B) is incorrect. In severe turbulence, the angle of attack will fluctuate due to the wind shears and wind shifts that cause the turbulence.

41. The most important rule to remember in the event of a power failure after becoming airborne is to

A. immediately establish the proper gliding attitude and airspeed.

B. quickly check the fuel supply for possible fuel exhaustion.

C. determine the wind direction to plan for the forced landing.

Answer (A) is correct. *(AFH Chap 5)*
DISCUSSION: In the event of a power failure after becoming airborne, the most important rule to remember is to maintain best glide airspeed. This will usually require a pitch attitude slightly lower than level flight. Invariably, with a power failure, one returns to ground, but emphasis should be put on a controlled return rather than a crash return. Many pilots attempt to maintain altitude at the expense of airspeed, resulting in a stall or stall/spin.
Answer (B) is incorrect. Checking the fuel supply should only be done after a glide has been established and a landing site has been selected. Answer (C) is incorrect. Landing into the wind may not be possible, depending upon altitude and field availability.

13.11 Taxiing Technique

42. When taxiing with strong quartering tailwinds, which aileron positions should be used?

A. Aileron down on the downwind side.

B. Ailerons neutral.

C. Aileron down on the side from which the wind is blowing.

Answer (C) is correct. *(AFH Chap 2)*
DISCUSSION: When there is a strong quartering tailwind, the aileron should be down on the side from which the wind is blowing (when taxiing away from the wind, turn away from the wind) to help keep the wind from getting under that wing and flipping the airplane over.
Answer (A) is incorrect. The aileron should be down on the upwind (not downwind) side. Answer (B) is incorrect. The aileron positions help control the airplane while taxiing in windy conditions.

43. When taxiing an airplane with strong quartering tailwinds, which aileron position should be used?

A. Neutral.

B. Aileron down on the side from which the wind is blowing.

C. Aileron up on the side from which the wind is blowing.

Answer (B) is correct. *(AFH Chap 2)*
DISCUSSION: When there is a strong quartering tailwind, the aileron should be down on the side from which the wind is blowing (when taxiing away from the wind, turn away from the wind) to help keep the wind from getting under that wing and flipping the airplane.
Answer (A) is incorrect. Varying the aileron position appropriately will help control the airplane while taxiing in windy conditions. Positioning the aileron down on the side from which a strong quartering tailwind is blowing will prevent the wind from getting under that wing and flipping the airplane. Answer (C) is incorrect. The aileron should be down, not up, on the side from which a quartering tailwind is blowing. This will help to keep the wind from getting under that wing and flipping the airplane.

44. Which aileron positions should a pilot generally use when taxiing in strong quartering headwinds?

A. Aileron up on the side from which the wind is blowing.

B. Aileron down on the side from which the wind is blowing.

C. Ailerons neutral.

Answer (A) is correct. *(AFH Chap 2)*
DISCUSSION: When there is a strong quartering headwind, the aileron should be up on the side from which the wind is blowing to help keep the wind from getting under that wing and blowing the aircraft over. (When taxiing into the wind, turn into the wind.)
Answer (B) is incorrect. The aileron should be up (not down) on the side from which the wind is blowing (i.e., upwind). Answer (C) is incorrect. The aileron positions help control the airplane while taxiing in windy conditions.

45. Which wind condition would be most critical when taxiing a nosewheel equipped high-wing airplane?

  A. Quartering tailwind.

  B. Direct crosswind.

  C. Quartering headwind.

Answer (A) is correct.   *(AFH Chap 2)*
  DISCUSSION: The most critical wind condition when taxiing a nosewheel-equipped high-wing airplane is a quartering tailwind, which can flip a high-wing airplane over on its top. This should be prevented by holding the elevator in the down position, i.e., controls forward, and the aileron down on the side from which the wind is coming.
  Answer (B) is incorrect. A direct crosswind will probably not flip an airplane over. However, it may weathervane the airplane into the wind. Answer (C) is incorrect. A headwind is aerodynamically the condition an airplane is designed for, i.e., wind from the front.

46. (Refer to Figure 109 below.) (Refer to area A.) How should the flight controls be held while taxiing a tricycle-gear equipped airplane into a left quartering headwind?

  A. Left aileron up, elevator neutral.

  B. Left aileron down, elevator neutral.

  C. Left aileron up, elevator down.

Answer (A) is correct.   *(AFH Chap 2)*
  DISCUSSION: Given a left quartering headwind, the left aileron should be kept up to spoil the excess lift on the left wing that the crosswind is creating. The elevator should be neutral to keep from putting too much or too little weight on the nosewheel.
  Answer (B) is incorrect. Lowering the left aileron will increase the lift on the left wing. Answer (C) is incorrect. It describes the control setting for a right tailwind in a tailwheel airplane.

47. (Refer to Figure 109 below.) (Refer to area C.) How should the flight controls be held while taxiing a tricycle-gear equipped airplane with a left quartering tailwind?

  A. Left aileron up, elevator neutral.

  B. Left aileron down, elevator down.

  C. Left aileron up, elevator down.

Answer (B) is correct.   *(AFH Chap 2)*
  DISCUSSION: With a left quartering tailwind, the left aileron should be down so the wind does not get under the left wing and flip the airplane over. Also, the elevator should be down, i.e., controls forward, so the wind does not get under the tail and blow the airplane tail over front.
  Answer (A) is incorrect. It describes the control setting for a left headwind. Answer (C) is incorrect. It describes the control setting for a right tailwind.

48. (Refer to Figure 109 below.) (Refer to area B.) How should the flight controls be held while taxiing a tailwheel airplane into a right quartering headwind?

  A. Right aileron up, elevator up.

  B. Right aileron down, elevator neutral.

  C. Right aileron up, elevator down.

Answer (A) is correct.   *(AFH Chap 2)*
  DISCUSSION: When there is a right quartering headwind, the right aileron should be up to spoil the excess lift on the right wing that the crosswind is creating. The elevator should be up to keep weight on the tailwheel to help maintain maneuverability.
  Answer (B) is incorrect. The elevator should be up (not neutral) and the right aileron up (not down) when taxiing a tailwheel airplane in a right quartering headwind. Answer (C) is incorrect. The elevator should be up (not down) when taxiing in a right quartering headwind.

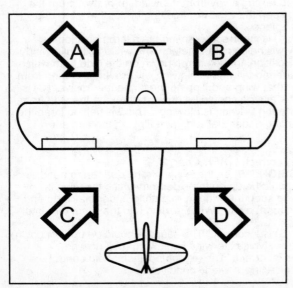

Figure 109. – Control Position for Taxi.

49. (Refer to Figure 109 on page 258.) (Refer to area C.) How should the flight controls be held while taxiing a tailwheel airplane with a left quartering tailwind?

   A. Left aileron up, elevator neutral.

   B. Left aileron down, elevator neutral.

   C. Left aileron down, elevator down.

Answer (C) is correct. *(AFH Chap 2)*
   DISCUSSION: When there is a left quartering tailwind, the left aileron should be held down so the wind does not get under the left wing and flip the airplane over. Also, the elevator should be down, i.e., controls forward, so the wind does not get under the tail and blow the airplane tail over front.
   Answer (A) is incorrect. The left aileron should be down (not up) and the elevator down (not neutral). Answer (B) is incorrect. The elevator should be down when taxiing with a tailwind.

13.12 Starting the Engine

50. What should be the first action after starting an aircraft engine?

   A. Adjust for proper RPM and check for desired indications on the engine gauges.

   B. Place the magneto or ignition switch momentarily in the OFF position to check for proper grounding.

   C. Test each brake and the parking brake.

Answer (A) is correct. *(AFH Chap 2)*
   DISCUSSION: After the engine starts, the engine speed should be adjusted to the proper RPM. Then the engine gauges should be reviewed, with the oil pressure being the most important gauge initially.
   Answer (B) is incorrect. This check is normally done just prior to engine shutdown. Answer (C) is incorrect. This check is done during taxi.

51. Should it become necessary to handprop an airplane engine, it is extremely important that a competent pilot

   A. call "contact" before touching the propeller.

   B. be at the controls in the cockpit.

   C. be in the cockpit and call out all commands.

Answer (B) is correct. *(AFH Chap 2)*
   DISCUSSION: Because of the hazards involved in handstarting airplane engines, every precaution should be exercised. It is extremely important that a competent pilot be at the controls in the cockpit. Also, the person turning the propeller should be thoroughly familiar with the technique.
   Answer (A) is incorrect. The person handpropping the airplane yells "gas off, switch off, throttle closed, brakes set" before touching the propeller initially. Contact means the magnetos are on, i.e., "hot." This is not done until starting is attempted. Answer (C) is incorrect. The person handpropping the airplane (not the person in the cockpit) calls out the commands.

END OF STUDY UNIT

STUDY UNIT FOURTEEN
AIRPLANE PERFORMANCE AND WEIGHT AND BALANCE

(7 pages of outline)

This study unit contains outlines of major concepts tested, sample test questions and answers regarding airplane performance and weight and balance, and an explanation of each answer. The table of contents above lists each subunit within this study unit, the number of questions pertaining to that particular subunit, and the pages on which the outlines and questions begin, respectively.

CAUTION: Recall that the **sole purpose** of this book is to expedite your passing the FAA pilot knowledge test for the sport pilot certificate. Accordingly, all extraneous material (i.e., topics or regulations not directly tested on the FAA pilot knowledge test) is omitted, even though much more information and knowledge are necessary to fly safely. This additional material is presented in the *Pilot Handbook* and *Sport Pilot Flight Maneuvers and Practical Test Prep*, available from Gleim Publications, Inc. See the order form on page 327.

14.1 DENSITY ALTITUDE COMPUTATIONS

1. Density altitude is determined most easily by finding the pressure altitude (indicated altitude when your altimeter is set to 29.92) and adjusting for the temperature.

   a. The adjustment may be made using your flight computer or a density altitude chart. This part of the FAA test requires you to use a density altitude chart.

2. When using a density altitude chart (see Figure 108 on page 269),

   a. Adjust the airport elevation to pressure altitude by adding or subtracting the conversion factor for the current altimeter setting.

   b. To adjust the pressure altitude for nonstandard temperature, plot the intersection of the actual air temperature (listed on the horizontal axis of the chart) with the pressure altitude lines that slope diagonally upward. Move left horizontally from the intersection to read density altitude on the vertical axis of the chart.

c. EXAMPLE: Outside air temperature 90°F
Altimeter setting 30.20" Hg
Airport elevation 4,725 ft.

Referring to Figure 108 on page 269, you determine the density altitude to be approximately 7,400 ft. This is found as follows:

1) The altimeter setting of 30.20" requires a –257 altitude correction factor.
2) Subtract 257 ft. from field elevation of 4,725 ft. to obtain pressure altitude of 4,468 ft.
3) Locate 90°F on the bottom axis of the chart and move up to intersect the diagonal pressure altitude line of 4,468 ft.
4) Move horizontally to the left axis of the chart to obtain the density altitude of about 7,400 ft.
5) Note that, while true altitude (i.e., airport elevation) is 4,725 ft., density altitude is about 7,400 ft.
6) Finally, note that you may determine the effects of temperature changes on density altitude simply by following the above chart procedure and substituting different temperatures.

14.2 TAKEOFF DISTANCE

1. Conditions that reduce airplane takeoff and climb performance are
   a. High altitude
   b. High temperature
   c. High humidity

2. Takeoff distance performance is displayed in the airplane operating manual either
   a. In chart form or
   b. On a graph.

3. If a graph, it is usually presented in terms of density altitude. Thus, one must first adjust the airport elevation for nonstandard pressure and temperature.
   a. In the graph used on this exam (see Figure 141 on page 271), the first section on the left uses outside air temperature and pressure altitude to obtain density altitude.
      1) The curved line on the left portion is standard atmosphere, which you use when the question calls for standard temperature.
   b. The second section of the graph, to the right of the first reference line, takes the weight in pounds into account.
   c. The third section of the graph, to the right of the second reference line, takes the headwind or tailwind into account.
   d. The fourth section of the graph, at the right margin, takes obstacles into account.
   e. EXAMPLE: Given an outside air temperature of 15°C, a pressure altitude of 5,650 ft., a takeoff weight of 2,950 lb., and a headwind component of 9 kt., find the ground roll and the total takeoff distance over a 50-ft. obstacle. Use Figure 141 on page 271.
   f. The solution to the example problem is marked with the dotted arrows on the graph. Move straight up from 15°C (which is also where the standard temperature line begins) to the pressure altitude of 5,650 ft. and then horizontally to the right to the first reference line. It is not necessary to adjust for weight because the airplane is at maximum weight of 2,950 lb. Continuing to the next reference line, the headwind component of 9 kt. means an adjustment downward in the wind component section (parallel to the guidelines). Finally, moving straight to the right gives the ground roll of 1,375 ft. The total takeoff distance over a 50-ft. obstacle, following parallel to the guideline up and to the right, is 2,300 ft.

4. An uphill runway slope increases takeoff distance.

14.3 CLIMB PERFORMANCE AND THRUST

1. The effect of winds can be especially important in takeoff performance considerations and may have a substantial impact on takeoff distance required.

    a. A tailwind that is 10% of the takeoff airspeed can increase the takeoff distance by as much as 19%.

2. Climb performance depends on the excess power (reserve power or thrust).

    a. Reserve power can be defined as the excess available power over and above that required to maintain horizontal flight at a given speed.

14.4 RANGE AND ENDURANCE

1. The recommended long-range cruise performance will provide an aircraft's maximum design-operating radius, or range.

    a. This condition will also allow the aircraft to travel a shorter distance with a maximum fuel reserve remaining.

2. Maximum endurance occurs when the airplane consumes minimum fuel and allows the airplane to fly for the longest amount of time.

    a. This is achieved by using the minimum power setting required to maintain steady, level flight.

14.5 CRUISE POWER SETTINGS

1. Cruise power settings are found by use of a table (see Figure 136 on page 274).

    a. It is based on 65% power.

    b. It consists of three sections to adjust for varying temperatures:

        1) Standard temperature (in middle)
        2) ISA –20°C (on left)
        3) ISA +20°C (on right)

    c. Values found in the table based on various pressure altitudes and temperatures include

        1) Engine RPM
        2) Manifold pressure (in. Hg)
        3) Fuel flow in gal. per hr. (with the expected fuel pressure gauge indication in pounds per square inch)
        4) True airspeed (kt. and MPH)

2. The test questions will gauge your ability to find values on the chart and interpolate between lines (see Figure 136 on page 274).

    a. EXAMPLE: A value for 9,500 ft. would be 75% of the distance between the number for 8,000 ft. and the number for 10,000 ft.

    b. EXAMPLE: At a pressure altitude of 6,000 ft. and a temperature of 26°C and with no wind, a 1,000-NM trip would take 71.42 gal. of fuel [(1,000 ÷ 161 kt. = 6.21 hr.); (6.21 hr. × 11.5 gph = 71.42 gal.)].

14.6 CROSSWIND COMPONENTS

1. Airplanes have a limit to the amount of direct crosswind in which they can land. When the wind is not directly across the runway (i.e., quartering), a crosswind component chart may be used to determine the amount of direct crosswind. Variables on the crosswind component charts are

   a. Angle between wind and runway
   b. Wind velocity

   NOTE: The coordinates on the vertical and horizontal axes of the graph will indicate the headwind and crosswind components of a quartering wind.

2. Refer to the crosswind component graph, which is Figure 137 on page 275.

   a. Note the example on the chart of a 40-kt. wind at a 30° angle.
   b. Find the 30° wind angle line. This is the angle between the wind direction and runway direction, e.g., runway 18 and wind from 210°.
   c. Find the 40-kt. wind velocity arc. Note the intersection of the wind arc and the 30° angle line.

      1) Drop straight down to determine the crosswind component of 20 kt.; i.e., landing in this situation would be like having a direct crosswind of 20 kt.
      2) Move horizontally to the left to determine the headwind component of 35 kt.; i.e., landing in this situation would be like having a headwind of 35 kt.
      3) EXAMPLE: You have been given 20 kt. as the maximum crosswind component for the airplane, and the angle between the runway and the wind is 30°. What is the maximum wind velocity without exceeding the 20-kt. crosswind component? Find where the 20-kt. crosswind line from the bottom of the chart crosses the 30° angle line, and note that it intersects the 40-kt. wind velocity line. This means you can land an airplane with a 20-kt. maximum crosswind component in a 40-kt. wind from a 30° angle to the runway.

14.7 GLIDES AND GLIDE SPEED

1. A glide is a basic maneuver in which the airplane loses altitude with little or no engine power; forward motion is maintained by gravity, and descent rate is controlled by the pilot based on a given pitch.

2. Airplanes with a higher glide ratio will travel farther during a glide.

   a. The **glide ratio** of an airplane is the horizontal distance the airplane will travel in relation to the altitude lost.

      1) EXAMPLE: A glide ratio of 10 to 1 means that a plane will travel 10,000 feet forward for every 1,000 feet of altitude lost.

   b. Wind speed and direction affect the glide ratio.

      1) With a headwind, the airplane will not glide as far forward because of the slower groundspeed.
      2) With a tailwind, the airplane will glide farther than normal because of the higher groundspeed.

3. The best glide speed is the airspeed at which the airplane will travel the greatest horizontal (forward) distance for a given loss of altitude.

   a. The purpose of a best glide speed is to lose as little altitude as possible while maximizing the glide distance.

   b. This speed corresponds to an angle of attack that results in the least drag on the airplane.

4. To maintain a constant airspeed, the pitch attitude must be adjusted as necessary.

    a. Any change in airspeed will result in a proportionate change in glide ratio.

    b. **Any** speed, slower or faster, other than the best glide speed will result in an increase in drag.

        1) This will result in an increased rate of descent and a decreased glide distance.

5. During the approach and landing phase, too fast a glide will result in floating over the ground or even overshooting a runway. Too slow a glide causes undershooting and hard touchdowns.

14.8 LANDING DISTANCE

1. Required landing distances differ at various altitudes and temperatures due to changes in air density.

    a. However, indicated airspeed for landing is the same at all altitudes.

2. Landing distance information is given in airplane operating manuals in chart or graph form to adjust for headwind, temperature, and dry grass runways.

3. It is imperative that you distinguish between distances for clearing a 50-ft. obstacle and distances without a 50-ft. obstacle at the beginning of the runway (the latter is described as the ground roll).

4. See Figure 138 on page 278 for an example landing distance graph. It is used in the same manner as the takeoff distance graph (Figure 141) discussed on page 262 and printed on page 271.

5. Refer to Figure 139 on page 280, which is a landing distance table.

    a. It has been computed for landing with no wind, at standard temperature, and at pressure altitude.

    b. The bottom "notes" tell you how to adjust for wind, nonstandard temperature, and a grass runway.

        1) Note 1 says to decrease the distance for a headwind. Note that tailwind hurts much more than headwind helps, so you cannot use the headwind formula in reverse.

    c. EXAMPLE: Given standard air temperature, 8-kt. headwind, and pressure altitude of 2,500 ft., find both the ground roll and the landing distance to clear a 50-ft. obstacle.

        1) According to the table (Figure 139), for 2,500 ft. at standard temperature with no wind, the ground roll is 470 ft. and the distance to clear a 50-ft. obstacle is 1,135 ft. These amounts must be decreased by 20% because of the headwind (8 kt. ÷ 4 × 10% = 20%). Therefore, the ground roll is 376 ft. (470 × 80%), and the distance to clear a 50-ft. obstacle is 908 ft. (1,135 × 80%).

14.9 WEIGHT AND BALANCE DEFINITIONS

1. **Empty weight** consists of the airframe, engine, and all items of operating equipment permanently installed in the airplane, including optional special equipment, fixed ballast, hydraulic fluid, unusable fuel, and undrainable (or, in some aircraft, all) oil.

2. Standard weights have been established for numerous items involved in weight and balance computations.

    a. The standard weight for aviation gasoline (AVGAS) is 6 lb./gal.

        1) EXAMPLE: 90 lb. of gasoline is equal to 15 gal. (90 ÷ 6).

3.   The **center of gravity** (CG) is the point of balance along the airplane's longitudinal axis. By multiplying the weight of each component of the airplane by its arm (distance from an arbitrary reference point, called the reference datum), that component's moment is determined. The CG of the airplane is the sum of all the moments divided by the total weight.

14.10 CENTER OF GRAVITY GRAPHS

1.   The only way to determine the airworthiness of a loaded airplane is to perform a complete weight and balance calculation before every flight.

    a.   If any changes are made to the loading condition of the airplane after a weight and balance calculation has been made, a new calculation should be completed to ensure you are within both weight and balance limits.

2.   The **loading graph** may be used to determine the load moment. (See top graph in Fig. 135 on page 283.)

    a.   On most graphs, the load weight in pounds is listed on the vertical axis. Diagonal lines represent various items such as fuel, baggage, pilot and front seat passengers, and back seat passengers.

        1)   Move horizontally to the right across the chart from the amount of weight to intersect the line which represents the particular item.

        2)   From the point of intersection of the weight with the appropriate diagonal line, drop straight down to the bottom of the chart to the moments displayed on the horizontal axis. Note that each moment shown on the graph is actually a moment index, or moment/1,000. This reduces the moments to smaller, more manageable numbers.

    b.   Then total the weights and moments for all items being loaded.

    c.   EXAMPLE: Determine the load (total) moment/1,000 in the following situation:

	Weight (lb.)	Moment/1,000 (lb.-in.)
Empty weight	1,350	51.5
Pilot & front seat passenger	400	?
Baggage	120	?
Usable fuel (38 gal. × 6 lb./gal.)	228	?
Oil (8 qt.)	15	−0.2

        1)   Compute the moment of the pilot and front seat passenger by referring to the loading graph, and locate 400 on the weight scale. Move horizontally across the graph to intersect the diagonal line representing the pilot and front passenger, and then to the bottom scale, which indicates a moment of approximately 15.0.

        2)   Locate 120 on the weight scale for the baggage. Move horizontally across the graph to intersect the diagonal line that represents baggage, then down vertically to the bottom scale, which indicates a moment of approximately 11.5.

        3)   Locate 228 on the weight scale for the usable fuel. Move horizontally across the graph to intersect the diagonal line representing fuel, then down vertically to the bottom scale, which indicates a moment of 11.0.

        4)   Notice a −0.2 moment for the engine oil (see note 2 on Fig. 135). Add all moments except this negative moment, and obtain a total of 89.0. Then subtract the negative moment to obtain a total aircraft moment of 88.8.

d.   Now add all the weights to determine that the airplane's maximum gross weight is not exceeded.

	Weight (lb.)	Moment/1,000 (lb.-in.)
Empty weight	1,350	51.5
Pilot & passengers	400	15.0
Baggage	120	11.5
Fuel	228	11.0
Oil	15	−0.2
	2,113	88.8

3.   The **center of gravity moment envelope chart** (see bottom graph in Fig. 135 on page 283) is a graph showing CG moment limits for various gross weights. Acceptable limits are established as an area on the graph. This area is called the envelope. Weight is on the vertical axis and moments are on the horizontal axis.

a.   Identify the center of gravity point on the center of gravity moment envelope graph by plotting the total loaded aircraft weight across to the right.

b.   Plot the total moment upward from the bottom.

c.   The intersection will be within the CG moment envelope if the airplane has been loaded within limits.

d.   EXAMPLE: Using the data above, locate the weight of 2,113 lb. on the vertical axis, and then move across the chart to the moment line of 88.8. The point of intersection will indicate that the aircraft is within both CG (i.e., normal category) and gross weight (i.e., less than 2,300 lb.) limits.

14.11 CENTER OF GRAVITY TABLES

1.   Another approach to determining weight and CG limits is to use tables.

2.   First, determine the total moment from the Useful Load Weights and Moments Table (Fig. 133 on page 286).

a.   Moments can be read directly from the table for a specific weight.

b.   If weight is between values, you can use the basic formula to determine the moment:

$$Weight \times Arm = Moment$$

1)   Then divide by 100 to determine moment/100.

3.   Then use the Moment Limits vs. Weight Table (Fig. 134 on page 287) to see if the total moment is within maximum and minimum limits for the gross weight.

QUESTIONS AND ANSWER EXPLANATIONS

All of the sport pilot knowledge test questions chosen by the FAA for release as well as additional questions selected by Gleim relating to the material in the previous outlines are reproduced on the following pages. These questions have been organized into the same subunits as the outlines. To the immediate right of each question are the correct answer and answer explanations. You should cover these answers and answer explanations while responding to the questions. Refer to the general discussion in the Introduction on how to take the FAA pilot knowledge test.

Remember that the questions from the FAA pilot knowledge test bank have been reordered by topic and organized into a meaningful sequence. Also, the first line of the answer explanation gives the citation of the authoritative source for the answer.

QUESTIONS

14.1 Density Altitude Computations

1. (Refer to Figure 108 on page 269.) Determine the density altitude for these conditions:

Altimeter setting 30.35
Runway temperature . . . . +25°F
Airport elevation . . . . 3,894 ft. MSL

    A. 2,000 feet MSL.

    B. 2,900 feet MSL.

    C. 3,500 feet MSL.

Answer (A) is correct. *(PHAK Chap 10)*
    DISCUSSION: With an altimeter setting of 30.35" Hg, 394 ft. must be subtracted from a field elevation of 3,894 ft. to obtain a pressure altitude of 3,500 feet. Note that the higher-than-normal pressure of 30.35 means the pressure altitude will be less than true altitude. The 394 ft. was found by interpolation: 30.3 on the graph is –348, and 30.4 was –440 feet. Adding one-half the –92-ft. difference (–46 ft.) to –348 ft. results in –394 feet. Once you have found the pressure altitude, use the chart to plot 3,500 ft. pressure altitude at 25°F to reach 2,000 ft. density altitude. Note that, since the temperature is lower than standard, the density altitude is lower than the pressure altitude.
    Answer (B) is incorrect. The density altitude would be 2,900 ft. MSL if you added (not subtracted) 394 ft. to 3,894 feet. Answer (C) is incorrect. Pressure (not density) altitude is 3,500 ft. MSL.

2. (Refer to Figure 108 on page 269.) What is the effect of a temperature increase from 30 to 50°F on the density altitude if the pressure altitude remains at 3,000 feet MSL?

    A. 900-foot increase.

    B. 1,100-foot decrease.

    C. 1,300-foot increase.

Answer (C) is correct. *(PHAK Chap 10)*
    DISCUSSION: Increasing the temperature from 30°F to 50°F, given a constant pressure altitude of 3,000 ft., requires you to find the 3,000-ft. line on the density altitude chart at the 30°F level. At this point, the density altitude is approximately 1,650 feet. Then move up the 3,000-ft. line to 50°F, where the density altitude is approximately 2,950 feet. There is an approximate 1,300-ft. increase (2,950 – 1,650 ft.). Note that 50°F is just about standard and pressure altitude is very close to density altitude.
    Answer (A) is incorrect. A 900-ft. increase would be caused by a temperature increase of 14°F (not 20°F). Answer (B) is incorrect. A decrease in density altitude would be caused by a decrease, not an increase, in temperature.

3. (Refer to Figure 108 on page 269.) What is the effect of a temperature increase from 25 to 50°F on the density altitude if the pressure altitude remains at 5,000 feet?

    A. 1,200-foot increase.

    B. 1,400-foot increase.

    C. 1,650-foot increase.

Answer (C) is correct. *(PHAK Chap 10)*
    DISCUSSION: Increasing the temperature from 25°F to 50°F, given a pressure altitude of 5,000 ft., requires you to find the 5,000-ft. line on the density altitude chart at the 25°F level. At this point, the density altitude is approximately 3,850 feet. Then move up the 5,000-ft. line to 50°F, where the density altitude is approximately 5,500 feet. There is about a 1,650-ft. increase (5,500 – 3,850 ft.). As temperature increases, so does density altitude; i.e., the atmosphere becomes thinner (less dense).
    Answer (A) is incorrect. A 1,200-ft. increase would result from a temperature increase of 18°F (not 25°F). Answer (B) is incorrect. A 1,400-ft. increase would result from a temperature increase of 20°F (not 25°F).

4. (Refer to Figure 108 on page 269.) Determine the pressure altitude at an airport that is 3,563 feet MSL with an altimeter setting of 29.96.

    A. 3,527 feet MSL.

    B. 3,556 feet MSL.

    C. 3,639 feet MSL.

Answer (A) is correct. *(PHAK Chap 10)*
    DISCUSSION: Note that the question asks only for pressure altitude, not density altitude. Pressure altitude is determined by adjusting the altimeter setting to 29.92" Hg, i.e., adjusting for nonstandard pressure. This is the true altitude plus or minus the pressure altitude conversion factor (based on current altimeter setting). On the chart, an altimeter setting of 30.0 requires you to subtract 73 ft. to determine pressure altitude (note that at 29.92, nothing is subtracted because that is pressure altitude). Since 29.96 is halfway between 29.92 and 30.0, you need only subtract 36 (–73 ÷ 2) from 3,563 ft. to obtain a pressure altitude of 3,527 ft. (3,563 – 36). Note that a higher-than-standard barometric pressure means pressure altitude is lower than true altitude.
    Answer (B) is incorrect. You must subtract 36 (not 7) from 3,563 ft. to obtain the correct pressure altitude. Answer (C) is incorrect. You must subtract 36 (not add 76) from 3,563 ft. to obtain the correct pressure altitude.

5. (Refer to Figure 108 below.) Determine the pressure altitude at an airport that is 1,386 feet MSL with an altimeter setting of 29.97.

A. 1,341 feet MSL.

B. 1,451 feet MSL.

C. 1,562 feet MSL.

Answer (A) is correct. *(PHAK Chap 10)*

DISCUSSION: Pressure altitude is determined by adjusting the altimeter setting to 29.92" Hg. This is the true altitude plus or minus the pressure altitude conversion factor (based on current altimeter setting). Since 29.97 is not a number given on the conversion chart, you must interpolate. Compute 5/8 of –73 (since 29.97 is 5/8 of the way between 29.92 and 30.0), which is 45. Subtract 45 ft. from 1,386 ft. to obtain a pressure altitude of 1,341 feet. Note that if the altimeter setting is greater than standard (e.g., 29.97), the pressure altitude (i.e., altimeter set to 29.92) will be less than true altitude.

Answer (B) is incorrect. You must subtract 45 ft. (not add 65) from 1,386 ft. to obtain the correct pressure altitude.
Answer (C) is incorrect. You must subtract 45 ft. (not add 176) from 1,386 ft. to obtain the correct pressure altitude.

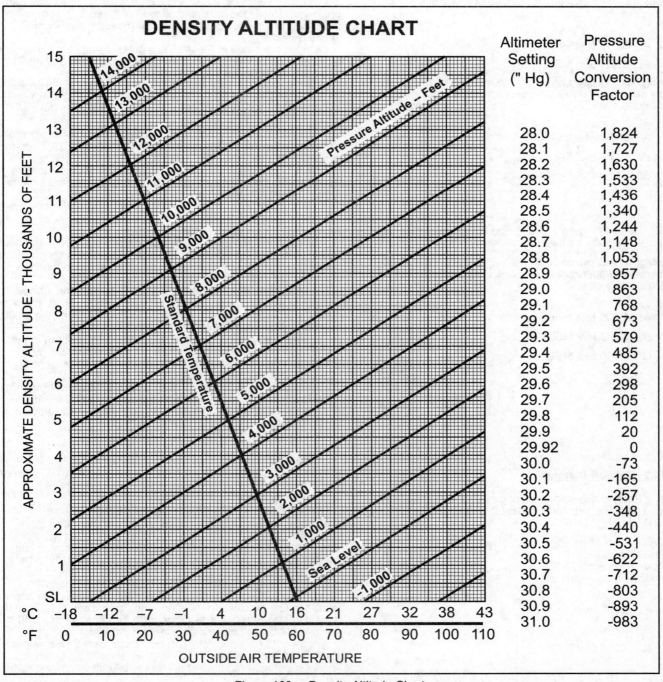

Figure 108. – Density Altitude Chart.

6. (Refer to Figure 108 on page 269.) What is the effect of a temperature decrease and a pressure altitude increase on the density altitude from 90°F and 1,250 feet pressure altitude to 55°F and 1,750 feet pressure altitude?

    A. 1,700-foot increase.

    B. 1,300-foot decrease.

    C. 1,700-foot decrease.

Answer (C) is correct. *(PHAK Chap 10)*
    DISCUSSION: The requirement is the effect of a temperature decrease and a pressure altitude increase on density altitude. First, find the density altitude at 90°F and 1,250 ft. (approximately 3,600 ft.). Then find the density altitude at 55°F and 1,750 ft. pressure altitude (approximately 1,900 ft.). Next, subtract the two numbers: 3,600 ft. minus 1,900 ft. equals a 1,700-ft. decrease in density altitude.
    Answer (A) is incorrect. Such a large decrease in temperature would decrease, not increase, density altitude. Answer (B) is incorrect. Density altitude would decrease 1,300 ft. if the temperature decreased to 60°F (not 55°F).

7. (Refer to Figure 108 on page 269.) Determine the pressure altitude with an indicated altitude of 1,380 feet MSL with an altimeter setting of 28.22 at standard temperature.

    A. 3,010 feet MSL.

    B. 2,991 feet MSL.

    C. 2,913 feet MSL.

Answer (B) is correct. *(PHAK Chap 10)*
    DISCUSSION: Pressure altitude is determined by adjusting the altimeter setting to 29.92" Hg, i.e., adjusting for nonstandard pressure. This is the indicated altitude of 1,380 ft. plus or minus the pressure altitude conversion factor (based on the current altimeter setting).
    On the right side of Fig. 108 is a pressure altitude conversion factor schedule. Add 1,533 ft. for an altimeter setting of 28.30 and 1,630 ft. for an altimeter setting of 28.20. Using interpolation, you must subtract 20% of the difference between 28.3 and 28.2 from 1,630 ft. (1,630 – 1,533 = 97 × .2 = 19). Since 1,630 – 19 = 1,611, add 1,611 ft. to 1,380 ft. to get the pressure altitude of 2,991 feet.
    Answer (A) is incorrect. Adding the conversion factor for an altimeter setting of 28.20, not an altimeter setting of 28.22, to the indicated altitude, results in 3,010 ft. MSL. Answer (C) is incorrect. Adding the conversion factor for an altimeter setting of 28.30, not an altimeter setting of 28.22, to the indicated altitude, results in 2,913 ft. MSL.

8. (Refer to Figure 108 on page 269.) Determine the density altitude for these conditions:

Altimeter setting 29.25
Runway temperature . . . . +81°F
Airport elevation . . . . 5,250 ft MSL

    A. 4,600 feet MSL.

    B. 5,877 feet MSL.

    C. 8,500 feet MSL.

Answer (C) is correct. *(PHAK Chap 10)*
    DISCUSSION: With an altimeter setting of 29.25" Hg, about 626 ft. (579 plus 1/2 the 94-ft. pressure altitude conversion factor difference between 29.2 and 29.3) must be added to the field elevation of 5,250 ft. to obtain the pressure altitude, or 5,876 feet. Note that barometric pressure is less than standard, and pressure altitude is greater than true altitude. Next, convert pressure altitude to density altitude. On the chart, find the point at which the pressure altitude line for 5,876 ft. crosses the 81°F line. The density altitude at that spot shows somewhere in the mid-8,000s of feet. The closest answer choice is 8,500 feet. Note that, when temperature is higher than standard, density altitude exceeds pressure altitude.
    Answer (A) is incorrect. If 650 ft. were subtracted from, not added to, 5,250 ft., pressure altitude would be 4,600 ft. MSL. Answer (B) is incorrect. Pressure altitude, not density altitude, is 5,877 ft. MSL.

14.2 Takeoff Distance

9. (Refer to Figure 141 on page 271.) Determine the total distance required for takeoff to clear a 50-foot obstacle.

OAT . . . . Std
Pressure altitude . . . . 4,000 ft
Takeoff weight . . . . 2,800 lb
Headwind component . . . . Calm

    A. 1,500 feet.

    B. 1,750 feet.

    C. 2,000 feet.

Answer (B) is correct. *(PHAK Chap 10)*
    DISCUSSION: The takeoff distance to clear a 50-ft. obstacle is required. Begin on the left side of the graph at standard temperature (as represented by the curved line labeled "ISA"). From the intersection of the standard temperature line and the 4,000-ft. pressure altitude, proceed horizontally to the right to the first reference line, and then move parallel to the closest guideline to 2,800 pounds. From there, proceed horizontally to the right to the third reference line (skip the second reference line because there is no wind), and move parallel to the closest guideline all the way to the far right. You are at 1,750 ft., which is the takeoff distance to clear a 50-ft. obstacle.
    Answer (A) is incorrect. The total distance required with a 10-kt. headwind would be 1,500 feet. Answer (C) is incorrect. The total distance required at maximum takeoff weight would be 2,000 feet.

10. (Refer to Figure 141 below.) Determine the approximate ground roll distance required for takeoff.

OAT . . . . 100°F
Pressure altitude . . . . 2,000 ft
Takeoff weight . . . . 2,750 lb
Headwind component . . . . Calm

   A. 1,150 feet.

   B. 1,300 feet.

   C. 1,800 feet.

Answer (A) is correct. *(PHAK Chap 10)*
   DISCUSSION: Begin on the left section of Fig. 141 at 100°F (see outside air temperature at the bottom). Move up vertically to the pressure altitude of 2,000 feet. Then proceed horizontally to the first reference line. Since takeoff weight is 2,750 lb., move parallel to the closest guideline, to 2,750 pounds. Then proceed horizontally to the second reference line. Since the wind is calm, proceed again horizontally to the right-hand margin of the diagram (ignore the third reference line because there is no obstacle; i.e., ground roll is desired), which will be at 1,150 feet.
   Answer (B) is incorrect. The ground roll distance required at maximum takeoff weight would be 1,300 feet. Answer (C) is incorrect. The total distance required to clear a 50-ft. obstacle would be 1,800 feet.

11. (Refer to Figure 141 below.) Determine the total distance required for takeoff to clear a 50-foot obstacle.

OAT . . . . Std
Pressure altitude . . . . Sea level
Takeoff weight . . . . 2,700 lb
Headwind component . . . . Calm

   A. 1,000 feet.

   B. 1,400 feet.

   C. 1,700 feet.

Answer (B) is correct. *(PHAK Chap 10)*
   DISCUSSION: Begin in the left section of Fig. 141 by finding the intersection of the sea-level pressure altitude and standard temperature (59°F) and proceed horizontally to the right to the first reference line. Then proceed parallel to the closest guideline to 2,700 pounds. From there, proceed horizontally to the right to the third reference line. You skip the second reference line because the wind is calm. Then proceed upward, parallel to the closest guideline to the far right side. To clear the 50-ft. obstacle, you need a takeoff distance of about 1,400 feet.
   Answer (A) is incorrect. The total distance required at 2,200-lb. takeoff weight would be 1,000 feet. Answer (C) is incorrect. The total distance required at maximum takeoff weight would be 1,700 feet.

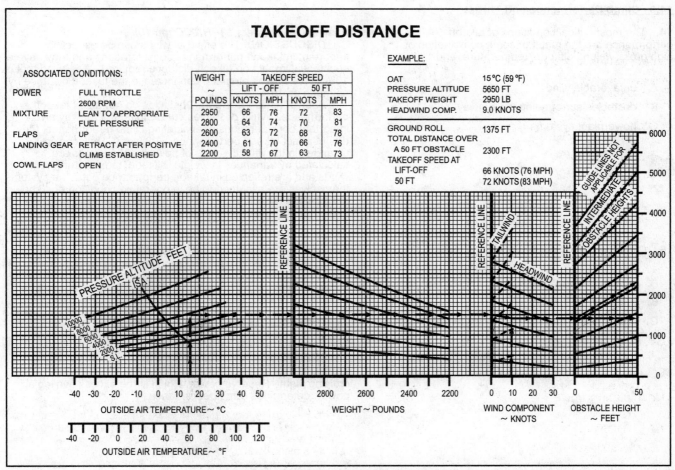

Figure 141. – Airplane Takeoff Distance Graph.

12. (Refer to Figure 141 on page 271.) Determine the approximate ground roll distance required for takeoff.

OAT . . . . 90°F
Pressure altitude . . . . 2,000 ft
Takeoff weight . . . . 2,500 lb
Headwind component . . . . 20 kts

    A. 650 feet.

    B. 850 feet.

    C. 1,000 feet.

Answer (A) is correct. *(PHAK Chap 10)*
    DISCUSSION: Begin with the intersection of the 2,000-ft. pressure altitude curve and 90°F in the left section of Fig. 141. Move horizontally to the right to the first reference line, then parallel to the closest guideline to 2,500 pounds. Next, move horizontally to the right to the second reference line, then parallel to the closest guideline to the right to 20 knots. Finally, move horizontally to the right directly to the right margin because there is no obstacle clearance. You should end up at about 650 ft., which is the required ground roll when there is no obstacle to clear.
    Answer (B) is incorrect. The ground roll distance required if the wind were calm would be 850 feet. Answer (C) is incorrect. The ground roll distance required at maximum takeoff weight would be 1,000 feet.

13. What effect does an uphill runway slope have upon takeoff performance?

    A. Decreases takeoff speed.

    B. Increases takeoff distance.

    C. Decreases takeoff distance.

Answer (B) is correct. *(PHAK Chap 10)*
    DISCUSSION: The upslope or downslope of a runway (runway gradient) is quite important when runway length and takeoff distance are critical. Upslope provides a retarding force that impedes acceleration because the engine has to overcome gravity, as well as surface friction and drag, resulting in a longer ground run, or takeoff distance.
    Answer (A) is incorrect. The indicated speed is the same on a level, downhill, or uphill runway at a given density altitude. Answer (C) is incorrect. A downhill, not uphill, slope will decrease the takeoff distance.

14.3 Climb Performance and Thrust

14. The most critical conditions of takeoff performance are the result of some combination of high gross weight, altitude, temperature, and

    A. unfavorable wind.

    B. obstacles surrounding the runway.

    C. powerplant systems.

Answer (A) is correct. *(PHAK Chap 10)*
    DISCUSSION: The effect of winds can be especially important in takeoff performance considerations and may have a substantial impact on takeoff distance required. A tailwind that is 10% of the takeoff airspeed can increase the takeoff distance by as much as 19%.
    Answer (B) is incorrect. Obstacles do not affect takeoff performance. While obstacles surrounding the runway are important considerations in evaluating climb performance, they do not affect takeoff performance. Answer (C) is incorrect. Changes in the effectiveness of powerplant systems are calculated by variances in weight, altitude, temperature, and winds and are reflected in takeoff performance data; the systems themselves are assumed to be in operating condition and should not alter the takeoff performance. Unfavorable winds will affect takeoff performance substantially.

15. Climb performance depends upon the

    A. reserve power or thrust.

    B. maximum L/D ratio.

    C. cruise power setting.

Answer (A) is correct. *(PHAK Chap 10)*
    DISCUSSION: Reserve power can be defined as the excess available power over and above that required to maintain horizontal flight at a given speed. Thus, climb performance depends on the excess power (reserve power or thrust).
    Answer (B) is incorrect. The maximum L/D ratio provides the speed for minimum drag, not climb performance. Reserve power, or excess available power, will determine climb performance. An aircraft will be unable to climb at its maximum L/D ratio if reserve power or thrust is unavailable. Answer (C) is incorrect. The cruise power setting is simply the power used in cruising flight. Reserve power, which is the excess available power, determines climb performance.

14.4 Range and Endurance

16. When range and economy of operation are the principal goals, the pilot must ensure that the airplane will be operated at the recommended

    A. specific endurance.

    B. long-range cruise performance.

    C. equivalent airspeed.

Answer (B) is correct. *(PHAK Chap 10)*
    DISCUSSION: The recommended long-range cruise performance will provide an aircraft's maximum design-operating radius, or range; this condition will also allow the aircraft to travel a shorter distance with a maximum fuel reserve remaining.
    Answer (A) is incorrect. Specific endurance is simply a term that refers to a calculation of time in air efficiency; it only refers to time flown, not to distance flown (range). Answer (C) is incorrect. Appropriate airspeeds may change across the course of a flight due to changes in weather conditions; specifically, equivalent airspeed is airspeed correct for installation and position errors and may vary with pressure.

17. Maximum endurance is obtained at the point of minimum power to maintain the aircraft

    A. in steady, level flight.

    B. in a long range descent.

    C. at its slowest possible indicated airspeed.

Answer (A) is correct. *(PHAK Chap 10)*
    DISCUSSION: Maximum endurance conditions allow the airplane to fly for the longest amount of time. This is achieved by using the minimum power setting required to maintain steady, level flight (in order to consume the least fuel).
    Answer (B) is incorrect. Maximum endurance occurs at the minimum power setting to maintain the airplane in steady, level flight, not long-range descent. At this power setting, the airplane will consume minimum fuel. Answer (C) is incorrect. Flying at the slowest possible indicated airspeed does not provide maximum endurance. Maximum endurance is the minimum power setting required to maintain steady, level flight.

14.5 Cruise Power Settings

18. (Refer to Figure 136 on page 274.) What fuel flow should a pilot expect at 11,000 feet on a standard day with 65 percent maximum continuous power?

    A. 10.6 gallons per hour.

    B. 11.2 gallons per hour.

    C. 11.8 gallons per hour.

Answer (B) is correct. *(PHAK Chap 10)*
    DISCUSSION: Note that the entire chart applies to 65% maximum continuous power (regardless of the throttle), so use the middle section of the chart, which is labeled a standard day.
    The fuel flow at 11,000 ft. on a standard day would be 1/2 of the way between the fuel flow at 10,000 ft. (11.5 GPH) and the fuel flow at 12,000 ft. (10.9 GPH). Thus, the fuel flow at 11,000 ft. would be 11.5 – 0.3, or 11.2 GPH.
    Answer (A) is incorrect. You must add (not subtract) 0.3 to 10.9 to obtain the correct fuel flow. Answer (C) is incorrect. You must subtract (not add) 0.3 from 11.5 to obtain the correct fuel flow.

19. (Refer to Figure 136 on page 274.) What is the expected fuel consumption for a 1,000-nautical mile flight under the following conditions?

Pressure altitude	8,000 ft
Temperature	22°C
Manifold pressure	20.8" Hg
Wind	Calm

    A. 60.2 gallons.

    B. 70.1 gallons.

    C. 73.2 gallons.

Answer (B) is correct. *(PHAK Chap 10)*
    DISCUSSION: To determine the fuel consumption, you need to know the number of hours the flight will last and the gallons per hour the airplane will use. The chart is divided into three sections. They differ based on air temperature. Use the right section of the chart as the temperature at 8,000 ft. is 22°C.
    At a pressure altitude of 8,000 ft., 20.8" Hg manifold pressure, and 22°C, the fuel flow is 11.5 GPH and the true airspeed is 164 knots. Given a calm wind, the 1,000-NM trip will take 6.09 hr. (1,000 NM ÷ 164 kt).

$$6.09 \text{ hr.} \times 11.5 \text{ GPH} = 70.1 \text{ gal.}$$

    Answer (A) is incorrect. The expected fuel consumption for a 1,000-NM flight with a true airspeed of 189 (not 164) kt. is 60.2 gallons. Answer (C) is incorrect. The expected fuel consumption for a 1,000-NM flight with a true airspeed of 157 (not 164) kt. is 73.2 gallons.

CRUISE POWER SETTINGS

65% MAXIMUM CONTINUOUS POWER (OR FULL THROTTLE)
2800 POUNDS

| PRESS ALT. | ISA –20 °C (–36 °F) | | | | | | | STANDARD DAY (ISA) | | | | | | | ISA +20 °C (+36 °F) | | | | | | |
| | IOAT | | ENGINE SPEED | MAN. PRESS | FUEL FLOW PER ENGINE | | TAS | IOAT | | ENGINE SPEED | MAN. PRESS | FUEL FLOW PER ENGINE | | TAS | IOAT | | ENGINE SPEED | MAN. PRESS | FUEL FLOW PER ENGINE | | TAS |
FEET	°F	°C	RPM	IN HG	PSI	GPH	KTS	MPH	°F	°C	RPM	IN HG	PSI	GPH	KTS	MPH	°F	°C	RPM	IN HG	PSI	GPH	KTS	MPH
SL	27	-3	2450	20.7	6.6	11.5	147	169	63	17	2450	21.2	6.6	11.5	150	173	99	37	2450	21.8	6.6	11.5	153	176
2000	19	-7	2450	20.4	6.6	11.5	149	171	55	13	2450	21.0	6.6	11.5	153	176	91	33	2450	21.5	6.6	11.5	156	180
4000	12	-11	2450	20.1	6.6	11.5	152	175	48	9	2450	20.7	6.6	11.5	156	180	84	29	2450	21.3	6.6	11.5	159	183
6000	5	-15	2450	19.8	6.6	11.5	155	178	41	5	2450	20.4	6.6	11.5	158	182	79	26	2450	21.0	6.6	11.5	161	185
8000	-2	-19	2450	19.5	6.6	11.5	157	181	36	2	2450	20.2	6.6	11.5	161	185	72	22	2450	20.8	6.6	11.5	164	189
10000	-8	-22	2450	19.2	6.6	11.5	160	184	28	-2	2450	19.9	6.6	11.5	163	188	64	18	2450	20.3	6.5	11.4	166	191
12000	-15	-26	2450	18.8	6.4	11.3	162	186	21	-6	2450	18.8	6.1	10.9	163	188	57	14	2450	18.8	5.9	10.6	163	188
14000	-22	-30	2450	17.4	5.8	10.5	159	183	14	-10	2450	17.4	5.6	10.1	160	184	50	10	2450	17.4	5.4	9.8	160	184
16000	-29	-34	2450	16.1	5.3	9.7	156	180	7	-14	2450	16.1	5.1	9.4	156	180	43	6	2450	16.1	4.9	9.1	155	178

NOTES: 1. Full throttle manifold pressure settings are approximate.
2. Shaded area represents operation with full throttle.

Figure 136. – Airplane Power Setting Table.

20. (Refer to Figure 136 above.) What is the expected fuel consumption for a 500-nautical mile flight under the following conditions?

Pressure altitude . . . . 4,000 ft
Temperature . . . . +29°C
Manifold pressure . . . . 21.3" Hg
Wind . . . . Calm

    A. 31.4 gallons.

    B. 36.1 gallons.

    C. 40.1 gallons.

Answer (B) is correct. *(PHAK Chap 10)*
DISCUSSION: At 4,000 ft., 21.3" Hg manifold pressure, and 29°C (use the section on the right), the fuel flow will be 11.5 GPH, and the true airspeed will be 159 knots. The 500-NM trip will take 3.14 hr. (500 NM ÷ 159 kt).

3.14 hr. × 11.5 GPH = 36.1 gal.

Answer (A) is incorrect. The expected fuel consumption for a 500-NM flight with a true airspeed of 183 (not 159) kt. is 31.4 gallons. Answer (C) is incorrect. The expected fuel consumption for a 500-NM flight with a true airspeed of 143 (not 159) kt. is 40.1 gallons.

21. (Refer to Figure 136 above.) Determine the approximate manifold pressure setting with 2,450 RPM to achieve 65 percent maximum continuous power at 6,500 feet with a temperature of 36°F higher than standard.

    A. 19.8" Hg.

    B. 20.8" Hg.

    C. 21.0" Hg.

Answer (C) is correct. *(PHAK Chap 10)*
DISCUSSION: The part of the chart on the right is for temperatures 36°F greater than standard. At 6,500 ft. with a temperature of 36°F higher than standard, the required manifold pressure change is 1/4 of the difference between the 21.0" Hg at 6,000 ft. and the 20.8" Hg at 8,000 ft., or slightly less than 21.0. Thus, 21.0 is the best answer given. The manifold pressure is closer to 21.0 than 20.8.
Answer (A) is incorrect. This manifold pressure would achieve 65% power at 36°F below (not above) standard temperature. Answer (B) is incorrect. The manifold pressure at 6,500 ft. is closer to 21.0 than 20.8.

22. (Refer to Figure 136 above.) Approximately what true airspeed should a pilot expect with 65 percent maximum continuous power at 9,500 feet with a temperature of 36°F below standard?

    A. 178 MPH.

    B. 181 MPH.

    C. 183 MPH.

Answer (C) is correct. *(PHAK Chap 10)*
DISCUSSION: The left part of the chart applies to 36°F below standard. At 8,000 ft., TAS is 181 MPH. At 10,000 ft., TAS is 184 MPH. At 9,500 ft., with a temperature 36°F below standard, the expected true airspeed is 75% above the 181 MPH at 8,000 ft. toward the 184 MPH at 10,000 ft., i.e., approximately 183 MPH.
Answer (A) is incorrect. The expected TAS at 6,000 ft. is 178 MPH. Answer (B) is incorrect. The expected TAS at 8,000 ft. is 181 MPH.

14.6 Crosswind Components

23. (Refer to Figure 137 below.) What is the crosswind component for a landing on Runway 18 if the tower reports the wind as 220° at 30 knots?

A. 19 knots.

B. 23 knots.

C. 30 knots.

Answer (A) is correct. *(PHAK Chap 10)*
DISCUSSION: The requirement is the crosswind component, which is found on the horizontal axis of the graph. You are given a 30-kt. wind speed (the wind speed is shown on the circular lines or arcs). First, calculate the angle between the wind and the runway (220° − 180° = 40°). Next, find the intersection of the 40° line and the 30-kt. headwind arc. Then, proceed downward to determine a crosswind component of 19 knots.
　　NOTE: The crosswind component is on the horizontal axis, and the headwind component is on the vertical axis.
　　Answer (B) is incorrect. The headwind (not crosswind) component is 23 knots. Answer (C) is incorrect. The total wind (not crosswind component) is 30 knots.

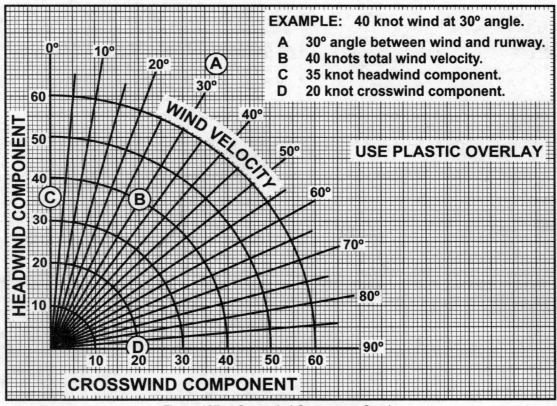

EXAMPLE: 40 knot wind at 30° angle.

A　30° angle between wind and runway.
B　40 knots total wind velocity.
C　35 knot headwind component.
D　20 knot crosswind component.

USE PLASTIC OVERLAY

Figure 137. – Crosswind Component Graph.

24. (Refer to Figure 137 above.) Determine the maximum wind velocity for a 45° crosswind if the maximum crosswind component for the airplane is 25 knots.

A. 25 knots.

B. 29 knots.

C. 35 knots.

Answer (C) is correct. *(PHAK Chap 10)*
DISCUSSION: Start on the bottom of the graph's horizontal axis at 25 kt. and move straight upward to the 45° angle between wind direction and flight path line (halfway between the 40° and 50° lines). Note that you are halfway between the 30 and 40 arc-shaped wind speed lines, which means that the maximum wind velocity for a 45° crosswind is 35 kt. if the airplane is limited to a 25-kt. crosswind component.
　　Answer (A) is incorrect. The maximum wind velocity for a 90° (not 45°) crosswind would be 25 knots. Answer (B) is incorrect. The maximum wind velocity for a 60° (not 45°) crosswind would be 29 knots.

25. (Refer to Figure 137 on page 275.) What is the headwind component for a landing on Runway 18 if the tower reports the wind as 220° at 30 knots?

A. 19 knots.

B. 23 knots.

C. 26 knots.

Answer (B) is correct. *(PHAK Chap 10)*
DISCUSSION: The headwind component is on the vertical axis (left-hand side of the graph). Find the same intersection as in the preceding question, i.e., the 30-kt. wind speed arc and the 40° angle between wind direction and flight path (220° – 180°). Then move horizontally to the left and read approximately 23 knots.
Answer (A) is incorrect. The crosswind (not headwind) component is 19 knots. Answer (C) is incorrect. If the wind were 30° (not 40°) off the runway, the headwind component would be 26 knots.

26. (Refer to Figure 137 on page 275.) With a reported wind of north at 20 knots, which runway (6, 29, or 32) is acceptable for use for an airplane with a 13-knot maximum crosswind component?

A. Runway 6.

B. Runway 29.

C. Runway 32.

Answer (C) is correct. *(PHAK Chap 10)*
DISCUSSION: If the wind is from the north (i.e., either 360° or 0°) at 20 kt., runway 32, i.e., 320°, would provide a 40° crosswind component (360° – 320°). Given a 20-kt. wind, find the intersection between the 20-kt. arc and the angle between wind direction and the flight path of 40°. Dropping straight downward to the horizontal axis gives 13 kt., which is the maximum crosswind component of the example airplane.
Answer (A) is incorrect. Runway 6 would have a crosswind component of approximately 17 knots. Answer (B) is incorrect. Runway 29 would have a crosswind component of 19 knots.

27. (Refer to Figure 137 on page 275.) What is the maximum wind velocity for a 30° crosswind if the maximum crosswind component for the airplane is 12 knots?

A. 16 knots.

B. 20 knots.

C. 24 knots.

Answer (C) is correct. *(PHAK Chap 10)*
DISCUSSION: Start on the graph's horizontal axis at 12 kt. and move upward to the 30° angle between wind direction and flight path line. Note that you are almost halfway between the 20 and 30 arc-shaped wind speed lines, which means that the maximum wind velocity for a 30° crosswind is approximately 24 kt. if the airplane is limited to a 12-kt. crosswind component.
Answer (A) is incorrect. The maximum wind velocity for a 50° (not 30°) crosswind would be 16 knots. Answer (B) is incorrect. The maximum wind velocity for a 40° (not 30°) crosswind would be 20 knots.

28. (Refer to Figure 137 on page 275.) With a reported wind of south at 20 knots, which runway (10, 14, or 24) is appropriate for an airplane with a 13-knot maximum crosswind component?

A. Runway 10.

B. Runway 14.

C. Runway 24.

Answer (B) is correct. *(PHAK Chap 10)*
DISCUSSION: If the wind is from the south at 20 kt., runway 14, i.e., 140°, would provide a 40° crosswind component (180° – 140°). Given a 20-kt. wind, find the intersection between the 20-kt. arc and the angle between wind direction and the flight path of 40°. Dropping straight downward to the horizontal axis gives 13 kt., which is the maximum crosswind component of the example airplane.
Answer (A) is incorrect. Runway 10 would have a crosswind component of 20 knots. Answer (C) is incorrect. Runway 24 would have a crosswind component of approximately 17 knots.

14.7 Glides and Glide Speed

29. The best speed to use for a glide is one that will result in the greatest glide distance for a given amount of

A. altitude.

B. fuel.

C. drag.

Answer (A) is correct. *(AFH Chap 3)*
DISCUSSION: The purpose of a best glide speed is to lose as little altitude as possible while maximizing the glide distance.
Answer (B) is incorrect. A glide is an operation that uses little or no engine power; fuel is not a factor here, as the engine may not be operating in a glide. Answer (C) is incorrect. The objective of a glide is maximum distance with minimum altitude loss; drag will be minimized during a glide.

30. What is descent rate controlled by during a glide?

    A. Wind speed and direction.

    B. The pitch of the airplane.

    C. The glide ratio of the airplane.

Answer (B) is correct. *(AFH Chap 3)*
    DISCUSSION: During a glide, the descent rate is controlled by the pilot based on a given pitch.
    Answer (A) is incorrect. Wind speed and direction affect the glide ratio, not the descent rate. Answer (C) is incorrect. Glide ratio is the horizontal distance the airplane will travel in relation to the altitude lost.

31. Gliding too fast during the approach and landing phase could result in what?

    A. Undershooting the runway.

    B. Overshooting the runway.

    C. A hard touchdown.

Answer (B) is correct. *(AFH Chap 3)*
    DISCUSSION: During the approach and landing phase, too fast a glide will result in floating over the ground or even overshooting a runway.
    Answer (A) is incorrect. Too slow a glide causes under-shooting of the runway. Answer (C) is incorrect. Too slow a glide causes hard touchdowns.

32. Glide ratio is defined as

    A. the horizontal distance the airplane will travel in relation to the altitude lost.

    B. the vertical distance the airplane will lose in relation to the relative wind.

    C. the airspeed at which the airplane will travel the greatest forward distance for a a given loss of altitude.

Answer (A) is correct. *(AFH Chap 3)*
    DISCUSSION: The glide ratio of an airplane is the horizontal distance the airplane will travel in relation to the altitude lost.
    Answer (B) is incorrect. Glide ratio is concerned with the horizontal, or forward, distance an airplane travels, not the vertical distance. Answer (C) is incorrect. The best glide speed is the airspeed at which the airplane will travel the greatest horizontal (forward) distance for a given loss of altitude.

14.8 Landing Distance

33. (Refer to Figure 138 on page 278.) Determine the total distance required to land.

```
OAT . . . . . . . . . . . . . . . . . . . . . . . . . . . . . . Std
Pressure altitude . . . . . . . . . . . . . . . . 10,000 ft
Weight . . . . . . . . . . . . . . . . . . . . . . . . 2,400 lb
Wind component . . . . . . . . . . . . . . . . . . . Calm
Obstacle . . . . . . . . . . . . . . . . . . . . . . . . 50 ft
```

    A. 750 feet.

    B. 1,925 feet.

    C. 1,450 feet.

Answer (B) is correct. *(PHAK Chap 10)*
    DISCUSSION: The landing distance graphs are very similar to the takeoff distance graphs. Begin with the pressure altitude line of 10,000 ft. and the intersection with the standard temperature line which begins at 20°C and slopes up and to the left; i.e., standard temperature decreases as pressure altitude increases. Then move horizontally to the right to the first reference line. Proceed parallel to the closest guideline to 2,400 pounds. Proceed horizontally to the right to the second reference line. Since the wind is calm, proceed horizontally to the third reference line. Given a 50-ft. obstacle, proceed parallel to the closest guideline to the right margin to determine a distance of approximately 1,900 feet.
    Answer (A) is incorrect. This amount is the total distance required to land with a 30-kt. headwind, not a calm wind, and without an obstacle, not with a 50-ft. obstacle. Answer (C) is incorrect. This amount is the approximate total distance required to land at a pressure altitude of 2,000 ft., not 10,000 ft., and a weight of 2,300 lb., not 2,400 pounds.

34. (Refer to Figure 138 on page 278.) Determine the approximate total distance required to land over a 50-ft. obstacle.

```
OAT . . . . . . . . . . . . . . . . . . . . . . . . . . . . . 90°F
Pressure altitude . . . . . . . . . . . . . . . . . . 4,000 ft
Weight . . . . . . . . . . . . . . . . . . . . . . . . 2,800 lb
Headwind component . . . . . . . . . . . . . . . . 10 kts
```

    A. 1,525 feet.

    B. 1,775 feet.

    C. 1,950 feet.

Answer (B) is correct. *(PHAK Chap 10)*
    DISCUSSION: To determine the total landing distance, begin at the left side of Fig. 138 on the 4,000-ft. pressure altitude line at the intersection of 90°F. Proceed horizontally to the right to the first reference line. Proceed parallel to the closest guideline to 2,800 lb., then straight across to the second reference line. Since the headwind component is 10 kt., proceed parallel to the closest headwind guideline to the 10-kt. line, then move directly to the right to the third reference line. Given a 50-ft. obstacle, proceed parallel to the closest guideline for obstacles to find the total distance of approximately 1,775 feet.
    Answer (A) is incorrect. A distance of 1,525 ft. would be the total distance required with an 18-kt. headwind, not a 10-kt. headwind. Answer (C) is incorrect. A distance of 1,950 ft. would be the total distance required with calm wind conditions, not with a 10-kt. headwind.

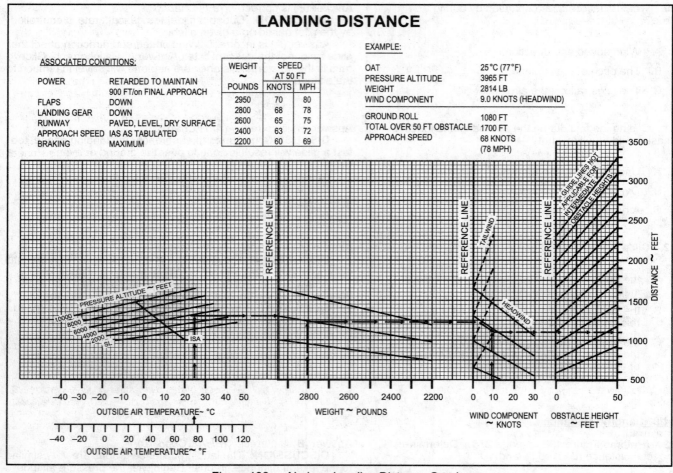

Figure 138. – Airplane Landing Distance Graph.

35. (Refer to Figure 138 above.) Determine the total distance required to land.

OAT . . . . 90°F
Pressure altitude . . . . 3,000 ft
Weight . . . . 2,900 lb
Headwind component . . . . 10 kts
Obstacle . . . . 50 ft

A. 1,450 feet.

B. 1,550 feet.

C. 1,725 feet.

Answer (C) is correct. *(PHAK Chap 10)*
DISCUSSION: To determine the total landing distance, begin with pressure altitude of 3,000 ft. (between the 2,000- and 4,000-ft. lines) at its intersection with 90°F. Proceed horizontally to the right to the first reference line, then parallel to the closest guideline to 2,900 pounds. From that point, proceed horizontally to the second reference line. Since there is a headwind component of 10 kt., proceed parallel to the closest headwind guideline down to 10 kt., then horizontally to the right to the third reference line. Given a 50-ft. obstacle, proceed parallel to the closest guideline for obstacles to find the landing distance of approximately 1,725 feet.
　　Answer (A) is incorrect. A distance of 1,450 ft. would be the total distance required with a 20-kt., not 10-kt., headwind. Answer (B) is incorrect. A distance of 1,550 ft. would be the total distance required at a pressure altitude of 2,000 ft., not 3,000 feet.

36. (Refer to Figure 138 on page 278.) Determine the total distance required to land.

OAT	32°F
Pressure altitude	8,000 ft
Weight	2,600 lb
Headwind component	20 kts
Obstacle	50 ft

    A. 850 feet.

    B. 1,400 feet.

    C. 1,750 feet.

Answer (B) is correct. *(PHAK Chap 10)*
    DISCUSSION: To determine the total landing distance, begin with the pressure altitude of 8,000 ft. at its intersection with 32°F (0°C). Proceed horizontally to the first reference line, then parallel to the closest guideline to 2,600 pounds. From that point, proceed horizontally to the second reference line. Since there is a headwind component of 20 kt., follow parallel to the closest headwind guideline down to 20 kt., then horizontally to the right to the third reference line. Given a 50-ft. obstacle, proceed parallel to the closest guideline for obstacles to find the landing distance of approximately 1,400 feet.
    Answer (A) is incorrect. A distance of 850 ft. would be the ground roll with no obstacle. Answer (C) is incorrect. A distance of 1,750 ft. would be the total distance required at maximum landing weight.

37. (Refer to Figure 139 on page 280.) Determine the approximate landing ground roll distance.

Pressure altitude	Sea level
Headwind	4 kts
Temperature	Std

    A. 356 feet.

    B. 401 feet.

    C. 490 feet.

Answer (B) is correct. *(PHAK Chap 10)*
    DISCUSSION: At sea level, the ground roll is 445 ft. The standard temperature needs no adjustment. According to Note 1 in Fig. 139, the distance should be decreased 10% for each 4 kt. of headwind, so the headwind of 4 kt. means that the landing distance is reduced by 10%. The result is 401 ft. (445 ft. × 90%).
    Answer (A) is incorrect. A distance of 356 ft. would be the ground roll with an 8-kt., not a 4-kt., headwind. Answer (C) is incorrect. Ground roll is reduced, not increased, to account for headwind.

38. (Refer to Figure 139 on page 280.) Determine the total distance required to land over a 50-ft. obstacle.

Pressure altitude	3,750 ft
Headwind	12 kts
Temperature	Std

    A. 794 feet.

    B. 836 feet.

    C. 816 feet.

Answer (C) is correct. *(PHAK Chap 10)*
    DISCUSSION: The total distance to clear a 50-ft. obstacle for a 3,750-ft. pressure altitude is required. Note that this altitude lies halfway between 2,500 ft. and 5,000 feet. Halfway between the total distance at 2,500 ft. of 1,135 ft. and the total distance at 5,000 ft. of 1,195 ft. is 1,165 feet. Since the headwind is 12 kt., the total distance must be reduced by 30% (10% for each 4 kt.).

$$70\% \times 1,165 = 816 \text{ ft.}$$

    Answer (A) is incorrect. A distance of 794 ft. would be the total distance to land at a pressure altitude of 2,500 ft., not 3,750 ft., with a 12-kt. headwind and standard temperature. Answer (B) is incorrect. A distance of 836 ft. would be the total distance to land at a pressure altitude of 5,000 ft., not 3,750 ft., with a 12-kt. headwind and standard temperature.

39. (Refer to Figure 139 on page 280.) Determine the approximate landing ground roll distance.

Pressure altitude	5,000 ft
Headwind	Calm
Temperature	101°F

    A. 495 feet.

    B. 545 feet.

    C. 445 feet.

Answer (B) is correct. *(PHAK Chap 10)*
    DISCUSSION: The ground roll distance at 5,000 ft. is 495 feet. According to Note 2 in Fig. 139, since the temperature is 60°F above standard, the distance should be increased by 10%.

$$495 \text{ ft.} \times 110\% = 545 \text{ ft.}$$

    Answer (A) is incorrect. A distance of 495 ft. would be ground roll if the temperature were 41°F, not 101°F. Answer (C) is incorrect. A distance of 445 ft. is obtained by decreasing, not increasing, the distance for a temperature 60°F above standard.

40. (Refer to Figure 139 on page 280.) Determine the approximate landing ground roll distance.

Pressure altitude	1,250 ft
Headwind	8 kts
Temperature	Std

    A. 275 feet.

    B. 366 feet.

    C. 470 feet.

Answer (B) is correct. *(PHAK Chap 10)*
    DISCUSSION: The landing ground roll at a pressure altitude of 1,250 ft. is required. The difference between landing distance at sea level and 2,500 ft. is 25 ft. (470 − 445). One-half of this distance (12) plus the 445 ft. at sea level is 457 feet. The temperature is standard, requiring no adjustment. The headwind of 8 kt. requires the distance to be decreased by 20%. Thus, the distance required will be 366 ft. (457 × 80%).
    Answer (A) is incorrect. The distance should be decreased by 20% (not 40%). Answer (C) is incorrect. A distance of 470 ft. is required at 2,500 ft. in a calm wind.

41. (Refer to Figure 139 below.) Determine the total distance required to land over a 50-foot obstacle.

Pressure altitude . . . . 7,500 ft
Headwind . . . . 8 kts
Temperature . . . . 32°F
Runway . . . . Hard surface

    A. 1,004 feet.

    B. 1,205 feet.

    C. 1,506 feet.

Answer (A) is correct. *(PHAK Chap 10)*
    DISCUSSION: Under normal conditions, the total landing distance required to clear a 50-ft. obstacle is 1,255 feet. The temperature is standard (32°F), requiring no adjustment. The headwind of 8 kt. reduces the 1,255 by 20% (10% for each 4 kt.). Thus, the total distance required will be 1,004 ft. (1,255 × 80%).
    Answer (B) is incorrect. A distance of 1,205 ft. results from incorrectly assuming that an adjustment for a dry grass runway is necessary and then applying that adjustment (an increase of 20%) to 1,004 ft. rather than to the total landing distance required to clear a 50-ft. obstacle as stated in Note 3, which is 1,255 feet. Answer (C) is incorrect. A distance of 1,506 ft. is obtained by increasing, not decreasing, the distance for the headwind.

LANDING DISTANCE									FLAPS LOWERED TO 40° - POWER OFF HARD SURFACE RUNWAY - ZERO WIND	
		AT SEA LEVEL & 59°F		AT 2500 FT & 50°F		AT 5000 FT & 41°F		AT 7500 FT & 32°F	
GROSS WEIGHT LB	APPROACH SPEED, IAS, MPH	GROUND ROLL	TOTAL TO CLEAR 50 FT OBS	GROUND ROLL	TOTAL TO CLEAR 50 FT OBS	GROUND ROLL	TOTAL TO CLEAR 50 FT OBS	GROUND ROLL	TOTAL TO CLEAR 50 FT OBS
1600	60	445	1075	470	1135	495	1195	520	1255

NOTES: 1. Decrease the distances shown by 10% for each 4 knots of headwind.
          2. Increase the distance by 10% for each 60 °F temperature increase above standard.
          3. For operation on a dry, grass runway, increase distances (both "ground roll" and "total to clear 50 ft obstacle") by 20% of the "total to clear 50 ft obstacle" figure.

Figure 139. – Airplane Landing Distance Table.

42. (Refer to Figure 139 above.) Determine the total distance required to land over a 50-foot obstacle.

Pressure altitude . . . . 5,000 ft
Headwind . . . . 8 kts
Temperature . . . . 41°F
Runway . . . . Hard surface

    A. 837 feet.

    B. 956 feet.

    C. 1,076 feet.

Answer (B) is correct. *(PHAK Chap 10)*
    DISCUSSION: Under standard conditions, the distance to land over a 50-ft. obstacle at 5,000 ft. is 1,195 feet. The temperature is standard, requiring no adjustment. The headwind of 8 kt., however, requires that the distance be decreased by 20% (10% for each 4 kt. of headwind). Thus, the landing ground roll will be 956 ft. (80% of 1,195).
    Answer (A) is incorrect. The distance should be decreased by 20% (not 30%). Answer (C) is incorrect. The distance should be decreased by 20% (not 10%).

14.9 Weight and Balance Definitions

43. Which items are included in the empty weight of an aircraft?

    A. Unusable fuel and undrainable oil.

    B. Only the airframe, powerplant, and optional equipment.

    C. Full fuel tanks and engine oil to capacity.

Answer (A) is correct. *(PHAK Chap 9)*
    DISCUSSION: The empty weight of an airplane includes airframe, engines, and all items of operating equipment that have fixed locations and are permanently installed. It includes optional and special equipment, fixed ballast, hydraulic fluid, unusable fuel, and undrainable oil.
    Answer (B) is incorrect. Unusable and undrainable fuel and oil and permanently installed optional equipment are also included in empty weight. Answer (C) is incorrect. Usable fuel (included in full fuel) and full engine oil are not components of basic empty weight.

44. If an aircraft is loaded 90 pounds over maximum certificated gross weight and fuel (gasoline) is drained to bring the aircraft weight within limits, how much fuel should be drained?

    A. 10 gallons.

    B. 12 gallons.

    C. 15 gallons.

Answer (C) is correct. *(PHAK Chap 9)*
    DISCUSSION: Since fuel weighs 6 lb./gal., draining 15 gal. (90 lb. ÷ 6) will reduce the weight of an airplane that is 90 lb. over maximum gross weight to the acceptable amount.
    Answer (A) is incorrect. Fuel weighs 6 (not 9) lb./gal. Answer (B) is incorrect. Fuel weighs 6 (not 7.5) lb./gal.

45. GIVEN:

	WEIGHT (LB)	ARM (IN)	MOMENT (LB-IN)
Empty weight	1,495.0	101.4	151,593.0
Pilot and passengers	380.0	64.0	---
Fuel (30 gal usable no reserve)	---	96.0	---

The CG is located how far aft of datum?

A. CG 92.44.

B. CG 94.01.

C. CG 119.8.

Answer (B) is correct. *(PHAK Chap 9)*
DISCUSSION: To compute the CG, you must first multiply each weight by the arm to get the moment. Note that the fuel is given as 30 gallons. To get the weight, multiply the 30 by 6 lb. per gal. (30 × 6) = 180 pounds.

	Weight (lb.)	Arm (in.)	Moment (lb.-in.)
Empty weight	1,495.0	101.4	151,593.0
Pilot and passengers	380.0	64.0	24,320.0
Fuel (30 × 6)	180.0	96.0	17,280.0
	2,055.0		193,193.0

Now add the weights and moments. To get CG, you divide total moment by total weight (193,193 ÷ 2,055.0 = a CG of 94.01 in.).
Answer (A) is incorrect. The total moment must be divided by the total weight to obtain the correct CG. Answer (C) is incorrect. The total moment must be divided by the total weight to obtain the correct CG.

46. (Refer to Figure 135 on page 283.) What is the maximum amount of fuel that may be aboard the airplane on takeoff if loaded as follows?

	WEIGHT (LB)	MOM/1000
Empty weight	1,350	51.5
Pilot and front passenger	340	---
Rear passengers	310	---
Baggage	45	---
Oil, 8 qt.	---	---

A. 24 gallons.

B. 32 gallons.

C. 40 gallons.

Answer (C) is correct. *(PHAK Chap 9)*
DISCUSSION: To find the maximum amount of fuel this airplane can carry, add the empty weight (1,350), pilot and front passenger weight (340), rear passengers (310), baggage (45), and oil (15), for a total of 2,060 lb. [Find the oil weight and moment by consulting Note (2) on Fig. 135. It is 15 lb. and –0.2 moments.] Gross weight maximum on the center of gravity moment envelope chart is 2,300. Thus, 240 lb. of weight (2,300 – 2,060) is available for fuel. Since each gallon of fuel weighs 6 lb., this airplane can carry 40 gal. of fuel (240 ÷ 6 lb. per gal.) if its center of gravity moments do not exceed the limit. Note that long-range tanks were not mentioned; assume they exist.
Compute the moments for each item. The empty weight moment is given as 51.5. Calculate the moment for the pilot and front passenger as 12.5, the rear passengers as 22.5, the fuel as 11.5, the baggage as 4.0, and the oil as –0.2. These total to 101.8, which is within the envelope, so 40 gal. of fuel may be carried.

	Weight	Moment/1000 lb.-in.
Empty weight	1,350	51.5
Pilot and front seat passenger	340	12.5
Rear passengers	310	22.5
Baggage	45	4.0
Fuel (40 gal. × 6 lb./gal.)	240	11.5
Oil	15	–0.2
	2,300	101.8

Answer (A) is incorrect. More than 24 gal. of fuel may be carried. Answer (B) is incorrect. More than 32 gal. of fuel may be carried.

47. An aircraft is loaded 110 pounds over maximum certificated gross weight. If fuel (gasoline) is drained to bring the aircraft weight within limits, how much fuel should be drained?

A. 15.7 gallons.

B. 16.2 gallons.

C. 18.4 gallons.

Answer (C) is correct. *(PHAK Chap 9)*
DISCUSSION: Fuel weighs 6 lb./gal. If an airplane is 110 lb. over maximum gross weight, 18.4 gal. (110 lb. ÷ 6) must be drained to bring the airplane weight within limits.
Answer (A) is incorrect. Fuel weighs 6 (not 7) lb./gal. Answer (B) is incorrect. Fuel weighs 6 (not 6.8) lb./gal.

14.10 Center of Gravity Graphs

48. If a pilot were to load a modern aircraft with full fuel, a full passenger load, and full baggage,

   A. The aircraft would be loaded in excess of its maximum gross weight.

   B. The aircraft will remain within design limits.

   C. Its airworthiness could only be determined by completing weight and balance computations.

Answer (C) is correct. *(PHAK Chap 4)*
   DISCUSSION: Weight and balance computations should be part of every preflight briefing. Never assume passengers are of equal weight. Perform a full computation of all items to be loaded on the aircraft, including baggage, pilot, passengers, and fuel. A competent pilot understands and respects the effects of CG and weight on an aircraft.
   Answer (A) is incorrect. The aircraft may be below its maximum gross weight but outside of its CG limits. Always perform a full computation of all items to be loaded on the aircraft, including baggage, pilot, passenger, and fuel. A competent pilot understands and respects the effects of CG and weight on the aircraft. Answer (B) is incorrect. There is no way to know if the aircraft remains within design limits without doing a complete weight and balance computation.

49. (Refer to Figure 135 on page 283.) What is the maximum amount of baggage that may be loaded aboard the airplane for the CG to remain within the moment envelope?

	WEIGHT (LB)	MOM/1000
Empty weight	1,350	51.5
Pilot and front passenger	250	---
Rear passengers	400	---
Baggage	---	---
Fuel, 30 gal.	---	---
Oil, 8 qt.	---	-0.2

   A. 105 pounds.

   B. 110 pounds.

   C. 120 pounds.

Answer (A) is correct. *(PHAK Chap 9)*
   DISCUSSION: To compute the amount of weight left for baggage, compute each individual moment by using the loading graph and add them up. First, compute the moment for the pilot and front seat passenger with a weight of 250 pounds. Refer to the loading graph and the vertical scale at the left side and find the value of 250. From this position, move to the right horizontally across the graph until you intersect the diagonal line that represents pilot and front passenger. From this point, move vertically down to the bottom scale, which indicates a moment of about 9.2.
   To compute rear passenger moment, measure up the vertical scale of the loading graph to a value of 400, horizontally across to intersect the rear passenger diagonal line, and down vertically to the moment scale, which indicates approximately 29.0.
   To compute the moment of the fuel, you must recall that fuel weighs 6 lb. per gallon. The question gives 30 gal., for a total fuel weight of 180 pounds. Now move up the weight scale on the loading graph to 180, then horizontally across to intersect the diagonal line that represents fuel, then vertically down to the moment scale, which indicates approximately 8.7.
   To get the weight of the oil, see Note (2) at the bottom of the loading graph section of Fig. 135. It gives 15 lb. as the weight with a moment of –.2.
   Now total the weights (2,195 lb. including 15 lb. of engine oil). Also total the moments (98.2 including engine oil with a negative 0.2 moment).
   With this information, refer to the center of gravity moment envelope chart. Note that the maximum weight in the envelope is 2,300 pounds. The total of 2,300 lb. – 2,195 lb. leaves a maximum possible 105 lb. for baggage. However, you must be sure 105 lb. of baggage does not exceed the 109 moments allowed at the top of the envelope. On the loading graph, 105 lb. of baggage indicates approximately 10 moments.
   Thus, a total of 108.2 moments (98.2 + 10) is within the 109 moments allowed on the envelope for 2,300 lb. of weight. Therefore, baggage of 105 lb. can be loaded.

	Weight	Moment/1000 lb.-in.
Empty weight	1,350	51.5
Pilot and front seat passenger	250	9.2
Rear passengers	400	29.0
Baggage	?	?
Fuel (30 gal. × 6 lb./gal.)	180	8.7
Oil	15	–0.2
	2,195	98.2
		(without baggage)

   Answer (B) is incorrect. This amount of baggage would exceed the airplane's maximum gross weight. Answer (C) is incorrect. This amount of baggage would exceed the airplane's maximum gross weight.

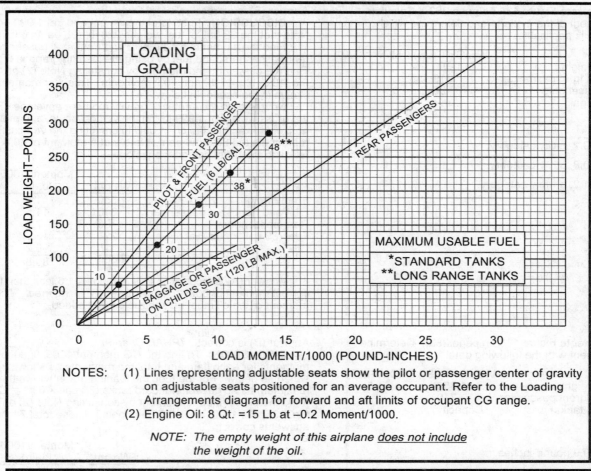

NOTES: (1) Lines representing adjustable seats show the pilot or passenger center of gravity
                on adjustable seats positioned for an average occupant. Refer to the Loading
                Arrangements diagram for forward and aft limits of occupant CG range.
          (2) Engine Oil: 8 Qt. =15 Lb at –0.2 Moment/1000.

          *NOTE: The empty weight of this airplane does not include
                  the weight of the oil.*

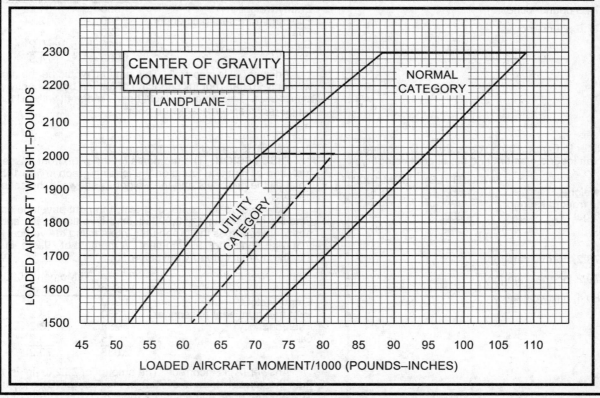

Figure 135. – Airplane Weight and Balance Graphs.

50. (Refer to Figure 135 on page 283.) Calculate the moment of the airplane and determine which category is applicable.

	WEIGHT (LB)	MOM/1000
Empty weight	1,350	51.5
Pilot and front passenger	310	---
Rear passengers	96	---
Fuel, 38 gal.	---	---
Oil, 8 qt.	---	−0.2

    A. 79.2, utility category.

    B. 80.8, utility category.

    C. 81.2, normal category.

Answer (B) is correct. *(PHAK Chap 9)*
DISCUSSION: First, total the weight and get 1,999 pounds. Note that the 38 gal. of fuel weighs 228 lb. (38 gal. × 6 lb./gal.).
Find the moments for the pilot and front seat passengers, rear passengers, and fuel by using the loading graph in Fig. 135. Find the oil weight and moment by consulting Note (2) on Fig. 135. It is 15 lb. and −0.2 moments. Total the moments as shown in the schedule below.
Now refer to the center of gravity moment envelope. Find the gross weight of 1,999 lb. on the vertical scale, and move horizontally across the chart until intersecting the vertical line that represents the 80.8 moment. Note that a moment of 80.8 lb.-in. falls into the utility category envelope.

	Weight	Moment/1000 lb.-in.
Empty weight	1,350	51.5
Pilot and front seat passenger	310	11.5
Rear passengers	96	7.0
Fuel (38 gal. × 6 lb./gal.)	228	11.0
Oil	15	−0.2
	1,999	80.8

Answer (A) is incorrect. This amount is 1.6 less than the correct moment of 80.8 lb.-in. Answer (C) is incorrect. The moment of the oil must be subtracted, not added.

51. (Refer to Figure 135 on page 283.) Determine the moment with the following data:

	WEIGHT (LB)	MOM/1000
Empty weight	1,350	51.5
Pilot and front passenger	340	---
Fuel (std tanks)	Capacity	---
Oil, 8 qt.	---	---

    A. 69.9 pound-inches.

    B. 74.9 pound-inches.

    C. 77.6 pound-inches.

Answer (B) is correct. *(PHAK Chap 9)*
DISCUSSION: To find the CG moment/1000, find the moments for each item and total the moments as shown in the schedule below. For the fuel, the loading graph shows the maximum as 38 gal. for standard tanks (38 gal. × 6 lb. = 228 lb.). [Find the oil weight and moment by consulting Note (2) on Fig. 135; it is 15 lb. and −0.2. moments.] These total 74.9, so this answer is correct.

	Weight	Moment/1000 lb.-in.
Empty weight	1,350	51.5
Pilot and front seat passenger	340	12.6
Fuel	228	11.0
Oil	15	−0.2
	1,933	74.9

Answer (A) is incorrect. This amount would be the moment with only 20 gal. (not full capacity) of fuel on board. Answer (C) is incorrect. This amount would be the moment with full long-range (not standard) tanks on board.

52. (Refer to Figure 135 on page 283.) Determine the aircraft loaded moment and the aircraft category.

	WEIGHT (LB)	MOM/1000
Empty weight	1,350	51.5
Pilot and front passenger	380	---
Fuel, 48 gal	288	---
Oil, 8 qt.	---	---

    A. 78.2, normal category.

    B. 79.2, normal category.

    C. 80.4, utility category.

Answer (B) is correct. *(PHAK Chap 9)*
DISCUSSION: The moments for the pilot, front passenger, fuel, and oil must be found on the loading graph in Fig. 135. Total all the moments and the weight as shown in the schedule below.
Now refer to the center of gravity moment envelope graph. Find the gross weight of 2,033 lb. on the vertical scale, and move horizontally across the graph until intersecting the vertical line that represents the 79.2 moment. A moment of 79.2 lb.-in. falls into the normal category envelope.

	Weight	Moment/1000 lb.-in.
Empty weight	1,350	51.5
Pilot and front seat passenger	380	14.2
Fuel (capacity)	288	13.7
Oil	15	−0.2
	2,033	79.2

Answer (A) is incorrect. The amount of 78.2 lb.-in. is 1.0 less than the correct moment of 79.2 lb.-in. Answer (C) is incorrect. The amount of 80.4 lb.-in. is 1.2 more than the correct moment of 79.2 lb.-in.

14.11 Center of Gravity Tables

53. (Refer to Figure 133 on page 286 and Figure 134 on page 287.) Determine if the airplane weight and balance is within limits.

Front seat occupants . . . . 340 lb
Rear seat occupants . . . . 295 lb
Fuel (main wing tanks) . . . . 44 gal
Baggage . . . . 56 lb

    A. 20 pounds overweight, CG aft of aft limits.

    B. 20 pounds overweight, CG within limits.

    C. 20 pounds overweight, CG forward of forward limits.

Answer (B) is correct. *(PHAK Chap 9)*
DISCUSSION: Both the total weight and the total moment must be calculated. As in most weight and balance problems, you should begin by setting up a schedule as below. Note that the empty weight in Fig. 133 is given as 2,015 lb. with a moment/100 in. of 1,554 (note the change to moment/100 on this chart) and that empty weight includes the oil.
The next step is to compute the moment/100 for each item. The front seat occupants' moment/100 is 289 (340 × 85 ÷ 100). The rear seat occupants' moment/100 is 357 (295 × 121 ÷ 100). The fuel (main tanks) weight of 264 lb. and moment/100 of 198 is read directly from the table. The baggage moment/100 is 78 (56 × 140 ÷ 100).
The last step is to go to the Moment Limits vs. Weight chart (Fig. 134) and note that the maximum weight allowed is 2,950, which means that the plane is 20 lb. over. At a moment/100 of 2,476, the plane is within the CG limits because the moments/100 may be from 2,422 to 2,499 at 2,950 pounds.

	Weight	Moment/100 lb.-in.
Empty weight with oil	2,015	1,554
Front seat	340	289
Rear seat	295	357
Fuel (44 gal. × 6 lb/gal)	264	198
Baggage	56	78
	2,970	2,476

Answer (A) is incorrect. The total moment of 2,476 lb.-in. is less (not more) than the aft limit of 2,499 lb.-in. at 2,950 pounds. Answer (C) is incorrect. The total moment of 2,476 lb.-in. is more (not less) than the forward limit of 2,422 lb.-in. at 2,900 pounds.

54. (Refer to Figure 133 on page 286 and Figure 134 on page 287.) Calculate the weight and balance and determine if the CG and the weight of the airplane are within limits.

Front seat occupants . . . . 350 lb
Rear seat occupants . . . . 325 lb
Baggage . . . . 27 lb
Fuel . . . . 35 gal

    A. CG 81.7, out of limits forward.

    B. CG 83.4, within limits.

    C. CG 84.1, within limits.

Answer (B) is correct. *(PHAK Chap 9)*
DISCUSSION: Total weight, total moment, and CG must all be calculated. As in most weight and balance problems, you should begin by setting up the schedule as shown below.
Next, go to the Moment Limits vs. Weight chart (Fig. 134), and note that the maximum weight allowed is 2,950 lb., which means that this airplane is 23 lb. under maximum weight. At a total moment of 2,441, it is also within the CG limits (2,399 to 2,483) at that weight.
Finally, compute the CG. Recall that Fig. 133 gives moment per 100 inches. The total moment is therefore 244,100 (2,441 × 100). The CG is 244,100/2,927 = 83.4.

	Weight	Moment/100 lb.-in.
Empty weight with oil	2,015	1,554
Front seat	350	298
Rear seat	325	393
Fuel, main (35 gal.)	210	158
Baggage	27	38
	2,927	2,441

Answer (A) is incorrect. The correct moment of 2,441 lb.-in./100 is within CG limits. Answer (C) is incorrect. You must divide the total moment by the total weight to arrive at the correct CG of 83.4 inches.

USEFUL LOAD WEIGHTS AND MOMENTS

OCCUPANTS

FRONT SEATS ARM 85		REAR SEATS ARM 121	
Weight	Moment 100	Weight	Moment 100
120	102	120	145
130	110	130	157
140	119	140	169
150	128	150	182
160	136	160	194
170	144	170	206
180	153	180	218
190	162	190	230
200	170	200	242

BAGGAGE OR 5TH SEAT OCCUPANT ARM 140

Weight	Moment 100
10	14
20	28
30	42
40	56
50	70
60	84
70	98
80	112
90	126
100	140
110	154
120	168
130	182
140	196
150	210
160	224
170	238
180	252
190	266
200	280
210	294
220	308
230	322
240	336
250	350
260	364
270	378

USABLE FUEL

MAIN WING TANKS ARM 75

Gallons	Weight	Moment 100
5	30	22
10	60	45
15	90	68
20	120	90
25	150	112
30	180	135
35	210	158
40	240	180
44	264	198

AUXILIARY WING TANKS ARM 94

Gallons	Weight	Moment 100
5	30	28
10	60	56
15	90	85
19	114	107

*OIL

Quarts	Weight	Moment 100
10	19	5

*Included in basic Empty Weight

Empty Weight ~ 2015

MOM / 100 ~ 1554

MOMENT LIMITS vs WEIGHT

Moment limits are based on the following weight and center of gravity limit data (landing gear down).

WEIGHT CONDITION	FORWARD CG LIMIT	AFT CG LIMIT
2950 lb (takeoff or landing)	82.1	84.7
2525 lb	77.5	85.7
2475 lb or less	77.0	85.7

Figure 133. – Airplane Weight and Balance Tables.

MOMENT LIMITS vs WEIGHT (Continued)

Weight	Minimum Moment 100	Maximum Moment 100	Weight	Minimum Moment 100	Maximum Moment 100
2100	1617	1800	2600	2037	2224
2110	1625	1808	2610	2048	2232
2120	1632	1817	2620	2058	2239
2130	1640	1825	2630	2069	2247
2140	1648	1834	2640	2080	2255
2150	1656	1843	2650	2090	2263
2160	1663	1851	2660	2101	2271
2170	1671	1860	2670	2112	2279
2180	1679	1868	2680	2123	2287
2190	1686	1877	2690	2133	2295
2200	1694	1885	2700	2144	2303
2210	1702	1894	2710	2155	2311
2220	1709	1903	2720	2166	2319
2230	1717	1911	2730	2177	2326
2240	1725	1920	2740	2188	2334
2250	1733	1928	2750	2199	2342
2260	1740	1937	2760	2210	2350
2270	1748	1945	2770	2221	2358
2280	1756	1954	2780	2232	2366
2290	1763	1963	2790	2243	2374
2300	1771	1971			
2310	1779	1980	2800	2254	2381
2320	1786	1988	2810	2265	2389
2330	1794	1997	2820	2276	2397
2340	1802	2005	2830	2287	2405
2350	1810	2014	2840	2298	2413
2360	1817	2023	2850	2309	2421
2370	1825	2031	2860	2320	2428
2380	1833	2040	2870	2332	2436
2390	1840	2048	2880	2343	2444
			2890	2354	2452
2400	1848	2057	2900	2365	2460
2410	1856	2065	2910	2377	2468
2420	1863	2074	2920	2388	2475
2430	1871	2083	2930	2399	2483
2440	1879	2091	2940	2411	2491
2450	1887	2100	2950	2422	2499
2460	1894	2108			
2470	1902	2117			
2480	1911	2125			
2490	1921	2134			
2500	1932	2143			
2510	1942	2151			
2520	1953	2160			
2530	1963	2168			
2540	1974	2176			
2550	1984	2184			
2560	1995	2192			
2570	2005	2200			
2580	2016	2208			
2590	2026	2216			

Figure 134. – Airplane Weight and Balance Tables.

55. (Refer to Figure 133 on page 286 and Figure 134 on page 287.) What is the maximum amount of baggage that can be carried when the airplane is loaded as follows?

Front seat occupants	387 lb
Rear seat occupants	293 lb
Fuel	35 gal

    A. 45 pounds.

    B. 63 pounds.

    C. 220 pounds.

Answer (A) is correct. *(PHAK Chap 9)*
    DISCUSSION: The maximum allowable weight on the Moment Limits vs. Weight chart (Fig. 134) is 2,950 pounds. The total of the given weights is 2,905 lb. (including the empty weight of the airplane at 2,015 lb. and the fuel at 6 lb./gal.), so baggage cannot weigh more than 45 pounds.
    It is still necessary to compute total moments to verify that the position of these weights does not move the CG out of CG limits.
    The total moment of 2,460 lies safely between the moment limits of 2,422 and 2,499 on Fig. 134, at the maximum weight, so this airplane can carry as much as 45 lb. of baggage when loaded in this manner.

	Weight	Moment/100 lb.-in.
Empty weight with oil	2,015	1,554
Front seat	387	330
Rear seat	293	355
Fuel, main (35 gal.)	210	158
Baggage	45	63
	2,950	2,460

    Answer (B) is incorrect. This amount of baggage would load the airplane above its maximum gross weight. Answer (C) is incorrect. This amount of baggage would load the airplane above its maximum gross weight.

56. (Refer to Figure 133 on page 286 and Figure 134 on page 287.) Determine if the airplane weight and balance is within limits.

Front seat occupants	415 lb
Rear seat occupants	110 lb
Fuel, main tanks	44 gal
Fuel, aux. tanks	19 gal
Baggage	32 lb

    A. 19 pounds overweight, CG within limits.

    B. 19 pounds overweight, CG out of limits forward.

    C. Weight within limits, CG out of limits.

Answer (C) is correct. *(PHAK Chap 9)*
    DISCUSSION: Both the weight and the total moment must be calculated. Begin by setting up the schedule shown below. The fuel must be separated into main and auxiliary tanks, but weights and moments for both tanks are provided in Fig. 133.
    Since 415 lb. is not shown on the front seat table, simply multiply the weight by the arm shown at the top of the table (415 lb. × 85 in. = 35,275 lb.-in.) and divide by 100 for moment/100 of 353 (35,275 ÷ 100 = 352.75). The rear seat moment must also be multiplied (110 lb. × 121 in. = 13,310 lb.-in.). Divide by 100 to get 133.1, or 133 lb.-in. ÷ 100. The last step is to go to the Moment Limits vs. Weight chart (Fig. 134). The maximum weight allowed is 2,950 lb., which means that the airplane weight is within the limits. However, the CG is out of limits because the minimum moment/100 for a weight of 2,950 lb. is 2,422.

	Weight	Moment/100 lb.-in.
Empty weight with oil	2,015	1,554
Front seat	415	353
Rear seat	110	133
Fuel, main	264	198
Fuel, aux.	114	107
Baggage	32	45
	2,950	2,390

57. (Refer to Figure 133 on page 286 and Figure 134 on page 287.) Which action can adjust the airplane's weight to maximum gross weight and the CG within limits for takeoff?

Front seat occupants . . . . 425 lb
Rear seat occupants . . . . 300 lb
Fuel, main tanks . . . . 44 gal

   A. Drain 12 gallons of fuel.

   B. Drain 9 gallons of fuel.

   C. Transfer 12 gallons of fuel from the main tanks to the auxiliary tanks.

Answer (B) is correct. *(PHAK Chap 9)*
   DISCUSSION: First, determine the total weight to see how much must be reduced. As shown below, this original weight is 3,004 pounds. Fig. 134 shows the maximum weight as 2,950 pounds. Thus, you must adjust the total weight by removing 54 lb. (3,004 – 2,950). Since fuel weighs 6 lb./gal., you must drain at least 9 gallons.
   To check for CG, recompute the total moment using a new fuel moment of 158 (from the chart) for 210 pounds. The plane now weighs 2,950 lb. with a total moment of 2,437, which falls within the moment limits on Fig. 134.

	Original Weight	Adjusted Weight	Moment/100 lb.-in.
Empty weight with oil	2,015	2,015	1,554
Front seat	425	425	362
Rear seat	300	300	363
Fuel	264	210	158
	3,004	2,950	2,437

   Answer (A) is incorrect. It is not necessary to drain 12 gal., only 9 gallons. Answer (C) is incorrect. Transferring fuel to auxiliary tanks will only affect the moment, not the total weight.

58. (Refer to Figure 133 on page 286 and Figure 134 on page 287.) With the airplane loaded as follows, what action can be taken to balance the airplane?

Front seat occupants . . . . 411 lb
Rear seat occupants . . . . 100 lb
Main wing tanks . . . . 44 gal

   A. Fill the auxiliary wing tanks.

   B. Add a 100-pound weight to the baggage compartment.

   C. Transfer 10 gallons of fuel from the main tanks to the auxiliary tanks.

Answer (B) is correct. *(PHAK Chap 9)*
   DISCUSSION: You need to calculate the weight and moment. The weight of the empty plane including oil is 2,015, with a moment of 1,554. The 411 lb. in the front seats has a total moment of 349.35 [411 × 85 (ARM) = 34,935 ÷ 100 = 349.35]. The rear seat occupants have a weight of 100 lb. and a moment of 121.0 [100 × 121 (ARM) = 12,100 ÷ 100 = 121.0]. The fuel weight is given on the chart as 264 lb. with a moment of 198.

	Weight	Moment/100 lb.-in.
Empty weight	2,015	1,554
Front seat	411	349.35
Rear seat	100	121.0
Fuel	264	198.0
	2,790	2,222.35

On the Fig. 134 chart, the minimum moment for 2,790 lb. is 2,243. Thus, the CG of 2,222.35 is forward. Evaluate A, B, and C to see which puts the CG within limits.

	Weight	Moment/100
A	+114	+107
B	+100	+140
C	+60	+56
	−60	−45
	0	+11

This answer choice is correct because, at 2,890 lb. (2,790 + 100), moment/100 of 2,362.35 (2,222.35 + 140) is over the minimum moment/100 of 2,354.
   Answer (A) is incorrect. At 2,904 lb. (2,790 + 114), the calculated moment/100 of 2,329.35 (2,222.35 + 107) does not reach the minimum required moment/100 of 2,370 for that weight. Answer (C) is incorrect. At 2,790 lb., an increase of 11 moment/100 does not reach the minimum of 2,243.

59. (Refer to Figure 133 on page 286 and Figure 134 on page 287.) Upon landing, the front passenger (180 pounds) departs the airplane. A rear passenger (204 pounds) moves to the front passenger position. What effect does this have on the CG if the airplane weighed 2,690 pounds and the MOM/100 was 2,260 just prior to the passenger transfer?

   A. The CG moves forward approximately 3 inches.

   B. The weight changes, but the CG is not affected.

   C. The CG moves forward approximately 0.1 inch.

Answer (A) is correct. *(AWBH Chap 2)*

   DISCUSSION: The requirement is the effect of a change in loading. Look at Fig. 133 for occupants. Losing the 180-lb. passenger from the front seat reduces the MOM/100 by 153. Moving the 204-lb. passenger from the rear seat to the front reduces the MOM/100 by about 74 (247 – 173). The total moment reduction is thus about 227 (153 + 74). As calculated below, the CG moves forward from 84.01 to 81.00 inches.

$$\text{Old CG} = \frac{226{,}000\ \text{lb.-in.}}{2{,}690\ \text{lb.}} = 84.01\ \text{in.}$$

$$\text{New CG} = \frac{203{,}300\ \text{lb.-in.}}{2{,}510\ \text{lb.}} = 81.00\ \text{in.}$$

   Answer (B) is incorrect. Intuitively, one can see that the CG will be affected. Answer (C) is incorrect. Intuitively, one can see that the CG will move forward more than only 0.1 inch.

60. (Refer to Figure 133 on page 286 and Figure 134 on page 287.) What effect does a 35-gallon fuel burn (main tanks) have on the weight and balance if the airplane weighed 2,890 pounds and the MOM/100 was 2,452 at takeoff?

   A. Weight is reduced by 210 pounds and the CG is aft of limits.

   B. Weight is reduced by 210 pounds and the CG is unaffected.

   C. Weight is reduced to 2,680 pounds and the CG moves forward.

Answer (A) is correct. *(AWBH Chap 2)*

   DISCUSSION: The effect of a 35-gal. fuel burn on weight balance is required. Burning 35 gal. of fuel will reduce weight by 210 lb. and moment by 158. At 2,680 lb. (2,890 – 210), the 2,294 MOM/100 (2,452 – 158) is above the maximum moment of 2,287; i.e., CG is aft of limits. This is why weight and balance should always be computed for the beginning and end of each flight.

   Answer (B) is incorrect. Intuitively, one can see that the CG would be affected. Answer (C) is incorrect. Although the moment has decreased, the CG (moment divided by weight) has moved aft.

END OF STUDY UNIT

APPENDIX A
SPORT PILOT PRACTICE TEST

The following 40 questions have been randomly selected from the questions in our sport pilot test bank. You will be referred to figures (charts, tables, etc.) throughout this book. Be careful not to consult the answers or answer explanations when you look for and at the figures. Topical coverage in this practice test is similar to that of the FAA pilot knowledge test. Use the correct answer listing on page 294 to grade your practice test.

NOTE: Our **FAA Test Prep Online** provides you with unlimited study and test sessions for your personal use. See the discussion on pages 17 through 20 in the Introduction of this book.

1. Aeronautical Decision Making (ADM) is a

A — systematic approach to the mental process used by pilots to consistently determine the best course of action for a given set of circumstances.
B — decision making process which relies on good judgment to reduce risks associated with each flight.
C — mental process of analyzing all information in a particular situation and making a timely decision on what action to take.

2. (Refer to Figure 53 on page 138.) The wind direction and velocity at KJFK is from

A — 180° true at 4 knots.
B — 180° magnetic at 4 knots.
C — 040° true at 18 knots.

3. (Refer to Figure 59 on page 178.) (Refer to area 1.) Identify the airspace over Lowe Airport.

A — Class G airspace -- surface up to but not including 1,200 feet AGL; Class E airspace -- 1,200 feet AGL up to but not including 18,000 feet MSL.
B — Class G airspace -- surface up to but not including 18,000 feet MSL.
C — Class G airspace -- surface up to but not including 700 feet MSL; Class E airspace -- 700 feet to 14,500 feet MSL.

4. (Refer to Figure 66 on page 181.) (Refer to area 3.) The vertical limits of that portion of Class E airspace designated as a Federal Airway over Magee Airport are

A — 1,200 feet AGL to 17,999 feet MSL.
B — 700 feet MSL to 12,500 feet MSL.
C — 7,500 feet MSL to 17,999 feet MSL.

5. (Refer to Figure 57 on page 176.) (Refer to area 2.) The floor of Class B airspace at Addison Airport is

A — at the surface.
B — 3,000 feet MSL.
C — 3,100 feet MSL.

6. (Refer to Figure 57 on page 176.) (Refer to area 4.) The floor of Class B airspace overlying Hicks Airport (T67) north-northwest of Fort Worth Meacham Field is

A — at the surface.
B — 3,200 feet MSL.
C — 4,000 feet MSL.

7. (Refer to Figure 56 on page 175.) (Refer to area 3.) Determine the approximate latitude and longitude of Currituck County Airport.

A — 36°24'N – 76°01'W.
B — 36°48'N – 76°01'W.
C — 47°24'N – 75°58'W.

8. For a complete listing of information provided in an Airport/Facility Directory (A/FD) and how the information may be decoded, refer to the

A — "Directory Legend Sample" located in the front of each A/FD.
B — Aeronautical Information Manual (AIM).
C — legend on sectional, VFR terminal area, and world aeronautical charts.

9. A series of judgmental errors that can lead to a human factors-related accident is sometimes referred to as the

A — error chain.
B — course of action.
C — DECIDE model.

10. What is the one common factor which affects most preventable accidents?

A — Structural failure.
B — Mechanical malfunction.
C — Human error.

11.   Pilots who become apprehensive for their safety for any reason should

A — request assistance immediately.
B — reduce their situational awareness.
C — change their mindset.

12.   The Federal Aviation Administration publication that provides the aviation community with basic flight information and Air Traffic Control procedures for use in the National Airspace System of the United States is the

A — Aeronautical Information Manual (AIM).
B — Airport/Facility Directory (A/FD).
C — Advisory Circular Checklist (AC 00-2).

13.   What effect, if any, does high humidity have on aircraft performance?

A — It increases performance.
B — It decreases performance.
C — It has no effect on performance.

14.   What is density altitude?

A — The height above the standard datum plane.
B — The pressure altitude corrected for nonstandard temperature.
C — The altitude read directly from the altimeter.

15.   Density altitude, and its effect on landing performance, is defined by

A — pressure altitude and ambient temperature.
B — headwind and landing weight.
C — humidity and braking friction forces.

16.   "Runway hold position" markings on the taxiway

A — identify where aircraft hold short of the runway.
B — identify areas where aircraft are prohibited.
C — allows an aircraft permission onto the runway.

17.   A below glide slope indication from a pulsating approach slope indicator is a

A — pulsating white light.
B — steady white light.
C — pulsating red light.

18.   Airspace at an airport with a part-time control tower is classified as Class D airspace only

A — when the prevailing visibility is below 3 statute miles.
B — when the associated control tower is in operation.
C — when the associated Flight Service Station is in operation.

19.   The normal radius of the outer area of Class C airspace is

A — 5 nautical miles.
B — 15 nautical miles.
C — 20 nautical miles.

20.   (Refer to Figure 59 on page 178.) (Refer to area 2.) What hazards to aircraft may exist in areas such as Devils Lake East MOA?

A — Unusual, often invisible, hazards to aircraft such as artillery firing, aerial gunnery, or guided missiles.
B — Military training activities that necessitate acrobatic or abrupt flight maneuvers.
C — High volume of pilot training or an unusual type of aerial activity.

21.   (Refer to Figure 59 on page 178.) (Refer to area 3.) When flying over Arrowwood National Wildlife Refuge, a pilot should fly no lower than

A — 2,000 feet AGL.
B — 2,500 feet AGL.
C — 3,000 feet AGL.

22.   Which is true regarding flight operations to a satellite airport, without an operating control tower, within Class C airspace area?

A — Prior to entering that airspace, a pilot must contact the FSS.
B — Prior to entering that airspace, a pilot must contact the tower.
C — Prior to entering that airspace, a pilot must establish and maintain communication with the ATC serving facility.

23.   After landing at a tower-controlled airport a pilot should contact ground control

A — when advised by the tower.
B — prior to turning off the runway.
C — after reaching a taxiway that leads directly to the parking area.

24.   The suffix "nimbus," used in naming clouds, means

A — a cloud with extensive vertical development.
B — a rain cloud.
C — a middle cloud containing ice pellets.

25.   What is the first step in neutralizing a hazardous attitude in the ADM process?

A — Dealing with improper judgment.
B — Recognition of hazardous thoughts.
C — Recognition of invulnerability in the situation.

26. Time-critical information on airports and changes that affect the national airspace system are provided by

A — Notices to Airmen (NOTAMs).
B — the Airport/Facilities Directory (A/FD).
C — Advisory Circulars (ACs).

27. Which incident requires an immediate notification be made to the nearest NTSB field office?

A — An overdue aircraft that is believed to be involved in an accident.
B — An in-flight radio communications failure.
C — An in-flight generator or alternator failure.

28. If a certificated pilot changes permanent mailing address and fails to notify the FAA Airmen Certification Branch of the new address, the pilot is entitled to exercise the privileges of the pilot certificate for a period of only

A — 30 days after the date of the move.
B — 60 days after the date of the move.
C — 90 days after the date of the move.

29. An ATC clearance means an authorization by ATC for an aircraft to proceed under specified conditions within

A — controlled airspace.
B — uncontrolled airspace.
C — published Visual Flight Rules (VFR) routes.

30. Which aircraft has the right-of-way over the other aircraft listed?

A — Glider.
B — Airship.
C — Aircraft refueling other aircraft.

31. What action is required when two aircraft of the same category converge, but not head-on?

A — The faster aircraft shall give way.
B — The aircraft on the left shall give way.
C — Each aircraft shall give way to the right.

32. How many passengers is a sport pilot allowed to carry on board?

A — One.
B — Two.
C — Three.

33. Preflight action, as required for all flights away from the vicinity of an airport, shall include

A — the designation of an alternate airport.
B — a study of arrival procedures at airports of intended use.
C — an alternate course of action if the flight cannot be completed as planned.

34. Basic day visual flight rules (VFR) minimum flight visibility for Class E airspace less than 10,000 feet mean sea level (MSL) is

A — 2,000 feet horizontal.
B — 3 statute miles.
C — 3 nautical miles.

35. During operations within Class E airspace at altitudes of less than 1,200 feet AGL, the minimum horizontal distance from clouds requirement for VFR flight is

A — 1,000 feet.
B — 1,500 feet.
C — 2,000 feet.

36. Thunderstorms reach their greatest intensity during the

A — mature stage.
B — downdraft stage.
C — cumulus stage.

37. Thunderstorms which generally produce the most intense hazard to aircraft are

A — squall line thunderstorms.
B — steady-state thunderstorms.
C — warm front thunderstorms.

38. A steady red light from the tower, for an aircraft on the ground indicates

A — Give way to other aircraft and continue circling.
B — Stop.
C — Taxi clear of the runway in use.

39. What wind condition prolongs the hazards of wake turbulence on a landing runway for the longest period of time?

A — Direct headwind.
B — Direct tailwind.
C — Light quartering tailwind.

40. When landing behind a large aircraft, the pilot should avoid wake turbulence by staying

A — above the large aircraft's final approach path and landing beyond the large aircraft's touchdown point.
B — below the large aircraft's final approach path and landing before the large aircraft's touchdown point.
C — above the large aircraft's final approach path and landing before the large aircraft's touchdown point.

PRACTICE TEST LIST OF ANSWERS

Listed below are the answers to the practice test. To the immediate right of each answer is the page number on which the question, as well as correct and incorrect answer explanations, can be found.

Q. #	Answer	Page	Q. #	Answer	Page	Q. #	Answer	Page	Q. #	Answer	Page
1.	A	106	11.	A	108	21.	A	158	31.	B	78
2.	A	138	12.	A	207	22.	C	165	32.	A	67
3.	A	158	13.	B	198	23.	A	42	33.	C	75
4.	A	159	14.	B	198	24.	B	122	34.	B	87
5.	B	161	15.	A	198	25.	B	108	35.	C	88
6.	C	162	16.	A	32	26.	A	207	36.	A	117
7.	A	169	17.	C	37	27.	A	94	37.	A	118
8.	A	208	18.	B	47	28.	A	67	38.	B	53
9.	A	106	19.	C	48	29.	A	61	39.	C	40
10.	C	110	20.	B	158	30.	A	78	40.	A	40

APPENDIX B
INTERPOLATION

The following is a tutorial based on information that has appeared in the FAA's *Pilot's Handbook of Aeronautical Knowledge*. Interpolation may be required in several questions found in this book.

A. To interpolate means to compute intermediate values between a series of given values.

    1. In many instances when performance is critical, an accurate determination of the performance values is the only acceptable means to enhance safe flight.

    2. Guessing to determine these values should be avoided.

B. Interpolation is simple to perform if the method is understood. The following are examples of how to interpolate, or accurately determine the intermediate values, between a series of given values.

C. The numbers in column A range from 10 to 30, and the numbers in column B range from 50 to 100. Determine the intermediate numerical value in column B that would correspond with an intermediate value of 20 placed in column A.

A	B
10	50
20	X = Unknown
30	100

    1. It can be visualized that 20 is halfway between 10 and 30; therefore, the corresponding value of the unknown number in column B would be halfway between 50 and 100, or 75.

D. Many interpolation problems are more difficult to visualize than the preceding example; therefore, a systematic method must be used to determine the required intermediate value. The following describes one method that can be used.

    1. The numbers in column A range from 10 to 30 with intermediate values of 15, 20, and 25. Determine the intermediate numerical value in column B that would correspond with 15 in column A.

A	B
10	50
15	
20	
25	
30	100

    2. First, in column A, determine the relationship of 15 to the range between 10 and 30 as follows:

$$\frac{15-10}{30-10} = \frac{5}{20} \text{ or } 1/4$$

        a. It should be noted that 15 is 1/4 of the range between 10 and 30.

3.   Now determine 1/4 of the range of column B between 50 and 100 as follows:

$$100 - 50 = 50$$
$$1/4 \text{ of } 50 = 12.5$$

   a.   The answer 12.5 represents the number of units, but to arrive at the correct value, 12.5 must be added to the lower number in column B as follows:

$$50 + 12.5 = 62.5$$

4.   The interpolation has been completed and 62.5 is the actual value which is 1/4 of the range of column B.

E.   Another method of interpolation is shown below:

1.   Using the same numbers as in the previous example, a proportion problem based on the relationship of the number can be set up.

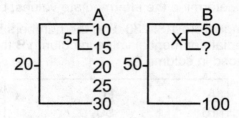

Proportion: $\dfrac{5}{20} = \dfrac{X}{50}$

$$20X = 250$$
$$X = 12.5$$

   a.   The answer, 12.5, must be added to 50 to arrive at the actual value of 62.5.

F.   The following example illustrates the use of interpolation applied to a problem dealing with one aspect of airplane performance:

Temperature (°F)	Takeoff Distance (ft.)
70	1,173
80	1,356

1.   If a distance of 1,173 feet is required for takeoff when the temperature is 70°F and 1,356 feet is required at 80°F, what distance is required when the temperature is 75°F? The solution to the problem can be determined as follows:

$$\begin{array}{c} 10\!-\!\begin{cases} 5\!-\!\begin{cases} 70° \\ 75° \end{cases} 183\!-\!\begin{cases} X\!-\!\begin{cases} 1{,}173 \\ ? \end{cases} \\ 1{,}356 \end{cases} \\ 80° \end{cases} \end{array}$$

$$\dfrac{5}{10} = \dfrac{X}{183}$$
$$10X = 915$$
$$X = 91.5$$

   a.   The answer, 91.5, must be added to 1,173 to arrive at the actual value of 1,264.5 ft.

APPENDIX C
FAA FIGURES WITHOUT ASSOCIATED QUESTIONS

The FAA has not released any sample questions associated with the following figures included in the FAA's *Computer Testing Supplement for Sport Pilot*. However, you may encounter one or more questions that reference the figures. These questions may be "pretest" questions (see page 6) or simply not published by the FAA. If you notice a question NOT covered by Gleim, please let us know. Email (aviation@gleim.com) or call (800-874-5346) us with your recollection of the question so we may improve our efforts to prepare future students and instructors.

```
METAR KAMA 301651Z 05016KT 5/8SM R04/3000FT BR OVC007 11/9 A3013
RMK DZB26DZE40

METAR KAUS 301651Z 12008KT 4SM -RAHZ BKN010 BKN023 OVC160 21/17
A3005 RMK RAB25

METAR KBRO 301655Z 15015G20KT 7SM SCT020 SCT130 TCU OVC250 29/19
A2997 RMK RAB19RAE25

METAR KDAL 301649Z 00000KT 3SM BRHZ OVC009 22/17 A3010

METAR KFTW 301654Z 09004KT 1/2SM HZFU VV006 21/17 A3010

METAR KTYR 301650Z AUTO 08004KT 3SM BR SCT015 24/19 A2999
```

Figure 3. – Aviation Routine Weather Reports (METAR).

1. The METARs in Figure 3 are decoded as follows:

a. METAR KAMA 301651Z 05016KT 5/8SM R04/3000FT BR OVC007 11/9 A3013 RMK DZB26DZE40

1) METAR – Aviation Routine Weather Report
2) KAMA – Rick Husband Amarillo International Airport, TX
3) 301651Z – Report issued on the 30th of the month, at 1651 UTC
4) 05016KT – Wind from 050° true at 16 knots
5) 5/8SM – Visibility is 5/8 of a statute mile
6) R04/3000FT – Runway 04, runway visual range 3,000 ft.
7) BR – Mist restricting visibility from 5/8 to 6 statute miles
8) OVC007 – Overcast layer of cloud at 700 ft. AGL
9) 11/9 – Temperature is 11°C and dew point is 9°C
10) A3013 – Altimeter setting is 30.13 inches of mercury
11) RMK – Remarks
12) DZB26DZE40 – Drizzle began 26 past the hour, drizzle ended 40 past the hour

b. METAR KAUS 301651Z 12008KT 4SM -RAHZ BKN010 BKN023 OVC160 21/17 A3005 RMK RAB25

1) METAR – Aviation Routine Weather Report
2) KAUS – Austin-Bergstrom International Airport
3) 301651Z – Report issued on the 30th of the month at 1651 UTC
4) 12008KT – Wind from 120° true at 8 knots
5) 4SM – Visibility 4 statute miles
6) -RAHZ – Light rain and haze present
7) BKN010 – Layer of broken cloud at 1000 ft. AGL
8) BKN023 – Layer of broken cloud at 2300 ft. AGL
9) OVC160 – Overcast layer of cloud at 16,000 ft. AGL
10) 21/17 – Temperature is 21°C and dewpoint is 17°C
11) A3005 – Altimeter setting is 30.5 inches of mercury
12) RMK – Remarks
13) RAB25 – Rain began at 25 past the hour

c.   METAR KBRO 301655Z 15015G20KT 7SM SCT020 SCT130 TCU OVC250 29/19 A2997 RMK RAB19RAE25

    1) METAR – Aviation Routine Weather Report
    2) KBRO – Brownsville/South Padre Island International Airport, TX
    3) 301655Z – Report issued on the 30th of the month at 1655 UTC
    4) 15015G20KT – Wind from 150° true at 15 knots gusting to 20 knots
    5) 7SM – Visibility 7 statute miles
    6) SCT020 – Layer of scattered cloud at 2,000 ft. AGL
    7) SCT130 – Layer of scattered cloud at 13,000 ft. AGL
    8) TCU – Towering cumulus clouds
    9) OVC250 – Overcast layer of cloud at 25,000 ft. AGL
    10) 29/19 – Temperature is 29°C and dewpoint is 19°C
    11) A2997 – Altimeter setting is 29.97 inches of mercury
    12) RMK – Remarks
    13) RAB19RAE25 – Rain began 19 past the hour, rain ended 25 past the hour

d.   METAR KDAL 301649Z 00000KT 3SM BRHZ OVC009 22/17 A3010

    1) METAR – Aviation Routine Weather Report
    2) KDAL – Dallas Love Field Airport, TX
    3) 301649Z – Report issued on the 30th of the month at 1649 UTC
    4) 00000KT –Wind less than three knots, which is reported as calm
    5) 3SM – Visibility 3 statute miles
    6) BRHZ – Mist and haze
    7) OVC009 – Overcast layer of cloud at 900 ft. AGL
    8) 22/17 – Temperature is 22°C and dewpoint is 17°C
    9) A3010 – Altimeter setting is 30.10 inches of mercury

e.   METAR KFTW 301645Z 09004KT 1/2SM HZFU VV006 21/17 A3010

    1) METAR – Aviation Routine Weather Report
    2) KFTW – Fort Worth Meacham International Airport, TX
    3) 301654Z – Report issued on the 30th of the month at 1645 UTC
    4) 09004KT – Wind from 090° true at 4 knots
    5) 1/2SM – Visibility 1/2 statute mile
    6) HZFU – Haze and smoke
    7) VV006 – Vertical visibility 600 ft.
    8) 21/17 – Temperature is 21°C and dewpoint is 17°C
    9) A3010 – Altimeter setting is 30.10 inches of mercury

f.   METAR KTYR 301650Z AUTO 08004KT 3SM BR SCT015 24/19 A2999

    1) METAR – Aviation Routine Weather Report
    2) KTYR – Tyler Pounds Regional Airport, TX
    3) 301650Z – Report issued on the 30th of the month at 1650 UTC
    4) AUTO – Automated weather station
    5) 08004KT – Wind from 080° true at 4 knots
    6) 3SM BR – Visibility 3 statute miles, mist
    7) SCT015 – Layer of scattered cloud at 1,500 ft. AGL
    8) 24/19 – Temperature is 24°C and dewpoint is 19°C
    9) A2999 – Altimeter setting is 29.99 inches of mercury

2.   Figure 8 shows a symbol from a surface analysis chart. The surface analysis chart is a computer-prepared report showing areas of high and low pressure, fronts, temperatures, dew points, wind directions and speeds, local weather, and visual obstructions.

   a.   The symbol in Figure 8 is a squall.

   NOTE: The FAA has not released any questions on this figure; however, you may encounter some on your knowledge test. To prepare for such questions, study the explanation with Figure 8 until you are familiar with the interpretation of the symbol in the figure.

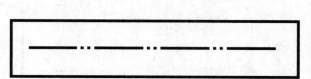

Figure 8. – Surface Analysis Chart Symbol.

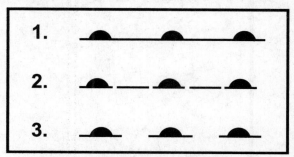

Figure 9. – Surface Analysis Chart Symbols.

3.   Figure 9 shows three surface analysis chart symbols.

   a.   Symbol number 1 indicates a warm front.
   b.   Number 2 is a warm frontolysis, which is the end of a front, when pressure and temperature differences have equalized.
   c.   Number 3 is a warm frontogenesis, which is the generation of a front, when there are increasing air density contrasts between the two air masses.

   NOTE: The FAA has not released any questions on this figure; however, you may encounter some on your knowledge test. To prepare for such questions, study the explanation with Figure 9 until you are familiar with the interpretation of each element in the figure.

4.   The symbols in Figure 10 show the cloud and visibility conditions from a reporting station.

   a.   The solid circle means that there is an overcast layer of cloud at the reporting station.
   b.   The "35" denotes cloud height in hundreds of feet, so the overcast layer of cloud is at 3,500 ft. AGL.
   c.   The sideways "8" means there is haze.
   d.   The "5" means that visibility is 5 statute miles.

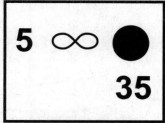

Figure 10. – Weather
Depiction Chart Symbol.

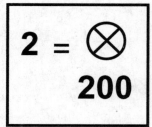

Figure 11. – Weather
Depiction Chart Symbol.

5.   The symbols in Figure 11 show the cloud and visibility conditions from a reporting station.

   a.   The circle with the "X" inside means that the sky is obscured.
   b.   The "200" represents cloud height in hundreds of feet, so there is a layer of cloud at 20,000 ft. AGL.
   c.   The "=" symbol means that there is fog or ground fog.
   d.   The "2" means that visibility is 2 statute miles.

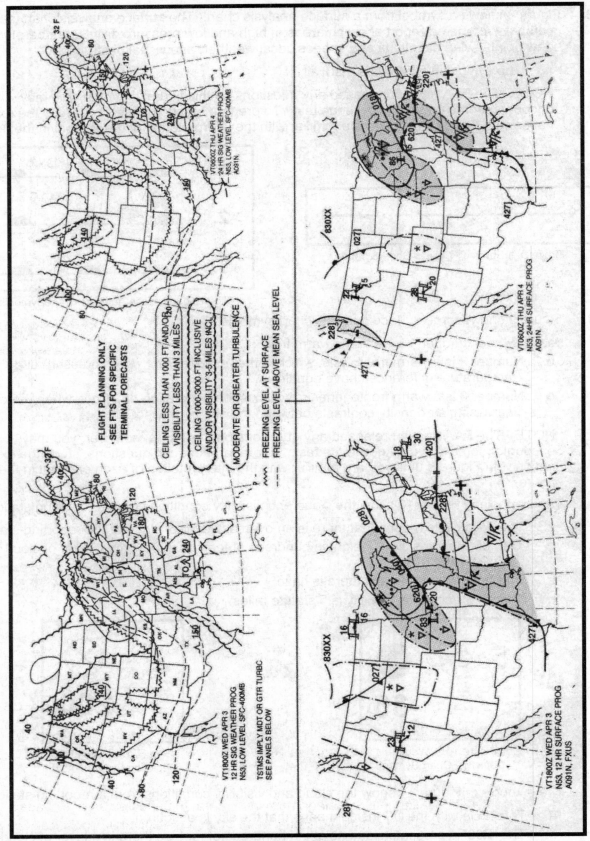

Figure 14. – Significant Weather Prognostic Chart.

6. Figure 14 on the previous page shows a low-level significant weather prognostic chart. The low-level significant weather prognostic chart (called a "prog" for brevity) is a four-panel chart.

   a. The two lower panels are 12- and 24-hr. surface progs (SFC PROG).

   b. The two upper panels are 12- and 24-hr. progs of significant weather (SIG WX) from the surface to 24,000 ft. MSL.

   c. The charts show conditions as they are forecast to be at the valid time (VT) of the chart.

   d. This prog is issued four times daily with the 12- and 24-hr. forecasts based on the 0000Z, 0600Z, 1200Z, and 1800Z synoptic data.

   e. The two surface prog panels use standard symbols for weather, fronts, significant troughs, and pressure centers.

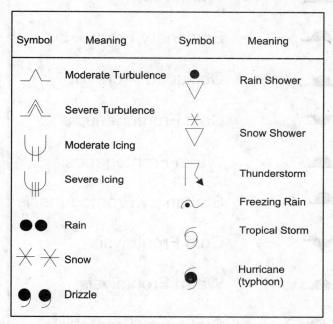

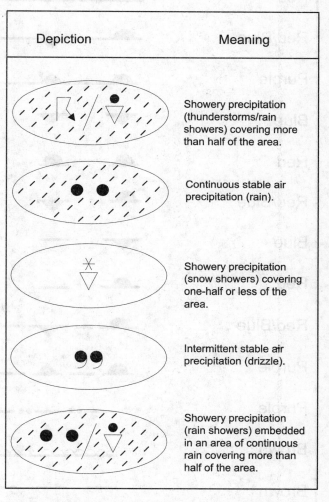

   1) High and low pressure centers are depicted by an "H" or "L," respectively.

   2) The surface prog also outlines areas of forecast precipitation and/or thunderstorms.

   3) Symbols are used to indicate precipitation type and character.

   4) If precipitation affects half or more of an area, the affected area is shaded.

   5) The absence of shading denotes more sparse precipitation, specifically coverage of less than half of the area.

   f. The upper panels depict IFR, MVFR, turbulence, and freezing levels.

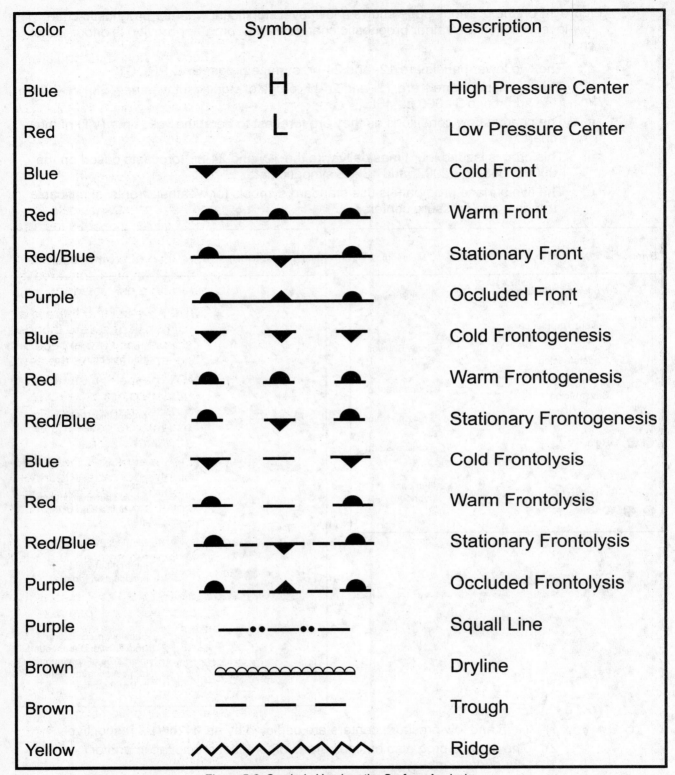

Color	Symbol	Description
Blue	H	High Pressure Center
Red	L	Low Pressure Center
Blue		Cold Front
Red		Warm Front
Red/Blue		Stationary Front
Purple		Occluded Front
Blue		Cold Frontogenesis
Red		Warm Frontogenesis
Red/Blue		Stationary Frontogenesis
Blue		Cold Frontolysis
Red		Warm Frontolysis
Red/Blue		Stationary Frontolysis
Purple		Occluded Frontolysis
Purple		Squall Line
Brown		Dryline
Brown		Trough
Yellow		Ridge

Figure 5-2. Symbols Used on the Surface Analysis.

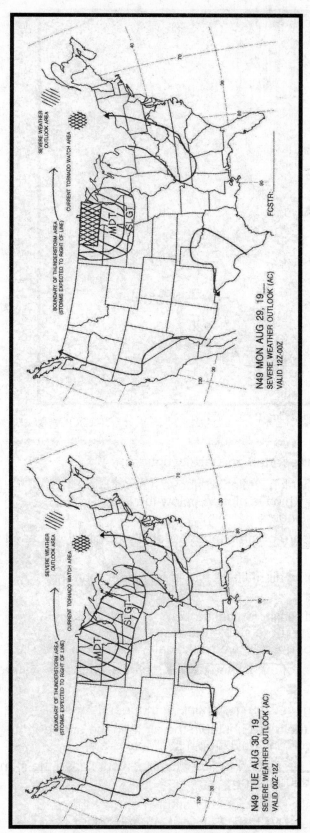

Figure 15. – Severe Weather Outlook Chart.

7. Figure 15 is a severe weather outlook chart.

a. The severe weather outlook chart is a 48-hr. outlook for thunderstorm activity presented in two panels.

b. The left-hand panel covers the first 24-hr. period beginning at 1200Z (12Z) and depicts areas of possible general and severe thunderstorm activity in the continental U.S.

   1) A line with an arrowhead delineates an area of probable thunderstorm activity located to the right of the line when facing in the direction of the arrow.

   2) If severe thunderstorm activity is expected in an area, that area is labeled with a risk category.

      a) **SLGT** means that there is a slight risk of severe thunderstorms; they are expected to cover 2% to 5% of the area.

      b) **MDT** means that there is a moderate risk of severe thunderstorms; they are expected to cover 6% to 10% of the area.

      c) **HIGH** means that there is a high risk of severe thunderstorms; they are expected to cover more than 10% of the area.

c. If general (i.e., non-severe) thunderstorm activity is expected in an area, that area is not labeled with a risk category.

   1) **NO SVR TSTMS FCST** means that the chart depicts no forecast areas of severe thunderstorms.

d. The right-hand panel covers the following day beginning at 1200Z and is similar to the left-hand panel, except that it is issued less frequently.

e. The severe weather outlook chart is strictly for advanced planning. It alerts all interests to the possibility of future storm development.

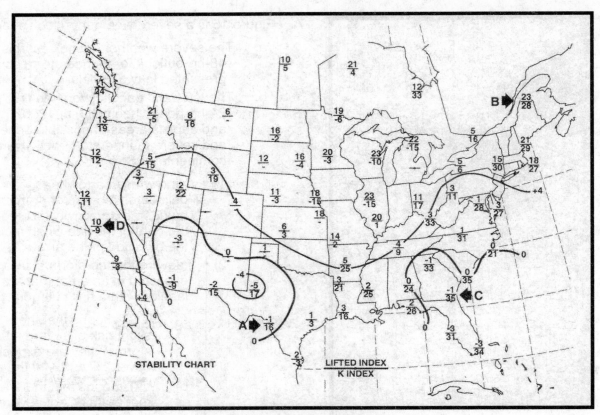

Figure 16. – Stability Chart.

8.   Figure 16 is a stability chart.

   a.   There are two stability indices that are reported on stability charts.

      1)   The top value is the lifted index, which is plotted above a short line.
      2)   The bottom value is the K index, which is plotted below the line.
      3)   An "M" indicates the value is missing.

   b.   The lifted index (LI) is a common measure of atmospheric stability. Stability is based on the lifted index only.

      1)   A positive LI means that a parcel of air, if lifted, would be colder than the surrounding air at 500 mb/hPa.

         a)   The air is stable and would resist vertical motion.
         b)   The more positive the LI, the more stable the air.
         c)   Large positive values (+8 or greater) would indicate very stable air.

      2)   A negative LI means that a parcel of air, if lifted to 500 mb/hPa, would be warmer than the surrounding air.

         a)   The air is unstable and suggests the potential for thunderstorms.
         b)   The more negative the LI, the more unstable the air, and the stronger the updrafts are likely to be with any developing thunderstorms.

      3)   A zero LI means that a parcel of air, if lifted to 500 mb/hPa, would have the same temperature as the actual air at 500 mb/hPa.

         a)   The air is said to be neutrally stable (neither stable nor unstable).

      4)   Contour lines are drawn for values of +4 and below at intervals of 4 (+4, 0, –4, –8, etc.).

NOTE: The FAA has not released any questions on Figure 16; however, you may encounter some on your knowledge test. To prepare for such questions, study the explanation with Figure 16 until you are familiar with the interpretation of the figure.

```
BOSC FA 241845
SYNOPSIS AND VFR CLDS/WX
SYNOPSIS VALID UNTIL 251300
CLDS/WX VALID UNTIL 250800...OTLK VALID 250800-251400
ME NH VT NA RI CT NY LO NJ PA OH LE WV MD DC DE VA AND CSTL WTRS

SEE AIRMET SIERRA FOR IFR CONDS AND MTN OBSCN.
TS IMPLY SEV OR GTR TURB SEV ICE LLWS AND IFR CONDS.
NON MSL HGTS DENOTED BY AGL OR CIG.

SYNOPSIS...19Z CDFNT ALG A 160NE ACK-ENE LN...CONTG AS A QSTNRY
FNT ALG AN END-50SW MSS LN. BY 13Z...CDFNT ALG A 140ESE ACK-HTO
LN...CONTG AS A QSTNRY FNT ALG A HTO-SYR-YYZ LN. TROF ACRS CNTRL
PA INTO NRN VA.  ...REYNOLDS...

OH LE
NRN HLF OH LE...SCT-BKN025 OVC045. CLDS LYRD 150. SCT SHRA. WDLY
    SCT TSRA. CB TOPS FL350. 23-01Z OVC020-030.  VIS 3SM BR. OCNL -
    RA. OTLK...IFR CIG BR FG.
SWRN QTR OH...BKN050-060 TOPS 100. OTLK...MVFR BR.
SERN QTR OH...SCT-BKN040 BKN070 TOPS 120. WDLY SCT -TSRA. 00Z
    SCT-BKN030 OVC050. WDLY SCT -TSRA. CB TOPS FL350. OTLK...VFR
    SHRA.

CHIC FA 241945
SYNOPSIS AND VFR CLDS/WX
SYNOPSIS VALID UNTIL 251400
CLDS/WX VALID UNTIL 250800...OTLK VALID 250800-251400
ND SD NE KS MN IA MO WI LM LS MI LH IL IN KY

SEE AIRMET SIERRA FOR IFR CONDS AND MTN OBSCN.
TS IMPLY SEV OR GTR TURB SEV ICE LLWS AND IFR CONDS.
NON MSL HGTS DENOTED BY AGL OR CIG.

SYNOPSIS...LOW PRES AREA 20Z CNTRD OVR SERN WI FCST MOV NEWD INTO
LH BY 12Z AND WKN. LOW PRES FCST DEEPEN OVR ERN CO DURG PD AND
MOV NR WRN KS BORDER BY 14Z. DVLPG CDFNT WL MOV EWD INTO S CNTRL
NE-CNTRL KS BY 14Z ..SMITH..

UPR MI LS
WRN PTNS...AGL SCT030 SCT-BKN050. TOPS 080. 02-05Z BECMG CIG
    OVC010 VIS 3-5SM BR. OTLK...IFR CIG BR.
ERN PTNS...CIG BKN020 OVC040. OCNL VIS 3-5SM -RA BR. TOPS FL200.
    23Z CIG OVC010 VIS 3-5SM -RA BR. OTLK...IFR CIG BR.

LWR MI LM LH
CNTRL/NRN PTNS...CIG OVC010 VIS 3-5SM -RA BR. TOPS FL200.
    OTLK...IFR CIG BR.

SRN THIRD...CIG OVC015-025. SCT -SHRA. TOPS 150. 00-02Z BECMG CIG
    OVC010 VIS 3-5SM BR. TOPS 060. OTLK...IFR CIG BR.

IN
NRN HALF...CIG BKN035 BKN080. TOPS FL200. SCT -SHRA. 00Z CIG
    BKN-SCT040 BKN-SCT080. TOPS 120. 06Z AGL SCT-BKN030. TOPS 080.
    OCNL VIS 3-5SM BR. OTLK...MVFR CIG BR.
SRN HALF...AGL SCT050 SCT-BKN100. TOPS 120. 07Z AGL SCT 030
    SCT 100. OTLK...VFR.
```

Figure 41. – Area Forecast.

9.   Figure 41 is an identical copy of Figure 6 on page 142 and may also appear on your test. All relevant material is covered in Study Unit 8, Subunit 5, "Aviation Area Forecast."

```
TAF

KMEM   121720Z 121818 20012KT 5SM HZ BKN030 PROB40 2022 1SM TSRA OVC008CB
       FM2200 33015G20KT P6SM BKN015 OVC025 PROB40 2202 3SM SHRA
       FM0200 35012KT OVC008 PROB40 0205 2SM -RASN BECMG 0608 02008KT BKN012
       BECMG 1012 00000KT 3SM BR SKC TEMPO 1214 1/2SM FG
       FM1600 VRB06KT P6SM SKC=

KOKC   051130Z 051212 14008KT 5SM BR BKN030 TEMPO 1316 1 1/2SM BR
       FM1600 18010KT P6SM SKC BECMG 2224 20013G20KT 4SM SHRA OVC020
       PROB40 0006 2SM TSRA OVC008CB BECMG 0608 21015KT P6SM SCT040=
```

Figure 42. – Terminal Aerodrome Forecasts (TAF).

10.   Figure 42 is an identical copy of Figure 5 on page 144 and may also appear on your test. All
      relevant material is covered in Study Unit 8, Subunit 6, "Terminal Aerodrome Forecast
      (TAF)."

```
FD WBC 151745
DATA BASED ON 151200Z
VALID 1600Z FOR USE 1800-0300Z.  TEMPS NEG ABV 24000
```

FT	3000	6000	9000	12000	18000	24000	30000	34000	39000
ALS			2420	2635–08	2535–18	2444–30	245945	246755	246862
AMA		2714	2725+00	2625–04	2531–15	2542–27	265842	256352	256762
DEN			2321–04	2532–08	2434–19	2441–31	235347	236056	236262
HLC		1707–01	2113–03	2219–07	2330–17	2435–30	244145	244854	245561
MKC	0507	2006+03	2215–01	2322–06	2338–17	2348–29	236143	237252	238160
STL	2113	2325+07	2332+02	2339–04	2356–16	2373–27	239440	730649	731960

Figure 43. – Winds and Temperatures Aloft Forecast.

11.   Figure 43 is an identical copy of Figure 7 on page 151 and may also appear on your test. All
      relevant material is covered in Study Unit 8, Subunit 10, "Wind and Temperature Aloft
      Forecasts (FB)."

> UA /OV OKC–TUL /TM 1800 /FL 120 /TP BE90 /SK 018 BKN 055 /
> /072 OVC 089 /CLR ABV /TA –9/WV 0921/TB MDT 055–072 /IC LGT–MDT
> CLR 072–089.

Figure 52. – Pilot Weather Report.

12. Figure 52 is a pilot weather report. It is decoded as follows:

    a. UA – Routine PIREP

    b. /OV OKC-TUL – In relation to the Oklahoma Will RGS W VOT and the Tulsa VORTAC

    c. /TM 1800 – Time of report 1800 UTC

    d. /FL 120 – Reported from altitude FL120

    e. /TP BE90 – Reporting aircraft BE90

    f. /SK 018 BKN 055 / – Sky cover layer of broken cloud at 1,800 ft. MSL, tops at 5,500 ft. MSL

    g. /072 OVC 089 /CLR ABV – Overcast layer of cloud at 7,200 ft. MSL, tops at 8,900 ft. MSL, clear above this layer

    h. /TA – Temperature –9°C

    i. /WV – Wind from 090°M at 21 knots

    j. /TB MDT 055-072 – Moderate turbulence 5,500 ft. MSL - 7,200 ft. MSL

    k. /IC LGT – MDT CLR 072-089 – Icing – light to moderate clear ice 7,200 ft. MSL - 8,900 ft. MSL

> UA/OV KOKC-KTUL/TM 1800/FL120/TP BE90//SK BKN018-TOP055/OVC072-
> TOP089/CLR ABV/TA M7/WV 08021/TB LGT 055-072/IC LGT-MOD RIME 072-089

Figure 52A. – Pilot Weather Report.

13. Figure 52A is an identical copy of Figure 4 on page 140 and may also appear on your test. Relevant material is covered in Study Unit 8, Subunit 4, "Pilot Weather Report (PIREP)."

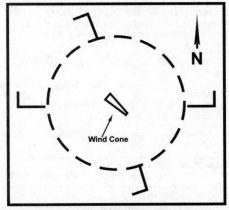

Figure 54. – Traffic Pattern Indicator.

14. Figure 54 is a traffic pattern indicator. It is similar to Figure 64 on page 34, with the one exception that no 18/36 runway is indicated. However, it does indicate Runway 35 with left circuits and Runway 17 with right circuits. All relevant material on traffic pattern indicators is covered in Study Unit 1, Subunit 3, "Airport Traffic Patterns."

TEXAS   156

DALLAS LOVE FLD (DAL) 5 NW UTC-6(-5DT) N32°50.83' W96°51.11'   DALLAS-FT. WORTH
  487 B S4 FUEL 100LL, JET A OX 1, 2, 3, 4 LRA ARFF Index B   H-2E, 4F, 5B, L-13C, A
  RWY 13R-31L: H8800X150 (CONC)   S-100, D-200, DT-350 HIRL,CL   IAP
    RWY 13R: VASI(V4L)—GA 3.0° TCH 53.' Thld dsplcd 490'. Tree. Rgt tfc.
    RWY 31L: MALSR. TDZ. Building.

  RWY 13L-31R: H7753X150 (CONC-GRVD)   S-100, D-200, DT-350 HIRL, CL
    RWY 13L: MALSR. TDZ. Tree.   **RWY 31R:** MALSR. VASI(V4L)—GA 3.0° TCH 38'. Pole. Rgt tfc.

  RWY 18-36: H6149X150 (ASPH)   S-50, D-74, DT-138 HIRL
    RWY 18: VASI(V4L)—GA 3.0° TCH 52'. Rgt tfc.   **RWY 36:** VASI(V4L)—GA 3.0° TCH 52'. REIL. Tree. Rgt tfc.
  RUNWAY DECLARED DISTANCE INFORMATION
    RWY 13L: ' TORA–7753   TORA–7753   ASDA–7753   LDA–7753
    RWY 31R: TORA–7753   TORA–7753   ASDA–7753   LDA–7753
    RWY 13R: TORA–8800   TORA–8800   ASDA–8800   LDA–8310
    RWY 31L: TORA–8800   TORA–8800   ASDA–8800   LDA–8800
    RWY 18:   TORA–6149   TORA–6149   ASDA–6149   LDA–6149
    RWY 36:   TORA–6149   TORA–6149   ASDA–6149   LDA–6149
  AIRPORT REMARKS: Attended continuously. Birds on and invof arpt. 260' AGL crane 1 mile south AER 3 1L SR-SS. 180'
  marked crane 4000' south AER 31L dalgt hours. Ldg Rwy 18 & takeoff Rwy 36 not authorized to aircraft over 60,000 lbs
  gross weight unless crosswind NW-SE rwys exceed acft safe operating capability. Noise sensitive areas all quadrants,
  noise abatement procedures in effect for fixed and rotary wing tfc, for information call arpt ops 214-670-6610. Private pilot
  certificate or better required to takeoff or land, no student solo flights permitted. Rwy 36 VASI OTS indef. Rwy 31R VASI
  OTS indef. Twy B7 clsd indef. Twy A has a 500' lgtd barricade 3600' apch end Rwy 13L. Twy M edge lgts out of svc between
  Twy B and Rwy 18, reflectors in place. Twy K clsd thru traffic. Flight Notification Service (ADCUS) available. NOTE: See Land
  and Hold Short Operations Section.
  COMMUNICATIONS: ATIS 120.15   **UNICOM** 122.95
    FORT WORTH FSS (FTW) TF 1-800-WX-BRIEF. NOTAM FILE DAL.
    DALLAS RCO 122.3 (FORT WORTH FSS)
  ⑂**REGIONAL APP CON** 125.2 (South) 124.3 (North)
    LOVE TOWER 118.7   **GND CON** 121.75   **CLNC DEL** 127.9
  ⑂**REGIONAL DEP CON** 118.55
  RADIO AIDS TO NAVIGATION: NOTAM FILE DAL.
    DALLAS - FT WORTH (H) VORTACW 117.0 DFW Chan 117 N32°51.96' W97°01.68'
      089° 9.0 NM to fld. 560/8E
    CONIS NDB (LOM) 275   LV   N32°46.48' W96°46.51'   311° 5.8 NM to fld.
    ILS/DME 111.5 I-DAL Chan 52 Rwy 13L.
    ILS/DME 111.1 I-DPX Chan 48 Rwy 13R. LOC unusable beyond 25° right side of course.
    ILS/DME 111.1 I-LVF Chan 48 Rwy 31L. LOM CONIS NDB. BC unusable.
    ILS/DME 111.5 I-OVW Chan 52 Rwy 31R.
    ASR

REDBIRD (RBD) 6 SW UTC-6(-5DT) N32°40.85' W96°52.09'   DALLAS-FT. WORTH
  660 B S4 FUEL 100LL, JET A OX 1, 2   COPTER
  RWY 13-31: H6451X150 (CONC) S-35, D-60, DT-110 MIRL 0.3% up NW   H-2E, 4F, 5B, L-13C, 17A, A
    RWY 13: REIL. VASI(V4L)—GA 3.0° TCH 50'. Trees.   IAP
    RWY 31: LDIN. VASI(V4L)—GA 3.0° TCH 47'. Road.
  RWY 17-35: H3801X150 (CONC) S-35, D-60, DT-110 MIRL
    RWY 17: REIL. PAPI (P4R)—GA 3.0° TCH 43'.   **RWY 35:** REIL.
  AIRPORT REMARKS: Attended 1400-0300Z . Birds on and in vicinity of arpt. When twr closed ACTIVATE LDIN Rwy 31
  VASI Rwy 13 and PAPI RWY 17—120.3. NOTE: See Land and Hold Short Operations Section.

  WEATHER DATA SOURCES: ASOS 126.925 (214) 330-5317. LAWRS.
  COMMUNICATIONS: CTAF 120.3   **ATIS** 126.35 **UNICOM** 122.95
    FORT WORTH FSS (FTW) TF 1-800-WX-BRIEF. NOTAM FILE RBD.
  ⑂**REGIONAL APP/DEP CON** 125.2
    TOWER 120.3 (1400-0300z)
    GND CON 121.7   **CLNC DEL** 125.45
  AIRSPACE: CLASS D svc effective 1400-0300Z other times CLASS G.
  RADIO AIDS TO NAVIGATION: NOTAM FILE DFW.
    DALLAS-FT WORTH (H) VORTACW 117.0 DFW Chan 117 N32°51.96' W97°01.68'
      136°13.7 NM to fld. 560/08E.
    NDB (HW) 287 RBD N32°40.62' W96°52.27' at fld. NOTAM FILE RBD.
    ILS 108.5 I-RBD Rwy 31. Unmonitored when tower closed.

DAN E. RICHARDS MUNI (See PADUCAH)

DAVID HOOKS   N30°07.53' W95°33.96' NOTAM FILE DWH.   HOUSTON
  NDB (MHW) 521   DWH   164° 3.9 NM to David Wayne Hooks Mem. Unmonitored.   L-17B

DAVID WAYNE HOOKS MEM (See HOUSTON)

Figure 55. – Airport/Facility Directory.

15. Figure 55 is an *A/FD* excerpt for Dallas Love Field and Redbird airports, Texas. Legend 2. –
     Airport/Facility Directory on page 197 decodes all of the elements in this excerpt. Study
     Figure 55 along with Legend 2 until you are familiar with the elements in the *A/FD* excerpt.

FAA LISTING OF
LEARNING STATEMENT CODES

Pages 309 through 311 contain the FAA's learning statement codes relating to questions found in this book. These are the codes that will appear on your Airman Computer Test Report. See the illustration on page 13. Your test report will list the learning statement code of each question answered incorrectly.

When you receive your Airman Computer Test Report, you can trace the learning statement codes listed on it to pages 309 through 311 to find out which topics you had difficulty with. You should discuss your test results with your CFI.

Additionally, you should trace the learning statement codes on your Airman Computer Test Report to our cross-reference of sport pilot test questions beginning on page 312. Determine which Gleim subunits you need to review.

Effective September 30, 2007, all knowledge test grade reports ceased to offer subject matter knowledge codes. The FAA has introduced learning statements that have taken the place of the previous knowledge code system. These statements are designed to represent the knowledge test topic areas in clear verbal terms and encourage applicants to study the entire area of identified weakness instead of merely studying a specific question area.

The learning statements listed below are all used in this test bank. The FAA will periodically revise the existing learning codes and add new ones.

To determine the knowledge area in which a particular question was incorrectly answered, compare the learning statements code(s) on your Airman Computer Test Report to the listing that follows. The total number of test items missed may differ from the number of learning statement codes shown on your test report because you may have missed more than one question in a certain knowledge area.

Code	Description
PLT005	Calculate aircraft performance - density altitude
PLT008	Calculate aircraft performance - landing
PLT011	Calculate aircraft performance - takeoff
PLT012	Calculate aircraft performance - time/speed/distance/course/fuel/wind
PLT013	Calculate crosswind / headwind components
PLT015	Calculate flight performance / planning - range
PLT018	Calculate load factor / stall speed / velocity / angle of attack
PLT019	Calculate pressure altitude
PLT021	Calculate weight and balance
PLT022	Define Aeronautical Decision Making (ADM)
PLT023	Define altitude - absolute / true / indicated / density / pressure
PLT025	Define Bernoulli's principle
PLT026	Define ceiling
PLT039	Interpret airport landing indicator
PLT041	Interpret altimeter - readings / settings
PLT059	Interpret information on a METAR / SPECI report
PLT061	Interpret information on a PIREP
PLT063	Interpret information on a Radar Summary Chart
PLT064	Interpret information on a Sectional Chart
PLT072	Interpret information on a Terminal Aerodrome Forecast (TAF)
PLT074	Interpret information on a Velocity/Load Factor Chart
PLT075	Interpret information on a Weather Depiction Chart
PLT076	Interpret information on a Winds and Temperatures Aloft Forecast (FB)
PLT077	Interpret information on an Airport Diagram
PLT078	Interpret information on an Airport Facility Directory (AFD)
PLT081	Interpret information on an Aviation Area Forecast (FA)
PLT095	Recall aerodynamics - longitudinal axis / lateral axis
PLT097	Recall aeromedical factors - effects of carbon monoxide poisoning
PLT098	Recall aeromedical factors - fitness for flight
PLT099	Recall aeromedical factors - scanning procedures
PLT103	Recall Aeronautical Decision Making (ADM) - hazardous attitudes
PLT104	Recall Aeronautical Decision Making (ADM) - human factors
PLT112	Recall aircraft controls - proper use / techniques
PLT114	Recall aircraft design - construction / function
PLT115	Recall aircraft engine - detonation/backfiring/after firing, cause/characteristics
PLT116	Recall aircraft general knowledge / publications / AIM / navigational aids
PLT118	Recall aircraft instruments - gyroscopic
PLT120	Recall aircraft limitations - turbulent air penetration
PLT122	Recall aircraft operations - checklist usage
PLT124	Recall aircraft performance - atmospheric effects
PLT125	Recall aircraft performance - climb / descent
PLT126	Recall aircraft performance - cold weather operations
PLT127	Recall aircraft performance - density altitude
PLT129	Recall aircraft performance - effects of runway slope / slope landing
PLT130	Recall aircraft performance - fuel
PLT131	Recall aircraft performance - ground effect
PLT132	Recall aircraft performance - instrument markings / airspeed / definitions / indications
PLT133	Recall aircraft performance - normal climb / descent rates
PLT134	Recall aircraft performance - takeoff

PLT141   Recall airport operations - markings / signs / lighting

PLT146   Recall airport operations - traffic pattern procedures / communication procedures

PLT147   Recall airport operations - visual glideslope indicators

PLT149   Recall airport preflight / taxi operations - procedures

PLT150   Recall airport traffic patterns - entry procedures

PLT161   Recall airspace classes - limits / requirements / restrictions / airspeeds / equipment

PLT162   Recall airspace requirements - operations

PLT163   Recall airspace requirements - visibility / cloud clearance

PLT166   Recall altimeter - settings / setting procedures

PLT167   Recall altimeters - characteristics / accuracy

PLT168   Recall angle of attack - characteristics / forces / principles

PLT170   Recall approach / landing / taxiing techniques

PLT171   Recall ATC - reporting

PLT172   Recall ATC - system / services

PLT173   Recall atmospheric conditions - measurements / pressure / stability

PLT185   Recall basic instrument flying - fundamental skills

PLT186   Recall basic instrument flying - pitch instruments

PLT187   Recall basic instrument flying - turn coordinator / turn and slip indicator

PLT189   Recall carburetor - effects of carburetor heat / heat control

PLT190   Recall carburetor ice - factors affecting / causing

PLT191   Recall carburetors - types / components / operating principles / characteristics

PLT192   Recall clouds - types / formation / resulting weather

PLT194   Recall collision avoidance - scanning techniques

PLT198   Recall course / heading - effects of wind

PLT200   Recall dead reckoning - calculations / charts

PLT201   Recall departure procedures - ODP / SID

PLT205   Recall effects of alcohol on the body

PLT206   Recall effects of temperature - density altitude / icing

PLT207   Recall electrical system - components / operating principles / characteristics / static bonding and shielding

PLT208   Recall emergency conditions / procedures

PLT213   Recall flight characteristics - longitudinal stability / instability

PLT215   Recall flight instruments - magnetic compass

PLT219   Recall flight operations - maneuvers

PLT225   Recall flight plan - requirements

PLT226   Recall fog - types / formation / resulting weather

PLT235   Recall forces acting on aircraft - aerodynamics

PLT241   Recall forces acting on aircraft - drag / gravity / thrust / lift

PLT242   Recall forces acting on aircraft - lift / drag / thrust / weight / stall / limitations

PLT243   Recall forces acting on aircraft - propeller / torque

PLT245   Recall forces acting on aircraft - stalls / spins

PLT247   Recall forces acting on aircraft - thrust / drag / weight / lift

PLT248   Recall forces acting on aircraft - turns

PLT249   Recall fuel - air mixture

PLT251   Recall fuel characteristics / contaminants / additives

PLT253   Recall fuel system - components / operating principles / characteristics / leaks

PLT257   Recall glider performance - speed / distance / ballast / lift / drag

PLT263   Recall hazardous weather - fog / icing / turbulence

PLT271   Recall human factors (ADM) - judgment

PLT274   Recall icing - formation / characteristics

PLT280   Recall inflight illusions - causes / sources

PLT281   Recall information in an Airport Facility Directory

PLT290   Recall information on AIRMETS / SIGMETS

PLT291   Recall information on an Aviation Area Forecast (FA)

PLT301   Recall inversion layer - characteristics

PLT305   Recall leading edge devices - types / effect / purpose / operation

PLT309   Recall load factor - angle of bank

PLT311   Recall load factor - effect of airspeed

PLT312   Recall load factor - maneuvering / stall speed

PLT313   Recall loading - limitations

PLT320   Recall navigation - true north / magnetic north

PLT323   Recall NOTAMs - classes / information / distribution

PLT324   Recall oil system - types / components / functions / oil specifications

PLT328   Recall performance planning - aircraft loading

PLT330   Recall physiological factors - cause / effects of hypoxia

PLT332   Recall physiological factors - hyperventilation

PLT334   Recall physiological factors - spatial disorientation

PLT335   Recall pilotage - calculations

PLT337   Recall pitot-static system - components / operating principles / characteristics

PLT340   Recall positive exchange of flight controls

PLT342   Recall powerplant - controlling engine temperature

PLT343   Recall powerplant - operating principles / operational characteristics / inspecting

PLT346   Recall primary / secondary flight controls - types / purpose / functionality / operation

PLT351   Recall propeller system - types / components / operating principles / characteristics

PLT366   Recall regulations - accident / incident reporting and preserving wreckage

PLT369   Recall regulations - aerobatic flight requirements

PLT373   Recall regulations - aircraft operating limitations

PLT374   Recall regulations - aircraft owner / operator responsibilities

PLT375   Recall regulations - aircraft return to service

PLT376   Recall regulations - airspace special use / TFRS

PLT377   Recall regulations - airworthiness certificates / requirements / responsibilities

PLT378   Recall regulations - Airworthiness Directives

PLT381   Recall regulations - altimeter settings

PLT383   Recall regulations - basic flight rules

PLT384   Recall regulations - briefing of passengers

PLT387   Recall regulations - change of address

PLT395   Recall regulations - definitions

PLT399   Recall regulations - display / inspection of licenses and certificates

PLT400   Recall regulations - documents to be carried on aircraft during flight

PLT401   Recall regulations - dropping / aerial application / towing restrictions

PLT402   Recall regulations - ELT requirements

PLT403   Recall regulations - emergency deviation from regulations

PLT404   Recall regulations - emergency equipment

PLT405   Recall regulations - equipment / instrument / certificate requirements

PLT414   Recall regulations - general right-of-way rules

PLT425   Recall regulations - maintenance reports / records / entries

PLT426   Recall regulations - maintenance requirements

PLT427   Recall regulations - medical certificate requirements / validity

PLT430	Recall regulations - minimum safe / flight altitude
PLT431	Recall regulations - operating near other aircraft
PLT434	Recall regulations - operational procedures for a controlled airport
PLT435	Recall regulations - operational procedures for an uncontrolled airport
PLT441	Recall regulations - pilot briefing
PLT442	Recall regulations - pilot currency requirements
PLT443	Recall regulations - pilot qualifications / privileges / responsibilities / crew complement
PLT444	Recall regulations - pilot-in-command authority / responsibility
PLT445	Recall regulations - preflight requirements
PLT446	Recall regulations - preventative maintenance
PLT448	Recall regulations - privileges / limitations of pilot certificates
PLT461	Recall regulations - use of aircraft lights
PLT463	Recall regulations - use of narcotics / drugs / intoxicating liquor
PLT464	Recall regulations - use of safety belts / harnesses (crew member)
PLT465	Recall regulations - use of seats / safety belts / harnesses (passenger)
PLT467	Recall regulations - visual flight rules and limitations
PLT473	Recall secondary flight controls - types / purpose / functionality
PLT475	Recall squall lines - formation / characteristics / resulting weather
PLT477	Recall stalls - characteristics / factors / recovery / precautions
PLT478	Recall starter / ignition system - types / components / operating principles / characteristics
PLT479	Recall starter system - starting procedures
PLT485	Recall taxiing / crosswind / techniques
PLT493	Recall the dynamics of frost / ice / snow formation on an aircraft
PLT494	Recall thermals - types / characteristics / formation / locating / maneuvering / corrective actions
PLT495	Recall thunderstorms - types / characteristics / formation / hazards / precipitation static
PLT497	Recall transponder - codes / operations / usage
PLT501	Recall turbulence - types / characteristics / reporting / corrective actions
PLT502	Recall universal signals - hand / light / visual
PLT503	Recall use of narcotics / drugs / intoxicating liquor
PLT509	Recall wake turbulence - characteristics / avoidance techniques
PLT510	Recall weather - causes / formation
PLT511	Recall weather associated with frontal activity / air masses
PLT512	Recall weather conditions - temperature / moisture / dewpoint
PLT514	Recall weather reporting systems - briefings / forecasts / reports
PLT515	Recall weather services - EFAS / TIBS / TPC / WFO / AFSS / HIWAS
PLT516	Recall winds - types / characteristics
PLT517	Recall winds associated with high / low-pressure systems
PLT518	Recall windshear - characteristics / hazards / power management
PLT520	Calculate density altitude

CROSS-REFERENCES TO
THE FAA LEARNING STATEMENT CODES

Pages 312 through 318 contain a listing of all of the questions that appear in this book. The questions are in Learning Statement Code (LSC) sequence. To the right of each LSC, we present our study unit/question number and our answer. For example, note that in one instance below, PLT005 is cross-referenced to 14-1, which represents our Study Unit 14, question 1; the correct answer is A.

Pages 309 through 311 contain a complete listing of all the FAA Learning Statement Codes associated with all of the questions presented in this book. Use this list to identify the specific topic associated to each Learning Statement Code.

The first line of each of our answer explanations in Study Units 1 through 14 contains

1. The correct answer.
2. A reference for the answer explanation, e.g., *PHAK Chap 1*. If this reference is not useful, use the following chart to identify the learning statement code to determine the specific reference appropriate for the question.

FAA Learning Code	Gleim SU/ Q. No.	Gleim Answer	FAA Learning Code	Gleim SU/ Q. No.	Gleim Answer	FAA Learning Code	Gleim SU/ Q. No.	Gleim Answer
PLT005	14-1	A	PLT012	14-22	C	PLT021	14-49	A
PLT005	14-2	C	PLT013	10-32	B	PLT021	14-50	B
PLT005	14-3	C	PLT013	14-23	A	PLT021	14-51	B
PLT008	14-33	B	PLT013	14-24	C	PLT021	14-52	B
PLT008	14-34	B	PLT013	14-25	B	PLT021	14-53	B
PLT008	14-35	C	PLT013	14-26	C	PLT021	14-54	B
PLT008	14-36	B	PLT013	14-27	C	PLT021	14-55	A
PLT008	14-37	B	PLT013	14-28	B	PLT021	14-56	C
PLT008	14-38	C	PLT015	14-17	A	PLT021	14-57	B
PLT008	14-39	B	PLT018	11-43	C	PLT021	14-58	B
PLT008	14-40	B	PLT018	11-44	C	PLT021	14-59	A
PLT008	14-41	A	PLT018	11-45	B	PLT021	14-60	A
PLT008	14-42	B	PLT018	11-46	C	PLT022	6-22	A
PLT011	14-9	B	PLT018	11-47	A	PLT022	6-25	A
PLT011	14-10	A	PLT018	11-48	B	PLT022	6-27	C
PLT011	14-11	B	PLT018	11-49	A	PLT023	12-28	B
PLT011	14-12	A	PLT019	14-4	A	PLT023	12-29	A
PLT012	10-14	A	PLT019	14-5	A	PLT023	12-30	B
PLT012	10-15	B	PLT019	14-7	B	PLT023	12-31	C
PLT012	14-18	B	PLT021	14-44	C	PLT023	12-32	B
PLT012	14-19	B	PLT021	14-45	B	PLT023	12-33	B
PLT012	14-20	B	PLT021	14-46	C	PLT023	12-34	B
PLT012	14-21	C	PLT021	14-47	C	PLT023	12-35	C

FAA Learning Code	Gleim SU/ Q. No.	Gleim Answer	FAA Learning Code	Gleim SU/ Q. No.	Gleim Answer	FAA Learning Code	Gleim SU/ Q. No.	Gleim Answer
PLT025	13–18	B	PLT064	9–31	C	PLT076	8–61	C
PLT026	8–11	B	PLT064	9–35	B	PLT076	8–62	B
PLT039	1–25	A	PLT064	9–37	B	PLT076	8–63	C
PLT039	1–27	B	PLT064	9–38	C	PLT076	8–64	C
PLT041	12–24	C	PLT064	9–39	C	PLT077	1–1	B
PLT041	12–25	C	PLT064	9–41	C	PLT077	1–2	B
PLT041	12–26	A	PLT064	9–42	C	PLT077	1–3	A
PLT041	12–27	B	PLT064	9–43	A	PLT077	1–4	C
PLT059	8–12	A	PLT064	9–44	C	PLT078	10–50	A
PLT059	8–13	C	PLT064	9–45	A	PLT078	10–51	B
PLT059	8–14	A	PLT064	9–47	B	PLT078	10–52	B
PLT059	8–15	B	PLT064	9–48	C	PLT078	10–53	A
PLT059	8–16	B	PLT064	9–49	C	PLT078	10–54	A
PLT061	8–21	A	PLT064	9–50	C	PLT081	8–27	A
PLT061	8–22	C	PLT064	9–52	B	PLT081	8–29	C
PLT061	8–23	A	PLT064	9–53	A	PLT081	8–30	B
PLT061	8–24	C	PLT064	9–54	B	PLT081	8–31	C
PLT061	8–25	C	PLT064	9–55	A	PLT081	8–32	A
PLT063	8–48	C	PLT064	9–56	C	PLT081	8–33	A
PLT063	8–49	B	PLT064	9–57	B	PLT095	11–5	B
PLT063	8–50	B	PLT064	9–58	B	PLT097	6–20	B
PLT063	8–51	A	PLT064	9–59	A	PLT097	6–21	A
PLT063	8–52	C	PLT064	10–24	C	PLT098	6–14	A
PLT063	8–53	A	PLT064	10–25	B	PLT098	6–46	A
PLT063	8–54	B	PLT072	8–34	A	PLT099	1–49	B
PLT064	9–3	A	PLT072	8–35	A	PLT099	6–17	A
PLT064	9–4	A	PLT072	8–36	A	PLT099	6–18	C
PLT064	9–5	A	PLT072	8–37	C	PLT103	6–26	A
PLT064	9–6	C	PLT072	8–38	B	PLT103	6–33	B
PLT064	9–9	A	PLT072	8–39	B	PLT103	6–37	A
PLT064	9–14	C	PLT072	8–40	B	PLT103	6–38	C
PLT064	9–16	B	PLT072	8–41	B	PLT103	6–39	C
PLT064	9–17	B	PLT074	11–50	C	PLT103	6–40	C
PLT064	9–20	B	PLT075	8–42	A	PLT103	6–41	C
PLT064	9–21	C	PLT075	8–43	B	PLT103	6–42	B
PLT064	9–22	B	PLT075	8–44	B	PLT103	6–43	C
PLT064	9–23	B	PLT075	8–45	A	PLT103	6–44	B
PLT064	9–24	C	PLT075	8–46	C	PLT103	6–48	A
PLT064	9–26	A	PLT075	8–47	A	PLT103	6–49	B
PLT064	9–28	C	PLT076	8–58	B	PLT104	6–23	C
PLT064	9–29	B	PLT076	8–59	B	PLT104	6–24	A
PLT064	9–30	C	PLT076	8–60	A	PLT104	6–29	A

FAA Learning Code	Gleim SU/ Q. No.	Gleim Answer	FAA Learning Code	Gleim SU/ Q. No.	Gleim Answer	FAA Learning Code	Gleim SU/ Q. No.	Gleim Answer
PLT104	6–34	A	PLT127	14–6	C	PLT146	1–30	A
PLT104	6–45	C	PLT129	14–13	B	PLT147	1–31	B
PLT104	6–47	C	PLT130	13–35	A	PLT147	1–32	C
PLT112	13–43	B	PLT130	13–36	A	PLT147	1–33	A
PLT114	11–3	A	PLT131	11–27	A	PLT147	1–34	C
PLT114	11–8	A	PLT131	11–28	A	PLT147	1–35	B
PLT115	13–30	C	PLT131	11–29	B	PLT147	1–36	B
PLT115	13–31	A	PLT131	11–30	B	PLT147	1–37	B
PLT115	13–32	B	PLT132	12–13	C	PLT147	1–38	B
PLT115	13–33	C	PLT132	12–14	C	PLT147	1–39	B
PLT116	1–18	B	PLT132	12–15	C	PLT147	1–40	B
PLT116	2–30	A	PLT132	12–16	C	PLT149	1–57	B
PLT116	2–41	A	PLT132	12–17	A	PLT150	9–46	A
PLT116	2–42	B	PLT132	12–18	C	PLT150	9–51	A
PLT116	2–43	C	PLT132	12–19	C	PLT161	2–1	C
PLT116	6–35	A	PLT132	12–20	B	PLT161	2–2	C
PLT116	9–15	A	PLT132	12–21	C	PLT161	2–3	B
PLT116	9–18	A	PLT132	12–22	C	PLT161	2–4	B
PLT116	10–26	C	PLT132	12–23	B	PLT161	2–5	C
PLT116	10–27	B	PLT133	14–30	B	PLT161	2–6	B
PLT116	10–28	C	PLT133	14–32	A	PLT161	2–7	C
PLT116	10–29	B	PLT134	14–14	A	PLT161	2–8	A
PLT116	10–40	B	PLT141	1–5	A	PLT161	2–9	C
PLT116	10–41	C	PLT141	1–6	C	PLT161	2–10	C
PLT116	10–42	A	PLT141	1–7	B	PLT161	2–11	C
PLT116	10–43	B	PLT141	1–8	A	PLT161	3–40	B
PLT116	10–44	A	PLT141	1–9	C	PLT161	9–7	B
PLT116	10–45	A	PLT141	1–10	B	PLT161	9–8	A
PLT116	10–49	A	PLT141	1–11	B	PLT161	9–32	C
PLT118	12–44	C	PLT141	1–12	A	PLT161	9–33	B
PLT120	13–40	C	PLT141	1–13	A	PLT162	2–12	C
PLT122	6–30	A	PLT141	1–14	A	PLT162	9–1	B
PLT122	6–31	A	PLT141	1–15	C	PLT162	9–2	A
PLT124	10–4	B	PLT141	1–16	B	PLT162	9–11	B
PLT124	10–30	A	PLT141	1–17	B	PLT162	9–12	B
PLT124	10–31	A	PLT141	1–19	A	PLT162	9–13	B
PLT125	14–15	A	PLT141	1–20	B	PLT162	9–36	C
PLT126	11–24	A	PLT141	1–26	C	PLT163	5–3	B
PLT127	10–2	B	PLT146	1–21	A	PLT166	12–37	C
PLT127	10–3	A	PLT146	1–22	C	PLT167	12–38	C
PLT127	10–7	B	PLT146	1–23	A	PLT167	12–39	B
PLT127	10–8	C	PLT146	1–24	C	PLT167	12–40	C

FAA Learning Code	Gleim SU/ Q. No.	Gleim Answer	FAA Learning Code	Gleim SU/ Q. No.	Gleim Answer	FAA Learning Code	Gleim SU/ Q. No.	Gleim Answer
PLT167	12–41	A	PLT192	7–46	C	PLT226	7–39	C
PLT167	12–42	A	PLT194	1–50	C	PLT235	11–35	B
PLT168	11–14	A	PLT194	1–51	A	PLT241	11–12	A
PLT168	11–15	A	PLT194	1–52	B	PLT241	11–13	C
PLT168	11–16	B	PLT194	1–53	B	PLT242	14–48	C
PLT168	11–17	C	PLT194	1–54	A	PLT243	11–37	A
PLT170	1–28	A	PLT194	1–55	B	PLT243	11–38	B
PLT170	14–31	B	PLT194	2–27	A	PLT243	11–39	B
PLT171	2–18	A	PLT194	6–16	C	PLT245	11–23	A
PLT171	2–19	A	PLT194	12–47	B	PLT247	11–10	A
PLT171	2–20	B	PLT194	12–48	C	PLT247	11–11	A
PLT171	2–21	C	PLT198	10–23	C	PLT248	11–31	A
PLT171	2–22	C	PLT200	10–13	C	PLT249	13–27	A
PLT171	2–23	B	PLT201	1–29	C	PLT249	13–28	B
PLT171	2–24	A	PLT205	6–8	C	PLT249	13–29	A
PLT171	2–25	C	PLT206	10–1	A	PLT251	13–37	C
PLT171	2–26	C	PLT206	10–5	B	PLT253	13–38	B
PLT171	2–28	A	PLT207	10–9	C	PLT253	13–39	C
PLT172	1–56	A	PLT207	13–1	C	PLT257	14–29	A
PLT172	1–58	B	PLT207	13–2	B	PLT263	7–21	C
PLT172	2–29	A	PLT207	13–3	C	PLT263	7–22	C
PLT173	7–47	A	PLT207	13–4	C	PLT263	7–23	B
PLT173	7–48	A	PLT208	13–41	A	PLT263	7–24	A
PLT185	12–46	C	PLT213	11–32	B	PLT263	7–25	A
PLT186	12–43	C	PLT213	11–33	A	PLT271	6–32	B
PLT187	12–45	A	PLT215	12–1	C	PLT271	6–36	B
PLT189	13–24	A	PLT215	12–2	C	PLT274	7–19	C
PLT189	13–25	B	PLT215	12–3	A	PLT274	7–20	C
PLT189	13–26	B	PLT215	12–4	C	PLT280	6–19	A
PLT190	13–16	A	PLT215	12–5	B	PLT281	9–10	B
PLT190	13–19	C	PLT215	12–6	B	PLT281	10–55	A
PLT190	13–20	C	PLT215	12–7	C	PLT281	10–56	A
PLT190	13–21	C	PLT215	12–8	C	PLT290	8–17	C
PLT190	13–22	A	PLT219	11–18	C	PLT290	8–18	B
PLT190	13–23	C	PLT225	10–33	A	PLT290	8–19	A
PLT191	13–17	B	PLT225	10–34	C	PLT290	8–20	C
PLT192	7–40	B	PLT225	10–35	B	PLT291	8–26	A
PLT192	7–41	B	PLT225	10–36	B	PLT291	8–28	A
PLT192	7–42	B	PLT226	7–35	A	PLT301	7–57	A
PLT192	7–43	B	PLT226	7–36	C	PLT301	7–58	A
PLT192	7–44	C	PLT226	7–37	B	PLT301	7–59	C
PLT192	7–45	B	PLT226	7–38	A	PLT301	7–60	A

FAA Learning Code	Gleim SU/ Q. No.	Gleim Answer	FAA Learning Code	Gleim SU/ Q. No.	Gleim Answer	FAA Learning Code	Gleim SU/ Q. No.	Gleim Answer
PLT305	12–36	C	PLT342	13–13	A	PLT395	3–2	B
PLT309	11–41	B	PLT343	13–10	C	PLT395	3–3	A
PLT311	11–40	B	PLT346	11–4	A	PLT395	3–4	B
PLT312	11–42	A	PLT346	11–6	A	PLT395	3–5	B
PLT313	10–18	A	PLT346	11–7	B	PLT395	3–6	C
PLT313	10–19	B	PLT346	11–9	A	PLT395	3–7	A
PLT313	11–34	B	PLT351	10–6	B	PLT395	3–8	A
PLT313	11–36	A	PLT366	5–37	A	PLT395	3–9	B
PLT320	10–12	A	PLT366	5–38	A	PLT395	3–10	A
PLT323	10–10	B	PLT366	5–39	B	PLT395	3–39	A
PLT323	10–11	A	PLT366	5–40	C	PLT399	3–19	C
PLT323	10–46	A	PLT366	5–41	B	PLT400	5–13	C
PLT323	10–47	A	PLT366	5–42	C	PLT401	4–7	B
PLT323	10–48	A	PLT366	5–43	C	PLT402	2–39	B
PLT324	13–5	A	PLT366	5–44	C	PLT402	2–40	C
PLT324	13–8	A	PLT366	5–45	C	PLT402	5–14	B
PLT328	14–43	A	PLT369	5–18	B	PLT402	5–15	B
PLT330	6–1	A	PLT369	5–19	A	PLT402	5–16	A
PLT330	6–2	C	PLT369	5–20	B	PLT403	4–35	B
PLT330	6–3	A	PLT369	5–21	B	PLT403	4–36	B
PLT332	6–4	A	PLT373	4–6	B	PLT404	5–22	B
PLT332	6–5	C	PLT373	5–25	B	PLT405	5–23	C
PLT332	6–6	B	PLT373	5–26	B	PLT405	5–24	A
PLT332	6–7	B	PLT374	5–27	B	PLT414	4–21	A
PLT332	6–15	C	PLT374	5–28	A	PLT414	4–22	C
PLT334	6–11	A	PLT375	5–31	B	PLT414	4–23	A
PLT334	6–12	A	PLT376	9–40	B	PLT414	4–24	C
PLT334	6–13	B	PLT377	3–11	C	PLT414	4–25	B
PLT334	6–28	A	PLT377	10–38	B	PLT414	4–26	B
PLT335	10–20	A	PLT378	3–12	B	PLT414	4–27	B
PLT335	10–21	A	PLT378	3–13	C	PLT414	4–28	B
PLT335	10–22	A	PLT381	4–33	A	PLT425	3–14	C
PLT337	12–9	C	PLT381	4–34	B	PLT425	5–29	A
PLT337	12–10	C	PLT383	5–9	C	PLT425	5–30	A
PLT337	12–11	B	PLT383	5–10	C	PLT425	5–33	B
PLT337	12–12	C	PLT383	5–11	B	PLT425	5–34	C
PLT340	10–17	A	PLT383	5–12	B	PLT425	5–35	A
PLT342	13–6	A	PLT384	4–15	B	PLT425	5–36	C
PLT342	13–7	C	PLT384	4–18	A	PLT426	5–32	C
PLT342	13–9	B	PLT384	4–19	A	PLT427	3–23	C
PLT342	13–11	C	PLT387	3–32	A	PLT427	3–24	B
PLT342	13–12	A	PLT395	3–1	A	PLT427	3–25	C

FAA Learning Code	Gleim SU/ Q. No.	Gleim Answer	FAA Learning Code	Gleim SU/ Q. No.	Gleim Answer	FAA Learning Code	Gleim SU/ Q. No.	Gleim Answer
PLT427	3–26	C	PLT463	4–9	A	PLT495	7–16	B
PLT427	3–27	B	PLT463	6–9	B	PLT495	7–17	A
PLT430	4–29	A	PLT464	4–13	A	PLT495	7–18	A
PLT430	4–30	A	PLT464	4–14	C	PLT497	2–13	C
PLT430	4–31	C	PLT465	4–16	B	PLT497	2–14	A
PLT430	4–32	B	PLT465	4–17	A	PLT497	2–15	A
PLT430	9–34	B	PLT467	5–1	A	PLT497	2–16	A
PLT431	4–20	C	PLT467	5–2	B	PLT497	2–17	B
PLT434	4–38	A	PLT467	5–4	B	PLT501	14–16	B
PLT434	4–39	C	PLT467	5–5	C	PLT502	2–31	B
PLT434	4–40	A	PLT467	5–6	B	PLT502	2–32	A
PLT435	4–37	B	PLT467	5–7	B	PLT502	2–33	B
PLT441	4–12	B	PLT467	5–8	C	PLT502	2–34	C
PLT442	3–28	C	PLT467	9–25	C	PLT502	2–35	B
PLT442	3–29	A	PLT467	9–27	A	PLT502	2–36	A
PLT442	3–30	C	PLT473	11–1	A	PLT502	2–37	B
PLT442	3–31	C	PLT473	11–2	C	PLT502	2–38	A
PLT443	3–17	C	PLT475	7–11	B	PLT503	6–10	B
PLT443	3–18	C	PLT477	11–19	C	PLT509	1–41	C
PLT443	3–33	A	PLT477	11–20	C	PLT509	1–42	A
PLT443	3–34	B	PLT477	11–21	B	PLT509	1–43	C
PLT443	3–35	A	PLT477	11–22	A	PLT509	1–44	C
PLT443	3–36	B	PLT478	13–14	A	PLT509	1–45	C
PLT443	4–1	B	PLT478	13–15	A	PLT509	1–46	B
PLT444	4–2	C	PLT478	13–34	B	PLT509	1–47	B
PLT444	4–3	A	PLT479	13–50	A	PLT509	1–48	A
PLT444	4–4	B	PLT479	13–51	B	PLT510	7–1	C
PLT444	4–5	B	PLT485	13–42	C	PLT510	7–2	A
PLT444	9–19	A	PLT485	13–44	A	PLT511	7–6	C
PLT444	10–37	A	PLT485	13–45	A	PLT511	7–7	C
PLT445	4–10	C	PLT485	13–46	A	PLT511	7–8	A
PLT445	4–11	C	PLT485	13–47	B	PLT511	7–9	A
PLT445	10–39	B	PLT485	13–48	A	PLT511	7–49	C
PLT446	3–15	A	PLT485	13–49	C	PLT511	7–50	B
PLT446	3–16	B	PLT493	11–25	C	PLT511	7–51	A
PLT448	3–37	C	PLT493	11–26	A	PLT511	7–52	C
PLT448	3–38	C	PLT494	7–5	C	PLT511	7–53	C
PLT461	5–17	C	PLT495	7–10	B	PLT511	7–54	A
PLT463	3–20	B	PLT495	7–12	A	PLT511	7–55	B
PLT463	3–21	C	PLT495	7–13	B	PLT511	7–56	A
PLT463	3–22	A	PLT495	7–14	A	PLT512	7–30	C
PLT463	4–8	C	PLT495	7–15	B	PLT512	7–31	C

FAA Learning Code	Gleim SU/ Q. No.	Gleim Answer
PLT512	7–32	B
PLT512	7–33	A
PLT512	7–34	B
PLT514	8–5	C
PLT514	8–6	B
PLT515	8–1	C
PLT515	8–2	C
PLT515	8–3	C
PLT515	8–4	A
PLT515	8–7	A
PLT515	8–8	C
PLT515	8–9	A
PLT515	8–10	A
PLT515	8–55	A
PLT515	8–56	C
PLT515	8–57	A
PLT515	10–16	A
PLT516	7–4	C
PLT517	7–3	B
PLT518	7–26	C
PLT518	7–27	C
PLT518	7–28	B
PLT518	7–29	A
PLT520	14–8	C

ABBREVIATIONS AND ACRONYMS IN
SPORT PILOT FAA KNOWLEDGE TEST

A/FD	*Airport/Facility Directory*		MB	magnetic bearing
AAH	*Advanced Avionics Handbook*		MC	magnetic course
AC	Advisory Circular		MEF	maximum elevation figure
ACL	Aeronautical Chart Legend		METAR	aviation routine weather report
AD	Airworthiness Directive		MH	magnetic heading
ADF	automatic direction finder		MOA	Military Operations Area
AFH	*Airplane Flying Handbook*		MSL	mean sea level
AFSS	Automated Flight Service Station		MTR	Military Training Route
AGL	above ground level		MVFR	marginal VFR
AIM	*Aeronautical Information Manual*		NDB	nondirectional radio beacon
AIRMET	Airman's Meteorological Information		NFCT	nonfederal control tower
AME	aviation medical examiner		NM	nautical mile
ANDS	accelerate north, decelerate south		NOTAM	notice to airmen
AOE	airport of entry		NPRM	Notice of Proposed Rulemaking
ARTS	Automated Radar Terminal System		NTSB	National Transportation Safety Board
ASEL	airplane single-engine land		OAT	outside air temperature
ATA	actual time of arrival		OBS	omnibearing selector
ATC	Air Traffic Control		PAPI	precision approach path indicator
ATIS	Automatic Terminal Information Service		PCL	pilot-controlled lighting
AvW	*Aviation Weather*		*PHAK*	*Pilot's Handbook of Aeronautical Knowledge*
AWBH	*Aircraft Weight and Balance Handbook*		PIC	pilot in command
AWS	*Aviation Weather Services*		PIREP	Pilot Weather Report
CDI	course deviation indicator		RB	relative bearing
CDT	central daylight time		SFC	surface
CFI	Certificated Flight Instructor		SIGMET	Significant Meteorological Information
CG	center of gravity		SM	statute mile
CH	compass heading		STC	supplemental type certificate
CT	control tower		SVFR	special VFR
CTAF	Common Traffic Advisory Frequency		TACAN	Tactical Air Navigation
DME	distance measuring equipment		TAF	terminal aerodrome forecast
DT	daylight time		TAS	true airspeed
DUAT	Direct User Access Terminal		TC	true course
EFAS	En Route Flight Advisory System		TH	true heading
ELT	emergency locator transmitter		TWEB	Transcribed Weather Broadcast
ETA	estimated time of arrival		UHF	ultra high frequency
ETD	estimated time of departure		UTC	Coordinated Universal Time
FA	area forecast		V_A	maneuvering speed
FAA	Federal Aviation Administration		VASI	visual approach slope indicator
FAR	Federal Aviation Regulations		V_{FE}	maximum flap extended speed
FB	winds and temperatures aloft forecast		VFR	visual flight rules
FBO	Fixed-Base Operator		VHF	very high frequency
FCC	Federal Communications Commission		VHF/DF	VHF direction finder
Fl Comp	Flight Computer		V_{LE}	maximum landing gear extended speed
FL	flight level		V_{NE}	never-exceed speed
FSDO	Flight Standards District Office		V_{NO}	maximum structural cruising speed
FSS	Flight Service Station		VOR	VHF omnidirectional range
GPH	gallons per hour		VORTAC	collocated VOR and TACAN
Hg	mercury		VOT	VOR test facility
HP	horsepower		VR	visual route
IAS	indicated airspeed		V_{S0}	stalling speed or the minimum steady flight speed in the landing configuration
ICAO	International Civil Aviation Organization			
IFH	*Instrument Flying Handbook*		V_{S1}	stalling speed or the minimum steady flight speed obtained in a specific configuration
IFR	instrument flight rules			
IR	instrument route		V_X	speed for best angle of climb
ISA	International Standard Atmosphere		V_Y	speed for best rate of climb
LLWAS	lowlevel wind-shear alert system		WCA	wind correction angle
mb	millibar		Z	Zulu or UTC time

INDEX OF LEGENDS AND FIGURES

INDEX

AUTHORS' RECOMMENDATIONS

The Experimental Aircraft Association, Inc., is a very successful and effective nonprofit organization that represents and serves those of us interested in flying, in general, and in sport aviation, in particular. We personally invite you to enjoy becoming a member. Visit their website at www.eaa.org.

Types of EAA Memberships:

$40 - Individual (includes subscription to *EAA Sport Aviation* magazine)
$50 - Family (extends all benefits to member's spouse and children under 18, except for an additional EAA magazine subscription)
Free - Student (for those age 18 or under who have completed the EAA Young Eagles program)
$1,295 - Lifetime

Write: EAA Aviation Center
3000 Poberezny Rd.
Oshkosh, Wisconsin 54902

Call: (920) 426-4800
(800) JOIN-EAA
Email: membership@eaa.org

The annual EAA Oshkosh AirVenture is an unbelievable aviation spectacular with over 10,000 airplanes at one airport and virtually everything aviation-oriented you can imagine! Plan to spend at least 1 day (not everything can be seen in a day) in Oshkosh (100 miles northwest of Milwaukee). Visit the AirVenture website at www.airventure.org.

Convention dates: 2014 -- July 28 through August 3
2015 -- July 27 through August 2

The annual Sun 'n Fun EAA Fly-In is also highly recommended. It is held at the Lakeland, FL (KLAL), airport (between Orlando and Tampa). Visit the Sun 'n Fun website at www.sun-n-fun.org.

Convention dates: 2014 -- April 1 through April 6
2015 -- April 21 through April 26
2016 -- April 5 through April 10

AIRCRAFT OWNERS AND PILOTS ASSOCIATION

AOPA is the largest, most influential aviation association in the world, with more than 415,000 members--two thirds of all pilots in the United States. AOPA's most important contribution to the world's most accessible, safest, least expensive, friendliest, easiest-to-use general aviation environment is their lobbying on our behalf at the federal, state, and local levels. AOPA also provides legal services, advice, and other assistance to the aviation community.

We recommend that you become an AOPA member, which costs only $45 annually. To join, call 1-800-USA-AOPA or visit the AOPA website at www.aopa.org.

LET'S GO FLYING!

The Aircraft Owners and Pilots Association (AOPA) hosts an informational web page on getting started in aviation. "Let's Go Flying!" contains information for those still dreaming about flying, those who are ready to begin, and those who are already making the journey.

The goal of this program is to encourage people to experience their dreams of flying through an introductory flight. Interested individuals can order a FREE copy of *Let's Go Flying: Your Invitation to Fly*, which explains how amazing it is to be a pilot. Other resources are available, such as a flight school finder, a guide on what to expect throughout training, an explanation of pilot certification options, a FREE monthly flight training newsletter, and much more. To learn more, visit www.aopa.org/letsgoflying.

INSTRUCTOR CERTIFICATION FORM
SPORT PILOT KNOWLEDGE TEST

Name: _____

      I certify that I have reviewed the above individual's preparation for the FAA Sport Pilot—General knowledge test [covering the topics specified in 14 CFR 61.309(a) through (l)] using the *Sport Pilot FAA Knowledge Test* book, software, and/or online course by Irvin N. Gleim and find him/her competent to pass the knowledge test.

| _____ | _____ | _____ | _____ | _____ |
| Signed | Date | Name | CFI Number | Exp. Date |

GLEIM Pilot Training Kits with Online Ground School

Sport	$199.95	_____
Private	$249.95	_____
Instrument	$249.95	_____
Commercial	$174.95	_____
Instrument/Commercial	$341.95	_____
Sport Pilot Flight Instructor	$174.95	_____
Flight/Ground Instructor	$174.95	_____
ATP	$189.95	_____

Also Available:

Flight Engineer Online Ground School	$99.95	_____
Flight Engineer Test Prep Online	$64.95	_____

Shipping (nonrefundable): **$20 per kit** $ _____
(Alaska and Hawaii please call for shipping price)
Add applicable sales tax for shipments within the state of Florida. $ _____
For orders outside the United States, please visit our website at
www.gleim.com/aviation/products.php to place your order.   TOTAL $ _____

Reference Materials and Other Accessories Available by Contacting Gleim.

TOLL FREE: 800.874.5346 ext. 471
WEBSITE: gleim.com

LOCAL: 352.375.0772 ext. 471
FAX: 352.375.6940
EMAIL: aviationteam@gleim.com

Gleim Publications, Inc.
P.O. Box 12848
Gainesville, FL 32604

NAME (please print) _____

ADDRESS_____ Apt. _____
          (street address required for UPS)

_____

CITY _____ STATE _____ ZIP _____

_____ MC/VISA/DISC _____ Check/M.O.   Daytime Telephone (____) ____ - _____

Credit Card # _____ - _____ - _____ - _____

Exp. ____ / ____   Signature _____
     Mo./Yr.

Email Address _____

If you see topics covered on your FAA knowledge test that are not contained in this book, please email us at aviation@gleim.com or mail us this form to report your experience and help us fine-tune our test preparation materials.

This form can be mailed to **Irvin N. Gleim • c/o Gleim Publications, Inc. • P.O. Box 12848 • University Station • Gainesville, Florida • 32604.** Please include your name and address so we can properly thank you for your interest.

1. _____

2. _____

3. _____

4. _____

5. _____

6. _____

7. _____

8. _____

9. _____

10. _____

11. _____

12. _____

13. _____

14. _____

15. _____

16. _____

17. _____

18. _____

Name: _____

Address: _____

City/State/Zip: _____

Telephone: Home: _____ Work: _____ Fax: _____

Email: _____